D1104418

RESPONSIBLE DRIVING

Heathrow, Florida

Glencoe
McGraw-Hill

New York, New York   Columbus, Ohio   Woodland Hills, California   Peoria, Illinois

REVIEWERS

Ray Kracik, Past President
ILLINOIS DRIVER EDUCATION ASSOCIATION

Dale E. Roe, Past President
VIRGINIA DRIVER EDUCATION TEACHER'S
ASSOCIATION

Lou Autry, Director, Driver Education
REGION 10 ASSOCIATION SERVICE CENTER
TEXAS

F. Michael Willard, President
NORTH CAROLINA DRIVER TRAFFIC SAFETY
EDUCATION ASSOCIATION
WEST FORSYTH HIGH SCHOOL
NORTH CAROLINA

James Lewis, President
CALIFORNIA ASSOCIATION OF SAFETY
EDUCATORS

Richard Mikulik, Driver Education
Instructor
MISSION HIGH SCHOOL
SAN FRANCISCO, CALIFORNIA

Barbara Brody, Past President
AMERICAN DRIVER TRAFFIC SAFETY EDUCATION
ASSOCIATION (ADTSEA)

John Svensson, President
TRAINING AND RESEARCH INSTITUTE FOR ADVANCED DRIVER
DEVELOPMENT (TRIADD)
GUELPH, ONTARIO, CANADA

Pat Venditte, Driver Education Instructor
CORNHUSKER DRIVING SCHOOL
OMAHA, NEBRASKA

Thomas Cardarella, Driver Education
Instructor
M & N DRIVING SCHOOL
ENFIELD, CONNECTICUT

Scott Callahan, Driver Education Instructor
KITTITAS HIGH SCHOOL
KITTITAS, WASHINGTON

Craig Dill, Driver Improvement Coordinator
CALIFORNIA STATE AUTO ASSOCIATION
SAN FRANCISCO, CALIFORNIA

Editorial and Production services by Visual Education Corporation,
Princeton, New Jersey

Glencoe/McGraw-Hill

A Division of The McGraw·Hill Companies

Copyright © 2000 by the American Automobile Association. All rights reserved. Originally
copyrighted © 1997, 1993, 1987, 1980, 1975, 1970, 1965, 1961, 1955, 1948, 1947, by the
American Automobile Association under the title *Sportsmanlike Driving*. Except as permitted
under the United States Copyright Act, no part of this publication may be reproduced or
distributed in any form or by any means, or stored in a database retrieval system, without
prior permission of the publisher.

Printed in the United States of America.

Send all inquiries to:
Glencoe/McGraw-Hill
21600 Oxnard Street, Suite 500
Woodland Hills, California 91367

ISBN: 0-02-653384-7
   2 3 4 5 6 7 8 9 071 05 04 03 02 01 00 99

TEACHER'S WRAPAROUND EDITION

CONTENTS

ABOUT THE AUTHORS

Dr. Francis C. Kenel

Responsible Driving was prepared under the direction of Dr. Francis C. Kenel. Dr. Kenel received a Ph.D in traffic safety and police traffic administration from Michigan State University. He has worked in driver education and has taught driver education teachers for more than 35 years. He has developed learning modules in areas such as risk management, perceptual development, and information processing. Before becoming director of the Traffic Safety Department of AAA, Dr. Kenel was professor and chairman for Traffic Safety and Accident Prevention, first at Illinois State University and then at the University of Maryland. He also served at the Highway Traffic Safety Center at Michigan State University and as a consultant on the Safe Performance Curriculum Project. Dr. Kenel was awarded the 1991 Richard Kaywood Award for his contributions in the field of driver education. Currently, Dr. Kenel serves as a consultant for AAA and the AMVETS/Toyota Safe Driving Challenge program. He is an adjunct professor at St. Cloud State University in Minnesota; Northern Virginia Community College in Annandale, Virginia; and University of New Mexico. He is also on the board of directors of the American Driver and Traffic Safety Education Association.

Dr. James E. Aaron

Dr. James E. Aaron received his B.S. and M.S. from the University of Illinois and his Ph.D. from New York University. He has taught and supervised high school driver education programs and was formerly professor and coor-dinator of the Safety Center at Southern Illinois University. Dr. Aaron has written nine textbooks on the subjects of driver and safety education. A past president of the American Driver and Traffic Safety Education Association, he was a charter member of the American Academy of Safety Education in the Illinois High School and College Driver Education Association. He serves as a chair in the Safety and Health Hall of Fame International and as a member of the National Highway Safety Advisory Committee to the Secretary of Transportation. As a teacher and lecturer, Dr. Aaron has consulted in Saudi Arabia, China, and Africa. He has been the recipient of over 80 state and federally funded research and training grants.

Dr. John W. Palmer

Dr. John W. Palmer received his B.S. in education from Illinois State University and his M.S. in educational administration and social science from the College of Racine. He received his Ph.D. in educational administration from the University of Minnesota. He has served as department chair for the Department of Health, Education, and Traffic Safety at St. Cloud University for nine years. His articles have been published in *Driver Education Digest, Journal of Traffic Safety Education, Traffic Safety*, and various state traffic safety publications. Currently, he is a member of the board of directors of both the Minnesota Safety Council and the National Safety Council. Dr. Palmer is a fellow of the American Academy of Safety Education. He is also a past president of the American Driver and Traffic Safety Education Association.

Dr. Maurice E. Dennis

Dr. Maurice E. Dennis earned his Ph.D. from Florida State University. He is currently a professor at Texas A&M University and is coordinator of the university's safety education program. He also develops curriculum and is an instructor in the teacher preparation program of the Texas DWI education program. Dr. Dennis is a past president of the Texas Alcohol Traffic Safety Education Association. He is a fellow of the American Academy of Safety Education and has served as president of the Texas Driver and Traffic Safety Education Association and the American Driver and Traffic Safety Education Association. Dr. Dennis has conducted workshops and written many articles on the subject of driver education.

Richard M. Russell

Richard M. Russell is a graduate of the Nova Scotia Institute of Technology. He owns and operates Advanced Driving Concepts, which conducts a variety of driver training programs. He is a member of the Society of Automotive Engineers and the Canadian Association of Road Safety Professionals. Mr. Russell is a founding member and a director of the Automobile Journalists Association of Canada and is technical editor of *CarGuide Magazine*. He writes traffic safety and automobile industry columns for a variety of national publications. Mr. Russell is a consultant to AAA in curriculum development, instructor training, and the establishment and operation of driving schools.

Charles A. Butler

Charles A. Butler received his B.S. degree in accident prevention, health, and physical education from the University of Maryland in 1972. He has taught in the District of Columbia public schools and at Howard University in Washington, D.C. He joined AAA over 20 years ago. As director of Driver Safety Services at AAA, Mr. Butler oversees the research, development, marketing, and distribution of programs, materials, and services for educational and consumer purposes. He is the lead instructor for AAA driver education teacher preparation courses and driver improvement instructor and instructor/leader courses throughout the United States. Mr. Butler also directed the development of the Teaching Your Teens to Drive parent involvement program as well as the revision of the AAA driver education textbooks *Responsible Driving* and *How to Drive*. He is a member of the American Driver Safety Education Association, Association of Driver Educators for the Disabled, and the Driving School Association of the Americas.

A PHILOSOPHY OF RISK MANAGEMENT

Risk is real and it is always present—this is without question the most significant fact that drivers must take into account whenever they get behind the wheel. Yet, surveys show that a vast majority of today's drivers have unrealistic assumptions about the possibility of their being involved in a risk situation that will result in a collision. In a recent study funded by the federal government, over one-third of the respondents predicted that the likelihood of their being in a collision in any year was 1 in 1000. Statistics show that the actual likelihood is approximately 1 in 9. This misperception increases risk. Individuals are unlikely to make decisions that reduce risk unless they first perceive risk.

Any discussion of the perception of risk must also take into account the driver's attitude toward his or her ability to control events. Typically, drivers underestimate risk because they overestimate their ability to prevent collisions. Many drivers feel that they can take chances and still avoid a collision because of their driving ability. For example, drivers who follow another vehicle too closely may think that they can stop in time should the driver ahead stop short. All too often this cannot be done and the result is a collision. However, it would be a mistake to infer from this example that drivers cannot exercise control over events on the roadway. The whole idea of risk management is based on the premise that drivers can exercise control, not by assuming that they can avoid risk when it arises, but by anticipating risk and acting to minimize it.

AN ORGANIZING PRINCIPLE FOR MANAGING RISK

Guidelines for risk management can be daunting for students. However, by viewing all driving situations as an interaction of visibility, time, and space factors relative to the traction available on the roadway, students have at their fingertips an organizing principle that they can consistently apply to the driving task.

In the context of managing visibility, time, and space, students can:

- Evaluate the probability that a dangerous event will occur.
- Consider what options they have for responding to the event if it does occur.
- Consider and compare the likely consequences of each option.
- Decide on the course of action that will minimize risk.

Consider this example. A driver is traveling along a multiple-lane highway at 50 mph in moderate traffic. To manage risk, the driver gathers and interprets information based on visibility, time, and space factors. In terms of visibility, the driver searches the roadway and checks mirrors to learn the position of nearby and approaching vehicles. In terms of time, the driver notes the speed of his or her own vehicle and other vehicles and considers how long it would take vehicles traveling at this speed to stop. In terms of space, the driver will evaluate whether there is sufficient distance between his or her vehicle and the vehicle ahead, and whether there is space to steer evasively if need be.

Armed with the information that a visibility-time-space orientation has provided, the driver can now consider the possibilities. What if the vehicle ahead has a blowout? What if the vehicle in the next lane swerves or cuts in? The driver can then weigh response options, such as braking or steering evasively to the left or right.

The driver has information to make a reasonable judgment about the likely consequences of each option. For example, steering left might result in a collision, while steering right would take the driver safely onto the highway shoulder. By considering options and consequences, the driver can take appropriate action to minimize risk.

What if a situation arises in which the driver has anticipated risk but still cannot avoid a collision? Drivers trained in risk-management strategies will not only have considered the probability of risk, they will also have planned ahead for how to manage a dangerous event if it should occur. Suppose, for example, that a driver is traveling east on a two-lane highway. Traffic is light in both directions. Suddenly, a vehicle in the westbound lane swerves directly into the driver's path of travel. A head-on collision appears imminent. The driver in the eastbound lane, however, has searched the roadside and knows that there is an area of grass and low shrubs to the right. By steering toward this area and adjusting speed up or down as necessary, the driver may not be able to avoid a collision, but he or she may be able to change both the angle and point of impact, thus significantly reducing the severity of the crash.

Drivers trained in the philosophy of risk management are in control of events. They exert control by continually gathering and interpreting visibility, time, and space data; evaluating the probability of dangerous events occurring; planning how to avoid danger if it should occur; and considering the consequences of their driving actions.

Responsible Driving provides examples of risk management in virtually every lesson. These examples underscore that risk is ever present, but it can be minimized through sound driving strategies.

ABOUT THE PROGRAM

A driver education course that is aimed at teens must take into account the frightening fact that this population is disproportionately at risk of being involved in motor vehicle crashes—both as drivers and as passengers. According to statistics compiled by the Insurance Institute for Highway Safety, teens represented 7 percent of the population in 1997 but 14 percent of all motor vehicle deaths.

Built upon the experience derived from Glencoe's work on ten editions of *Sportsmanlike Driving, Responsible Driving* has been carefully designed to appeal to the teen driver. Its primary goal is to help the student become a responsible driver, well aware of—and better able to manage—the risks of driving. With this goal in mind, *Responsible Driving* also addresses such issues as resisting harmful peer and social pressures, exercising emotional control, and developing social responsibility. Students are encouraged to assess their own level of maturity.

Responsible Driving provides students with an opportunity to learn the meaning of risk, how to avoid high-risk situations if possible, and how to minimize them if unavoidable. Throughout the text, students are given practical driving instruction, helpful tips and information, and risk-man-

agement strategies. Typical driving situations are described to engage students in evaluating and considering how they would manage risk. As students learn about the factors that have an impact on the driving task, they will gain the confidence necessary to become safe, responsible drivers.

The *Responsible Driving* program consists of the following components:

- **Student Text**
- **Teacher's Wraparound Edition**
- **Teacher's Classroom Resources, including transparencies, traffic charts, software, videotape cassettes, and other materials, including the following:**
  - Study Guide
  - Tests booklets
  - Lesson Plans
  - Information Masters
  - Understanding the Dangers of Alcohol and Other Drugs booklet
  - Car Care Manual
  - Behind-the-Wheel Checklist
  - Parent Involvement booklet
  - CD-ROM: *Teaching Your Teens to Drive*

STUDENT TEXT

Responsible Driving is divided into four units with a total of 18 chapters. Unit 1 presents students with an opportunity for self-assessment and an introduction to the concept of risk management. It also includes comprehensive guidance for taking the state driving test. The second unit moves into a discussion of basic driving skills, and the third unit progresses to more complex skills and driving issues. The final unit encourages students to plan for the future.

ORGANIZATION

Unit Openers

Each unit begins with a two-page spread that includes a photograph, an introduction designed to relate the unit theme to realistic student goals, and a list of the chapters in the unit.

Chapter Openers

Each chapter begins with a two-page spread that includes a list of the lesson titles.

Chapters

Each chapter contains four lessons, each developing one aspect of the overall topic of the chapter.

Lessons

Each lesson is designed to comprise appropriate reading and activities for one class period. Each lesson has two or more objectives and a list of key terms that are listed in the order they appear in the lesson.

Lesson Review Questions

Every lesson ends with questions keyed to each of the lesson objectives and designed to assess student understanding.

What Would You Do?

At the close of each lesson, a photograph depicting a related driving scenario is presented along with a thought-provoking question designed to assess students' decision-making ability.

Skills Lesson

This one-page lesson develops map reading skills or provides cross-curricular skills development in math, science, social studies, language arts, and other areas that are related to the driving experience.

Chapter Review

This single page contains a Key Points section that summarizes each lesson of the chapter based on the lesson objectives. It also contains two chapter projects and an internet project that offer practical ideas and activities to enhance students' knowledge and understanding of driving-related matters.

Chapter Test

This single-page test contains multiple-choice and fill-in questions designed to evaluate student learning of all the chapter's objectives, as well as a Driver's Log essay question formulated to provide an alternate assessment of students' understanding of the major concept of the chapter.

Unit Test

Each of the four units closes with a two-page multiple-choice cumulative test comprised of questions that might be found on state driving tests.

SPECIAL FEATURES IN THE STUDENT TEXT

In addition to numerous photographs, schematic drawings, and charts, *Responsible Driving* contains the following special features:

CONNECTIONS	Many chapters have a short, informative feature designed to provide a link between the content of driver education and other curricular areas such as science, mathematics, or social studies.
TIPS FOR NEW DRIVERS	This is a special feature directed at solving the special problems experienced by every new driver.
ADVICE FROM THE EXPERTS	At the end of the last lesson of every chapter, driving professionals provide their personal advice to new drivers. This advice is offered from driver education instructors and consultants, members of the highway patrol, and motor vehicle officials nationwide.
SAFETY TIPS	Important safety information appears regularly in the side columns throughout each chapter.
FYI	Bits of special, high-interest information, including up-to-date statistics, are included periodically in side columns.
Energy Tips	Tips to help students remember that the conservation of energy is in everyone's self-interest appear in the side columns throughout each chapter.
PROJECTS	These activities, which include an internet project, help students become more aware of the laws within their states, improve their driving skills, and increase their understanding of driving-related issues.
GLOSSARY	Every major vocabulary term is listed and defined in the glossary.
INDEX	A comprehensive index is provided to assist students in finding particular topics.

TEACHER'S WRAPAROUND EDITION

The Teacher's Wraparound Edition provides teaching suggestions printed in the margin beside the actual student text pages.

CHAPTER OVERVIEW

To provide the teacher with a concise preview of chapter content, a two-page chapter overview has been developed and placed in the Teacher's Wraparound Edition directly preceding every chapter. The following information can be found on the overview spread.

Theme Development

A concise paragraph provides an overview of the major chapter themes.

Lesson Titles and Objectives

These columns provide an idea of individual lesson goals.

Chapter Features

A brief lesson-by-lesson description of special features is included, as well as a description of the chapter projects and skills lesson.

Teacher's Classroom Resources

A list of Glencoe teaching resources that are available for the specific chapter is provided.

Other Program Resources

A list of optional materials produced by Glencoe and correlated with the program is included.

CHAPTER OPENER PAGES

The two-page spread that opens each chapter contains the following elements.

Chapter Overview

A lesson-by-lesson description outlines the major concepts covered.

Chapter Vocabulary

Vocabulary words are listed in alphabetical order.

What's on the Road Ahead?

Suggestions are given to help students use the photographs in their textbook as motivation to begin to think about the content of the chapter.

Background

Relevant material and up-to-date statistics place the chapter content in a broader context.

Relating to Prior Knowledge

Ideas are provided to engage students in a discussion of their own experience in relation to the content of the chapter.

Concept of the Driving Task

Suggestions that provide students with a way of viewing the driving task appear at the bottom of the first page of each chapter opener.

The Big Idea

At the bottom of the second page of each chapter opener spread, an idea is provided for students to keep in mind as they read.

LESSON PAGES

Each lesson in the Teacher's Wraparound Edition is based on a sound pedagogical approach exemplified by the following four-step learning cycle.

FOCUS

A motivational section sets the purpose for the lesson and lists the objectives and lesson vocabulary. Suggestions for teaching resources are also provided.

TEACH

Teaching suggestions specific to each objective are provided in addition to a modeling suggestion designed to help students focus on the concept about which they will be learning.

ASSESS

Students' answers to objective-linked questions will provide an assessment of their learning. Answers are provided at the end of each lesson.

High-interest, cooperative learning activities are provided for students who demonstrate difficulty with the lesson content. Challenging Study Guide activities are provided to allow students to learn on their own and to expand their basic learning.

CLOSE

The final section provides an opportunity for students to summarize their learning in the context of a class discussion; also, students have an opportunity to make an entry in their own Driver's Log.

END-OF-CHAPTER PAGES

The three pages that end each chapter contain teaching suggestions, objectives, and answers for skills lessons. Answers to Chapter Test questions are also provided.

SPECIAL FEATURES IN THE TEACHER'S WRAPAROUND EDITION

In addition to teaching suggestions, modeling ideas, and cooperative learning activities, the Teacher's Wraparound Edition has the following special features.

It's a Fact

High-interest, up-to-date statistical data and relevant factual information is provided to share with students.

State-by-State

Important information relating to variations in laws and guidelines among the states is provided.

The International Scene

International driving guidelines, with special emphasis on Canada and Mexico, are given to improve awareness of international differences.

Driving Tip

Timely driving hints are included for instructors to share with students.

Meeting Student Diversity

Specific ideas are included to help students who are challenged physically, emotionally, or mentally, or have limited English proficiency.

Learning Models

Examples of driving situations are schematically displayed for teachers to replicate in order to graphically explain concepts in the teaching cycle.

Cooperative Learning Suggestions

Projects and reteaching activities are provided to be done by partners or in small group settings.

Answers to Lesson Review Questions

Concise answers are consistently positioned at the end of each lesson.

Teaching Tips for Student-Text Features

Specific ideas are suggested for helping students get the maximum benefit from featured material. These suggestions are positioned at point-of-use and share design aspects of the student-text feature for quick identification.

TEACHER'S CLASSROOM RESOURCES

The following teaching materials have been designed to accompany *Responsible Driving*.

Information Masters

A booklet with perforated pages contains materials suitable for reproduction. There are two types of materials in the booklet: (1) information sheets to be reproduced and distributed to students, such as traffic safety statistics, charts and checklists, and Tips for New Drivers from *Responsible Driving* and (2) management materials designed for the instructor's use, including observation checklists for predriving and behind-the-wheel maneuvers.

Transparencies

An array of 32 color and 18 black-and-white transparencies are provided to support instructional presentations. Based on the highly graphic illustrations in *Responsible Driving*, the transparencies provide an excellent visual catalyst for classroom discussion.

Lesson Plans

The lesson plan booklet provides a handy summary of each of the lessons plus an overview of the four-step lesson structure contained in the Teacher's Wraparound Edition.

Tests

The Tests booklets (Version A and Version B) provide additional opportunities to assess student understanding of important concepts. A variety of test formats is utilized, including multiple choice, true-false, short answer, and matching. The tests also provide students with test-taking review and practice for the knowledge or written portion of the state driving test. For each chapter, two pages of material for the A test and two pages of material for the B test have been developed. Additionally, four pages of comprehensive testing are provided in an A and B format for use at the end of the course.

Study Guide

The Study Guide is a softcover booklet that contains one page of material for each lesson. The booklet is provided to help students work through the major concepts of the lesson. Each Study Guide page closes with an activity titled Find Out More. This open-ended exploratory activity gives students a chance to extend their understanding of the lesson concepts with thought-provoking projects and activities. These activities may include observations of or interviews with other drivers, the analysis of traffic problems, or research on state laws pertaining to the subject of the lesson.

Study Guide Teacher's Edition

The teacher's version of the student Study Guide contains answers to Study Guide questions.

Behind-the-Wheel Checklist

A booklet of blackline masters contains 30 pages of checklists that outline proper safety, vehicle-check, and driving procedures. The checklists have four purposes. First, students can use them to review procedures prior to in-vehicle practice. Second, the checklists provide a positive and concrete way for parents to assist their children. Third, the teacher can use the checklists as an organizer for feedback to students after observing students' driving. Fourth, students riding in the vehicle with a student driver can use the checklists as a basis for recording observations about the student driver's skills.

Traffic Charts

Two 23- by 35-inch vinyl charts, printed on both sides, can be used to show a variety of roadway configurations, such as intersections, two-lane highways, and others. A variety of attachable figures including cars, trucks, traffic signs, and lights provide the elements needed to effectively model typical driving situations for the class.

Car Care Manual

Step-by-step guidelines for caring for a vehicle are described in this 16-page booklet, designed specifically for the new driver. Important maintenance and safety checks are emphasized.

Understanding the Dangers of Alcohol and Other Drugs

A 32-page booklet helps students recognize and avoid the dangers of alcohol and other drugs. The booklet includes detailed fact sheets and thought-provoking activities, as well as realistic "what would you do?" scenarios for students to explore individually and in groups.

Parent Involvement

Designed to help parents support and encourage their teens as they learn to be responsible drivers, this 32-page booklet contains chapter-by-chapter information and suggestions linked with the textbook. The booklet enables parents to take an active role in guiding and reinforcing students' understanding of risk-management principles.

Testmaker

The Testmaker software contains an array of test questions from which instructors can draw.

Posters

Posters provide basic information that students need, including a depiction of important signs and markings.

Videotape Cassettes

From the high-impact productions of AAA come two important video components. Students are able to see for themselves the importance of learning to manage risk while driving.

Software Program

Because of the critical relationship between alcohol, other drugs, and student risk while driving, a nationally recognized software program has been included in the program. It provides students with a private forum in which they can explore the answers to important questions related to alcohol and other drugs.

CD-ROM

The *Teaching Your Teens to Drive* CD-ROM presents material that parents or guardians can use to help their teens become safe drivers.

DRIVER EDUCATION INSTRUCTION

Driver education and driver training are not the same. Students are eager to learn how to drive; what instructors must teach them is how to be responsible drivers.

The first goal of a sound driver education course is to make it clear to students that what they are learning involves much more than simply operating controls. Students are learning how to think behind the wheel, how to plan ahead and anticipate the actions of other roadway users, and how to control their vehicle in order to minimize risk to themselves and others.

Instructional Aims

For maximum instructional effectiveness, driver education should be a well-integrated and coordinated blend of classroom instruction and structured laboratory experience. All learning activities should be carefully organized and goal-oriented. To help ensure student success, instructors should aim for the following:

- **Relevance.** Students should understand not only what content is being taught in each lesson, but also why it is being taught.
- **Active student involvement in the learning process.** Students will develop cognitive driving skills much more readily by participating in teacher-led and small-group discussions, by projecting themselves into specific driving situations, by brainstorming solutions to realistic driving problems and challenges; and by having ample opportunity to ask questions.
- **Effective coordination of classroom learning and laboratory instruction.** Students should be able to transfer their "book learning" to practical application at the earliest possible opportunity. Promptly putting theory into practice enhances comprehension and provides maximum reinforcement.
- **Integration of complementary instructional media.** Carefully coordinating a variety of instructional media with lesson content can help to motivate students while aiding comprehension. Media may range from videotapes and transparencies to traffic-situation display charts.

Classroom Instruction

To become competent and responsible drivers, students must acquire a wide range of knowledge and skills. Instruction that progresses in a clear and logical manner and consistently engages student interest can best accomplish the learning goals. To that end, effective classroom instruction should incorporate certain key elements:

- **Clear and specific performance objectives.** Students should understand exactly what they are learning, why they are learning it, and what level of mastery they are expected to demonstrate.
- **Realistic driving situations.** Students should have an opportunity to explore coping strategies for the wide range of challenges that they will face as drivers. Discussion of situations should not be limited only to traffic and roadway factors, but should also incorporate the physical, psychological, and emotional factors that can have a significant impact on driver safety.
- **Emphasis on the dangers of alcohol and other drugs.** No driver education program can be complete without making vividly clear to students the extreme hazards of using alcohol and other drugs.
- **Motivational and thought-provoking activities.** Instructors may use a variety of means to gain and hold student interest, such as whole-class and small-group discussion of open-ended driving problems, demonstrations using models and visual aids, and hands-on projects that build on or extend classroom learning.
- **Opportunities for assessment.** Both instructor and students should have frequent opportunities for learning assessment. Such opportunities may be provided through both oral and written questioning as well as periodic testing. Assessment should focus on factual knowledge, key concepts, and the cognitive skills required for safe and responsible driving.

- **Periodic review.** Rare indeed is the student who will not benefit from content review. Moreover, for many students a single presentation of instructional content may not be sufficient to ensure comprehension, much less retention. Students should therefore have frequent opportunities to review what they have learned, to link that content with newly acquired knowledge, and to apply their cumulative knowledge to a variety of driving situations.

- **Integration of instructional content.** Textbooks progress chapter by chapter, but the challenge that driver education students face when they get behind the wheel is to integrate everything they have learned. To help students meet that challenge, instructional content should be integrated and reinforced whenever possible. For example, pavement markings might first be taught in the context of rules of the road, then covered a second time in the context of highway driving, and reviewed once again in the context of expressway driving. Similarly, students should be given opportunities to think through their handling of driving situations that involve a combination of elements—night driving in the rain on a winding road, for example.

- **Cogent statistics and facts.** Up-to-date statistics and factual information can help to shape students' attitudes by highlighting specific driving hazards (such as the correlation between drinking and collisions) and underscoring ways of reducing risk (such as wearing safety belts and motorcycle helmets).

Laboratory Instruction

Laboratory instruction—actual in-vehicle experience, simulation, or a combination of the two—provides students with the opportunity to apply what they have learned and to "get the feel" of driving. To be effective, laboratory instruction—like classroom instruction—should incorporate certain basic elements:

- **Close timing of laboratory experience with related classroom instruction.** Classroom learning and related laboratory instruction should occur as close in time as possible. Ideally, students should be able to apply what they learn in class almost immediately in a laboratory session. While this ideal may be difficult to achieve, it represents, nevertheless, a goal to strive for. When such close proximity is impossible, students should, at the very least, be given an opportunity to review key points of directly related classroom content just prior to their laboratory session.

- **Careful coordination of classroom and laboratory instructional content.** Classroom and laboratory instruction should be linked as closely as possible in order to facilitate and reinforce learning. Driving strategies and maneuvers should be carried out in the laboratory session in a manner that is consistent with classroom instruction. Terminology used should be similarly consistent. Fundamental principles—such as managing visibility, time, and space to minimize driving risk—should be stressed in both classroom and laboratory settings.

- **Maximum active student participation.** Active participants learn much more readily than passive observers. With this in mind, instructors should seek ways to maximize active student involvement. For example, while one student is practice-driving a vehicle, two student passengers riding in the backseat might use checklists or other structured materials to monitor driver performance. Backseat observers might also participate in an ongoing discussion of the driver's thinking process in minimizing risk or an analysis of strategies for handling specific traffic situations encountered.

- **Structured driving experience.** Laboratory sessions should be clearly focused and carefully structured. Whether the goal is parallel parking on a busy city street or making a left turn at a rural intersection, students should understand in advance the environment in which they will be driving and know what specific procedures they will be putting into practice.

- **Progression from simple to complex.** Students should gradually build on and expand their driving knowledge and abilities. An instructional sequence that moves from simple to complex will help to accomplish this. For example, students should master basic steering and speed control before moving on to more complex maneuvers such as passing another vehicle.

Parent Participation

Parents, as well as other adult family members, can play an important role in driver education. They can share the responsibility for helping students develop the skills and judgment needed for responsible driving.

Parents should be encouraged to give their teens as much supervised practice-driving time as possible. To this end, driver education instructors should send parents:

- A brief letter that describes the driver education program, explains the importance of practice-driving time, and asks for parental support

- A detailed checklist of basic driving maneuvers, designed to guide parents in supervising their children's practice sessions

- An end-of-course evaluation of student abilities, highlighting specific areas in which the student requires additional supervised practice in order to attain mastery

Instructors should also encourage parents to read the *Responsible Driving* Parent Involvement booklet and to use the guide to help their teens become responsible and skilled drivers.

Pacing Suggestions for *Responsible Driving*

Each lesson of *Responsible Driving* is crucial to students' understanding of the driving task. It is recommended that all lessons be taught. The pacing chart below assumes that a two-semester course will meet once a week, a one-semester course will meet twice weekly, and a nine-week course will meet four times a week. It is further assumed that classes will last for 50 minutes. For the six-week course, it is assumed that classes will meet daily for 1 hour and 15 minutes. In addition to class time, integrated laboratory instruction is recommended to allow students to put theory into practice.

COURSE TIME	TWO SEMESTERS	ONE SEMESTER	NINE WEEKS	SIX WEEKS
Recommended Lessons per Week	2	4	8	10

INFUSING MULTICULTURALISM INTO DRIVER EDUCATION

Helping students to recognize and celebrate the variety of cultural influences and contributions to their lives is an important goal of education. Students who belong to specific cultural groups are empowered by identifying with positive role models who share their cultural background. At the same time, students who are made aware of the accomplishments of cultures other than their own are enriched by this knowledge. Fostering multicultural awareness is a powerful tool to help all students feel a personal connection to their learning.

A driver education classroom provides students with an opportunity to consider the implications of their behavior and attitudes on their ability to be responsible drivers. Many will realize the need to modify behaviors and attitudes that they might have thought acceptable or never thought of at all. It is highly appropriate to seize this opportunity to extend students' self-evaluation to attitudes that they might have about cultures other than their own.

Responsible Driving honors the contributions of a wide variety of cultural groups to the history and technology of transportation. Advice from the Experts, a feature appearing in every chapter, offers advice from driving professionals from varied cultural groups. In a multicultural link titled Cultural Crossroads, students are introduced to people such as Garrett Morgan, the African American inventor of the three-way traffic light; Kitty O'Neil, a woman descended from the Cherokee who overcame deafness to become a successful stunt driver; and the Inuits of Alaska, whose lives have been changed by the discovery of oil in the waters of the Northwest Passage. Cultural Crossroads also acknowledges the cultural contributions of the past, such as the invention of the wheel by the ancient Sumerians and the construction of roads in ancient China.

Cultural Crossroads is fully integrated into the *Responsible Driving* program. Using it as a springboard, instructors can engage students in a discussion of the role that a wide variety of cultural groups have played in our lives. Instructors may want to encourage students to find out more about the people and cultures introduced in Cultural Crossroads.

STUDENTS WITH SPECIAL NEEDS

A basic objective of *Responsible Driving* is to foster a responsible attitude toward driving and help develop mastery of basic driving skills. Mastering driving skills is important to all students, including those in the mainstream as well as those with learning differences and other special needs. *Responsible Driving* has been designed to address the needs of all students. However, the following suggestions will help create a positive learning experience for students with special needs by fostering self-esteem and enhancing students' perception of their ability to perform tasks successfully.

The Physically Challenged

Students who have physical disabilities should be evaluated by a certified diagnostic center, such as a rehabilitation hospital. Once their physical needs have been analyzed, special equipment can be recommended to enable them to operate a vehicle. Even if in-vehicle instruction is not practical, these students will benefit by knowing such devices exist. In addition, a lesson in Chapter 3 of *Responsible Driving* is devoted to this information.

The Learning Disabled

Students who have learning difficulties will benefit from an emphasis on concrete and iconic examples such as photographs and schematics in the text and situations displayed on the traffic charts. They will also profit from group activities in which they are paired with more able students and encouraged to express themselves verbally. The What Would You Do? activities in the Student Text and the Driver's Log in the Teacher's Wraparound Edition offer opportunities for verbal expression. Activities involving group interaction are suggested in the Reteaching section on the lesson pages of the Teacher's Wraparound Edition.

The Visually Impaired

Students with visual impairments should be given vision tests to ensure that they see well enough to drive with corrective lenses. These students should be warned never to drive without their glasses or contact lenses, and they should be encouraged to keep an extra pair of glasses in the car in case of loss, breakage, or problems with contact lenses.

The Hearing Impaired

Students with hearing impairments will need to practice recognizing visual cues, using searching techniques, and using their vehicle's mirrors to compensate for hearing problems. A lesson in Chapter 3 of *Responsible Driving* discusses compensation techniques for this population. Instruction may be greatly enhanced by the use of hand signals that have been developed to be used in the driver education vehicle with hearing-impaired students. These signals are pictorially displayed in the booklet of information masters.

CHAPTER	LESSON	OBJECTIVES
1	One	Limited English Proficiency: suggested word substitutions
	Two	Visually Impaired: advice on dark or tinted glasses
2	Two	Limited English Proficiency: knowledge-test interpreters
3	One	Emotionally Challenged: controlling emotional reactions
	Two	Physically Challenged: searching tips
4	Three	Limited English Proficiency: clarifying terminology
5	One	Limited English Proficiency: special vocabulary of signs
	Three	Orientation Dysfunction: right/left difficulty
	Four	Visually Impaired: compensating for color blindness
6	Two	Limited English Proficiency: terminology substitution
7	Two	Physically Challenged: left/right perceptual problems
8	Two	Limited English Proficiency: vehicle system terminology
	Four	Orientation Dysfunction: steering in reverse
9	Three	Limited English Proficiency: acting-out concepts
10	Three	Hearing Impaired: visual cues
	Four	Limited English Proficiency: simplifying parking terms
		Physically Challenged: special parking permits
11	One	Orientation Dysfunction: following directions
	Four	Limited English Proficiency: identifying signs while driving
12	Four	Learning Disabled: visualization
13	One	Limited English Proficiency: substituting vocabulary
14	One	Limited English Proficiency: substituting vocabulary
15	Two	Learning Disabled: modeling jump-starting a vehicle
	Four	Learning Disabled: first aid
16	Two	Limited English Proficiency: consumer language
	Three	Learning Disabled: concept of interest
	Four	Physically Challenged: obtaining vehicle insurance
17	One	Learning Disabled: making a checklist
	Two	Limited English Proficiency: engine-related terminology
18	Two	Limited English Proficiency: travel-related terminology

Students with Limited English Proficiency

These students may not have difficulty mastering the content, but they may encounter trouble with the language. Students for whom English is a second language will benefit by being paired in group activities with English-proficient students. Simplifying the language by substituting simpler words for more complex ones, such as "look around" for "search," may be helpful. In addition, these students may also benefit from the use of hand signals designed for the hearing impaired.

The Teacher's Wraparound Edition offers specific instructional suggestions for working with special needs students. These suggestions appear in the feature titled Meeting Student Diversity as detailed in the chart on the previous page.

EVALUATION

"How am I doing?" is a question that students will be asking as they move through this course. The assessment activities in *Responsible Driving* are designed to provide formative evaluation tools as students progress toward the learning objectives and summative evaluation tools to determine if students have mastered the objectives at prescribed intervals in the learning experience. The following is a list of assessment tools that are found in *Responsible Driving* with suggestions for their use.

STUDENT TEXT

End of Lesson

Lesson Review Questions Questions that are correlated with the lesson objectives assess students' comprehension. These questions may be used as the basis for a class discussion or assigned for written answers.

What Would You Do? Students' responses to these decision-making questions will assess their ability to apply the information in the lesson to a real-life driving situation. These questions have been designed to test students' ability to identify options, prioritize, and identify and evaluate consequences in order to make a choice. Instructors may want to use What Would You Do? as a group discussion activity, a whole-class discussion activity, or an independent writing activity. Evaluation of students' responses to Lesson Review questions and What Would You Do? will help determine assignment of reteaching or enrichment activities.

End of Chapter

End-of-Chapter Tests appear in the textbook to evaluate students' understanding of the chapter. Multiple-choice questions test student's comprehension. The open-ended answer required for the Driver's Log question tests students' critical thinking and provides them with an opportunity for self-assessment.

End of Unit

End-of-Unit Tests are cumulative and are comprised of multiple-choice questions similar to those found on state driving tests. Thus, at four points in the course, instructors will have an opportunity to make a summative evaluation of student learning.

TEACHER'S WRAPAROUND EDITION

Driver's Log

At the conclusion of every lesson, metacognitive questions are posed to help students summarize their learning, assess their own difficulties and devise possible solutions, or create personal checklists of points to remember. Students' answers to Driver's Log questions are a useful evaluation tool that will show what they think is important or difficult, and in so doing, will provide insight into their learning.

Instructors may wish to use these questions as the basis of class or small-group discussion, or they may wish to have students set aside a portion of a three-ring binder as their personal Driver's Log.

ANCILLARIES

Behind-the-Wheel Checklist

Designed as an aid to in-vehicle instruction, the materials in this booklet cover a wide range of basic driving maneuvers and provide an organized way of ensuring that students have either mastered a maneuver or require more practice. Also included in the booklet is a student progress chart for evaluating overall student competence.

Tests (Version A and Version B)

Blackline masters are provided to be assigned at the end of each chapter. Each test covers basically the same material in a different sequence.

SUPPLIERS

The organizations listed below supply materials and information relating to motor vehicles and driver education. The types of materials offered by each organization vary over time.

AAA
Traffic Safety Department
1000 AAA Drive
Heathrow, FL 32746

AAA Foundation for Traffic Safety
1440 New York Avenue, NW
Suite 201
Washington, DC 20005

Advanced Driving Skills Institute
4660 Brayton Terrace South
Palm Harbor, FL 34605

American Driver and Traffic Safety Education Association
c/o Indiana University of Pennsylvania
Highway Safety Center
Indiana, PA 15705

American Insurance Association
1130 Connecticut Avenue, NW
Washington, DC 20036

American Road and Transportation Builders
1010 Massachusetts Avenue, NW
Washington, DC 20001

Car Care Council
One Grand Lake Drive
Port Clinton, OH 43452

Consumers Union
101 Truman Avenue
Yonkers, NY 10703

Doron Precision Systems, Inc.
P.O. Box 400
Binghamton, NY 13902

Ford Motor Company
Department of Educational Affairs
The American Road
Dearborn, MI 48121

General Motors Corporation
Department of Public Relations
3044 West Grand Boulevard
Detroit, MI 48202

Institute of Transportation Engineers
525 School Street, SW
Suite 410
Washington, DC 20024

Insurance Institute for Highway Safety
1005 North Globe Road
Arlington, VA 22201

Mothers Against Drunk Driving (MADD)
511 East John Carpenter Freeway
Irving, TX 75062

National Safety Council
Traffic Department
1121 Spring Lake Drive
Itasca, IL 60143

Shell Oil Company
Community Activities Division
One Shell Plaza
Houston, TX 77001

Smith System, Inc.
1106 West Pioneer Parkway
Arlington, TX 76013

Students Against Destructive Decisions (SADD)
P.O. Box 800
Marlboro, MA 01752

Texas Department of Public Safety
P.O. Box 4087
Austin, TX 78773

Texas Transportation Institute
Communications Program
Suite 101 CE/TTI Tower
Texas A&M University
College Station, TX 77843

RESPONSIBLE DRIVING

Heathrow, Florida

 **Glencoe McGraw-Hill**

New York, New York   Columbus, Ohio   Woodland Hills, California   Peoria, Illinois

REVIEWERS

James Lewis, President
CALIFORNIA ASSOCIATION OF SAFETY EDUCATORS

Richard Mikulik, Driver Education Instructor
MISSION HIGH SCHOOL
SAN FRANCISCO, CALIFORNIA

Barbara Brody, Past President
AMERICAN DRIVER TRAFFIC SAFETY EDUCATION
ASSOCIATION (ADTSEA)

John Svensson, President
TRAINING AND RESEARCH INSTITUTE FOR
ADVANCED DRIVER DEVELOPMENT, INC. (TRIADD)
GUELPH, ONTARIO, CANADA

Pat Venditte, Driver Education Instructor
CORNHUSKER DRIVING SCHOOL
OMAHA, NEBRASKA

Thomas Cardarella, Driver Education Instructor
M & N DRIVING SCHOOL
ENFIELD, CONNECTICUT

Scott Callahan, Driver Education Instructor
KITTITAS HIGH SCHOOL
KITTITAS, WASHINGTON

Craig Dill, Driver Improvement Coordinator
CALIFORNIA STATE AUTO ASSOCIATION
SAN FRANCISCO, CALIFORNIA

Editorial and Production services by Visual Education Corporation,
Princeton, New Jersey

Glencoe/McGraw-Hill

*A Division of The **McGraw·Hill** Companies*

Copyright © 2000 by the American Automobile Association. All rights reserved. Originally
copyrighted © 1997, 1993, 1987, 1980, 1975, 1970, 1965, 1961, 1955, 1948, 1947, by the
American Automobile Association under the title *Sportsmanlike Driving.* Except as permitted
under the United States Copyright Act, no part of this publication may be reproduced or
distributed in any form or by any means, or stored in a database retrieval system, without
prior permission of the publisher.

Printed in the United States of America.

Send all inquiries to:
Glencoe/McGraw-Hill
21600 Oxnard Street, Suite 500
Woodland Hills, California 91367

ISBN: 0-02-653382-0 (Student's Edition; casebound)
2 3 4 5 6 7 8 9   071   05 04 03 02 01 00 99

ISBN: 0-02 653383-9 (Student's Edition; softbound)
2 3 4 5 6 7 8 9   071   05 04 03 02 01 00 99

COORDINATING AUTHOR

Dr. Francis C. Kenel
STAFF DIRECTOR OF TRAFFIC SAFETY (RETIRED)
AMERICAN AUTOMOBILE ASSOCIATION
HEATHROW, FLORIDA

CONSULTING AUTHORS

Dr. James Aaron
DRIVER PERFORMANCE CONSULTANT
PALM HARBOR, FLORIDA

Dr. John W. Palmer
ASSOCIATE PROFESSOR
ST. CLOUD STATE UNIVERSITY
ST. CLOUD, MINNESOTA

Dr. Maurice E. Dennis
COORDINATOR AND PROFESSOR
TEXAS A&M UNIVERSITY
COLLEGE STATION, TEXAS

Richard Russell
ADVANCED DRIVING CONCEPTS
DARTMOUTH, NOVA SCOTIA, CANADA

Charles A. Butler
DIRECTOR, SAFETY SERVICES
AAA TRAFFIC SAFETY DEPARTMENT
HEATHROW, FLORIDA

iii

PREFACE

Well, this is it. You're going to learn to drive, and you're probably in a big hurry to get behind the wheel. However, driving is something that you cannot rush into. There is a great deal of essential driving information that you need to know first. It's important that you understand that risk is always present for the driver but that good drivers learn more effectively to manage risk. Good drivers reduce risk by managing visibility, time, space, and the available traction. We want you to be a good driver.

We've spent many years working on safe driving strategies and attitudes and at the same time working with young people such as you who can't wait to drive. *Responsible Driving* has been written with you in mind. We want you to know the rules and the facts about driving, but we also want you to know why they are important. This book tells you the *What* and *How* about driving, and it always tells you the *Why*.

The American Automobile Association, which you probably know as the AAA or Triple A, is part of the team that helped put *Responsible Driving* together. The AAA is an organization that has the greatest resources in the world on driving. We have used these resources in *Responsible Driving* to help you understand what driving is all about.

As you begin reading *Responsible Driving,* you'll see that the first unit is titled "Starting with You." It begins that way because we care about you, the AAA cares about you, and we want you to care about yourself and those with whom you will share the roadway. You're at the beginning of a very big moment in your life—the day you get your driver's license. We're happy to have the opportunity to help you learn how to use it safely and responsibly.

DR. FRANCIS C. KENEL
DR. JAMES AARON
DR. JOHN W. PALMER
DR. MAURICE E. DENNIS
RICHARD RUSSELL
CHARLES A. BUTLER

CONTENTS

UNIT 3   Moving onto the Road   173

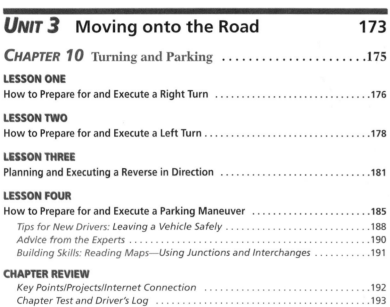

UNIT 4 Planning for Your Future   295

SPECIAL CONTENTS

CULTURAL CROSSROADS

TIPS FOR NEW DRIVERS

CHAPTER

CONNECTIONS

CHAPTER

BUILDING SKILLS: READING MAPS

BUILDING CURRICULUM SKILLS

UNIT 1

Starting with You

UNIT THEME

In Unit 1, students are challenged to explore how their own attitudes and behaviors affect their ability to be safe and responsible drivers. Students will learn how to prepare for their state driving test. They will learn to recognize the dangers posed by peer pressure, alcohol or other drug use, and underestimation of risk.

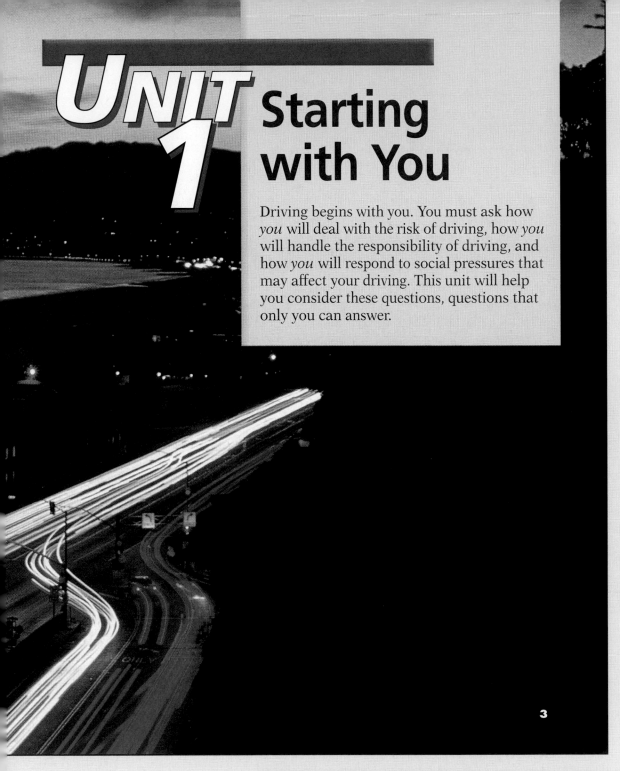

UNIT 1

Starting with You

Driving begins with you. You must ask how *you* will deal with the risk of driving, how *you* will handle the responsibility of driving, and how *you* will respond to social pressures that may affect your driving. This unit will help you consider these questions, questions that only you can answer.

3

TEACHING YOUR TEENS TO DRIVE

AAA's *Teaching Your Teens to Drive: A Partnership for Survival* helps new drivers, with their parents' assistance, develop their driving skills. The program is available as a videotape or CD-ROM, both with a handbook.

Assessing and Managing Risk Overview

THEME DEVELOPMENT Responsible drivers recognize that risk is a reality inherent in driving. The SIPDE process and Smith System offer organized strategies for minimizing risk. Driver education provides instruction on risk management and the responsibilities of a driver.

LESSON	PAGES	LESSON OBJECTIVES	STATE/LOCAL OBJECTIVES
1 The Highway Transportation System and Risk Management	6–10	1. Name the three parts of the highway transportation system. 2. Explain how and by whom the highway transportation system is regulated. 3. Describe five ways that you can reduce risk when using the highway transportation system.	
2 Understanding and Applying the SIPDE Process	11–14	1. Define and explain the steps of the SIPDE process, including the approximate time/distance needed to *search, identify, predict, decide,* and *execute.* 2. Describe how the SIPDE process can be applied while you are driving.	
3 Understanding and Using the Smith System	15–16	1. Explain the importance of the Smith System. 2. Describe the guidelines of the Smith System, including Aim high and look ahead, Keep your eyes moving, Get the big picture, Make sure others see you, and Leave yourself a way out.	
4 The Value of Taking a Driver Education Course	17–18	1. Describe the advantages to be gained from a driver education course regarding knowledge and the ability to manage time, space, and visibility. 2. Name some factors that might affect your ability to drive safely.	
Building Skills	19		
Review: Chapter Summary	20		
Chapter Test	21		

CHAPTER FEATURES	TCR COMPONENTS

CONNECTIONS
Math

Understanding the interstate highway numbering system.

Study Guide, p. 1
Lesson Plan, p. 3
Information Masters
1, 2, 5, and 8

TIPS **FOR NEW DRIVERS**

Identifying information about pedestrians, roadway markings and conditions, and other vehicles.

Study Guide, p. 2
Lesson Plan, p. 3
Information Master 19

Study Guide, p. 3
Lesson Plan, p. 4

ADVICE FROM THE EXPERTS

The importance of positioning the vehicle properly and using safety features in order to manage risk.

Study Guide, p. 4
Lesson Plan, p. 4

BUILDING SKILLS: READING MAPS

Using the Map Scale

PROJECTS

1. Read your state driver's manual.
2. Predict the behavior of other drivers.

Test A, pp. 1–2
Test B, pp. 1–2

OTHER PROGRAM RESOURCES

Testmaker software
Teaching Your Teens to Drive: Introduction, video or CD-ROM, AAA, 1998
Traffic charts

ADDITIONAL RESOURCES

Breaking the Accident Chain of Events, Video 403, AAA Foundation
Managing Space and Time for Safe Driving, Video 449, AAA Foundation
Heavenly Debate, Video 434, AAA Foundation
Using Your Eyes Effectively, Video 488, AAA Foundation
Young Driver Attitude Scale, Computer Program 371, AAA Foundation

---

NAME _____ DATE _____

Assessing and Managing Risk

TEST A

Read each statement below. If it is true, place a T in the space to the left of the statement. If the statement is false, place an F next to it.

__T__ 1. The highway transportation system consists of vehicles, roadways, and people.

__T__ 2. The main goal of the highway transportation system is to move people from place to place as efficiently and safely as possible.

__T__ 3. A moped is considered a motor vehicle.

__F__ 4. A vehicle equipped with an air bag is less safe in a collision than a vehicle equipped with only a safety belt.

__T__ 5. An interstate highway sign with an odd number means that the interstate goes in a north/south direction.

__T__ 6. An interstate sign numbered 90 means that the interstate goes in an east/west direction in the northern part of the United States.

__T__ 7. Federal, state, and local governments all work together to regulate the highway transportation system.

__T__ 8. About 35 percent of the deaths of 15- to 20-year-olds occur through vehicle crash injuries.

__T__ 9. One way of reducing the risk of possible injury in a collision is always to anticipate the actions of other drivers.

__F__ 10. The SIPDE process does not help you manage visibility, time, and space.

__F__ 11. The risk of being involved in a collision in any given year is 1 in 100.

__F__ 12. Good drivers need very little space between them and other vehicles because they have much better reactions than other drivers.

__F__ 13. More than half of all traffic deaths occur in single-car collisions.

__F__ 14. Your emotional state has very little effect on your ability to drive.

© AAA and Glencoe/McGraw-Hill

NAME _____ DATE _____

Look at the interstate highway signs below and write the letter of the sign that goes with the statement.

A   B   C   D

__C__ 15. This interstate highway goes in a north/south direction in the western United States.

__B__ 16. This is the most southern of the interstate highways above that goes in an east/west direction.

__D__ 17. Of the interstate highways above that go in an east/west direction, this one is in the most northern part of the United States.

__A__ 18. This interstate highway goes in a north/south direction in the eastern United States.

Select the phrase that best completes each sentence below. Write the letter of the answer you have chosen to the left of each statement.

__C__ 19. The SIPDE process includes
a. searching, identifying, positioning, dropping, and elevating.
b. aiming high, predicting, getting the big picture, and deciding.
c. searching, identifying, predicting, deciding, and executing.
d. keeping your eyes moving, leaving yourself an out, and predicting.

__d__ 20. When you use the Smith System in driving, you
a. get the big picture.
b. keep your eyes moving.
c. make sure others see you.
d. do all of the above.

__b__ 21. "Aim high" means
a. to keep your eyes moving.
b. to look 20 to 30 seconds ahead of you.
c. to always steer straight ahead.
d. none of the above.

22. What benefits can you gain by taking a driver education course?

Answers may include: Understanding the ways emotions and maturity affect driving; understanding

how to maneuver and control your car; getting insight into how drugs and alcohol affect driving;

knowledge of traffic laws and rules of the road; how to buy, insure, and maintain a car; knowledge of

how a car works; and what to do in case of an emergency on the road.

© AAA and Glencoe/McGraw-Hill

NAME _____ DATE _____

Assessing and Managing Risk

TEST B

Read each statement below. If it is true, place a T in the space to the left of the statement. If the statement is false, place an F next to it.

__T__ 1. The highway transportation system consists of motor vehicles, roadways, and people.

__T__ 2. A vehicle's performance, such as the ability to stop quickly, is determined in part by how the vehicle is cared for.

__F__ 3. Interstate highway signs with larger, odd numbers go in an east/west direction in the southern part of the United States.

__T__ 4. The rules governing vehicle registration, driver's licensing, and highway maintenance can be found in the National Highway Safety Act.

__F__ 5. The highway transportation system is regulated only by local agencies.

__T__ 6. State governments have the right to enact certain laws, such as the age at which a person is allowed to drive.

__F__ 7. The risk of being involved in a collision in any given year is 1 in 500.

__T__ 8. Turning on your low-beam headlights during daylight hours increases the distance your vehicle can be seen from 2,500 feet away to 4,700 feet.

__F__ 9. It is the responsibility of the vehicle manufacturer to keep your brakes in good working order.

__F__ 10. Good drivers need very little space between them and other vehicles because they have much better reactions than other drivers.

__F__ 11. You should confine your visual search while you are driving to what is directly in front of you.

__T__ 12. "Leave yourself a way out" is part of the Smith System.

__F__ 13. More than half of all traffic deaths occur in single-car collisions.

© AAA and Glencoe/McGraw-Hill

NAME _____ DATE _____

Look at the interstate highway signs below and write the letter of the sign that goes with the statement.

A   B   C   D

__A__ 14. This highway goes in a north/south direction in the eastern United States.

__B__ 15. This highway goes in an east/west direction in the southern United States.

__D__ 16. This highway goes in an east/west direction in the northern United States.

__C__ 17. This highway goes in a north/south direction in the western United States.

Write the letter of the answer you have chosen to the left of each question.

__d__ 18. What is one way to make sure that the other person sees you, as described in the Smith System?
a. Always drive with your low-beam headlights on.
b. Tap your brakes to let following drivers know you are stopping or slowing.
c. Signal your intention to turn.
d. All of the above.

__b__ 19. What does "aim high" mean?
a. Keep your eyes moving.
b. Look 20 to 30 seconds ahead of you.
c. Always steer straight ahead.
d. None of the above.

__a__ 20. What is a good example of "leaving yourself a way out," as described in the Smith System?
a. Position your car so that you have space in one of the lanes next to you and can move there to avoid a collision.
b. Have your brakes adjusted.
c. Always know the route that you will follow on a trip to avoid getting lost.
d. Keep your car seat clear in case you need to get out the other door if you get into a collision.

21. Describe The National Traffic and Motor Vehicle Safety Act.

The National Traffic and Motor Vehicle Safety Act requires vehicle manufacturers to build safety

features such as safety belts into their vehicles. The law requires manufacturers to correct vehicle

defects after a vehicle has been sold.

© AAA and Glencoe/McGraw-Hill

NAME _____ DATE _____

CHAPTER 1 Assessing and Managing Risk

STUDY GUIDE FOR CHAPTER 1   LESSON 1

The Highway Transportation System

A. The National Highway Safety Act controls the regulations for vehicle registration, road construction and maintenance, and driver licensing. What do you think the effects on the following would be if suddenly we had no National Highway Safety Act?

Roads and Highways: Inconsistent, possibly unsafe road construction and maintenance from state to state.

Drivers and Pedestrians: Dangerous conditions at intersections and on roads due to different laws from state to state.

Cars and Trucks: With different inspection standards from state to state, or no standards in some states, increased pollution and higher accident rates could occur.

B. Although each state has its own laws governing the use of motor vehicles, the federal government has also set national highway and driving standards. Tell by marking S or F next to the provision whether it is a state or a federal law.

___F___ **1.** Establishes 65 MPH as the maximum speed that may be driven anywhere.

___F___ **2.** Sets national standards for all motor vehicle equipment.

___S___ **3.** Regulates vehicle inspection.

___S___ **4.** Enforces traffic laws.

___F___ **5.** Tells what highway maintenance the state must provide.

___S___ **6.** Regulates vehicle registration.

___F___ **7.** Instructs automobile manufacturers about what safety devices they must provide.

___S___ **8.** Assigns points to driver's record for traffic violations.

___S___ **9.** Regulates driver licensing.

___F___ **10.** Requires the vehicle manufacturer to recall a vehicle and correct any defects discovered after a vehicle is sold.

C. FIND OUT MORE. Interview somebody you know who is a driver. Ask that person what he or she does personally to reduce risk when driving. What does the driver do to keep the vehicle in good, safe condition? What does she or he do to anticipate the actions of others? Do the driver and all passengers wear seat belts? Has the driver ever driven while very tired or sick? What has the driver done in the last year to improve his or her driving skills? Write your findings on a separate piece of paper.

NAME _____ DATE _____

STUDY GUIDE FOR CHAPTER 1   LESSON 2

Understanding and Applying the SIPDE Process

A. Driving is a complex task that involves many elements. Although you can become comfortable at the wheel only by practicing, learning a strategy that you can use right away will help you a lot. Name the elements of the SIPDE process, and write a brief description of each.

1. S   Search the roadway and offroad areas 20 to 30 seconds ahead for information that can help you select a planned path of travel.

2. I   Identify objects or conditions 12 to 15 seconds ahead that could interfere with planned path.

3. P   Predict any actions or changes in conditions that could increase the level of risk.

4. D   Decide what action to take 4 to 5 seconds ahead to reduce the level of risk.

5. E   Execute what you have decided to do.

B. For each sentence below, circle T if the statement is true and F if it is false. Correct each false statement in the space below.

1. You should look ahead 20 to 30 seconds on the roadway for information that can help you select your path of travel.   (T)   F

_____

2. Using the SIPDE process makes you a less safe driver because you are concentrating on the process, not on driving.   T   (F)

Using the SIPDE process makes you a safer driver.

3. Using the SIPDE process trains you to identify possible problems in the roadway at least 6 to 8 seconds ahead.   T   (F)

Using the SIPDE process trains you to identify problems in the roadway 12 to 15 seconds ahead.

4. The final step in the SIPDE process usually involves making a routine maneuver.   (T)   F

_____

5. The most important part of the SIPDE process is to practice applying it in your driving.   (T)   F

_____

C. FIND OUT MORE. Interview someone you know who drives. Ask the person what information he or she collects about the road while driving in order to avoid collisions. Does the person use the SIPDE process or a version of it?

Review student's work.

NAME _____ DATE _____

STUDY GUIDE FOR CHAPTER 1   LESSON 3

Understanding the Smith System

A. Give some examples of applying each of the Smith System habits. Imagine that you are actually driving. What will you be specifically looking for and doing?

Smith System Habit

Aim high and look ahead, not down.

Answers may include: Look ahead for curves, intersections, stop signs, stop lights, brake lights indicating traffic slowing, lanes closing ahead, traffic merging.

Keep your eyes moving.

Continually change what your eyes are looking at, from the road far ahead to close by, to the mirrors, to the speedometer, to the offroad areas, and back to the road.

Get the big picture.

Look at the whole scene: the flow of traffic, the pedestrian traffic, school buses, children, heavy traffic, weather conditions, signs.

Make sure that others can see you.

Drive with low-beam headlights on, stay out of other drivers' blind spots, tap your brake lights when slowing, signal intention to turn well in advance.

Leave yourself a way out.

Keep aware of all space around you. Have lane to left or right open in case you have to move to avoid a collision, and enough space in front to stop safely.

B. FIND OUT MORE. The next time you are in a vehicle, take notes on what some drivers do to make sure that other drivers see them. How do they communicate their intentions to other drivers? What special things do bus drivers or truck drivers do to be seen?

Review student's work.

_____

_____

_____

NAME _____ DATE _____

STUDY GUIDE FOR CHAPTER 1   LESSON 4

The Value of Taking a Driver Education Course

A. Driver education courses have many great benefits. What do you think the results would be in the long run, say in 20 years, on the following rates and statistics if there were no driver education courses?

1. Insurance rates   would increase greatly because of more accidents. This could make insurance too expensive for the average young person to purchase.

2. Accident rates   would increase greatly, especially for newer, younger drivers.

3. Drinking and driving conviction rates   would probably rise, especially for younger drivers, who might not learn about the reasons not to drink and drive.

4. Traffic deaths   would increase greatly, especially for younger drivers.

B. Describe briefly your personality as you think it will affect your driving. What is your maturity level? Do you get upset easily? What kinds of situations annoy you?

Review student's answers.

_____

_____

_____

C. FIND OUT MORE. Call a local vehicle insurance company and ask if you can take a few minutes to ask some questions. Ask what the insurance rates will be for you when you are ready to drive. Also, ask what the rates would be for someone your age who is not taking any driver education classes. What will the rates be when you are 25 years old? What are they for a person without driver education? What are they for someone convicted of driving while intoxicated?

Review student's work.

_____

_____

_____

_____

Assessing and Managing Risk

CHAPTER OVERVIEW

LESSON ONE

The parts of the highway transportation system are defined, and its regulation is explained. Students are introduced to the concept of reducing risk and managing visibility, time, and space.

LESSON TWO

The SIPDE process is defined and explained as an organized way to approach the driving task and to manage risk.

LESSON THREE

The Smith System is explained and related to SIPDE as a coordinated method of minimizing risk.

LESSON FOUR

The benefits of a driver education course are previewed, with an emphasis on a responsible approach to operating a vehicle, maintaining it, and understanding the emotional and physical factors that affect driving.

VOCABULARY

collision
highway transportation system
  (HTS)
margin of space
risk
SIPDE process
Smith System
visibility

CONCEPT OF THE DRIVING TASK

Explain that driving is not just a physical task. In fact, it is primarily a mental and social one. It is mental because responsible drivers must make sound judgments and decisions based on an intelligent assessment of the traffic situation; it is social because drivers share the roadway with other drivers and with pedestrians.

CHAPTER 1

Assessing and Managing Risk

Whenever you walk or ride on our nation's streets and roadways, you become part of the highway transportation system. It is important to learn how to use the system safely and responsibly.

CHAPTER 1   *Assessing and Managing Risk*   **5**

PRESENTING THE BIG IDEA ———

Individuals are not likely to make decisions that reduce risk unless they first recognize that risk is real.

INTRODUCING THE CHAPTER

What's on the Road Ahead?

Have students read the lesson titles and objectives. Briefly discuss the topic of each lesson. Tell students that in this chapter, they will be introduced to one of the most important driving skills: learning how to anticipate, minimize, and manage risk.

Background: The Larger Picture

The following 1997 statistics will help give students a sense of the ever-increasing size of the driving community and the risk that drivers face:

- more than 211 million registered vehicles in the United States
- more than 180 million licensed drivers in the United States
- more than 6.7 million police-reported collisions
- almost 42,000 traffic fatalities and more than 3.5 million disabling injuries

Relating to Prior Knowledge

Have students discuss what they know about risky driving situations and how they think a course in driver education will help them avoid these situations.

The Big Idea

Discuss students' reactions to the Big Idea statement. Suggest that they keep this idea in mind as they read Chapter 1.

The Highway Transportation System and Risk Management

(pages 6–10)

FOCUS

Objectives

- Name the three parts of the highway transportation system.
- Explain how and by whom the highway transportation system is regulated.
- Describe five ways that you can reduce risk when using the highway transportation system.

Resources

 Study Guide, page 1

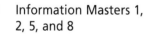 Traffic charts

Information Masters 1, 2, 5, and 8

Vocabulary

highway transportation system (HTS)
collision
risk
visibility
margin of space

Motivator

Ask students what they think the chances are that they will be involved in a collision each year that they drive. (Accept student answers without comment; 1 in 9.)

Pose the following situation and question: You will be driving daily from your home to an interstate highway to a city where you will drive through rush-hour traffic to a job. How can you reduce risk to yourself and others on the

LESSON ONE

OBJECTIVES

1. Name the three parts of the highway transportation system.
2. Explain how and by whom the highway transportation system is regulated.
3. Describe five ways that you can reduce risk when using the highway transportation system.

KEY TERMS

highway transportation system (HTS)
collision
risk
visibility
margin of space

The Highway Transportation System and Risk Management

A vast network of highways, streets, and roads crisscrosses the United States. Each day, millions of drivers travel these roadways.

As you prepare to join the other drivers on our nation's roads, remember that your goal is not just to learn to drive. It is to learn to drive safely and responsibly.

What Is the Highway Transportation System?

Motor vehicles, streets and highways, drivers, cyclists, and pedestrians—these are all part of the **highway transportation system,** or the **HTS.** The main goal of this complex system is to enable people and goods to move from place to place as safely and efficiently as possible.

Highway Concept and Design

Early American roads were built along the routes of existing trails and were constructed with little or no planning. Nowadays an army of engineers is needed just to plan today's more complex highways.

Engineers must plan the route of a highway, the construction of bridges along the route, exit and entrance ramps, where traffic signs are going to be located, and anything else pertaining to the highway. Curves must be planned carefully to make sure they are banked, or tilted, properly.

More than 206 million registered vehicles travel within the HTS, ranging from large vehicles, such as tractor-trailers and buses, to small vehicles, such as motorcycles and mopeds. There are vehicles of every imaginable description, from flashy new luxury cars to battered old pickup trucks.

Motor vehicles in the HTS differ in more than just appearance and age, however. They also vary in how they handle. A heavy truck, for instance, does not accelerate, steer, or brake the same way that a lightweight sports car does. How well an owner cares for his or her vehicle also affects its performance.

Motor vehicles vary, too, in safety features and in their ability to provide protection to drivers and passengers in case of a **collision,** or crash.

IT'S A FACT

When asked what their chances of being in a collision were during one year, slightly more than one-tenth of the drivers gave the correct answer: 1 in 9. Fewer than one-fourth of the respondents predicted the likelihood as 1 in 10 or greater, and almost one-third answered that the likelihood was 1 in 1,000. These responses are particularly meaningful since research shows that drivers who feel risk-free also feel that they have total control over whether or not they will be involved in a collision.

For example, drivers of solidly built vehicles equipped with air bags are far less vulnerable to injury than are motorcyclists or the drivers of most subcompact cars.

Roadways

Nearly 4 million miles of roadways link the states, counties, cities, and towns of the United States. These roadways range from multilane superhighways to twisting country roads to vehicle-choked city streets.

Some roadways are smooth and well maintained, while others are peppered with cracks, bumps, and potholes. Driving the great assortment of roads found in the HTS is a challenge, especially at night and in poor weather.

People

The people who use the highway transportation system include more than 180 million licensed drivers, passengers, cyclists, and pedestrians—in other words, just about everyone! Most of these people act responsibly when using the roads, whether driving, riding, or walking.

Some people, however, behave in an unsafe or irresponsible manner. They drive recklessly, cross streets without looking, and weave their bikes through heavy traffic. Such people pose a serious danger to other roadway users. This is just a sample of the behaviors that drivers must anticipate and learn to cope with.

How Is the HTS Regulated?

Federal, state, and local governments work together to regulate the highway transportation system. For example, federal law established a

FYI

During daylight hours, you can see the low beams of an oncoming vehicle from 4,700 feet away, or a little less than a mile. You can see an oncoming vehicle without headlights only from 2,500 feet away, or about half a mile.

Math

The way highways in the highway transportation system are numbered can tell you something about the road on which you're traveling. If you know your numbers, such signs can give additional information.

If the number on a highway sign is odd, it means that the road goes north and south. An even-numbered sign means that the road goes east and west.

Interstate numbers range from 4 to 99. The greater the even number, the farther north you are. The greater the odd number, the farther east you are.

Imagine that you are on Interstate 90. That's an even number and close to 99, so you are traveling either east or west in the northern part of the United States.

THE INTERNATIONAL SCENE

Canada

All vehicles manufactured since 1991 for sale in Canada must have daytime running lights (DRLs), which automatically turn on the low beams whenever the ignition is on. Statistics show that driving with these lights on reduces the risk of death as a result of a frontal crash by 28 percent.

CONNECTIONS
Math

To check student understanding, you may wish to ask the following: On which route would you be farther south—Route 80 or Route 90? (Route 80)

roadway you will be traveling? (Sample answer: Recognize risk is real; keep a well-maintained vehicle; anticipate the actions of other drivers and pedestrians; wear safety belts; drive with low-beam lights on; drive only when physically and mentally sound; develop and improve good driving skills; learn how to manage visibility, time, and space.)

TEACH

Explain

OBJECTIVE 1: Most students will have no difficulty understanding the makeup of the highway transportation system. However, many drivers do not understand how vehicle differences affect the safety of other drivers on the HTS. An important factor in managing risk is being aware of the positive and negative features of other vehicles on the roadway.

OBJECTIVE 2: Students should be aware that although all states follow the federal uniform standard laws, individual states, cities, and towns may also impose their own laws.

OBJECTIVE 3: Students may benefit from a discussion of minimizing risk to both themselves and other roadway users by taking such actions as these:

• recognizing and adjusting to the risk inherent in poor road or weather conditions
• maintaining the vehicle
• using safety belts to ensure that in the event of a collision, the driver and any passengers will have the best chance of survival
• ensuring that other drivers can see the vehicle that you are driving by keeping the low-beam headlights on at all times
• driving only when you are in good mental and physical condition
• constantly evaluating and improving driving skills and abilities
• effectively managing time, space, and visibility

Teaching Model

The purpose of this model is to help students begin to think about risk reduction, not to discuss passing rules.

Display this situation:

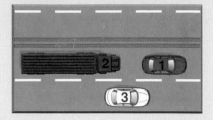

Tell students the following: You are in vehicle 1 traveling at 50 mph. Note that the truck behind you is following you too closely. Model the thinking process that you will go through to manage risk in this situation. (You will do the following.

• Recognize that it takes a truck almost twice as long to stop as it takes a passenger car; therefore, you would want to get out of the truck's way because it is following you too closely.

• Decide to move to the right-hand lane so that the truck can pass you.

• Speed up to put enough space between you and the car in the right-hand lane (vehicle 3) so that you can safely go in front of it.

• Signal to indicate to the drivers of both the car and the truck your intention to switch lanes.

• Then switch lanes when it is safe to do so.)

maximum speed limit of 55 miles per hour in 1974. This law was changed in 1995 to allow the individual states to set their own highway speed limits. Enforcing speed limits and other traffic laws is the job of state and local police.

Federal and State Requirements

To set uniform standards for various aspects of vehicle and driver safety, the federal government passed two other important laws.

The National Traffic and Motor Vehicle Safety Act requires automakers to build certain safety features, such as safety belts and shatterproof windows, into their motor vehicles. This law also requires manufacturers to correct vehicle defects discovered after vehicle models are sold.

The National Highway Safety Act established specific guidelines for state motor vehicle safety programs. Each state must follow these guidelines. They govern such matters as vehicle registration and inspection, driver licensing, traffic laws and traffic courts, and highway construction and maintenance.

The National Highway Safety Act allows each state to set its own statutes, or laws, that concern highway safety. Many of these statutes are of special interest to teenage drivers. In 12 states, for example, teens under a certain age—usually 17 or 18—are not allowed to drive at night. In other states, teenagers must be enrolled in high school before they can get and keep their driver's licenses.

Cities and towns, too, pass driving regulations that must be obeyed within their limits. For example, in many cities, drivers may turn right at red lights except where expressly prohibited.

◆ Risk is always present. The chances that you will be in a collision within the year are 1 in 9.

How Can You Reduce Risk Within the HTS?

Driving involves **risk**—the chance of injury to yourself or others and the chance of damage to vehicles and property. The first important step toward responsible driving is realizing that this risk is *real*—probably much more real than you think.

• In any given year, the likelihood of your being involved in a collision is about 1 in 9. Your chances of suffering an injury that is serious enough to disable you are about 1 in 83.

Driving Tip

Explain to students that a mature driver recognizes that there are risks involved in driving. Tell them that one way a driver can manage risk is by driving defensively and being alert to what other drivers might do.

- About 35 percent of the deaths of 15- to 20-year-olds occur through motor vehicle crash injuries.
- Eighty-five percent of traffic deaths occur in the first collision in which the vehicle's occupants are involved.
- More than 39 percent of vehicle occupant deaths in 1997 involved only one vehicle.

No matter how confident you may feel or how well you've mastered the basics of driving, the risk of being involved in a collision is always present. There are, however, actions you can take to maximize your control over driving situations and to minimize the risk.

Understanding and Reducing Risk

Many factors contribute to the degree of risk when you drive. Some are obvious, such as bad weather or poor roads. Others, such as the condition of your vehicle, may be less obvious, but they are just as important to consider.

Driving responsibly means assessing the risk and doing all you can to reduce or control it. Here are five ways to do that.

Keep your vehicle in top condition. Are your brakes working properly? Are your tires properly inflated and your windows clean? The better the condition of your vehicle, the more control you have when you're driving.

Anticipate the actions of others. Wise drivers drive defensively. They identify cues to behavior that help them predict how other roadway users will act or react. Because drivers and pedestrians often act without thinking or communicating, you must learn to search for clues.

Take steps to protect yourself and others. Wearing safety belts can save you and your passengers from death or serious injury. Turning on your low-beam headlights at all times, even during daylight hours if your vehicle is not equipped with automatic daytime running lights (DRLs), reduces risk by increasing the ability of others to see you.

Drive only when you're in sound physical and mental condition. Are you feeling alert and clearheaded? Are you concentrating on

◆ Most drivers overestimate their ability to manage risk and underestimate actual risk.

◆ Poor weather can be a contributing factor in the degree of risk that drivers face.

CHAPTER 1   Assessing and Managing Risk   **9**

Ask

Ask students to discuss the risks involved in remaining in front of the truck.

Read

Have students read Lesson 1 to learn their connection to the highway transportation system, the factors that drivers must be aware of to use the system safely, and ways in which drivers can anticipate and manage risk as they use the HTS.

ASSESS

Guided Practice

Have students answer the Lesson 1 Review questions. The answers are provided below.

Reteaching

Have students work together in groups of four to list risk management strategies and to brainstorm situations in which those strategies might forestall a dangerous driving situation. If students have difficulty recalling risk management ideas, encourage them to locate the ideas again in their textbooks.

After groups have completed this task, have them take part in a class discussion about the benefits of risk management strategies. Encourage group participants to share what they have developed in the group with the rest of the class.

MEETING STUDENT DIVERSITY

Limited English Proficiency

Substitute more basic words for a student who has a limited vocabulary or who has difficulty understanding terminology. For example, substitute *seeing and being seen* for *visibility*.

Enrichment

Assign the Study Guide for Lesson 1. The Find Out More section encourages students to expand their basic learning of the lesson concepts.

CLOSE

Summarize

Return to the first part of the Motivator question. Discuss the implications of students' initial perceptions of the likelihood that they might be involved in a collision during a year. Help students summarize the meaning of perceived versus actual risk by discussing this question:

How does it benefit you as a driver to be aware that the likelihood that you will be involved in a collision during a year is 1 in 9?

Discuss the situation that was developed in the second part of the Motivator section. Recall students' initial responses, and have students add what they have learned in this lesson to their risk-management ideas.

DRIVER'S LOG

Discuss how following each tip will reduce risk. For example, identifying vehicles or pedestrians that might enter the driver's path reduces the risk of being surprised by an unanticipated maneuver.

WHAT WOULD YOU DO?

Sample answer: Bad weather and poor visibility contribute to risk. Wear a safety belt, and turn on your headlights.

FYI

Many commuters enjoy the benefits of carpooling, or ridesharing. By driving less frequently, an individual in a car pool cuts the cost of gas, oil, vehicle upkeep, tolls, and parking. Having fewer cars on the road also makes carpooling an environmentally sound idea.

WHAT WOULD YOU DO?

What factors are contributing to risk? What steps can you take to reduce risk?

---

your driving—or thinking about tomorrow night's date? To drive safely, you need to be 100 percent behind the wheel.

Make a conscious effort to develop your driving skills. Working to improve your driving habits and abilities will help protect you and your passengers.

Managing Visibility, Time, and Space

As you learn to drive, you will learn numerous guidelines to help you make sound driving decisions. One basic principle underlies virtually all of these guidelines: the wise management of visibility, time, and space.

Visibility refers to what you can see from behind the wheel and how well you see it and to the ability of others—pedestrians and other drivers—to see you. When you are driving, reduced visibility means increased risk. On the other hand, when you take steps to increase visibility, you decrease risk.

Time and space come into constant play when you are driving. Time can refer to the ability to judge your speed and the speed of other vehicles. It can also refer to how long it will take your vehicle or another vehicle to stop or intersect paths.

Space refers to distance. Wise drivers keep a **margin of space** between their vehicles and other vehicles when they drive. This allows them room to maneuver.

You will read about visibility, time, and space throughout this book, because all three are crucial elements in safe and responsible driving. In fact, managing the various factors related to visibility, time, and space is the key to reducing risk when you drive.

Lesson 1 Review

1. What are the three parts of the highway transportation system?
2. Who regulates the highway transportation system? Give examples.
3. What are some ways that you can reduce driving risk when using the highway transportation system?

Lesson 1 Review

Answers

1. Motor vehicles, roadways, and people.
2. Federal, state, and local governments; federal sets uniform standards for vehicle safety; state and local pass driving regulations for their state or city limits and enforce traffic laws passed by the federal government.
3. Keep your vehicle in top condition; anticipate the actions of others; take steps to protect yourself and others; drive only when you are in sound physical and mental condition; make an effort to develop driving skills.

Understanding and Applying the SIPDE Process

Driving is challenging because you need to do many tasks at once. You have to control the vehicle, watch the roadway and off-road areas, read signs, and be alert for the sudden actions of other road users.

Although as a young driver you will have good reflexes, you will not have the skills of experienced drivers. You need to develop visual skills, decision-making skills, and vehicle-handling skills to become a safe driver.

Because you have so much to keep track of when you're driving, it is helpful to use an organized system to gather and process information. An organized system will help you make sound decisions and reduce driving risk.

What Is SIPDE?

One easy-to-use system for dealing with the challenge of driving is known as the **SIPDE process**—short for *search, identify, predict, decide,* and *execute.* SIPDE is a five-step process.

1. *Search* the roadway and the off-road areas 20 to 30 seconds ahead for information that can help you plan a path of travel. (Twenty to 30 seconds equals about 1½ to 2 blocks at 25 to 30 mph in the city and about ⅓ to ½ mile at 50 to 65 mph on the highway.)
2. *Identify* objects or conditions within 12 to 15 seconds ahead that could interfere with your planned path of travel.
3. *Predict* what actions or changes in conditions on or near the roadway could increase the level of risk.

OBJECTIVES

1. Define and explain the steps of the SIPDE process, including the approximate time/distance needed to *search, identify, predict, decide,* and *execute.*
2. Describe how the SIPDE process can be applied while you are driving.

KEY TERM

SIPDE process

◆ *The SIPDE process can help you to manage risk in many different situations.*

Driving Tip

Explain to students that the SIPDE process will be very important to them when they begin driving. The steps in this process should be considered in *every* driving situation, not only in ones where potential conflict might arise. Explain that good drivers use this process instinctively because it gives them an organized way to think about the driving task. Also stress that, as in all driving procedures that students will learn, SIPDE will take time and practice before it becomes instinctive to them.

Understanding and Applying the SIPDE Process

(pages 11–14)

FOCUS

Objectives

- Define and explain the steps of the SIPDE process, including the approximate time/distance needed to *search, identify, predict, decide,* and *execute.*
- Describe how the SIPDE process can be applied while you are driving.

Resources

📁 Study Guide, page 2

📁 Traffic charts

📁 Information Master 19

Vocabulary

SIPDE process

Motivator

Pose the following: You are driving on a one-way, tree-lined, shaded residential street behind two bicyclists. They are in the middle of the street, and both sides of the street are occupied by parked motor vehicles. You can see beyond the bicyclists. They are approaching a sun-drenched intersection. What plan of action will you take to assess and manage this situation? (Students may mention search the roadway to choose a planned path of travel; identify objects that could interfere with your path; predict what the bicyclists might do; decide on the actions you will take; execute your decision.)

TEACH

Explain

OBJECTIVE 1: Students should have little difficulty remembering the individual steps that the SIPDE acronym stands for.

OBJECTIVE 2: Students will benefit from understanding that the SIPDE process gives drivers time to react to a situation and thereby reduce risk.

Teaching Model

Display this situation:

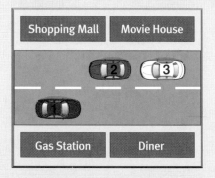

Tell students the following: You are in vehicle 1 traveling east; vehicles 2 and 3 are traveling west. Model the thinking process that you will go through to manage this situation. (You will do the following.

- Search the roadway ahead and to the side, and check your rearview mirror.
- Identify the fact that the broken lines in the road mean oncoming vehicles are permitted to make a left turn or vehicles behind you may pass. Note that there are businesses on your right.
- Predict that the driver of vehicle 2 might make a left turn into the gas station.
- Decide that you will slow down a little in anticipation.
- Execute your plan.)

◆ *Use your rearview and side mirrors to help you search all around your vehicle.*

4. *Decide* what action or actions to take (such as reduce speed, increase speed, steer, brake, or steer and brake simultaneously) at least 4 to 5 seconds ahead of time to control or reduce risk.
5. *Execute* your decision.

Let's see how you can use the SIPDE process to manage visibility, time, and space.

Search

When you search, you should try to gather as much information as possible about what is happening on or near the roadway.

Use a systematic search pattern to gather information. First, search the road 20 to 30 seconds ahead, then look to the sides. Then glance in your rearview and sideview mirrors to check for traffic behind you. Next, check the sides of the road again. Then again survey the road ahead for ongoing and oncoming traffic.

Identify

To identify information important to you as a driver, you need to do more than simply look. You have to think about what you're looking for. Your aim is to identify as early as possible any objects or conditions that could become a threat to your path of travel.

Much as a detective investigates a crime scene seeking important clues, a driver needs to investigate the roadway and identify possible problems as far in advance as possible—at least 12 to 15 seconds ahead.

Suppose you are driving on a narrow two-way street in a residential neighborhood. Vehicles are parked along the street, vehicles are behind you, vehicles are coming toward you in the other lane, and people are on the sidewalk. Along your side of the street, you identify a young girl on a bicycle. As you get nearer to her, you can see that she is wobbling and having trouble steering the bicycle.

FOR NEW DRIVERS

Identifying Information

Identify these objects and conditions as you drive:
- vehicles, pedestrians, or objects that are in your path or could enter your path
- vehicles, pedestrians, or objects close to the back or sides of your vehicle
- vehicles, objects, or roadway features that limit your visibility and may conceal objects or conditions
- signs, signals, and roadway markings
- roadway surface conditions

State BY State

Some states offer driver examinations in languages other than English. In these states, a qualified interpreter can administer the driver's test. If your state offers this alternative, informing students of this option may allay anxiety about taking the driving test for students for whom English is a second language.

Predict

As you search the roadway and note the position of vehicles, pedestrians, and objects, you try to predict what might happen and prepare for it.

In the situation with the young girl on the bicycle, you might predict the possibility of her veering into your path or falling off her bike in front of your vehicle.

Decide

Once you have identified a potentially threatening object or condition and predicted what might happen, you can decide how best to minimize the risk of a collision.

Keep in mind that most situations allow you a choice of actions. As with any decision, you need to weigh the possibilities. What are the likely consequences of the actions you're considering? Which actions will be most effective in minimizing risk to yourself and others? The purpose of using the SIPDE process is to give yourself as much time as possible to make a wise decision.

What will you decide to do as you get closer to the girl on the bike? Remember that a slight change of speed or position is usually better than a major change in either speed or position.

You could steer closer to oncoming vehicles while passing her. You could tap your horn lightly to warn the girl that you are behind her. You could reduce your speed. You decide to combine all three of these actions in order to minimize risk.

Execute

The final step in the SIPDE process is to execute the decision you have made. In most instances, executing a decision simply means making a routine maneuver. Occasionally, however, you may have to take some kind of emergency action.

Here are the steps you would execute to avoid colliding with the girl on the bicycle. First, slow down and prepare to stop if necessary. Next, wait for a break in the oncoming traffic. Then, lightly tap your horn. Honking loudly might frighten the girl into losing control of her bike.

Energy Tips

Use the SIPDE process to help you judge when to reduce speed or increase following distance and thereby avoid unnecessary stops. Each time you stop and then accelerate again, you burn extra fuel.

◆ *Bicyclists and parked vehicles present potentially threatening conditions to the driver.*

Ask

Ask students to discuss the steps they would take if they were driving a vehicle that was behind vehicle 1.

Read

Have students read Lesson 2 to develop an understanding of how the SIPDE process provides an organized method of gathering and processing the information needed to make sound driving decisions and to reduce driving risk.

ASSESS

Guided Practice

Have students answer the Lesson 2 Review questions. The answers are provided below.

Reteaching

Pair a more able student with one who is experiencing difficulty with this lesson. Present them with the following situation, and ask them to demonstrate how the SIPDE process would help them assess and manage potential risk:

You are in vehicle 1. Vehicle 2 is disabled. Vehicle 3 is moving out of its lane to pass vehicle 2. A pedestrian is standing at X.

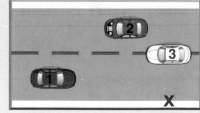

MEETING STUDENT DIVERSITY

Visually Impaired

Students who wear corrective eyeglasses should be cautioned to keep an extra pair of glasses in the vehicle. They should also be advised against wearing dark glasses or tinted contact lenses when driving at night.

TIPS FOR NEW DRIVERS

Discuss how following each tip will reduce risk. For example, identifying vehicles or pedestrians that might enter the driver's path reduces the risk of being surprised by an unanticipated maneuver.

Enrichment

Assign the Study Guide for Lesson 2. The Find Out More section encourages students to expand their basic learning of the lesson concepts.

CLOSE

Summarize

Return to the Motivator question, and discuss the situation again in light of what students have learned about the SIPDE process. Have them describe what they would recognize in the search and identify steps, predict what might happen, and explain how they would decide to react in order to minimize risk. Compare this analysis with their initial response to the situation, and discuss how the SIPDE process helped them organize their thoughts.

DRIVER'S LOG

How will you use the SIPDE process to help you manage time, space, and visibility when you drive?

WHAT WOULD YOU DO?

Sample answer: First, search the intersection to gather information. Next, identify potential hazards such as the vehicle coming from the right. Then predict the possibility that other vehicles or pedestrians might enter the intersection and collide with you. Decide what actions you could take to avoid a collision in such a situation. If necessary, execute these actions at the proper time.

SAFETY TIPS

"Better to be safe than sorry" is a maxim with special relevance for drivers. Never assume that a driver, cyclist, or pedestrian sees you and will not enter your path of travel. When appropriate, tap your horn or flash your lights. Always be prepared to steer or brake to avoid a collision.

Using the SIPDE process, explain how you would manage risk in this situation.

Finally, cautiously pass the bicyclist, allowing her as much space as possible. By waiting for a break in the traffic flow before steering around the girl, you will minimize the risk of colliding with an oncoming vehicle.

Applying the SIPDE Process

The SIPDE process fosters safe driving by enabling you to manage visibility, time, and space. While it is important to understand what the process is, it is far more important to practice applying it.

When you're behind the wheel, simply knowing what the letters SIPDE stand for won't help you drive safely. What *will* help you is making the principles of this process an automatic part of your own thinking—and driving.

For example, you can minimize risk by using the SIPDE process to identify threatening objects or conditions as far in advance as possible. The sooner you realize that you may be faced with a threatening situation, the sooner you can take action to reduce the risk.

Similarly, you can keep threatening objects or conditions apart by using the SIPDE process to help you separate one from another. For instance, suppose you are driving along a two-lane road. Up ahead, you see a bus approaching. At the same time you also see a group of boys walking along your side of the road. Rather than pass both the boys and the bus at the same time, you should adjust your speed so that you pass each one separately. By passing them separately in this way, you have simplified the situation and reduced the risk of a collision.

Lesson 2 Review

1. What are the steps of the SIPDE process?
2. How can the SIPDE process be applied while driving?

Lesson 2 Review

Answers

1. The steps are search, identify, predict, decide, and execute.
2. *Search* the roadway for information to help select a planned path of travel; *identify* objects or conditions that could interfere with that path; *predict* what actions or changes in conditions on or near the roadway could increase the level of risk; *decide* what action or actions to take to minimize risk; and *execute* that decision.

Understanding and Using the Smith System

Like the SIPDE process, the **Smith System** is a series of principles designed to help you drive safely and defensively.

What Is the Smith System?

The Smith System consists of five driving guidelines, which are discussed in the following sections. Understanding and using these guidelines is far more important than memorizing their exact wording.

Aim High and Look Ahead, Not Down

Look well ahead of your vehicle as you drive. Do not look down at the road directly in front of you. As a general rule, try to look about 20 to 30 seconds ahead. Remember that 20 to 30 seconds ahead means about 1½ to 2 blocks at 25 to 30 mph in the city and about ⅓ to ½ mile at 50 to 65 mph on the highway. Note that aiming high and looking ahead is similar to the first step, search, in SIPDE.

Keep Your Eyes Moving

Roadway and off-road conditions are always changing. Search the scene constantly. Stay alert for changes on or near the roadway or potentially dangerous conditions that might require you to adjust the speed or position of your vehicle.

Get the Big Picture

Search the whole scene, not just a part of it. As you approach an intersection, for example, you need to search for vehicles and pedestrians

◆ *Spot possible dangers early by aiming high and looking well ahead, not down.*

CHAPTER 1   *Assessing and Managing Risk*   **15**

LESSON THREE

OBJECTIVES
1. Explain the importance of the Smith System.
2. Describe the guidelines of the Smith System, including Aim high and look ahead, Keep your eyes moving, Get the big picture, Make sure others see you, and Leave yourself a way out.

KEY TERM
Smith System

FOCUS

Objectives
- Explain the importance of the Smith System.
- Describe the guidelines of the Smith System, including Aim high and look ahead, Keep your eyes moving, Get the big picture, Make sure others see you, and Leave yourself a way out.

Resources
📁 Study Guide, page 3
📁 Traffic charts

Vocabulary
Smith System

Motivator
Pose the following: You are driving through a residential neighborhood with many children playing in it. What can you do in addition to using SIPDE to manage risk? (Students may mention look well ahead; scan the roadway for possible changes; make sure others see you; plan a way out of possible risk.)

TEACH

Explain
OBJECTIVE 1: Emphasize that the Smith System steps take more time to implement than to read about or recite.

OBJECTIVE 2: Explain that the Smith System, like the SIPDE process, is an organizational skill.

Driving Tip

Explain that the Smith System and the SIPDE process are not mutually exclusive but should be used in conjunction with each other. Tell students that both of these methods provide them with an organized way of approaching the driving task.

Teaching Model

Describe the following: As you approach a four-way intersection, you see pedestrians, a bicyclist, and several vehicles approaching from different directions. Model your thinking process. (You see the possibility that the bicyclist or the pedestrians might enter the roadway. You note the vehicles and look for their drivers to signal their intentions.)

Ask

What if the cyclist suddenly enters your intended path of travel?

Read

Have students read Lesson 3 to learn how to use the Smith System.

ASSESS

Guided Practice

Have students answer the Lesson 3 Review questions. The answers are provided below.

Reteaching

Have groups brainstorm risks that each step of the Smith System can forestall.

Enrichment

Assign the Study Guide for Lesson 3. The Find Out More section encourages students to expand their basic learning of the lesson concepts.

CLOSE

Summarize

Return to the Motivator question. Discuss how using the Smith System would change students' initial answers.

DRIVER'S LOG

Which step in the Smith System is the most difficult one for you to understand how to implement? How will you overcome this difficulty?

◆ Driving with your low-beam headlights on insures that others will be able to see you.

WHAT WOULD YOU DO?

How would you use the Smith System in this situation?

16 UNIT 1 *Starting with You*

moving in all directions, for traffic-control devices, and for anything that might block your vision or otherwise increase risk.

Make Sure Others See You

Communicate with drivers and pedestrians. If your vehicle is not equipped with automatic daytime running lights, drive with your low-beam headlights on, even during daylight hours. Position your vehicle so that others can see you, signal your intention to turn, and tap the brake pedal so that your brake lights warn following drivers that you're slowing or stopping.

Leave Yourself a Way Out or a Margin of Safety

Always leave yourself a path of escape—a way to avoid a collision. Position your vehicle so that you keep a margin of space around it. In the earlier example of the girl riding the bicycle, for example, leaving yourself a way out meant waiting for a break in the oncoming traffic before steering around her.

Lesson *3* Review

1. What is the importance of the Smith System?
2. What are the guidelines of the Smith System?

WHAT WOULD YOU DO?

Sample answer: Aim high and look ahead, keep your eyes moving, make sure other drivers see you, and leave yourself a path of escape.

Lesson *3* Review

Answers

1. A series of principles designed to help you drive safely and defensively.
2. Aim high and look ahead, not down; keep your eyes moving; get the big picture; make sure others see you; leave yourself a way out or a margin of safety.

The Value of Taking a Driver Education Course

The responsibility for operating your vehicle safely is yours. Driver education will help you meet that responsibility.

What Can You Gain from a Driver Education Course?

Driver education helps you become an alert and knowledgeable driver capable of dealing successfully with a wide range of driving situations.

Knowledge

Through driver education, you will gain:
- an understanding of the ways in which your personality, emotions, and maturity affect your driving.
- an understanding of how to maneuver and control your vehicle so as to minimize risk in different driving environments.
- an insight into the ways in which alcohol and other drugs impair driving and a knowledge of the penalties for their use.
- a knowledge of traffic laws, rules of the road, signs and signals, and roadway markings.
- a foundation of consumer information, such as guidelines for buying, insuring, and maintaining a vehicle and tips for trip planning.
- an understanding of how a vehicle works.
- a knowledge of what to do in case of emergency.
- an awareness of limiting factors for yourself and your vehicle.

Ability to Manage Visibility, Time, and Space

Driver education will increase your awareness of the roadway and its surroundings. You will learn how to better manage visibility, time, and space. You'll learn to better maximize your own safety as well as that of your passengers, other drivers, and pedestrians.

◆ Driver education will help you learn to become a responsible driver.

IT'S A FACT

Teenage drivers are both inexperienced behind the wheel and immature—key factors that contribute to their high crash risk. Teenage licensure ages vary from state to state; statistics show that delayed licensing reduces teenage crash rates considerably. Age (maturity) and experience factors play a major role in crash risk.

OBJECTIVES

1. Describe the advantages to be gained from a driver education course regarding knowledge and the ability to manage time, space, and visibility.
2. Name some factors that might affect your ability to drive safely.

LESSON FOUR

The Value of Taking a Driver Education Course

(pages 17–18)

FOCUS

Objectives

- Describe the advantages to be gained from a driver education course, regarding knowledge and the ability to manage time, space, and visibility.
- Name some factors that might affect your ability to drive safely.

Resources

📁   Study Guide, page 4

Motivator

What must you know besides how to operate a vehicle to be a safe driver? (Students may mention that you must understand emotions, traffic laws, and vehicle maintenance.)

TEACH

Explain

OBJECTIVE 1: Explain that an A or a B in a driver education course may entitle a student to a discount on motor vehicle insurance.

OBJECTIVE 2: Have students discuss in more detail some of the factors that might interfere with their ability to drive.

Teaching Model

Describe the following: You are picking up a friend to drive to a meeting. You're angry because the friend is late. Model your thinking
continued on page 18

Have students discuss factors that might help manage risk.

process. (You recognize that anger can increase driving risk; you express your anger to your friend in words and not through driving.)

Ask

How can you profit from controlling emotional situations?

Read

Have students read Lesson 4 to preview their learning in driver education.

ASSESS

Guided Practice

Have students answer the Lesson 4 Review questions. The answers are provided below.

Reteaching

Have groups create a five-point TV ad promoting driver education as more than learning how to operate a vehicle.

Enrichment

Assign the Study Guide for Lesson 4. The Find Out More section encourages students to expand their basic learning of the lesson concepts.

CLOSE

Summarize

Return to the Motivator question. Discuss with students how their ideas about driving were changed by this lesson.

DRIVER'S LOG

What factors affecting responsible driving had never occurred to you before?

ADVICE FROM THE EXPERTS

Dr. Francis C. Kenel
Staff Director of Safety (Retired), AAA

Risk means the chance of injury, damage, or loss. The purpose of this book is to help you develop the knowledge, skills, and habits that can enable you to manage risk.

The most important skill of good drivers is positioning the vehicle so that their ability to see and the ability of others to see them is maximized. When a vehicle is positioned properly, adjusting speed becomes easier. Equally important is using safety belts and restricting driving if you are not in top physical condition.

Driver education will help you evaluate and respond to the constantly changing driving environment more effectively. You will learn how to better manage and minimize risk by thinking ahead and by preparing for threatening situations that may develop.

Awareness of Limiting Factors

To become a safe and responsible driver, you need more than driving skill. You also need to understand that there are factors that can seriously interfere with your ability to drive, such as:

- the feeling that there is little or no risk involved in driving and that if a collision occurs, it's "the other person's fault."
- the effects of an illness or injury—or the side effects of the medicine you may be taking for it.
- your emotional state.
- the effects of alcohol and other drugs.

The knowledge you gain through driver education and the experience you acquire behind the wheel will develop your driving skills and decision-making abilities. How you use these skills and abilities, however, is up to you. Only you can decide to be a *responsible* driver.

WHAT WOULD YOU DO?

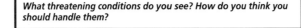

What threatening conditions do you see? How do you think you should handle them?

Lesson 4 Review

1. How can a driver education course be of value to you?
2. What factors might interfere with your ability to drive safely?

WHAT WOULD YOU DO?

Sample answer: Threatening conditions include possible merging traffic, reduced space, and construction workers and equipment. Use the SIPDE process.

Lesson 4 Review

Answers

1. Provide you with knowledge of vehicles; develop your ability to make sound driving decisions; provide awareness of emotional and physical factors that can impede driving ability; provide knowledge about vehicle maintenance and traffic laws.
2. Your emotional state; effects of illness or injury; side effects of medications; effects of alcohol and other drugs; the feeling that there is little or no risk involved in driving.

Using the Map Scale

People drive to get from one place to another. But they don't always know how to get there or how far they will have to drive. One way to make sure of your destination and the distance you'll need to travel is to use a road map.

Suppose you want to drive from San Jacinto, California, to Indio, California. You'll travel north on highway 79 to Route 10 and then southwest to Indio. Now you know how you're going to drive there, but how can you determine approximately how many miles you'll be traveling?

Look at the map scale to help you figure out the distance. The numbers along the top show the distance in miles. The scale shows you that 1 inch on the map is equal to about 25 miles.

You can use a ruler or a piece of string to estimate your traveling distance. Just find out how many inches long your route on the map is, and then multiply by 25.

Try It Yourself

1. About how far is it from San Jacinto to Indio along highways 79 and 10?
2. If you travel at an average speed of 50 miles an hour, how long will it take to get from San Jacinto to Indio?
3. Driving at the same average speed, how long will it take you to get from Perris to La Jolla?

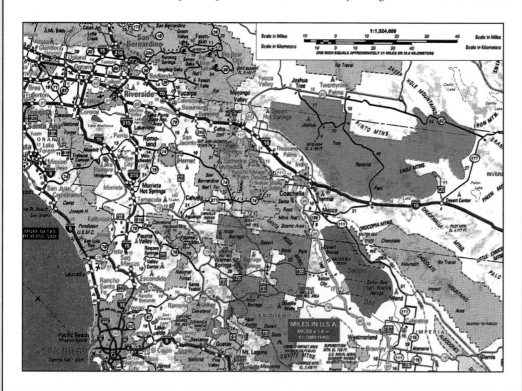

Objective

Demonstrate an ability to use a map scale to determine distance.

Teaching the Skill

- Be sure students understand that the distances should be measured to and from the dot symbols on the map that indicate cities or towns.
- Tell students that some maps have a miles-to-kilometers ratio rather than a miles-to-inches ratio. In that case, they will need to measure to determine if the scale represents an inch.
- Alert students to the fact that maps differ in terms of the ratio of miles to inches or of kilometers to centimeters.

ANSWERS TO
Try It Yourself Questions

1. about 64 miles
2. about $1\frac{1}{4}$ hours
3. about $1\frac{3}{4}$ hours

CHAPTER SUMMARY

Key Points

Have students read the Key Points to review the major concepts of the chapter.

PROJECTS

Cooperative Learning:

Students will benefit by working with a partner on one or both projects. When the assignment is completed, the whole class will profit by sharing and comparing results.

CHAPTER 1 REVIEW

KEY POINTS

Lesson One

1. Motor vehicles, roadways, and people make up the highway transportation system. The main goal of this system is to enable people and goods to move from place to place as safely and as efficiently as possible.
2. Federal, state, and local governments work together to regulate the highway transportation system.
3. Five ways that you can reduce driving risk are to keep your vehicle in top condition, anticipate the actions of others, take steps to protect yourself and others, drive only when you're in sound physical and mental condition, and make a conscious effort to develop your driving skills.

Lesson Two

1. SIPDE is short for *search, identify, predict, decide,* and *execute.*
2. Using SIPDE, drivers search the roadway and off-road areas 20 to 30 seconds ahead for information that can help them select a planned path of travel, identify objects or conditions 12 to 15 seconds ahead that could interfere with their planned path of travel, predict what actions or changes in conditions on or near the roadway could increase the level of risk, decide at least 4 to 5 seconds ahead what action or actions to take to control or reduce risk, and then execute their decision.

Lesson Three

1. The Smith System is a series of principles designed to help you drive safely and defensively.
2. There are five guidelines to the system. Aim high and look ahead. Keep your eyes moving. Search the whole scene to get the big picture. Make sure others see you. Leave yourself a path of escape in order to avoid a collision.

Lesson Four

1. Through a driver education course you can gain a knowledge of vehicles and driving and develop your ability to manage visibility, time, and space.
2. You can become aware of factors that can seriously interfere with driving ability, such as your emotional state, the effects of an illness or injury, or the effects of alcohol and drugs.

PROJECTS

1. Obtain a copy of your state driver's manual. Read the table of contents, then take some time to skim through the book. What topics are emphasized? What charts and illustrations are included? Are sample test questions included?
2. As a passenger, identify objects on or near the road ahead. What actions might you take to minimize driving risk? Try to predict what other drivers will do. Compare your predictions with what actually happens.

Search the Glencoe Web site to find statistics on the safety and driving issues in your state.
drivered.glencoe.com

Visit Glencoe's Driver Education Web site for student activities that relate to this chapter.
drivered.glencoe.com

CHAPTER TEST

Write the letter of the answer that best completes each sentence.

1. The highway transportation system is made up of
   a. motor vehicles, people, and buildings.
   b. roadways, people, and motor vehicles.
   c. cars, trains, and airplanes.

2. Searching the road 20 to 30 seconds ahead
   a. is equal to looking about ½ mile ahead at 25 to 30 mph in the city.
   b. is equal to looking about ⅓ to ½ mile ahead at 50 to 65 mph on the highway.
   c. is equal to looking about ½ block ahead at 25 to 30 mph in the city.

3. Driving with your headlights on during daylight hours
   a. increases your chances of being seen.
   b. increases engine efficiency.
   c. allows you to pass in a no-passing zone.

4. When you gather information about the roadway and surroundings, you
   a. execute.
   b. predict.
   c. search.

5. Under the National Traffic and Motor Vehicle Safety Act, automakers must
   a. provide for vehicle registration.
   b. build safety features into their vehicles.
   c. offer a choice of models to customers.

6. Risk in driving
   a. does not pertain to good drivers.
   b. depends on the confidence of the driver.
   c. is always present.

7. The Smith System
   a. is a three-step process.
   b. is regulated by the National Motor Vehicle Safety Act.
   c. are principles that help you drive safely.

8. Driver education can provide you with
   a. a knowledge of the rules of the road.
   b. discounts on vehicle purchases.
   c. automobile insurance.

9. The HTS is regulated by
   a. the National Highway Safety Act.
   b. the FBI.
   c. federal, state, and local governments.

10. *Visibility* refers to your ability to
    a. see and be seen.
    b. judge the speed of your vehicle.
    c. drive without wearing eyeglasses.

Write the word or phrase that best completes each sentence.

Smith System	designers	SIPDE
visibility	HTS	

11. The goal of the _____ is to enable people and goods to move safely and efficiently.

12. When you drive, reduced _____ means increased risk.

13. "Make sure others see you" is a basic principle of the _____.

14. _____ is a system designed to help you gather information in an organized way.

DRIVER'S LOG

In this chapter, you have learned about ways to manage risk while driving. Write three paragraphs that give your personal view on the following:

- How would you evaluate the possibility of your being involved in a collision? Explain.
- What kinds of situations do you feel hold the greatest risk for you as a driver?
- What steps will you take to manage the risks that you consider the most serious?

CHAPTER 1 REVIEW

CHAPTER TEST

Assign the Chapter Test to all students.

Answers

1. b
2. b
3. a
4. c
5. b
6. c
7. c
8. a
9. c
10. a
11. HTS
12. visibility
13. Smith System
14. SIPDE

DRIVER'S LOG

Students' responses will reflect their personal viewpoints. However, their answers should provide an assessment of their understanding of perceived versus actual risk and ways in which drivers can manage risk.

Evaluate

- Test A, pages 1–2 or Test B, pages 1–2 📁
- Testmaker software

RETURN TO THE BIG IDEA

In light of what students have learned in this chapter about risk management, discuss the notion that individuals are not likely to make decisions that reduce risk unless they first recognize that risk is real.

Getting Ready: Your State Driving Test Overview

THEME DEVELOPMENT To obtain a driver's license, prospective drivers must show their knowledge of driving regulations and their ability to operate a vehicle safely and responsibly. Careful preparation for driving knowledge and in-vehicle tests will ensure satisfactory test performance. In states with graduated driver licensing, students will spend additional time practicing driving skills before becoming fully licensed.

CHAPTER FEATURES	TCR COMPONENTS
TIPS FOR NEW DRIVERS Creating a plan based on GDL.	Study Guide, p. 5 Lesson Plan, p. 5
TIPS FOR NEW DRIVERS Practicing for the in-vehicle test.	Study Guide, p. 6 Lesson Plan, p. 5 Information Master 25
TIPS FOR NEW DRIVERS Choosing a vehicle for the in-vehicle test.	Study Guide, p. 7 Lesson Plan, p. 6 Behind-the-Wheel Checklists 1 and 2 Information Master 25
ADVICE FROM THE EXPERTS How to prepare for and pass a driver's license test.	Study Guide, p. 8 Lesson Plan, p. 6
BUILDING SKILLS: CRITICAL THINKING The High Cost of Fuel	Test A, pp. 3–4 Test B, pp. 3–4

PROJECTS

1. Write five questions that you think might be on your state's knowledge test.
2. Interview people who have just acquired their licenses.

OTHER PROGRAM RESOURCES

Testmaker software
Teaching Your Teens to Drive: video or CD-ROM, AAA, 1998
Traffic charts

ADDITIONAL RESOURCES

Journal of Traffic Safety Education, American Driver Traffic Safety Education Association
Your state driver's manual
Study Skills, M. Hosler, Glencoe, 1991
Studying for a Driver's License, Francis C. Kenel, Peoples Publishing Group, 1994

NAME _____ DATE _____

CHAPTER 2   Getting Ready: Your State Driving Test

TEST A

Select the phrase that best completes each sentence below. Write the letter of the answer you have chosen to the left of each statement.

d 1. With graduated driver licensing, you
   a. need to have an adult with you at all times when you drive.
   b. do not need to take a vision test.
   c. do not need to take a driver education course.
   d. need to pass your state's written knowledge test.

b 2. A good way to study for the knowledge test would be to
   a. ask a friend what to study.
   b. take a sample test from the driver's manual if it has one.
   c. ask your parents what to study.
   d. do none of the above.

a 3. Some states require that you bring _____ to the test.
   a. proof that you have completed a driver education course
   b. one of your parents or an adult
   c. your state driver's manual
   d. a certificate of title

b 4. When taking the knowledge test, the best thing to do if you have a tough question is to
   a. raise your hand.
   b. relax, keep going, and come back to the question later.
   c. not do anything until you answer the question.
   d. hold your breath to help relax.

d 5. Ideally, the in-vehicle test should be taken in
   a. the same vehicle you will be driving after you get the license.
   b. a vehicle with a manual transmission.
   c. a vehicle with an automatic transmission.
   d. the same vehicle you have practiced in.

d 6. For the in-vehicle test, your state may require you to present
   a. your driver's permit.
   b. the vehicle's registration.
   c. the vehicle's insurance identification card.
   d. all of the above.

b 7. If you're not going to take the test in the school's driver-training car,
   a. the state will have to provide one.
   b. you will have to provide the vehicle.
   c. you will not be able to get a license.
   d. none of the above applies.

NAME _____ DATE _____

Read each statement below. If it is true, place a T in the space to the left of the statement. If the statement is false, place an F next to it.

F 8. The procedure for obtaining a driver's license is the same from state to state.

F 9. In all states, you will take your in-vehicle test in the same vehicle you used in your driver education class.

T 10. All states have now adopted some form of graduated driver licensing.

T 11. To prove your age and identity, you should bring your birth certificate.

F 12. In all states, the in-vehicle test is given on an off-road closed course.

T 13. Your in-vehicle test may test your ability to parallel park.

T 14. You should not bring a vehicle to your in-vehicle test that you have never driven.

T 15. Part of your predriving check before the test is to make sure your lights are clean.

T 16. Before taking the in-vehicle test, make sure your safety belts are working.

F 17. In most states, it is acceptable to commit one traffic violation during the in-vehicle test and still pass.

T 18. Being nervous is natural and can be mentioned to the examiner.

In each space below, write the correct word or words that best complete the sentence.

19. The answer to all questions on your knowledge test can be found in your state's ___driver's manual___

20. Your in-vehicle test is sometimes called a ___road___ test.

21. When you take the road test, what adjustments should you make before you start the engine?
Make sure the seat is adjusted so that you have a clear view of the road and can reach the pedals comfortably. Make sure the head restraint is adjusted properly. Rear- and sideview mirrors should be adjusted for maximum visibility. Make sure no objects inside the car are blocking your views. Fasten your safety belt.

NAME _____ DATE _____

CHAPTER 2   Getting Ready: Your State Driving Test

TEST B

Select the phrase that best completes each sentence below. Write the letter of the answer you have chosen to the left of each statement.

b 1. With graduated driver licensing, you will
   a. need to have an adult with you at all times when you drive.
   b. need to pass your state's written knowledge test.
   c. not need to take a vision test.
   d. not need to take a driver education course.

b 2. In most states, if you violate a traffic law or commit a dangerous act during your in-vehicle test,
   a. you may not get a good score.
   b. you will automatically fail.
   c. you can have your vehicle taken away from you.
   d. none of the above applies.

d 3. When taking the in-vehicle test, you should make sure that
   a. your headlights are on.
   b. your radio is on.
   c. your radio is off.
   d. both a and c apply.

c 4. During the in-vehicle test, you should.
   a. use hand signals only when turning to demonstrate your knowledge of them.
   b. talk a lot with the examiner.
   c. not chat with the examiner.
   d. ask the examiner what your scores are as you are driving.

d 5. To help you in taking the knowledge test, you should
   a. study the material in advance.
   b. be well rested when you take the test.
   c. think carefully before answering the questions.
   d. do all of the above.

d 6. To earn a driver's license, you have to show that
   a. you know the traffic laws in your state.
   b. you can demonstrate basic control of a motor vehicle.
   c. your vision is adequate to drive.
   d. all of the above apply.

c 7. The real purpose of studying the driver's manual is to
   a. improve your reading skills.
   b. read it because it is required.
   c. learn driving rules and safe practice.
   d. help you pass the test.

NAME _____ DATE _____

Read each statement below. If it is true, place a T in the space to the left of the statement. If the statement is false, place an F next to it.

F 8. When an examiner is making notes during your in-vehicle test, it probably means that you have failed the test.

T 9. In all states, the in-vehicle test will be done in an off-road closed course.

T 10. One of the best defenses against making mistakes during the in-vehicle test is practice.

T 11. In some cases, you can take your in-vehicle test in the same vehicle you used in your driver education course.

T 12. You should study ahead of time to prevent forgetting what you learned.

F 13. It is important to take your in-vehicle test on an empty stomach so that you don't get sleepy.

T 14. The best proof of your age and identity is your birth certificate.

F 15. If you are going to be taking a vehicle with a manual transmission to the in-vehicle test, you should practice using an automatic transmission.

T 16. Before you take your in-vehicle test, you may be required to prove that the vehicle is insured.

T 17. You should check your windshield wipers before you take your in-vehicle test.

F 18. If your examiner is talking to you, do not listen and keep concentrating on driving.

In each space below, write the word or words that best complete the sentence.

19. Deep breathing can help you to be ___relaxed___ if you become nervous before or during the exam.

20. The answers to questions on your knowledge test can be found in your state's ___driver's manual___ .

21. On what items should you make a predriving check on the day before the test?
On the day before the test, check the brakes, clutch and gas pedals, lights, horn, fluid levels, tire pressure, and windshield wipers.

On the day of the test?
On the day of the test, clean the windows, adjust and clean the mirrors, clean the lights, and check your fuel level.

STUDY GUIDE

Panel 1 (Page 5)

NAME _____ DATE _____

CHAPTER 2 Getting Ready: Your State Driving Test

STUDY GUIDE FOR CHAPTER 2   LESSON 1

Introducing Graduated Driver Licensing

A. For each sentence below, circle T if the statement is true and F if it is false. Correct each false statement in the space below.

1. There are generally three stages in a graduated driver licensing system.   ⓣ   F

2. The American Automobile Association (AAA) offers guidelines to states that want to set up graduated driver licensing systems.   ⓣ   F

3. The first stage of graduated driver licensing lasts for a year.   T   ⓕ
The first stage lasts four to six months.

4. During the first stage of graduated driver licensing, the new driver must be supervised at all times by a licensed driver over the age of 30.   T   ⓕ
The licensed driver must be at least 21 years old.

5. In all stages of graduated driver licensing, new drivers are penalized less severely for traffic infractions than experienced drivers.   T   ⓕ
New drivers are penalized more severely than experienced drivers.

6. States with graduated driver licensing have experienced a reduction in traffic violations and accidents.   ⓣ   F

B. Talk to two people you know who have been driving for ten years or more. Find out if they are familiar with graduated driver licensing. Ask them what they think about this relatively new way of licensing drivers. Discuss with them how they would have liked this system when they were learning to drive. Summarize their responses below.
Review student's work.

_____

_____

_____

_____

_____

© AAA and Glencoe/McGraw-Hill   RESPONSIBLE DRIVING STUDY GUIDE CHAPTER 2   ◆ **5**

Panel 2 (Page 6)

NAME _____ DATE _____

STUDY GUIDE FOR CHAPTER 2   LESSON 2

Getting Ready for the Knowledge Test and the In-Vehicle Test

A. For each sentence below, circle T if the statement is true and F if it is false. Correct each false statement in the space below.

1. It's easier to wait until the last minute to study for your written knowledge test.   T   ⓕ
You should prepare well ahead of time for your written test.

2. The only purpose of studying the driver's manual is to pass the written test.   T   ⓕ
Study the driver's manual to learn driving rules and safe practices so that you can be a
responsible driver.

3. If you are going to use a vehicle with a manual transmission for the in-vehicle test, you should practice in that vehicle.   ⓣ   F

4. You should not eat any meals on the day of the in-vehicle test to ensure that you do not get sleepy while driving.   T   ⓕ
You should not skip any meals before the test.

5. The best advice for preparing for the in-vehicle test is to practice.   ⓣ   F

6. All states will test your driving skills in actual traffic, not on off-street courses.   T   ⓕ
Some states may test you on off-road courses.

B. FIND OUT MORE. Consult your state driver's manual. What papers do you need to bring to the department of motor vehicles when you go to take the in-vehicle test? How much money do you need to bring for fees?
Review student's work.

_____

_____

_____

_____

6 ◆ RESPONSIBLE DRIVING STUDY GUIDE CHAPTER 2   © AAA and Glencoe/McGraw-Hill

---

Panel 3 (Page 7)

NAME _____ DATE _____

STUDY GUIDE FOR CHAPTER 2   LESSON 3

Getting the Vehicle Ready for the Test

A. The chapter lists some characteristics of vehicles that are not recommended for taking your in-vehicle test. What are they?
One that is in poor condition, one you have seldom or never driven, one that frequently stalls,
one that restricts your ability to see, doesn't have safety belts, has muffler problems.

_____

B. When you make your predriving check before the day of the in-vehicle test, what will you be checking on the car?
Brakes, defroster/defogger, clutch and gas pedals, lights, horn, fluid levels, tire pressure and
windshield wipers.

Why do you think you should do this before the day of the test and not the same day?
You should look at these the day before the test because you may need time to fix some items.

_____

_____

C. What should you look at when you make your predriving check on the day of the exam?
Be sure that the interior and windows are clean, mirrors are clean and properly adjusted, lights
are clean, and the vehicle has enough fuel.

_____

D. FIND OUT MORE. Use the same vehicle or one very similar to the one that you will be using for your driving test. Make the same predriving check as you would the day before the test. What did you find?
Review student's work.

_____

_____

_____

© AAA and Glencoe/McGraw-Hill   RESPONSIBLE DRIVING STUDY GUIDE CHAPTER 2   ◆ **7**

Panel 4 (Page 8)

NAME _____ DATE _____

STUDY GUIDE FOR CHAPTER 2   LESSON 4

Taking the In-Vehicle Test

A. For each sentence below, circle T if the statement is true and F if it is false. Correct each false statement in the space below.

1. In most states, you are allowed to commit two dangerous acts during the in-vehicle test before you fail the test.   T   ⓕ
In most states, one dangerous act during the in-vehicle test can cause you to fail.

2. Fasten your safety belt before you start the engine.   ⓣ   F

3. During the in-vehicle test, turn on your low-beam headlights.   ⓣ   F

4. Revving the engine when the vehicle is stopped helps to conserve fuel.   T   ⓕ
Revving the engine at a stop light wastes fuel.

5. If the examiner writes anything down during the in-vehicle test, it probably means that you have failed the test.   T   ⓕ
The examiner has to write notes, and they may not mean anything at all.

6. It is good to admit to yourself that you are nervous about the in-vehicle test, but you should never admit it to the examiner.   T   ⓕ
If you are nervous, it may be a good idea to admit it to the examiner.

7. If you are nervous, holding your breath will help to make you calm.   T   ⓕ
If you are nervous, breathing deeply will help.

8. You should keep the radio off during the in-vehicle test.   ⓣ   F

B. FIND OUT MORE. The chapter says that it takes about five years to gain the experience necessary to make quality driving judgments. Talk to someone you know who has driven for a long time, and ask how long it took for that person to become a good driver. Summarize the response below.
Review student's work.

_____

Did the driver have any collisions in the first five years of driving? How did they happen?

_____

_____

8 ◆ RESPONSIBLE DRIVING STUDY GUIDE CHAPTER 2   © AAA and Glencoe/McGraw-Hill

---

Getting Ready: Your State Driving Test

CHAPTER OVERVIEW

LESSON ONE
Information on the new system of graduated driver licensing is provided.

LESSON TWO
How students should prepare for the knowledge test and the in-vehicle driving test is described.

LESSON THREE
How to select and prepare a vehicle for the in-vehicle driver's test is explained.

LESSON FOUR
Guidelines and suggestions for taking the in-vehicle test are provided.

VOCABULARY

graduated driver licensing (GDL)

22

CONCEPT OF THE DRIVING TASK

Point out that taking the state driving test can be stressful even when the test taker has studied and practiced. Learning to deal with stress and maintaining concentration are important parts not only of test taking but also of driving itself.

CHAPTER 2

Getting Ready: Your State Driving Test

You will learn a great deal about driving that will help you with your state driving test. It is important that you know how to prepare yourself and your vehicle for the test. Knowing how to prepare will help you succeed.

PRESENTING THE BIG IDEA

Careful advance preparation will help ensure success on both the state knowledge test and in-vehicle driving test.

INTRODUCING THE CHAPTER

What's on the Road Ahead?

Have students read the lesson titles and objectives. Briefly discuss the topic of each lesson. Tell students that in this chapter, they will learn how to prepare themselves and their vehicle for the state driving test they will need to pass in order to obtain a driver's license.

Background: Driver's Licenses

Licenses to operate a motor vehicle have been required since about 1910. Today all 50 states have laws setting the age at which a person may first apply for a driver's license. State laws may also restrict a teenager's driving privileges and/or require a course in driver education in order to obtain a license before the age of 18. In 22 states, teenagers younger than a certain age are not allowed to drive during high-risk hours, usually between midnight and 5 A.M. In 46 states, drivers under 21 years of age who are stopped for cause and are found to have a blood alcohol level of between 0.00 percent and 0.02 percent may have their license suspended or another penalty imposed.

Relating to Prior Knowledge

Have students discuss what they know about test-taking strategies and how they think a driver education course will help them prepare for their state driving test.

The Big Idea

Discuss students' reactions to the Big Idea statement. Suggest that they keep this idea in mind as they read Chapter 2.

Introducing Graduated Driver Licensing

(pages 24–25)

FOCUS

Objectives
- Discuss the purpose of graduated driver licensing.
- Name the three stages of the graduated driver licensing system.

Resources
 Study Guide, page 5

Vocabulary
graduated driver licensing (GDL)

Motivator
Pose the following question: What kinds of driving conditions do you need to experience before you can be considered a safe driver? (Students may mention weather conditions, different kinds of traffic, highway driving, and driving at night.)

TEACH

Explain
OBJECTIVE 1: Point out that there is a lower crash rate because the extra practice time allows the new driver to gain experience and confidence on the road.

OBJECTIVE 2: Note that the three stages of the GDL mentioned are guidelines from the AAA. Actual state GDL laws may vary. Also point out that GDL has not been adopted in all states.

LESSON ONE

OBJECTIVES
1. Discuss the purpose of graduated driver licensing.
2. Name the three stages of the graduated licensing system.

KEY TERM
graduated driver licensing (GDL)

Introducing Graduated Driver Licensing

No matter how much you have practiced, you cannot go from being a beginner to a fully experienced, safe driver overnight. For this reason, some states are introducing a system called **graduated driver licensing (GDL).** It is based on the idea that a teen with a new driver's license needs time and guidance to gain driving experience and skills in reduced-risk settings.

The Stages of the GDL System

In some states, a person will have full driving privileges as soon as he or she passes the driving tests. In states with a GDL system, newly licensed drivers will graduate from one licensing stage to the next as they achieve the goals at each level. AAA offers guidelines to states setting up a GDL system. Most GDL systems include three stages.

Stage 1: The Learner's Permit
The first stage in the GDL system lasts four to six months. The new driver practices basic driving skills and safe driving practices under totally supervised conditions.

Recommendations for eligibility To qualify for Stage 1, the new driver should:
- be the minimum age required by the state.
- have a parent's written permission.
- have passed the state's vision and written knowledge tests.

Recommended components Stage 1 drivers should be:
- in possession of a learner's permit.
- supervised at all times by a licensed driver who is at least 21 years old.
- required to take a basic driver education course.
- provided with 30 to 50 hours of behind-the-wheel driving certified by a parent, guardian, or licensed instructor.

TIPS **FOR NEW DRIVERS**

Don't Rush Yourself

If your state has not implemented a graduated driver licensing system, you might want to consider creating a plan of your own based on the GDL recommendations in the lesson. For several months after you have received your license, continue to practice driving only with a licensed adult in the vehicle. Then drive unsupervised for another 50 hours, limiting your driving to the hours between 5 A.M. and midnight. Remember that when you are behind the wheel, you have assumed responsibility for yourself and for others. Take that responsibility seriously: Lives depend on it.

24   UNIT 1   *Starting with You*

 FOR NEW DRIVERS

Caution students not to let peer pressure tempt them into driving beyond their capabilities. For example, students should avoid driving on highways at night until they are comfortable with daytime highway driving.

DRIVER'S LOG

Have students describe what the recommendations for eligibility are for each stage of the GDL system.

- required to remain free of any at-fault crashes or moving violations for at least six months before progressing to the next stage.
- penalized more for traffic violations than are experienced drivers.

Stage 2: Intermediate/Probationary License

During unsupervised, low-risk driving practice, the new driver is exposed to more demanding situations than those in Stage 1.

Recommendations for eligibility To qualify for Stage 2, the driver should:
- be at least the minimum age required by the state.
- have completed a minimum of four to six months of supervised driving.
- have successfully completed Stage 1.
- have passed the road test given by an approved agency.

Recommended components Stage 2 drivers should be:
- required to pass an advanced driver education course.
- required to complete 50 more hours of behind-the-wheel driving.
- restricted from driving between midnight and 5 A.M., unless accompanied by an adult who is at least 21 years old.
- required to remain free of any at-fault crashes or moving violations for at least 12 months or until age 18.
- penalized more for traffic infractions than are experienced drivers.

Stage 3: Full License

This license allows the driver unrestricted driving privileges.

Recommendations for eligibility To qualify for Stage 3, the driver should:
- be at least 18 years of age.
- have successfully completed Stage 2.
- have passed a final road test.

Additional recommendations for the GDL system include the mandatory use of seat belts and a limit on the number of passengers, which in no case should exceed the number of seat belts in the vehicle.

FYI

States with GDL laws have experienced crash and traffic violation reductions of 5 to 16 percent.

WHAT WOULD YOU DO?

This new driver lives in a state with a GDL system. What rules in Stage 1 is she observing?

Lesson 1 Review

1. What is the purpose of graduated driver licensing?
2. What are the three stages of the GDL licensing system?

WHAT WOULD YOU DO?

Sample answer: The teen is being supervised by a licensed driver at least 21 years old and is getting practice toward 30 to 50 hours of behind-the-wheel driving.

Lesson 1 Review

Answers

1. To help new drivers increase driving skills gradually and gain experience driving in reduced-risk settings.
2. Stage 1 is the learner's permit stage: the new driver practices under totally supervised conditions. Stage 2 is the intermediate/probationary stage: the new driver is exposed to more demanding situations. Stage 3 is the full license stage: the driver receives unrestricted driving privileges.

Teaching Model

Describe the following situation: You have just gotten your learner's permit. You live in a state that has graduated driver licensing. Model steps you will take in the next few months to become a fully licensed driver. (You will have to be supervised by an adult, take a basic driver education course, and have 30 to 50 hours of behind-the-wheel driving in Stage 1. In Stage 2, you would be able to drive unsupervised. You might have to pass an advanced driver education course and complete an additional 50 hours of behind-the-wheel driving. Your driving hours would be restricted. In Stage 3, you would pass a road test and become a fully licensed driver.)

Ask

Ask students to think about how teens might gradually gain experience driving in conditions with different levels of risk.

Read

Have students read Lesson 1 to learn about the GDL.

ASSESS

Guided Practice

Have students answer the Lesson 1 Review questions. The answers are provided below.

Reteaching

Have students work in small groups to describe the stages of GDL.

Enrichment

Assign the Study Guide for Lesson 1. The Find Out More section encourages students to expand their basic learning of the lesson concepts.

CLOSE

Summarize

Return to the Motivator question. Recall students' initial responses, and discuss how the GDL system would allow them to become safe drivers.

Getting Ready for the Knowledge Test and the In-Vehicle Test

(pages 26–29)

FOCUS

Objectives

• Name four ways in which you can prepare yourself for the knowledge test, and describe how you would go about implementing each.

• List three preparations you can make for the in-vehicle test, and explain how to carry out each of the preparations.

Resources
Study Guide, page 6
Information Master 25

Motivator

Pose the following question: How will you prepare for your knowledge test and your in-vehicle or road test? (Sample answer: For the knowledge or written test, study the driver's manual and review the material with a friend. For the in-vehicle test, practice driving, get a good night's sleep, eat a good breakfast, bring necessary documents, and bring items you may need, such as a seat cushion.)

OBJECTIVES

1. Name four ways in which you can prepare yourself for the knowledge test, and describe how you would go about implementing each.
2. List three preparations you can make for the in-vehicle test, and explain how to carry out each of the preparations.

Getting Ready for the Knowledge Test and the In-Vehicle Test

In addition to a vision test, you must pass a knowledge or written test and a driving performance test. Application and testing procedures for obtaining a driver's license vary from state to state. To find out what the requirements are where you live, check your state driver's manual or ask your driver education instructor.

In a number of states, your driver education teacher will administer the in-vehicle performance test, or road test, after you have passed a knowledge test. In some states, your teacher will arrange for an examiner to come to your school to give the test. In both of these cases, you will take your in-vehicle performance test in the vehicle you've been using during the driver education course. In other states, you must make your own arrangements with the department of motor vehicles to take all the necessary tests.

How Can You Prepare for the Knowledge Test?

Getting ready to take the knowledge test for your driver's license is not much different from preparing for a test in school. Study the material in advance, be well rested when you take the test, and think carefully before answering the questions.

Study Wisely

Your state driver's manual contains the information that you will need in order to study for the knowledge test. Follow these guidelines for studying the manual.

• Read one section at a time. Use a marker to highlight important information you think may be on the test, or keep a notebook in which you write this information.

 FOR NEW DRIVERS

Practicing for the In-Vehicle Test

When practicing your driving, here are some of the skills you may need to demonstrate. You will learn about these skills in Chapters 8, 9, and 10:

- parallel parking
- starting and stopping smoothly
- shifting gears
- backing up safely
- turning
- passing
- following at a safe distance
- signaling
- executing turnabouts

THE INTERNATIONAL SCENE

Europe

A U.S. driver's license is valid in Europe. Before going abroad, a U.S. citizen might also want to obtain an international driving permit, available from the American Automobile Association.

- Reread the section and summarize it for yourself. Write your summary in your notebook.
- Study with someone else who is going to take the test, or ask a friend or family member to quiz you on information from the manual.
- Take the sample test, if there is one in your state's manual. If there is anything in the manual that you don't understand, ask your driver education instructor to explain it to you.
- Review the chapter and unit tests in this book. Look up the answers if you don't remember them.

Budget your study time. Don't wait until the last minute and then try to cram for the test. Figure out how much time you have to study. Then decide how much time you'll devote to studying each day or week, perhaps leaving additional study time just before you take the knowledge test.

Keep in mind that the real purpose of studying the driver's manual is not just to pass the test. Your true goal is to learn driving rules and safe practices so that you can be a responsible driver.

Get Yourself Ready Physically

Get a good night's sleep before the test. No matter how much you have learned, you'll never pass the test if you're too sleepy to think clearly.

Don't skip meals before taking the test. Eating right will keep your energy level high and help you focus your thoughts.

Bring the Necessary Papers

If you have to go to the department of motor vehicles office to take your test, you will have to bring several documents with you. You'll need proof of age and identity. The best proof of both is your birth certificate.

Some states require that you bring proof that you have satisfactorily completed a course in driver education if you are under age 18 or 19. In most cases, a parent or some other adult who has a driver's license will have to accompany you.

FYI

While most states still give road tests in actual traffic, some states do all their testing on closed courses. These tests usually emphasize parallel parking, turns, and turnabouts.

◆ *Before taking your knowledge test, ask a friend or family member to quiz you on the material in the manual.*

TEACH

Explain

OBJECTIVE 1: Students may benefit from a review of test-preparation techniques.

OBJECTIVE 2: Stress the importance of taking the test in the same vehicle used for practice.

Teaching Model

Describe the following situation: You have scheduled an appointment for the in-vehicle test. Model how you will prepare. (You will schedule some time each day to practice driving, eat properly and get enough sleep prior to the test, gather necessary documents, and make sure you have the items you need.)

Ask

Ask students to think about how the information they learned for the written test can help them when they take the in-vehicle test.

Read

Have students read Lesson 2 to understand how to prepare themselves for the knowledge test and the in-vehicle test.

ASSESS

Guided Practice

Have students answer the Lesson 2 Review questions. The answers are provided below.

Reteaching

Have students work in groups, sharing suggestions for how to get ready for both tests.

FYI

The first drivers' licenses in the United States were issued by the Board of Examiners of Operators of Automobiles in Chicago, Illinois, on July 6, 1899.

Check the driver's manual or call the department of motor vehicles beforehand to find out the specific documents your state requires. People who work for a state's department of motor vehicles usually allow no exceptions to the rules. If the manual says to bring your Social Security card with you, then be sure to do so. Failure to bring necessary documents may result in your not being able to take the test.

Stay Calm

As you prepare for the knowledge test and on the day that you actually take it, stay calm. Read each question carefully, and take time to think before selecting your answer. If you get stuck on a question, skip it and return to it later.

Don't let a tough question throw off your concentration. Just relax and keep going. Generally, there is no time limit on how long you have to complete the test (so long as it is before the department's closing time).

How Can You Prepare for the In-Vehicle Test?

To pass the in-vehicle or road test, you need to show the examiner that you have a working knowledge of the rules of the road and that you have mastered basic driving skills. As with most tests, the key to success is advance preparation.

◆ *Practice the manuevers you find especially difficult, such as backing or three-point turns.*

Know What You Are Doing

Practice, practice, practice—that's the best advice for preparing for the in-vehicle test. The more hours you spend behind the wheel, the more skilled and confident you will become as a driver.

When you practice driving, ask the person you're with to point out any areas in which you might need improvement. Spend extra time perfecting any maneuvers you find difficult.

Be alert for road signs as you practice. Be sure you understand what each sign means and what procedures you should follow at each. Review your driver's manual if you're uncertain about any sign or traffic rule.

MEETING STUDENT DIVERSITY

Limited English Proficiency

Explain to students who have language difficulty that they should find out from the local driver-testing center whether they can take the test with the aid of an interpreter.

FOR NEW DRIVERS

To review, you may want to have students describe how each maneuver is performed and discuss related risk-reduction techniques.

Remember, too, that driving is more than just a series of physical movements. Becoming a good driver means exhibiting sound judgment and decision-making skills. In other words, knowing how to make a left turn is important, but knowing when it is safe to make the turn is even more important.

If possible, practice driving in the same vehicle in which you will take your test. Ideally, this should also be the vehicle you'll be driving *after* you get your driver's license. At the very least, your practice vehicle should be similar to the one you'll be using. If, for example, you'll be using a stick shift on the day of the test, be sure to practice driving in a stick-shift vehicle.

Be Alert and Ready

Many of the same suggestions made earlier about preparing yourself for the knowledge test apply for the in-vehicle test. To be at your best, get a solid night's sleep before the day of the test, and don't skip meals before the test.

Bring What You Need

For the in-vehicle test, you will need certain documents. Your state may require you to present your valid driver's permit as well as proof of vehicle registration and adequate insurance for the vehicle you're driving. You may also need proof that the vehicle has been properly inspected and has passed an emissions test. Check your state driver's manual to learn what documents your state requires.

Also bring enough money or a check to pay the licensing fees, and any other items you may need, such as a seat or back cushion and your prescription glasses or sunglasses, if you need to wear them when you drive.

Lesson *2* Review

1. How can you plan to study for the knowledge test?
2. What preparations can you make for the in-vehicle test?

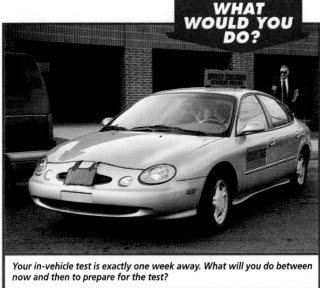

WHAT WOULD YOU DO?

Your in-vehicle test is exactly one week away. What will you do between now and then to prepare for the test?

Enrichment

Assign the Study Guide for Lesson 2. The Find Out More section encourages students to expand their basic learning of the lesson concepts.

CLOSE

Summarize

Return to the Motivator question. Recall students' initial responses, and discuss any additional techniques they have learned.

DRIVER'S LOG

Have students make a list of what they would do to prepare for the in-vehicle test.

WHAT WOULD YOU DO?

Sample answer: Practice driving as much as possible in similar traffic conditions, especially those maneuvers that seem most difficult.

Lesson *2* Review

Answers

1. Study the driver's manual, review with friends, get a good night's sleep, and eat a good breakfast.
2. Practice driving, get a good night's sleep, eat well, and bring necessary documents to the test.

Getting the Vehicle Ready for the Test

(pages 30–31)

FOCUS

Objectives

• Name two ways in which you can prepare your vehicle for the in-vehicle test.

• List the actions you should take before and on the day of the test.

Resources

 Study Guide, page 7

 Behind-the-Wheel Checklists 1 and 2

 Information Master 25

Motivator

Pose the following question: How will you prepare your vehicle for the in-vehicle test? (Sample answer: Make sure the vehicle is in good operating condition; clean the windows; adjust the mirrors; make sure the comfort and control systems work; check directional signals, horn, and headlights.)

TEACH

Explain

OBJECTIVE 1: Stress the need to check the vehicle well in advance, so that any necessary repairs may be made.

OBJECTIVE 2: Discuss briefly a few of the suggestions given in Chapters 7 and 17.

Teaching Model

Pose the following situation: You are trying to decide which of your parents' vehicles to use for the in-vehicle test. You have practice

---

OBJECTIVES

1. Name two ways in which you can prepare your car for the in-vehicle test.
2. List the actions you should take before and on the day of the test.

Getting the Vehicle Ready for the Test

If you are not going to take your in-vehicle test in the school's driver-training car, you will have to provide the vehicle. Be sure the one you use is as ready for the test as you are.

How Can You Get the Test Vehicle Ready?

The vehicle you drive for your test should be in top condition. It should be clean inside and out. All windows should be in good condition, and the door handles should work properly. In addition, the vehicle should be in good mechanical condition. The last thing you need on the day of your test is a mechanical or other problem.

Choose Your Vehicle Wisely

If you have a choice of what vehicle to use for your test, choose one that is in good all-around condition and that you feel comfortable driving.

Remember that you may have to show proof that the vehicle is registered and insured and that it has been properly inspected and has passed an emissions test. Do *not* bring to the test a vehicle that:

• you have seldom or never driven.
• frequently stalls.
• restricts your ability to see.
• does not have safety belts.
• has muffler problems.
• you have difficulty getting into or out of.

TIPS FOR NEW DRIVERS

Choosing a Vehicle for the Test

Suppose you have practiced in and are equally comfortable driving two cars, both of which are in good mechanical condition. Which car should you choose to use for your in-vehicle test? Here are some tips that may make your decision easier.

• Choose a car with an automatic transmission over one with a manual transmission. Nervousness can make you have trouble coordinating the clutch, the gearshift, and the accelerator.
• Choose a smaller car over a larger car. Smaller cars are generally easier to maneuver.
• Choose a conservative, family-type car over a sports car or "souped-up" vehicle. Make a good first impression on the examiner.

State BY State

Each state has specific requirements for taking a road test. New Jersey, for example, requires a licensed driver in attendance, a valid driver's permit, current vehicle registration and insurance identification cards, and a valid vehicle inspection sticker.

TIPS FOR NEW DRIVERS

Have students discuss the benefits of each tip.

Check Out the Vehicle in Advance

Before the day of the test, conduct basic predriving checks of the following items:

- defroster/defogger
- brakes
- clutch and gas pedals
- all lights
- horn
- fluid levels
- tire pressure
- windshield wipers and windshield washer fluid

By checking out the test vehicle in advance, you can make sure that whatever is not in good working order will be fixed in time for the test. Be sure you know where all the controls are and how to operate them.

On the day of the test:

- Clean the interior of the vehicle.
- Clean the windows.
- Adjust and clean the mirrors.
- Clean the lights.
- Verify that you have enough fuel.

Remove any obstructions from inside the car, such as packages or hanging ornaments. Be sure your vehicle's safety belts are working properly.

To review other suggestions for advance preparation of your vehicle, see Chapters 7 and 17.

Lesson 3 Review

1. Why is it important to check out your vehicle in advance of taking the test?
2. What predriving checks should you make on your vehicle before you take the test?

◆ *Be sure that your mirrors—inside and outside—are clean and that you adjust them properly.*

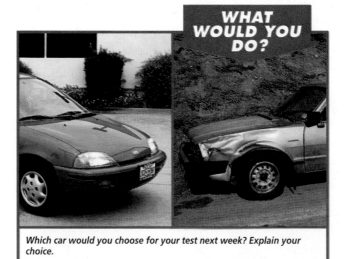

WHAT WOULD YOU DO?

Which car would you choose for your test next week? Explain your choice.

driven both cars. Your father's car is six years old and has an automatic transmission. Your mother's car is almost new, has a standard transmission, and is very sporty looking. Model the thinking process for deciding which car to use. (You recognize that although your mother's car is new and sporty looking, it will be easier for you to drive a car with an automatic transmission—especially if you're nervous on the day of the test.)

Ask

Ask students to discuss other factors to consider when choosing between two vehicles.

Read

Have students read Lesson 3 to learn how to select and prepare a vehicle for the in-vehicle test.

ASSESS

Guided Practice

Have students answer the Lesson 3 Review questions. The answers are provided below.

Reteaching

Have pairs or groups make a checklist for preparing a vehicle for an in-vehicle test.

Enrichment

Assign the Study Guide for Lesson 3. The Find Out More section encourages students to expand their basic learning of the lesson concepts.

CLOSE

Summarize

Return to the Motivator question, and review how to prepare a vehicle for the road test. Discuss this question: Why is it important to choose wisely the vehicle you will use for the test?

DRIVER'S LOG

Have students list items they will need to check in the vehicle they use for their in-vehicle test.

WHAT WOULD YOU DO?

Sample answer: Choose the vehicle that is in better condition so that you won't have vehicle problems when you take the test.

Lesson 3 Review

Answers

1. It avoids vehicle problems on the day of the test.
2. Before the day of the test, check equipment in the vehicle, such as defroster, brakes, lights, and horn. Check tire pressure. On the day of the test, clean the vehicle's interior, clean windows, adjust mirrors, and check safety belts.

Taking the
Final Test: The
In-Vehicle Test

(pages 32–34)

FOCUS

Objectives

• Name at least four guidelines to keep in mind when taking the in-vehicle test.

• Describe in detail what each guideline entails.

Resources

📁 Study Guide, page 8

📁 Traffic charts

Motivator

Pose the following: The day of your in-vehicle test has finally arrived. You open the driver's door and slide behind the wheel. The examiner enters the vehicle. How should you conduct yourself before and after you start the vehicle's engine? (Sample answer: Make necessary adjustments in the seat, head restraint, and mirrors; fasten your safety belt; try to remain calm; be polite and attentive to the examiner; turn on low-beam headlights; use defroster and windshield wipers if necessary; check mirrors and blind spots.)

TEACH

Explain

OBJECTIVES 1 AND 2: Students should understand the importance of listening carefully to the examiner and not anticipating instructions or making assumptions. If in doubt, students should ask the examiner to repeat what he or she said.

OBJECTIVES
1. Name at least four guidelines to keep in mind when taking the in-vehicle test.
2. Describe in detail what each guideline entails.

Taking the Final Test:
The In-Vehicle Test

The big day has finally arrived: You're about to take the in-vehicle test for your driver's license. You've practiced driving for many hours, but you feel nervous just the same. You want to pass the test on your first try.

What Should You Do Once You Are Sitting Behind the Wheel?

The examiner who rides with you during your test will evaluate your skill at handling the vehicle as well as your ability to drive safely and responsibly. In most states, you will fail the test automatically if you violate a traffic law or commit a dangerous act.

Make All Necessary Adjustments First

Before you start the engine, recheck your vehicle to see if any adjustments are needed.

• Make sure your seat is adjusted so that you have a clear view of the road and can reach the accelerator and brake pedals comfortably. If you use a seat or back cushion, put it in place.

◆ *Concentrate on your driving and the examiner's instructions during the in-vehicle test.*

• Make sure your head restraint on the back of your seat is correctly adjusted.
• Make sure the rearview and sideview mirrors are positioned for maximum visibility.
• Make certain that no objects inside the vehicle are blocking your view.
• Fasten your safety belt.

Follow these procedures after you've started the engine.

• If necessary, turn on window defrosters and windshield wipers.
• Turn on the low-beam headlights.
• If the radio is on, turn it off.
• Check your mirrors and blind spots before starting to drive.

32   UNIT 1   *Starting with You*

IT'S A FACT

Each state offers several different licenses for which a person may apply. A basic license is required for all types of motor vehicles registered except motorcycles, which require a special license. A special license is also required to operate agricultural vehicles and heavy commercial vehicles, such as tractor-trailers.

Concentrate on What You Are Doing

Follow these guidelines for keeping your mind on your driving during the in-vehicle test.

Listen carefully to any instructions. Follow the examiner's instructions exactly. If you don't understand something the examiner says, ask for clarification.

Don't chat with the examiner. During the test, the examiner may say very little to you. Don't let it bother you if your examiner is the silent type. This may just be his or her personality. On the other hand, if your examiner is talkative and asks a lot of questions, don't let that distract you from concentrating on driving.

Don't worry about what the examiner is writing. During the test, expect the examiner to be writing and making notes on a form. Don't assume the examiner is being critical. Many categories have to be tested and noted. The examiner may be writing favorable comments too.

Don't let a mistake throw you. If you make a mistake, maintain your concentration. Don't let a minor error rattle you so much that you make a worse mistake. If you're going through a complicated maneuver, move the vehicle slowly, paying special attention to the gear you're in, the direction your wheels are turned, and the obstacles and traffic around you.

Stay Calm

Because this is an important test and you care about the results, you are going to be nervous. This is natural. But you can do some things to minimize your nervousness and help you concentrate on your driving.

Be well prepared. If you have practiced a great deal, you should be prepared for the in-vehicle test. Thorough preparation is the best defense against making mistakes during the test.

Admit that you're nervous. It's helpful to admit that you're nervous in a situation that is making you tense. Even though you're prepared, be aware of how you feel, and don't be afraid to tell your examiner. Don't be disappointed, however, if the examiner does not reassure you.

Have a positive attitude. Remember that you are well prepared. Be confident that you are going to do your best.

Bring support. The licensed driver who drives you to the test should be positive, optimistic, supportive, and calm. However, do not expect that person to be allowed to accompany you while you are taking the in-vehicle test.

SAFETY TIPS

If your vehicle has automatic shoulder belts, be sure you also fasten your lap belt for maximum protection.

Energy Tips

Don't rev the engine when you are stopped at a stop sign or red light or while you are stopped in traffic. Revving the engine wastes fuel and may annoy the examiner.

State BY State

All states have some sort of point system for keeping track of a driver's record. When a driver is convicted of a moving violation, points are added to his or her record; the more serious the violation, the more points. A certain number of points may cause the driver to be fined, to lose his or her license, or to be required to take a safe-driving course.

Teaching Model

Display this situation:

Tell students the following: You are in vehicle 1 with the examiner in the passenger seat. You have just finished demonstrating how to parallel park, which is the maneuver you find most difficult. The examiner is making notes and has just told you to pull back into traffic and continue driving. Model the thinking process you go through to manage this situation. (You do the following.

- Take a deep breath, and do not worry about any mistakes you may have made.
- Do not be preoccupied with what the examiner is writing.
- Respond politely and prepare to move.
- Put on your left signal and check for traffic before pulling out.)

Ask

Ask students to discuss the importance of maintaining concentration while taking the in-vehicle test.

Read

Have students read Lesson 4 to become familiar with techniques to help them take and pass the in-vehicle test.

ASSESS

Guided Practice

Have students answer the Lesson 4 Review questions. The answers are provided below.

*Have students discuss
the four categories: con-
trol, observation, position,
and signaling.*

Reteaching

Have students work in pairs or small groups to discuss strategies for taking the in-vehicle test. After groups have completed this task, have students create a class list of do's and don'ts for taking the in-vehicle test.

Enrichment

Assign the Study Guide for Lesson 4. The Find Out More section encourages students to expand their basic learning of the lesson concepts.

CLOSE

Summarize

Return to the Motivator question, and reexamine students' initial ideas about how they should conduct themselves during the in-vehicle test in light of what they have learned in this lesson. Extend the discussion by having students review in their own words the guidelines for taking the in-vehicle test successfully.

DRIVER'S LOG

Have students list practical tips for taking the in-vehicle test.

ADVICE FROM THE EXPERTS

Judy L. Alton
Sergeant, Texas Department of Public Safety

When you take the in-vehicle test, try to relax. Imagine that the examiner is your best friend. In Texas we grade on four categories: control, observation, position, and signaling. Controlling the vehicle is knowing how to handle it. Observation is making sure you look at all times—turn your head so the examiner can tell when you are looking. Position has to do with always maintaining the proper lane position. You should signal to make a turn or lane change and also with your horn if you need to give a warning.

Breathe deeply. Pay attention to the way you're breathing. When people are anxious, they tend to hold their breath. Deep breathing will keep the oxygen moving through your system and help you stay calm.

Exercise Good Judgment

Show the examiner that you are a mature, responsible person. Always be courteous, both to the examiner and to the pedestrians and other drivers you may meet on the roadway. Above all, do not smoke while you are taking the in-vehicle test.

Demonstrate the skills you learned in your driver education course. Allow yourself plenty of time to pull out into traffic. Search the path ahead for any object or condition that could raise the level of risk. Follow other vehicles at a proper distance. Be alert for traffic control devices, and remember to signal your intentions.

WHAT WOULD YOU DO?

The examiner is ready for you to begin the in-vehicle test. What actions will you take before starting the engine?

Lesson 4 Review

1 What adjustments will you need to make to your vehicle before you start your engine?

2 How can you concentrate and stay calm during the in-vehicle test?

WHAT WOULD YOU DO?

Sample answer: Make sure your seat, head restraint, and mirrors are correctly adjusted and that no objects block your view. Fasten your safety belt.

Lesson 4 Review

Answers

1. Adjust seat, head restraint, mirrors, safety belts; turn off radio.
2. Listen carefully; don't chat with the examiner; don't worry about what the examiner is writing; don't let making a mistake throw off your concentration; have a positive attitude.

The High Cost of Fuel

Oil, the precious resource that is the source of the gasoline that powers our motor vehicles, has been the cause of a confusing mix of benefits and drawbacks to the Inuits of Alaska. In the 1800s, these native people witnessed the exploration of their homeland by navigators searching for a quick Arctic sea route from the New World to the wealth of Asia. This sea route, the Northwest Passage, was finally traveled in 1903 by the Norwegian explorer Roald Amundsen.

Today the Inuits are affected by another exploration—the search for oil in the waters of the Northwest Passage. With the discovery of oil at Prudhoe Bay on Alaska's north coast, human-made oil-drilling islands have been built amidst the 18,000 islands of the 4,000-mile-long Northwest Passage.

The trans-Alaska pipeline carries the oil from Prudhoe Bay to ports in southern Alaska, where it is transferred to huge ice-breaking tankers that carry the oil to refineries outside of Alaska.

For many Inuits, the frozen-over sea is like the land. Driving a ship through it is like driving a bulldozer across a farmer's field. The tankers also pose a danger to the environment, such as that caused when the *Exxon Valdez* struck a reef and poured 10.9 million gallons of crude oil into Prince William Sound. The oil destroyed wildlife that lived in these waters and was absorbed in the gravel beaches along the shoreline.

The threat to the environment and to the Inuit way of life are somewhat balanced by the increased income and other material gains that oil has brought to these Native Americans of Alaska. In the Alaskan Native Claims Settlement Act of 1971, the U.S. government gave Alaskans with at least one Native American grandparent a share in the oil-rich lands.

The Inuits are in the forefront of a movement that while recognizing the need for oil and its economic benefit, also recognizes the need to protect the environment. The threat of pollution has been an important topic in the five Inuit Circumpolar Conferences that have been held since 1977 to discuss the future of Arctic peoples.

What Do You Think Now?

How can the need for oil and the economic advantages it brings be balanced by the need to protect and preserve the environment?

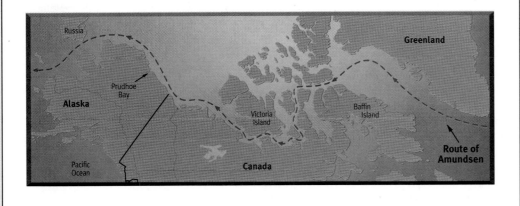

Objective:
Demonstrate an ability to analyze information, understand differing viewpoints, and form an opinion.

Teaching the Skill

- On a world map, have students locate the "New World"—that is, the Western Hemisphere—the Arctic, Asia, Alaska, the Atlantic Ocean, and the Pacific Ocean.
- Be sure students understand that the Northwest Passage was a sea route from the Atlantic Ocean to the Pacific Ocean through the Arctic. Have them trace the Northwest Passage on the map.
- Have students discuss how the native peoples of Alaska have been harmed and helped by the quest for oil.
- You may want to mention that Roald Amundsen was also the first explorer to reach the South Pole, in 1911.

ANSWER TO What Do You Think Now Question

Students' answers will vary, but they should reflect students' understanding that there are no easy solutions to the conflict.

CHAPTER SUMMARY

Key Points

Have students read the Key Points to review the major concepts of the chapter.

PROJECTS

Cooperative Learning:

Students will benefit by working with a partner on one or both projects. When the assignment is completed, the whole class will profit by sharing and comparing results.

CHAPTER 2 REVIEW

KEY POINTS

Lesson One

1. No matter how much you practice for your driving test, you can't go from being a complete beginner to being an experienced driver overnight. For this reason, some states have implemented a system called graduated driver licensing (GDL).
2. GDL is a three-stage system that gives people time to increase their driving skills gradually in low-risk settings. A GDL system generally includes beginning, intermediate, and full licensing stages.

Lesson Two

1. To prepare for the knowledge test, study your state driver's manual thoroughly. Read one section at a time and summarize it, study with a friend, and take any sample tests. Go for the test well rested, and take with you any documents you may need. When you take the test, stay calm, read each question carefully, and take time to think before selecting your answer.
2. To prepare for the in-vehicle test, practice driving as much as you can, preferably in the same vehicle in which you will take your test.

Be alert and ready by getting a good night's sleep before the day of the test. Bring what you need, including correct documentation, money or a check, and other necessary items, such as sunglasses and a cushion.

Lesson Three

1. Be sure the vehicle you choose for the test is in top condition. Check out your vehicle before you take the test.
2. Conduct predriving checks the day before the in-vehicle test. Check the brakes, fluid levels, pedals, lights, horn, tires, defoggers, and windshield wipers. On the day of the test, make sure that your vehicle's windows, mirrors, lights, and interior are clean.

Lesson Four

1. When taking the in-vehicle test, first make all necessary adjustments before you start to drive: seat, head restraint, mirrors, and safety belt. Stay calm. Be prepared, admit you're nervous, be positive, and breathe deeply.
2. Concentrate on what you are doing while you are driving. Listen carefully to the examiner, don't chat with him or her, and try not to worry.

PROJECTS

1. Write five questions that you think may be on your knowledge test. Exchange questions with a partner in your class. Try to answer your partner's questions. Check all answers in your driver's manual.
2. Interview two people who have acquired their licenses in the past year. What maneuvers were they required to make during the in-vehicle test? What was easiest and hardest about the test. Discuss your findings with your class.

*inter*NET
CONNECTION

Drive through the Web to learn more about graduated driver licensing, including the status of GDL in your state.
drivered.glencoe.com

*inter*NET
CONNECTION

Visit Glencoe's Driver Education Web site for student activities that relate to this chapter.
drivered.glencoe.com

CHAPTER TEST

Write the letter of the answer that best completes each sentence.

1. With a graduated driver licensing system, you
   a. must be 21 years old to drive alone.
   b. increase your driving skills and privileges gradually.
   c. are penalized less severely than an experienced driver for traffic violations.

2. Your goal in studying for the knowledge test is to
   a. learn the rules of the road so that you can be a responsible driver.
   b. pass your driving test.
   c. answer all the questions correctly.

3. Three ways to prepare for your knowledge test are to
   a. eat right, sleep well, and study.
   b. study, bring documents, and exercise.
   c. eat right, read, and check the brakes.

4. If you are not going to take your test in the school's driver education car,
   a. the driving instructor will provide a car.
   b. you will have to pay more for your license.
   c. it will be up to you to provide the vehicle.

5. If possible, practice driving in
   a. many different vehicles.
   b. the same vehicle in which you will take your test.
   c. a rental car.

6. One way to stay calm during the in-vehicle test is to
   a. rev the engine.
   b. breathe deeply.
   c. take the sample test.

7. When taking your in-vehicle test, it is
   a. okay to tell the examiner that you are nervous.
   b. a good idea to chat with the examiner.
   c. helpful to play audiocassettes.

8. You should check your car's fluid levels
   a. the day before your in-vehicle test.
   b. in the presence of the examiner.
   c. during the knowledge test.

9. If you violate a traffic law while taking your in-vehicle test, you
   a. will automatically fail the test in most states.
   b. can usually still pass the test.
   c. will be banned from driving for one year.

10. Your best proof of age is your
    a. parent's sworn testimony.
    b. birth certificate.
    c. driver's permit.

Write the word or phrase that best completes each sentence.

clarification	documents	license
emissions inspection	responsible	

11. Being a(n) _____ driver means exhibiting sound judgment and decision-making skills.

12. You may need proof that the vehicle you bring for the test has passed a(n) _____.

13. If you do not understand something the examiner says, ask for _____.

14. Take with you to the test all the _____ that you will need.

DRIVER'S LOG

In this chapter, you have learned how to prepare yourself and your vehicle for the state driving test. Do you think you will have more difficulty with the in-vehicle test or the knowledge test? Write two paragraphs in which you analyze the reasons for the difficulty and explain what you will do to remedy the situation.

CHAPTER 2 REVIEW

CHAPTER TEST

Assign the Chapter Test to all students.

Answers

1. b
2. a
3. a
4. c
5. b
6. b
7. a
8. a
9. a
10. b
11. responsible
12. emissions inspection
13. clarification
14. documents

DRIVER'S LOG

Students' responses will reflect their personal viewpoints. However, their answers should provide an assessment of their understanding of the preparation needed in order to take the in-vehicle test.

Evaluate

• Test A, pages 3–4 or Test B, pages 3–4 📁
• Testmaker software

RETURN TO THE BIG IDEA ———

Discuss the idea that careful advance preparation can help ensure success on the state driving test.

CHAPTER 3 — Knowing Yourself Overview

THEME DEVELOPMENT Self-knowledge is vital to safe and responsible driving. Drivers must be aware of the impact that emotions have on their behavior, be able to recognize when they are being influenced by their emotions, and have the strength to control their emotions. Drivers must also understand how physical limitations, both temporary and long-term, can affect the driving task and possibly endanger their safety and the safety of other roadway users. Understanding these limitations and their effects can help drivers learn how to compensate for such conditions. However, the first step is self-knowledge.

CHAPTER FEATURES	TCR COMPONENTS
	Study Guide, p. 9 Lesson Plan, p. 7
FOR NEW DRIVERS Compensating for reduced visibility at night.	Study Guide, p. 10 Lesson Plan, p. 7 Information Master 18
TIPS FOR NEW DRIVERS Fighting fatigue.	Study Guide, p. 11 Lesson Plan, p. 8 Information Master 17
ADVICE FROM THE EXPERTS Keeping one's emotions from interfering with driving.	Study Guide, p. 12 Lesson Plan, p. 8
BUILDING SKILLS: CRITICAL THINKING Kitty O'Neil	Test A, pp. 5–6 Test B, pp. 5–6

PROJECTS

1. Identify ways to control emotions.

2. Identify sounds and sensations in a moving vehicle.

OTHER PROGRAM RESOURCES

Testmaker software

ADDITIONAL RESOURCES

Young Driver Attitude Scale, Computer Program 371, AAA Foundation

Heavenly Debate, Video 434, AAA Foundation

Breaking the Accident Chain of Events, Video 403, AAA Foundation

Night Driving, Video 453, AAA Foundation

Wake Up!, Brochure 368, AAA Foundation

Short Cut to Experience, Video SS2, Smith System

NAME _____ DATE _____

CHAPTER 3 Knowing Yourself

TEST A

Select the phrase that best completes each sentence below. Write the letter of the answer you have chosen to the left of each statement.

__d__ 1. If your visual acuity is 20/40, it means that
a. you read an eye chart at 20 feet away with one eye and at 40 feet with the other.
b. you can read an eye chart at 20 feet away with glasses and at 40 feet without them.
c. at the age of 20, you have the vision of a person 40 years of age.
d. a sign that you should read at 40 feet is only readable to you at 20 feet.

__d__ 2. Driver fatigue can be caused by
a. boredom.
b. overwork.
c. exposure to too much sun.
d. all of the above.

__d__ 3. The reason that you should turn your engine off if you have to pull over in a rest area for sleep is to
a. prevent a robbery of your vehicle.
b. prevent driver fatigue.
c. prevent the noise of the vehicle's engine from disturbing anyone.
d. prevent carbon monoxide poisoning.

__c__ 4. Accurate depth perception is critical for
a. checking tire tread depth.
b. checking dashboard indicators.
c. passing a vehicle on a two-lane highway.
d. focusing on roadway signs.

__b__ 5. Of all your senses that you use while driving, the most important one is your sense of
a. hearing.
b. sight.
c. smell.
d. taste.

__b__ 6. The best remedy for driving fatigue is
a. fresh air.
b. rest.
c. singing loudly.
d. coffee.

__c__ 7. The vision that enables you to detect movement not directly in front of you is
a. field vision.
b. central vision.
c. peripheral vision.
d. none of the above.

NAME _____ DATE _____

Read each statement below. If it is true, place a T in the space to the left of the statement. If the statement is false, place an F next to it.

__T__ 8. Fatigue can impair your vision.

__T__ 9. Exercise is one remedy for fatigue.

__T__ 10. Your sense of hearing can help you if a vehicle is in your blind spot.

__F__ 11. If you are upset, one good remedy is to go on a long drive.

__T__ 12. It is a good idea to wear sunglasses to protect your eyes against the sun's glare.

__T__ 13. Color-blind people can get driver's licenses even if they can't tell the difference between a red and a green light.

__T__ 14. People with physical disabilities can drive if they prove that they are able to drive safely.

__T__ 15. A hand-operated brake and accelerator can help people without the full use of their legs to drive.

__T__ 16. *Prosthetic device* is another term for an artificial limb.

In each space below, write the word or words that best complete the sentence.

17. Poisoning from fumes from your vehicle's gasoline engine is called ____carbon monoxide____ poisoning.

18. The vision that you have in a narrow beam straight ahead of you is called ____area of central____ vision.

19. ____Depth____ perception helps you to judge the distance that objects are away from you.

20. You should switch your headlights from high beam to low beam when an approaching vehicle gets no closer than ____500____ feet away from you.

21. How can you fight fatigue before you drive and while you are driving?

Answers may include: The best way to control fatigue is to get rest. Before you drive: get lots of rest; don't eat fatty foods or drink alcoholic beverages. While driving: have a good flow of air; wear sunglasses if needed; take turns driving if possible; turn on the radio, talk, sing; stop regularly to get rest and exercise.

NAME _____ DATE _____

CHAPTER 3 Knowing Yourself

TEST B

Select the phrase that best completes each sentence below. Write the letter of the answer you have chosen to the left of each statement.

__c__ 1. Accurate depth perception is critical for
a. checking tire tread depth.
b. checking dashboard indicators.
c. passing a vehicle on a two-lane highway.
d. focusing on roadway signs.

__d__ 2. If you must stop along a roadway to rest, you should
a. try to find a lighted area, then pull over as far off the road as possible.
b. lock all doors but keep the window open a little.
c. turn on your parking lights but turn off all other accessories.
d. do all of the above.

__c__ 3. In order to control your emotions when driving, you should NOT
a. Plan ahead.
b. Drive when your emotions are even.
c. Expect everybody to know the rules.
d. Maintain a mature attitude.

__d__ 4. Driver fatigue can be caused by
a. overwork.
b. boredom.
c. exposure to too much sun.
d. all of the above.

__a__ 5. Fatigue can be best overcome by
a. rest.
b. a good flow of fresh air.
c. stopping regularly.
d. exercise.

__d__ 6. The function of depth perception is
a. to give three-dimensional perspective.
b. to help to judge the distance between two things.
c. to help to judge the distance an object is from you.
d. all of the above.

__b__ 7. The best action to take when you see a vehicle coming toward you with its high beams on is to
a. turn your high beams on at the oncoming vehicle.
b. direct your attention to the right edge of the roadway, keeping the oncoming vehicle in your peripheral vision.
c. pull your vehicle over to the side of the road.
d. never take your eyes off the oncoming vehicle.

NAME _____ DATE _____

Read each statement below. If it is true, place a T in the space to the left of the statement. If the statement is false, place an F next to it.

__T__ 8. If you have a temporary injury, such as a pinched nerve, the pain can distract your attention from the road.

__T__ 9. A person with cerebral palsy may be able to get a driver's license.

__F__ 10. The most important sense you use in driving is your sense of hearing.

__T__ 11. Your field of vision is what you see looking straight ahead and at angles to your left and right.

__T__ 12. Color-blind people can drive safely.

__F__ 13. Anger is the only emotion that can really interfere with your ability to drive safely.

__T__ 14. A cold can affect the way that you drive.

__T__ 15. Any person with a physical disability can drive if the person can prove that he or she can drive safely.

__F__ 16. Night blindness is a problem when your visual acuity falls below 20/20.

In each space below, write the word or words that best complete the sentence.

17. A color-blind driver can tell the meaning of traffic lights by their ____shape or position____ .

18. ____Depth perception____ gives a three-dimensional perspective and is helpful in letting you know when it is safe to pass another vehicle.

19. Poisoning from fumes from your vehicle's gasoline engine is called ____carbon monoxide____ poisoning.

20. You should be ____500____ feet away from an oncoming vehicle before you switch your headlights from high to low beams.

21. What steps do you need to take to compensate for reduced visibility while driving at night?

Answers may include: Drive more slowly than you would during the day. Increase your following distance to at least 3 seconds. Keep your eyes moving; don't stare at brightly lit areas. Make sure your windshield and headlights are clean. Use high beams whenever safe to do so, and avoid driving at your usual bedtime.

NAME _____ DATE _____

STUDY GUIDE FOR CHAPTER 3   LESSON 1

CHAPTER 3 Knowing Yourself

Emotions Affect Your Driving Ability

A. Strong emotions are a part of life. Being a good driver means knowing yourself well enough not to let your emotions interfere with your driving, and sometimes this means not driving at all. Indicate which of the guidelines below would be appropriate for each of the situations described. (Some situations can have more than one guideline.)

Guidelines

a. Identify situations that can lead to upsets.

b. Plan your trip to allow enough time.

c. Expect other drivers to make mistakes.

d. Delay driving when upset.

Situations

__a/d__ 1. The person you had been dating started going out with your best friend last week. You have been having a hard time sleeping and doing your homework.

__a/d__ 2. You just got your license and are getting ready to take your mother for a ride. Your mother tells you that she cannot pay for your car insurance as she had promised.

__a/b__ 3. It is Thanksgiving Day. You have to drive 100 miles in a snowstorm and arrive by noon.

__c__ 4. The vehicle in front of you stops short, and you brake with a jolt.

__a__ 5. You have a summer job delivering newspapers by car. Your boss and some of your customers often irritate you.

__d__ 6. The check you expected in the mail is not there. You owe your friend money, which you had promised you would pay back today. You feel panicky.

__b__ 7. You know that you are going to start a new job on Monday, and you are going away for the weekend.

__a/b__ 8. Construction has started on a bridge along your route. You dread the drive home.

__d__ 9. You are driving home after a basketball game in which you made a dumb play. You cannot stop thinking about the game.

__c__ 10. The vehicle in front of you drives very slowly up to a signal and then speeds up through the yellow light. You have to stop for the red light.

B. FIND OUT MORE. Interview five people who drive. What kinds of situations or emotions set them off? What makes them lose their concentration while driving?

Review student's work.

NAME _____ DATE _____

STUDY GUIDE FOR CHAPTER 3   LESSON 2

How Vision Affects Your Ability to Drive

A. Match the following terms by placing the letter of the clue in the right column next to the item in the left column.

__c__ 1. visual acuity   a. gives three-dimensional perspective to objects

__d__ 2. field of vision   b. estimating distance between yourself and an object

__e__ 3. area of central vision   c. ability to see clearly

__f__ 4. peripheral vision   d. what you see looking straight ahead and at an angle to the left and right

__a__ 5. depth perception   e. vision clearest in a narrow cone-shaped area directly in front of you

__b__ 6. distance judgment   f. enables you to notice objects and movement to the side

B. For each sentence below, circle T if the statement is true and F if it is false. Correct each false statement in the space below.

1. About 90 percent of all decisions that you make while driving are based on information gathered with your eyes. (T)   F

2. A color-blind person cannot legally drive.   T   (F)
   A color-blind person can safely and legally drive.

3. When driving at night, you should increase your following distance to 1 second.   T   (F)
   At night, increase your following distance to a minimum of 3 seconds.

4. You should switch on your high beams in city traffic.   T   (F)
   You should switch on your high beams on long stretches of empty highway.

5. The light from an oncoming vehicle's headlights cause your eyes' pupils to become larger.
   T   (F)
   An oncoming car's headlights cause the pupils of your eyes to become narrower.

C. FIND OUT MORE. Look in your state driver's manual. What visual acuity do you need to pass the vision test? What can be done to get your license if your visual acuity is low?
   Review student's answers.

NAME _____ DATE _____

STUDY GUIDE FOR CHAPTER 3   LESSON 3

Temporary Physical Conditions

A. For each sentence below, circle T if the statement is true and F if it is false. If the statement is false, correct it in the space below.

1. "Down time," or the time when people are less alert than usual, occurs for most people between the hours of 1 p.m. and 5 p.m. (T)   F

2. The best way to fight fatigue is to stop what you are doing and get some coffee.   T   (F)
   The best way to fight fatigue is to rest.

3. Having a steady flow of fresh air in your vehicle can help you fight fatigue. (T)   F

4. If you have to pull off the road at night, your windows should be lowered at least halfway to avoid carbon monoxide poisoning.   T   (F)
   Your windows should be opened slightly, just enough to get a flow of fresh air.

5. You can drive after taking any medication prescribed by a doctor.   T   (F)
   You can drive if the medication does not have side effects that interfere with driving.

6. Temporary injuries can make it risky for you to drive. (T)   F

B. Fatigue is a major cause of accidents on the highways. Write in the spaces below what your personal plan will be to avoid fatigue before going on a road trip as well as what your precautions will be during the trip to keep yourself awake and alert.
   Examples of possible answers: Get plenty of rest before driving, avoid fatty foods, avoid
   alcohol before driving, play the radio, sing, talk, let someone else drive, pull over every 2 hours
   for 15 minutes of rest and exercise, and keep a fresh flow of air in the car.

C. FIND OUT MORE. What if you had a cold and had to go on a trip? What kind of medication could you safely use? To find out, go to a local drugstore and look at the packages of cold remedies that they sell. Make a list of the ones that say they do not cause drowsiness.
   Review student's answers.

NAME _____ DATE _____

STUDY GUIDE FOR CHAPTER 3   LESSON 4

Long-Term Physical Conditions

A. Many physically challenged, or disabled, people can now drive motor vehicles with the aid of certain improvements that have been made in technology and science. Some physical challenges are listed below. In the space next to each physical challenge, describe what can be used to make it possible for the person to drive.

1. people without full use of their legs **hand-operated brakes and accelerator**

2. people without arms **prosthetic devices and special controls**

3. people who use wheelchairs **specially equipped vans with wheelchair lifts**

4. people who can't turn their heads or shoulders **extra-large rearview mirrors**

B. For each sentence below, circle T if the statement is true and F if it is false. Correct each false statement in the space below.

1. A person with a spinal cord injury cannot get a license to drive.   T   (F)
   A person with a spinal cord injury can get a driver's license as long as he or she can drive safely.

2. Another term for an artificial limb is *prosthetic device*. (T)   F

3. People between the ages of 50 and 75 have the highest pedestrian death rates.   T   (F)
   People 75 years and older have the highest pedestrian death rates.

4. Anybody with a physical challenge can now get a driver's license.   T   (F)
   You must first prove that you can drive safely before you can get a driver's license.

5. An older person generally has a slightly faster reaction time than a younger person.
   T   (F)
   An older person generally has a slower reaction time than a younger person.

C. FIND OUT MORE. Call your state's department of motor vehicles and ask them what the procedure is for a physically challenged person to get a driver's license in your state. How are the tests administered? For what length of time are the licenses issued?
   Review student's answers.

Knowing Yourself

CHAPTER OVERVIEW

LESSON ONE
The effects of emotions on driving are described along with several strategies to control these emotions.

LESSON TWO
Several dimensions of vision are defined, and their particular application to driving is discussed. Suggestions for strategies to help compensate for certain visual deficits are also provided.

LESSON THREE
Temporary conditions such as fatigue, short-term illnesses, and injuries affecting driving are described as well as techniques to deal with these conditions.

LESSON FOUR
Long-term physical factors such as hearing loss, aging, disability, and chronic illnesses are discussed along with strategies and devices specifically designed to compensate for these conditions.

VOCABULARY

area of central vision
carbon monoxide
color blindness
contrast sensitivity
depth perception
night blindness
peer pressure
peripheral vision
vertical field of vision
visual acuity

38

CONCEPT OF THE DRIVING TASK

Driving is a task that involves all facets of a human being—mental, physical, and emotional. To evaluate and manage risk effectively in all driving situations, drivers must be able to understand and control or compensate for emotions and physical shortcomings that can have a significant impact on driving decisions and the ability to manage visibility, time, and space.

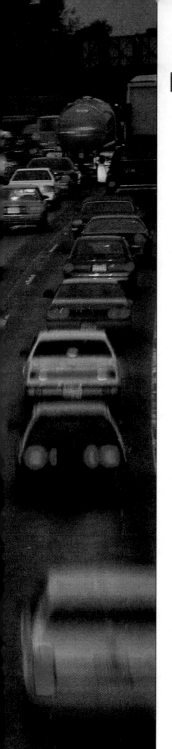

CHAPTER 3

Knowing Yourself

Whenever you get behind the wheel of a vehicle, you must be certain that you are both physically and emotionally fit to drive. It is important to recognize and control physical and emotional factors that might impair the driving task.

LESSON ONE
Emotions Affect Your Driving Ability

LESSON TWO
How Vision Affects Your Ability to Drive

LESSON THREE
Temporary Physical Conditions That Affect
Your Ability to Drive

LESSON FOUR
Long-Term Physical Factors That Affect
Driving Ability

CHAPTER 3 *Knowing Yourself* **39**

PRESENTING THE BIG IDEA ———

Concentration is a crucial element in the driving task. A driver must concentrate on the roadway, other drivers, and the vehicle while being alert to the risk inherent in all driving situations. Understanding and controlling or overcoming any impediments to this concentration are vital.

What's on the Road Ahead?

Have students read the lesson titles and objectives. Briefly discuss the topic of each lesson. Tell students that in this chapter, they will explore the role that emotions and physical factors play in the driving task.

Background: Understanding Emotions

Emotional responses have a strong effect on the mind and body. Understanding emotions can help students recognize how uncontrolled emotional responses can affect drivers.

- Strong emotions cause the nervous system to send signals to the body's organs and glands, alerting them to defend the body.
- In the presence of fear or anger, the adrenal gland empties adrenaline into the bloodstream, causing an increase in breathing rate, heartbeat, and blood pressure.
- Anger also causes the release of a hormone called noradrenalin, which causes a reddening of the face and an excess production of stomach juices. These excess stomach juices can produce a painful stomachache. In the long term, they can cause ulcers.

Relating to Prior Knowledge

Have students name and describe emotions and physical illnesses with which they are familiar. Encourage them to discuss how they think these emotions and conditions might affect the process of driving a vehicle.

The Big Idea

Discuss students' reactions to the Big Idea statement. Suggest that they keep this idea in mind as they read Chapter 3.

Emotions Affect Your Driving Ability

(pages 40–42)

FOCUS

Objectives

• Describe three effects your emotions can have on your driving.

• Describe at least six ways to control the effects your emotions may have on your driving.

Resources

 Study Guide, page 9

Vocabulary

peer pressure

Motivator

Ask students to imagine the following scenario: You are in a terrible mood—you got a bad grade on a test, you lost your leather jacket, and you had an argument with a friend. Now imagine that you have to get into your vehicle and drive home. How does your mood put you at risk, and how can you manage that risk? (Students may respond that concentrating on the day's problems can cause inattention to the driving task; risk may be managed by recognizing that emotions affect driving, waiting until feelings settle down, trying to control emotional reactions until an appropriate time.)

TEACH

Explain

OBJECTIVE 1: Students may benefit from a discussion of how inattention, lack of concentration, and inability to process information pose specific risks for drivers.

LESSON ONE

OBJECTIVES

1. Describe three effects your emotions can have on your driving.
2. Describe at least six ways to control the effects your emotions may have on your driving.

KEY TERM

peer pressure

Emotions Affect Your Driving Ability

Responsibility. Maturity. Self-control. No doubt you've heard these words spoken many times by parents, teachers, and other adults.

As a new driver, those same words will again take on important meaning for you. When you're driving, it's not just skill that matters. It's your ability to think clearly and make sound, responsible driving decisions.

How Do Emotions Affect Your Driving?

Everyone experiences strong feelings, both positive and negative: joy, sadness, anger, fear. Such feelings are part of what it means to be alive.

When you experience a strong negative emotion, you may feel the need to do something forceful. If you're driving, you may have an impulse to act out your emotion by driving aggressively—a very dangerous and irresponsible attitude to take. Aggressive driving incidents have increased so much that there is even a term—*road rage*—to describe the violence sometimes associated with these incidents.

◆ **Strong emotions can have an effect on your driving. They can interfere with your ability to manage risk.**

Inattention

Strong feelings may focus your attention on one thing. If you've just won a tough game, maybe you review the big play over in your mind. Maybe you're thinking about your boyfriend or girlfriend.

Emotions can interfere with your driving by taking your attention away from the road. You may be so preoccupied that you speed or take other risks, without even realizing what you are doing.

Lack of Concentration

Sometimes you can't seem to concentrate on anything. You may feel anxious about a date or excited about getting an A on a test. Let someone else drive or wait until you're better able to focus on the driving task.

THE INTERNATIONAL SCENE

Mexico

In Mexico and other Spanish-speaking countries, stop signs have the same color and shape as those in the United States. The word displayed on the sign is *Parar*, which is the Spanish word for *stop*. Other road signs may not be recognizable by shape or color, so it is helpful to understand Spanish words such as *mantenerse a la derecha* (keep to the right) and *mantenerse a la izquierda* (keep to the left).

Ability to Process Information

Safe driving is a full-time job for your mind as well as for your body. You have to see and hear the signs and signals of the roadway. You also have to use good judgment based on the information you gather.

If you are having a strong emotion, your ability to process roadway information may be diminished. This decreases your ability to manage risk.

How Can You Control Emotions?

Though sometimes it may not seem possible, you *can* learn to control your emotions when you have to. You can also take steps to avoid or minimize problems relating to your emotional state.

Maintain a Responsible Attitude

You exhibit a responsible attitude when you show respect for order and safety and take responsibility for your actions. You should assume a responsible attitude and put aside strong emotions while you drive. Be courteous even if you happen to feel angry. Concentrate on driving safely.

Avoid Triggering Aggressive Driving

Put your angry feelings aside, or you may act in ways that cause other drivers to act aggressively. You can avoid doing so by practicing common courtesy. Here are some examples.
- Keep a safe distance from the vehicles ahead.
- Apologize with an appropriate gesture when you make a mistake.
- Always signal when changing lanes.
- Keep your cool. Don't make obscene gestures or flash your headlights.

Identify Troublesome Situations

Identify situations that may upset or annoy you, and deal with them in a responsible way. When a situation is likely to bother you—an unexpected traffic jam, for example—take a few deep breaths; say to yourself, "I won't let this get to me"; and focus your attention on driving.

You know, for example, that traffic is heavy at rush hour. If you must drive then, you have a choice to make. You can grit your teeth and snarl at the traffic. Or you can tell yourself, "I know traffic is going to be slow now, but this won't last forever. I'm not going to let this bother me." Then you can drive safely and patiently.

◆ *Don't let your emotions get the better of you. Instead, learn ways to control your emotions.*

MEETING STUDENT DIVERSITY

Emotionally Challenged

Some students who are generally more restless, impulsive, and aggressive than others may find it particularly hard to envision controlling their emotions when driving. Work with these students to role-play solutions to emotional situations. Identify the activity as problem solving and not emotional control.

OBJECTIVE 2: Students may profit from a discussion of strategies that will help them focus on the task at hand and put aside emotional considerations. Particular attention should be paid to identifying driving-related situations, such as traffic jams or the reckless driving of other drivers, that can cause sudden and strong emotional reactions.

Teaching Model

Describe the following situation: You have circled a 7-block area repeatedly searching for a parking space. When you finally find one and are preparing to park, another vehicle comes up behind you and "steals" your space. You try to persuade the driver that this was your space, but with no success. As you pull away to look for another spot, you are so angry that your hands are shaking. Model the thinking process that you go through to manage risk by confronting and controlling your anger. (You do the following.

- Realize that you are upset, and take a deep breath to clear your head.
- Recognize that what has happened is over and nothing that you can do will change the result.
- Concentrate on the task at hand—finding a parking space—rather than on what has happened.)

Ask

Ask students to discuss the risks that they might have faced if they had not taken steps to calm down and instead had allowed their anger to take charge.

Read

Have students read Lesson 1 to learn how emotions can affect driving decisions and lead to risk. Also have them read to learn strategies for controlling these emotions.

ASSESS

Guided Practice

Have students answer the Lesson 1 Review questions. The answers are provided below.

Reteaching

Have student pairs develop situations in which strong emotions interfere with the driving task. Suggest that partners meet with other student pairs to share the situations that they have developed. Then have these groups discuss the risks involved in each situation and possible strategies to minimize those risks by managing emotional responses.

Enrichment

Assign the Study Guide for Lesson 1. The Find Out More section encourages students to expand their basic learning of the lesson concepts.

CLOSE

Summarize

Return to the Motivator question, and discuss it again in light of what students have learned in this lesson. Ask students to summarize in their own words the link between emotions and the driving task.

Also have them talk about strategies that can help manage emotions. You may wish to use this question to help center student responses: How can understanding that emotions affect the way you perceive situations help you manage risk in driving?

DRIVER'S LOG

Have students describe what they find most difficult about controlling their emotions and what they might do to overcome this difficulty.

SAFETY TIPS

Don't let conversation with passengers distract you while driving. If you have a serious or emotional matter to discuss with a companion, do so after you've parked the car.

WHAT WOULD YOU DO?

You're already late. How will you deal with your emotions and with getting to your destination in this situation?

WHAT WOULD YOU DO?

Sample answer: Tell yourself that the delay won't last forever, and concentrate on driving.

Plan Ahead

Advance planning can reduce stress and avoid problems. Will your route take you near a stadium at the time that sports fans are crowding the roadways? You can leave home earlier. Will you be traveling on a highway that is partially closed for repair? Try to find an alternate route.

Always allow enough time to get where you are going—extra time if you know you'll be traveling in heavy traffic or bad weather.

Expect Mistakes from Others

Rather than let yourself get irritated by every instance of bad driving you encounter, accept the fact that everyone makes mistakes at one time or another. Drivers may be distracted, inexperienced, or even intoxicated. Never assume that other drivers will drive safely or obey all rules.

Don't Drive When Upset or Depressed

Anger or other strong emotions may be disturbing you. You may also have feelings of grief or intense anxiety that could last for several days. It may be dangerous to drive. Think twice and stay off the road until these feelings subside. It's better to wait until your feelings settle down and you're able to concentrate.

Don't Give In to Negative Peer Pressure

Peer pressure, or the influence of friends who are in your age group, can be very strong. After all, you want to be accepted. However, friends may sometimes encourage you to act in risky ways. For example, peer pressure can lead teens to believe risky driving is cool. Let your friends know that you think too much of yourself to give in to such pressure.

Train Yourself Always to Use Correct Procedures

Get into the habit of using safe driving procedures. Make such procedures automatic, no matter what your emotional state may be.

Lesson **1** Review

1. How can emotions affect your driving?
2. How can you control your emotions when you drive?

Lesson **1** Review

Answers

1. They cause inattention and lack of concentration; they affect your ability to process information.
2. Maintain a mature attitude; plan ahead in order to identify troublesome situations in advance; expect mistakes from others; do not drive when depressed; recognize when you are upset as a first step to dealing with your emotions; train yourself to use safe driving procedures so that they become second nature and are not affected by your emotions.

How Vision Affects Your Ability to Drive

Your sense of sight is the most important of the senses that affect your ability to drive. In fact, about 90 percent of the decisions you make while driving are based on information you gather with your eyes. If you are having trouble seeing, your ability to drive safely is in serious jeopardy.

Why Is Good Vision Critical to Driving Ability?

Being able to see well means more than simply having "20/20 vision." It means being able to see straight ahead and to the sides and being able to perceive depth as well as color.

If your ability to see clearly is impaired, you will have difficulty adjusting your car's speed and position to minimize risk. You will not be able to search the roadway far enough ahead to spot a threatening condition early. You will also have trouble identifying signs, signals, and roadway markings.

To check your ability to see clearly, you should be tested for **visual acuity** (clear vision) by a health care professional or by your local department of motor vehicles. The visual acuity test measures how well you can see and whether or not you need to wear glasses or contact lenses to improve your vision.

Field of Vision

When you are standing still and looking straight ahead, you can see what is directly ahead and also what is at an angle to your right and left. This is your field of vision.

Your vision is clearest in a narrow cone-shaped area directly in front of you, your **area of central vision.** Vision at angles to your right and left is called **peripheral vision.** This vision enables you to notice objects and movement to your sides. Your vision up and down, called your **vertical field of vision,** allows you to see traffic lights overhead and pavement

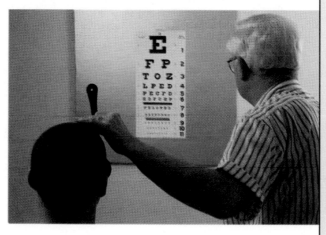

OBJECTIVES

1. Explain why good vision is critical to driving ability.
2. Explain how to compensate for such vision problems as poor depth perception, color blindness, and night blindness.

KEY TERMS

visual acuity
area of central vision
peripheral vision
vertical field of vision
depth perception
contrast sensitivity
color blindness
night blindness

◆ *Have your vision tested regularly. Good vision is crucial to risk management. Traveling at 30 mph, with 20/20 visual acuity, you can read a 6-inch-high street sign from a distance of about 180 to 225 feet, or 4 to 5 seconds away. With 20/40 vision, you would have to be within 90 to 135 feet, or 2 to 3 seconds away, to read the same sign. With 20/100 vision, you would have less than 1 second to read and respond to the sign.*

CHAPTER 3   *Knowing Yourself*   **43**

Driving Tip

Explain to students that one way to compensate for poor depth perception is to practice judging distances by using time along with familiar units of space, such as the length of a vehicle, a city block, or the distance between utility poles.

LESSON TWO

How Vision Affects Your Ability to Drive

(pages 43–45)

FOCUS

Objectives

• Explain why good vision is critical to driving ability.
• Explain how to compensate for such vision problems as poor depth perception, color blindness, and night blindness.

Resources

📁 Study Guide, page 10
📁 Traffic charts
📁 Information Master 18

Vocabulary

visual acuity
area of central vision
peripheral vision
vertical field of vision
depth perception
contrast sensitivity
color blindness
night blindness

Motivator

Ask students which one of the five senses affects 90 percent of the decisions that a person makes while driving. (vision)

Have students discuss what it means to see well and why good vision is needed to drive safely. (Students may mention to have good central and peripheral vision and depth and color perception; good vision is crucial to adjusting speed and position and to identify signs, signals, and roadway markings.)

TEACH

Explain

OBJECTIVE 1: Students should readily recognize the importance of good vision. However, they may benefit from an activity in which they are deprived of one of the elements of good vision—such as peripheral vision.

OBJECTIVE 2: Students may profit from a discussion of the strategies suggested to compensate for vision problems.

- Poor depth perception. Increase following distance and practice comparing relative speeds of approaching vehicles by counting to measure time gaps in traffic.
- Color blindness. Use position, shape, and wording of signs to identify their meaning.
- Night blindness. Don't look directly into glaring headlights but look beyond them, to the right edge of the roadway, and use peripheral vision.

Teaching Model

Describe the following situation: You are driving at night on a two-lane roadway. Model the thinking process that you go through to manage risk. (You do the following.)

- Realize that your vision is reduced at night. Slow down and increase following distance.
- Recognize that lights of oncoming vehicles can cause temporary blindness, so you don't look directly into the lights but over to the right edge of the road and use your peripheral vision.
- Recognize that other drivers may be having trouble driving at night, so you use low beams when following or meeting oncoming vehicles.)

Ask

Ask students to discuss risk factors when driving at night.

Read

Have students read Lesson 2 to learn how vision affects driving and to learn strategies to help compensate for visual deficits.

SAFETY TIPS

If you are driving with your high beams on, you can blind drivers coming toward you. Switch to low beams when oncoming traffic is within 500 feet.

TIPS FOR NEW DRIVERS

Driving at Night

When you drive at night, you need to compensate for reduced visibility. Here are some steps to take.

- Drive more slowly than you would during the day. Adjust your speed to the range of your headlights. Increase your following distance to 3 or 4 seconds or more.
- Keep your eyes moving. Don't stare at brightly lit areas. Keep your attention on the street-level activities around you and in the direction in which you are heading.
- Make sure your windshield and headlights are clean.
- Use your headlights wisely. Use your high beams when possible, such as on long stretches of empty road. Switch to low beams for city driving and when following vehicles or meeting oncoming vehicles.
- Avoid driving near your usual bedtime. Your level of alertness is low at this time.

---

markings, such as crosswalks or arrows in turn lanes. When you are in forward motion as you drive, your field of vision narrows. You need to move your eyes from side to side and up and down to detect any potentially dangerous conditions.

How Can You Compensate for Vision Problems?

If you have a problem with depth perception, distance judgement, contrast sensitivity, color blindness, or night blindness, you can compensate for the problem when you drive.

Poor Depth Perception

Depth perception gives a three-dimensional perspective to objects. It helps you judge the relative distance between two objects. Whenever you look at an object far away, you are using depth perception. You use distance judgment to estimate the distance between yourself and the object.

Depth perception and distance judgment work together. They are especially important when you drive because they help you control your following distance and adjust your position in traffic.

To compensate for poor depth perception, give yourself extra margins of space and time. For example, you can increase your following distance. You can also compare the relative speeds of the cars coming toward you.

Contrast Sensitivity

Contrast sensitivity helps you see details in the driving environment. Any time you face the glare of headlights or drive when it is dark, you are using contrast sensitivity. If you have trouble seeing details because of glare or darkness, slow down and adjust your position in traffic.

Color Blindness

The most commonly used colors in traffic are red, green, and yellow. If you have normal color vision, you won't have

---

MEETING STUDENT DIVERSITY

Physically Challenged

Some students may need extra help in developing simple visual skills. Have them practice searching for objects in their area of central vision and identifying objects in their peripheral vision.

a problem recognizing these colors when you see them. Some people, however, have **color blindness.** These people are unable to tell the difference between red and green or between blue and yellow.

Color-blind people *can* drive safely. They can tell the meaning of signs and signals by their shape and position or by reading the words printed on them.

Night Blindness

Even if you have 20/20 vision, you do not see as well at night as you do during the day. At night your visual acuity, field of vision, depth perception, contrast sensitivity, and color vision are all reduced. For some people, seeing at night is even more difficult.

If seeing at night poses a particular problem for you, you may have a condition known as **night blindness.** Have your eyes checked, and avoid driving at night.

One of the biggest problems in night driving is glare caused by the sudden brightness of the headlights of oncoming vehicles. Whether you look directly at the approaching beams or not, the pupils of your eyes narrow to adjust to the brightness. Your eyes then take a moment to readjust to the darkness of night. During this time, you may be temporarily blinded.

Here are some ways to deal with the danger of glare.

- Do not look directly at the headlights of an oncoming car. Instead, look beyond them and direct your attention to the right edge of the roadway, keeping the approaching car in your peripheral vision.
- Reduce your speed if you are momentarily blinded by glare.
- Keep alert to possible glare situations that may arise, as on curved or hilly roadways. When you anticipate such a situation, turn your eyes slightly away from it, keeping it in your peripheral vision.

Lesson 2 Review

1. Why is good vision important to driving ability?
2. What can you do to compensate for poor depth perception? For night blindness?

WHAT WOULD YOU DO?

You are driving at night and are having trouble seeing the road. How can you ensure the safety of yourself and your passengers?

Lesson 2 Review

Answers

1. Ninety percent of driving decisions are based on information gathered with the eyes.
2. To compensate for poor depth perception, increase the distance between your vehicle and the one you are following, and compare relative speeds of approaching vehicles by counting to measure time gaps in traffic; to compensate for night blindness, don't look directly at oncoming headlights, look to the right, use peripheral vision, and avoid driving at night.

TIPS FOR NEW DRIVERS

Check students' understanding by having them put these night-driving suggestions into their own words.

ASSESS

Guided Practice

Have students answer the Lesson 2 Review questions. The answers are provided below.

Reteaching

Have students work in groups to test their vision at 20 feet under the brightest light available in the room. Suggest that they look at an object with letters readable at that distance. Then have them repeat the test under diminished lighting conditions. Have groups discuss strategies to use when driving under such conditions.

Enrichment

Assign the Study Guide for Lesson 2. The Find Out More section encourages students to expand their basic learning of the lesson concepts.

CLOSE

Summarize

Return to the Motivator questions, and discuss them again. Help students summarize the importance of all elements of good vision and compensation techniques for vision problems.

DRIVER'S LOG

Have students observe a roadway scene in daylight and then again at night to describe possible risks that a night driver would face that might not be risks in daytime.

WHAT WOULD YOU DO?

Sample answer: Avoid looking directly into oncoming headlights, reduce speed, and keep alert to possible glare situations.

Temporary Physical Conditions That Affect Your Ability to Drive

(pages 46–47)

FOCUS

Objectives

• Describe how fatigue affects driving ability and how to fight fatigue.

• Explain the ways that short-term illnesses and injuries may affect driving.

Resources

 Study Guide, page 11

 Information Master 17

Vocabulary

carbon monoxide

Motivator

Pose the following: While driving, you grow drowsy. What actions can you take to minimize driving risk? (Students may mention rolling down a window for air; turning on the radio; looking for a safe place to pull over and stop to rest.)

TEACH

Explain

OBJECTIVES 1 AND 2: Students will profit from discussing how various physical symptoms can increase driving risk.

LESSON THREE

OBJECTIVES

1. Describe how fatigue affects driving ability and how to fight fatigue.
2. Explain the ways that short-term illnesses and injuries may affect driving.

KEY TERM

carbon monoxide

Temporary Physical Conditions That Affect Your Ability to Drive

At times, you will have to decide whether or not you feel physically well enough to drive—or whether it is safe to ride with another driver. Conditions such as fatigue, a cold, the flu, or an injury may be temporary, but these conditions can affect your ability to make good decisions while driving.

You've already read about two important factors affecting a driver's ability to operate a vehicle: emotional state and vision. Various other physical factors can limit or impair driving ability.

In some instances, you can compensate for a limiting physical condition. At other times, your wisest course of action is not to drive at all.

TIPS FOR NEW DRIVERS

Fighting Fatigue

Fatigue is usually temporary and easily overcome. The best way to overcome fatigue is to stop doing whatever you are doing and get some rest.

Before You Drive
• Get plenty of rest.
• Avoid heavy, fatty foods.
• Do not drink alcoholic beverages.

While You Drive
• Make sure there is a good flow of fresh air in the car. If your car is overheated or poorly ventilated, you may become sleepy.
• Wear sunglasses to cope with glare from sun and snow.
• Take turns driving with someone else.
• Turn on the radio. Sing, whistle, or talk to yourself.
• Stop regularly, get out of the car, and walk, jog, or do other light exercise for a few minutes.

How Does Fatigue Affect Your Driving Ability?

Nearly everyone experiences fatigue at times. Fatigue may be brought on by lack of sleep, boredom, illness, or stress. Overeating, drinking alcoholic beverages, or riding in an overheated vehicle all compound the effects of fatigue. The body's natural rhythms cause nearly everyone to be less alert in the late afternoon.

Fatigue is dangerous if you're driving. Your senses are impaired. You may not see objects clearly. You may miss critical information—signs, lights, sounds. You may misjudge speed and distance or take needless risks. You may drift into a state of "highway hypnosis" or even fall asleep at the wheel.

Lack of sleep is now recognized as perhaps the leading cause of traffic fatalities—even ahead of drinking. Combining too little sleep with alcohol consumption virtually guarantees a crash.

MEETING STUDENT DIVERSITY

Limited English Proficiency

For students who have difficulty with English, you may want to substitute the word *tired* for *fatigued*. You may also want to ask students to offer other words in both English and their native language that have a similar meaning.

TIPS FOR NEW DRIVERS

Have students discuss how each tip can help a driver prevent or fight fatigue.

When you feel tired, you're clearly in no condition to begin a long drive. If you are already on the road and find yourself getting sleepy, you're better off pulling over than trying to continue driving. Although it is usually not a good idea to sleep in your car at the side of the road, here are some tips if you have no choice but to stop and rest.

- At night, stop at a well-lit roadside rest area. If you cannot find such an area, make sure you are as far off the highway as possible.
- Roll down a window just enough so that fresh air enters the vehicle but not enough that someone might be able to enter it.
- Turn off the engine to avoid being poisoned by **carbon monoxide,** a colorless, odorless gas.
- Lock all the doors.
- Leave your parking lights on, but turn off all other electrical equipment.
- Before you begin to drive again, get out of the car and make sure you are fully awake.

How Do Short-Term Illnesses or Injuries Affect Your Driving?

A temporary illness, such as a cold, the flu, or an allergy, can make it risky for you to drive. So can an injury, such as a broken bone or a pinched nerve. The discomfort or pain you experience can distract your attention from the road and lessen your ability to manage visibility, time, and space.

If you cannot avoid driving when you're ill, at least try to minimize the amount of driving you do. Allow extra time to get where you're going. Drive more slowly than you normally would, and keep your attention focused on driving, not on how you feel.

Be especially careful about driving if you are taking any medication. Always read the information that appears on medicine containers. Some labels specifically warn against driving. Indeed, some medications for common illnesses can cause drowsiness, nausea, headache, or dizziness—conditions that are extremely dangerous for the driver of a vehicle.

Lesson **3** Review

1. How can fatigue affect your driving? How can you fight fatigue?
2. What effect can temporary illness or injury have on your driving?

SAFETY TIPS

All vehicles emit carbon monoxide gas. It can make you physically ill or even kill you. Have your vehicle's exhaust system checked regularly. Avoid driving a vehicle that has an exhaust leak or a broken tailpipe. Such defects allow harmful exhaust gases to be trapped beneath the vehicle, even when it is moving. These gases may leak into the vehicle's interior.

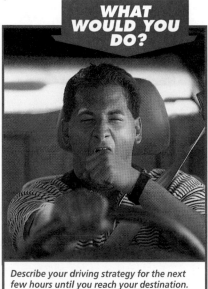

WHAT WOULD YOU DO?

Describe your driving strategy for the next few hours until you reach your destination.

Teaching Model

Describe the following: You must drive, but you have a bad cold. Model your thinking process. (You recognize that your cold may impair concentration, so you will drive more slowly than usual, allow extra time, and avoid taking medicine that may cause drowsiness.)

Ask

Ask students to discuss how a cold might hamper driving ability.

Read

Have students read Lesson 3 to learn the effects of temporary physical conditions on ability to drive.

ASSESS

Guided Practice

Have students answer the Lesson 3 Review questions. The answers are provided below.

Reteaching

Have partners design a poster warning drivers of the dangers posed by temporary physical conditions. Have them include tips to compensate for these conditions.

Enrichment

Assign the Study Guide for Lesson 3. The Find Out More section encourages students to expand their basic learning of the lesson concepts.

CLOSE

Summarize

Reexamine the Motivator question in light of what students learned in this lesson.

DRIVER'S LOG

Have students keep a record for a week of the times of day when they experience fatigue.

WHAT WOULD YOU DO?

Sample answer: Ensure proper ventilation, turn on the radio, or stop to rest if possible.

Lesson **3** Review

Answers

1. Fatigue impairs the senses and may cause a driver to miss critical information, misjudge speed and distance, and even fall asleep at the wheel; to fight fatigue, drivers can roll down a window for fresh air, stop at a lighted rest area, stop regularly to get out of the vehicle and stretch the muscles.
2. The discomfort or pain of a temporary illness or injury can cause drivers to become distracted and lose concentration on the driving task.

Long-Term Physical Factors That Affect Driving Ability

(pages 48–50)

FOCUS

Objectives

- Describe the ways that hearing loss affects driving ability.
- Identify several ways that drivers can compensate for physical disabilities.
- Describe how aging and chronic illness can affect driving ability.

Resources

 Study Guide, page 12

Motivator

Pose the following: While driving, you find yourself behind a vehicle that is being driven by a person who appears to be quite old. What do you need to know about older drivers that can help you manage risk? How should you behave when you encounter an older driver on the roadway? (Students may mention that older drivers may have slower reaction times, less acute vision, and may be compensating for these limitations by driving more slowly. Other drivers should slow down as well, exhibit patience, and be respectful of an older driver's age and experience.)

LESSON FOUR

OBJECTIVES
1. Describe the ways that hearing loss affects driving ability.
2. Identify several ways that drivers can compensate for physical disabilities.
3. Describe how aging and chronic illnesses can affect driving ability.

KEY TERM
driver evaluation facility

Long-Term Physical Factors That Affect Driving Ability

Some people face long-term or permanent physical challenges. Science and medicine, along with advances in technology, have greatly improved the driving potential of such individuals.

How Does Hearing Loss Affect Driving Ability?

◆ Special devices enable many people to drive who would otherwise be unable to do so.

Your sense of hearing is an important guide to conditions on the roadway and within your own car. The sound of a siren, horn, or train signal warns you of possible danger. You may hear the sound of a vehicle before you actually see the vehicle. Sounds from your own vehicle may alert you to engine, muffler, or tire trouble.

Drivers with a hearing loss may be able to compensate by wearing hearing aids. They can rely more on their vision, frequently searching the roadway and making good use of the rearview and sideview mirrors.

How Can Challenges Caused by Physical Disabilities Be Met?

A few years ago, it would have been virtually impossible for a person with cerebral palsy or a spinal cord injury to drive. Such challenges, called physical disabilities, often created obstacles that were impossible to overcome. With the development of modern science and technology, however, such disabilities are no longer permanent barriers. Although the severity of a person's physical disability still has an impact on driving ability, new types of equipment,

---

State BY State

In an increasing number of states, it is illegal to drive while wearing stereo headphones. Regardless of whether or not it is illegal in your state, students should be aware that driving while wearing these devices is extremely dangerous because they drown out traffic sounds vital to the driving task.

such as joystick driving systems, voice-activated controls, and modified vehicles, can greatly increase his or her driving potential.

For example, many people who do not have full use of their legs are able to drive with the aid of such special devices as hand-operated brakes and gas pedals. People without arms can utilize special rings that are attached to the steering wheel, dashboard controls, door locks, radio controls, and so forth. Artificial limbs, called prosthetic devices, enable these drivers to grasp the rings and operate the vehicle.

Special vans are made for people who use wheelchairs. These vans are equipped with wheelchair lifts that can be operated from inside or outside the vehicle, as well as with extra space that permits the driver to smoothly transfer from a wheelchair to a special power seat.

Drivers who have no ability to turn their heads or shoulders can use extra-large rearview mirrors to extend their vision over a wider area.

Anyone with a physical disability who wants to drive a car, and is able to show that he or she can do so safely, can get a license. Usually, such individuals are required to undergo a comprehensive medical assessment that determines their potential to drive. A special center, called a **driver evaluation facility,** is designed specifically for this purpose.

How Do Aging and Chronic Illnesses Affect Driving Ability?

Aging and chronic illnesses are other long-term physical factors that can affect a person's ability to drive.

Aging

As a young person, your reaction time is likely to be faster and your sense of sight keener than that of an older person. Older people, however, can call on their driving experience to help them reduce risk and anticipate threatening conditions. They can also compensate for possible age-related limitations by reducing driving speed and by avoiding heavily traveled roadways.

As you encounter older drivers and pedestrians, be respectful of their age and experience. Slow down and be patient. Someone will do the same for you one day.

FYI

Be especially careful when you see elderly pedestrians. People 75 years of age and older have the highest pedestrian death rates.

◆ Older drivers can call on their experience to help them manage risk.

IT'S A FACT

The time needed to regain vision after being temporarily blinded by bright headlights varies dramatically according to age. For people under 50, the recovery of vision time is about 3 to 4 seconds. At 50 mph, 3 to 4 seconds translates to 225 feet, or three-quarters of the length of a football field. For people over 50, 5 to 12 seconds is a more common recovery time.

TEACH

Explain

OBJECTIVE 1: Most students will have no trouble realizing the problems faced by drivers who have a hearing impairment. However, they may profit from a discussion of ways that drivers with normal hearing can face the same sorts of problems. For example, playing a vehicle's radio too loudly can diminish a driver's ability to hear vital traffic sounds.

OBJECTIVE 2: Students will have little difficulty understanding problems faced by drivers who are physically challenged. However, they may be unfamiliar with the fact that specially equipped vehicles can offer these individuals the ability to drive.

OBJECTIVE 3: Encourage students to discuss the limitations posed by chronic illnesses and aging. Ask them to describe how each of these limitations can affect the driving task.

Teaching Model

Describe the following: Your aunt has epilepsy, which is controlled by medication. She has not had a seizure in more than ten years and would like to apply for a driver's license, but she does not know if she is eligible because of her illness and is embarrassed to find out. Share your thinking process as you model what you will tell your aunt to reassure her about applying. (You will tell her that chronic illnesses are nothing to be embarrassed about and that she should ask her doctor for a letter stating that her illness is under control and that the medication she is taking will not impair her ability to drive; she can take the letter to the motor vehicle department to help her obtain a license.)

Ask

Ask students to discuss why state motor vehicle departments are concerned about drivers with chronic illnesses.

ADVICE FROM THE EXPERTS

Have students discuss strategies for coping with distractions and for keeping emotions in check.

Read

Have students read Lesson 4 to learn the effects of aging and chronic illness on driving and to learn about ways to compensate for these conditions.

ASSESS

Guided Practice

Have students answer the Lesson 4 Review questions. The answers are provided below.

Reteaching

Pair a student who experiences difficulty with this lesson with a more able student. Have them work together to write and present a public service television commercial informing either individuals who are physically challenged or those with chronic illnesses of their options if they want to obtain a driver's license and/or a vehicle.

Enrichment

Assign the Study Guide for Chapter 3. The Find Out More section encourages students to expand their basic learning of the lesson concepts.

CLOSE

Summarize

Review the Motivator section, and have students discuss other limiting conditions and compensation strategies.

DRIVER'S LOG

Have students write about the most useful or surprising information they learned in this lesson.

ADVICE FROM THE EXPERTS

Sue MacNeil
Injury Prevention Specialist, Little World Road Safety and Injury Prevention, Kinburn, Ontario, Canada

To evaluate and manage risk, you have to be honest with yourself. Are you feeling upset or angry about something? Is your mind focused on some disturbing event that just occurred? If so, you may be wise to put off driving until you feel calmer and can better concentrate.

Sometimes events that upset you occur while you are driving. For example, another driver may cut in front of you. Resist the urge to let your emotions affect your driving. Don't let outside pressures interfere with your ability to manage risk.

Chronic Illnesses

A chronic illness is one that lasts over a long period of time or one that recurs often.

Some chronic illnesses, such as epilepsy, arthritis, diabetes, and asthma, can be treated and controlled by medication. However, the medication itself can result in such side effects as drowsiness, dizziness, headache, and nausea, that interfere with safe driving. To obtain a driver's license, people with chronic illnesses must furnish proof that the illnesses are under control and that medication won't cause side effects that impair driving ability.

WHAT WOULD YOU DO?

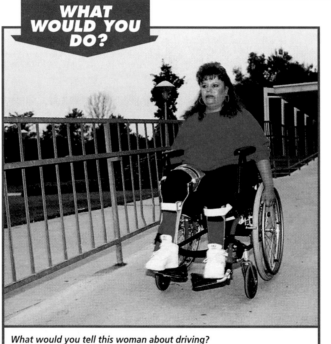

What would you tell this woman about driving?

Lesson **4** Review

1. How can impaired hearing affect your ability to drive?
2. How can drivers who have a physical disability compensate for that disability?
3. What effect do aging and chronic illnesses have on driving ability?

WHAT WOULD YOU DO?

Sample answer: Special equipment is available to accommodate drivers who are physically challenged.

Lesson **4** Review

Answers

1. Impaired hearing can prevent a driver from getting crucial signals such as sirens, horns, and train whistles, as well as vehicle sounds that can alert drivers to possible vehicle trouble.
2. Physically disabled drivers can compensate by using vehicles equipped with devices such as hand-operated brakes and accelerators, and wheelchair-lift-equipped vans.
3. Aging and chronic illness can affect reaction time and vision; medication used may have dangerous side effects.

Kitty O'Neil

Kitty O'Neil is 5 feet 3 inches tall and weighs only 98 pounds, but her accomplishments are giant-sized. She has held the women's world land speed driving record of 512 mph and has gone on to become the second-fastest human, with a land speed of 618 mph. Of course, both of these records were accomplished in specially designed cars driven at test sites and not on highways.

O'Neil has also set records as a champion drag boat racer and water-skier, and she is a former American Athletic Union national diving champion. She uses the skills that enabled her to set these records in her work as a movie stunt woman. Among other things, she has jumped off six-story buildings, pretended to be drowning, and been set on fire.

Why does Kitty O'Neil do these things? As she says, one reason is to prove that physically challenged people "can do anything." Kitty O'Neil has been deaf since she was four months old. She believes that she owes her will to succeed to her mother, a woman of Cherokee descent who died when Kitty was 21 years old. She taught Kitty how to talk and play the cello and the piano and rewarded Kitty whenever she perfected a new skill. O'Neil says that she would like to show others that her mother's encouragement and support "has paid off beyond anyone's hopes."

What Do You Think Now?

Does the story of Kitty O'Neil change or confirm your opinion of the capabilities of people who are physically challenged? Explain your answer.

BUILDING SKILLS: CRITICAL THINKING

Objective

Demonstrate the ability to think critically about the capabilities of physically challenged individuals.

Teaching the Skill

- Discuss with students why hearing is a sense that is needed for driving.
- Have students consider how a person with a hearing impairment can be a safe and accomplished driver.
- Discuss how Kitty O'Neil's deafness might have contributed to her success.

ANSWER TO
What Do You
Think Now Question

Accept reasonable responses. Students may express surprise and admiration for O'Neil's courage and accomplishments. They may state that the ability to overcome a physical challenge indicates a determination to succeed in other areas that call for courage and stamina.

CHAPTER SUMMARY

Key Points

Have students read the Key Points to review the major concepts of the chapter.

Cooperative Learning:
Students will benefit by working with a partner on one or both projects. When the assignment is completed, the whole class will profit by sharing and comparing results.

CHAPTER 3 REVIEW

KEY POINTS

Lesson One

1. Emotions such as joy, sadness, anger, and fear can cause you to be inattentive, interfere with your ability to concentrate, and hinder your ability to process information while driving.
2. You can make an effort to control your emotions by maintaining a responsible attitude and identifying situations that may cause you to become upset.

Lesson Two

1. You must have good vision in order to adjust your car's speed and position to minimize risk. Good vision also enables you to identify signs, signals, and roadway markings.
2. To compensate for poor depth perception, practice judging the distance between two objects; for color blindness, learn the meaning of signs and signals by their shape and position; for low-contrast situations and night blindness, drive more slowly than you would during the day.

Lesson Three

1. Fatigue impairs your senses. It could cause you to fall asleep while driving, miss critical information, take risks, or misjudge speed and distance. Fight fatigue by getting plenty of rest, avoiding alcoholic beverages and heavy foods, opening the windows to get fresh air, and taking turns driving with someone else.
2. Short-term illness or injury can cause pain or discomfort, which can distract your attention from the road and lessen your ability to manage visibility, time, and space.

Lesson Four

1. Hearing loss may prevent you from being aware of sounds that warn you of possible danger, such as the sounds of sirens or horns, and can prevent you from being aware of problems within your own car.
2. People without full use of their legs can drive with the aid of devices such as hand-operated brakes and accelerators. With the aid of prosthetic devices, people without arms can drive using special rings and dashboard controls. Those who use wheelchairs can use specially equipped vehicles.
3. Aging can affect a driver's reaction time and eyesight. Medications for chronic illnesses may have side effects that interfere with safe driving.

PROJECTS

1. Emotional factors play an important part in the way people drive. What are some ways that people could be reminded to maintain a responsible attitude and to be courteous and patient while driving?
2. While you are a passenger, close your eyes. Use your other senses to gather information. Can you identify the sounds you hear? Can you tell whether the car is speeding up, slowing down, or making a turn?

*inter*NET CONNECTION

Use the Internet to investigate the problems of aggressive driving, which may also be called road rage.
drivered.glencoe.com

*inter*NET CONNECTION

Visit Glencoe's Driver Education Web site for student activities that relate to this chapter.
drivered.glencoe.com

CHAPTER TEST

Write the letter of the answer that best completes each sentence.

1. Strong emotions can
   a. affect your night vision.
   b. help you drive safely.
   c. interfere with your driving judgment.

2. If you are severely fatigued, you should
   a. avoid driving.
   b. drive with your high beams on.
   c. drive quickly to your destination.

3. A physical factor that may affect driving ability is
   a. the effects of medication.
   b. the color of your eyes.
   c. a feeling of sadness.

4. A person who cannot see well at angles to the left and right has difficulty with
   a. night vision.
   b. depth perception.
   c. peripheral vision.

5. One way to deal with headlight glare is to
   a. look right at the car's headlights.
   b. look at the right edge of the road.
   c. increase speed to get past the car quickly.

6. As a driver, it is your responsibility to drive
   a. your friends to school.
   b. only when you are able to concentrate.
   c. no matter how you are feeling.

7. Drivers who are unable to turn their head or shoulders can use
   a. revolving seats.
   b. extra-large rearview mirrors.
   c. a thickly padded seat cushion.

8. To control your emotions in traffic
   a. yell at other drivers.
   b. daydream about pleasant events.
   c. expect others to make mistakes.

9. If you use correct procedures, you will
   a. reduce risk no matter how you may feel.
   b. never have a collision.
   c. be able to drive without paying attention.

10. Most of the information you gather about traffic situations comes from
    a. other drivers.
    b. your vision.
    c. your sense of hearing.

Choose the phrase that best completes each sentence.

field of vision	wheelchair lifts
responsible attitude	lack of concentration
depth perception	sense of hearing

11. Your _____ helps you judge the distance between cars.

12. Having a(n) _____ means respecting others' well-being and an awareness of the consequences of your actions.

13. Your _____ includes what you can see directly in front of you, up and down, and at an angle to the sides.

14. Strong emotions can lead to a(n) _____ when you drive.

15. Modified vehicles for people who are physically disabled may include _____.

DRIVER'S LOG

In this chapter, you have learned about how emotional and physical factors can affect driving. Write at least two paragraphs giving your ideas on the following questions.
- What "sets you off" emotionally?
- How will you control these factors and your emotions?

CHAPTER 3 REVIEW

CHAPTER TEST

Assign the Chapter Test to all students.

Answers
1. c
2. a
3. a
4. c
5. b
6. b
7. b
8. c
9. a
10. b
11. depth perception
12. responsible attitude
13. field of vision
14. lack of concentration
15. wheelchair lifts

DRIVER'S LOG

Students' responses will reflect their personal viewpoints. However, their answers should provide an assessment of their understanding of the impact that emotional responses can have on the driver and the driving task.

Evaluate
- Test A, pages 5–6 or Test B, pages 5–6 📁
- Testmaker software

RETURN TO THE BIG IDEA

Discuss the concept that concentration is crucial to the driving task and that drivers are responsible for recognizing and controlling any factors that interfere with their ability to concentrate.

Handling Social Pressures Overview

THEME DEVELOPMENT Alcohol and other drugs impair driving ability and put driver, passengers, and others at risk. Responsible drivers use neither alcohol nor drugs, and discourage others from using these dangerous substances. Drivers should also recognize that distractions can impair driving ability and increase risk.

LESSON	PAGES	LESSON OBJECTIVES	STATE/LOCAL OBJECTIVES
1 Alcohol's Effect on One's Health and One's Future	56–57	**1.** Describe the effects of alcohol. **2.** Name some responsibilities regarding drinking. **3.** Explain how to identify a problem drinker.	
2 Alcohol and Its Effects on Driving Ability	58–62	**1.** Explain how alcohol affects driving ability. **2.** Name the laws about and penalties for driving while intoxicated.	
3 How Other Drugs Affect Driving Ability	63–65	**1.** Describe some kinds of drugs other than alcohol. **2.** Explain how these drugs affect driving ability.	
4 Distractions Can Increase Driving Risk	66–68	**1.** Name some distractions that increase driving risk. **2.** Describe how these distractions can hinder your driving ability.	
Building Skills	69		
Review: Chapter Summary	70		
Chapter Test	71		

CHAPTER FEATURES	TCR COMPONENTS
	Study Guide, p. 13
	Lesson Plan, p. 9
	Information Masters 3 and 5
 **CONNECTIONS** Social Studies The origin and social impact of Students Against Destructive Decisions (SADD).	Study Guide, p. 14 Lesson Plan, p. 9 Information Masters 4, 6, and 15
TIPS FOR NEW DRIVERS Recognizing when other drivers are under the influence of alcohol or drugs.	Study Guide, p. 15 Lesson Plan, p. 10
ADVICE FROM THE EXPERTS The importance of avoiding driving situations that involve drinking.	Study Guide, p. 16 Lesson Plan, p. 10
BUILDING SKILLS: READING MAPS Using the Mileage Chart	Test A, pp. 7–8 Test B, pp. 7–8

PROJECTS

1. Find out about local chapters of MADD and SADD.

2. Interview a police officer about teenage drivers and DUI or DWI.

OTHER PROGRAM RESOURCES

Testmaker software
Responsible Driving software: Alcohol and Other Drugs

ADDITIONAL RESOURCES

Just Another Friday Night, Film 455, AAA Foundation
Parents Discuss Kids, Cars, Alcohol, Film 583, AAA Foundation

---

NAME _____   DATE _____

CHAPTER 4 Handling Social Pressures

TEST A

Match the following terms by placing the letter of the definition to the left of the item.

__c__1. alcohol   a. a drug that greatly alters the mind

__a__2. hallucinogen   b. permission to have yourself tested for alcohol use any time you drive

__d__3. stimulant   c. the most widely abused drug

__e__4. inhibitions   d. a drug that speeds up the central nervous system

__b__5. implied consent   e. elements of our personality that hold back certain behaviors

Select the phrase that best completes each sentence below. Write the letter of the answer you have chosen to the left of each statement.

__d__6. A hallucinogen that makes a user drowsy and distorts reaction time and judgment of time and space is
    a. cocaine.
    b. PCP.
    c. a barbiturate.
    d. marijuana.

__c__7. Regarding alcohol and driving, it is false that
    a. 40 percent of all highway deaths are alcohol related.
    b. about one in five drivers aged 16 to 20 who die in highway crashes is intoxicated.
    c. one or two drinks will not affect one's night vision.
    d. about three in ten Americans will be involved in an alcohol-related crash at some time in their lives.

__c__8. The alcoholic content of a 5-ounce glass of wine, a 12-ounce bottle of beer, or $1\frac{1}{2}$ ounces of whiskey is
    a. greatest in the whiskey.
    b. greatest in the glass of wine.
    c. about the same.
    d. least in the bottle of beer.

__a__9. Alcohol is classified as a
    a. depressant.
    b. stimulant.
    c. hallucinogen.
    d. narcotic.

__d__10. The way to sober up a person who has had too much to drink is to
    a. give the person black coffee.
    b. make the person take a cold shower.
    c. make the person exercise.
    d. give the alcohol time to wear off.

__d__11. A person's _____ is affected by alcohol.
    a. vision
    b. judgment
    c. coordination
    d. all of the above

Read each statement below. If it is true, place a T in the space to the left of the statement. If the statement is false, place an F next to it.

__T__12. It is not always safe to drive after taking an over-the-counter drug.

__F__13. Stimulants have a slowing-down effect on the central nervous system.

__F__14. In all states, a person must have an alcohol level of 10 percent or greater in the bloodstream to be considered intoxicated.

__F__15. It is safe to drive after a few drinks as long as you are able to stay within the speed limit.

__T__16. DWI stands for "driving while intoxicated."

__F__17. In 1997, more than 100,000 highway deaths were alcohol related.

__F__18. The main reason that you should not play loud music in the car is that it is rude to other passengers.

__T__19. Driving with an animal in the car can be a dangerous distraction unless you have the animal in a pet carrier or the animal is restrained by a passenger.

__T__20. In most states it is illegal to wear stereo headphones while you drive.

__T__21. Peer pressure can influence the way that you dress and the way you talk.

__F__22. You have to drink heavily for at least 10 years before you can be considered an alcoholic.

23. What is your responsibility to a friend who has been drinking and wants to drive?

Do not let someone you know drive if that person has been drinking. Take the keys and drive the

person to his or her destination, call your parents or the friend's parents, or call a taxi.

24. What are the symptoms of a problem drinker?

Look for changes in a person's behavior or situation, such as loss of initiative, frequent lateness and

absences from school, behavior problems, a decline in grades, a change or loss of friends, or trouble

with the law.

CHAPTER 4 Handling Social Pressures

TEST B

Match the following terms by placing the letter of the definition to the left of the item.

__c__1. blood alcohol concentration   a. a drug that speeds up the central nervous system

__d__2. depressant   b. a kind of hallucinogen

__a__3. stimulant   c. the percentage of alcohol in a person's blood

__e__4. hallucinogen   d. a drug that slows down the central nervous system

__b__5. LSD   e. a drug that greatly alters the mind

Select the phrase that best completes each sentence below. Write the letter of the answer you have chosen to the left of each statement.

__d__6. Drivers who choose to drink should
    a. ask a nondrinking friend to drive.
    b. call a cab or take a bus.
    c. drive if they feel in control.
    d. do either a or b.

__b__7. A false statement about drinking is that
    a. it is illegal for people under age 21 to consume alcohol.
    b. one or two drinks will affect a person's vision very minimally.
    c. about one in five drivers aged 16 to 20 who dies in highway collisions is intoxicated.
    d. alcohol is the most used and abused drug in the world.

__b__8. A can of beer, a glass of wine, and $1\frac{1}{2}$ ounces of liquor
    a. have greatly different alcohol contents.
    b. have almost equal alcohol contents.
    c. will not show any level of alcohol on a Breathalyzer test.
    d. are not absorbed into the bloodstream if you have eaten a big meal.

__c__9. The only way to get sober after drinking too much alcohol is to
    a. take a cold shower.
    b. exercise or walk around.
    c. allow enough time to let the alcohol wear off.
    d. drink black coffee.

__c__10. Alcohol is classified as a(n)
    a. amphetamine.
    b. barbiturate.
    c. depressant.
    d. stimulant.

__d__11. Use of alcohol affects
    a. a person's coordination.
    b. a person's vision.
    c. a person's judgment.
    d. all of the above.

__b__12. A symptom of a problem drinker is
    a. lots of speeding tickets.
    b. a loss of initiative.
    c. always being on time.
    d. drinking less than was planned.

Read each statement below. If it is true, place a T in the space to the left of the statement. If the statement is false, place an F next to it.

__T__13. Marijuana makes a person drowsy.

__T__14. A person may be charged with a DWI even without a BAC of 0.10 percent or greater.

__F__15. Reasoning is about the last of the driver's abilities to be affected by alcohol.

__F__16. You are safe to drive after one or two drinks but unsafe after three drinks.

__T__17. Adults can be considered intoxicated in some states if their BAC is 0.08 percent.

__T__18. You can be considered a problem drinker even if you are a teenager.

__T__19. About one-fifth of drivers aged 15 to 20 who were killed in crashes were intoxicated.

__T__20. DWI stands for "driving while intoxicated."

__F__21. It is always safe to drive after taking over-the-counter medications.

__T__22. Peer pressure can influence what music you listen to and how you dress.

__T__23. Using a cellular phone while driving is unsafe.

24. What can you do if you or someone you know is a problem drinker?

You can contact Alcoholics Anonymous (AA), a support group for recovering alcoholics, or Alateen, a

support group for people who have an alcoholic parent, sibling, or friend.

NAME _____   DATE _____

STUDY GUIDE FOR CHAPTER 4   LESSON 1

Alcohol's Effect on One's Health and One's Future

A. For each sentence below, circle T if the statement is true and F if it is false. Correct each false statement in the space below.

1. Peer pressure can influence the way you walk and talk.   **T**   F

2. Alcohol is a powerful drug.   **T**   F

3. There are ways to tell before you start drinking if it will eventually become a problem for you.   T   **F**
There is no way to tell beforehand whether you will become a problem drinker.

4. Choosing not to drink guarantees that you will not become addicted to alcohol.   **T**   F

5. Frequent lateness and absences from school are not a sign of problem drinking.   T   **F**
Frequent lateness and absences from school can be a sign of problem drinking.

6. People have no responsibility to protect themselves and others from the threat of people who drink and drive.   T   **F**
People always have a responsibility to protect themselves and others from drivers who drink.

7. A support group for young people who have an alcoholic friend, parent, or sibling is Alateen.   **T**   F

8. Alcohol abuse can cause malnutrition.   **T**   F

B. FIND OUT MORE. Go to your library. Look up any information that you can find on teenage alcoholism, and write what you find below.

Review student's work.

_____
_____
_____
_____

NAME _____   DATE _____

STUDY GUIDE FOR CHAPTER 4   LESSON 2

Alcohol and Its Effects on Driving

A. Check the facts in the graph below and answer the questions. The graph is based on the effects of alcohol on a 150-pound adult male who has had four or more years of experience driving and who is an experienced drinker as well.

ELIMINATION RATE
Blood Alcohol Level (BAL)

1. For how long does alcohol remain in a person's blood? 12 hours

2. Between what hours should the person in the graph not drive? Between 5 p.m. and 5 a.m.

3. For approximately how long is this person legally impaired? 6 hours, 45 minutes

4. Between what hours is the person legally intoxicated? Between 8:30 p.m. and 10:15 p.m.

5. For how long after the person stops drinking is he legally impaired? 5 ¹/₄ hours

6. What is the alcohol level at the time elimination starts? .12 percent

7. How long does it take for the alcohol to be eliminated? 8 hours

8. Is the person legally impaired for a longer period while absorbing the alcohol or while eliminating the alcohol? Eliminating

B. FIND OUT MORE. Search your local newspaper for one week. Keep a list of all accidents related to alcohol, and describe one of them below.

Review student's work.

NAME _____   DATE _____

STUDY GUIDE FOR CHAPTER 4   LESSON 3

How Other Drugs Affect Driving Ability

A. For each sentence below, circle T if the statement is true and F if it is false. Correct each false statement in the space below.

1. Over-the-counter drugs are drugs that you can purchase only with a prescription.   T   **F**
Over-the-counter drugs are drugs that you can purchase without a doctor's prescription.

2. Over-the-counter drugs will not interfere with your driving ability.   T   **F**
Some over-the-counter drugs can make you drowsy or can have other side effects.

3. A depressant slows down the central nervous system.   **T**   F

4. Alcohol is a stimulant.   T   **F**
Alcohol is a depressant.

5. Stimulants can make users think that they are more alert than usual.   **T**   F

6. The chemicals in marijuana can stay in your body for as long as 6 hours.   T   **F**
The chemicals in marijuana can stay in your system for up to 6 weeks.

7. LSD is a kind of depressant.   T   **F**
LSD is a kind of hallucinogen.

8. Marijuana can make the user feel drowsy.   **T**   F

B. FIND OUT MORE. Collect your local newspaper for a week. Write a brief summary of any articles that you find about the problems associated with drugs and alcohol. Pay particular attention to what is happening in your community.

Review student's work.

_____
_____
_____
_____
_____
_____
_____

NAME _____   DATE _____

STUDY GUIDE FOR CHAPTER 4   LESSON 4

Distractions Can Increase Driving Risk

A. There are many sources of distractions for drivers that can make it unsafe to drive. How would you handle the following distractions?

Radio, cassette or CD player Examples of possible answers: Keep the volume low; don't look for or change cassettes or CDs while driving.

Headphones Headphones in vehicles are illegal in many states and should never be worn while driving because they block out sounds the driver may need to hear.

Cellular phones Do not use cellular phones while driving; pull over to place or answer calls.

Loud, rowdy passengers It is your responsibility to tell passengers to be quiet and to sit still.

Restless children Tell children the rules before starting out. Bring games, toys, or tapes to keep them from becoming bored.

Animals in the vehicle Keep all animals in carrying cases, have a friend hold the animal by its leash, or get a pet safety belt.

Toll roads Get the change ready before starting out, or have a passenger be in charge of the change. Never look for change while the vehicle is in motion.

B. FIND OUT MORE. Call your local pet store. What devices are sold to keep dogs and cats restrained in vehicles?

Review student's work.

Handling Social Pressures

CHAPTER OVERVIEW

LESSON ONE
The dangers of alcohol are described, and responsibilities to self and others are discussed.

LESSON TWO
The physical and mental effects of alcohol on driving ability are explained, and drinking-related laws, tests, and penalties are discussed.

LESSON THREE
The effects on driving ability of drugs other than alcohol are described.

LESSON FOUR
Distractions that can impair driving ability are discussed.

VOCABULARY

blood-alcohol concentration
 (BAC)
driving under the influence (DUI)
driving while intoxicated (DWI)
implied consent
inhibitions

54

CONCEPT OF THE DRIVING TASK

Explain that drivers must take responsibility for their actions. There are no "good reasons" for driving with impaired ability or otherwise driving in an unsafe manner. Getting behind the wheel of a vehicle means accepting the responsibility to operate the vehicle in a safe manner at all times.

CHAPTER 4

Handling Social Pressures

As a driver, you will be responsible for your safety as well as that of your passengers and other roadway users. It is important to learn how to base your decisions on good judgment and not on a desire to "go along" with the crowd.

LESSON ONE
Alcohol's Effect on One's Health and One's Future

LESSON TWO
Alcohol and Its Effects on Driving Ability

LESSON THREE
How Other Drugs Affect Driving Ability

LESSON FOUR
Distractions Can Increase Driving Risk

PRESENTING THE BIG IDEA

Driving with one's ability impaired—whether by prescription medication, alcohol, or for any other reason—is both irresponsible and dangerous.

INTRODUCING THE CHAPTER

What's on the Road Ahead?

Have students read the lesson titles and objectives. Briefly discuss the topic of each lesson. Tell students that in this chapter, they will learn how alcohol and other drugs seriously impair driving ability.

Background: Drinking and Driving

Statistics paint a grim portrait of the costs and dangers of drinking and driving.

- Alcohol is involved in about 40 percent of all highway deaths. In 1997 alone, alcohol-related crashes claimed more than 16,000 lives—well over 300 per week. About a third of those killed were under 25 years of age.
- About half the people killed in alcohol-related collisions are not the ones who were drinking.
- Drinking one or two drinks makes a teenage driver more than 40 times more likely to be involved in a fatal collision than a sober driver of any age.

Relating to Prior Knowledge

Have students discuss how taking medication or using alcohol or drugs can affect a person's ability to function.

The Big Idea

Discuss students' reactions to the Big Idea statement. Suggest that they keep this idea in mind as they read Chapter 4.

Alcohol's Effect on One's Health and One's Future

(pages 56–57)

FOCUS

Objectives
- Describe the effects of alcohol.
- Name some responsibilities regarding drinking.
- Explain how to identify a problem drinker.

Resources

 Study Guide, page 13

 Information Masters 3 and 5

 Understanding the Dangers of Alcohol and Other Drugs

Motivator
You think one of your friends may be developing a drinking problem. What warning signs should you watch for? (Students may mention changes in the person's behavior or life situation, such as loss of initiative, frequent absences from school, or trouble with the law.)

TEACH

Explain
OBJECTIVE 1: Stress that no one ever sets out to become a problem drinker.

OBJECTIVE 2: Explain to students that a true friend is willing to "hassle" a friend about drinking.

OBJECTIVE 3: Students should note that behavioral changes may be gradual.

OBJECTIVES
1. Describe the effects of alcohol.
2. Name some responsibilities regarding drinking.
3. Explain how to identify a problem drinker.

FYI

No one is alone. If a person or someone he or she knows has a drinking problem, he or she can contact:

Alcoholics Anonymous
P.O. Box 459
Grand Central Station
New York, NY 10163

Alateen
P.O. Box 862
Midtown Station
New York, NY 10018

Both of these organizations have listings in local phone directories.

Alcohol's Effect on One's Health and One's Future

You are at an exciting, yet confusing, time in your life. Sometimes people treat you as an adult and at other times as a child. Learning to cope with this partial independence is a natural stage of growing up. It is the time when you are very vulnerable to peer pressure.

Peer pressure can influence the way you dress, your taste in music, and even the way you talk. This is usually harmless. However, peer pressure can also influence you in ways that can damage you and your future, such as influencing you to experiment with drinking alcohol. Understanding how alcohol can destroy your hopes, dreams, and ambitions can help you resist destructive peer pressure.

What Are the Effects of Alcohol?

Alcohol is a powerful and dangerous drug—it can change the way people act, think, and feel. Many people experiment with alcohol to overcome feelings of shyness, inhibition, or unhappiness or because it makes them feel like part of the group. Alcohol addiction can creep up slowly and take control of a person's life. School, work, friends, family, plans for the future become meaningless to the problem drinker. He or she becomes psychologically and physically dependent on alcohol.

Annually, fatalities associated with alcohol use claim five times more people than heroin, cocaine, marijuana, and all other illegal drugs combined. The high number of traffic fatalities involving young people is the reason why every state has passed laws to make it illegal for people under age 21 to buy, possess, or consume alcohol. In 1997, more than 16,000 people died in alcohol-related crashes in the United States.

For people age 21 or over, excessive drinking is no longer tolerated. Recently enacted laws that prohibit open containers of alcoholic beverages in vehicles, lower permissible blood alcohol levels, and increase fines and penalties encourage responsible drinking for people 21 and older.

What Are a Person's Responsibilities Regarding Drinking?

There is no such thing as responsible drinking for an underage person. There are, however, responsibilities that everyone has regarding alcohol drinking and drinkers.

IT'S A FACT

In 1997, 16,189 people were killed in alcohol-related motor vehicle collisions. More than 327,000 people were injured.

- People have a responsibility to protect themselves from the threat that drinking poses to their health and well-being. They also have a responsibility to protect themselves and others from the risk posed by people who drink and drive.
- If you are with someone who has been drinking, don't let that person drive. You can help by taking the car keys, driving yourself, calling your parents for a ride, calling a taxi, or making other arrangements.
- There are support groups to help problem drinkers and their relatives and friends. These groups keep any information confidential. Two such groups are Alcoholics Anonymous, or AA, and Alateen.

AA is an organization for people who feel or know that they may have a problem with alcohol and need help. Alateen is a support group for young people who have an alcoholic parent, sibling, or friend.

What Are the Symptoms of a Problem Drinker?

People must be able to recognize the signs of problem drinking. Look for changes in a person's behavior or life situation such as loss of initiative, frequent lateness and absences from school, behavior problems at school, a decline in grades, a change of friends, leisure activities that focus on alcohol, and trouble with the law. A person with a drinking problem often denies having a problem, drinks alone, has trouble sleeping, and may suffer from memory loss or blackouts.

Other symptoms can be seen in health problems that can afflict the problem drinker, such as liver failure, heart disease, cancer, brain damage, convulsions, and malnutrition.

Alcoholism is a disease. Its consequences are devastating and include loss of self-esteem, loss of friends and family, and even loss of life. The best defense against this disease is to say no when you are offered that first drink.

WHAT WOULD YOU DO?

You and a friend are offered a drink. You say no but your friend wants to try one. What will you say to your friend?

Lesson 1 Review

1. What can be the consequences of alcohol use?
2. What responsibilities do people have to themselves and to friends regarding drinking?
3. How would you recognize the signs of a problem drinker, and what might you do to help that person?

WHAT WOULD YOU DO?

Sample answer: It's better not to drink, but if you do, don't drive.

Lesson 1 Review

Answers
1. It can change the way you act, think, and feel and cause health and social problems.
2. Don't drink and drive or let friends drive if they've been drinking; seek help from a support group.
3. Look for changes in behavior or life situation; talk to that person about support groups.

Teaching Model

Describe the following situation: Your friend has been drinking at a party. You don't think he should drive home. Model the thinking process that you will use in this situation. (You will insist on driving yourself, call your parents or a taxi for a ride, or make other arrangements.)

Ask

Ask students to discuss the risks of letting the person drive.

Read

Have students read Lesson 1 to learn some of the dangers of alcohol use.

ASSESS

Guided Practice

Have students answer the Lesson 1 Review questions. The answers are provided below.

Reteaching

Have students work in small groups to create a "Dangers of Alcohol" poster.

Enrichment

Assign the Study Guide for Lesson 1. The Find Out More section encourages students to expand their basic learning of the lesson concepts.

CLOSE

Summarize

Return to the Motivator question, and discuss each of the warning signs.

DRIVER'S LOG

How can you help a friend who has a drinking problem?

Alcohol and Its Effects on Driving Ability

(pages 58–62)

FOCUS

Objectives

- Explain how alcohol affects driving ability.
- Name the laws about and penalties for driving while intoxicated.

Resources

 Study Guide, page 14

 Information Masters 4, 6, and 15

Understanding the Dangers of Alcohol and Other Drugs

Vocabulary

blood-alcohol concentration (BAC)
inhibitions
implied consent
driving while intoxicated (DWI)
driving under the influence (DUI)

Motivator

Elicit from students, or else provide, some familiar drinking-and-driving messages. For example: drinking and driving don't mix; one drink can be too many; friends don't let friends drive drunk. Write these messages on the chalkboard for later reference. Then pose this question to students: You've heard and read that drinking and driving greatly increases your risk of having a collision. Exactly how does alcohol interfere with your ability to drive? (Students may respond that alcohol slows down the part of the brain that controls muscle movement and reflexes. It also

LESSON TWO

OBJECTIVES
1. Explain how alcohol affects driving ability.
2. Name the laws about and penalties for driving while intoxicated.

KEY TERMS
blood-alcohol concentration (BAC)
inhibitions
implied consent
driving while intoxicated (DWI)
driving under the influence (DUI)

Alcohol and Its Effects on Driving Ability

When you are behind the wheel of a motor vehicle, all of your senses must be on alert. You need to react quickly to potentially threatening conditions and then make split-second decisions. Being a good driver takes skill and judgment. No matter how good a driver you are, however, alcohol *will* decrease your skill and *will* damage your judgment.

How Does Alcohol Affect Driving Ability?

Even one drink might be enough to impair your ability to drive safely. From the moment alcohol enters your bloodstream, you begin to lose your ability to think clearly. Even a small amount of alcohol causes changes in your coordination. It should not come as a surprise that approximately 40 percent of all highway deaths are alcohol related.

Facts About Alcohol and Driving

These facts tell you why drinking and driving is a recipe for disaster.
- The 16,189 fatalities in alcohol-related crashes during 1997 represent an average of one alcohol-related fatality every 32 minutes.
- In 1997, 14 percent (7,670) of the 56,602 drivers who were involved in fatal crashes who had a 0.10 percent or greater **blood-alcohol**

CONNECTIONS
Social Studies
CULTURAL CROSSROADS

In 1981 a high school in Wayland, Massachusetts, lost two of its students in alcohol-related crashes in one week. From these needless deaths began a movement by Robert Anastas, the high school's health director, that resulted in the formation of Students Against Driving Drunk (SADD). Mr. Anastas wanted to find a way to help his students confront the dangers of drinking and driving. By the end of 1982, SADD had become a national organization.

Recently, SADD changed its name to Students Against Destructive Decisions. Why? SADD's message now includes viewpoints on issues affecting the health and safety of youth. While its biggest message is still about drinking and driving, SADD is also concerned with drugs and drug prevention, seat-belt use, teen pregnancy, suicide, and gangs. The new name better reflects all the issues SADD is now dedicated to helping.

IT'S A FACT

Alcohol involvement in motor vehicle crashes peaks at night and is higher on weekends than on weekdays. Among passenger vehicle drivers who are fatally injured between 6 P.M. and 6 A.M., more than half have blood-alcohol concentrations (BACs) at or above 0.10 percent. More than 40 percent of the drivers who are fatally injured on weekends have BACs of 0.10 percent or more.

concentration (BAC), or percentage of alcohol in the blood, were young drivers 15 to 20 years old.

- In 1997, 21 percent of young drivers 15 to 20 years old who were killed in crashes were intoxicated.
- More than 327,000 people were injured in crashes where police reported that alcohol was present—an average of one person injured about every 2 minutes.
- About three in every ten Americans will be involved in an alcohol-related crash at some time in their lives.

In spite of these terrible statistics, alcohol is the most widely used and abused drug in the world. Yes, it is a drug, and it is deadly.

Even one drink of alcohol causes changes in the body. That is because alcohol is not digested, as food is. Rather, it is absorbed into the bloodstream through the walls of the stomach and small intestine. Once in the bloodstream, alcohol is quickly carried to all parts of the body. Alcohol has the greatest effect on the brain because that is the organ that controls all body functions. A drinker's mental and physical abilities become diminished.

PROBABILITY OF A FATAL COLLISION

Relative risk of fatal crash as a function of BAC and age

16 to 19 year olds
+55 year olds
20 to 24 year olds
25 to 54 year olds

Relative risk of fatal crash (%)

Blood alcohol concentration (mg%)

◆ This graph shows how age, blood alcohol concentration (BAC), and the probability of being in a crash are related.

Myths and Facts About Alcohol

Alcohol is one of the most misunderstood and widely used drugs. The truth about alcohol is the best weapon against it.

There are plenty of myths about alcohol. Let's look at the facts.

Myth Beer is not as intoxicating as hard liquor.
Fact Not true! Sure, there is more alcohol in an ounce of liquor than in an ounce of beer. However, each of these standard drinks—a 12-ounce bottle of beer, a 5-ounce glass of wine, or a 1½ ounce shot of 80 proof liquor—contains about the same amount of alcohol.

Myth You can't get drunk on a full stomach.
Fact A full stomach just means the alcohol is absorbed into the bloodstream a little more slowly. *All* of that alcohol will still get into the bloodstream and travel to the brain and other parts of your body.

clouds judgment. Alcohol slows reaction time, impairs coordination as well as vision, and interferes with the perception of depth, distance, and speed.)

TEACH

Explain

OBJECTIVE 1: Students will benefit from a discussion of how alcohol affects driving ability in terms of the SIPDE process introduced in Chapter 1. By impairing vision and depth perception, for example, alcohol limits a driver's ability to search the roadway and identify threatening conditions and objects. By impairing judgment, alcohol hampers a driver's ability to predict the possible actions of other drivers and decide on an appropriate course of action. By impairing coordination, alcohol makes it difficult for a driver to execute the proper response.

OBJECTIVE 2: Students should note that even a BAC as low as 0.03—one drink—affects driving ability and crash likelihood. For drivers 16 to 19 years of age, one drink increases the chances of a fatal crash $2\frac{1}{2}$ times; two drinks increase the chances $7\frac{1}{2}$ times. Consuming three drinks increases the probability 40 times. The probability of a crash begins to increase significantly, even for adults, at 0.05 percent BAC and climbs rapidly after about 0.08 percent. For all drivers with BACs above 0.15 percent, the likelihood of being killed in a single-vehicle crash can be nearly 400 times greater than it is for a person who does not drink.

State BY State

People convicted of alcohol-impaired driving are subject to a variety of legal sanctions. All states except New Hampshire and Wisconsin permit jail sentences for first offenders. Eleven states mandate jail or community service after a first conviction for alcohol-impaired driving.

CONNECTIONS
Social Studies

CULTURAL CROSSROADS

Discuss with students the implications of SADD's expanding its areas of concern.

Teaching Model

Describe the following situation: A friend drives you to a party in her vehicle. At the party, you notice that your friend has two drinks. You make a comment to her about not drinking and driving, but she laughs and says, "Everyone does it." Then she adds, "Besides, I had a big dinner, and it's impossible to get drunk on a full stomach." Model the thinking process that you will use to handle this situation. (You will do the following.)

- Know that *not* "everyone does it," and even if everyone did, that still would be no reason to risk your life.
- Realize that while having a full stomach may mean that alcohol is absorbed a little more slowly, a full stomach does not keep a person from getting drunk.
- Decide that you must make other arrangements to get home—and that you must try to keep your friend from driving.)

Ask

Ask students to discuss how to keep from drinking in a situation where some of their peers are drinking.

Read

Have students read Lesson 2 to find out how alcohol affects driving ability and to learn about laws, tests, and penalties pertaining to driving while intoxicated.

FYI

The body can't eliminate much more than ½ ounce of alcohol in an hour. It will take about 2 hours for the body to get rid of a standard-sized drink. This figure will vary, however, depending on the gender, weight, and size of the person.

◆ An intoxicated driver will have difficulty focusing on the pen as the officer moves it.

Myth Drinking and driving is not dangerous.
Fact Motor vehicle crashes are the single largest health risk for people under 28 and the number 1 killer of teenagers.

Myth You must drink because friends want you to even though you are the driver.
Fact Real friends would not want you to hurt yourself or others. Tell them the facts about alcohol.

Myth Black coffee, a cold shower, lots of exercise, or all three together can quickly sober up a drinker.
Fact No way! The body cannot burn up much more than ½ ounce of alcohol in an hour. Nothing can speed up the process.

Myth Alcohol makes you feel better when you're down in the dumps.
Fact Not really. Alcohol is a depressant, or "downer." It may make a person feel worse than before.

Myth Sometimes, because of peer pressure at a party, there is no other choice but to drink.
Fact You do have a choice. Don't drink. Abstinence is the only responsible action for anyone under 21.

The Physical Effects of Alcohol

Drinking drivers 16 to 19 years old have a higher fatal crash probability than any other age group. For instance, young drivers with a blood-alcohol concentration of between 0.08 and 0.10 percent are 40 times more likely to be involved in a fatal crash than a sober driver. Why does this occur?

The answer is that people who have little or no driving experience have a higher risk of being involved in a fatal crash.

Reaction time After two or more drinks, a driver becomes physically slower and less alert. In fact, for some people, reaction time may be impaired after only one drink.

Coordination Movement gets sloppy and uncoordinated. Drivers who have been drinking are less able than others to make critical decisions. They have trouble steering and may step on the brake pedal too late or miss it entirely.

Distance (depth) perception Alcohol affects the ability to judge distance, or depth. Drinking drivers may perceive something as farther away than it really is. They cannot tell where the vehicles around them really are or how far away road signs or signals are.

IT'S A FACT

Nearly three out of every five holiday traffic fatalities are alcohol related.

Speed perception Drinking drivers often cannot tell how fast another vehicle is approaching. Such drivers also have a distorted sense of how fast they are going, which is not surprising when you consider that alcohol severely dulls the senses.

Vision Alcohol affects the reflex action of the eyes that causes pupils to become smaller in bright light and larger as light diminishes. Drinkers' eyes are not protected against headlight glare because pupils don't return to normal size quickly enough once the headlights have passed. Temporary blindness results. Alcohol also impairs side, color, and night vision, eye focus, and it may cause double vision.

The Mental Effects of Alcohol

Alcohol doesn't just affect the part of your brain that controls your physical reactions. It also affects the part of the brain that controls the ability to reason.

As if that isn't bad enough, alcohol affects your judgment and, consequently, can make you feel as if you are thinking more clearly than usual. This false message makes drinking drivers even more dangerous because they do not have the judgment to realize that something is wrong. A driver in this condition is apt to make poor decisions—even fatal ones.

Alcohol affects your **inhibitions,** the elements of your personality that stop you from behaving without regard to possible consequences. In drivers, the loss of inhibition can be very dangerous and can cause them to take chances they would normally avoid.

What Are the Laws, Tests, and Penalties for Drinking and Driving?

Drinking and driving causes countless tragedies. All states have laws regulating the minimum drinking age and laws against drinking and driving. In all states, it is illegal for people under age 21 to buy, possess, or drink alcoholic beverages.

Implied Consent Laws

When you use public roads, you agree to give law enforcement officials permission to test you for alcohol use if you are arrested on suspicion of drinking and driving. This permission is known as **implied consent,** and it is the law in all 50 states. The test will determine your blood-alcohol concentration (BAC).

◆ *Blurred or double vision is often the result of a driver's having had too much to drink.*

FYI

Most states and the District of Columbia have enacted administrative license suspension (ALS) laws. A driver's license can be suspended if a person refuses to take a test for blood-alcohol concentration or if a person fails the test. This is in addition to any fines or penalties connected with conviction for driving while intoxicated or under the influence.

ASSESS

Guided Practice

Have students answer the Lesson 2 Review questions. The answers are provided below.

Reteaching

Have students work together in small groups to list physical and mental ways in which alcohol can affect a driver. After groups have completed their lists, have them share and compare their work with the whole class. Encourage students to discuss specific examples of how alcohol can impair judgment and driving ability in various situations.

Enrichment

Assign the Study Guide for Lesson 2. The Find Out More section encourages students to expand their basic learning of the lesson concepts.

Driving Tip

Designated drivers and other nondrinkers should be aware of the variety of nonalcoholic beverages that they may purchase in addition to juices and soft drinks. Advise students that various alcohol substitutes are available in restaurants and stores, ranging from nonalcoholic beers to simple tonic water.

Summarize

Refer back to the drinking-and-driving messages on the chalkboard. Discuss the thinking behind these messages in light of what students have learned in this lesson. Return to the Motivator question. Ask students to summarize alcohol's physical and mental effects and give examples of how these effects increase driving risk.

DRIVER'S LOG

How does drinking impair a driver's ability to use the SIPDE process? What are the legal penalties for driving while intoxicated (DWI) or driving under the influence (DUI)?

WHAT WOULD YOU DO?

Sample answer: They can ride with a friend who has not been drinking; they can take the keys from the driver; they should not let the driver drive.

FYI

As of January 1997, 47 states and the District of Columbia had established lower BACs for young drivers. Federal legislation passed in 1995 encourages states to adopt and enforce "zero tolerance" (0.00 percent to 0.02 percent BAC maximum) for drivers under 21.

In many states, adult drivers with a BAC of 0.10 percent or higher can be charged with **driving while intoxicated (DWI).** Some states call this **driving under the influence (DUI).**

Tests for Intoxication

Chemical analysis of blood or urine can measure a person's BAC, or a breath-testing device can measure the percentage of alcohol in the breath. In an increasing number of states, a reading of 0.08 percent or higher is enough to convict adult drivers of DWI or DUI and to take away their license. In most states, teenage drivers with any BAC over 0.00 up to 0.02 percent violate 21-year-old minimum drinking age laws—sometimes referred to as zero tolerance laws.

Even if a driver's BAC is lower than the legal limit, he or she can still be charged with DWI or DUI. The police can stop anyone whose driving appears to be impaired. They can give a field sobriety test by asking the driver to perform simple tasks, such as standing on one leg or walking a line.

If you are ever stopped for suspicion of DWI or DUI, be courteous and cooperate with the police officer. Drivers who refuse to submit to a chemical test for BAC can have their licenses suspended whether they are convicted or not.

Penalties and Consequences

The penalties for DWI or DUI differ in each state. A license can be suspended, a fine can be assessed, and a jail term can be imposed. If injury or death results from a collision in which the driver has been drinking, the driver can be prosecuted for more serious offenses, such as vehicular homicide. Drivers convicted of DWI or DUI pay higher insurance premiums once their licenses are restored, and may have to attend education and counseling programs.

In addition to legal penalties, there may be other consequences. Drunk drivers involved in crashes have to live with the emotional consequences of having caused injury or death. Civil suits, permanent physical disabilities and long-term health problems to both the driver and passengers may also result.

WHAT WOULD YOU DO?

The driver has been drinking steadily. How can his companions get home? What is their responsibility to the driver?

Lesson 2 Review

1. How does alcohol affect a driver?
2. What should you know about the laws, tests, and penalties for driving while intoxicated?

Lesson 2 Review

Answers

1. It impairs ability to think, as well as coordination and reflexes; increases reaction time; impairs perception of depth, distance, and speed; impairs vision.

2. It is illegal to buy, possess, or drink alcohol if you are under 21; law enforcement officials have the right to test drivers for alcohol use; drinking and driving can cause you to lose your license, pay a fine, and even go to jail.

How Other Drugs Affect Driving Ability

LESSON THREE
OBJECTIVES
1. Describe some kinds of drugs other than alcohol.
2. Explain how these drugs affect driving ability.

Alcohol is not the only drug that can impair your ability to drive. Almost any drug can have a harmful effect on your driving skill.

There are many different kinds of drugs. Some can be bought only by prescription. Others can be bought over the counter without a prescription. Some drugs are against the law but can be bought illegally.

What Drugs Affect Driving Ability?

How a drug affects you depends on the drug itself. Some drugs can decrease your ability to make sound decisions and respond well to situations. Other drugs can change the way you think. It is important that you know about these drugs and their effects on driving. Once you understand the danger of combining drugs and driving, you can take steps to avoid putting yourself and others at risk.

Synergism

Synergism is the interaction of one drug with another to enhance the effect of one or both. For example, if a person drinks alcohol and takes a depressant, the combination could produce an effect on the person greater than the individual effects of either substance when taken alone. Even a nonprescription drug such as an antihistamine can be dangerous when mixed with alcohol. It is very important, therefore, to avoid combining alcohol and other drugs or combining any drugs unless prescribed by a physician.

TIPS · FOR NEW DRIVERS

Under the Influence

Be aware of signs that other drivers on the road may be under the influence of alcohol or other drugs. Various signs indicate possible problems.

Traveling at Erratic Speeds—Either Too Fast or Too Slowly
Alcohol-impaired drivers often have trouble driving at a steady speed.

Running over Curbs or Turning into the Wrong Lane
Alcohol-impaired drivers are often unable to turn smoothly.

Weaving from Side to Side
Alcohol-impaired drivers suffer from loss of coordination and attention, which affects their ability to steer smoothly.

Ignoring or Overshooting Traffic Signs
Alcohol-impaired drivers suffer impaired reflexes and vision loss.

If you find yourself on the same roadway as a driver who shows any of these signs, increase the amount of space between your vehicles. Be alert to the fact that there is an impaired driver sharing the roadway with you. If possible, inform a police officer of what you have noticed.

CHAPTER 4   *Handling Social Pressures*   **63**

Driving Tip

Be sure students understand that when they travel in a vehicle with other people, they share responsibility for what goes on in that vehicle. Thus, if a passenger in the vehicle is using an illegal drug, the other riders are risking legal consequences whether or not they use the drug. If it is the driver who is using the drug, the passengers are risking their lives as well.

LESSON THREE

How Other Drugs Affect Driving Ability
(pages 63–65)

FOCUS

Objectives
- Describe some kinds of drugs other than alcohol.
- Explain how these drugs affect driving ability.

> ### Resources
> 📁 Study Guide, page 15
> 📁 *Understanding the Dangers of Alcohol and Other Drugs*

Motivator
You have a bad cold. To lessen the symptoms, you buy an over-the-counter cold remedy at the pharmacy. Before driving your vehicle, what precautions should you take? (Students may respond that you should read the package label to see whether the product might cause drowsiness, dizziness, or other side effects that could interfere with driving ability; you might also check with the pharmacist.)

TEACH

Explain
OBJECTIVE 1: Stress that the term *drugs* has a wide range of meaning.

OBJECTIVE 2: Students should understand that any medication or drug may have side effects and that those side effects may distract a driver, impair judgment or concentration, or otherwise hinder driving ability.

continued on page 64

Students should also note that side effects may be subtle and may come on gradually. Moreover, students should be aware that two drugs taken in combination may produce side effects that neither drug causes individually.

Teaching Model

Describe the following situation: You're at a party where someone starts boasting that he can drive perfectly well while "stoned" on marijuana. Model the thinking process that you will use to refute this claim. (You will realize that marijuana can affect the user's perception of speed, time, and distance; understand that marijuana can cause someone to stare at something to the point of becoming unaware of anything else going on.)

Ask

Ask students to discuss the risks of driving while under the influence of various drugs.

Read

Have students read Lesson 3 to learn how various drugs affect driving ability.

ASSESS

Guided Practice

Have students answer the Lesson 3 Review questions. The answers are provided below.

Reteaching

Have students work together in small groups to list the effects of over-the-counter drugs, prescription drugs, depressants, stimulants, hallucinogens, and narcotics.

TIPS FOR NEW DRIVERS

Advise students that if they are being followed by an erratically driven vehicle, they should let the driver pass.

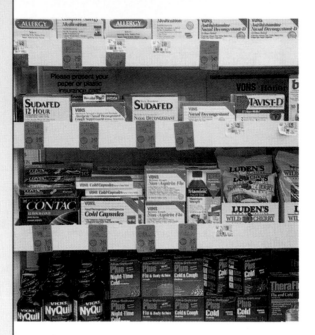

◆ *Many of the capsules, tablets, and syrups commonly found in medicine cabinets are over-the-counter drugs.*

Over-the-Counter Drugs

Over-the-counter drugs are drugs that can be purchased legally without a doctor's prescription. You may not even think of them as drugs. They are used for colds, flu, headaches, allergies, and other everyday ailments. It's important to read the package label of these drugs, which may warn that their use may "cause drowsiness or dizziness," or "Do not drive after using." Pay attention to these warnings! It is your responsibility as a driver to know what side effects any medications you are taking might cause.

Prescription Drugs

You can buy prescription drugs at a pharmacy if your doctor prescribes them for you. Remember to ask your doctor or the pharmacist if you can drive safely while you are taking any prescription medication.

Many prescription drugs have warnings on the package or the bottle. Look carefully. It is your responsibility as a driver to know what drugs you are taking and what effects they can have.

Depressants

Depressants slow down, or depress, the central nervous system. Doctors order depressants for patients who are experiencing a great deal of tension, who are very anxious, or who are being treated for high blood pressure.

While depressants can help with these symptoms, they also slow down the patient's mental and physical activity. Like alcohol, which is also a depressant, these drugs slow down reflexes and have a harmful effect on coordination.

DRUGS THAT AFFECT DRIVING ABILITY

Narcotics	Depressants	Stimulants	Hallucinogens
Heroin	Alcohol	Amphetamines (speed)	Marijuana
Codeine	Barbiturates	Cocaine (crack or rock)	LSD
Morphine	Methadone		PCP (angel dust)
	Sleeping pills		Hashish
	Tranquilizers		

MEETING STUDENT DIVERSITY

Limited English Proficiency

Drug-related terminology can be confusing for students with limited English proficiency. Be sure all students understand the difference between an over-the-counter drug and a prescription drug. You may also need to take some time to explain common slang terms for various illicit drugs.

Stimulants

Stimulants speed up, or stimulate, the central nervous system. Some drivers misuse these drugs and take them to keep awake when driving long distances.

Stimulants can give users a false feeling of well-being and make them think that they are superalert. These drugs often cause drivers to take foolish and life-threatening risks. When the effect of stimulants wears off, which can happen very suddenly, users can become very tired quickly. Many stimulants are illegal.

Hallucinogens

Hallucinogens are so dangerous that selling or using them is against the law. They are called mind-altering drugs for a good reason. Hallucinogens change the way a person thinks, sees, and acts.

Marijuana Marijuana may make a user drowsy. It can affect people's awareness of how fast or slow they are driving and their ability to judge time and space. People who use marijuana may just sit and stare and be completely unaware of anything that is going on around them. No one really knows when the effects of marijuana wear off. The chemicals in this drug can stay in the body for as long as four to six weeks. Drivers may think that the effects have worn off when they are still under the influence of marijuana.

LSD and PCP The strongest hallucinogens are LSD and PCP (angel dust). While using LSD or PCP, people can forget who they are, where they are, and what they are doing. These drugs can cause drivers to lose the ability to judge space and the speed at which they are driving.

Narcotics

Narcotics have a strong depressant effect. They can cause stupor, coma, and even death.

Lesson 3 Review

1. What are some other kinds of drugs besides alcohol?
2. How do these drugs affect your ability to drive?

FYI

Marijuana masks the feeling of nausea that accompanies intoxication. Drinkers who mix marijuana and alcohol may not realize how much alcohol they have consumed. They may continue drinking until they suffer alcohol poisoning, which can result in coma or even death.

WHAT WOULD YOU DO?

You are taking a prescription medicine. Can you drive your sister to the movies? How will you decide if it is safe for you to drive?

After groups have completed their lists, have them share and compare their work with the whole class. Encourage students to discuss specific examples of how drug use can impair a person's ability to operate a vehicle safely.

Enrichment

Assign the Study Guide for Lesson 3. The Find Out More section encourages students to expand their basic learning of the lesson concepts.

CLOSE

Summarize

Return to the Motivator question. Recall students' initial responses, and have students summarize the additional information that they have gained from this lesson. You also may want to point out that medication does not affect everyone the same way. One person may experience no side effects from a given medicine, while another person may have a strong reaction.

DRIVER'S LOG

What kinds of drugs can affect driving ability? What are the dangers of driving while taking medication?

WHAT WOULD YOU DO?

Sample answer: Before driving, check with a doctor or pharmacist; also check for warning labels on the bottle.

Lesson 3 Review

Answers

1. Over-the-counter drugs, prescription drugs, depressants, stimulants, hallucinogens, narcotics.
2. Decrease ability to make sound judgments; change the way you think; depress or speed up the central nervous system.

Distractions Can Increase Driving Risk

(pages 66–68)

FOCUS

Objectives

• Name some distractions that increase driving risk.
• Describe how these distractions can hinder your driving ability.

Resources

 Study Guide, page 16

Motivator

Pose the following: You're driving home from the beach with your two young nephews. The kids, who are in the backseat, start to argue about something. Before long they are yelling and hitting each other. You tell them to stop, but they don't listen. How does this situation increase driving risk? What can you do to reduce that risk? (Students may respond that the kids distract you, causing you to focus attention on them rather than on the driving task. To reduce risk, you must settle down the kids, even if you have to pull off the road to do so. You might also separate them by having one sit in the front.)

TEACH

Explain

OBJECTIVE 1: Students should understand that anything—or anyone—that diverts their attention from the task of driving increases risk. You may want to have the class brainstorm a list of possible

LESSON FOUR

OBJECTIVES
1. Name some distractions that increase driving risk.
2. Describe how these distractions can hinder your driving ability.

Distractions Can Increase Driving Risk

There is much to pay attention to when you drive. You have to see what is going on around you. You need to be sure that other drivers know where you are and what you plan to do. You have to keep adjusting your speed and vehicle position to driving conditions. You have to be alert to any surprises that might turn into emergencies.

With all of this going on, you need to be sure that no distractions inside your vehicle will take your attention away from your driving and increase your risk.

SAFETY TIPS

When driving with infants and small children, be sure they are in safety seats and that the seats are securely fastened in place in the backseat. Do not allow small children to ride in the front seat of vehicles equipped with passenger-side air bags. The powerful force of an inflating air bag can injure or kill small children.

How Can Distractions Hinder Your Driving Ability?

Imagine that you are driving along a busy highway. Suddenly you see an antique car driving beside you. You have never seen a vehicle like this before, so you take your eyes off the road ahead for just a second to get a closer look. Just then another vehicle pulls ahead of you, and you have to brake hard. You have let yourself become distracted from your driving responsibilities. You almost crashed into another vehicle.

Many events can distract you as you drive. It is important to be aware of these distractions so that you can be a safe and responsible driver.

A Vehicle Audio System Can Distract You

Most vehicles have radios, cassette players, or CD players, but do not become so interested in the music that you forget to pay attention to your driving. Remember, too, that loud music can mask useful information.

A radio can be distracting if it is too loud. Keep volume at a reasonable level. Your concentration must be focused on driving. Looking for and changing tapes or CDs is also distracting—and very dangerous. Risk is increased anytime you take your eyes off the road or drive with only one hand on the wheel.

Headphones Can Be Dangerous

In most states, it is against the law to wear stereo headphones while you drive. You need information when you drive—and that includes roadway sounds.

THE INTERNATIONAL SCENE

Ontario, Canada

The driver and all passengers in a vehicle are required by law to wear seat belts in Toronto and all other cities of the province of Ontario. Travelers who violate this law are subject to large fines.

If you're wearing headphones, you may not be able to hear another vehicle honking its horn at you. You may lose your concentration if you're too absorbed in what you're hearing. Put them away. Your job now is to pay attention to your driving.

Cellular Phones Can Distract You

Using a cellular phone while driving is not recommended. Statistics show that cell phones are distracting and increase the risk of a crash. Dialing and talking divert a driver's attention away from controlling the vehicle and watching the road.

Cellular phones *can* provide some safety benefits for a motorist. You can, for instance, use a cell phone to get help if your vehicle malfunctions or to report a crash.

Keep your phone in the glove compartment with the ringer off. If you must place or receive a phone call, even in an emergency, do so only when stopped, preferably in an off-road location. Never try to talk while driving. Remember that you need to give driving your full attention.

Passengers Can Distract You

Sometimes the people in your vehicle want you to pay more attention to them than to your driving. They may ask you to turn around and look at what they're doing. Sometimes they can be talking loudly. They may try to roughhouse in the vehicle or hang out the windows.

You are responsible for the safety of your passengers, and it is your responsibility to tell them to sit still or be quiet. You're not being rude—you're being a safe, responsible driver.

Little children can become bored or restless on long trips. They may start fighting with each other or try to take off their safety belts. You can make sure that children behave by telling them the rules before you start driving and by keeping them quietly occupied.

Make sure you have some tape cassettes for them to listen to or quiet games for them to play in the vehicle. You can also stop more often than you normally would and let the children get out and stretch their legs.

Other Distractions

Driving with animals in your vehicle can be dangerous. A dog may suddenly jump on your lap, or a cat may crawl under your feet and land on the gas pedal. You have to plan ahead if you are going to take an animal in

◆ **If you talk on a cellular phone while you are driving, you increase your chances of having an accident, because your full attention is not on driving.**

◆ **Don't let passengers distract you. Tell them how you expect them to behave before they enter your car.**

---

distractions. Encourage students to think of distractions that may occur when riding with peers.

OBJECTIVE 2: Students might discuss each distraction and suggest ways of coping with it.

Teaching Model

Describe the following situation: You're driving to the shopping mall with a close friend. Your friend is looking at a sports magazine and repeatedly holding up photographs for you to look at. Model the thinking process that you will use to reduce driving risk in this situation. (You will recognize that taking your eyes off the road, even for a moment, is dangerous because it diverts your attention from the driving task; wait until you've stopped the vehicle before looking at the photographs.)

Ask

Ask students to discuss the risks of taking one's eyes off the road.

Read

Have students read Lesson 4 to learn how distractions can hinder driving ability.

ASSESS

Guided Practice

Have students answer the Lesson 4 Review questions. The answers are provided below.

Reteaching

Have students work together in small groups to list possible distractions, discuss the risks posed by these distractions, and brainstorm ways for a driver to maintain or regain concentration.

After students complete this task, you may want to have them role-play some common situations to show how they could handle distractions to minimize driving risk.

Driving Tip

Explain to students that when they travel to a place where they haven't been before, they should familiarize themselves with directions for getting there *before* driving, not while the vehicle is moving. Looking away from the roadway to read a map or handwritten instructions can have fatal consequences.

Have students discuss what they can do to oppose the use of alcohol and other drugs.

Enrichment

Assign the Study Guide for Lesson 4. The Find Out More section encourages students to expand their basic learning of the lesson concepts.

CLOSE

Summarize

Return to the Motivator question. Have students expand their initial answers with additional information and insights gained from this lesson. Encourage students to be as specific as possible in their responses.

DRIVER'S LOG

What kinds of distractions can increase driving risk? What can you do to minimize risk?

WHAT WOULD YOU DO?

Sample answer: Explain to passengers your need to concentrate and ask for their cooperation.

ADVICE FROM THE EXPERTS

William F. Cullinane
Executive Director, Students Against Destructive Decisions (SADD)

Most young people have rejected the social pressure to drink and drive. Next, they must reject the pressure to use alcohol and other drugs. They must realize that to solve this problem, they first have to see themselves as part of it.

For young people to recognize their involvement in the problem, they need to receive honest feedback from others who care. SADD students across the country are providing alcohol-free and drug-free alternatives for their peers. They are offering a caring hand, not an enabling one.

your vehicle. Think about putting the animal in a carrying case, or ask a friend to come with you and hold the animal by its leash. If you travel with pets frequently, you should be aware that pet safety belts are available at specialty shops.

Many drivers become distracted in traffic jams. They get stuck for a long time and lose their concentration. Remember, even when you are stopped, that it is important to pay attention to everything that is going on around you.

When you are driving on a toll road, you will need change to pay the toll. Make sure you know how much change you will need, and look for change *before* you start out on your trip. Plan ahead. Have a container with plenty of change in it within reach so that you don't have to search through your pockets when you should be concentrating on driving.

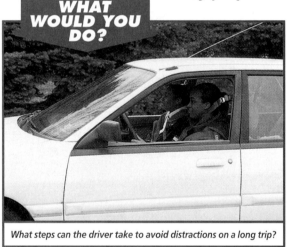

WHAT WOULD YOU DO?

What steps can the driver take to avoid distractions on a long trip?

Drivers who smoke are distracted when they search for or light cigars, cigarettes, or pipes. A lit cigarette falling on the seat or in the driver's lap is dangerous. Don't smoke and drive—especially in a closed vehicle, where passengers can inhale the smoke.

Remember, your job is to concentrate on your driving. Being prepared to handle distractions is part of that job.

Lesson 4 Review

1. What distractions can increase your driving risk?
2. How can these distractions hinder your driving ability?

Lesson 4 Review

Answers

1. Radio, headphones, tape or CD player, passengers, pets in the vehicle, traffic jams, smoking.
2. They hinder your paying attention to driving; with loud music you may not hear a horn honking at you or the siren on an emergency vehicle.

Using the Mileage Chart

Suppose you are planning to drive from Abilene to El Paso. How many miles would you be traveling? One way to find out would be to use a mileage chart such as the one on this page. Using a mileage chart is easy.

First look at the names of cities down the left side of the chart. Find Abilene, and put your left finger over it.

Then look at the cities across the top of the chart. Put your right finger on El Paso.

Now move your left finger across the chart until it reaches the box below El Paso. The number in the box is the distance in miles between Abilene and El Paso. The distance is 450 miles. That's quite a trip.

To estimate how long it will take you if you drive at an average speed of 55 miles per hour, divide 450 by 55. The trip will take between 8 and 9 hours. But don't forget to add in some time for rest stops. Therefore, you can figure on about a 10-hour trip.

Try It Yourself

1. How many miles is it between San Angelo and Eagle Pass?
2. If you are traveling at 55 miles an hour, how long will it take you to drive from El Paso to Pecos?
3. Which trip would be longer—one from Odessa to Houston or one from Lubbock to San Antonio?

MILEAGE CHART	Abilene	Amarillo	Dallas	Eagle Pass	El Paso	Houston	Lubbock	Midland	Odessa	Pecos	San Angelo	San Antonio
Abilene		273	180	302	450	355	171	148	180	245	92	250
Amarillo	273		351	517	421	597	134	237	258	330	310	513
El Paso	450	421	646	479		751	345	312	289	210	415	555
Lubbock	171	134	318	394	345	530		121	142	219	202	406
Odessa	180	258	352	301	289	507	142	20		75	132	345
San Angelo	92	310	262	215	415	374	202	113	132	210		215

Objective

Demonstrate an ability to use a mileage chart to determine distance.

Teaching the Skill

- Explain that using a mileage chart to determine distance is faster and easier than using a map scale. However, only certain cities appear on a mileage chart, so use of the chart is limited.
- Point out that the distance between two places not on the mileage chart may be estimated by finding the distance between cities shown on the chart that are near the two places.
- Advise students that when they are finding or comparing distances, they should always check to see whether the distances are in miles or kilometers.

ANSWERS TO
Try It Yourself Questions

1. 215 miles
2. a little less than 4 hours
3. from Odessa to Houston (101 miles longer)

CHAPTER SUMMARY

Key Points

Have students read the Key Points to review the major concepts of the chapter.

PROJECTS

Cooperative Learning:

Students will benefit by working with a partner on one or both projects. When the assignment is completed, the whole class will profit by sharing and comparing results.

CHAPTER 4 REVIEW

KEY POINTS

Lesson One

1. Drinking alcohol can change a person's actions, thoughts, and feelings. It can become addictive so that the need for alcohol becomes more important than friends, family, and future plans.
2. People's responsibilities include protecting themselves from the hazards that drinking poses to their health and well-being, as well as protecting themselves and others from the threat of people who drink and drive.
3. Some symptoms that indicate a problem drinker are loss of initiative, frequent lateness and absence from school, trouble with the law, sleeplessness, and memory loss.

Lesson Two

1. Some ways that alcohol affects driving ability are that it reduces inhibitions, reduces ability to react quickly, impairs coordination, and has a negative effect on a driver's judgment.
2. When people use public roads, they agree to give law enforcement officials the right to test them for alcohol use if they suspect the drivers of drinking and driving. This is the law of

implied consent. In many states, a driver over age 21 is considered intoxicated if his or her blood-alcohol concentration is 0.08 percent or greater. Most states have enacted lower BAC limits (0.00 percent to 0.02 percent) for people under age 21. Penalties for DWI or DUI may include driver's license suspension, assessment of a fine, and a term in jail.

Lesson Three

1. Over-the-counter drugs, prescription drugs, depressants, stimulants, hallucinogens, and narcotics can affect driving ability.
2. Depressants slow down the central nervous system; stimulants speed it up. Hallucinogens are illegal mind-altering drugs. Narcotics are illegal drugs that have a strong depressant effect.

Lesson Four

1. Distractions can hinder your driving ability by drawing your attention away from the road.
2. Distractions include radios, tape decks, CD players, stereo headphones, cell phones, noisy passengers, disruptive children, animals, traffic jams, toll payments, and smoking.

PROJECTS

1. Many organizations work to educate drivers about the dangers of drinking and driving. Besides SADD, Mothers Against Drunk Driving (MADD) is probably the best known. Find information about MADD.
2. Refer to your state driver's manual or interview a police officer. Discover the circumstances under which a teenage driver can be convicted of DUI or DWI in your state. Find out about the penalties for conviction as well.

*inter*NET
CONNECTION

Explore the Web for other statistics on drinking and driving.
drivered.glencoe.com

*inter*NET
CONNECTION

Visit Glencoe's Driver Education Web site for student activities that relate to this chapter.
drivered.glencoe.com

CHAPTER 4 REVIEW

CHAPTER 4 REVIEW

CHAPTER TEST

Write the letter of the answer that best completes each sentence.

1. Distractions can
   a. slow reflexes.
   b. decrease risk.
   c. increase risk.

2. Drinking alcohol
   a. does not affect your mental abilities.
   b. often helps you think more clearly.
   c. slows down the part of your brain that controls muscles and reflexes.

3. Over-the-counter drugs
   a. may be used when driving short distances.
   b. may impair driving ability.
   c. must be ordered for you by a doctor.

4. You can reduce the effects of alcohol if you
   a. take a very cold shower.
   b. exercise.
   c. allow several hours to pass.

5. Implied consent means that you
   a. agree to be tested if you are suspected of drinking and driving.
   b. agree to obey the rules of the road.
   c. have the right to be uncooperative if you are stopped by police.

6. You can reduce distractions while driving by
   a. putting on a set of stereo headphones.
   b. looking at the scenery.
   c. keeping radio volume low and asking passengers to speak quietly.

7. To get help with a drinking problem
   a. drink just once a week.
   b. drink only beer.
   c. join a support group.

8. Alcohol is
   a. a harmless substance.
   b. a powerful drug.
   c. nonaddictive.

9. In most states, drivers over age 21 are considered intoxicated if their BAC is greater than
   a. 0.10 percent.
   b. 0.07 percent.
   c. 0.04 percent.

10. Even a small amount of alcohol can affect your
    a. long-term memory.
    b. ability to judge distance and speed.
    c. hearing.

Write the word or phrase that best completes each sentence.

| prescription | stimulants | concentration |
| depressants | inhibitions | peer pressure |

11. _____ stop you from behaving without regard to possible consequences.

12. Drugs that slow down the central nervous system are called _____.

13. _____ drugs must be ordered by a doctor.

14. _____ often give drivers a false sense of self-confidence and cause them to take foolish and life-threatening risks.

15. The influence of your friends is called _____.

DRIVER'S LOG

In this chapter, you have learned about how social pressures can cause you to behave in ways that will put you and others at risk. Imagine that a friend has been drinking and wants to drive you home. Your friend says, "Don't worry, I'm just fine." What will you say? How might your friend respond? Write a dialogue showing what might happen.

CHAPTER 4 REVIEW

CHAPTER TEST

Assign the Chapter Test to all students.

Answers
1. c
2. c
3. b
4. c
5. a
6. c
7. c
8. b
9. a
10. b
11. Inhibitions
12. depressants
13. Prescription
14. Stimulants
15. peer pressure

DRIVER'S LOG

Students' responses will reflect their personal viewpoints. However, their answers should provide an assessment of their understanding of the dangers of drinking and driving.

Evaluate
• Test A, pages 7–8 or Test B, pages 7–8 📁
• Testmaker software

RETURN TO THE BIG IDEA

Discuss why driving with one's ability impaired is both irresponsible and dangerous. Include in the discussion the dangers that impaired drivers pose to pedestrians.

UNIT 1

This review tests students' knowledge of the material in Chapters 1 through 4. Use the review to help students study for their state driving test.

Answers

1. b
2. b
3. a
4. b
5. b
6. c
7. a
8. b
9. c
10. a
11. b
12. b
13. a
14. a

UNIT 1 CUMULATIVE REVIEW

This review tests your knowledge of the material in Chapters 1–4. Use the review to help you study for your state driving test. Choose the answer that best completes each statement.

1. The best way to fight fatigue is to
   a. use a stimulant.
   b. rest.
   c. look at the scenery.
   d. drink coffee.

2. *BAC* stands for
   a. brain alcohol content.
   b. blood-alcohol concentration.
   c. basic automobile collision.
   d. body alcohol content.

3. In 1 hour, the adult human body can burn
   a. about ½ ounce of alcohol.
   b. about 1 ounce of alcohol.
   c. about 2 ounces of alcohol.
   d. about 3 ounces of alcohol.

4. Traffic laws are enforced by
   a. the CIA.
   b. state and local police.
   c. the department of motor vehicles.
   d. United States marshals.

5. Over 39 percent of all occupant fatalities
   a. involve more than one vehicle.
   b. involve only one vehicle.
   c. are "fender-benders."
   d. involve pedestrians.

6. Marijuana remains in the body for
   a. up to one week.
   b. up to two weeks.
   c. up to six weeks.
   d. up to ten weeks.

7. A visual acuity test measures
   a. how well you can see.
   b. pupil dilation.
   c. convex vision.
   d. headlight power.

8. Over-the-counter medications
   a. never affect driving ability.
   b. sometimes produce side effects.
   c. improve concentration.
   d. must be prescribed by a doctor.

9. The area of vision directly ahead of a person is called
   a. side vision.
   b. convex vision.
   c. the area of central vision.
   d. peripheral vision.

10. The second stage of the graduated driver licensing (GDL) system is
    a. an intermediate/probationary license.
    b. supervised driving at all times.
    c. a learner's permit.
    d. full driving privileges.

11. Each year, a driver's chance of being involved in a collision is
    a. 1 in 15.
    b. 1 in 9.
    c. 1 in 3.
    d. 1 in 2.

12. The influence of one's friends is called
    a. maturity.
    b. peer pressure.
    c. HTS.
    d. SIPDE.

13. One way to reduce driving risk is to
    a. anticipate the actions of others.
    b. always use high-beam headlights.
    c. join a support group.
    d. close the windows.

14. Through driver education, students learn
    a. how to maneuver and control a vehicle.
    b. the traffic laws of all 50 states.
    c. how to drive without paying attention.
    d. how to join a support group.

15. If you are temporarily blinded by headlight glare, you should
    a. look down.
    b. see a doctor.
    c. reduce your speed.
    d. close your eyes.

16. Some people with physical disabilities are able to drive by using
    a. prosthetic devices.
    b. a breathalyzer.
    c. peripheral vision.
    d. narcotics.

17. To be eligible for Stage 1 of the GDL program, a teen should
    a. complete six months' supervised driving.
    b. have a parent's written permission.
    c. be at least 18 years old.
    d. pass the road test.

18. Alcohol affects
    a. judgment.
    b. traffic laws.
    c. the HTS.
    d. the automotive industry.

19. A person who is feeling angry or upset should
    a. let someone else drive.
    b. turn on the radio.
    c. talk to passengers.
    d. sing.

20. You must provide a vehicle for the
    a. Smith System.
    b. knowledge test.
    c. in-vehicle test.
    d. visual acuity test.

21. Playing loud music will reduce your ability to sense
    a. a pedestrian crossing in front of you.
    b. warning signs of danger such as sirens.
    c. 90 percent of your driving decisions.
    d. the relative distance of two objects.

22. To prove your identity at the department of motor vehicles, you can take
    a. a birth certificate.
    b. your parent's tax return.
    c. a phone bill.
    d. a report card.

23. Make sure that the vehicle you use to take your in-vehicle test
    a. has a standard shift.
    b. is registered and insured.
    c. is the school's driver-training vehicle.
    d. has a working stereo system.

24. As of 1995, maximum speed limits on highways are set by
    a. local police.
    b. the federal government.
    c. the individual states.
    d. the Uniform Vehicle Code.

25. Roads are part of the
    a. highway transportation system.
    b. Smith System.
    c. administrative system.
    d. uniform vehicle network.

26. Stimulants
    a. improve concentration.
    b. impair judgment.
    c. depress the central nervous system.
    d. improve reflexes.

27. One problem common to night driving is
    a. moon blindness.
    b. pedestrians.
    c. headlight glare.
    d. color blindness.

28. To make wise driving decisions, use
    a. the SIPDE process.
    b. the Uniform Vehicle Code.
    c. an HTS.
    d. risk.

Answers

15. c
16. a
17. b
18. a
19. a
20. c
21. b
22. a
23. b
24. c
25. a
26. b
27. c
28. a

Learning the Basics

UNIT THEME

In Unit 2, students examine the fundamentals of driving. Students will recognize that these basic elements form the foundation of safe, responsible driving. They will develop respect for the rights of other drivers, understand the rules of the road, and begin to familiarize themselves with the primary requisites and maneuvers for safely operating a vehicle.

UNIT 2

Learning the Basics

The fundamentals of driving are second nature to good drivers. These basics should become second nature to you as well. This unit will help you learn the first steps toward becoming a good driver.

75

TEACHING YOUR TEENS TO DRIVE

AAA's *Teaching Your Teens to Drive: A Partnership for Survival* helps new drivers, with their parents' assistance, develop their driving skills. The program is available as a videotape or CD-ROM, both with a handbook.

Signs, Signals, and Markings Overview

THEME DEVELOPMENT Traffic signs, signals, and markings are designed to facilitate the smooth flow of traffic and to make roadway users aware of possible dangers, road conditions, traffic rules, and various kinds of information. In order for the highway transportation system to work effectively, all drivers must understand and obey these signs, signals, and markings.

CHAPTER FEATURES	TCR COMPONENTS
	Study Guide, p. 17
	Transparencies 1 and 2
	Posters
	Lesson Plan, p. 11

CONNECTIONS History

The origin of the three-way traffic signal.

Study Guide, p. 18
Transparencies 3–5
Posters
Lesson Plan, p. 11

 FOR NEW DRIVERS

Using shared left-turn lanes.

Study Guide, p. 19
Posters
Lesson Plan, p. 12

ADVICE FROM THE EXPERTS

The importance of recognizing and understanding roadway signs, signals, and markings.

Study Guide, p. 20
Transparencies 6 and 7
Posters
Lesson Plan, p. 12

BUILDING SKILLS: MATH

Reading and Interpreting a Bar graph

Test A, pp. 9–10
Test B, pp. 9–10

PROJECTS

1. Explore the advantages and disadvantages of right turn on red laws.
2. Evaluate signs, signals, and pavement markings.

OTHER PROGRAM RESOURCES

Testmaker software
Responsible Driving,
    Video 1: Lessons 3 and 4
Traffic charts

ADDITIONAL RESOURCES

Getting Safely Past the Orange Barrels, Video 433, AAA Foundation
Signs, Signals, and Markings: Understanding the Language of the Road, Video 469, AAA Foundation
Dangerous Crossings: A Second Thought, Video 412, AAA Foundation

---

NAME _____ DATE _____

CHAPTER 5 Signs, Signals, and Markings

TEST A

Read each statement below. If it is true, place a T in the space to the left of the statement. If the statement is false, place an F next to it.

__F__ 1. A stop sign is shaped like a triangle.

__F__ 2. A blue sign with white lettering indicates a recreational area, a state or national park, or a historic site.

__T__ 3. A broken yellow line means that you can pass if it is safe to do so.

__F__ 4. If you see a railroad advance warning sign, the best thing to do is to get across the railroad tracks as fast as possible.

Select the phrase that best completes each sentence below. Write the letter of the answer you have chosen to the left of each statement.

__c__ 5. A brown sign with white lettering can tell you about
a. speed limits.
b. roadside services.
c. state parks.
d. mileage to your destination.

__c__ 6. Traffic that is traveling in the same direction is separated by
a. a yellow line.
b. double solid yellow lines.
c. broken white lines.
d. none of the above.

__b__ 7. At an intersection with a traffic signal and a police officer directing traffic, you should obey
a. the traffic signal.
b. the officer.
c. the light first, then the officer.
d. none of the above.

__b__ 8. If you come to a yield sign,
a. stop 10 feet past the sign.
b. yield to traffic in the cross street.
c. do not pay attention to it.
d. stop to check if there is traffic behind you.

NAME _____ DATE _____

Look over the following signs. In the space below the sign, write in the letter that best describes what kind of sign it is.

A = Regulatory   B = Warning   C = International   D = Informational

__A__ 9. (DO NOT ENTER)   __B__ 10. (winding road)   __D__ 11. (CAMPING)

__C__ 12. (no left turn)   __A__ 13. (ONLY right turn)   __B__ 14. (DETOUR)

__B__ 15. (pedestrian)   __D__ 16. (ROCKY MOUNTAIN NAT'L PARK)   __D__ 17. (EXIT)

18. Explain what shared left-turn lanes are, and describe how to use them safely.

A shared left-turn lane allows traffic going in either direction to enter the lane to make a left turn. You should not get into this lane too soon. Watch for cars pulling out of entrances and side streets. You should never use this lane for anything but turning left.

NAME _____ DATE _____

CHAPTER 5 Signs, Signals, and Markings

TEST B

Read each statement below. If it is true, place a T in the space to the left of the statement. If the statement is false, place an F next to it.

__F__ 1. At a stop sign, when there are two white lines crossing the roadway, you must stop at the second line you come to.

__T__ 2. A brown sign with white lettering indicates a recreational area, a state or national park, or a historic site.

__T__ 3. A broken white line means that you can move into the lane next to you once it is safe to do so.

__F__ 4. If you see a railroad advance warning sign, the best thing to do is to get across the railroad tracks as fast as possible.

Select the phrase that best completes each sentence below. Write the letter of the answer you have chosen to the left of each statement.

__b__ 5. A blue sign with white lettering tells you about
a. speed limits.
b. roadside services.
c. state parks.
d. mileage to your destination.

__a__ 6. Traffic that is traveling in opposite directions on a two-lane highway is separated by
a. yellow lines.
b. solid white lines.
c. broken white lines.
d. none of the above.

__b__ 7. At an intersection with a traffic signal and a police officer directing traffic, you should obey
a. the traffic signal.
b. the officer.
c. the light first, then the officer.
d. none of the above.

__b__ 8. If you come to a stop sign and there is no white line on the road, stop
a. 10 feet past the stop sign.
b. even with the stop sign or just before it.
c. 10 feet before the stop sign.
d. anywhere as long as you stop.

NAME _____ DATE _____

Look over the following signs. In the space below the sign, write in the letter that best describes what kind of sign it is.

A = Regulatory   B = Warning   C = International   D = Informational

__A__ 9. (SPEED LIMIT 50)   __A__ 10. (railroad crossing)   __D__ 11. (CAMPING)

__C__ 12. (no left turn)   __A__ 13. (EXIT 25 M.P.H.)   __B__ 14. (DETOUR)

__B__ 15. (crossing)   __D__ 16. (ROCKY MOUNTAIN NAT'L PARK)   __D__ 17. (BUSINESS LOOP 22)

18. Explain what shared left-turn lanes are, and describe how to use them safely.

A shared left-turn lane allows traffic going in either direction to enter the lane to make a left turn. You should not get into this lane too soon. Watch for vehicles pulling out of entrances and side streets. You should never use this lane for anything but turning left.

NAME _____ DATE _____

CHAPTER 5 Signs, Signals, and Markings

STUDY GUIDE FOR CHAPTER 5   LESSON 1

Understanding Regulatory and Warning Signs

A. Look at the shapes of the signs below. Under each sign, explain what kind of sign it is and what it means.

1. regulatory/stop sign

2. regulatory/yield sign

3. regulatory/speed limit sign

4. regulatory/railroad crossbuck

5. regulatory/do not enter

6. warning/curve

B. FIND OUT MORE. In the next week, take notes on your way to and from school. What regulatory and warning signs are there on this route?

Review student's work.

NAME _____ DATE _____

STUDY GUIDE FOR CHAPTER 5   LESSON 2

Guide and International Signs

A. Write the letter of the statement that defines each sign below.

A = Route Marker   B = Destination Sign   C = International Sign
D = Recreational Area Sign   E = Roadside Services

1. A   **2.** A   **3.** B

4. E   **5.** D   **6.** C

7. A   **8.** C   **9.** E

B. In the next week, look over the roads in your area. What international signs, if any, exist where you live? Where are they located?

Review student's work.

NAME _____ DATE _____

STUDY GUIDE FOR CHAPTER 5   LESSON 3

Understanding the Purpose of Pavement Markings

A. Select the phrase that best completes each sentence below. Write the letter of the answer you have chosen to the left of each question.

___a___ **1.** Yellow lines separate traffic going
    a. in opposite directions.   **c.** off an exit ramp.
    b. in the same direction.   **d.** around a curve.

___b___ **2.** A solid yellow line to your left on the road means that you are in or at
    a. a railroad crossing.   **c.** a one-way street.
    b. a no-passing zone.   **d.** an intersection.

___b___ **3.** White lines parallel to the roadway
    a. separate traffic going in opposite directions.   **c.** separate parking spaces.
    b. separate traffic going in the same direction.   **d.** separate traffic around curves.

___c___ **4.** On divided highways, a single solid yellow line
    a. marks the right edge of the roadway.   **c.** marks the left edge of the roadway.
    b. means that you may not pass.   **d.** means none of the above.

B. In the space below, three passing situations are described. In the space above the descriptions, draw in the roadway markings that would show the passing situation. With arrows, indicate the direction in which your vehicle is moving.
Review student's work.

Do not pass in either direction. Pass only in your direction. Legal only for oncoming vehicles to pass.

C. FIND OUT MORE. In the next week, see if you can find an example of an area that has diagonal "zebra" lines on the pavement. Where did you find this marking? What do the lines mean?

Review student's work.

NAME _____ DATE _____

STUDY GUIDE FOR CHAPTER 5   LESSON 4

Responding to Traffic Control Signals

A. Look at the following lane use lights. Describe what they mean in the space below.

1. Red X   **2.** Green arrow   **3.** Yellow X   **4.** Flashing yellow X

Red X   Do not drive in this lane.

Green arrow   You are permitted to drive in this lane.

Yellow X   Vacate this lane because it soon will be a red X.

Flashing yellow X   Use with caution for left turn movements only.

B. Describe the steps that you should take to turn right on a red light. If it is illegal to do so at that light, how would you know?

1. Who invented the automatic traffic signal?   Garrett A. Morgan

2. When was the automatic traffic signal invented?   1923

3. How much did the inventor earn from General Electric? $40,000

4. What other invention is the inventor responsible for?   The gas inhalator.

C. FIND OUT MORE. Call your state's department of motor vehicles and ask them what the procedure is for a physically challenged person to get a driver's license in your state. How are the tests administered? For what length of time are the licenses issued?

Review student's research.

CHAPTER 5

Signs, Signals, and Markings

CHAPTER OVERVIEW

LESSON ONE
Regulatory and warning signs are described, illustrated, and explained.

LESSON TWO
Informational signs and international signs and symbols are described, illustrated, and explained.

LESSON THREE
Roadway markings are described, illustrated, and explained.

LESSON FOUR
Traffic signals are described, illustrated, and explained.

VOCABULARY

guide sign
international sign
lane-use lights
pedestrian
regulatory sign
shared left-turn lane
traffic control signal
warning sign
yield sign

76

CONCEPT OF THE DRIVING TASK

Communication is a crucial element of the driving task. Drivers need information about the roadway ahead. They need to be warned of hazards on the highway and rules that apply at specific places or times. Signs, signals, and markings provide such information. Drivers need to understand how this information affects not only them but all other roadway users as well.

CHAPTER 5

Signs, Signals, and Markings

Good drivers understand the role of communication. The signs, signals, and markings you see on the roadway are a vital means of communication. It is important that you understand the messages that they communicate.

PRESENTING THE BIG IDEA ———

Every state highway department is responsible for communicating important information to highway users. Roadway users, in turn, are responsible for paying attention to signs, signals, and roadway markings. Tuning in to the information we are given is crucial to managing risk on the highway.

INTRODUCING THE CHAPTER

What's on the Road Ahead?

Have students read the lesson titles and objectives. Briefly discuss the topic of each lesson. Tell students that in this chapter, they will be introduced to key communication tools of the highway transportation system: signs, signals, and markings.

Background: The Larger Picture

The following information will help students realize that because millions of vehicles are on the nation's roads, a consistent system of signs, signals, and markings that all drivers understand is needed to ensure that traffic flows smoothly and efficiently.

- The United States has almost 4 million miles of streets, roads, and highways.
- U.S. drivers are estimated to travel about 3 trillion miles a year.
- The average passenger vehicle in the United States travels about 13,000 miles a year.

Relating to Prior Knowledge

Have students discuss how, as pedestrians, they use traffic signals. Ask them how they think that traffic signals, signs, and markings help drivers.

The Big Idea

Discuss students' reactions to the Big Idea statement. Suggest that they keep this idea in mind as they read Chapter 5.

Understanding Regulatory and Warning Signs

(pages 78–82)

FOCUS

Objectives

- Identify and describe the purpose of regulatory signs.
- Describe the actions to take at regulatory signs.
- Identify the purpose of warning signs.
- Describe how to respond to warning signs.

Resources

 Study Guide, page 17

 Traffic charts

 Transparencies 1 and 2

Vocabulary

regulatory sign
yield sign
warning sign

Motivator

Ask students to name the road signs with which they are familiar. Have them discuss what these road signs mean. (Students may mention stop sign, which indicates a driver must come to a full stop; yield sign, which indicates a vehicle on another roadway has the right-of-way; speed limit sign, which indicates the maximum and minimum speeds; railroad crossing; and various warning signs.)

LESSON ONE

OBJECTIVES
1. Identify and describe the purpose of regulatory signs.
2. Describe the actions to take at regulatory signs.
3. Identify the purpose of warning signs.
4. Describe how to respond to warning signs.

KEY TERMS
regulatory sign
yield sign
warning sign

◆ Stop signs are most frequently placed at one or more corners of an intersection.

Understanding Regulatory and Warning Signs

Highways and streets would be difficult to use without signs that give drivers information and warnings and tell them what to do and what not to do. If there were no signs, how would you know you were on the right road? Imagine how difficult it would be to manage risk if there were no speed limits or rules regulating when or where to yield. Roadway signs provide important information about where you are, where you are going, and what rules or laws to follow.

What Are Regulatory Signs?

A **regulatory sign** regulates or controls the movement of traffic. These signs tell you and other drivers what you must do and what you must not do when you drive. Regulatory signs are red, white, black, green on white, or white on black. Most regulatory signs have square, vertical rectangular, or horizontal rectangular shapes. A red circle with a red slash on any of these signs means *NO*. You can recognize regulatory signs by their color and shape.

What Actions Should You Take at Regulatory Signs?

Regulatory signs give commands or set limits. When you see a stop sign, you must stop. When you see a **yield sign,** you must slow and yield (give way) to traffic on the crossroad or the road onto which you are merging. A speed limit sign indicates the maximum speed you may drive under ideal conditions.

Stop Signs

Most often you will see a stop sign at the intersection of two roadways. There may be stop signs on all four corners or on only one or two corners of an intersection. In

78   UNIT 2   *Learning the Basics*

THE INTERNATIONAL SCENE

Canada

In the province of Manitoba, it is illegal to ride a bicycle or a horse while under the influence of alcohol. Offenders may be fined or even imprisoned.

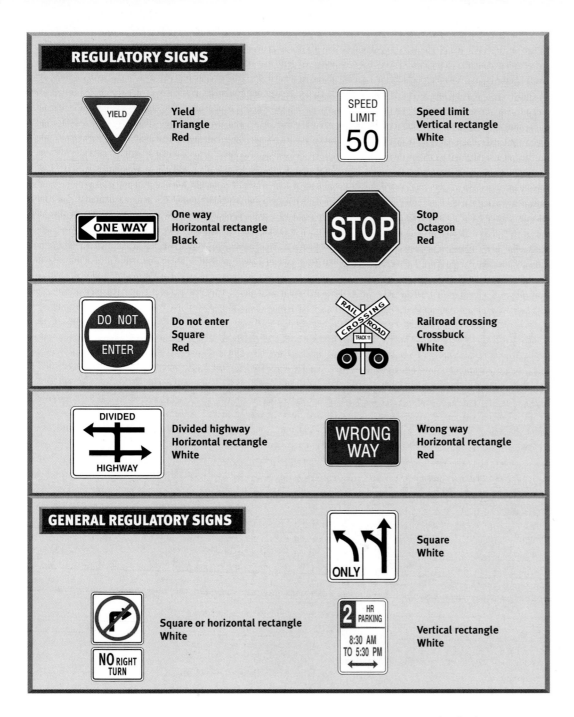

REGULATORY SIGNS

YIELD
Yield
Triangle
Red

SPEED LIMIT 50
Speed limit
Vertical rectangle
White

ONE WAY
One way
Horizontal rectangle
Black

STOP
Stop
Octagon
Red

DO NOT ENTER
Do not enter
Square
Red

RAIL CROSSING ROAD TRACK 11
Railroad crossing
Crossbuck
White

DIVIDED HIGHWAY
Divided highway
Horizontal rectangle
White

WRONG WAY
Wrong way
Horizontal rectangle
Red

GENERAL REGULATORY SIGNS

ONLY
Square
White

NO RIGHT TURN
Square or horizontal rectangle
White

2 HR PARKING 8:30 AM TO 5:30 PM
Vertical rectangle
White

State BY State

Students should be aware that although states govern their own traffic laws, the same basic traffic signs and controls are used throughout the nation.

TEACH

Explain

OBJECTIVE 1: Students should recognize that the shapes of regulatory signs have meaning. It may be helpful for them to categorize the signs by shape. Square or rectangular signs generally tell what to do or not to do; an octagon is reserved for stop signs; and a triangle pointing down always indicates a yield sign. You may also want to point out that the colors and shapes of these signs are subject to change pending decisions by the Federal Highway Administration.

OBJECTIVE 2: Students should be aware that they cannot assume that all drivers will obey regulatory signs. Indeed, students should understand that to manage risk, they should anticipate that other drivers will *not* obey signs.

OBJECTIVE 3: Students should be aware of the significance of the shape and color of warning signs. They can be categorized as follows:

- diamond shape, yellow with black letters: warns of possible hazards ahead
- pentagon shape, yellow with black letters: warns that there is a school crossing or school zone ahead
- pennant shape, yellow with black letters: marks the beginning of a no-passing zone
- round, yellow with black letters: gives advance warning of a railroad crossing
- orange, with black letters: warns of construction or repair activity

These signs are also subject to change by the Federal Highway Administration.

OBJECTIVE 4: Most students will have little difficulty remembering what the warning signs mean. However, they may feel that if they can't see the danger, it isn't there. An important factor in managing risk is being prepared for risks that cannot be seen immediately. Warning signs help.

Teaching Model

The purpose of this model is to help students begin to think about how to react to warning signs.

Display this situation:

Tell students the following: You are in vehicle 1 traveling at 35 mph, it is 3 P.M. on a weekday afternoon, and it is raining very hard. Model the thinking process that you will go through to manage risk in this situation. (You will do the following.

• Recognize that you are approaching a school zone at about the time that school lets out.

• Take into account the poor weather conditions, and recognize that children may be using umbrellas that block their vision.

• Be especially alert for the sudden appearance or unexpected action of a child in the roadway.

• Slow down to give yourself more time to watch for children and to warn the driver behind you.

• Proceed with extreme caution, and recognize that even after passing the school zone, you need to be on the lookout for children walking home.)

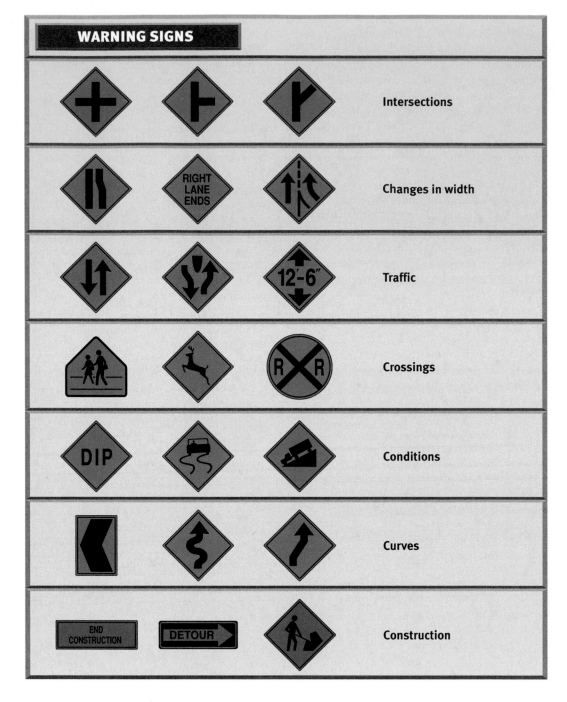

MEETING STUDENT DIVERSITY

Limited English Proficiency

For your students who have difficulty with English, stress the shape of the signs in relation to their purpose so that students will be able to anticipate what these signs say. Provide extra practice in the special vocabulary of the signs.

some places, stop signs are located in the middle of the block; these indicate crosswalks.

You must come to a full stop at a stop sign. Often a white stop line is painted on the pavement in line with the sign. There may be two white lines indicating a pedestrian crosswalk just beyond the stop line, or there may be walk lines and no stop line. You are required to stop in front of the first white line you come to. If there are no lines, stop just in front of or in line with the sign.

After you stop, if there is no traffic from the right or left you may proceed. When there is traffic on the other roadway, you must decide what to do. If there are stop signs for cross traffic and another vehicle has reached its stop sign before you reach yours, you must let it go first. If you and the other vehicle arrive at the same time, the driver on the left must let the vehicle on the right go first. If you are the driver of the vehicle on the right, make sure the driver of the vehicle on the left is going to wait. Then proceed cautiously.

Yield Signs

At a yield sign, you move from one roadway onto or across another one. As you approach the yield sign, slow down and check oncoming traffic and the traffic behind you. Search right and left for cross and oncoming traffic. If a vehicle is coming toward you, you'll have to judge its distance and speed and decide whether you can safely enter or cross the road. You may need to stop and wait until the roadway is clear of traffic before you proceed.

Speed Limit Signs

Speed limit signs show the maximum, or fastest, speed allowed on a roadway. Driving faster than the posted speed is illegal. Some speed limit signs also post minimum speeds. These signs are usually on expressways. You should not travel more slowly than the minimum speed posted, unless road or weather conditions make it unsafe to travel at that speed.

Railroad Crossbuck

A railroad crossing crossbuck is located where railroad tracks cross the roadway. On multiple-lane roadways and in heavy traffic areas, signal bells, flashing red lights, and railroad gates may also warn and protect drivers. Regardless of whether or not lights or gates are present, if a train is coming, you must stop.

◆ Yield signs and speed limit signs are two examples of regulatory traffic signs.

CHAPTER 5   *Signs, Signals, and Markings*   **81**

IT'S A FACT

Drivers make up nearly seven out of every ten vehicle occupants killed in vehicle crashes.

Ask

Ask students to discuss why it is important to react immediately to warning signs and not wait until encountering the situation warned about.

Read

Have students read Lesson 1 to learn about how to identify and respond to regulatory and warning signs.

ASSESS

Guided Practice

Have students answer the Lesson 1 Review questions. The answers are provided below.

Reteaching

Pair a more able student with one who has experienced difficulty with this lesson. Have them work together to make road signs and then test each other by holding up the signs and explaining what they stand for. After students have identified the signs, have them discuss how they would react to each one.

Enrichment

Assign the Study Guide for Lesson 1. The Find Out More section encourages students to expand their basic learning of the lesson concepts.

CLOSE

Summarize

Return to the Motivator question. Discuss the meaning of the regulatory and warning signs. Lead a class discussion on the risk management aspects of signs and drivers' responsibility to respond to signs in a safe manner in order to protect themselves and others.

DRIVER'S LOG

How does becoming familiar with the relationship between the shape of a sign and its message help a driver manage risk?

WHAT WOULD YOU DO?

Sample answer: The chevron sign means there is a curve coming up. Slow down and proceed with caution.

◆ *A railroad advance warning sign is placed well before a railroad crossing crossbuck.*

What Are Warning Signs?

A **warning sign** alerts you to changes in the condition or use of the road ahead. Warning signs include those that tell you about road construction and maintenance, school zones and crossings, railroad crossings, curves, intersections, changes in road width, and deer crossings. All warning signs are either yellow or orange with black symbols or letters, and most are diamond-shaped.

What Actions Should You Take at Warning Signs?

When you see a warning sign, increase your level of alertness to changes in the roadway, in traffic, or in environmental conditions. Always proceed with caution. Be especially careful when you see a school zone sign or a railroad advance warning sign.

School Area Signs

When you see a school zone or school crossing sign, you must slow down and proceed with caution. Children may be playing nearby and may dart into the street. At a school crossing sign, stop and wait for children to cross the roadway.

Railroad Advance Warning Signs

Be especially careful when you come to a railroad advance warning sign. Slow down before you reach the tracks, and be prepared to stop. Look in both directions to see if a train is approaching.

WHAT WOULD YOU DO?

The symbol on this sign is called a chevron. What does the sign mean? What would you do in this situation?

Lesson 1 Review

1. How can you tell which roadway signs are regulatory signs?
2. What should you do when you see a stop sign? A yield sign? A railroad crossbuck?
3. How do you know which signs are warning signs?
4. How should you proceed at school zone or school crossing signs and railroad advance warning signs?

Lesson 1 Review

Answers

1. By shape and color; they generally tell you what to do or not to do.
2. At a stop sign: stop; at a yield sign: give other vehicles the right-of-way; at a railroad crossbuck: stop if a train is coming.
3. Warning signs are either yellow or orange with black symbols or letters; most are diamond shaped.
4. Slow down and proceed with caution.

Guide and International Signs

LESSON TWO

OBJECTIVES

1. Identify and describe the purpose of informational or guide signs.
2. Identify and describe the design and function of three international signs used in the United States.

KEY TERMS

guide sign
international sign

Highway signs do more than just warn you and tell you what you can and cannot do. Signs can provide information about where you are, where you are going, how to get there, how far you have to go, and what services and sites are available to help make your trip comfortable and enjoyable.

As you drive, you will see signs that convey information through color, shape, and symbols instead of words.

What Are the Functions of Guide Signs?

As you travel along the roadways, you'll see four kinds of guide signs. A **guide sign** gives information about roadways and routes; the mileage to certain destinations; roadside services such as rest stops, service stations, and campsites; and recreational areas and nearby points of interest.

Route Markers

Routes are the numbered roadways that crisscross the continent. Interstate routes that lead *into* cities have three digits and begin with an odd digit (195, 395, and so on). If a three-digit route begins with an even digit (295, 684), the route goes *around* a city or connects to interstate highways at both ends.

Destination and Mileage Signs

You will often see destination and mileage signs mounted over highway lanes. They tell you where you are, which lane to take to get to your destination, what exits are coming up, and how far away the exits are. Smaller

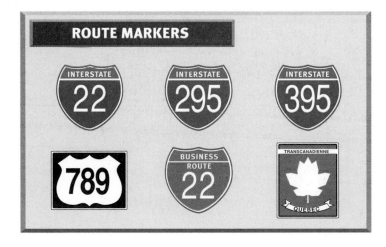

ROUTE MARKERS

INTERSTATE 22 · INTERSTATE 295 · INTERSTATE 395

789 · BUSINESS ROUTE 22 · TRANSCANADIENNE QUEBEC

IT'S A FACT

Traffic signs date back to the early Roman roads. Today New York City alone has nearly a million road signs.

LESSON TWO

Guide and International Signs

(pages 83–85)

FOCUS

Objectives

- Identify and describe the purpose of informational or guide signs.
- Identify and describe the design and function of three international signs used in the United States.

> **Resources**
>
> Study Guide, page 18
>
> Transparencies 3–5

Vocabulary

guide sign
international sign

Motivator

Ask students what other kinds of road signs they can think of besides the regulatory and warning signs studied in Lesson 1. What purpose do these signs serve? (Students may mention route markers, destination signs, roadside-services signs, international signs. These signs provide information.)

TEACH

Explain

OBJECTIVE 1: Signs that convey information are called guide signs or informational signs. Students will benefit from recognizing that drivers often slow down to read these signs, which can contribute to risk.

OBJECTIVE 2: Students should note that a red circle with a diagonal bar through it indicates a prohibited action. You may also want to explain that there are other international signs besides those shown in the textbook.

Teaching Model

Describe the following situation: You are planning a trip with a friend to an unfamiliar part of the country. Model the thinking process that you go through to be sure you do not miss route and destination signs. (You do the following.

• Plan out your route on a map.

• Write down road numbers and exits you will need to watch for.

• Give your passenger responsibility for checking route and destination signs.)

Ask

What risks can be avoided by the travel plan you have outlined?

Read

Have students read Lesson 2 to learn about informational signs and international road signs.

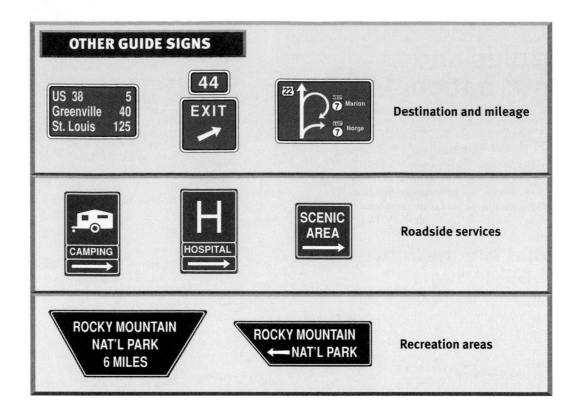

State BY State

Drivers moving to a new state must apply for a license in that state. For example, a new Texas resident has three days after moving into the state to secure a Texas license.

CONNECTIONS
History

You may want to note that Garrett Morgan lived from 1877 to 1963. Although his traffic signal did not look the same as modern signals, it did have green, red, and yellow lights.

![CONNECTIONS History — CULTURAL CROSSROADS]

CONNECTIONS
History

One of the most important traffic safety devices is the automatic traffic signal. It is responsible for the orderly movement of millions of vehicles and pedestrians in today's cities and towns. The three-way traffic signal was invented in 1923 by Garrett A. Morgan. He sold the rights to his invention to the General Electric Company for $40,000.

Morgan earned a far more important reward for another of his safety devices. In 1916, two dozen men were trapped by an explosion in a tunnel 228 feet below Lake Erie near Cleveland, Ohio. The tunnel was filled with smoke, natural gases, dust, and debris. The situation seemed hopeless because no one could survive going down into the tunnel to rescue the trapped men. However, by using his new invention—the gas inhalator, an early gas mask—Morgan was able to lead a rescue party to reach the men and to save the lives of many of them. In 1963, the city of Cleveland awarded this courageous African American a gold medal for his heroism.

signs on the side of the road also tell you how far you are from different places. Destination and mileage signs are either white or green.

Roadside Services

When you want to stop for gas or food or make a phone call, look for blue signs with white lettering.

Recreational Areas

Some informational signs are brown with white lettering. These signs guide you to state and national parks, historic sites, and other places of interest.

What International Signs Are Used in the United States?

An **international sign** is one that you can understand without knowing another language. The meaning is conveyed by colors, shapes, symbols, and numbers.

Lesson 2 Review

1. Which signs are guide signs?
2. What kinds of international signs are used in the United States?

WHAT WOULD YOU DO?

What does the sign mean? What should you be alert to when you see this sign?

ASSESS

Guided Practice

Have students answer the Lesson 2 Review questions. The answers are provided below.

Reteaching

Have partners test each other's recognition of signs by asking such questions as: "If you need gasoline, what symbol would you look for?"

Enrichment

Assign the Study Guide for Lesson 2. The Find Out More section encourages students to expand their basic learning of the lesson concepts.

CLOSE

Summarize

Return to the Motivator question, and discuss how this lesson added to students' knowledge of signs and symbols.

DRIVER'S LOG

How can you minimize risk caused by other drivers' unfamiliarity with road signs?

WHAT WOULD YOU DO?

Sample answer: A slippery surface may create a road hazard.

Lesson 2 Review

Answers

1. Signs that give information about roadways and routes, the mileage to certain destinations, roadside services, and recreational areas.
2. Those for a first aid station, telephone, gas station, no U-turn, and others.

Understanding the Purpose of Pavement Markings

(pages 86–89)

FOCUS

Objectives

• Identify the meaning of yellow and white roadway lane markings.

• Describe the meaning of arrows and other nonlane roadway markings.

Resources

📁 Study Guide, page 19

📁 Traffic charts

Vocabulary

shared left-turn lane

Motivator

Draw the following on the board:

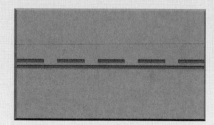

Ask students if they have ever noticed this marking painted on a roadway. Have them discuss what they think it means. Encourage students to talk about other roadway markings that they have noticed and what meaning they think these markings have. (Students may mention that yellow lines divide traffic going in opposite directions; white ones separate same-direction traffic

LESSON THREE

OBJECTIVES

1. Identify the meaning of yellow and white road-way lane markings.
2. Describe the meaning of arrows and other non-lane roadway markings.

KEY TERM

shared left-turn lane

Understanding the Purpose of Pavement Markings

You have probably noticed lines, arrows, and words painted on streets and highways. These markings give drivers and pedestrians important information, directions, and warnings about roadway travel. You need to understand pavement markings in order to control and reduce risk.

What Do Yellow or White Lines on the Roadway Mean?

Yellow and white roadway lines provide directions or warnings for drivers. Yellow lines divide traffic traveling in opposite directions. White lines parallel to the roadway separate same-direction traffic into lanes. White lines perpendicular to the roadway indicate crosswalks, railroad crossings, and stop signs at intersections.

◆ *Double broken yellow lines mark lanes in which traffic changes direction at different times of the day.*

Yellow Lines

Traffic that is traveling in opposite directions on a roadway is separated by a broken yellow line, double solid yellow lines, or a combination of broken and solid yellow lines. On divided highways, a single solid yellow line marks the left edge of the roadway.

If the solid line of the combination solid-broken yellow lines is the first one to your left, you may not cross it to pass another vehicle. If the broken yellow line is the first one to your left, you may cross it (and the solid yellow line) to pass a vehicle

MEETING STUDENT DIVERSITY

Orientation Dysfunction

Some students have trouble with the concept of left and right. Give these students practice by having them walk toward signs that you hold up and turn to the left or right as the signs indicate.

when it is safe to do so. When two solid yellow lines divide a road, neither you nor drivers traveling in the opposite direction can cross them to pass another vehicle. You may, however, turn left across them to turn into a driveway.

White Lines

White lines that are parallel to the roadway mark the lanes for traffic moving in the same direction. If the lines are broken, you can move from lane to lane when it is safe to do so. Single white lines between lanes of traffic moving in the same direction are meant to discourage passing at high-risk locations but do not prohibit passing.

Solid white lines are used to indicate the right side of the roadway. These lines are especially helpful at night because they mark the outer edges of the road, which are otherwise hard to see. A solid white line may also mark a bicycle or breakdown lane on the right side of the roadway.

◆ *You may not pass on a two-way road divided by solid yellow lines.*

◆ *The broken white lines indicate that you may change lanes or pass. This solid white edge line marks a breakdown lane. You should not travel in a breakdown lane.*

Driving Tip

Emphasize to students that roadway markings are only one factor to consider before changing lanes, passing, or turning. Drivers must also consider traffic and road and weather conditions before making any maneuver.

into lanes; a broken yellow line means that passing is allowed; broken white lines mean that drivers can change lanes. Other markings include white lines perpendicular to the roadway indicating crosswalks; stop lines; white arrows directing drivers into lanes from which they can drive straight ahead or turn right or left; road exit ramps; high-occupancy vehicle lanes; reversible lanes.)

TEACH

Explain

OBJECTIVE 1: Students will benefit from recognizing that yellow and white roadway lane markings provide advance warning not only of what they can do but of what other drivers can do as well. Students should realize that managing risk always involves being aware of what other drivers might do.

OBJECTIVE 2: Students may benefit from a discussion in which they identify and explain the meaning of the following pavement markings as you display them:

- white arrows—direct drivers into lanes from which they can drive straight ahead, turn left, or turn right
- white arrows pointing alternately right and left (found on some three-lane highways)—shared left-turn lanes indicating that vehicles moving in either direction can use the lane to make a left turn into another road or entrance
- reversible lanes—at different times of day may be used by traffic moving in opposite directions
- high occupancy vehicle (HOV) lanes—set aside for use by vehicles carrying more than one occupant

Teaching Model

Display the following:

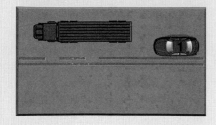

Describe this situation to students: You are in vehicle 1. In front of you is a slow-moving truck that you want to pass. You see no vehicles coming from the other direction. Model your thinking process as you decide whether or not to pass. (You do the following.

- See that traffic appears clear in the oncoming lane.
- Note that the double solid line indicates that you cannot pass.
- Note that the broken yellow line ahead indicates where you can pass.
- Decide to wait to pass until you are alongside the broken line.)

Ask

What other hazards might the truck pose in this situation?

Read

Have students read Lesson 3 to learn the meaning of markings painted on the roadway.

ASSESS

Guided Practice

Have students answer the Lesson 3 Review questions. The answers are provided below.

Reteaching

Have students work in groups to make up slogans or acronyms to help them remember what the lines painted on the roadway indicate.

◆ *Other roadway markings include lines, arrows, symbols, and lettering that help guide drivers and pedestrians.*

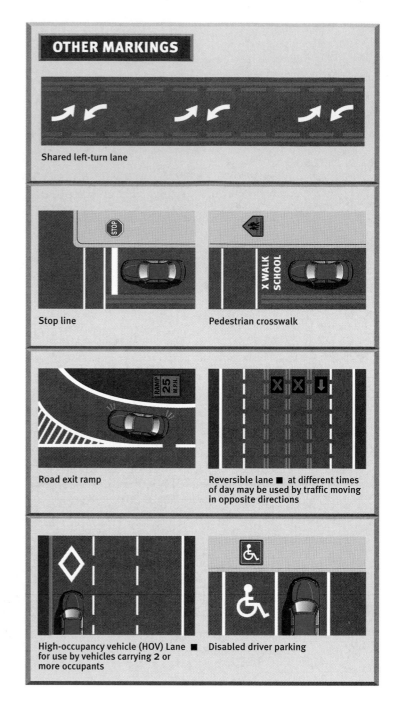

OTHER MARKINGS

Shared left-turn lane

Stop line

Pedestrian crosswalk

Road exit ramp

Reversible lane ■ at different times of day may be used by traffic moving in opposite directions

High-occupancy vehicle (HOV) Lane ■ for use by vehicles carrying 2 or more occupants

Disabled driver parking

State BY State

In 28 states and the District of Columbia, a driver's license is valid for four years. In 21 states, the time period between renewals varies from one to eight years. In one state—Arizona—a driver's initial license is valid until the driver's 60th birthday.

What Do Other Markings on the Roadway Mean?

Other roadway markings may include lines, arrows, symbols, and lettering designed to guide drivers and pedestrians.

Arrows

White arrows on the roadway identify lanes from which you can drive straight ahead or turn right or left. On some three-lane roadways, the center lane is marked by parallel solid and broken yellow lines with white arrows that point alternately left and right. This lane is called a **shared left-turn lane.** Vehicles moving in either direction can use these lanes to make left turns onto another road or into an entrance. Drivers who want to make left turns onto the roadway can also move into the shared left-turn lane and wait for a gap in traffic.

Other Markings

On the opposite page are other pavement markings whose meaning and purpose you should know.

Lesson 3 Review

1. Which pavement markings let you know that it is legal to pass? That it is illegal to pass?
2. How is a shared left-turn lane marked? How would you use it?

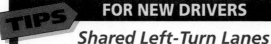

TIPS

FOR NEW DRIVERS

Shared Left-Turn Lanes

Here are tips for using shared left-turn lanes safely.
- Do not move into the lane too soon. The longer you stay in the lane, the more likely it is you will meet someone coming in the opposite direction.
- Watch for cars pulling out of entrances and side streets. They may cross in front of you, cutting you off.
- Do not use a shared left-turn lane for anything but turning left.

WHAT WOULD YOU DO?

You are driving alone. Are you allowed to use this lane? Why or why not?

Enrichment

Assign the Study Guide for Lesson 3. The Find Out More section encourages students to expand their basic learning of the lesson concepts.

CLOSE

Summarize

Return to the Motivator question, and have students use it as a lead-in to a review of what they have learned in this lesson.

DRIVER'S LOG

What roadway markings indicate that it is legal to pass or to change lanes? What markings indicate that it is not legal to do so?

WHAT WOULD YOU DO?

Sample answer: No, because the vehicle must be carrying more than one person.

TIPS

FOR NEW DRIVERS

To check students' understanding, you may wish to have them discuss risks related to each of the tips given.

Lesson 3 Review

Answers

1. Legal: broken white or yellow lines, combination solid-broken yellow lines if the broken line is the first on your left; illegal: solid yellow lines, combination solid-broken yellow lines if the solid line is the first one on your left.
2. Solid and broken yellow lines with white arrows that point alternately left and right; to make a left turn.

Responding to Traffic Control Signals

(pages 90–92)

FOCUS

Objectives

• Describe traffic signals and the meanings of their colors.
• Describe the colors and meanings of lane-use lights.

Resources

 Study Guide, page 20

 Traffic charts

 Transparencies 6 and 7

Vocabulary

traffic control signal
pedestrian
lane-use light

Motivator

Pose the following: A red arrow is pointing left on a traffic signal. Can you make a left turn? (No.)

Have students discuss the various traffic signals and explain what they mean. (Students may mention red—stop; flashing red—stop until it is safe to proceed; yellow—do not enter the intersection; flashing yellow—slow down and proceed with caution; green—go when it is safe; green arrow—traffic moving in that direction may proceed if path is clear; yellow arrow—appears after a green arrow to indicate signal is about to change; red arrow—traffic not allowed to turn in that direction. Lane signals: red X— may not drive in that lane; yellow X—vacate lane because it will soon be controlled by red X.)

LESSON FOUR

OBJECTIVES
1. Describe traffic signals and the meanings of their colors.
2. Describe the colors and meanings of lane-use lights.

KEY TERMS
traffic control signal
pedestrian
lane-use light

Responding to Traffic Control Signals

A **traffic control signal** keeps traffic moving in an orderly manner. Except in large cities, most signals operate automatically, using a timer system to change the lights through the green-yellow-red sequence. In many large cities, signals are linked electronically to and are controlled by computer. This sets up a gridwork that allows traffic to move smoothly and adjusts to changes in traffic volume.

How Do You Know When to Stop or Move Your Vehicle Through Traffic?

As a user of the highway transportation system, your movement, whether you're a driver or pedestrian, is controlled by a series of traffic signals, arrows, flashing lights, pedestrian signals, or the directions of a traffic officer.

Traffic Signals

Traffic signals are usually located at intersections where the level of risk increases. Special-use signals may operate during specific hours or on demand at school zones, fire stations, or factories. Traffic signals may be vertical or horizontal, and may have one to five or more separate lenses that give information to roadway users. The most common lenses are red, yellow, and green circles.

At a flashing signal you must either stop or slow down, depending on the color of the light. If you see a flashing red signal this means that

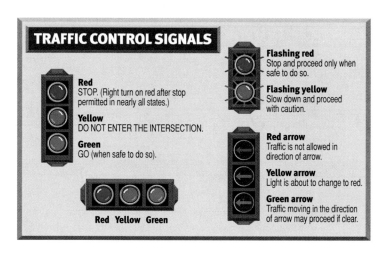

TRAFFIC CONTROL SIGNALS

Red
STOP. (Right turn on red after stop permitted in nearly all states.)

Yellow
DO NOT ENTER THE INTERSECTION.

Green
GO (when safe to do so).

Red Yellow Green

Flashing red
Stop and proceed only when safe to do so.

Flashing yellow
Slow down and proceed with caution.

Red arrow
Traffic is not allowed in direction of arrow.

Yellow arrow
Light is about to change to red.

Green arrow
Traffic moving in the direction of arrow may proceed if clear.

MEETING STUDENT DIVERSITY

Visually Impaired

Color-blind students should know that light positions are standardized: in vertical signals, red is on top, yellow in the middle, and green on the bottom; in horizontal signals, red is at the left, yellow in the middle, and green at the right.

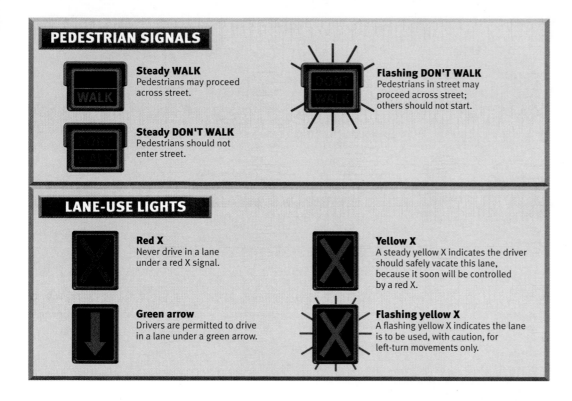

PEDESTRIAN SIGNALS

Steady WALK
Pedestrians may proceed across street.

Steady DON'T WALK
Pedestrians should not enter street.

Flashing DON'T WALK
Pedestrians in street may proceed across street; others should not start.

LANE-USE LIGHTS

Red X
Never drive in a lane under a red X signal.

Green arrow
Drivers are permitted to drive in a lane under a green arrow.

Yellow X
A steady yellow X indicates the driver should safely vacate this lane, because it soon will be controlled by a red X.

Flashing yellow X
A flashing yellow X indicates the lane is to be used, with caution, for left-turn movements only.

you must come to a full stop, just as you would at a stop sign. You must slow down at a flashing yellow signal.

Pedestrian Signals

In the city, you'll find pedestrian signals at busy intersections. Some are also located in the middle of the block. They may have either words or signals telling **pedestrians,** or people on foot, how to proceed.

If you're driving and the pedestrian signal starts to flash an orange "Don't walk," you can expect that your traffic signal is going to turn from green to yellow to red. However, don't just watch the pedestrian signals. Pay attention to the pedestrians and the traffic signal controlling vehicle traffic.

Traffic Officer's Signals

Keep in mind that a police officer can take the place of and overrule traffic control signals. Thus, when an officer *is* present and directing traffic, you should follow the officer's signals even if they go against those of an automatic traffic signal or stop sign.

Energy Tips

Save fuel by letting up on the accelerator well in advance of a red light, stop sign, or yield sign.

State BY State

Explain to students that the time interval between a yellow light and the subsequent red light varies from city to city. To manage risk, drivers traveling in an unfamiliar area should not assume that the time interval will be the same as they are accustomed to; it may be considerably shorter.

TEACH

Explain

OBJECTIVES 1 AND 2: Students should have little difficulty in understanding what the traffic and lane signals stand for. However, as with all signals, students should be aware that they must always perform a visual check to minimize risk. For example, drivers who have a green light cannot proceed automatically without checking for pedestrians and other vehicles. Risk management requires that drivers never assume that all roadway users will necessarily obey traffic signals.

Teaching Model
Display the following:

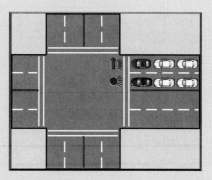

Explain to students: You are in vehicle 2. The light is red. The light above vehicle 1 has a green arrow indicating that a right turn is permitted. You want to turn right. Model your thinking process.

• You know you are not in the turn lane.

• You realize that you cannot get over to the turn lane without causing a risk situation.

• You wait for a green light and then proceed to turn at the next intersection, or you go around the block to return to the turn lane of this intersection.

Ask

How do you know which light applies to your vehicle?

Read

Have students read Lesson 4 to learn about the meaning of traffic signals.

ADVICE FROM THE EXPERTS

Have students discuss the importance of being attentive to road signs and signals and how inattention poses a risk to all drivers.

ASSESS

Guided Practice

Have students answer the Lesson 4 Review questions. The answers are provided below.

Reteaching

Have students work in groups to test their understanding of traffic lights and signals. Each group should make up a traffic situation involving a signal or lane light and decide how to manage risk in that situation. Groups should then exchange situations and come up with risk management strategies.

Enrichment

Assign the Study Guide for Lesson 4. The Find Out More section encourages students to expand their basic learning of the lesson concepts.

CLOSE

Summarize

Return to the Motivator question, and discuss students' original answers in light of what they have learned in this lesson. Have students summarize the basic rules of traffic signals.

DRIVER'S LOG

If you were asked to write one safety tip involving traffic lights and signals, what would it be?

ADVICE FROM THE EXPERTS

James E. Weaver
Highway Engineer, Traffic Control Division, Federal Highway Administration

Highway and traffic engineers design traffic control devices to convey a uniform, clear, and simple message to all highway users. It is your responsibility as a driver to recognize and fully understand the meaning of these devices by their color, shape, legend, and placement. This is important so that you will be able to respond properly and take the actions needed to maneuver your car safely in different traffic, terrain, and weather conditions.

Are There Signals That Let You Know Which Lanes You Can Use?

On heavily traveled multiple-lane roadways, you may see **lane-use lights** mounted above the roadway. It is important for you to know what to do in response to these signals because they are used when lane traffic is reversed during rush hours. Lane-use lights indicate which lane(s) you can use at any given time.

Lesson 4 Review

1. What are the colors and the meanings of the colors of traffic signals?
2. What are the meanings of the different colors of lane-use lights?

WHAT WOULD YOU DO?

You are stopped at a red light and want to turn right. Should you make the turn now?

WHAT WOULD YOU DO?

Sample answer: No. Wait until there is no vehicle coming from your left and no pedestrians crossing.

Lesson 4 Review

Answers

1. Green: go; yellow: slow down, do not enter the intersection; red: stop.
2. Do not drive in a lane with a red X; you can drive in a lane with a green arrow or X; vacate a lane with a steady yellow X; use a lane with a flashing yellow X only for turning.

Reading and Interpreting a Bar Graph

A bar graph presents information in a way that makes it easy to compare quantities.

The bar graph below shows the number of licensed vehicle drivers in different years. The numbers along the vertical axis, going up the left side of the graph, stand for tens of millions. So 1 equals 10 million, 5 equals 50 million, and so on.

The years in which the number of drivers are being compared are written along the bottom of the graph, on the horizontal axis.

Try It Yourself

1. About how many licensed drivers were there in 1962? In 1997?

2. About how many more licensed drivers were there in 1975 than in 1955? About how many more were there in 1975 than in 1962?

3. Which year shown on the graph had the smallest increase in the number of new drivers?

4. Between which two years shown did the number of licensed drivers nearly double?

5. What is the approximate average number of new licensed drivers each year? (Figure the difference between the last and the first years shown. Then divide by the number of years.)

6. If the trend in numbers of licensed drivers continues, about how many would you expect in the year 2010?

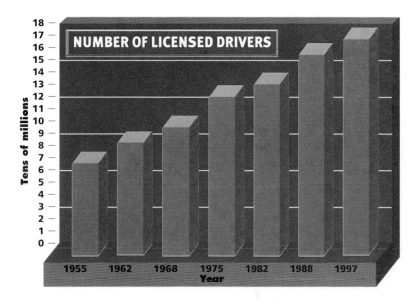

NUMBER OF LICENSED DRIVERS

Objective

Demonstrate understanding of how to read and interpret information presented on a bar graph.

Teaching the Skill

- Help students see that the units along the vertical axis are presented at regular intervals.

- Suggest that students follow the bar up with one finger and the units across with another finger until both fingers join.

- Before students answer the questions, discuss the kinds of questions that require numerical answers and those that can be answered by visual comparisons.

- Discuss how looking at the graph can help people recognize a trend without knowing the exact numerical information.

ANSWERS TO Try It Yourself Questions

1. 90 to 92 million; about 180 million
2. about 55 million; about 40 million
3. 1982
4. 1955 and 1982 or 1962 and 1997
5. 3 million
6. more than 190 million

CHAPTER SUMMARY

Key Points

Have students read the Key Points to review the major concepts of the chapter.

PROJECTS

Cooperative Learning:

Students will benefit by working with a partner on one or both of the projects. When the assignment is completed, the whole class will profit by sharing and comparing results.

CHAPTER 5 REVIEW

KEY POINTS

Lesson One

1. Regulatory signs control the movement of traffic. They can be red, white, black, green on white, or white on black. A red circle with a red slash on any of these signs means *NO*.
2. You must come to a full stop at stop signs, yield to cross traffic at yield signs, drive no faster than the limit posted on speed limit signs, and be prepared to stop at railroad crossbuck signs.
3. Warning signs alert you to changes in road conditions. They are black on yellow or orange and are usually diamond-shaped. Some warning signs are construction, school area, and railroad advance warning signs.
4. Respond to warning signs by increasing your level of alertness, slowing down, and proceeding with caution.

Lesson Two

1. Informational, or guide, signs include route signs, destination and mileage signs, roadside service signs, and recreational area signs.
2. International signs communicate their meaning by symbols. Some international signs used in the United States are First Aid Station and Telephone.

Lesson Three

1. Yellow lane markings divide traffic moving in opposite directions. White lane markings separate traffic traveling in the same direction. If the first line on the pavement to your left is a yellow or white broken line, you may pass another vehicle when it is safe to do so. If the line is solid, you may not pass.
2. Arrows direct drivers into lanes from which they can turn. Other road markings include lines, symbols, and words to guide drivers and pedestrians.

Lesson Four

1. Traffic signals have from one to five or more lenses. Those with three lenses can be either vertical or horizontal. The most common lenses are red (Stop), yellow (Do not enter intersection), and green (Go when safe to do so).
2. A red X signal indicates that you should not drive in that lane. A green arrow indicates that you are permitted to drive in that lane. A steady yellow X indicates that you should vacate the lane as soon as possible, and a flashing yellow X indicates that the lane may be used with caution to make left turns.

PROJECTS

1. Find out how intersections in your state are marked where right turns on red lights are prohibited. Describe what you believe to be the advantages and disadvantages of allowing right turns on red lights. Find intersections where right on red is prohibited. Determine what each one has in common.
2. Do you find certain signs, signals, or pavement markings confusing? How would you improve them? How would you change their location, shape, size, color, symbols, lettering, numbering, timing, and how often they appear?

*inter*NET CONNECTION

Take a trip to the Web to find more information on international traffic signs.
drivered.glencoe.com

*inter*NET CONNECTION

Visit Glencoe's Driver Education Web site for student activities that relate to this chapter.
drivered.glencoe.com

CHAPTER TEST

Write the letter of the answer that best completes each sentence.

1. White lines parallel to the road separate
   a. traffic moving in the same direction.
   b. traffic moving in opposite directions.
   c. vans from trucks.

2. When a police officer is giving hand signals at an intersection, you should
   a. always follow the officer's directions.
   b. follow the traffic signals.
   c. proceed with caution.

3. A yield sign indicates that a driver
   a. has the right of way.
   b. may need to stop and wait until the roadway is clear of traffic before proceeding.
   c. must move to a different lane.

4. When you approach a stop sign and observe no other vehicles around, you should
   a. slow down but continue moving past the sign.
   b. come to a full stop at the sign.
   c. blow your horn and increase your speed.

5. Two solid yellow lines on a roadway indicate that
   a. passing is permitted in either direction.
   b. the left lane may be used only for left turns.
   c. no passing is permitted in either direction.

6. When approaching a flashing red traffic signal, you should
   a. slow down and proceed with caution.
   b. respond as if it were a stop sign.
   c. immediately turn right.

7. A steady yellow X posted above a highway lane indicates that
   a. vehicles should move slowly.
   b. vehicles should move to a different lane.
   c. the lane will become an exit ramp.

8. Blue signs with white lettering indicate
   a. roadside services.
   b. roadway conditions.
   c. construction areas.

9. Shared left-turn lanes are marked by
   a. solid yellow lines.
   b. white arrows that point in the same direction.
   c. parallel broken yellow lines with white arrows that point left and right.

10. A red arrow indicates
    a. a detour.
    b. a one-way street.
    c. traffic is not allowed in the direction of the arrow.

Write the word or phrase that best completes each sentence.

advance warning	regulatory
pavement markings	breakdown lanes
high-occupancy vehicle	

11. You may be permitted to drive in _____ lanes if your vehicle has two or more occupants.

12. A(n) _____ sign indicates what a driver must or must not do.

13. Traffic signals, signs, and _____ provide drivers with information.

14. A railroad _____ sign is round and yellow with black markings.

DRIVER'S LOG

In this chapter you have learned about the signs, signals, and pavement markings that communicate information to drivers. Take 5 minutes to list all that you can remember and explain what they mean. Which ones did you leave out? Write about how you will remember them in the future.

CHAPTER TEST

Assign the Chapter Test to all students.

Answers

1. a
2. a
3. b
4. b
5. c
6. b
7. b
8. a
9. c
10. c
11. high-occupancy vehicle
12. regulatory
13. pavement markings
14. advance warning

DRIVER'S LOG

Students' responses will reflect their personal viewpoint. However, their answers should provide an assessment of their understanding of the meaning and importance of signs, signals, and markings.

Evaluate

- Test A, pp. 9–10 or Test B, pp. 9–10 📁
- Testmaker software

RETURN TO THE BIG IDEA ——

Discuss how drivers can manage risk on the roadway by tuning in to information communicated through signs, signals, and roadway markings.

Rules of the Road Overview

THEME DEVELOPMENT Responsible drivers know and observe the rules of the road, including administrative laws, right-of-way rules, speed limits, and legal obligations.

CHAPTER FEATURES	TCR COMPONENTS
	Study Guide, p. 21
	Lesson Plan, p. 13
	Information Master 1
	Study Guide, p. 22
	Transparencies 8–13
	Lesson Plan, p. 13

 FOR NEW DRIVERS

Procedures to follow if you are stopped by the police.

Study Guide, p. 23
Lesson Plan, p. 14
Information Master 17

 **CONNECTIONS** Social Studies

Converting miles to kilometers.

ADVICE FROM THE EXPERTS

Recognizing the leading causes of collisions.

Study Guide, p. 24
Lesson Plan, p. 14

BUILDING SKILLS: READING MAPS

Using Coordinates

Test A, pp. 11–12
Test B, pp. 11–12

PROJECTS

1. Compare driver's manuals from various states.
2. Investigate drivers' attitudes and knowledge about speeding and speed laws.

OTHER PROGRAM RESOURCES

Testmaker software
Traffic charts

ADDITIONAL RESOURCES

First on the Scene, Video 428, AAA Foundation
On the Scene: A Guide to Bystander Care at Roadside Emergency, Video 458, AAA Foundation
Digest of Motor Laws, AAA Foundation

CHAPTER 6
CHAPTER TEST

NAME _____ DATE _____

CHAPTER 6 Rules of the Road

TEST A

In each space below, write the word or words that best complete the sentence.

1. You give right-of-way to a person walking with a guide dog or who is using a **white cane** _____ no matter where the person is crossing the street.

2. Your vehicle registration usually must be renewed every _____ **year** _____.

3. The right-of-way laws that all states use are based on the _____ **Uniform Vehicle** _____ Code.

4. When an emergency vehicle is coming toward you with a siren on and its lights flashing, you should move your vehicle to the _____ **right** _____ side of the road.

5. At an intersection not controlled by a traffic sign or signal, a driver should yield to those on the _____ **right** _____.

6. Speed limits are determined after careful study by _____ **traffic** _____ engineers.

Select the phrase that best completes each sentence below. Write the letter of the answer you have chosen to the left of each statement.

a 7. The individual state's administrative laws set statewide standards for
   a. financial responsibilities.
   b. interstate highway maintenance.
   c. right-of-way.
   d. both b and c.

d 8. Before granting a driver's license, most states test for
   a. minimum visual requirements.
   b. knowledge of traffic laws.
   c. driving ability.
   d. all of the above.

c 9. A state has the power to
   a. issue you a driver's license.
   b. suspend your driver's license.
   c. do both a and b.
   d. do none of the above.

b 10. Most states use _____ to determine whether or not to suspend a driver's license.
   a. police discretion
   b. a point system
   c. a judge's discretion
   d. none of the above

© AAA and Glencoe/McGraw-Hill   ◆ 11

NAME _____ DATE _____

a 11. A certificate of title proves
   a. who owns a car.
   b. you have insurance.
   c. the car is registered in the state.
   d. your license plate is not stolen.

a 12. When turning left at an intersection, yield
   a. to all oncoming vehicles until you have the time and space to turn.
   b. only to traffic on the right.
   c. only to traffic on the left.
   d. only to emergency vehicles.

d 13. Before a speed limit is determined for a particular road, a study must be made of
   a. road surface.
   b. average amount of traffic.
   c. any hidden dangers.
   d. all of the above.

d 14. Maximum and minimum speed limits tell you
   a. how fast you must drive.
   b. the speed that cannot be exceeded.
   c. the minimum speed that you must go.
   d. both b and c.

a 15. At night, some states
   a. have lower speed limits.
   b. have higher speed limits.
   c. eliminate speed limits on rural roads.
   d. do both b and c.

Read each statement below. If it is true, place a T in the space to the left of the statement. If the statement is false, place an F next to it.

T 16. Anyone selling a vehicle must provide a certificate of title.

F 17. The certificate of title must always be carried in the car.

T 18. You must yield to traffic on through streets if you are at a stop sign.

F 19. The speed limit tells you the fastest speed that you may drive, but you can always go as slow as you want.

T 20. It is always illegal to drive faster than the posted speed limit.

21. An automobile collision has just occurred. You were not injured. What do you do?
   If you are involved in a collision, stop immediately. Warn others if possible. Give aid to the injured. Try to get medical help. Call the police. Exchange information. Stay at the scene. Make accident reports. Get names and addresses of witnesses.

12 ◆   © AAA and Glencoe/McGraw-Hill

NAME _____ DATE _____

CHAPTER 6 Rules of the Road

TEST B

In each space below, write the word or words that best complete the sentence.

1. At the scene of a collision, if you have them, you should set up reflective triangles or flares _____ **100** _____ feet ahead of and behind the collision.

2. If you are involved in a collision with a parked car, you should try to locate the _____ **car's owner** _____.

3. The document that proves who owns a vehicle is called a _____ **title** _____.

4. At a four-way stop, all traffic must yield to the vehicle that arrived _____ **first** _____.

5. In case you are involved in a collision, you should never admit _____ **fault** _____.

6. Wherever crossing the street, a blind person using a white cane or with a _____ **guide dog** _____ always gets the right-of-way.

Select the phrase that best completes each sentence below. Write the letter of the answer you have chosen to the left of each statement.

d 7. When driving, you must yield to
   a. any ambulance.
   b. any police vehicle.
   c. both a and b.
   d. any emergency vehicle with its siren on and emergency lights flashing.

d 8. You should drive slower than the posted speed limit
   a. in congested traffic.
   b. in bad weather conditions.
   c. when visibility is poor.
   d. in all of the above conditions.

c 9. It is legal to exceed the speed limit
   a. in an emergency.
   b. to pass a vehicle.
   c. on no occasion.
   d. when the speed limit is not posted.

a 10. If you are involved in a collision and nobody appears to be hurt, you should
   a. stop immediately and pull your vehicle off the roadway.
   b. accuse the other driver of causing the collision.
   c. keep on driving to the nearest phone and alert the police.
   d. do none of the above.

© AAA and Glencoe/McGraw-Hill   ◆ 11

NAME _____ DATE _____

d 11. To warn other drivers of a collision, you can
   a. turn on your four-way flashers.
   b. set flares or reflective triangles in front of and behind the collision scene.
   c. wave a flashlight or a light-colored cloth at oncoming traffic.
   d. do all of the above.

b 12. Fatality rates are highest for occupants of
   a. large cars.
   b. small pickup trucks.
   c. tractor-trailers.
   d. station wagons.

b 13. After being treated for minor injuries at a collision scene and being released by the police, you should
   a. continue to your destination.
   b. see a doctor.
   c. see your lawyer.
   d. file an accident report.

d 14. A certificate of title lists
   a. name of the owner.
   b. make of the vehicle.
   c. vehicle identification number (VIN).
   d. all of the above.

a 15. Your vehicle registration usually must
   a. be renewed yearly.
   b. be kept safely at home.
   c. show proof of insurance.
   d. show your driver's license number.

Read each statement below. If it is true, place a T in the space to the left of the statement. If the statement is false, place an F next to it.

T 16. Laws concerning learner's permits are set by the individual state.

T 17. On a two-lane, nondivided highway, a driver must always stop when meeting or overtaking a school bus that is either loading or unloading students.

F 18. One of the first things to do after a collision is to move the injured.

T 19. No matter what the posted speed limit is, you must always drive at a speed that is proper for existing conditions.

F 20. After being involved in a collision, you do not need to file an accident report if you have talked with police at the collision scene.

T 21. If you pass a collision scene that appears to be under control, you should keep on driving.

22. How should you act and what should you do if you are pulled over by the police?
   Stay calm, and remain in your vehicle, keeping both hands visible. Produce any requested documents quickly. Be courteous. Do not lie, cry, or make excuses. Never try to bribe a police officer.

12 ◆   © AAA and Glencoe/McGraw-Hill

96C   CHAPTER 6

NAME _____ DATE _____

CHAPTER 6 | Rules of the Road

STUDY GUIDE FOR CHAPTER 6   LESSON 1

Each State Has Administrative Laws

A. For each sentence below, circle T if the statement is true and F if it is false. If a statement is false, correct it in the space provided below.

1. Administrative laws apply only to traffic violations.   T   (F)

The laws apply to issuing driver's licenses and permits, registering vehicles, financial responsibilities, and safety equipment and care of vehicles.

2. A point system enables the state to keep track of a driver's violations.   (T)   F

3. A certificate of title is the same as a certificate of registration.   T   (F)
A certificate of title is different from a registration and proves who owns a vehicle.

4. Driving tests are designed and administered by the federal government.   T   (F)

Driving tests are designed and administered by each individual state.

5. You receive your license plates when you receive your certificate of title.   T   (F)

You receive license plates when you register your vehicle.

6. For your driver's license, you will be tested on traffic laws and knowledge of signs, car repair, and signals.   T   (F)

You will be tested on traffic laws, signals, safe driving, and visual acuity.

7. A driver's license that is suspended is usually taken away for a period of 10 to 15 days.   T   (F)

A driver's license is usually suspended for a period of 30 to 90 days.

B. FIND OUT MORE. Look in your state driver's manual and see whether your state uses a point system. If so, how many points does it take to lose your license? How many points are given for speeding at 15 miles per hour over the speed limit? If your state does not use a point system, what does the driver's manual say about guidelines the state uses to take away a driver's license?

Review student's work.

_____

_____

_____

_____

_____

_____

© AAA and Glencoe/McGraw-Hill   RESPONSIBLE DRIVING STUDY GUIDE CHAPTER 6 ◆ **21**

NAME _____ DATE _____

STUDY GUIDE FOR CHAPTER 6   LESSON 2

Right-of-Way Rules Are Essential

A. You are driving vehicle X. Who must yield right-of-way?   a, b, and X yield to the ambulance.

Why?   An emergency vehicle with lights flashing has priority.

B. You are driving vehicle X. Which vehicles may go through the intersection first?   Vehicles a, b, and c

Last?   Vehicle X.

Why?   Vehicle X has a stop sign in front of it and must wait for traffic to clear.

C. FIND OUT MORE. Go to a four-way stop in your area and bring a pencil and pad of paper. Count the total number of vehicles that pass through the intersection in 30 minutes. How many drivers proceeded through the four-way stop correctly? What percentage went through incorrectly?

Review student's answers.

22 ◆ RESPONSIBLE DRIVING STUDY GUIDE CHAPTER 6   © AAA and Glencoe/McGraw-Hill

---

NAME _____ DATE _____

STUDY GUIDE FOR CHAPTER 6   LESSON 3

Speed Limits Help in Reducing Risk

A. Explain the basic speed law, and give an example of how it works.

The basic speed law states that you should always drive at a speed that is reasonable and

proper for existing conditions. For example, a maximum posted speed limit may be 55 mph on a

highway. In a snowstorm, however, you could be ticketed for driving that fast because 55 mph

is too fast for the weather condition.

_____

_____

_____

_____

B. FIND OUT MORE. Using your state driver's manual, answer the following questions.

1. What is the maximum speed limit on the interstates in your state?
Review student's answer.

2. Does your state have a night speed limit on your interstate highways that is different from the day speed limit?
Review student's answer.

3. Does your state have a different speed limit for trucks than for other vehicles?
Review student's answer.

4. What, if any, is the minimum speed limit on your interstate highways?
Review student's answer.

5. What is the speed limit on state roads where the speed is not posted?
Review student's answer.

6. What is the speed limit for school zones in your state?
Review student's answer.

7. What is the speed limit in business or recreation areas in your state?
Review student's answer.

© AAA and Glencoe/McGraw-Hill   RESPONSIBLE DRIVING STUDY GUIDE CHAPTER 6 ◆ **23**

NAME _____ DATE _____

STUDY GUIDE FOR CHAPTER 6   LESSON 4

If You Are Involved in a Collision

A. You are driving at 55 mph in the right-hand lane of the freeway. Traffic ahead of you slows down to a near stop; since you see some highway construction warning signs, you figure that this is the reason for the slowdown. The vehicle directly behind you does not notice you slowing down and hits you from behind. You, in turn, hit the vehicle ahead of you. You are feeling fine, but your passenger says that her neck and back are hurting from the collision. The driver of the vehicle that hit you comes to your vehicle and acts very mad at you, saying that the accident was your fault because your brake lights were not working. What actions will you take at the accident scene, and in what order? What will you say to the driver of the vehicle that hit you?

Warn others, help your passenger and any other injured people, get medical help, call the police,

exchange information, stay at the scene, make accident reports, get names and addresses of

witnesses, and get your passenger to a doctor. You should remain calm when talking with the

driver of the vehicle that hit you from behind, and you should not admit guilt.

B. For each sentence below, circle T if the statement is true and F if it is false. Correct each false statement in the space below.

1. When a driver is involved in a collision, the driver should never move the vehicle until the police arrive.   T   (F)

If possible, a driver should move the vehicle off the roadway and out of traffic.

2. After a collision, reflective triangles should be set up no more than 50 feet in front of and behind a vehicle.   T   (F)
Reflective triangles should be set up at least 100 feet in front of and behind the vehicle.

3. If you are involved in a collision that results in serious injury or death, you must not leave the accident scene until the police allow you to go.   (T)   F

4. People involved in a collision should be moved immediately out of their vehicles to a safe spot on the side of the road.   T   (F)

If the people involved in the collision were injured, they should not be moved.

C. FIND OUT MORE. Look at your state driver's manual. Under what conditions must you file an accident report?
Review student's work.

24 ◆ RESPONSIBLE DRIVING STUDY GUIDE CHAPTER 6   © AAA and Glencoe/McGraw-Hill

Rules of the Road

CHAPTER OVERVIEW

LESSON ONE
Various state administrative laws are described, including those governing driver's licenses, vehicle ownership and registration, and insurance.

LESSON TWO
Right-of-way rules and procedures are described.

LESSON THREE
Speed limits are defined and explained along with the conditions under which they do and do not apply.

LESSON FOUR
Drivers' obligations in the event of a collision are described.

VOCABULARY

administrative laws
advisory speed limit
fixed speed limit
point system
revoke
right-of-way
suspend

96

CONCEPT OF THE DRIVING TASK

Explain that for the highway transportation system to work safely and efficiently, drivers must comply with the rules and regulations that govern all major aspects of driving and road use. Driver responsibility includes knowing not only what the rules and regulations are but also why they are needed.

CHAPTER 6
Rules of the Road

Drivers belong to the society of roadway users. In a smoothly running society, members agree to follow the rules. It is important that you learn the rules of the road in order to be a responsible member of the roadway community.

LESSON ONE
Each State Has Administrative Laws

LESSON TWO
Right-of-Way Rules Are Essential

LESSON THREE
Speed Limits Help in Reducing Risk

LESSON FOUR
If You Are Involved in a Collision

PRESENTING THE BIG IDEA ——

The efficiency and safety of any system depend on the degree to which all participants obey the rules of that system.

What's on the Road Ahead?

Have students read the lesson titles and objectives. Briefly discuss the topic of each lesson. Tell students that in this chapter, they will become familiar with important rules and regulations regarding use of the roadway.

Background: The Larger Picture

The following statistics will give students an idea of why rules and regulations are needed on America's roadways.

- A motor-vehicle-related fatality occurs in the United States about every 13 minutes.
- A motor-vehicle-related injury occurs in the United States about every 10 seconds.
- Collisions cost more than $170 billion annually.

Relating to Prior Knowledge

Have students discuss what they know about their state's rules and regulations concerning obtaining a driver's license, buying and selling a vehicle, and registering a vehicle.

The Big Idea

Discuss students' reactions to the Big Idea statement. Suggest that they keep this in mind as they read Chapter 6.

Each State Has Administrative Laws

(pages 98–99)

FOCUS

Objectives

• Identify the procedures that are regulated by administrative laws.

• Describe how to comply with administrative laws.

Resources

 Study Guide, page 21

 Information Master 1

Vocabulary

administrative laws
suspend
revoke
point system

Motivator

Pose the following: Imagine that you are ready to obtain your driver's license. What requirements might you expect to have to meet to get your license? (Students may mention taking a written or computerized test; taking a road test.)

TEACH

Explain

OBJECTIVE 1: Students will profit from a discussion of the implied purpose of administrative laws—to regulate and ensure smooth operation of the highway transportation system.

OBJECTIVE 2: Students should recognize the range of procedures that administrative laws cover.

OBJECTIVES

1. Identify the procedures that are regulated by administrative laws.
2. Describe how to comply with administrative laws.

KEY TERMS

administrative laws
suspend
revoke
point system

Each State Has Administrative Laws

Rules and laws are vital to society. Traffic laws and ordinances are important for a variety of reasons.

They provide rules for the behavior of drivers and help drivers predict what others on the road will do. They serve as a guide to police and courts, promote the orderly flow of traffic, and help prevent collisions.

What Are Administrative Laws?

Each state has laws that enable state officials to control the operation of the state's highway transportation system. Among the laws are **administrative laws,** which establish the procedures for issuing driver's licenses and learner's permits and registering motor vehicles. Other procedures cover the financial responsibilities of vehicle drivers and owners and the minimum safety equipment and care of a vehicle.

How Do You Comply with Administrative Laws?

To drive and own a vehicle, you must obey your state's motor vehicle laws—beginning with obtaining a license to drive.

Getting a Driver's License

Granting a license to operate a motor vehicle is a function of state government. To obtain a license, you must pass a series of tests. Each state tests vision; knowledge of signs, signals, and markings; traffic laws; and safe driving practices. Tests may be verbal, written, or computerized.

In most states, the last test is a road or in-vehicle test. This test demonstrates your basic vehicle control skills. If you pass these tests and pay the necessary fees, you will receive your license. If your state has a graduated driver licensing system, you may need to take more than one driving test.

States also have the power to take licenses away. States can **suspend,** or take away, licenses for a specified period of time—usually for 30 to 90 days, but fewer than 365 days. States can also **revoke** licenses. This means states can take licenses away for a year or more, after which the person whose license has been revoked can apply for another license.

Energy Tips

Excessive speed causes crashes and can cost you points. Excessive speed also wastes fuel. Be responsible!

State BY State

Some states, such as Florida and Kentucky, require young people between the ages of 15 and 18 who apply for a driver's license to provide proof of enrollment in high school or proof of graduation. In these states, students who drop out of high school before graduating cannot obtain a license or will lose their license if they already have one.

Violations and the Point System

How does a state decide when to take away a person's driver's license? Most states use a **point system.** Various traffic violations "cost" a number of points, depending on their seriousness. When a driver is ticketed for violating a traffic law and is convicted, a report is sent to the state's department of motor vehicles. The points are then put on the driver's record.

If a driver whose license has been suspended continues to get points when the suspension is lifted, the license can be revoked. Some violations are so serious that offenders can lose their licenses immediately upon conviction. These violations include driving under the influence of alcohol or other drugs, leaving the scene of a collision in which there has been an injury, and using a motor vehicle in the commission of a crime.

Certificate of Title

States issue a certificate of title when you buy a motor vehicle. This proves that you own the vehicle. The state keeps a copy of this title. Anyone selling a motor vehicle must supply a certificate of title to the buyer. The certificate lists the name of the owner and the make, style, vehicle identification number (VIN), and engine number of the vehicle.

Vehicle Registration

When purchasing a vehicle, you must register it with the state. You'll receive a registration form and license plate(s). If liability insurance is required, you must provide the name of your insurance company. Registration must be renewed every year or two. Keep your registration in the vehicle.

Insurance

Part of driving is the ability to prove financial responsibility. You must show that you can pay for damages you may cause if you are in a crash that results in death, injury, or property damage to others. You will learn more about automobile insurance in Chapter 16.

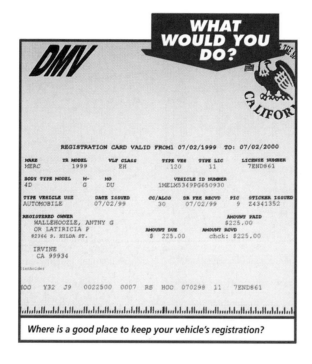

WHAT WOULD YOU DO?

REGISTRATION CARD VALID FROM1 07/02/1999 TO: 07/02/2000

Where is a good place to keep your vehicle's registration?

Lesson *1* Review

1. What administrative laws does every state have?
2. What do administrative laws require you to do?

Sample answer: Keep the vehicle's registration inside the vehicle.

Lesson *1* Review

Answers

1. Laws establishing procedures for issuing driver's licenses, registering vehicles, financial responsibilities of drivers and owners, and minimum safety equipment and care of a vehicle.
2. To obtain a driver's license, certificate of title, registration and insurance; to maintain an acceptable driving record.

Teaching Model

Tell students the following: You are buying a used vehicle from someone who advertised in the newspaper. Model your thinking as you prepare questions to ask the seller. (Sample answer: Do you have the certificate of title? Is the vehicle registration current?)

Ask

What would you do if the seller did not have the certificate of title?

Read

Have students read Lesson 1 to learn about administrative procedures and laws.

ASSESS

Guided Practice

Have students answer the Lesson 1 Review questions. The answers are provided below.

Reteaching

Have small groups review the administrative laws. Each group member should be responsible for leading a discussion of one law and the reasons behind it.

Enrichment

Assign the Study Guide for Lesson 1. The Find Out More section encourages students to expand their basic learning of the lesson concepts.

CLOSE

Summarize

Return to the Motivator question, and discuss students' initial answers in light of what they have learned. Discuss what would happen if there were no laws or traffic regulations.

DRIVER'S LOG

What administrative laws apply to drivers? What administrative laws apply to vehicle owners?

Right-of-Way Rules Are Essential

(pages 100–102)

FOCUS

Objectives

• Define the meaning of the term *right-of-way*.

• Identify when you should yield the right-of-way.

> ### Resources
>
> Study Guide, page 22
>
> Traffic charts
>
> Transparencies 8–13

Vocabulary

right-of-way

Motivator

Ask students what they think is one of the most common violations of traffic laws in fatal collisions. (Accept student answers without comment; a driver's failure to yield the right-of-way.)

TEACH

Explain

OBJECTIVE 1: Students should have little difficulty understanding that right-of-way rules are designed to set standards by which drivers can determine which driver should wait. However, it is crucial that students recognize that relying only on the rules can lead to potential risk. Drivers must remember that not all motorists obey the rules, and they must be prepared for such an eventuality.

LESSON TWO

OBJECTIVES

1. Define the meaning of the term *right-of-way*.
2. Identify when you should yield the right-of-way.

KEY TERM

right-of-way

Right-of-Way Rules Are Essential

When you drive, sometimes one or more drivers or pedestrians will want to use the same roadway space at the same time that you do. How can you avoid a collision? You can determine who should go first and who should wait. To do so, you need to know the rules about right-of-way.

What Is Right-of-Way?

As a good driver, you will sometimes have to yield the **right-of-way,** or let others go first. Never assume that you have the right-of-way. Right-of-way is *always given* by someone. Right-of-way laws are very clear in identifying who shall yield to whom in almost every situation. However, human beings make mistakes. The rule that you must yield the right-of-way in order to avoid a collision overrides all the other rules.

Right-of-way laws of all states are based on the Uniform Vehicle Code. Therefore, the laws about when drivers should yield the right-of-way are the same from state to state.

When Should You Yield the Right-of-Way?

Here are three situations in which you must yield the right-of-way.

• You must yield to any emergency vehicle, such as an ambulance, that has its sirens on and its lights flashing. Move to the far right of the road and stop if you are on a two-way, two-lane roadway or on a multiple-lane highway going in the same direction as the emergency vehicle. If you are going in the opposite direction on a multiple-lane road, you do not have to stop, but you should move to the right.

• You must yield to people who are blind and are carrying a white cane or using a guide dog, no matter where they cross.

• You must yield to any pedestrians at crosswalks.

On the following pages, you will find some of the right-of-way situations that occur most often. In each picture, the red car is required to yield. In all these situations, drivers must yield to pedestrians who are crossing at crosswalks.

At STOP signs, yield to traffic on the through street.

THE INTERNATIONAL SCENE

Great Britain

In Great Britain, 31 percent of all roadway deaths are pedestrian deaths resulting from pedestrian-vehicle collisions. This rate is more than twice that of the United States and France. In these two countries, 14 percent of roadway deaths are pedestrian deaths. Fatalities often result from pedestrian error or from drivers not yielding the right-of-way to pedestrians.

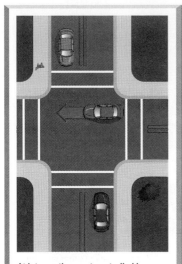
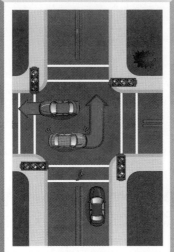

At intersections not controlled by traffic signs or signals, yield to vehicles already in the intersection. Drivers on the left must yield to those on their right.

At traffic lights, yield to vehicles still in the intersection when the light changes.

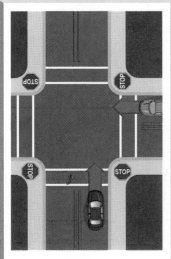
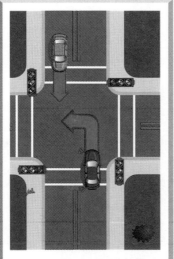

At four-way stops, yield to vehicles that arrive first. If you arrive at the same time, yield to a vehicle from the right.

When you are turning left at an intersection, yield to all oncoming vehicles until you have the time and space to make a turn.

FYI

A majority of drivers fail to stop at stop signs. It is important to keep this in mind when you try to anticipate the actions of other drivers.

MEETING STUDENT DIVERSITY

Limited English Proficiency

Students with limited English proficiency may have difficulty understanding terms such as *yield* and *right-of-way*. Clarify by adding, "or allow the other vehicle to go ahead first" each time you use these terms.

OBJECTIVE 2: Students will benefit from recognizing that if there is any doubt about who has the right-of-way, yielding and letting the other driver know that you intend to yield is always safest.

Teaching Model

Display this situation:

Tell students the following: You are in vehicle 1, traveling east. You notice that vehicle 2 is stalled and blocking the lane, so you have to pass around it, which means crossing over the broken line. At the same time, you see vehicle 3 coming in the opposite lane. Model your thinking process in this situation. (You do the following.

- Slow down and yield the right-of way to vehicle 3.
- Signal after vehicle 3 has passed, and pass vehicle 2 if no other oncoming vehicles are near.)

Ask

What actions should the driver of vehicle 2 have taken to reduce risk to his or her vehicle and other vehicles?

Read

Have students read Lesson 2 to learn about right-of-way rules.

ASSESS

Guided Practice

Have students answer the Lesson 2 Review questions. The answers are provided below.

Reteaching

Have students work in small groups, using model vehicles or cutouts to practice basic right-of-way procedures in various situations. Have students describe what they see in each situation and how they intend to proceed.

Enrichment

Assign the Study Guide for Lesson 2. The Find Out More section encourages students to expand their basic learning of the lesson concepts.

CLOSE

Summarize

Return to the Motivator question. Discuss how knowing that failure to obey right-of-way rules is one of the common causes of fatal collisions will help students manage risk. Help students summarize right-of-way rules by going through situations described in the lesson and having students explain who is required to yield.

DRIVER'S LOG

What should you expect of other drivers in a situation where you legally have the right-of-way?

WHAT WOULD YOU DO?

Sample answer: to vehicles already in the intersection, vehicles coming from the right cross street, and pedestrians; right-of-way rules.

SAFETY TIPS

When you are on a side street approaching a well-traveled road, stop at the intersection even if a stop sign is not present. Proceed when you are sure you have enough time and space to do so.

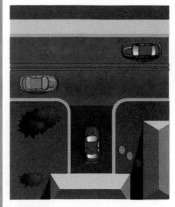

Coming out of a driveway or alley, yield to all vehicles in the roadway.

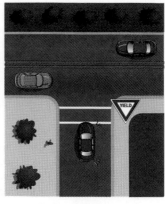

At all YIELD signs, yield to all vehicles on the cross street.

One of the most common violations in fatal collisions involving more than one car is a driver's failure to yield the right-of-way. Remember, just because you are on a major street or are on the right at a four-way stop, do not assume that others will yield to you. Be alert! Sometimes it is safer to yield even if the other driver is required by law to yield. To manage risk, you should remember that others will not always obey traffic signs and signals. Make yourself visible, and identify an escape route in case something goes wrong.

When signaling a move left or right into a lane being used by other drivers, you must yield to any vehicle that is passing or appears to be so close that it presents a danger.

On a nondivided highway, all drivers must stop when meeting or overtaking a school bus that is loading or unloading children. Laws vary from state to state, so it is important to know the school bus laws for states in which you will be traveling.

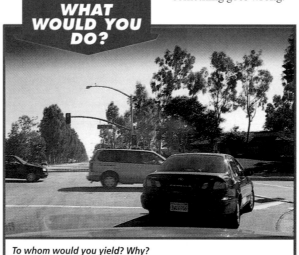

WHAT WOULD YOU DO?

To whom would you yield? Why?

Lesson 2 Review

1. What does right-of-way mean?
2. In which situations should you yield the right-of-way?

Lesson 2 Review

Answers

1. One driver is required to yield to another or to a pedestrian.
2. Yield to emergency vehicles, people who are blind, and vehicles in an intersection; yield at stop signs, four-way stops, and yield signs; yield when moving into another lane or when leaving an alley or driveway; yield to a stopped school bus with signals flashing.

Speed Limits Help in Reducing Risk

The most important requirements for safe driving are visibility, time, and space. Together they determine the speed at which you can travel safely. What is a safe speed? Posted maximum speed limits give guidelines to answer this question, but they only apply under ideal conditions.

Speed limits are chosen to protect you and other drivers. Traffic engineers study road conditions and evaluate the road surface, the average amount of traffic, and any hidden dangers. They also know how many collisions have happened at any given location. A speed limit is decided upon only after all these factors have been taken into consideration. Further studies may also be conducted to see if limits should be lowered as congestion increases.

What Kinds of Speed Limits Are There?

All states post speed limits on their roadways. These speed limit signs reflect the *maximum* speed at which you can drive under the best of conditions. For example, you would not drive at the maximum allowable

CONNECTIONS
Social Studies
CULTURAL CROSSROADS

If you drive in Mexico or Canada, you will see signs in Spanish or French. In both countries, another "language" is used on signs as well. It is the "language" of the metric system of measurement.

Distances on destination signs in Mexico and Canada are given in kilometers rather than in miles. Similarly, speed limit signs refer not to *miles per hour* but to *kilometers per hour*. The speed limit sign you see here means 100 kilometers per hour (km/h), or about 65 miles per hour. You can figure out whether you are traveling

within the allowable speed limit by converting kilometers per hour to miles per hour. To make a rough estimate, take half of the posted speed limit and add a little more. Half of 100 is 50, and a little more is 60 or 65. For a closer estimate, take ⅗ of the posted speed limit. Then check your speedometer to see whether you are traveling between 60 and 65 miles per hour.

When you are driving in another country, make sure you know whether or not that country uses the metric system of measurement. To help you out, the speedometers in many vehicle models record speeds both in miles per hour and in kilometers per hour.

LESSON THREE

OBJECTIVES
1. Define the meaning of the following kinds of speed limits: fixed, advisory, and day and night.
2. Explain under what conditions posted speed limits do not apply.

KEY TERMS
fixed speed limit
advisory speed limit

LESSON THREE

Speed Limits Help in Reducing Risk
(pages 103–105)

FOCUS

Objectives
- Define the meaning of the following kinds of speed limits: fixed, advisory, and day and night.
- Explain under what conditions posted speed limits do not apply.

Resources
- Study Guide, page 23
- Traffic charts
- Information Master 17

Vocabulary
fixed speed limit
advisory speed limit

Motivator
Pose the following situation: You are driving on a road where the regulatory signs indicate that drivers may not legally go faster than 55 mph or slower than 25 mph. As night falls, a heavy snowfall begins, and you can barely see ahead of you. Will you be breaking the law by driving slower than 25 mph? Explain your reasoning. (Students may respond that this is a situation in which the speed limit does not apply because even the minimum speed is unsafe under these conditions.)

Driving Tip

Explain to students that they should keep to the right when driving on a multiple-lane highway to allow faster-moving vehicles to pass on the left.

TIPS FOR NEW DRIVERS

To check students' understanding, have them discuss why they think each of the tips is important.

TEACH

Explain

OBJECTIVE 1: Students should recognize that speed laws are set for reasons—to control the flow of traffic and to minimize risk to all roadway users. Most students will understand reasons for not exceeding maximum speed limits. However, they will benefit from a discussion of the hazards of driving below the minimum speed limit.

OBJECTIVE 2: Students should understand that speed limit signs do not mean that drivers have to travel at the speeds posted. Although drivers must never exceed the maximum limit, at certain times the lower limits do not apply, such as during bad weather or hazardous road conditions.

Teaching Model

Describe this situation: You are driving on a highway where the maximum speed limit is 55 mph. You see warning signs indicating a curve ahead and a square yellow sign indicating a maximum speed limit of 35 mph. Model your thinking process as you proceed in this situation. (You do the following.

- Slow down to the 35 mph limit.
- Pay attention to how well you can control your vehicle on the curve at this speed.
- Reduce your speed even more if your control of visibility, time, and space requires it.)

Ask

Why is it a good idea to drive below the speed limit on curves, especially if weather or road conditions are bad?

Read

Have students read Lesson 3 to learn about posted speed limits and conditions under which a minimum posted speed limit does not apply.

◆ *Note the advisory speed limit sign. You should not exceed 15 mph on this curve.*

speed in the middle of a snowstorm, but you might do so on a clear day.

Posted speed limits do not tell you at what speed to drive. They only say you cannot safely go faster or, in special cases, more slowly than the speed shown. All states also have basic speed limits that mean you cannot drive at speeds slower or faster than conditions safely permit. What does this mean to you as a driver?

Fixed Speed Limit

A **fixed speed limit** is the maximum and minimum speed that a vehicle may be driven on a particular roadway. Drivers may never legally travel at a speed faster than the maximum posted speed. Drivers whose speed is greater than the posted maximum speed can be arrested and, if convicted, made to pay a fine.

Drivers can also be arrested and ticketed for driving too slowly. A vehicle traveling below the minimum posted speed limit can be dangerous to other drivers who must suddenly slow down when they approach this vehicle. Slow drivers can also make other drivers nervous or angry and in addition cause traffic tie-ups and congestion.

Advisory Speed Limit

All roads are not straight and flat. There are hills, curves, and other changes in the roadway. Drivers need to adjust their speed for these changes. An **advisory speed limit** interrupts normal driving speed for a limited time. It provides guidelines for adjusting speed.

For example, a warning sign is usually posted before a sharp curve and before an exit ramp. If the curve is very sharp, a square yellow advisory speed sign may be posted beneath the warning sign to advise you of the maximum safe speed for that curve. In addition, chevron-shaped markings may be used to emphasize the risk. Like all speed limits, advisory limits are based on ideal road conditions.

Day and Night Speed Limits

Some states have lower speed limits at night. Night driving is much more

---

TIPS **FOR NEW DRIVERS**

Being Pulled Over

What should you do if you are pulled over by the police?

- Stay calm.
- Remain in your vehicle, keeping your hands visible.
- Produce requested documents quickly and efficiently.
- Be courteous. Do not argue with, insult, or touch the officer.
- Do not lie, cry, or make excuses.
- *Never* try to bribe the officer. Bribery is illegal!

IT'S A FACT

Crashes on curves account for 45 percent of all deaths in roadside hazard crashes. Another 35 percent of the deaths involve crashes on hills.

CONNECTIONS
Social Studies

Check students' understanding by having them estimate and convert other speeds.

dangerous because it is hard to see in the dark. Driving at a lower speed gives drivers more time to search for visual clues and to identify objects or conditions that could increase risk.

What Are Basic Speed Laws?

No matter what speed limit is posted, all states have a basic speed rule in their traffic laws that says: Always drive at a speed that is reasonable and proper for existing conditions.

A safe speed at any particular time is determined by the type and condition of the road and by such factors as the traffic, weather, and light. Your ability to manage visibility, time, and space also determines what is a safe speed at any given time.

By law, drivers must go more slowly than the minimum posted speed if poor road or traffic conditions make that speed unsafe. In such cases, the arresting officer must show that the driver was going too fast for the weather, road, or traffic conditions at that time.

Driving faster than the posted speed limit is never safe or reasonable and is always illegal.

Take note of these facts about speed. The higher the speed:
- the less time the driver has to spot dangerous situations and take action.
- the greater the time and distance it takes to stop a vehicle.
- the greater the chance the vehicle will skid or roll over on a turn.
- the greater the force of impact will be in a collision.
- the greater the personal injuries and property damage will be in a collision.

Drivers can also be arrested for driving too slowly. In these cases, the officer must show that the speed was so slow that it caused danger to other drivers going at a reasonable speed.

Lesson 3 Review

1. What are the different kinds of speed limits?
2. What are the basic speed laws?

◆ A few interstate roads have speed limits as high as 75 mph. This speed may not be reasonable or proper in bad weather.

WHAT WOULD YOU DO?

Snow is on the ground and you see this sign. At what speed would you drive? Why?

CHAPTER 6   Rules of the Road   **105**

Lesson 3 Review

Answers

1. Fixed, advisory, day, and night.
2. Laws that state that one should always drive at a speed that is reasonable and proper for existing conditions.

ASSESS

Guided Practice

Have students answer the Lesson 3 Review questions. The answers are provided below.

Reteaching

Have students work in groups to brainstorm situations in which posted speed limits would not apply. Suggest that groups compare their ideas and prepare a list of guidelines that all groups agree upon.

Enrichment

Assign the Study Guide for Lesson 3. The Find Out More section encourages students to expand their basic learning of the lesson concepts.

CLOSE

Summarize

Return to the Motivator question, and discuss the situation again in light of what students have learned in this lesson. Have them discuss why the minimum speed limit does not apply in this case and in what other situations it might not apply.

DRIVER'S LOG

What factors should you consider in deciding on the speed at which you drive?

WHAT WOULD YOU DO?

Sample answer: more slowly than indicated by the posted speed; the basic speed rule.

If You Are Involved in a Collision

(pages 106–108)

FOCUS

Objectives

• Describe the actions that you should take if you are involved in a collision.

• Learn what the legal consequences of a collision might be.

Resources

 Study Guide, page 24

Motivator

Pose the following situation: You are involved in a collision with another vehicle. How should you respond, and what are your responsibilities? (Students may mention that you should stop immediately; move the vehicle to the side of the road; put on emergency flashers to warn other drivers; call the police; if there are injuries, get medical help; exchange information with the other driver; get names and addresses of witnesses; stay on the scene as necessary; make out accident reports; inform your insurance company.)

TEACH

Explain

OBJECTIVE 1: Students should understand that fulfilling their legal obligations in the event of a collision does not necessarily mean they are at fault.

OBJECTIVE 2: Students should know that if they fail to follow certain procedures after a collision, they can be legally prosecuted.

OBJECTIVES
1. Describe the actions that you should take if you are involved in a collision.
2. Learn what the legal consequences of a collision might be.

If You Are Involved in a Collision

No matter how good a driver you are, there is no guarantee that you can always avoid a collision. Human suffering, loss of time, legal problems, and great expense can result from a collision regardless of who is at fault.

What Should You Do If You Are in a Collision?

After a collision, some people may panic or react in strange ways. They may also be in a state of shock. If you are in a collision, you should try to remain calm. Remember that the collision scene is no place to begin arguing with the other driver or with the police. Do not accuse anyone of causing the collision and do not admit fault yourself. Sign only forms given to you by the police. Do not sign any other statements at the scene of the accident. You have the legal right to consult an attorney before making any statement.

If you are involved in a collision, you should do the following.

◆ Collisions are frightening, but knowing what to do if you are involved in one can help you to stay calm.

Stop immediately. Drivers who do not stop when involved in a collision are breaking the law. Unless someone was seriously injured or killed, and if you can still drive your vehicle, try to move it off the roadway and out of traffic. Turn off the ignition to prevent the risk of fire.

Warn others if possible. If you cannot move your vehicle out of traffic, you must do everything you can to notify other drivers that there is a problem ahead. Turn on your hazard flashers. If you have flares or reflecting triangles, set them up at least 100 feet ahead of and behind the collision scene. If you don't have them, ask someone, possibly another driver who offers to help, to stand at the side of the road out of traffic and wave a flashlight or light-colored cloth to warn oncoming traffic.

106 UNIT 2 *Learning the Basics*

IT'S A FACT

Crashes on wet or slippery roads account for 16 percent of all deaths in roadside hazard crashes. Sixty-three percent of the deaths in crashes on slippery roads occur at night; 42 percent occur on curves, and 39 percent occur on hills.

Give aid to the injured. Check for injured persons. Try to make them comfortable, but do not move them unless you know what you are doing. Moving an injured person can result in more serious injury. Do what you can to provide first aid. (You will learn more about first aid in Chapter 15.)

Try to get medical help. If you or someone who has stopped to help has a cellular phone or a CB (citizens-band radio), use it to call the police, who will ensure that other emergency services are also notified. Use 911 or other emergency numbers if available. Or try to flag down another driver to go for aid or to call the appropriate emergency services.

Call the police. By law, a collision resulting in injury, death, or property damage above a given dollar value must be reported to the police. A few states require that all collisions be reported no matter what the damages are.

Exchange information. Drivers involved in collisions should exchange information with the other driver and any passengers. You should exchange drivers' and passengers' names and addresses, driver's license information, names of insurance companies, and vehicle registration information. If you are involved in a collision with a parked car, you should try to locate the owner. If you cannot, leave a note under the windshield wiper blades containing the same information that you would exchange at any other collision scene. For your records, write down a description and the license number of the vehicle that was struck, plus the date, time, and place.

Get names and addresses of witnesses. You have already exchanged information with the other driver and passengers. If there are witnesses at the scene, write down their names and addresses too. You might need them to verify your account of the collision.

Stay at the scene. If you are uninjured, remain at the scene of the collision until your help is no longer needed. If people have been seriously injured or killed, remain at the scene until the police allow you to leave.

Make accident reports. Drivers involved in any collision that results in injury should make a written report to the police and to the department of motor vehicles. States have different laws about reporting property damage under certain amounts. Know what your state law requires. Check your state driver's manual or contact your motor vehicle department to get this information. If you do not file a report, your driver's license could be suspended

FYI

Death rates are higher for occupants of small pickup trucks and small utility vehicles than for any other type of passenger vehicles, including the smallest cars.

◆ *Make a written accident report to the police, even if you have talked with them at the collision scene.*

Driving Tip

Explain to students that a collision cannot always be avoided. Tell them that they may sometimes see one coming. Point out these hints: If you are about to be hit from the side, accelerate so that you will be hit behind the rear wheels. Steer to avoid a head-on collision. Always wear safety belts; they will keep you from being thrown against the inside of the vehicle or out of the vehicle in the event of a collision.

They should also recognize that getting the names and addresses of witnesses and going to see a doctor after a collision are often wise actions to take even though they have no legal obligation to do so.

Teaching Model

Describe the following situation: Your vehicle has skidded on a slippery road and hit a center rail, spinning your vehicle around and badly damaging the left front. No one was hurt. Model your thinking immediately after the collision. (You do the following.

- Stop the vehicle immediately.
- Turn on your emergency flashers.
- When safe to do so, find out if your vehicle can still move.
- Drive the vehicle off the roadway and out of traffic, if it can move.
- Set out flares, reflecting triangles, or other warning devices to alert other drivers.
- Call the police and remain there until they come.
- Make out an accident report.)

Ask

Even if another vehicle is not involved in the collision, why may it be necessary to make out a report?

Read

Have students read Lesson 4 to become familiar with procedures to follow in the event of a collision.

ASSESS

Guided Practice

Have students answer the Lesson 4 Review questions. The answers are provided below.

Reteaching

Have students work in small groups to list actions that they would take if they were involved in a collision. Have students work together to make a chart describing and illustrating procedures. Have groups compare charts to determine if all important steps were covered and to add any that were not.

ADVICE FROM THE EXPERTS

Have students discuss the "five leading causes of collisions" and explore strategies for avoiding these dangers.

Enrichment

Assign the Study Guide for Lesson 4. The Find Out More section encourages students to expand their basic learning of the lesson concepts.

CLOSE

Summarize

Return to the Motivator question, and discuss the situation in view of what students have learned in the lesson. Have them describe the steps they would take to fulfill their obligations at the scene of a collision. Ask how they would attempt to handle their emotions in this situation.

DRIVER'S LOG

Have students list procedures to follow in case of a collision.

WHAT WOULD YOU DO?

Sample answer: The police must be called if someone has been injured or if otherwise dictated by state law.

ADVICE FROM THE EXPERTS

William Coar
Traffic Safety Technician, AAA, National Office

Driving is a risky business. Every year in the United States more than 40,000 people are killed and over 3 million are injured in motor vehicle crashes. Speeding is one of the biggest contributors to these crashes. Other factors include: inattention, failure to obey stop signs and signals, failure to yield the right-of-way, and driving under the influence.

To reduce risk, drivers must effectively manage visibility, time, and space. This can be accomplished by looking well ahead of your vehicle, maintaining a proper following distance, and controlling your speed.

regardless of whether or not the collision was your fault. Of course, you should also inform your insurance company.

See a doctor. Even if you have been treated at the scene of the collision, be sure to see your own doctor. Some injuries do not appear right away. Be safe and get yourself checked out thoroughly.

Legal consequences of a collision can be very serious. If a collision is the result of your having broken a traffic law, you may, depending on the severity of the crash:

- be fined and have to pay court costs.
- have your license suspended or revoked.
- be sent to jail.

If it is found that you were intoxicated or under the influence of other drugs at the time of a collision, the penalties are even more severe.

If you pass a collision scene and help appears needed, you should stop well off the roadway and offer whatever assistance that you can. However, if the situation appears under control, keep going. Stopping at the scene of a collision when it is unnecessary for you to do so can cause additional hazards for others who are using the roadway.

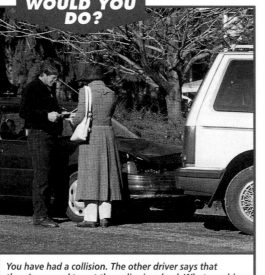

WHAT WOULD YOU DO?

You have had a collision. The other driver says that there's no need to get the police involved. What would you tell the driver?

Lesson 4 Review

1. What are your responsibilities if you are in a collision?
2. What may be the legal consequences of a collision?

Lesson 4 Review

Answers

1. Stop immediately, warn other drivers, aid the injured, call the police, try to get medical help, exchange information with the other driver, obtain the names and addresses of witnesses, stay at the scene, make out an accident report, see a doctor.
2. You may be fined, have your license suspended or revoked, be sent to jail.

Using Coordinates

You want to find Port Allen, Louisiana, on the map. How can you do that quickly?

First find Port Allen on the map index. It is listed alphabetically. Beside the name, you will see H-12. These are coordinates.

Look at the map. There are letters along the left side and numbers along the bottom. Find the H and put your left finger on it. Now find the 12. Move your left finger straight across the map until it is above the 12. Port Allen is in that area.

Notice the ◉ beside Port Allen. This means it is a county seat. A ○ stands for a town, a ■ stands for a city, and ✪ stands for the state capital. If you scan the map quickly, you can see that the names of cities and towns are written in different-size type. The larger the type, the greater the population.

Try It Yourself

1. Find Denson on the map. Is its population greater or less than the population of Port Allen?
2. Find Franklinton and Watson. Which is a county seat?
3. Find Baton Rouge and New Orleans. Which is the capital of Louisiana? Which has the smaller population?

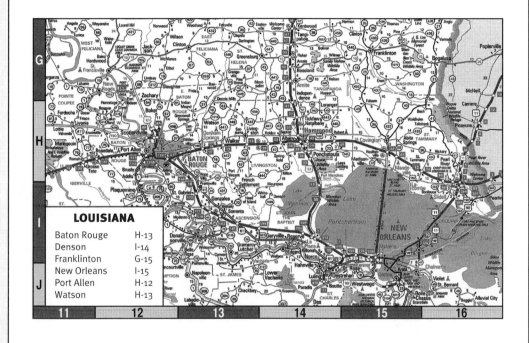

LOUISIANA

Baton Rouge	H-13
Denson	I-14
Franklinton	G-15
New Orleans	I-15
Port Allen	H-12
Watson	H-13

Objective

Demonstrate an ability to use a map index, coordinates, and typography to find and identify a specific location.

Teaching the Skill

- Be sure students recognize that a road map is divided into grids, each square of which is identified by a letter and a number—the coordinates—which help users locate places.
- Point out that once students find the area designated by the coordinates, they may have to search around in that area for the specific site they're trying to find.
- Draw students' attention to the map symbols and legend so that they recognize the meaning of the symbols.

ANSWERS TO Try It Yourself Questions

1. less than
2. Franklinton
3. Baton Rouge; Baton Rouge

CHAPTER SUMMARY

Key Points

Have students read the Key Points to review the major concepts of the chapter.

PROJECTS

Cooperative Learning:

Students will benefit by working with a partner on one or both projects. When the assignment is completed, the whole class will profit by sharing and comparing results.

CHAPTER 6 REVIEW

KEY POINTS

Lesson One

1. Every state has administrative laws that set standards for issuing driver's licenses and learner's permits, certificates of title, motor vehicle registration, and financial responsibility requirements.
2. To comply with the administrative laws, drivers must obtain a driver's license, maintain an acceptable driving record, obtain a certificate of title when buying a car, register their vehicle, and prove financial responsibility by obtaining vehicle insurance.

Lesson Two

1. Right-of-way means that one driver is required to yield when making a move in traffic.
2. You must yield the right-of-way to emergency vehicles, people who are blind, and pedestrians in crosswalks. At intersections not controlled by signals or signs, yield to vehicles already in the intersection. At stop or yield signs, yield to traffic on the cross street. At traffic lights, vehicles still in the intersection when the light changes must be given the right-of-way. When moving into a lane used by other drivers, yield to passing vehicles. Stop when a school bus stops to pick up or discharge students.

Lesson Three

1. Fixed speed limits are the maximum and minimum speeds that a vehicle may be driven on a particular roadway. Advisory speed limits provide guidelines when an adjustment in speed is needed, such as when approaching a sharp curve in the road.
2. Always drive at a speed that is reasonable and proper for existing conditions.

Lesson Four

1. Drivers involved in a collision must stop immediately and turn off the ignition, give aid to the injured, try to get medical help, call the police, exchange relevant information, get names and addresses of witnesses, stay at the scene, make accident reports, and see a doctor.
2. The legal consequences of a collision can be serious. If the collision is the result of your having broken a traffic law, you may, depending on the severity of the crash, be fined, have your license suspended or revoked, or be sent to jail.

PROJECTS

1. Find out the location of your area's department of motor vehicles. Visit it or write a letter asking for a copy of your state's driver's manual. Do the same with two neighboring states. Report on laws that are the same as the laws in your state and those that are different.
2. Ask at least four drivers if they can name five facts about roadway speed. Prepare a report on your findings. You may want to compare your report with the reports of others in your class and put together a combined report on drivers' attitudes and knowledge about speeding and speed laws.

inter **NET** CONNECTION

Search the Glencoe Web site for information on how to fill out a vehicle registration form.
drivered.glencoe.com

inter **NET** CONNECTION

Visit Glencoe's Driver Education Web site for student activities that relate to this chapter.
drivered.glencoe.com

CHAPTER 6 REVIEW

CHAPTER TEST

Write the letter of the answer that best completes each sentence.

1. If you are in a collision and the other driver is injured, you should
   a. go home and call an ambulance.
   b. stay at the scene until the police arrive.
   c. run away as fast as you can.

2. Posted speed limits
   a. tell you at what speed you must drive.
   b. are only on interstate highways.
   c. indicate you cannot safely go faster or slower than specified speeds.

3. The higher the speed, the more likely it is that a vehicle will
   a. develop engine problems.
   b. roll over on a turn.
   c. get excellent gas mileage.

4. Administrative laws set standards for
   a. rules of the road.
   b. minimum speed allowed.
   c. motor vehicle registration.

5. On a two-lane street, an ambulance is coming from behind with its siren blaring and lights flashing. You should
   a. pull over to the left and stop.
   b. pull over to the right and stop.
   c. increase your speed.

6. At an intersection, a person with a guide dog steps off the curb. You
   a. tap your horn and continue forward.
   b. stop to yield the right-of-way.
   c. drive around the person.

7. Your driver's license can be revoked if you
   a. are convicted of DUI or DWI.
   b. get into a collision.
   c. drive below the minimum speed limit.

8. Two drivers who have been in a collision should
   a. avoid any contact with each other or with witnesses.
   b. split the cost of any damages.
   c. exchange names and other information.

9. Right-of-way rules determine
   a. minimum speed limits in each state.
   b. procedures for turning right.
   c. who should yield the right-of-way.

10. You must pass a series of tests in order to
    a. increase your number of driving points.
    b. obtain a driver's license.
    c. obtain a certificate of title.

Write the word or phrase that best completes each sentence.

vehicle registration information
Uniform Vehicle Code   point system
accident report   basic speed rule

11. The _____ states that you should always drive at a speed that is reasonable and proper for existing conditions.

12. If you are involved in a collision, you should make a(n) _____.

13. Most states use a(n) _____ to keep track of traffic violations by individual drivers.

14. All states have right-of-way laws that are based on the _____.

DRIVER'S LOG

In this chapter, you have learned about the rules and laws that govern the roadways and the motorists who use them. Write about the five rules you think you will have the most trouble remembering. Explain what you will do to jog your memory.

CHAPTER 6 REVIEW

CHAPTER TEST

Assign the Chapter Test to all students.

Answers

1. b
2. c
3. b
4. c
5. b
6. b
7. a
8. c
9. c
10. b
11. basic speed rule
12. accident report
13. point system
14. Uniform Vehicle Code

DRIVER'S LOG

Students' responses will reflect their personal viewpoints. However, their answers should provide an assessment of their understanding of the rules and laws that drivers must know and obey.

Evaluate

- Test A, pp. 11–12 or Test B, pp. 11–12
- Testmaker software

RETURN TO THE BIG IDEA

Drawing on what students have learned in this chapter, discuss the idea that the efficiency and safety of any system depends on the degree to which participants obey the rules of that system.

Getting to Know Your Vehicle Overview

THEME DEVELOPMENT Vehicles are equipped with systems carefully designed to provide drivers with comfort, control, visibility, protection, information, and means of communication. These systems help drivers minimize risk to themselves and to other roadway users.

CHAPTER FEATURES	TCR COMPONENTS
	Study Guide, p. 25 Transparency 14 Lesson Plan, p. 15 Car Care Manual
CONNECTIONS Science Adjusting your mirrors to help reduce the size of blind spots.	Study Guide, p. 26 Transparencies 15 and 16 Lesson Plan, p. 15 Car Care Manual
	Study Guide, p. 27 Lesson Plan, p. 16 Car Care Manual
ADVICE FROM THE EXPERTS Checks and procedures to use before driving.	Study Guide, p. 28 Lesson Plan, p. 16 Car Care Manual Behind-the-Wheel Checklists 1 and 2
BUILDING SKILLS: SOCIAL STUDIES Making a Circle Graph **PROJECTS** 1. Read more about the systems discussed in Chapter 7. 2. Report on the comparative safety of various motor vehicles.	Test A, pp. 13–14 Test B, pp. 13–14

OTHER PROGRAM RESOURCES

Teaching Your Teens to Drive: Lesson 1, video or CD-ROM, AAA, 1998
Testmaker software
Traffic charts

ADDITIONAL RESOURCES

Vehicle and Personal Security, Video 492, AAA Foundation

CHAPTER 7
CHAPTER TEST

NAME _____ DATE _____

CHAPTER 7 Getting to Know Your Vehicle

TEST A

Select the phrase that best completes each sentence below. Write the letter of the answer you have chosen to the left of each statement.

__b__ 1. In cars without power seats, the driver's seat adjustment is usually located
a. on the steering column.
b. in the lower left or front of the driver's seat.
c. on the dashboard.
d. on the floorboards.

__a__ 2. The air conditioner is used to
a. lower humidity.
b. raise humidity.
c. defog windows.
d. do none of the above.

__d__ 3. The ignition switch is used to
a. turn on the car's electrical system.
b. start the engine.
c. turn off the electrical system.
d. do all of the above.

__a__ 4. A vehicle with an automatic transmission is usually started in Park because
a. the vehicle could roll if you started it in Neutral.
b. the vehicle could jump forward if you started it in Drive.
c. it is easier on the ignition switch.
d. it will not start in Neutral.

__d__ 5. Vehicles with manual transmissions have a clutch pedal
a. to the right of the accelerator.
b. between the accelerator and the brake pedal.
c. on the dashboard.
d. to the left of the brake pedal.

__a__ 6. Cruise control is a vehicle option that lets you
a. drive at a chosen speed without using the accelerator pedal.
b. drive safely in the snow.
c. keep moving safely in a traffic jam.
d. drive without having to use the brake pedal.

__d__ 7. The defroster is used to
a. clear moisture from the inside windows.
b. clear frost from the windows.
c. make it easier to scrape ice from the windows.
d. do all of the above.

__c__ 8. You can reduce the size of your blind spots by
a. adjusting your rearview mirror 30 degrees upward.
b. adjusting your sideview mirrors 45 degrees outward.
c. adjusting your rearview and sideview mirrors 15 degrees outward.
d. adjusting your visor.

__d__ 9. The function of a shoulder-lap safety belt is
a. to reduce by 50 percent the risk of being killed in a collision.
b. to help you stay in control of the car if you have to swerve or brake hard by keeping you close to the steering wheel.
c. to lessen the chance that you will be thrown through the windshield.
d. all of the above.

In each space below, write the word or words that best complete the sentence.

10. You control the vehicle's speed when you press on the ____accelerator____.

11. ____Power____ brakes require less foot power to stop the vehicle than regular brakes do.

12. You use the ____parking____ brake to keep your vehicle from rolling when it is stopped.

13. If your headlights are dirty, your visibility will be ____reduced____.

14. The best kind of safety belt is a ____shoulder-lap____ belt.

15. A(n) ____air bag____ is a device that inflates automatically in a frontal crash to help prevent injuries.

16. Your vehicle's ____alternator____ provides electricity to the car and the battery.

17. Your oil pressure gauge warns you if your car's oil pressure is too ____low____.

Read each statement below. If it is true, place a T in the space to the left of the statement. If the statement is false, place an F next to it.

__T__ 18. An overheated vehicle can cause drowsiness.

__T__ 19. A manual transmission's fifth gear can serve as an overdrive gear, saving fuel.

__T__ 20. One way to turn off your cruise control setting is to tap the brakes lightly.

__F__ 21. One advantage of power brakes is that they shorten the vehicle's braking distance by 50 percent.

22. What are some devices in a vehicle that are designed to make the driver more comfortable? Why go to the trouble to make the driver comfortable?

Seat-position controls, tilt steering wheel, air conditioner, heater, and air vents. Being uncomfortable is

not good for a driver of any vehicle because it detracts from the job of driving.

NAME _____ DATE _____

CHAPTER 7 Getting to Know Your Vehicle

TEST B

Select the phrase that best completes each sentence below. Write the letter of the answer you have chosen to the left of each statement.

__c__ 1. A padded head restraint is intended
a. to serve as a pillow only when you pull over to get rest.
b. to be used as a neck rest when driving to combat fatigue.
c. to help prevent neck injury when a vehicle is hit from behind.
d. to do all of the above.

__a__ 2. The function of an odometer is to
a. keep track of the number of miles that the vehicle has been driven.
b. keep track of the number of miles per gallon.
c. show how fast you are going.
d. tell you when your electrical system is failing.

__d__ 3. The function of an alternator is to
a. recharge the battery.
b. operate equipment like the radio.
c. provide electricity to keep the engine running.
d. do all of the above.

__c__ 4. You should pull your vehicle over and stop to avoid damage if
a. the temperature gauge or light says the engine is too hot.
b. the oil-pressure light or gauge says the oil pressure is low.
c. either a or b occurs.
d. the radio is too loud.

__c__ 5. The accessory position on the ignition switch allows you to
a. adjust the rearview mirror without turning on the engine.
b. start the vehicle and turn on the radio at the same time.
c. turn on the radio without turning on the engine.
d. turn off the cruise control system.

__b__ 6. If the parking brake light on your dashboard is on, you should
a. set the parking brake before moving.
b. release the parking brake before moving the vehicle.
c. get the brakes repaired.
d. put the vehicle in gear before shutting off the engine.

__a__ 7. If your vehicle has a breakdown and you need to warn other drivers that you are parked on the side of the road, you should
a. turn on your emergency flashers.
b. turn on your headlights.
c. turn on your parking lights.
d. honk your horn.

__b__ 8. You should check your vehicle's fluids (for example, engine oil, battery fluid, brake fluid)
a. at least once a day.
b. at least once a week.
c. at least once a month.
d. every six months.

__b__ 9. If you have the heater on and the vehicle gets very warm inside,
a. moisture will form on the insides of the windows.
b. you could become drowsy.
c. you are less likely to become drowsy.
d. you could severely damage the vehicle's engine.

In each space below, write the word or words that best complete the sentence.

10. You should always check your mirrors and look over your ____shoulder____ for blind spots.

11. On most vehicles, a safety-belt warning light and a ____buzzer____ remind you to fasten your seat belt.

12. You should have passengers enter your vehicle from the ____curb____ side when parked on the side of the street.

13. The ____air conditioner____ will lower the humidity of the vehicle's interior.

14. You start your vehicle by inserting and turning your key in the ____ignition____ switch.

15. A car with an automatic transmission will only start in Park and ____Neutral____.

16. You have to use a clutch with a ____manual____ transmission.

17. ____Cruise control____ is a device that lets you automatically maintain constant speed without using the accelerator pedal.

18. ____Air bags____ and safety belts are successful in preventing or reducing injuries in frontal crashes.

Read each statement below. If it is true, place a T in the space to the left of the statement. If the statement is false, place an F next to it.

__T__ 19. All 50 states require very young children to ride in approved car seats.

__T__ 20. All vehicles manufactured since 1986 have a third brake light in the center on their rear windows.

__F__ 21. Your air conditioner should be used to help clear fogged windows.

22. Describe some features of a vehicle that you use to communicate with others. What do they communicate?

Answers may include: Brake lights, backup lights, and turn indicators communicate that you are

stopping, slowing, backing, or turning.

NAME _____ DATE _____

CHAPTER 7 Getting to Know Your Vehicle

STUDY GUIDE FOR CHAPTER 7 LESSON 1

Comfort and Control Systems

A. Match the vehicle part on the left with a description of one of the part's functions on the right.

d	1. air conditioner	a.	turns on the vehicle's electrical system
g	2. air vents	b.	makes your vehicle stop without a lot of foot power
a	3. ignition switch	c.	maintains speed so that you do not have to use the accelerator
h	4. accelerator	d.	lowers the vehicle's humidity
f	5. emergency brake	e.	controls the direction in which the vehicle is going
b	6. power brakes	f.	keeps a stopped vehicle from rolling
c	7. cruise control	g.	allows outside air to flow into the vehicle
e	8. steering wheel	h.	controls speed

B. The ignition system has five positions. What are they, and what do they do?

1. On: turns on ignition, electrical systems, dashboard information gauges and warning lights.

2. Start: draws power from the battery to the engine.

3. Off: turns off the engine but does not allow the key to be removed.

4. Lock: locks the ignition switch and steering wheel.

5. Accessory: lets you use electrical equipment without running the engine.

C. FIND OUT MORE. Talk with somebody you know who has a vehicle with cruise control. Find out when this person uses cruise control. Does the person feel that less concentration is needed on the road because of cruise control?

Review student's work.

NAME _____ DATE _____

STUDY GUIDE FOR CHAPTER 7 LESSON 2

Visibility and Protective Systems of Your Vehicle

A. For each sentence below, circle T if the statement is true and F if it is false. Correct each false statement in the space below.

1. Your side-marker lights come on when you turn on your headlights.   Ⓣ   F

2. A good set of mirrors will eliminate all blind spots.   T   Ⓕ
Mirrors cannot eliminate all blind spots.

3. You can rely exclusively on your mirrors when backing up.   T   Ⓕ
You cannot rely only on mirrors when backing. You must turn your head to look over your shoulders.

4. If you are wearing a shoulder-lap seat belt at the time of a crash, your risk of being killed is reduced by 50 percent.   Ⓣ   F

5. An example of a passive safety device is an air bag.   Ⓣ   F

6. All states require very young children to ride in safety-tested and approved car seats.   Ⓣ   F

7. Air bags are most effective in preventing injury in rear-end crashes.   T   Ⓕ
Air bags are most effective in preventing injuries in frontal crashes.

8. Head restraints are valuable in preventing injuries to the head because the restraints prevent your head from hitting the steering wheel.   T   Ⓕ
Head restraints prevent injuries to the neck by stopping the head from snapping back.

B. FIND OUT MORE. Ask an adult to move a vehicle to an open area. Get into the driver's seat, and adjust the mirrors so that you can see as much of what is behind and next to you as possible. Have someone else in the class walk around the vehicle while you observe the person. Where are the blind spots in that vehicle? Draw a diagram below.
Review student's research.

NAME _____ DATE _____

STUDY GUIDE FOR CHAPTER 7 LESSON 3

Information and Communication Systems

A. For each sentence below, circle T if the statement is true and F if it is false. Correct each false statement in the space below.

1. If your alternator warning light comes on, you should turn off any unnecessary electrical devices and check with a mechanic as soon as possible.   Ⓣ   F

2. The oil-pressure gauge tells you if your vehicle is low on oil.   T   Ⓕ
The oil-pressure gauge tells you if the pressure at which the oil is being pumped is low.

3. If brake fluid is leaking, the brake warning light will come on.   Ⓣ   F

4. Your vehicle's backup lights are red or amber and come on when you shift into Reverse.   T   Ⓕ
Your vehicle's backup lights are white and come on when you put the vehicle in Reverse.

5. Vehicles are required by law to have a license-plate light.   Ⓣ   F

B. What does each of the following do?

1. Speedometer   Shows how fast the vehicle is moving.

2. Fuel gauge   Shows how full or empty the gas tank is.

3. High-beam indicator   Tells you whether your high-beam headlights are on or off.

4. Temperature gauge   Tells you if the engine temperature is too hot.

5. Alternator   Provides electricity to keep the engine running.

6. Oil pressure gauge   Warns when pressure of oil being pumped into engine is low.

7. Emergency flashers   Warn other drivers that a vehicle is stopped.

8. Odometer   Keeps track of miles driven.

C. FIND OUT MORE. Ask someone you know who drives what the effect would be on the vehicle's safety if each of the above did not work. Summarize the responses below.
Review student's work.

NAME _____ DATE _____

STUDY GUIDE FOR CHAPTER 7 LESSON 4

Checks and Procedures to Use Before Driving

A. For each sentence below, circle T if the statement is true and F if it is false. Correct each false statement in the space below.

1. Each year, about 200 children under the age of six are killed while playing in the family driveway.   Ⓣ   F

2. You should inspect the area around your vehicle after you get into it.   T   Ⓕ
You should inspect area around your vehicle before you get into it.

3. You should check the level of engine oil once a month.   T   Ⓕ
You should check level of engine oil at least once a week.

4. When checking the battery, you should check for corrosion.   Ⓣ   F

5. You should always load packages from the roadside of a parked vehicle.   T   Ⓕ
You should always load packages from the curbside of the car.

6. When entering a vehicle, you should walk around the front of the vehicle, facing traffic.   Ⓣ   F

B. What procedures should you follow for an inside-the-vehicle check before you start the vehicle?
Examples of possible answers: Close and lock all doors, put key in ignition, adjust seat so that you can see the roadway and are comfortable, adjust head restraints and have passengers adjust theirs also, adjust all mirrors, clean inside of windows, make sure that no packages or other objects are blocking the view or are loose, and familiarize yourself with controls. You and passengers should fasten seat belts.

C. FIND OUT MORE. For the next two weeks, keep a record of every time you ride in a vehicle as a passenger. How many times did the driver check to see that you were wearing a seat belt?
Review student's work.

Getting to Know Your Vehicle

CHAPTER OVERVIEW

LESSON ONE
Components of a vehicle's comfort and control systems are described in the context of managing driving risk.

LESSON TWO
A vehicle's visibility and protective systems are described, and how these systems reduce driving risk is explained.

LESSON THREE
Components of the information and communication systems of a vehicle are described, and the importance of these systems is explained.

LESSON FOUR
Predriving checks and procedures are described, with an emphasis on problem prevention.

VOCABULARY

accelerator
air bag
alternator
antitheft device
blind spot
brake pedal
cruise control
defroster
directional signal
emergency flashers
gear selector lever
gearshift
head restraint
odometer
overdrive
parking brake
passive safety device
power brakes
power steering
speedometer

112

CONCEPT OF THE DRIVING TASK

Explain that the various electronic and mechanical systems in a vehicle are designed to make the driving task safer and easier. To derive maximum benefit from these systems, a driver should understand their function and learn how to use them effectively.

CHAPTER 7

Getting to Know Your Vehicle

It is important for you to know and understand your vehicle's systems and the checks you should make before you start driving. Understanding the function and purpose of each system and what the lights and gauges can tell you will help you manage risk. To manage risk when driving, you must be able to quickly locate, read, understand, and operate all controls and switches without taking your eyes off the road ahead for more than one second at a time.

LESSON ONE
Comfort and Control Systems and Risk Management

LESSON TWO
The Visibility and Protective Systems of Your Vehicle

LESSON THREE
Information and Communication Systems

LESSON FOUR
Checks and Procedures to Use Before Driving

PRESENTING THE BIG IDEA ____

Proper use of a vehicle's various systems, such as those that communicate information to the driver and to other roadway users, helps minimize driving risk.

INTRODUCING THE CHAPTER

What's on the Road Ahead?

Have students look at the photographs and read the lesson titles and objectives. Briefly discuss the topic of each lesson. Tell students that in this chapter they will read about the various systems of a vehicle and learn how to use them to manage risk.

Background: Evolution of Vehicle Comfort

Driving comfort has come a long way since the early 1900s, when drivers were tossed, bounced, shaken, and often splattered with water and mud as they steered their open vehicles over rough roads. The self-starter was invented in 1911, and a wide range of comfort and control features were introduced in the 1920s and 1930s. These included fully enclosed vehicles, quieter engines, improved tires, shock absorbers, electric headlights, and factory-installed heaters and radios. The first fully automatic transmission appeared in 1939 in moderately priced Oldsmobiles made by General Motors.

Relating to Prior Knowledge

Have students discuss what they know about the purpose and use of a vehicle's gauges, warning lights, and instrument panel controls.

The Big Idea

Discuss students' reactions to the Big Idea statement. Suggest that they keep this idea in mind as they read Chapter 7.

Comfort and Control Systems and Risk Management

(pages 114–117)

FOCUS

Objectives

• Describe four devices that help make you comfortable in a vehicle.

• List six devices that enable you to control a vehicle, and explain what each one does.

Resources

 Study Guide, page 25

 Transparency 14

Car Care Manual

Vocabulary

gear selector lever
gearshift
overdrive
power steering
accelerator
cruise control
brake pedal
power brakes
parking brake

Motivator

Pose the following situation: You see a used vehicle you'd like to buy. You've never owned one before, but you've ridden in plenty of vehicles. Before you buy this vehicle, you want to check to see if it has most of the features you want. The salesperson tells you that the vehicle has good "comfort and control systems," but you want to see for yourself. What kinds of things do you look for? (Students may mention comfort

---

LESSON ONE

OBJECTIVES

1. Describe four devices that help make you comfortable in a vehicle.
2. List six devices that enable you to control a vehicle, and explain what each one does.

KEY TERMS

gear selector lever
gearshift
overdrive
power steering
accelerator
cruise control
brake pedal
power brakes
parking brake

SAFETY TIPS

Cruise control should not be used when driving where grip between the tires and road is low or where frequent speed adjustments are necessary.

Comfort and Control Systems and Risk Management

Suppose you're driving along and suddenly you see a light blink on your control panel. What does it mean? If you don't know the answer, it means that you don't know your vehicle. Not knowing puts you, your passengers, and other drivers at risk.

Vehicles are equipped with a variety of comfort and control devices. You have to know what these devices do, where they are located, and how they operate. For specific information, refer to the owner's manual.

What Devices Help Make You Comfortable in a Vehicle?

You must concentrate while driving, and being uncomfortable can distract you from the driving task. Vehicles have comfort devices to help you, but you have to know how to use them to their best advantage. Some comfort devices help reduce muscle strain. Others control the interior climate of your car and make driving less tiring.

Seat-Position Controls

The driver's seat must be comfortable, and it must suit the driver. It should provide good visibility and access to the controls.

Many vehicles have power seat-adjustment controls, which allow you to adjust the seat up or down, forward or back, or tilt the seat to better fit the vehicle to the driver.

In vehicles without power seats, the seat-adjustment lever is usually located on the lower left side or front of the driver's seat. Pulling back or up on the lever allows the driver to adjust the seat forward or back for better access to vehicle controls and switches.

In a vehicle with a steering wheel air bag, adjust the seat so you are at least 10 inches from the steering wheel.

Steering Wheel

The top of the steering wheel should be no higher than the top of the driver's shoulders. Many vehicles have an adjustable (tilt wheel)

THE INTERNATIONAL SCENE

Scandinavia

In the Scandinavian countries of Sweden, Norway, and Denmark, drivers must turn off the vehicle ignition if they stop for more than 2 minutes. This procedure helps minimize the amount of pollution that vehicles emit.

steering wheel. Drivers can adjust the steering wheel to a position that provides maximum comfort and control. In vehicles that do not have a tilt wheel, a driver may need to use a wedge-shaped driving cushion.

Air Conditioner and Heater

Use the air conditioner to cool the vehicle and lower the humidity, and use the heater to warm the vehicle interior and clear fogged windows. Never overheat your vehicle. An overheated vehicle can cause drowsiness.

Air Vents

Adjustable vents allow outside air to flow into the vehicle. They are usually located on the dashboard or on the front lower left and right sides.

How Can You Control the Movement of Your Vehicle?

The parts of a vehicle's control system enable you to start and stop the vehicle and control its speed and direction.

Ignition Switch

Inserting and turning the key in a vehicle's ignition switch starts the engine. This switch is usually found on the steering column. The ignition switch normally has five positions: Accessory, Lock, Off, On, and Start.

Selector Lever for Automatic Transmission

On vehicles that have automatic transmissions, you choose the gear you want by moving the **gear selector lever.** This lever is located either on the steering column or on the floor to the right of the driver's seat.

A vehicle with an automatic transmission will start only in Park or Neutral. Usually drivers start from Park, because Park is the gear in which they leave the car. In this position, a vehicle will not roll. A car in Neutral *will* roll on an incline.

FYI

The refrigerated truck was patented in 1949 by Frederick McKinley Jones, an African-American inventor. Until that time, fresh produce and other perishable food had to be transported by railroad. The refrigerated truck made it possible for towns not on railroad routes to receive regular deliveries of these products.

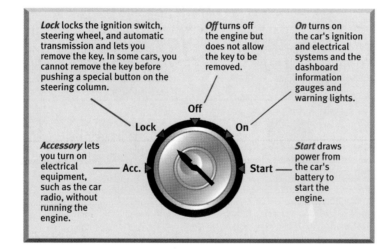

Lock locks the ignition switch, steering wheel, and automatic transmission and lets you remove the key. In some cars, you cannot remove the key before pushing a special button on the steering column.

Off turns off the engine but does not allow the key to be removed.

On turns on the car's ignition and electrical systems and the dashboard information gauges and warning lights.

Accessory lets you turn on electrical equipment, such as the car radio, without running the engine.

Start draws power from the car's battery to start the engine.

Off
Lock   On
Acc.   Start

Driving Tip

Explain to students that if their vehicle's air conditioner is blowing warm or hot air rather than cold air, the problem may be a lack of refrigerant—the same gas used in refrigerators. To extend the life of the refrigerant in a vehicle's air conditioner, it helps to run the unit for a few minutes every week, even in winter. Doing so circulates the lubricants throughout the system and helps keep the seals flexible.

system—seat position controls, steering wheel, heater and air conditioner, air vents; control system—ignition switch, transmission selector [for automatic transmission] or gearshift selector and clutch pedal [for manual transmission], steering wheel, accelerator or gas pedal, cruise control, brake pedal, parking brake.)

To check students' understanding, discuss the term *perishable*, and ask why Jones's invention was so significant.

TEACH

Explain

OBJECTIVE 1: Students should recognize that comfort is one of the important goals of vehicle design. Discuss the purpose of driver comfort—to allow drivers to keep their attention on the driving task.

OBJECTIVE 2: Students will probably be familiar with various control devices from having ridden in vehicles. The devices described in this lesson are the ignition switch, gear selector lever, gearshift and clutch pedal for manual transmission, steering wheel, accelerator or gas pedal, cruise control, brake pedal, and parking brake.

Teaching Model

Pose this situation: You are about to drive a vehicle that belongs to a friend of yours. Your friend is not as tall as you are, and you've never driven the vehicle before. Model the procedure that you go through to get comfortable after you enter the vehicle. (You do the following.

• Adjust the seat to give you the leg room you need and enable you to operate the floor pedals and vehicle controls and switches comfortably [if your friend were much taller than you, you might need to buy a wedge-shaped driving cushion and/or brake and accelerator extension pedals].

continued on page 116

- Adjust the steering wheel, if possible, for maximum comfort and vehicle control; you want the steering wheel and seat height positioned so that the top of the wheel is no higher than the top of your shoulders.
- Adjust the air conditioner or heater and the air vents if necessary.)

Ask

Ask students to discuss possible dangers of not being comfortable when driving.

Read

Have students read Lesson 1 to become familiar with the parts of the comfort and control systems and to learn how these systems assist drivers in managing risk. Encourage students to compare features described and illustrated in the text with features they have seen in vehicles.

ASSESS

Guided Practice

Have students answer the Lesson 1 Review questions. The answers are provided below.

Reteaching

Have students work together in small groups, using 3" × 5" cards to make identifying labels for each of the parts of the comfort and control systems described in this lesson. Then have them write brief corresponding descriptions for the parts on separate cards. Next, have students shuffle both groups of cards and match each part label with the appropriate description.

You may also want to have students look through advertisements in magazines to find photographs or descriptions of comfort and control system components. Have students cut out the advertisements and discuss the features shown or described.

Gearshift for Manual Transmission

On vehicles that have manual transmissions, you choose the gear you need by stepping down on the clutch pedal and moving the **gearshift** (or stick shift). The gearshift is usually located on the floor to the right of the driver's seat, although occasionally you'll find the gearshift on the side of the steering column.

The gearshift may have three, four, or five speed positions, plus a reverse position. The fifth gear serves as an **overdrive** gear, which allows the engine to run more slowly and fuel efficiently at high speeds.

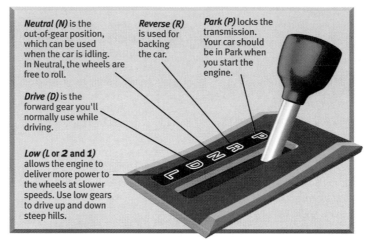

Neutral (N) is the out-of-gear position, which can be used when the car is idling. In Neutral, the wheels are free to roll.

Drive (D) is the forward gear you'll normally use while driving.

Low (L or 2 and 1) allows the engine to deliver more power to the wheels at slower speeds. Use low gears to drive up and down steep hills.

Reverse (R) is used for backing the car.

Park (P) locks the transmission. Your car should be in Park when you start the engine.

Clutch Pedal

Cars with manual transmissions have a clutch pedal located to the left of the brake pedal. In Chapter 8 you will read more about how to operate the clutch pedal and the gearshift.

Steering Wheel

You control the direction of your front wheels by turning the steering wheel. In cars equipped with **power steering,** it takes little effort to turn the wheel.

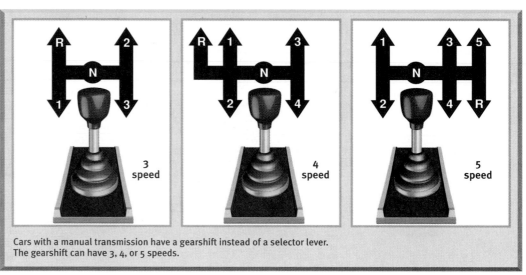

Cars with a manual transmission have a gearshift instead of a selector lever. The gearshift can have 3, 4, or 5 speeds.

MEETING STUDENT DIVERSITY

Limited English Proficiency

Students who have trouble remembering the names and functions of comfort and control devices may find it helpful to create a chart displaying key parts and briefly describing each part's purpose. Take extra time to ensure that students understand the meaning of key words, such as *transmission* and *clutch*.

Accelerator (Gas Pedal)

You move the vehicle and control its speed by pressing on the **accelerator,** or gas pedal, with your right foot. The greater the pressure you put on the accelerator, the more fuel the carburetor or fuel injectors feed to the engine. The more fuel that flows into the engine, the faster the vehicle will go.

Cruise Control

Cruise (or speed) **control** is an optional vehicle feature that lets you maintain a desired speed without keeping your foot on the accelerator. Cruise control is intended for highway driving, in situations where you can maintain a constant rate of speed.

To use cruise control, first accelerate to the speed of the traffic, then reduce speed by 2 or 3 mph. Set the control button or switch located on the turn-indicator arm or on the steering wheel. You can switch off cruise control whenever you choose, or you can cancel it by tapping the brake pedal.

Although cruise control is a convenience, think when you use it. Cruise control may lead you to be less alert than you should be.

Brake Pedal

You slow or stop the vehicle by pressing down on the **brake pedal. Power brakes** require less foot pressure to operate than non-power brakes. However, power brakes do *not* shorten the distance needed to stop the vehicle.

Parking Brake

The **parking brake,** frequently called the emergency or hand brake, is used to keep a parked vehicle from rolling. The parking brake control can be a small pedal located to the left side of the floor panel, a hand lever located under the left side of the dashboard, or a floor-mounted hand lever located to the right of the driver's seat.

Lesson *1* Review

1. What equipment is designed to make drivers comfortable?
2. What devices control the vehicle? What does each device do?

FYI

When a vehicle with power steering stalls, the power steering is lost. If the vehicle cannot be started and needs to be rolled off the road, the steering wheel will be very difficult to turn.

WHAT WOULD YOU DO?

You are driving in the right lane at 50 mph. What actions will you take to minimize risk? What vehicle controls will come into play?

Enrichment

Assign the Study Guide for Lesson 1. The Find Out More section encourages students to expand their basic learning of the lesson concepts.

CLOSE

Summarize

Return to the Motivator question, and discuss students' initial responses in view of what they have learned from this lesson. Have students summarize the components of the comfort and control systems and discuss why each component is important to drivers. Encourage students to be specific in their answers.

Also have students discuss how the control system of a vehicle with a manual transmission differs from the control system of a vehicle with an automatic transmission. Ask students what system components both kinds of vehicles have.

DRIVER'S LOG

How can a vehicle's comfort and control systems help drivers manage risk?

WHAT WOULD YOU DO?

Sample answer: Maintain a safe following distance, stay in lane, and drive at a safe speed. Vehicle controls that will come into play include the steering wheel, accelerator, brake pedal, and clutch pedal and gearshift (for a manual transmission).

Lesson *1* Review

Answers

1. Devices designed to increase comfort include seat-position controls, adjustable steering wheel, heater, air conditioner, and air vents.
2. The ignition switch starts the engine; the selector lever or gearshift is used to choose the gear; the clutch pedal in a vehicle with a manual transmission is used with the gearshift to change gears; the steering wheel controls the direction of the front wheels; the accelerator and brake pedals move or stop the vehicle; cruise control maintains a desired speed; the parking brake keeps a parked vehicle from rolling.

The Visibility and Protective Systems of Your Vehicle

(pages 118–122)

FOCUS

Objectives

- Name at least five aids to visibility.
- Describe four features that are designed to protect you and your passengers from injury.
- Name three antitheft devices.

Resources

 Study Guide, page 26

 Traffic charts

 Transparencies 15 and 16

Car Care Manual

Vocabulary

defroster
blind spot
passive safety device
air bag
head restraint
antitheft device

Motivator

It's a cold and snowy night. You'd rather be inside keeping warm, but you have to drive to the bus station to pick up your cousin, who's coming to visit. How do you use your vehicle's visibility and protective systems to help you manage the driving task successfully? (Sample answer: Turn on the headlights, adjust the dashboard lights, turn on the windshield wipers and defroster, check the rearview and sideview mirrors, adjust the head restraint, fasten the safety belt.)

LESSON TWO

OBJECTIVES

1. Name at least five aids to visibility.
2. Describe four features that are designed to protect you and your passengers from injury.
3. Name three antitheft devices.

KEY TERMS

defroster
blind spot
passive safety device
air bag
head restraint
antitheft device

SAFETY TIPS

Always be sure that your headlights and taillights are clean. Dirty lights reduce visibility.

◆ Glancing often in your rearview and sideview mirrors helps you to scan all around your car.

The Visibility and Protective Systems of Your Vehicle

Some safety features reduce driving risk by aiding visibility. Others reduce or control risk by protecting the driver and passengers from injury. Still others guard the vehicle against theft.

What Devices Aid Visibility?

Seeing and being seen are critical to controlling risk and making driving easier and safer. A vehicle's visibility system better enables you to see the roadway and maximizes the ability of others to see you.

Lights

Using your headlights helps other roadway users to see you both at night *and* during the *day*. Headlights help you see better at night, in dim light, and in bad weather. Taillights and side-marker lights better enable drivers and other highway users to see your vehicle.

Headlights can be switched to either low beams or more intense high beams. Most of the time you'll be using the low beams.

The switch to turn on your headlights is either on the dashboard or on a stem on the left side of the steering column. You either pull the lever toward you or push it away to change to high or low beams. In some older vehicles, the switch is a button located on the left side of the floor panel.

When you turn on your headlights, your taillights and side-marker lights also come on. In addition, the dashboard gauges, dials, and controls light up. You can dim or brighten these dashboard lights by turning a knob located on the instrument panel or turn-indicator lever.

In many vehicles, the same light switch knob used to turn on exterior lights can also control the brightness of the dashboard lights and turn on the interior dome light.

Windshield Wipers and Washer

Vehicles normally have two-, three-, or variable-speed windshield wipers. Some vehicles also have a wiper in the rear window.

State BY State

As of January 1, 1998, 49 states and the District of Columbia had safety-belt-use laws. Twelve states require all occupants to use safety restraints. In 37 states, only front-seat occupants must use them. In 15 states, failure to use safety restraints is a primary violation for which an offender can be stopped and ticketed. In the other states, such failure is a secondary offense for which a person can be ticketed if stopped for another violation. In most states, it is the driver's responsibility to ensure that occupants use restraints if required.

Variable-speed wipers allow the driver to set the wipers to move at a very slow or very rapid rate. This feature is useful when only an occasional wipe is needed to keep the window clear, as during a light drizzle. It is also helpful during a driving rain when a faster rate is needed.

The windshield washer squirts water or an antifreeze solution onto the windshield. The liquid is stored in a container under the hood.

Rearview and Sideview Mirrors

Your vehicle's rearview and sideview mirrors provide vision to the rear and sides of the roadway. Even when correctly adjusted, however, they cannot eliminate all **blind spots**—areas of the road that you cannot see in the mirrors. You must make a final check to the sides before you make any lateral move. Turning your head to use the side mirrors or to check over your shoulder should be limited to a quick glance to detect the presence of objects and not to gather detailed information.

Sun Visors

Sun visors can be moved up and down and turned to the side to prevent the sun from shining in the driver's eyes. However, be careful not to let the visors interfere with your view of the roadway or traffic to the side.

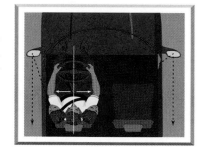

◆ Look over your shoulder for traffic in your blind spots before changing lanes, and try never to travel in another driver's blind spots. Adjust your mirrors carefully.

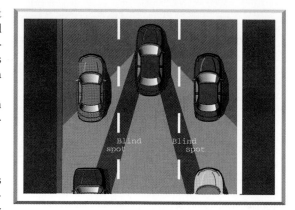

CONNECTIONS
Science

When you are planning to change lanes, you must be certain your blind spots are clear. One way you can reduce the size of blind spots is by adjusting your rearview and sideview mirrors 15 degrees outward.

Adjust the inside rearview mirror to take in as much as possible. You should be able to use this mirror with a shift of the eyes, not a turn of the head. Drivers 6 feet tall or more may find it helpful to turn the mirror 180 degrees so that the day/night switch is on the top of the mirror. This

action raises the mirror about 2 inches and eliminates a blind spot to the front.

Adjust the sideview mirrors to reduce side and rear blind spots as much as possible. To adjust the driver's side mirror, place your head against the window and set the mirror so you can just see the side of the car. For the passenger's side mirror, position your head in the middle of the car and adjust the mirror in the same way, so you can just see the side of the car. Remember, though, that even properly adjusted mirrors will not eliminate all blind spots. You will still need to check over your shoulder. See the illustration above.

IT'S A FACT

Drivers must cope with blind spots no matter what kind of vehicle they drive, although some vehicles have larger or more blind spots than others. Blind spots typically are located just beyond the range of rearview and sideview mirrors, but they may also result from a vehicle's structural design.

CONNECTIONS
Science

To check students' understanding, ask them to show what a 15-degree outward adjustment looks like. Discuss why it is important to try to reduce blind spots.

TEACH
Explain
OBJECTIVE 1: Students will probably recognize most of the aids to visibility. However, students will benefit from a detailed discussion of the capabilities and functions of each visibility system component. The idea that mirrors do not eliminate all blind spots is worthy of special note.

OBJECTIVE 2: Devices that protect drivers and passengers from injury should be familiar to most students. It will be helpful to distinguish those devices that are "passive" from those that require action on the part of the driver or passengers. Point out, too, that air bags inflate for only the briefest instant and that most are useful only in frontal impacts. Some vehicles now have side-impact air bags.

OBJECTIVE 3: Students should recognize that antitheft devices are useful only when the driver remembers to activate them. Students may also be interested to learn that many insurance companies offer a discount to vehicle owners whose vehicles are equipped with antitheft devices.

Display this situation:

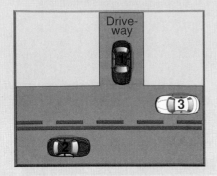

Tell students the following: You are in vehicle 1 about to drive forward out of your driveway. Vehicles 2 and 3 are traveling in opposite directions. It is a rainy night. Model the thinking process that you go through to manage risk in this situation. (You do the following.

- Lock your vehicle doors.
- Fasten your safety belt.
- Put on your low beams.
- Put on your windshield wipers and, if necessary, your defroster.
- Wait for approaching vehicles to pass before moving.
- Signal your intention to turn.)

Ask

Ask students to discuss how visibility and protective features reduce risk for the occupants of vehicles 2 and 3.

Read

Have students read Lesson 2 to learn about the components of a vehicle's visibility and protective systems and how these components function to help the driver manage risk.

ASSESS

Guided Practice

Have students answer the Lesson 2 Review questions. The answers are provided below.

All new cars equipped with air bags carry this warning: "Sitting too close to the steering wheel can result in injury in the event of a crash." Crash investigations have reported facial injuries and broken forearms. Such injuries usually occur when drivers using hand-over-hand steering have their forearm across the steering wheel at the moment the air bag inflates.

Defroster (Defogger)

Use the **defroster**—sometimes called the defogger—to clear moisture or frost from the front, rear, and side windows. Heat from the defroster can also make it easier to scrape ice from the windows. In most vehicles, front and rear defrosters have separate controls.

What Features Protect You and Your Passengers from Injury?

Your vehicle's protective features help reduce risk by guarding you and your passengers against injury in case of a collision or sudden emergency maneuver.

Some safety features, such as air bags, are passive safety devices. **Passive safety devices** operate without the user having to do anything. Other features, such as manual safety belts, require drivers and passengers to take some action to protect themselves.

Safety Belts

Drivers and passengers should always wear safety belts—preferably, shoulder-lap belts—whenever the vehicle is in motion. If you are wearing a shoulder-lap belt at the time of a crash, your risk of being killed is reduced by about 50 percent, and your risk of serious injury is reduced by 70 percent.

Properly worn safety belts protect the wearer against injury in a collision. They lessen the chance that you or your passengers will be thrown against the dashboard, through the windshield, or out a door that has sprung open in a crash. In addition, safety belts help keep you behind the wheel and in control of the vehicle if you have to swerve or brake abruptly or are struck by another vehicle.

Forty-nine states have passed laws that require the driver and front-seat passengers to wear safety belts. All 50 states have laws requiring very young children to ride only in special safety-tested and approved child safety seats.

Air Bags

Almost 79 million vehicles are now equipped with **air bags,** which inflate automatically in a frontal crash, then deflate again in a fraction of a second. Some vehicles also have air bags that inflate in a side collision. Air bags are very effective in preventing injuries, but they do not reduce the need for wearing a safety belt.

MEETING STUDENT DIVERSITY

Special Needs

Students with visual or perceptual problems may have difficulty distinguishing right from left in a mirror. To help these students, have a mirror available in the classroom for students to practice identifying objects behind them to the right and left. Encourage students to double-check positions by looking back over their shoulders, to the right and left.

Head Restraints

Head restraints are standard equipment on front-seat backs and optional on the rear seats of some vehicles. These padded restraints protect against whiplash (neck injury), especially when your vehicle is hit from behind. To get the maximum benefit from head restraints, make sure that they are properly adjusted. Head restraints should be high enough to make contact with the back of your head, not the base of your skull.

Door Locks

Keep vehicle doors locked. Locked doors not only are unlikely to open in a crash, but they also help prevent uninvited people from entering your car when you're stopped.

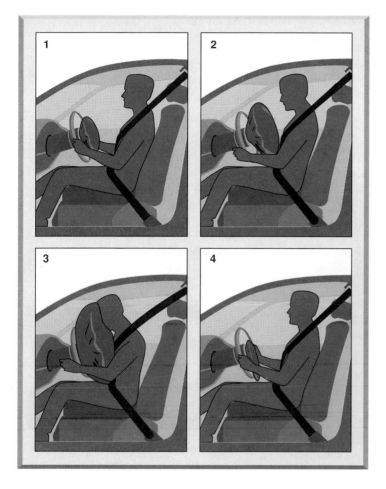

SAFETY TIPS

In cold weather, leave the blower off and turn the temperature control to the hottest setting for the first couple of minutes. This allows the air to warm up and prevents that initial ice-cold blast from freezing the inside of the windshield.

FYI

Nearly one out of seven recovered stolen vehicles still have the keys in them!

◆ *In less than one second, airbags (1) begin to inflate on impact, (2) become fully inflated, (3) cushion the driver from the frontal blow, and (4) deflate.*

Reteaching

Divide students into small groups, and have each student describe the function of one or more components of a vehicle's visibility and protective systems. Have the members of each group work together to make a chart of both systems, illustrating the components and describing their functions. Then have the groups display and compare their charts.

Enrichment

Assign the Study Guide for Lesson 2. The Find Out More section encourages students to expand their basic learning of the lesson concepts.

State BY State

Several states provide a special driver's guide for prospective drivers who have reading difficulties. Interested students may want to contact the motor vehicle department or the state or regional department of education to find out if such material is available in their state.

CLOSE

Summarize

Return to the Motivator question. Discuss procedures for driving safely in this situation in view of what students have learned about visibility and protective systems in this lesson. Help students compare passive and active protective systems by discussing the function and effectiveness of safety belts, head restraints, air bags, safety-glass windows, impact-resistant bumpers, and various antitheft devices.

DRIVER'S LOG

Have students list the parts of a vehicle's visibility and protective systems and describe how each serves to reduce risk to driver and passengers. Which parts require adjustment by driver or passengers? Which do not?

WHAT WOULD YOU DO?

Sample answer: The driver of the vehicle should be wearing a shoulder-lap safety belt, which would increase his chances of surviving a crash by 50 percent. Also, the driver is sitting too close to the steering wheel, limiting his ability to steer and increasing chances of injury in a crash. Finally, his head restraint should be higher.

FYI

Very soon some automotive manufacturers will put air bags in back seats. "Smart" air bags will also be installed in vehicles. During a crash, the size and weight of an individual will determine whether and how the air bag deploys.

WHAT WOULD YOU DO?

What is this driver doing wrong? What would you tell him?

Structural Features

Automotive manufacturers build a wide range of safety features into their vehicles. These features include tempered safety-glass windows, impact-resistant bumpers, protective padding on the dashboard and interior roof, energy-absorbing steering columns, and childproof door locks that are controlled by the driver. Factors such as a vehicle's size and weight also help determine how well occupants are protected in a crash.

What Devices Guard Against Vehicle Theft?

Vehicle theft is a nationwide problem. Various devices help protect your vehicle against thieves and vandals.

Ignition Buzzer

When your key is in the ignition switch and you open the driver's door, you will hear a buzz or other sound to remind you to take your key with you when you leave the vehicle.

Locks

Vehicles are now equipped with various locks, including door locks, a steering-column lock, and locks on the trunk, hood, and gas tank.

Alarms and Other Antitheft Devices

A wide range of **antitheft devices** are available for vehicles, ranging from elaborate alarm systems to disabling devices that keep the vehicle from starting or prevent the steering wheel from turning. Some vehicle security systems can be turned on or off by remote control using a key chain transmitter.

Lesson 2 Review

1. What vehicle devices aid your ability to see and be seen?
2. What features help protect you and your passengers from injury in the event of a collision?
3. What devices might prevent the theft of a vehicle?

Lesson 2 Review

Answers

1. Lights, windshield wipers and washer, sun visors, defroster (defogger), and rearview and sideview mirrors aid your ability to see and be seen.
2. Safety belts, air bags, head restraints, door locks, and various structural features protect you and your passengers from injury.
3. The ignition buzzer (reminding you to take your keys), door locks, alarm systems, and disabling devices may prevent vehicle theft.

Information and Communication Systems

As you drive, you gather information about other roadway users, the roadway itself, and off-road conditions by searching in all directions. You get information about the workings of your own vehicle by checking the instruments, gauges, and lights on the dashboard.

While you gather information, you are letting other roadway users know where you are and what you intend to do.

What Devices Provide Information About Your Vehicle?

Drivers need to know how fast they are going, how far they have gone, and how their vehicle systems are working. The instruments, gauges, and lights on your dashboard can give you this information.

Speedometer and Odometer

The **speedometer** shows, in miles per hour and kilometers per hour, how fast your vehicle is moving.

The **odometer** keeps track of the total number of miles the vehicle has been driven. Some vehicles also have a separate trip odometer, which can be reset to zero at any time.

Fuel Gauge

Your fuel gauge shows how close to full—or empty—your fuel tank is. Your owner's manual tells you how many gallons of fuel your tank holds.

Alternator Gauge or Warning Light

Your vehicle's **alternator** provides electricity to keep the engine running, recharge the battery, and operate such equipment as lights and radio. If the alternator does not produce enough power, the electricity stored in your battery will be drained. The alternator gauge will indicate "discharge" or a red warning light will come on.

When the alternator does not work properly, turn off unnecessary electrical devices and check with a mechanic as soon as possible. If you delay, your battery will die.

◆ *It is time to refuel when the needle on your fuel gauge reaches the red area.*

OBJECTIVES
1. Name at least seven devices that provide information about your vehicle.
2. Name and describe how at least five devices let you communicate with other drivers and pedestrians.

KEY TERMS
speedometer
odometer
alternator
directional signal
emergency flashers

LESSON THREE

Information and Communication Systems

(pages 123–125)

FOCUS

Objectives
• Name at least seven devices that provide information about your vehicle.
• Name and describe how at least five devices let you communicate with other drivers and pedestrians.

Resources
📁 Study Guide, page 27
📁 Car Care Manual

Vocabulary
speedometer
odometer
alternator
directional signal
emergency flashers

Motivator
You're driving along the highway. Suddenly you see a red light begin to glow on your dashboard. It's your temperature warning light. What does this red light mean? What will you do? How will you use your vehicle's information and communication systems? (Students may mention that the engine is overheating. They need to get off the road and communicate to other drivers that they are doing so; come to a stop as far off the road as possible; put on their emergency flashers; identify the problem.)

IT'S A FACT

The greatest mileage recorded for a vehicle was 1.2 million miles. This means the vehicle's odometer returned to 00,000 eleven times. The vehicle, a 1957 Mercedes 180D, was owned by Robert O'Reilley of Olympia, Washington. This feat was recorded in the *Guiness Book of World Records.*

Explain

OBJECTIVE 1: Students should recognize that gauges and warning lights typically indicate serious problems. If you delay responding to such problems it can be dangerous to driver and passengers and damaging to the vehicle.

OBJECTIVE 2: Students should understand that signaling turns and lane changes is more than a courtesy. Communicating intentions to other drivers (and pedestrians) helps minimize risk to all roadway users.

Teaching Model

Tell students the following: You are driving a friend home at night, in the city. To minimize risk, you know it's important to communicate with other roadway users. Model your thinking process as you drive through city streets, then park to let your friend out. (You do the following.

• Put on your lights. Headlights, taillights, and side-marker lights will enable other roadway users to see your vehicle.

• Use your directional signals when turning or changing lanes.

• Tap your brake pedal when possible to let drivers behind you know when you intend to slow down or stop.

• Put on your emergency flashers or parking lights to let other drivers know that you've stopped the vehicle along the road.

• Use your horn when necessary to warn other roadway users.)

Ask

Ask students what rear lights a vehicle is equipped with and what purpose each of these lights serves.

Read

Have students read Lesson 3 to become familiar with the information and communication systems of a vehicle and how these systems help drivers manage risk.

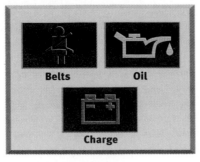

◆ *The safety-belt light turns red when you start the car to remind you to buckle up.*

SAFETY TIPS

A warning light flashing alerts you to a problem, but it does not tell you what is wrong. Take your vehicle to a mechanic as soon as possible. Do not drive any farther than you absolutely must.

Temperature Gauge or Warning Light

The temperature gauge or light lets you know if your engine temperature is too high. Overheating can damage your engine. Get off the road as soon as possible, turn off the engine, and have the problem checked.

Oil-Pressure Gauge or Warning Light

The oil-pressure gauge warns you when the pressure at which oil is being pumped to the engine is low. This means that the engine is not being lubricated properly. To avoid serious engine damage, stop driving immediately and consult a mechanic. Note that the oil-pressure gauge or light does not indicate how much oil is in the engine. You need to check the oil dipstick for that information.

Brake Warning Light

Most vehicles have a brake warning light. When it goes on, you might be low on brake fluid, the fluid is leaking, or the brakes are not working properly. Check with a mechanic immediately.

Other Dashboard Lights

Your parking-brake light reminds you to release the parking brake before moving the vehicle. A daytime running light indicator shows when your daytime running lights are on. A high-beam indicator light shows when your vehicle's high-beam headlights are on, and a safety-belt warning light and buzzer remind you to fasten your safety belt. There is also an air bag light and an antilock brake system (ABS) light.

How Can You Communicate with Other Roadway Users?

Other drivers need to know where you are and what you are planning to do. You cannot talk to them verbally, but your vehicle has a number of devices that you can use to communicate with other roadway users.

Taillights

Like headlights and side-marker lights, taillights help others see your vehicle. Taillights also help communicate your intentions.

In addition to red taillights, the back of your car is equipped with red brake lights, white backup lights, and red or amber turn indicators. All vehicles manufactured since 1986 also have a third centered high-mounted brake light located at the bottom or above the top of the rear window.

Driving Tip

Explain that the trip odometer makes it easy not only to record distance between two places but also to compute miles per gallon. Simply set the trip odometer to zero when filling the gas tank. Then, when next filling up the tank, divide the number of miles shown on the trip odometer by the number of gallons purchased. The quotient will be the miles per gallon traveled between fill-ups.

Brake lights go on when you step on the brake, to warn others that you are slowing or stopping. The backup lights signal that you've shifted into Reverse and intend to back up.

One other light on the back of your vehicle is the license-plate light, which comes on with headlights and parking lights. This light is required by law and aids in identifying vehicles.

Directional (Turn) Signals

Your flashing red or amber **directional**, or turn, **signal**—sometimes called a blinker—shows that you plan to turn or change lanes. To operate the signal, move the turn-indicator arm up for right and down for left.

Normally, the signal lever clicks into position, then clicks off when you straighten the wheel. If the signal doesn't stop flashing, move the lever back manually.

Emergency Flashers (Hazard Lights)

The emergency-flasher switch is usually located on the steering column or dashboard. **Emergency flashers** make all four turn-signal lights flash at the same time. Use your flashers to warn other drivers that your vehicle is stopped on or near the road or that you are moving very slowly.

Parking Lights

In addition to low- and high-beam headlights, your vehicle is equipped with parking lights. Use parking lights (or emergency flashers) to help other drivers see you when your car is stopped along the side of the road. Parking lights are *not* designed to light the roadway when your vehicle is in motion. In some states it is illegal to drive with parking lights on.

Horn

Use your vehicle's horn to alert drivers, pedestrians, or cyclists to your presence or to warn them of danger.

The horn is generally located on the steering wheel. Before driving any vehicle, it is wise to locate and try the horn.

Lesson 3 Review

1. What devices provide information about your vehicle?
2. What devices enable you to communicate with other roadway users?

FYI

Daytime running lights are now standard equipment on many U.S. vehicles. These headlights go on automatically when the driver starts the vehicle. Daytime running lights have been required on Canadian vehicles since 1989, resulting in an 11 percent decrease in two-vehicle, different-direction collisions, according to a recent study.

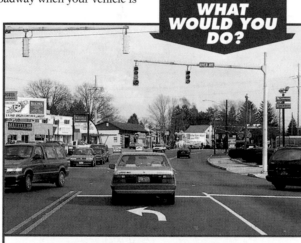

WHAT WOULD YOU DO?

You want to turn left, then pull over to the right side of the road. How will you communicate to others what you plan to do?

ASSESS

Guided Practice

Have students answer the Lesson 3 Review questions. The answers are provided below.

Reteaching

Have students work in small groups to make drawings, charts, or models of a vehicle's information and communication systems. Student's work should include all system components, along with a brief description of each component's function or purpose. Have groups share their drawings, charts, or models with the class as a whole.

Enrichment

Assign the Study Guide for Lesson 3. The Find Out More section encourages students to expand their basic learning of the lesson concepts.

CLOSE

Summarize

Return to the Motivator questions. Discuss what the warning light means and what procedure to follow when this warning light comes on or when a vehicle's temperature gauge indicates a problem. Extend the discussion by asking students to explain how a vehicle's information and communication systems help the driver manage risk. Also discuss the dangers of ignoring a warning light.

DRIVER'S LOG

Have students list the parts of a vehicle's information and communication systems and describe how each helps the driver minimize the risk of personal injury and damage to the vehicle. You may also want to have students draw a model instrument panel in their logs, labeling the various gauges and lights.

WHAT WOULD YOU DO?

Sample answer: The driver should switch on the left directional signal to turn left. After making the turn, the driver should use the right directional signal to indicate the intention to pull over to the right. The driver should also tap the brake pedal.

Lesson 3 Review

Answers

1. The vehicle's information system includes the speedometer and odometer, fuel gauge, alternator gauge or warning light, temperature gauge or warning light, oil-pressure gauge or warning light, brake warning light, and other dashboard lights.
2. You can communicate by using taillights, directional signals, emergency flashers, parking lights, and the vehicle horn.

Checks and Procedures to Use Before Driving

(pages 126–128)

FOCUS

Objectives

- Describe six checks you should make before entering your vehicle.
- Describe five checks you should make after entering your vehicle.

Resources

 Study Guide, page 28

 Traffic charts

 Behind-the-Wheel Checklists 1 and 2

 Car Care Manual

Motivator

Explain to students that many driving problems can be avoided by taking specific safety precautions before driving. Ask students what actions they might take before driving to minimize risk. (Students may mention checking the area surrounding the vehicle, the wheels, and the vehicle body; checking fluid levels and the battery connection; making sure doors are locked; adjusting seat, head restraint, and mirrors; making sure windows are clean and clear; knowing where all controls are located and how they work; removing any objects that block your view; fastening driver and passenger safety belts.)

TEACH

Explain

OBJECTIVE 1: Students should understand that the safety checks

LESSON FOUR

OBJECTIVES
1. Describe six checks you should make before entering your vehicle.
2. Describe five checks you should make after entering your vehicle.

Checks and Procedures to Use Before Driving

If you were a pilot, you wouldn't dream of taking off without thoroughly checking your airplane first. Safety and equipment checks are equally important when you're about to drive a motor vehicle. The best time to find out about a problem or potential problem is *before* your vehicle is moving.

What Should You Check Before Entering Your Vehicle?

You should inspect the vehicle and the area around it before you enter your vehicle. If you need to step into the roadway, check carefully for approaching traffic.

◆ *Check under your car for leaks, objects, and animals every time you plan to drive.*

Surrounding Area

- Look for children playing nearby. Each year about 200 children under the age of six are killed while playing in the family driveway.
- Look for animals that may be hiding under or walking or sleeping near the vehicle.
- Look for objects in the area of the vehicle and on the roadway that may interfere with safe movement or damage the tires.
- Check under the vehicle for fresh stains that could be indications of fluid leaks.

Wheels

- Check for underinflated tires and for tire wear or damage.
- Note which way your front wheels are turned. This is the direction in which your vehicle will go as soon as it begins moving.

Driving Tip

Explain to students that there are also various checks that are important to make *after* driving. For example, check to make sure you've turned off the headlights and locked the doors; check to see that your front wheels are turned toward the curb when you are parking downhill and away from the curb when parking uphill; check to see that you haven't blocked a driveway or parked too close to a fire hydrant.

Car Body

- Check for damaged or missing parts, and make sure that all lights and windows are clean and undamaged.
- In winter, scrape off snow and ice.

Under the Hood

- At least once a week or when you stop for gas, check the engine oil, radiator coolant, battery charge, brakes, transmission, and windshield-washer fluids.
- Check the battery connections. Are the cables tight? Are the terminals free from corrosion?

Getting into the Vehicle

Now you are ready to get into your vehicle. Do it safely.

- Load packages and have passengers enter from the curbside.
- Look carefully for approaching traffic before stepping into the roadway. Have your keys in hand.
- Walk around the front of the vehicle, facing oncoming traffic.
- Wait for a break in traffic before opening the door, and open it only far enough and long enough to allow you to get into the vehicle.

On a warm day, condensation from a vehicle's air-conditioning unit may form a puddle under the vehicle. It is important to be able to distinguish this puddle from those formed by fluid leaks.

◆ Adjust mirrors and seats, fasten your safety belt, and lock the doors before you move into traffic.

What Should You Check After Entering the Vehicle?

Get into the habit of making safety checks and adjustments as soon as you get into the vehicle. In addition to observing the following guidelines, consult your owner's manual for further information.

Inside-the-Vehicle Checks and Procedures

- Close and lock all doors.
- Place the key in the ignition.
- Adjust the seat so that you can clearly see the roadway and comfortably reach the floor pedals and other vehicle controls.

CHAPTER 7   *Getting to Know Your Vehicle*   **127**

IT'S A FACT

Fatal pedestrian-motor vehicle collisions occur most often between 6 P.M. and 10 P.M. Such collisions are more likely to occur on Fridays and Saturdays than on other days of the week. More than two-thirds of pedestrian fatalities occur in urban areas.

described are all checks they can make themselves in very little time. Caution students that objects near the tires may not be as harmless as they appear to be. A paper bag may contain a glass bottle.

OBJECTIVE 2: Stress the idea that anything that limits the driver's vision increases risk to driver, passengers, and other roadway users.

Teaching Model

Display this situation:

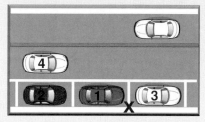

Tell students the following: You (X) intend to do a predriving check of your vehicle, vehicle 1, which is parked at the curb between vehicles 2 and 3. Model the thinking process that you use. (You do the following.

- Check under and near your vehicle.
- Wait for vehicle 4 to pass before stepping into the street.
- Check under the hood. Note: If the vehicle has an inside hood-release lever, you must enter the vehicle first to pull the lever.
- When ready to get in, have your keys in hand and walk around the front of the vehicle, facing approaching traffic.
- Wait until no vehicles are near, then open the driver's side door. Enter the vehicle quickly.)

Ask

Ask students to discuss risks involved in not checking traffic while doing a predriving check. Ask why it's safest to walk around the front of the vehicle rather than around the back.

Read

Have students read Lesson 4 to learn procedures for predriving checking and for entering the vehicle.

ADVICE FROM THE EXPERTS

Stress the idea that predriving adjustments are intended to help the driver operate the vehicle safely and comfortably.

ASSESS

Guided Practice

Have students answer the Lesson 4 Review questions. The answers are provided below.

Reteaching

Have students work together in small groups to prepare a checklist of items to check before driving. Then have groups compare their lists and create a master class list.

Enrichment

Assign the Study Guide for Lesson 4. The Find Out More section encourages students to expand their basic learning of the lesson concepts.

CLOSE

Summarize

Return to the Motivator question, and discuss students' responses in view of what they have learned from this lesson. Help students summarize the lesson content by discussing how predriving checks can help you reduce driving risk. Encourage students to be as specific as possible and to provide examples to support their answers.

DRIVER'S LOG

What problems or potential problems might a driver discover by checking his or her vehicle before driving? Why is it important to identify such problems *before* driving?

ADVICE FROM THE EXPERTS

Charles A. Butler
Director, Safety Services, AAA

How well you manage risk is determined by what you do before you start driving. Make sure all vehicle system devices are working properly, and know how to use and adjust them—especially mirrors, seat, lights, steering wheel, and occupant restraints. Vehicle system devices improve visibility and improve your ability to steer, accelerate, and brake. They also protect you in the event of a crash. Good risk managers always make predriving vehicle systems checks.

- Adjust the head restraint. Have passengers adjust theirs.
- Adjust rearview and left sideview mirrors so that you can use them with just your eyes and do not need to move your head. Adjust the right sideview mirror for the best vision with the least head movement.
- Check the inside of the windows. Then clean, defog, or defrost as necessary.

WHAT WOULD YOU DO?

You have never driven this vehicle before. What checks and procedures will you use before entering and driving it?

- Make sure there are no objects inside the vehicle that will block your view or tumble about as you drive.
- Familiarize yourself with the controls for any devices you may need to use. While moving, minimize the time you take to use any of these devices. Make any adjustments when traffic and roadway conditions do not pose a threat.
- Fasten your safety belt and make sure all passengers have fastened theirs.

Lesson 4 Review

1. What should you check before getting into your vehicle?
2. What should you check once you are inside the vehicle?

WHAT WOULD YOU DO?

Refer to Lesson 4 Review answers 1 and 2 and Behind-the-Wheel Checklists 1 and 2 for possible responses.

Lesson 4 Review

Answers

1. Check the surrounding area for children, animals, objects, or fluid leaks; check the tires; inspect the body of the vehicle, and clean the lights and windows; at least once a week, check the fluid levels.
2. Once inside the vehicle, lock the doors; adjust seat, head restraint, and mirrors; clean the windows; reposition objects that may block your view; familiarize yourself with controls; fasten safety belt.

Making a Circle Graph

A poll is a way of finding out what a group of people think about a certain topic. You've probably seen or heard of polls showing what people think about political events, celebrities, and economic situations.

Conduct a poll to find out what members of your class think are their chances of being involved in a collision.

Try It Yourself

Follow these steps.

1. Count the number of people in your class. This number represents 100 percent of the class.
2. Ask each person this question: *What do you think the chances are of your being in a collision?* Then ask each person to choose one of the following as a response:
   a. 1 in 5, **b.** 1 in 10, **c.** 1 in 50, **d.** 1 in 100, **e.** 1 in 500, **f.** 1 in 1,000, **g.** don't know

3. Tally the number of responses to each choice.
4. Divide the number of responses to a choice by the total number of people in the class to get the percentage of people who responded to that choice. For example, if four people said "1 in 10" and there are 27 people in the class, the fraction would be 4/27, or about 15 percent.
5. Make a circle graph to show the results. A full circle represents the whole class, or 100 percent. First divide the circle into fourths. Each fourth represents 25 percent. Then mark segments of the circle to show the approximate percentage of people who responded to each choice.
6. Your finished graph might look something like the one below.
   The chances of being in a traffic collision in any given year are actually 1 in 5. In a poll of 1,506 people, only 1 person out of 10 chose that rate. How does your class compare?

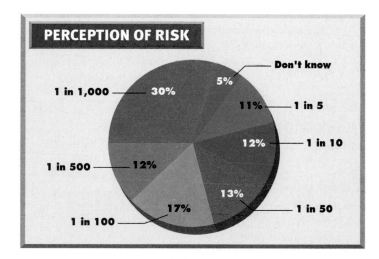

PERCEPTION OF RISK

- Don't know 5%
- 1 in 5 — 11%
- 1 in 10 — 12%
- 1 in 50 — 13%
- 1 in 100 — 17%
- 1 in 500 — 12%
- 1 in 1,000 — 30%

BUILDING SKILLS: SOCIAL STUDIES

Objective

Demonstrate the ability to conduct a poll and make a circle graph to show the results.

Teaching the Skill

- Be sure students understand the idea that the total number of people in their class represents 100 percent of the people polled and corresponds to the whole circle.
- Have students prepare a tally sheet with the question, possible responses, and space for marking the number of people who choose each answer.
- You may want to have students use calculators to help them calculate the percentages.

ANSWER TO
Try It Yourself Questions

Check students' graphs, and guide them in comparing their work to the graph shown on page 129 of the textbook. Point out to them that the proportions on their graphs may be different from the textbook examples.

CHAPTER 7 REVIEW

CHAPTER SUMMARY

Key Points

Have students read the Key Points to review the major concepts of the chapter.

PROJECTS

Cooperative Learning:

Students will benefit by working with a partner on one or both projects. When the assignment is completed, the whole class will profit by sharing and comparing results.

KEY POINTS

Lesson One

1. Devices that help make you comfortable in a vehicle include seat-position controls, adjustable steering wheel, heater, air conditioner, and air vents.
2. Devices that enable you to control a vehicle include the ignition switch, the gear-selector lever or gearshift, the steering wheel, cruise control, the accelerator, the brake pedal, and the parking brake.

Lesson Two

1. Devices that aid visibility include lights, windshield wipers and washer, sun visors, defroster, and rearview and sideview mirrors.
2. Car features that protect you and your passengers from injury include safety belts, air bags, head restraints, door locks, and various structural features such as safety-glass windows, impact-resistant bumpers, and protective padding on the dashboard.
3. Devices such as locks, alarms, and the audible key reminder can help prevent the theft of a vehicle.

Lesson Three

1. The speedometer, odometer, fuel gauge, alternator gauge, temperature gauge, oil-pressure gauge, brake warning lights, and various dashboard lights provide information about your vehicle.
2. Taillights, directional signals, emergency flashers, parking lights, and horn let you communicate with others.

Lesson Four

1. Before entering your vehicle, you should check the surrounding area for children, animals, objects, or fluid leaks; check the condition and direction of the tires; inspect the body of the vehicle for damage and clean the lights and windows; and regularly check the fluid levels and battery connections.
2. After entering the vehicle, lock the doors; adjust the seat, head restraint, and mirrors; clear the windows; reposition any objects inside the car that may block your view or tumble about; familiarize yourself with all controls; fasten your safety belt; and make sure passengers have fastened theirs.

PROJECTS

1. Obtain a vehicle owner's manual and read through the contents. Find the sections that deal with the various kinds of systems you've read about in this chapter. What information can you obtain from an owner's manual that you won't find in a textbook?
2. Research and report on the comparative safety of different makes and models of motor vehicles. Try to find out specific reasons why some vehicles are safer than others. Your librarian can help you identify sources of information.

You may also want to discuss this subject with insurance agents, mechanics, and other knowledgeable people.

*inter*NET CONNECTION

For the latest news on air bag safety, visit Glencoe's Web site.
drivered.glencoe.com

*inter*NET CONNECTION

Visit Glencoe's Driver Education Web site for student activities that relate to this chapter.
drivered.glencoe.com

CHAPTER TEST

Write the letter of the answer that best completes each sentence.

1. Three features that improve visibility are
   a. sun visors, bucket seats, and headlights.
   b. defroster, windshield wipers, and side-view mirrors.
   c. sunroof, air bags, and brake lights.

2. Head restraints should make contact with
   a. the base of your skull.
   b. the top of your head.
   c. the back of your head.

3. Cruise control
   a. increases your control of a vehicle.
   b. may lead you to be less alert.
   c. is best used in heavy inner-city traffic.

4. An odometer indicates
   a. the distance a vehicle has traveled.
   b. the speed at which a vehicle is traveling.
   c. the amount of current in your battery.

5. Three devices that control the speed and direction of your vehicle are the
   a. gearshift, brake pedal, and steering wheel.
   b. engine, battery, and accelerator.
   c. tires, air conditioner, and ignition switch.

6. Ice has formed on your windshield. You should
   a. pull the sun visor into the "up" position.
   b. turn on the air conditioner.
   c. turn on the defroster.

7. Each year approximately 200 children under the age of six are killed while playing
   a. on highways.
   b. in driveways.
   c. on sidewalks.

8. Taillights, emergency flashers, and parking lights
   a. are parts of a vehicle's communications system.
   b. cannot be activated with the ignition in the "off" position.
   c. are parts of a vehicle's information system.

9. Using a safety belt will
   a. protect you from getting whiplash.
   b. increase your chances of surviving a collision.
   c. decrease your chances of surviving a collision.

10. Directional signals
    a. are controlled by the turn-indicator arm.
    b. are controlled by a button on the dashboard.
    c. become activated whenever you turn the steering wheel.

Write the word or phrase that best completes each sentence.

safety check	blind spots	air bags
antitheft devices	automatic	manual

11. You should look over your shoulder when turning to detect anything in your_____.

12. Vehicles that have a(n) _____ transmission require you to use a clutch pedal.

13. _____ are considered passive safety devices because they operate automatically.

14. A(n) _____ enables you to find out about a problem before your vehicle is moving.

15. Alarm systems and audible key reminders are examples of _____.

DRIVER'S LOG

In this chapter, you have learned about the different systems of your vehicle and checks you should make before and after entering your vehicle. When you become a driver, what will you do to be sure that you do not forget to make these checks—even if you feel you're in too much of a hurry to take the time? Write a paragraph telling what you will do.

CHAPTER TEST

Assign the Chapter Test to all students.

Answers

1. b
2. c
3. b
4. a
5. a
6. c
7. b
8. a
9. b
10. a
11. blind spots
12. manual
13. Air bags
14. safety check
15. antitheft devices

DRIVER'S LOG

Students' responses will reflect their personal viewpoints. However, their answers should provide an assessment of their understanding of the reasons that systems checks are vital to safe driving.

Evaluate

- Test A, pages 13–14 or Test B, pages 13–14
- Testmaker software

RETURN TO THE BIG IDEA

In light of what students have learned in this chapter, discuss the idea that proper use of a vehicle's various systems helps minimize driving risk.

CHAPTER 8 — Starting, Steering, Stopping Overview

THEME DEVELOPMENT Whether driving a vehicle equipped with an automatic or a manual transmission, drivers must master such basic vehicle control procedures as starting the vehicle, putting the vehicle in motion, and stopping the vehicle. Drivers must also be able to steer a vehicle straight ahead, to the rear, and through turns. To maneuver a vehicle safely, drivers must understand how acceleration and deceleration are related to speed.

CHAPTER FEATURES	TCR COMPONENTS
	Study Guide, p. 29
	Transparencies 17 and 18
	Lesson Plan, p. 17
	Behind-the-Wheel Checklists 3 and 4

TIPS FOR NEW DRIVERS

Learning to move a vehicle with manual shift forward after stopping on an uphill grade.

Study Guide, p. 30
Transparencies 19–21
Lesson Plan, p. 17
Behind-the-Wheel Checklist 4
Information Master 22

CONNECTIONS
Math

Computing the average speed at which a vehicle has been traveling.

Study Guide, p. 31
Lesson Plan, p. 18

TIPS FOR NEW DRIVERS

Accelerating.

ADVICE FROM THE EXPERTS

The importance of maintaining adequate space around one's vehicle.

Study Guide, p. 32
Lesson Plan, p. 18
Behind-the-Wheel Checklists 5–7

BUILDING SKILLS: READING MAPS

Understanding Roadway Classifications

PROJECTS

1. Elicit driving tips from an experienced driver.
2. Explain the differences between hand-over-hand and push-pull-feed steering methods.

Test A, pp. 15–16
Test B, pp. 15–16

OTHER PROGRAM RESOURCES

Testmaker software
Traffic charts

ADDITIONAL RESOURCES

Don't Let Up!, Video 377, AAA Foundation
Starting Right, film, Doron Precision Systems
Teaching Your Teens to Drive: Lessons 1 and 2, video or CD-ROM, AAA, 1998

NAME _____ DATE _____

CHAPTER 8 | Starting, Steering, Stopping

TEST A

Read each statement below. If it is true, place a T in the space to the left of the statement. If the statement is false, place an F next to it.

__T__ 1. If your car is equipped with an automatic transmission, you should always start it in Park.

__T__ 2. If you are stopped at a light going up a hill, one way to move forward again is to hold your place with the parking brake and then accelerate a little as you release the parking brake.

__F__ 3. You should use the heel of your foot on the brake to stop the car whenever possible.

__T__ 4. When coming to a stop, it is a good practice to tap your brakes lightly to warn drivers behind you that you are about to stop.

__F__ 5. If it is done correctly, threshold braking will often result in your wheels locking.

__T__ 6. One difference between a manual and an automatic transmission is that an automatic transmission will shift the forward gears for you.

__F__ 7. When the clutch pedal is all the way down to the floor, the transmission and engine are engaged.

__T__ 8. Driving in high-heeled shoes may give you less control of the accelerator than flat-heeled shoes.

__T__ 9. The best way to get a feel for the vehicle's friction point is to practice in Reverse gear.

Select the phrase that best completes each sentence below. Write the letter of the answer you have chosen to the left of each statement.

__b__ 10. When backing your vehicle,
a. you should use your rearview mirror.
b. you look over your shoulder to see where you are going.
c. your vehicle's front swings in the same direction in which the steering wheel is turning.
d. you should do all of the above.

__d__ 11. You set a vehicle's automatic choke by
a. pressing the brake pedal once to the floor and then releasing it.
b. pressing the clutch pedal once to the floor and then releasing it.
c. having a mechanic give your vehicle a tune-up.
d. doing none of the above.

__a__ 12. After starting your engine, you should
a. check that the oil pressure system is working.
b. activate your turn signal.
c. pull into traffic.
d. check your oil dipstick.

NAME _____ DATE _____

__d__ 13. The amount of foot pressure required to stop a vehicle depends on
a. the size and weight of the vehicle.
b. the road surface.
c. the type of brakes on the vehicle.
d. all of the above.

__a__ 14. After coming to a red light while driving a vehicle with an automatic transmission, you
a. leave the vehicle in Drive.
b. shut the engine down.
c. put the car's transmission in Reverse.
d. put the car's transmission in Park.

__d__ 15. Locking your wheels in an emergency braking situation
a. decreases braking effectiveness.
b. can make you go into a skid.
c. increases your stopping distance.
d. can do all of the above.

__c__ 16. The effect of threshold braking is to
a. cause skids.
b. lock wheels.
c. prevent locking of wheels.
d. increase stopping distance.

__b__ 17. Vehicles with manual-shift transmissions
a. usually cost more than automatics.
b. can reduce fuel consumption if driven properly.
c. do not have clutches.
d. are easier to drive than vehicles with automatic transmissions.

__b__ 18. The friction point is
a. the place where the wheels meet the pavement.
b. the point where, as you let up on the clutch pedal, the transmission and engine engage.
c. the point where, as you push down on the brake, the vehicle begins to slow down.
d. the place where the brake shoes rub against the wheel drum.

19. What steps should you follow to put in motion a vehicle already running? The vehicle has an automatic transmission.

Press down on the brake pedal. Shift the gear selector to Drive or Reverse. Release the parking brake,

turn on the directional signal, and check in the mirrors for traffic. Look over your shoulder for traffic in

blind spots, remove your foot from the brake, and apply gradual pressure on the accelerator.

_____

_____

_____

_____

_____

NAME _____ DATE _____

CHAPTER 8 | Starting, Steering, Stopping

TEST B

Read each statement below. If it is true, place a T in the space to the left of the statement. If the statement is false, place an F next to it.

__T__ 1. "Riding the clutch" is when you hold your vehicle in place on a hill by using the accelerator and the clutch instead of a brake.

__T__ 2. You should start off in Low gear if the surface is icy or snowy.

__F__ 3. When downshifting, you can never skip a gear and move, for example, from Fourth gear to Second.

__T__ 4. When driving at 45 mph, your acceleration rate to 55 mph will be slower than your acceleration rate from 25 to 35 mph.

__F__ 5. When accelerating, a general rule is that you should accelerate rapidly in order to get to your desired speed as soon as possible.

__T__ 6. To keep your vehicle moving at a steady, legal speed, you should keep your eye on the road, making frequent glances at the speedometer.

__T__ 7. It often takes less time and space to steer away from an object than to brake to avoid it.

__T__ 8. When you are steering through a turn, your vehicle's rear wheels do not follow the same path as the front wheels.

__F__ 9. In push-pull-feed steering, only one hand at a time is on the steering wheel in a turn.

Select the phrase that best completes each sentence below. Write the letter of the answer you have chosen to the left of each statement.

__b__ 10. If you are in a vehicle with a manual transmission and it jerks forward while moving from a stop,
a. you need a tune-up.
b. you may have released the clutch too abruptly.
c. you could have pressed too hard on the clutch pedal.
d. both b and c apply.

__d__ 11. Downshifting can have the effect of making your vehicle
a. gain power.
b. steer effectively.
c. slow down.
d. do all of the above.

__b__ 12. When you want to downshift from Second gear to First,
a. don't.
b. you should be going very slowly, almost stopped.
c. your speed should be no more than 28 mph.
d. your speed should be no more than 22 mph.

NAME _____ DATE _____

__d__ 13. A vehicle's acceleration is determined partly by
a. the power of the engine.
b. the transmission and the differential gear ratios.
c. the weight of engine oil.
d. both a and b.

__a__ 14. In accelerating, the following general rule applies:
a. Accelerate gradually and save fuel.
b. Always accelerate to get to the speed limit as rapidly as possible.
c. Keep your heel on the accelerator.
d. Accelerate with your left foot on the brake pedal.

__b__ 15. Steering may often be the only way to avoid a crash at higher speeds because
a. braking can never help you avoid an object.
b. it may be impossible to stop your vehicle in time.
c. you need less time to stop the vehicle.
d. both a and b apply.

__a__ 16. You set the automatic choke when
a. starting a vehicle.
b. stopping a vehicle.
c. slowing a vehicle on a downhill grade.
d. slowing a vehicle on an uphill grade.

__d__ 17. The effect of threshold braking is to
a. cause skids.
b. lock wheels.
c. do both a and b.
d. prevent locking of wheels.

__b__ 18. The job of the clutch is to
a. shift gears.
b. break the connection between the transmission and the engine.
c. break the connection between the power train and the carburetor.
d. help stabilize the vehicle in turns.

19. What are the correct steps for putting a vehicle with an automatic transmission in motion? Assume that the vehicle has already been started.

Press down on the brake pedal. Shift gear selector to Drive or Reverse. Release parking brake, turn on

directional signal, and check in the mirrors for traffic. Look over shoulder for traffic in blind spots,

remove foot from brake, and apply gradual pressure on the accelerator.

_____

_____

_____

_____

_____

NAME _____ DATE _____

CHAPTER 8 Starting, Steering, Stopping

STUDY GUIDE FOR CHAPTER 8   LESSON 1

Automatic Transmissions

A. The following sentences are procedures for starting a car with an automatic transmission. However, they are in the wrong order. Write the number that identifies the correct order of each step in the space to the left.

- _5_ **a.** Turn the ignition key to the Start position. Release as soon as the engine starts.
- _3_ **b.** If you do not have an automatic fuel-injection system, set the automatic choke by pressing the accelerator pedal once to the floor and releasing it.
- _1_ **c.** Make sure that the gear selector lever is in Park.
- _4_ **d.** Press the accelerator lightly with your foot and hold it.
- _6_ **e.** As the engine idles, check your gauges to be sure that the oil-pressure system and other systems are working.
- _2_ **f.** Make sure that the parking brake is set.

B. For each sentence below, circle T if the statement is true and F if it is false. Correct each false statement in the space below.

1. For best control of both the accelerator and brake pedals, rest the heel of your foot on the floor.   (T)   F

2. To keep from rolling back after stopping on an uphill grade, use your right foot to press on the brake pedal while gently accelerating with your left foot.   T   (F)
   Press on the brake with your left foot and the accelerator with your right foot.

3. Threshold braking increases braking efficiency by locking the car's wheels in an emergency braking situation.   T   (F)
   Threshold braking increases braking efficiency by preventing your wheels from locking.

4. The amount of braking pressure required to stop a vehicle depends in part upon the surface of the road.   (T)   F

C. FIND OUT MORE. The chapter suggests purchasing a vehicle with antilock brakes. Call up a new vehicle dealer and ask if antilock brakes are an option with new vehicles; if so, how much do they cost?
   Review student's work.

NAME _____ DATE _____

STUDY GUIDE FOR CHAPTER 8   LESSON 2

Manual Transmissions

A. Correct each of the following statements. You do not have to repeat the sentence exactly.

1. When you make a downshift in an emergency, the first thing to do after you have pressed on the brake is to shift to Second gear.
   When you downshift in an emergency, the first thing to do after you have pressed on the brake
   is to press the clutch pedal to the floor.

2. The difference between driving an automatic vehicle and one with a manual transmission is that a manual shift requires the use of the clutch pedal to make the brakes work.
   The difference between driving an automatic vehicle and one with a manual shift is that a
   manual shift requires you to shift the gears yourself and to use a clutch pedal.

3. The friction point is the point at which the clutch and other parts of the engine separate.
   The friction point is the point at which the engine and transmission engage.

4. You hold a manual transmission vehicle in place on a hill by pressing on the gas pedal slightly while keeping the clutch near the friction point.
   You hold a vehicle in place on a hill by using the brakes.

5. The easiest way to get a feel for where the friction point is to practice using Fourth or Fifth gear.
   The easiest way to get a feel for the friction point is to practice using Reverse gear.

6. Glance at your feet from time to time as you are driving to be sure that they are on the correct pedals.
   If you are driving, your attention should be focused on the road, not on your feet.

B. FIND OUT MORE. Ask at least ten people you know who drive whether they prefer an automatic or a manual transmission. What reasons do they give for their choices?
   Review student's work.

NAME _____ DATE _____

STUDY GUIDE FOR CHAPTER 8   LESSON 3

Acceleration, Deceleration, and Speed

A. Complete the sentences below by filling in the blanks with the correct words.

1. The rate of acceleration is the __time__ it takes to accelerate from one speed to another.
2. You check your speed by giving quick glances at the __speedometer__.
3. As __speed__ varies, there is a difference in the car's vibration and level of sound.

B. Complete the following statements by circling the correct words in the parentheses.

1. (Gradual/Sudden) acceleration is recommended in most cases.
2. As the speed of a vehicle increases, the rate of acceleration is (higher/lower).
3. You need (more/less) time to pass another vehicle when traveling at 50 mph than at 30 mph.
4. A heavy truck needs (more/less) time and distance to decelerate than cars do.

C. For each sentence below, circle T if the statement is true and F if it is false. Correct each false statement in the space below.

1. One of the factors that affect a car's acceleration rate is the road surface.   (T)   F

2. Accelerating quickly saves fuel.   T   (F)
   Accelerating gradually saves fuel.

3. For best control while accelerating, you should press gently on the accelerator with the heel of your foot.   T   (F)
   For best control while accelerating, press gently on the accelerator with your toes.

4. It is safe to look at the speedometer while driving as long as you do it by taking quick glances.   (T)   F

D. FIND OUT MORE. The chapter's "Connections: Math" tells you how to figure out miles per hour on trips. Read and solve the following problem.

You and your family went on a long vacation. Your first leg of the trip took 6 hours and you traveled 330 miles. The next day, you went 522 miles and you drove for 11 hours. On the last day, you drove 360 miles in 8 hours. What was your average speed in miles per hour for the trip?
   1212 miles traveled divided by 25 hours of driving = 48.5 mph.

NAME _____ DATE _____

STUDY GUIDE FOR CHAPTER 8   LESSON 4

Learning How to Steer the Vehicle

A. For each sentence below, circle T if the statement is true and F if it is false. Correct each false statement in the space below.

1. It often takes more time and energy to brake to avoid hitting an object than to steer away from it.   (T)   F
   At speeds over 30 mph, the only way to avoid a collision may be to steer away from it.

2. At speeds over 25 or 30 mph, the only way to avoid a collision may be to step on the brakes.   T   (F)

3. Keeping your vehicle moving on the path of travel you have chosen is called tracking.   (T)   F

4. To track smoothly, you need to focus your attention directly in front of the vehicle you are driving.   T   (F)
   To track smoothly, direct your attention to points well ahead of your intended path.

5. Steering through a turn requires more steering wheel movement than does lane positioning.   (T)   F

6. In push-pull-feed steering, you have to cross your hands when turning the steering wheel.   T   (F)
   In push-pull-feed steering, your hands do not cross.

7. Backing while looking into the rearview mirror is not a good idea.   (T)   F

8. When backing, the rear of your vehicle moves in the opposite direction to the steering wheel.   T   (F)
   The rear of your vehicle moves in the same direction as the steering wheel.

B. FIND OUT MORE. Talk with somebody who drives frequently or with a professional driver such as a trucker, police officer, or bus driver. Ask the person what procedures she or he uses when backing up. What differences are there between the person's procedures and the one described in the chapter?
   Review student's work.

Starting, Steering, Stopping

CHAPTER OVERVIEW

LESSON ONE

Basic procedures for starting, moving, and stopping a vehicle equipped with an automatic transmission are explained.

LESSON TWO

Basic procedures for starting, moving, and stopping a vehicle that has a manual transmission are explained.

LESSON THREE

Acceleration and deceleration are defined, and their relation to speed is explored within the context of risk management.

LESSON FOUR

Basic procedures for steering straight ahead, to the rear, and through turns are described.

VOCABULARY

acceleration
antilock brake system (ABS)
clutch
deceleration
downshift
friction point
hand-over-hand steering
idle
manual shift
push-pull-feed steering
rate of acceleration
rate of deceleration
threshold braking
tracking
transmission

132

CONCEPT OF THE DRIVING TASK

Explain that driving skills, just like any other skills, require a combination of learning and practice. New as well as experienced drivers must continue to work to improve their ability to drive safely under various road and weather conditions.

CHAPTER 8

Starting, Steering, Stopping

Basic driving procedures are second nature to good drivers. It is important that you learn these procedures so that you can manage them safely and smoothly. Mastering the basics is crucial to the driving task.

LESSON ONE
Basic Operating Procedures:
Automatic Transmission

LESSON TWO
Basic Operating Procedures:
Manual Transmission

LESSON THREE
Acceleration, Deceleration, and Speed

LESSON FOUR
Learning How to Steer the Vehicle

INTRODUCING THE CHAPTER

What's on the Road Ahead?

Have students read the lesson titles and objectives. Briefly discuss the topic of each lesson. Tell students that in this chapter they will be introduced to basic procedures for operating a vehicle.

Background: The Automatic Transmission

Vehicle manufacturers experimented with automatic transmissions in the early 1900s. Not until the late 1930s, however, were fully automatic transmissions built into regular production-model vehicles. Interestingly, one early form of automatic transmission found in some vehicles as late as the 1960s required the driver to push buttons to shift gears.

Relating to Prior Knowledge

Have students discuss what they know about automatic versus manual transmissions and why drivers might choose to have one type rather than the other.

The Big Idea

Discuss students' reactions to the Big Idea statement. Suggest that they keep this idea in mind as they read Chapter 8.

PRESENTING THE BIG IDEA ─────

Driving is a complicated process. To master the necessary skills, drivers must learn and practice basic procedures and maneuvers—such as starting a vehicle, steering, and braking—until they become second nature. Once these procedures and maneuvers are mastered, drivers can then focus on the challenges—and risks—of interacting with other roadway users.

Basic Operating Procedures: Automatic Transmission

(pages 134–137)

FOCUS

Objectives

- Describe how to start a vehicle with an automatic transmission and how to put the vehicle in motion.
- Describe how to slow and stop a vehicle with an automatic transmission.

Resources

 Study Guide, page 29

 Transparencies 17 and 18

Behind-the-Wheel Checklists 3 and 4

Vocabulary

transmission
idle
threshold braking
antilock brake system (ABS)

Motivator

Write the words *Drive, Reverse,* and *Park* on the chalkboard. Ask students under what circumstances they would shift the gear selector lever of an automatic transmission into these gears. (Most students will probably recall the basic purpose of these gears from Chapter 7. Drive is the forward gear; Reverse is used to back the vehicle; Park is the gear the vehicle should be in when one starts the engine.)

LESSON ONE

OBJECTIVES

1. Describe how to start a vehicle with an automatic transmission and how to put the vehicle in motion.
2. Describe how to slow and stop a vehicle with an automatic transmission.

KEY TERMS

transmission
idle
threshold braking
antilock brake system (ABS)

◆ When you follow the steps for starting your car, warning lights come on briefly.

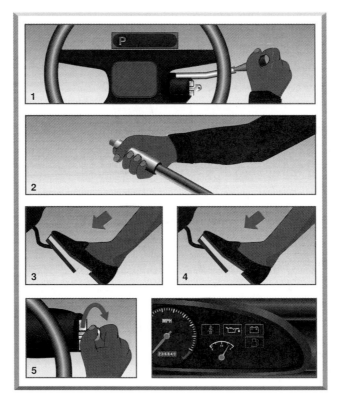

Basic Operating Procedures: Automatic Transmission

In Chapter 1, you learned a basic principle of responsible driving: To reduce risk, you need to manage visibility, time, and space. Your ability to put this principle into practice depends on how well you can control your vehicle. You control a vehicle through a set of gears called a **transmission.** The transmission enables you to move your vehicle forward or backward. The gear you select determines the direction.

Whether you drive a vehicle with an automatic transmission or one with a manual transmission, the key to becoming a skilled driver is the same: *practice.*

How Do You Start and Move a Vehicle with an Automatic Transmission?

It is important to start your vehicle's engine properly to avoid damaging the starter system or wasting fuel.

To start the engine of a vehicle with an automatic transmission, follow the steps below, one at a time. Practice doing these steps until they become habit.

1. Make sure the gear selector lever is in Park. If the selector lever is in Neutral, the car may roll if the parking brake has not been set.
2. Check that the parking brake is set.

   Note: If your car has an electronic fuel-injection (EFI) system or if the engine is warm from driving or very

---

IT'S A FACT

A driver's ability to operate a vehicle safely and responsibly is the single most important factor in minimizing driving risk. However, various other risk-related factors also come into play. For example, research shows that people traveling in small vehicles are injured more often and more severely in collisions than those riding in larger vehicles.

cold from the weather, Steps 3 and 4 may vary or may not be required at all. Check your vehicle's owner's manual for details.

3. Set the automatic choke by pressing the accelerator (gas pedal) once to the floor and releasing it.
4. Press the accelerator lightly with your right foot and hold it.
5. Turn the ignition key to the Start position. Release the key *as soon as* the engine starts.
6. As the engine **idles** (runs with no pressure on the accelerator), check the gauges and warning lights to be sure that the oil-pressure system and other systems are working properly.

Putting the Vehicle in Motion

Once your engine is running and you've checked the gauges, you're ready to put the vehicle in motion. Follow these steps.

1. Press down firmly on the brake pedal. Follow the advice of your driving instructor about which foot to use when braking.
2. Use your right hand to shift the gear selector lever to Drive or Reverse, depending on which way you intend to move.
3. Release the parking brake.
4. Check for traffic in your rearview and sideview mirrors. Be prepared to accelerate into the desired lane once the roadway is clear.
5. Turn on your directional signal to indicate the direction in which you want to move.
6. Look over your shoulder to check blind spots.
7. Remove your foot from the brake, and gradually apply pressure to the accelerator.

Working the accelerator properly takes practice if you use your right foot for both accelerating and braking. For best control of both the accelerator and brake pedals, rest the heel of your right foot on the floor in a position that lets you keep it there while

◆ *To put a car in motion, accelerate gently to avoid "jackrabbit" starts.*

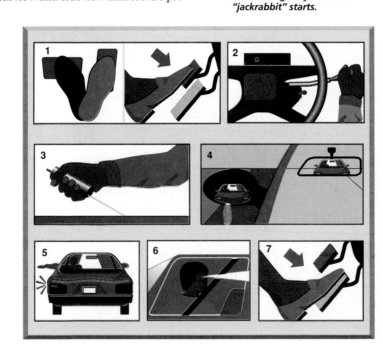

Explain

OBJECTIVE 1: Some students may feel overwhelmed at first by the many procedural details involved in starting and moving a vehicle. Reassure students that the best way to fight an "overload" feeling is to learn the basic procedures for operating a vehicle and then practice these procedures over and over until they become second nature.

OBJECTIVE 2: Stress that, through experience, students will get a feel for braking that they can't get simply from reading. Point out, too, that the brakes of different vehicles require varying amounts of foot pressure.

Teaching Model

Describe the following situation: You're seated behind the wheel of your vehicle (automatic), which is parked at the curb. You're ready to start the engine and drive away. Model the thinking process that you go through to start and move the vehicle. (You do the following.

• Make sure the gear selector is in Park and the parking brake is set.
• Set the choke by pressing the accelerator to the floor once. Then press the accelerator again and turn the ignition key. Note: If your vehicle is equipped with an electronic fuel-injection (EFI) system, the owner's manual may specify different starting procedures. Pressing the accelerator to the floor is not required.
• Step on the brake, and shift to Drive. Release the parking brake, turn on the directional signal, and check traffic. Remove your foot from the brake, and accelerate gradually.)

Ask

Have students discuss what steps they can take to ensure safety when starting and moving a vehicle.

Read

Have students read Lesson 1 to learn the procedures for safely starting, moving, and stopping a vehicle equipped with an automatic transmission.

ASSESS

Guided Practice

Have students answer the Lesson 1 Review questions. The answers are provided below.

Reteaching

Have students work together in small groups to create posters showing the step-by-step procedures for starting a vehicle with an automatic transmission, for putting the vehicle in motion, and for stopping it.

Enrichment

Assign the Study Guide for Lesson 1. The Find Out More section encourages students to expand their basic learning of the lesson concepts.

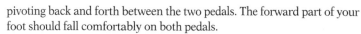

Energy Tips

Allowing your engine to run unnecessarily while your vehicle is stopped or parked wastes fuel and pollutes the air. In some cities, doing so is also against the law.

◆ *Identify in advance the need to stop by using the SIPDE process.*

pivoting back and forth between the two pedals. The forward part of your foot should fall comfortably on both pedals.

Moving forward after stopping on an uphill grade requires extra practice. To keep from rolling back, use your left foot to press the brake pedal while gently accelerating with your right foot. As soon as the vehicle starts to pull forward, take your left foot off the brake. (An alternative is to hold the vehicle in place by setting the parking brake, then releasing the brake as you accelerate.)

How Do You Slow and Stop a Vehicle with Automatic Transmission?

You will often have to slow down and stop your vehicle under both planned and unexpected circumstances. Red lights, stop signs, pedestrians running across streets, vehicles cutting in front of you—these and countless other situations will require you to apply your brakes.

Braking

For smooth braking, you need to develop a sense of timing and get a feel for applying the right amount of pressure on the brake pedal. Your goal is to stop in time, neither overshooting nor undershooting your desired stopping point. Moreover, whenever possible, you want to stop your vehicle gradually, not abruptly.

The amount of foot pressure required to brake to a stop depends on the size and weight of the vehicle, its type of brakes, your maneuvering space, and the road surface. As you practice driving and become more experienced, you'll become increasingly skilled at judging the distance needed to bring your vehicle to a smooth stop.

For effective control of brake pressure, position the heel of your foot between and in front of the accelerator and brake pedal. In this way, you'll be able to apply pressure with your toes, and you can easily increase or decrease pressure as needed. (See illustration on page 135.)

Driving Tip

Explain that new drivers often tend to step down too hard on the brake pedal, causing the vehicle to stop abruptly. Such braking also causes brakes and tires to wear out. Tell students that their ability to brake gradually and smoothly will improve with practice. Large parking lots, when not in use, provide a good place to practice brake control.

Follow these steps when preparing to brake to a stop.

1. Check your mirrors for any vehicles that may be following. Lightly tap the brake pedal: your flashing brake lights will warn following drivers that you intend to stop.
2. Apply smooth, steady, firm pressure to the brake pedal, easing up slightly as you come to a halt.
3. Leave the transmission in Drive if you plan to move ahead within a minute or so, as when you're stopped for a red light. If you'll be stopped longer, follow the parking procedures described in Chapter 10, and turn off your engine.

Emergency Braking

The procedures for stopping under emergency conditions differ slightly. If a driver or pedestrian suddenly enters your path of travel, you may need to stop the vehicle as quickly as possible. However, you don't want to slam on the brakes so hard that the wheels lock (stop turning). Locked wheels can increase your stopping distance and can also cause you to lose steering control and go into a skid.

To prevent the wheels from locking, press, or "squeeze," the brake pedal firmly to a point just *before* the wheels lock, and hold it there. This is called **threshold braking.** If the wheels start to skid, reduce pressure very slightly, then add pressure again as needed. Release pressure as the vehicle comes to a stop. For additional guidelines on braking and skid control, see Chapter 14.

When purchasing a vehicle, consider buying one that has antilock brakes. An **antilock brake system (ABS)** is made to keep the wheels from locking when the driver brakes abruptly.

Lesson 1 Review

1. What steps would you follow to start and move a vehicle with an automatic transmission?
2. How would you use your brakes to slow and stop a vehicle with an automatic transmission? How would you stop in an emergency?

WHAT WOULD YOU DO?

How can you enter the flow of traffic safely and smoothly?

CLOSE

Summarize

Return to the Motivator question. Discuss with students how this lesson has increased their understanding of the use of gears in a vehicle equipped with an automatic transmission.

DRIVER'S LOG

Have students begin a section on basic vehicle control procedures in their log. Direct them to divide their section into two parts: one for automatic transmission and one for manual transmission. Have students list the procedures for starting, moving, and stopping a vehicle with an automatic transmission.

WHAT WOULD YOU DO?

Sample answer: Signal, check traffic, watch for pedestrians, and proceed with care when it is safe to do so.

Lesson 1 Review

Answers

1. To start, make sure gear selector is in Park and parking brake is set; set choke and press accelerator if required (not required if vehicle has electronic fuel injection); turn key to Start. To move, step on brake; shift into gear; release parking brake; check traffic signal, remove foot from brake, and accelerate.
2. Check mirrors, and apply smooth, steady, firm pressure. In an emergency, use the technique of threshold braking.

Basic Operating Procedure: Manual Transmission

(pages 138–142)

FOCUS

Objectives

• Explain how manual and automatic transmissions differ.
• Describe how to start and move a vehicle with a manual transmission.
• Explain how to use each forward gear.

Resources

 Study Guide, page 30

 Transparencies 19–21

 Behind-the-Wheel Checklist 4

Information Master 22

Vocabulary

manual shift
clutch
friction point
downshift

Motivator

Ask students in what ways they think operating a vehicle with a manual transmission differs from operating a vehicle with an automatic transmission. Most students will probably recall the basic differences between automatic and manual transmissions from Chapter 7. Students may mention that an automatic transmission will shift forward gears for the driver. There are usually four or five forward gears. When operating a manual transmission, however, the driver has to change gears by

OBJECTIVES

1. Explain how manual and automatic transmissions differ.
2. Describe how to start and move a vehicle with a manual transmission.
3. Explain how to use each forward gear.

KEY TERMS

manual shift
clutch
friction point
downshift

♦ *Below are the gearshift positions for 4-speed and 5-speed manual transmissions.*

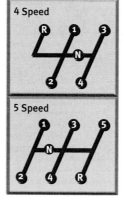

Basic Operating Procedures: Manual Transmission

Many people drive vehicles with manual transmissions because they enjoy shifting gears. Others prefer manual transmission vehicles because they usually cost less than the same models with automatic transmissions and, when properly driven, may reduce fuel consumption.

How Do Manual and Automatic Transmissions Differ?

In manual transmissions, there are usually three to five gears in forward and one in reverse. The choice of the forward gear determines the power delivered by the engine to the drive wheels.

An automatic transmission set in Drive will shift the forward gears for you. When you operate a manual transmission, or **manual shift,** you must shift the gears by moving the gearshift (or stick shift) by hand. You start in Low, or First, gear and shift to higher gears as you pick up speed. As you slow down, you shift back down from high to low.

To change gears, you break the connection between the engine and the transmission by pressing the **clutch** pedal to the floor. When the clutch pedal is up, the engine is again engaged to the transmission.

How Do You Operate a Vehicle with a Manual Transmission?

Learning to drive a vehicle equipped with a manual transmission is easier if you already know how to operate a vehicle with an automatic transmission. The key to driving a manual-shift vehicle is mastering the clutch, which you'll use each time you shift gears.

Starting the Engine

As when starting a vehicle with an automatic transmission, make sure the parking brake is set. Press the clutch pedal to the floor with your left foot, press the brake pedal with your right foot, and then shift

IT'S A FACT

Statistics continue to underscore the need for drivers to concentrate on the roadway and not allow themselves to be distracted. In 1994, for example, front-end impacts accounted for 51 percent of all passenger vehicle occupant deaths. Alert, defensive driving could have prevented many of these deaths.

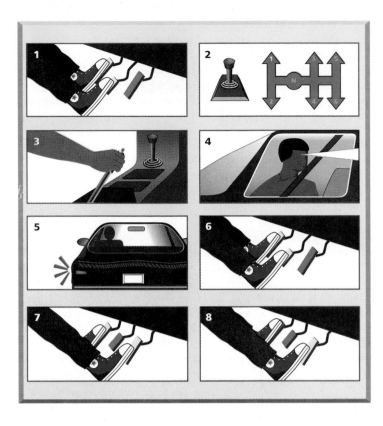

◆ You use both feet when you shift and move a car with a manual transmission.

into Neutral. (There is no gear position equivalent to Park on the gearshift for a vehicle with a manual transmission.) Now turn the ignition key to start.

Putting the Vehicle in Motion

To get a manual-shift vehicle to move—and to keep it moving—you must learn to coordinate the use of the clutch with that of the gearshift and the accelerator. Reading about how to do this will help you understand the process. Only through actual practice, however, can you gain the experience needed to master stick-shift driving.

Clutching and shifting actions should come to feel so natural to you that you

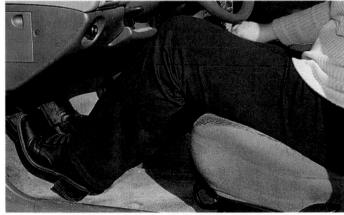

◆ It takes plenty of practice to use the clutch pedal to shift smoothly.

CHAPTER 8 *Starting, Steering, Stopping* **139**

hand. The driver's choice of forward gear determines the speed of the vehicle and the power delivered by the engine to the drive wheels.

To change gears in a vehicle equipped with a manual transmission, the driver must press the clutch pedal to the floor to break the connection between the engine and the transmission. In a vehicle with an automatic transmission, there is no clutch pedal to operate.

TEACH

Explain

OBJECTIVE 1: Students should note that while both manual and automatic transmissions have Neutral gear, only automatics have Park.

OBJECTIVES 2 and 3: Students may benefit from a discussion of the special challenges of driving a vehicle with a manual transmission, such as:

- coordinating the use of the gearshift with use of the floor pedals.
- coordinating the use of both feet in working clutch, accelerator, and brake pedals.
- learning to sense the friction point.
- starting out in First gear, then shifting to higher gears as the vehicle gains speed.
- downshifting as the vehicle's speed decreases.
- moving the vehicle forward after stopping on an uphill grade.

Driving Tip

Explain to students that when driving a vehicle equipped with a manual transmission, they should pay close attention to the sound of the engine, vehicle vibrations, and the speedometer. Any one or more of these factors can indicate that the engine is being overloaded, or lugging, and the driver needs to shift to a lower gear.

Teaching Model

Describe the following situation: You're seated behind the wheel of your vehicle, which has a manual transmission and is parked at the curb. You're ready to start the engine and drive away. Model the thinking process that you go through to start and move the vehicle, noting key differences from the procedure for starting and moving a vehicle with an automatic transmission. (You do the following.

- Make sure the parking brake is set.
- Press the clutch pedal to the floor, step on the brake, shift into Neutral, and turn the ignition key. With an automatic transmission, you'd start the engine in Park, and there would be no clutch to press.
- Shift into First gear, and release the parking brake. With an automatic transmission, you'd shift into Drive.
- Switch on your directional signal, and check traffic. As you let the clutch pedal up, move your right foot from the brake to the accelerator and press gently.)

TIPS — FOR NEW DRIVERS

Discuss with students why being able to hold the vehicle in place is so important. Have them discuss the dangers of rolling backward. Students should understand that if their vehicle rolls backward, it may hit a vehicle stopped too closely behind. Also, if a pedestrian happens to dart around the back of the vehicle, that person could be struck if the vehicle rolls.

---

scarcely need to think about them. After all, once you're on the roadway, you can't be looking down at your feet and hands.

The key to smooth clutch operation is learning to sense the **friction point.** This is the point when, as you let up the clutch pedal, the engine and the transmission engage. As you continue to let up the clutch, you must match the forward (or backward) motion of the vehicle with an increase in pressure on the gas pedal.

The easiest way to get a feel for the friction point is to practice by using Reverse gear. Because Reverse is a lower gear than First, you'll find it easier to sense the friction point.

Follow these steps to put the vehicle in motion.

1. Press the brake pedal with your right foot. With your left foot, press the clutch pedal to the floor.
2. Shift into First gear.
3. Release the parking brake.
4. Switch on your turn signal to indicate the direction you plan to move.
5. Check for traffic in your rearview and sideview mirrors. Look over your shoulder to check blind spots.
6. With your your right foot on the brake, slowly let the clutch up to the friction point. Look at the roadway, not down at your feet or hands!
7. Move your right foot from the brake to the accelerator.
8. Pressing down gently on the accelerator, slowly let the clutch pedal up.

If the car jerks forward, you either released the clutch too abruptly, or you pressed too hard on the gas pedal. If the vehicle lurches and the engine stalls, you have not fed the engine enough gas. Keep practicing until you can coordinate clutch and accelerator.

TIPS — FOR NEW DRIVERS

Holding the Vehicle in Place

Learning to move a manual-shift vehicle forward after stopping on an uphill grade takes practice. To keep the car from rolling backward, follow these steps.

1. Set the parking brake.
2. Press the clutch to the floor, and shift into First gear.
3. Let the clutch pedal up to the friction point, and press gently on the accelerator.
4. Release the parking brake as you begin to feel the car pulling forward.
5. Press the accelerator as you let up the clutch pedal.
6. Accelerate in First gear until you have gained enough speed to shift into Second gear.

Don't hold your vehicle in place on a hill by pressing the gas pedal slightly while keeping the clutch near the friction point. "Riding the clutch" this way wears your clutch needlessly. Always brake to keep your vehicle from rolling back.

How Can You Use Each Forward Gear?

Your selection of gears depends on the power and speed you need for various driving tasks.

Low, or First, gear gives the power needed to set a vehicle in motion.

Second gear lets you go as fast as 15 to 25 mph, depending on the horsepower of

---

MEETING STUDENT DIVERSITY

Limited English Proficiency

Terminology used to describe vehicles equipped with a manual transmission can be especially confusing for students with limited English proficiency. Explain to students that terms such as *manual transmis-* *sion, manual shift, standard transmission,* and *stick shift* all refer to essentially the same kind of vehicle—one in which you must change gears by hand.

the engine and on whether the transmission is a 3-, 4-, or 5-speed one. You can also use Second gear to start on ice or to drive in heavy snow.

Third gear, in vehicles with 3-speed transmissions, is used for all speeds over 25 mph. If a vehicle has a 4- or 5-speed transmission and a small engine, Third is used at speeds up to 30 or 40 mph.

Use Fourth gear for driving above 35 mph on flat roadway. When you are driving uphill, you may have to achieve 40 mph or more before shifting to Fourth or Fifth gear.

Keep in mind that power, speed, and the gear in use are strictly related. At a given speed, the power of an engine is greater in lower gear. For example, when starting up a steep grade, you generally shift to a lower gear to maintain power. When the roadway levels out, you can shift to a higher gear and keep up the same speed with less power.

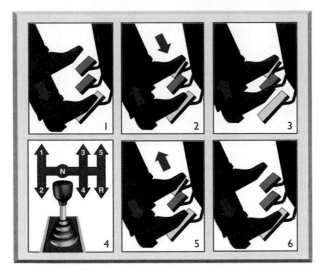

◆ *Coordinate using the clutch, gearshift, and gas pedal to shift gears.*

Shifting to a Higher Gear

To shift to a higher gear, follow these steps.

1. Accelerate to a speed appropriate for the gear you want to be in.
2. Press the clutch pedal to the floor.
3. Release the accelerator.
4. Shift to the next higher gear.
5. Press again on the accelerator. Release the clutch pedal slowly through the friction point.
6. Let the clutch pedal up all the way.

Downshifting

There are several reasons to **downshift,** or shift from a higher to a lower gear: to gain power, to accelerate, to steer effectively, to brake the vehicle on a downslope (except when the road is slippery), and to slow down or stop.

To shift to a lower gear, follow these steps.

1. Release the accelerator. (If you also want to slow down, press the brake pedal.)
2. Press the clutch pedal to the floor.

Ask

Ask students which basic procedures for starting and moving a vehicle are the same for both automatic and manual transmissions.

Read

Have students read Lesson 2 to learn the procedures for safely starting, moving, and stopping a vehicle equipped with a manual transmission.

ASSESS

Guided Practice

Have students answer the Lesson 2 Review questions. The answers are provided below.

Reteaching

Have students work together in small groups to create posters showing the step-by-step procedures for starting a vehicle with a manual transmission, for putting the vehicle in motion, and for stopping the vehicle.

After groups have completed this task, have them compare their posters with those they created for a vehicle with an automatic transmission in Lesson 1. Encourage participants to discuss procedural similarities and differences with the class.

Enrichment

Assign the Study Guide for Lesson 2. The Find Out More section encourages students to expand their basic learning of the lesson concepts.

Driving Tip

Explain that it is essential to master the coordination of clutch, gearshift, and accelerator before driving a vehicle with a manual transmission in traffic. When driving, drivers must focus their attention on the roadway. They cannot look down at their feet or at the gearshift.

CLOSE

Summarize

Return to the Motivator question. Discuss with students how this lesson has increased their understanding of how operating a vehicle with a manual transmission differs from operating a vehicle with an automatic transmission.

DRIVER'S LOG

Have students add to the section on vehicle control procedures they began in Lesson 1. Ask them to list the procedures for starting, moving, and stopping a vehicle with a manual transmission. Have them make special note of procedural differences between the two types of vehicles.

WHAT WOULD YOU DO?

Sample answer: Use clutch and brake pedals to stop, and use gearshift to shift into Neutral; use clutch and gearshift to shift to First gear, then accelerate when safe.

◆ *To downshift, brake. Then press the clutch to the floor, shift to the next lower gear, and press the accelerator.*

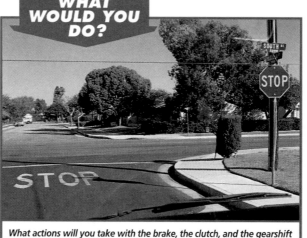

WHAT WOULD YOU DO?

What actions will you take with the brake, the clutch, and the gearshift as you approach, then pass through, this intersection?

3. Shift to the next lower gear. (Sudden decrease in speed may require shifting to an even lower gear—as when braking sharply and downshifting from Fourth gear to Second.)
4. Release the clutch pedal to the friction point. Press down on the accelerator as necessary.

Note that you do not have to downshift through each lower gear as you slow down or stop. In fact, routinely downshifting to stop will cause unnecessary wear on the clutch, an expensive part to replace.

It is easy to downshift from Fifth, Fourth, and Third gears to lower gears, but it is difficult to shift from Second to First. To downshift to First gear, you have to bring the vehicle almost to a complete stop.

Stopping

To stop from a low gear, follow these steps.
1. Check mirrors for traffic behind you.
2. Tap the brake pedal to flash your brake lights and signal drivers behind you that you intend to stop.
3. Press the brake pedal to reduce speed to 10 to 15 mph. Then press the clutch pedal to the floor to keep the vehicle from stalling.
4. Apply smooth, steady brake pressure to bring the vehicle to a stop.
5. Keep your foot on the brake pedal and shift to Neutral.

To make an emergency stop, press the clutch pedal to the floor, and use threshold braking.

Lesson 2 Review

1. How is a manual transmission different from an automatic transmission?
2. What steps would you follow to start and move a vehicle with a manual transmission?
3. How would you use the forward gears of a vehicle that has a manual transmission?

Lesson 2 Review

Answers

1. To operate a manual transmission, the driver must press a clutch pedal and shift gears by hand.
2. To start, make sure parking brake is set; press clutch and brake pedals; shift into Neutral; turn key to Start. To move, press brake and clutch pedals; shift into First; release parking brake; check traffic and signal; release clutch and accelerate.
3. First gear puts the vehicle in motion; Second lets you move 15 to 25 mph; Third is used up to 30 to 40 mph; Fourth is used for driving over about 35 mph.

Acceleration, Deceleration, and Speed

OBJECTIVES
1. Define acceleration and deceleration.
2. Explain how these terms are related to speed.

KEY TERMS
acceleration
rate of acceleration
deceleration
rate of deceleration

To minimize driving risk, you must be able to maneuver your vehicle safely. To do so, you have to know your vehicle's capabilities and limitations. When changing lanes or passing, for example, you need to judge how much time and distance your vehicle will require to move ahead of other vehicles. Learning about acceleration, deceleration, and speed can help you judge time and space more accurately, thus helping you to be a safe driver.

How Are Acceleration, Deceleration, and Speed Related?

Speed and acceleration are closely linked. When drivers say their vehicle has good **acceleration** (or "pickup"), they mean the vehicle is able to increase speed relatively quickly. The time it takes to accelerate from one speed to another is the **rate of acceleration.**

Deceleration, on the other hand, refers to decreasing speed, or slowing down. The time it takes to decelerate from one speed to another is the **rate of deceleration.**

Several factors affect a vehicle's acceleration, including the power of the engine, the transmission and differential gear ratios, adhesion between the drive wheels and the road surface, and the weight the engine is pulling. Your ability to drive safely and effectively depends in large part on the knowledgeable use of your vehicle's acceleration.

CONNECTIONS
Math

A speedometer tells you how fast you're traveling at a given moment, but to find out your average speed for a particular distance, you'll need to do a little math.

Average speed equals total distance traveled divided by total time traveled. Suppose, for example, the distance from your home to the beach is 70 miles. One afternoon, it takes you an hour and a half to drive there. Your average speed equals 70 (total miles driven) divided by 1½ (total time), or just over 46 miles per hour.

Driving Tip

Explain that accelerating can help avoid a collision. Suppose a driver is nearing an intersection and suddenly sees a vehicle moving toward him or her. Hard braking could bring the driver to a stop directly in the path of the threatening vehicle. A quick burst of speed, however, may remove the driver from the collision path.

CONNECTIONS
Math

To check student understanding, you may want to pose additional problems.

LESSON THREE

Acceleration, Deceleration, and Speed

(pages 143–145)

FOCUS

Objectives
• Define acceleration and deceleration.
• Explain how these terms are related to speed.

Resources
 Study Guide, page 31
 Traffic Charts

Vocabulary
acceleration
rate of acceleration
deceleration
rate of deceleration

Motivator
Pose the following: You're driving at 15 mph. To pass a vehicle, you accelerate to 25 mph. Later you're driving at 40 mph. To pass another vehicle, you accelerate to 50 mph. Which took longer—accelerating from 15 to 25 mph or from 40 to 50 mph? (Students may wrongly assume higher speeds mean faster acceleration. They should understand that at higher speeds, a vehicle's acceleration rate is lower.)

TEACH

Explain
OBJECTIVES 1 and 2: Students may benefit from a discussion of situations in which acceleration comes into play, such as passing, merging, and driving uphill.

Teaching Model

Display this situation:

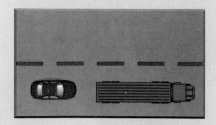

Tell students the following: You are driving the car, and you want to pass the truck. Model the thinking process you use to gauge risk in this situation. (You check the roadway; consider your speed and that of the truck; judge whether you have enough time and distance to pass safely.)

Ask

Ask students to discuss the danger of trying to pass without having enough time and distance to do so safely.

Read

Have students read Lesson 3 to learn why understanding speed, acceleration, and deceleration is important.

 **FOR NEW DRIVERS**

Accelerating gradually is particularly important when the road is wet. Abrupt acceleration can cause skidding.

ASSESS

Guided Practice

Have students answer the Lesson 3 Review questions. The answers are provided below.

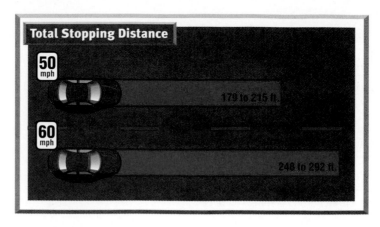

Total Stopping Distance

50 mph — 179 to 215 ft.

60 mph — 246 to 292 ft.

◆ *The greater the speed, the greater the distance needed to brake the car to a stop. Here the total stopping distance— which is the distance traveled from perception to response— for a car traveling at 50 mph ranges from 179 feet to 215 feet.*

TIPS **FOR NEW DRIVERS**

Accelerating

• For best control when accelerating, rest the heel of your foot on the floor, and press the pedal gently with your toes.

• As a general rule, accelerate gradually. Beginning drivers sometimes make errors when they increase speed quickly. Accelerating gradually also saves fuel.

• No two cars accelerate exactly the same way. When driving an unfamiliar vehicle, allow yourself time to get used to the feel of the gas pedal and to the vehicle's acceleration capability.

Acceleration and Deceleration Rates Vary

Rate of acceleration varies with speed. At higher speeds, a vehicle's rate of acceleration will be lower. As a result, it will generally take more time to accelerate from 45 mph to 55 mph than from 20 mph to 30 mph.

Understanding this principle is important for risk management. For example, the lower acceleration rate at high speeds means you must allow more time to pass when traveling at 50 mph than when moving at 30 mph.

Equally important to keep in mind is that deceleration rates, like acceleration rates, vary with speed. At higher speeds, your vehicle's rate of deceleration is lower. So a vehicle traveling at 60 mph needs a great deal more time and space to slow and brake to a stop than the same vehicle traveling at 30 mph.

A vehicle's rates of acceleration and deceleration also vary with weight. A heavy truck, for example, needs much more time and distance to accelerate or decelerate than does a passenger vehicle.

Maintaining a Constant Speed

The ability of vehicles to maintain a given speed varies greatly. Large passenger vehicles with high-horsepower, 6- or 8-cylinder engines and mid-size and sport sedans with turbo-charged small engines generally have good acceleration and can maintain their speed climbing a hill. An under-powered subcompact vehicle, however, may not be able to hold its speed because of its small engine.

Many large vehicles also have difficulty maintaining their speed. Tractor-trailer rigs and interstate buses have huge engines, but these large vehicles accelerate very slowly.

Monitoring Your Speed

New drivers find it difficult to control the speed of their vehicle simply by observing the

IT'S A FACT

Most serious pedestrian injuries result from striking the hood, windshield, or top of a vehicle—not from subsequent impact with the road or being run over.

speed of traffic around them. As a result, they frequently check the speedometer. Such checks should be made with quick glances, as traffic conditions permit.

With experience, you'll become more aware of clues to your vehicle's performance and speed. You'll notice, for example, that as speed varies, there's a difference in the vehicle's vibration and in the level of sound from the tires, the wind, and the engine. Drivers of vehicles with manual transmissions must make a special effort to learn to judge speed because they have to make speed-related decisions about shifting gears.

Note that it is harder to estimate your vehicle's speed immediately after you've made a sharp change in speed. If, for example, you've been driving at 20 mph and rapidly accelerate to 45 mph, you'll feel as though you're moving faster than you actually are.

On the other hand, if you've been traveling at highway speeds and suddenly enter a 25-mph zone, your tendency may be to slow down less than you should because you've become accustomed to moving at higher speeds. The best way to prevent yourself from speeding in such an instance is to check your speedometer.

◆ New drivers often increase speed without realizing it, so check your speedometer frequently.

Lesson 3 Review

1. What is acceleration? How are acceleration and speed related?
2. What is deceleration? How is deceleration related to speed?

WHAT WOULD YOU DO?

Which vehicle probably needs more time and distance to accelerate: the truck or the car? How would knowing this help you manage time and space to reduce risk?

Reteaching

Pair a more able student with one who is having difficulty. Have them work together using the clingboard to analyze the link between speed and acceleration.

Enrichment

Assign the Study Guide for Lesson 3. The Find Out More section encourages students to expand their basic learning of the lesson concepts.

CLOSE

Summarize

Return to the Motivator question. Guide students in concluding that it would take longer to accelerate from 40 mph to 50 mph than from 15 mph to 25 mph.

DRIVER'S LOG

How can a vehicle's inability to accelerate quickly add to the level of driving risk?

WHAT WOULD YOU DO?

Sample answer: The truck; if both vehicles move uphill, you will probably draw closer to the truck.

Lesson 3 Review

Answers

1. Acceleration means increasing speed; the rate at which a vehicle accelerates, or increases speed, is lower at higher speeds.
2. Deceleration means decreasing speed; the rate at which a vehicle decelerates, or decreases speed, is lower at higher speeds.

Learning How to Steer the Vehicle

(pages 146–150)

FOCUS

Objectives

• Describe the procedures for steering straight ahead and when turning.

• Explain how to steer in Reverse gear.

Resources

 Study Guide, page 32

 Traffic charts

 Behind-the-Wheel Checklists 5, 6, 7, and 12

Vocabulary

tracking
hand-over-hand steering
push-pull-feed steering

Motivator

You're driving straight ahead on a city street. In what position are your hands on the steering wheel? You approach an intersection and signal to make a right turn. As you make the turn, how does your hand position on the wheel change? (Students' answers will mainly reflect their past observation of drivers. The answers that follow can be expected after students complete the lesson. When steering in a straight line, position your hands as recommended by your driving instructor. Some instructors may, for example, recommend the 9 o'clock and 3 o'clock positions while others prefer the 7 o'clock and 5 o'clock positions. When turning, use either hand-over-hand steering or push-pull-feed steering.)

LESSON FOUR

OBJECTIVES

1. Describe the procedures for steering straight ahead and when turning.
2. Explain how to steer in Reverse gear.

KEY TERMS

tracking
hand-over-hand steering
push-pull-feed steering

FYI

The average driver takes ½ to ¾ of a second to step on the brake after identifying a dangerous situation. Thus, even at 20 mph, your vehicle would travel at least 20 feet before you could step on the brake.

Learning How to Steer the Vehicle

Many new drivers assume that they know all they need to know about steering a vehicle. After all, they think, they've been steering bicycles and sleds since they were children. Such activities do share elements in common with steering a motor vehicle. However, there are important differences new drivers must learn.

For one thing, unlike a bicycle or sled, a motor vehicle has power independent of the driver's own efforts—a great deal of power. Moreover, steering is not simply a matter of pointing the vehicle in the direction you want to go. Steering is a basic means of risk management.

How Can You Steer Your Vehicle Forward and Through Turns?

Suppose you're about to drive through an intersection. Suddenly another vehicle crosses in front of you. The best way to avoid a collision is to brake your vehicle, right? Not necessarily.

It often takes less time and space to steer away from an object than to brake to avoid hitting it. (Of course, to avoid a collision by steering, you must have previously identified an area into which you can safely steer.)

Steering plays a particularly important part in risk management when you're traveling at speeds over 25 or 30 mph. At such speeds, steering may often be your only way to avoid a collision, because higher speeds increase the distance and time needed to stop the vehicle.

Holding the Steering Wheel

When steering in a straight line or through a moderate curve, grasp the steering wheel firmly with your fingers. Many experienced drivers place their hands at 9 o'clock and 3 o'clock or at 8 o'clock and 4 o'clock positions. Others position their hands on the lower part of the wheel, in the 7 o'clock and 5 o'clock positions. Follow the recommendations of your instructor. No matter which hand position you use, your thumbs should rest on the wheel.

Tracking and Steering

Keeping your vehicle moving on the path of travel that you have chosen is called **tracking**. Tracking requires a driver to make whatever

Driving Tip

Explain to students that a responsible driver keeps both hands on the steering wheel at all times (except when shifting gears). Driving with only one hand on the wheel may look "cool," but doing so lessens the driver's control over the vehicle and reduces the driver's ability to cope with an emergency.

steering adjustments are needed to hold the desired course.

To track smoothly, learn to direct your attention to points 20 to 30 seconds ahead along your intended path of travel. Choose these points on the basis of where you want to go and traffic conditions.

If you're like many new drivers, you'll find steering a vehicle more challenging than you'd anticipated, particularly when traveling on winding roads. At first, you may not notice small changes in your vehicle's position in a traffic lane. You may fail to adjust your steering in time and then tend to overcorrect, causing the car to zigzag rather than move in a straight line. You'll tend to look at the right edge marker or center line while driving through curves. Doing so will also cause the vehicle to zigzag. However, with practice and concentration, you'll learn to look through curves and well ahead of your vehicle along your path of travel. You'll soon improve your ability to keep your vehicle on track with only minor steering adjustments.

◆ *Think of the steering wheel as the face of a clock so that you can position your hands correctly.*

Steering in a Straight Line

The steering adjustments you must make on a straight road are small but critical. Be on the alert for gradual changes in the position of your vehicle. It should not "wander" in its lane.

Steer toward a point in the center of your path of travel, looking well ahead as you drive. When you look to the point where you will steer, you will automatically steer in the proper direction.

◆ *Always look and steer toward a point in the center of your intended path of travel.*

As you drive, check your mirrors whenever you spot anything along your intended path of travel that could cause you to change speed or position.

To look in your rearview mirror, move just your eyes. To look in your sideview mirror, turn your head only slightly.

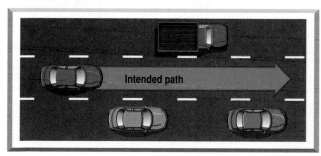

Intended path

CHAPTER 8   *Starting, Steering, Stopping*   **147**

TEACH

Explain
OBJECTIVE 1: Students should recognize the importance of keeping both hands on the steering wheel.

OBJECTIVE 2: Students may benefit from a discussion of the special dangers of backing up and actions they can take to minimize risk. Points to stress include these.

- Always back up slowly and cautiously.
- Monitor both the rear and the front of the vehicle. Remember, when steering in Reverse gear, the rear moves in the same direction that you turn the steering wheel, while the front moves in the opposite direction.
- Maximize visibility by removing any obstacles inside the vehicle.
- Turn to look; do not rely solely on rearview or sideview mirrors.
- Watch for pedestrians or vehicles unexpectedly entering your path of travel.
- Be especially alert for young children, whose small size makes them difficult to see through the rear window.
- Keep in mind that when you back up to one side or the other, the two points of your vehicle most likely to strike something are the rear side in the direction you're turning and the front side opposite that direction.

MEETING STUDENT DIVERSITY

Orientation Dysfunction

Driving in Reverse confuses some students. Review the procedure for turning the wheel—using visual aids or models—as often as needed until students understand the basics of driving in Reverse: turning the wheel to the right steers the back of the vehicle to the right; turning the wheel to the left steers it to the left.

Teaching Model

Describe the following situation: You're driving in a city in moderate traffic. You're approaching an intersection where you intend to turn left. Model the thinking process that you go through to make the turn safely. (You do the following.

- Look beyond the turn to the point you want to reach. You want to identify this point before you begin to turn.
- Position your vehicle in the proper lane.
- Turn on your left directional signal.
- Check the road ahead for traffic signs and signals, vehicles, and pedestrians.
- Check your rearview mirror and side mirrors before starting to turn.
- Use either hand-over-hand steering or push-pull-feed steering to make the turn.
- With your eyes directed toward the point you want to reach, steer back to the straight-ahead position when you're about midway through the turn by allowing the steering wheel to slide back through your fingers. This steering technique is generally accepted if done smoothly and under control.
- Check rearview and side mirrors again after completing the turn.)

Ask

Ask students to discuss the risks involved in making a turn in a busy city intersection and how they can reduce these risks.

Read

Have students read Lesson 4 to learn the procedures for safely steering a vehicle straight ahead, backward, and through turns.

Steering to Turn

Steering through a turn requires more steering-wheel movement than does lane positioning. To turn corners smoothly and safely, you need to develop a good sense of timing and make a habit of searching a wider area.

When steering through a turn, keep in mind that your vehicle's rear wheels do not follow the same path as the front wheels. They have a smaller turning radius, so you must allow ample space along the path you're turning. Without this space, your rear wheels may hit the curb or other objects.

Two specific steering techniques are effective for turning the wheel: hand-over-hand and push-pull-feed. The following procedures describe how to make a right turn; to make a left turn, reverse the movements.

Hand-over-hand steering To turn right using **hand-over-hand steering,** use your left hand to push the steering wheel up, around, and down. At the same time, bring your right hand across your left forearm to grip the wheel on the far side. Then use your right hand to pull the side of the wheel up, around, and down. Repeat this series of movements as often as needed to complete the turn, making any left or right steering corrections that may be required.

Hand-over-hand steering provides effective vehicle control when you're steering through tight-radius turns, such as hard turns and hairpin turns.

♦ *If you are not too tall or somewhat stout, you may find push-pull-feed steering more comfortable.*

Push-pull-feed steering Grasp the steering wheel with the right hand resting between 3 and 5 o'clock and the left hand between 7 and 9 o'clock. One hand pushes the wheel up toward 12 o'clock. (Use the left hand for right turns and vice versa.) At the same time, the other hand slides up to 1 o'clock for the right turn (or 11 o'clock for the left turn), grasps the wheel, and pulls it down. While the pulling hand goes down, the pushing hand releases its grip and returns to its original position to continue the process as needed.

Push-pull-feed steering lets you keep both your hands on the steering wheel at all times. The positioning of your hands causes less fatigue on longer drives and gives you better steering control in an

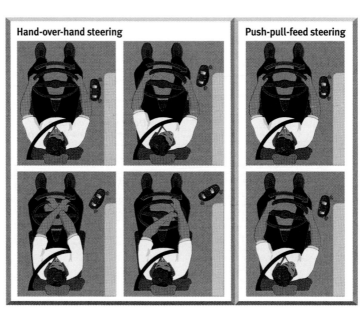

Hand-over-hand steering | Push-pull-feed steering

THE INTERNATIONAL SCENE

Germany

About 700 kilometers of roadway in Berlin are wired with infrared beacons at key stoplights, monitoring the flow and density of traffic. The beacons beam the information to a computerized control center, which then beams the data to special receivers in a select number of vehicles. These receivers communicate to drivers what is going on. They also display the most efficient route of travel.

emergency. Also, you can sit farther from the steering wheel. Since your arms never cross over the face of the steering wheel, there is less chance of injury if the driver's side air bag deploys.

Whichever steering method you choose, use the following guidelines when making a turn.

- Look beyond the turn to the point you want to reach. Identify this point before you start to turn.
- Always use your directional signal. Check the roadway ahead and both mirrors before starting to turn. Check the mirrors again after completing the turn, waiting if possible until you've straightened the wheels.
- On a hard turn, slow down to maintain control as you enter the turn. Accelerate gently about halfway through to pull out of the turn.
- With your eyes on the point you want to reach, start to steer back to the straight-ahead position when you're about midway through the turn. Do this by reversing the hand-over-hand or push-pull-feed movements.

How Do You Steer in Reverse?

When steering in Reverse gear, you have to learn where to look and how to control direction and speed. Always back slowly. When you steer left or right while backing, the vehicle's movements are more abrupt.

When you are backing a vehicle, visibility through the rear window is limited. Head restraints and passengers may further block your view. Backing while looking into the rearview mirror restricts your view even more.

To maximize your ability to see, turn your head and shoulders so that you can look back in the direction you want to move. When you move backward, the rear of your vehicle moves in the direction that you turn the steering wheel, while the front swings in the opposite direction.

Note, too, that when you back a vehicle, the two points most likely to hit something are the rear side of the vehicle in the direction in which you are turning and the front side of the vehicle opposite the direction in which you are turning.

Steering to the Rear

Follow these steps when backing a vehicle.

1. With your foot on the brake, shift into Reverse gear. If you are backing straight, place your left hand on the top of the

◆ Don't forget to look over both shoulders when you steer to the rear.

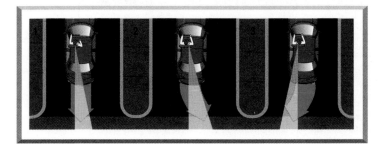

State BY State

Specific laws regarding the use of approved child safety seats while children are riding in a motor vehicle vary from state to state. *All* states, however, require children below certain ages to be seated securely in an approved child safety seat, ride in the rear, or in certain instances, use standard adult safety belts. Fines for violating child restraint laws run as high as $150 for a first offense.

ASSESS

Guided Practice
Have students answer the Lesson 4 Review questions. The answers are provided below.

Reteaching
Have students work together in small groups to create charts of procedural do's and don'ts for steering in a straight line, steering to the rear, and steering through a turn. Encourage students to provide explanatory drawings with their charts.

After groups have completed this task, have them share their work with the class. Encourage discussion of risk factors in each situation and driver actions to reduce risk.

Enrichment
Assign the Study Guide for Lesson 4. The Find Out More section encourages students to expand their basic learning of the lesson concepts.

CLOSE

Summarize

Return to the Motivator question. Discuss with students how this lesson has changed their understanding of how to position their hands on the steering wheel. You may want to extend the discussion by having students compare the hand-over-hand and push-pull-feed methods and demonstrate both methods on a model.

Also encourage students to think about how steering a vehicle equipped with a manual transmission differs from steering one with an automatic transmission. Students should understand the basic steering procedure is the same, except that the driver of the vehicle with a manual transmission must remove one hand from the steering wheel to shift gears as appropriate.

DRIVER'S LOG

Have students add to the section on basic vehicle control procedures they began in Lesson 1. Ask them to list the procedures for safely steering a vehicle straight ahead, backward, and through turns.

WHAT WOULD YOU DO?

Sample answer: Turn head and shoulders so that you can see in the direction you want to move; proceed slowly and cautiously, with quick glances to the front.

ADVICE FROM THE EXPERTS

Ron Hales
Professor of Safety Education, Central Safety Center, Central Washington University

When preparing to stop, always check your inside mirror for vehicles that are following you. Maintaining adequate space around your vehicle is very important, and knowing what is behind you is critical to your safety and that of your passengers.

When stopping behind another vehicle, maintain an adequate space cushion in front of your vehicle. The best way to do this is to make sure that from the driver's seated position, the rear tires of the vehicle ahead and a small portion of the roadway are completely visible to you.

steering wheel and your right arm across the top of the seat. Look over your right shoulder. If you are backing to the right or left, keep both hands on the wheel and look over your shoulder in the direction you want to move.

2. Ease pressure off the brake slowly. Give yourself plenty of time to monitor the rear and front of your vehicle. To move the vehicle slowly, apply only slight pressure, if any, to the accelerator.

3. Look at the point where you want to go so that you can identify and correct steering errors early. Turn the wheel as needed.

4. Concentrate your visual search out the rear window, with quick, repeated glances to the front. Keep alert to ensure that the vehicle is moving in the right direction and that the front end is not about to strike anything.

5. Continue to look out the rear window as you bring the vehicle to a stop.

WHAT WOULD YOU DO?

What procedures would you follow to back out of this driveway? What safety precautions should you take before moving the vehicle?

Lesson 4 Review

1. What procedures would you follow to steer a vehicle straight ahead? To turn?
2. How do you back a vehicle?

Lesson 4 Review

Answers
1. Steer toward a point in the center of your travel path, looking well ahead; to turn, use the hand-over-hand or push-pull-feed technique, and look beyond the turn to the point you want to reach.
2. With your foot on the brake, shift into reverse; move slowly and cautiously, looking at the point where you want to go.

Understanding Roadway Classifications

Maps help you get where you are going. They also tell about the kinds of roads you can use to get there. Most maps have a key such as this one. Find 🛣 at coordinates D, 5 on the map. The map key indicates that this is a no-toll, limited-access highway. See the dots along Route 2? The key tells you that this is a scenic route. Find Route 9. The key tells you that Route 9 is a paved secondary road that is not divided.

Try It Yourself

1. What can you tell about Route 7 between Pittsfield and Stockbridge?
2. What kind of road connects Adams and Savoy Center?
3. Describe the different kinds of roads you can take from Southampton to Pittsfield.

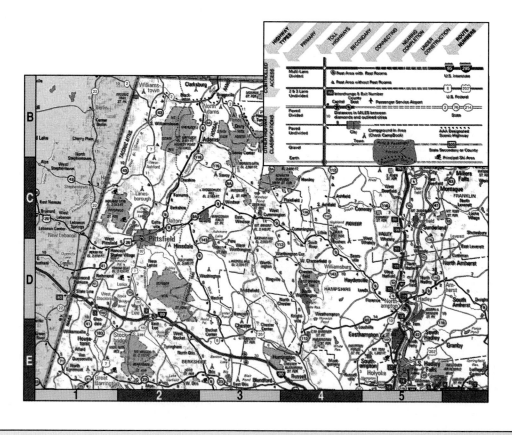

BUILDING SKILLS: READING MAPS

Objective

Demonstrate an ability to understand roadway classifications from the symbols on a map and map key.

Teaching the Skill

- Review with students how to use map coordinates to find a location on a road map.
- Discuss with students how knowing the type of road on which they will be traveling can help them plan time as well as distance.
- Have students explain how knowing whether a road is a toll or nontoll highway can help them plan a trip.

ANSWERS TO
Try It Yourself Questions

1. It is a paved two- and three-lane undivided highway, or secondary highway.
2. gravel road
3. One possible answer: You can take Route 10, a paved, undivided secondary highway, to Route 9, a paved, undivided designated scenic byway.

CHAPTER SUMMARY

Key Points

Have students read the Key Points to review the major concepts of the chapter.

PROJECTS

Cooperative Learning:

Students will benefit by working with a partner on one or both projects. When the assignment is completed, the whole class will profit by sharing and comparing results.

KEY POINTS

Lesson One

1. To start a vehicle with an automatic transmission, put the gear selector in Park. Set the automatic choke if it applies to your vehicle. Then press the accelerator and turn the key. To move the vehicle, step on the brake and shift to Drive or Reverse. Release the parking brake, take your foot off the brake, and accelerate gradually.
2. To slow and stop a vehicle with an automatic transmission, check your mirrors, tap your brake pedal, and apply steady pressure to the brake pedal, easing up slightly as you come to a halt.

Lesson Two

1. You need to change forward gears by manually shifting up or down in a manual transmission. An automatic transmission set in Drive will shift the forward gears for you.
2. To start a vehicle with a manual transmission, set the parking brake. Press the clutch to the floor, step on the brake, shift into Neutral, and turn the key. To move the vehicle, shift into First and release the parking brake. As you let the clutch up, move your right foot from the brake to the accelerator and press gently. To stop the vehicle, press the clutch to the floor,

and move your right foot to the brake. Apply smooth pressure until the vehicle stops.
3. First gear sets the vehicle in motion. Second gear is used for speeds up to 15 to 25 mph or to start on ice or to drive in heavy snow. Third gear is used for speeds over 25 mph (3-speed transmissions) or speeds up to 30 or 40 mph (4- or 5-speed transmissions). Fourth or Fifth gear is used for driving at higher speeds.

Lesson Three

1. Acceleration is an increase of speed. Deceleration means a slowing down.
2. The rate of acceleration or deceleration varies with speed. At higher speeds, a vehicle's acceleration and deceleration rates are lower.

Lesson Four

1. To steer your vehicle straight ahead, steer toward a point in the center of your path of travel. When steering to turn, look beyond the turn to the point you want to reach. Use the hand-over-hand or push-pull-feed steering method.
2. When backing, look over your right shoulder, place your left hand at the top of the steering wheel, and steer in the direction you want the vehicle to move. Proceed slowly and carefully, monitoring both the rear and front of your vehicle.

PROJECTS

1. Talk to someone who has been driving for several years. Ask what lessons this driver has learned through experience and what tips he or she might offer you as a beginning driver.
2. Demonstrate the difference between the hand-over-hand and push-pull-feed steering. Which technique seems easier to you? Why? Survey several drivers to find out which method they use and why.

*inter*NET
CONNECTION

Use the Internet to download information on how antilock brakes work. Investigate the advantages and disadvantages of an antilock brake system. **drivered.glencoe.com**

*inter*NET
CONNECTION

Visit Glencoe's Driver Education Web site for student activities that relate to this chapter. **drivered.glencoe.com**

CHAPTER TEST

Write the letter of the answer that best completes each sentence.

1. You can set an automatic choke by
   a. pumping the brake pedal.
   b. pressing the gas pedal to the floor once and then releasing it.
   c. turning the ignition key to "on."

2. One advantage of push-pull-feed steering is that
   a. your hands are on the wheel at all times.
   b. your hands are free to adjust the mirrors.
   c. you can back more easily.

3. With a manual transmission, the speed of the vehicle determines
   a. the tightness of the vehicle's turning radius.
   b. the choice of forward gear.
   c. the need for an occasional fuel injection.

4. A vehicle's rate of acceleration is lower at
   a. warmer engine temperatures.
   b. high speeds.
   c. low speeds.

5. To avoid rolling backward when starting on an uphill grade, you should
   a. set your parking brake firmly.
   b. lock the brakes.
   c. start the engine in third gear.

6. As you drive, you will develop the ability to estimate your speed by
   a. sensing the vehicle's friction point.
   b. riding the clutch.
   c. sensing a difference in the vehicle's vibrations.

7. To start a vehicle with an automatic transmission,
   a. first shift into Second gear.
   b. keep your foot on the brake pedal.
   c. make sure the gear selector lever is in Park.

8. To change gears in a vehicle with a manual transmission, you must
   a. press the clutch pedal to the floor.
   b. engage in threshold braking.
   c. rapidly decelerate.

9. When turning, always
   a. sound your horn.
   b. use your directional signal.
   c. shift into Reverse.

10. When driving around a curve, you should focus
    a. beyond the turn, on the point you want to reach.
    b. on the road directly in front of you.
    c. on objects in your rearview mirror.

Write the word or phrase that best completes each sentence.

acceleration	manual transmission
tracking	automatic transmission
clutch	rate of deceleration

11. _____ means an increase of speed.

12. A vehicle's _____ can have four or five forward gears.

13. The key to smooth _____ operation is sensing the friction point.

14. _____ means keeping your vehicle moving on the path that you have chosen to travel.

15. The time it takes for a vehicle to slow down is the _____.

DRIVER'S LOG

In this chapter, you have learned about the basic procedures you need to know to operate a vehicle. Write at least two paragraphs giving your ideas about why these procedures are almost second nature to experienced drivers and why they should become second nature to you.

RETURN TO THE BIG IDEA

In the context of what students have learned in this chapter, discuss why, to drive safely, drivers must practice basic procedures and maneuvers until they become second nature.

CHAPTER TEST

Assign the Chapter Test to all students.

Answers

1. b
2. a
3. b
4. b
5. a
6. c
7. c
8. a
9. b
10. a
11. Acceleration
12. manual transmission
13. clutch
14. Tracking
15. rate of deceleration

DRIVER'S LOG

Students' responses will reflect their personal viewpoints. However, their answers should provide an assessment of their understanding of the importance of mastering the basic driving skills.

Evaluate

- Test A, pages 15–16 or Test B, pages 15–16 📁
- Testmaker software

Basic Driving Skills

THEME DEVELOPMENT To reduce risk, drivers must manage visibility, time, and space factors when entering or leaving the flow of traffic, when driving on hills and mountains, when changing lanes, and when passing other vehicles.

LESSON	PAGES	LESSON OBJECTIVES	STATE/LOCAL OBJECTIVES
1 Moving from a Curb into Traffic and out of Traffic to a Curb	156–158	**1.** Describe procedures for steering away from the curb and entering traffic. **2.** Describe procedures for steering out of traffic and moving toward a curb.	
2 Managing Power and Speed on Hills and Mountains	159–161	**1.** Describe how to drive uphill and downhill. **2.** Describe safe procedures for driving on mountain roadways.	
3 Managing Visibility, Time, and Space When Changing Lanes	162–163	**1.** Describe several factors involved in planning a lane change correctly. **2.** Understand the steps involved in making a lane change.	
4 Passing Another Vehicle and Being Passed	164–166	**1.** Name conditions you should be aware of when you want to pass another vehicle. **2.** Describe the procedure for passing another vehicle. **3.** Describe what to do when another vehicle passes you.	

CHAPTER FEATURES	TCR COMPONENTS
TIPS FOR NEW DRIVERS Learning how to park beyond an intersection.	Study Guide, p. 33 Lesson Plan, p. 19 Behind-the-Wheel Checklists 7 and 8
	Study Guide, p. 34 Lesson Plan, p. 19 Behind-the-Wheel Checklist 29
TIPS FOR NEW DRIVERS Communicating with other drivers.	Study Guide, p. 35 Lesson Plan, p. 20 Behind-the-Wheel Checklist 9 Information Master 16
ADVICE FROM THE EXPERTS The importance of practicing on-road procedures.	Study Guide, p. 36 Transparency 22 Lesson Plan, p. 20 Behind-the-Wheel Checklist 21
BUILDING SKILLS: LANGUAGE Using Prefixes and Combining Forms	Test A, pp. 17–18 Test B, pp. 17–18

PROJECTS

1. Record driver communication.
2. Read a state driving manual to learn about mountain driving.

OTHER PROGRAM RESOURCES

Testmaker software
Responsible Driving,
    Video 1: Lessons 3 and 4
Traffic Charts

ADDITIONAL RESOURCES

*Managing Space and Time
    for Safe Driving,* Video
    449, AAA Foundation
*Using Your Eyes
    Effectively,* Video 488,
    AAA Foundation
*Teaching Your Teens to
    Drive*: Lessons 2, 4, 6,
    and 12, video or CD-
    ROM, AAA, 1998

NAME _____ DATE _____

CHAPTER 9 Basic Driving Skills

TEST A

Read each statement below. If it is true, place a T in the space to the left of the statement. If the statement is false, place an F next to it.

T 1. In higher altitudes, you could become short of breath or sleepy because there is less oxygen in the air.

T 2. When you are not moving with the flow of traffic, you face increased risks.

F 3. When driving uphill, you need less power because of the pull of gravity.

F 4. Using cruise control on hills is more fuel efficient than not using it.

F 5. When driving down a hill in a car that has a manual transmission, the only way to increase control is to apply the brakes.

F 6. In higher altitudes, decreased oxygen will not have an effect on your engine.

Select the phrase that best completes each sentence below. Write the letter of the answer you have chosen to the left of each statement.

c 7. The four basic kinds of road communication that drivers exchange are
a. intentions, nonverbal, silent, oral.
b. nonverbal, presence, electronic, oral.
c. intentions, warnings, presence, feedback.
d. warnings, passive, nonverbal, basic.

c 8. You know that it is illegal to pass another vehicle when
a. a warning sign says so.
b. a roadway marking says so.
c. both a and b occur.
d. none of the above occurs.

b 9. When parking in a space just beyond an intersection, you
a. signal before entering the intersection.
b. signal after you have entered the intersection.
c. signal when you are completely through the intersection.
d. do not signal at all. It is safer to avoid signaling in this case.

a 10. The most dangerous movement of the four listed below is
a. passing a vehicle on a two-lane, two-way highway.
b. passing a motorcycle on a freeway.
c. being passed by any vehicle on a two-lane, two-way highway.
d. passing a truck on a freeway.

b 11. If driving down a long, steep hill in a car with an automatic transmission,
a. use the brakes to slow down.
b. move the selector to a lower gear to slow down.
c. ease off the pressure on the accelerator to slow down.
d. do all of the above.

NAME _____ DATE _____

c 12. If you are driving on a mountain road behind a truck, you need to
a. pass the truck as soon as you can.
b. blink your lights.
c. increase your following distance.
d. do all of the above.

d 13. In driving on mountain roads, the altitude makes _____ especially dangerous.
a. snow
b. rain
c. fog
d. snow, rain, and fog

d 14. The first thing to do before changing lanes is to
a. steer smoothly into the next lane.
b. adjust your speed.
c. signal your intentions.
d. check your mirrors.

The following statements are procedures you go through when changing lanes. Number them in the order that you would perform them.

4 15. Adjust your speed up and down as needed.

6 16. Steer smoothly into the lane.

1 17. Check your mirrors.

5 18. Move only when you have the time and space to do so.

3 19. Check over your shoulder for blind spots.

2 20. Signal your intent to move.

21. Under what conditions should you not pass another vehicle?

You should not pass another vehicle if it is not legal or if the traffic, weather, or road

conditions are not safe for passing. You must be able to pass another vehicle without going

over the speed limit.

_____

_____

_____

_____

_____

_____

NAME _____ DATE _____

CHAPTER 9 Basic Driving Skills

TEST B

Read each statement below. If it is true, place a T in the space to the left of the statement. If the statement is false, place an F next to it.

T 1. Using cruise control is not fuel efficient when driving on hills.

F 2. Of all the kinds of roads, the most dangerous for passing another vehicle is a controlled-access highway.

T 3. To pass another vehicle, you typically need to go at least 10 mph faster than the vehicle in front of you.

F 4. The only time it is permitted to speed is when you are passing another vehicle on a two-lane road.

T 5. When driving downhill, you need to use less power because of gravity.

F 6. When driving in a vehicle equipped with a manual transmission, it is best to downshift after you have gone at least halfway down the hill.

T 7. When you are driving in high altitudes, you have to pay more attention to your engine overheating than you do in lower altitudes.

Select the phrase that best completes each sentence below. Write the letter of the answer you have chosen to the left of each statement.

b 8. When parking in a space just beyond an intersection, you
a. signal before entering the intersection.
b. signal after you have entered the intersection.
c. signal when you are completely through the intersection.
d. do not signal at all. It is safer to avoid signaling in this case.

c 9. The four basic kinds of road communication that drivers exchange are
a. intentions, nonverbal, silent, oral.
b. nonverbal, presence, electronic, oral.
c. intentions, warnings, presence, feedback.
d. warnings, passive, nonverbal, basic.

a 10. The most dangerous movement of the four listed below is
a. passing a vehicle on a two-lane, two-way highway.
b. passing a motorcycle on a freeway.
c. being passed by any vehicle on a two-lane, two-way highway.
d. passing a truck on a freeway.

c 11. You know that it is illegal to pass another vehicle when
a. a warning sign says so.
b. a roadway marking says so.
c. both a and b are true.
d. none of the above applies.

NAME _____ DATE _____

d 12. When you are going to pass another vehicle, you can communicate your intentions by
a. honking your horn.
b. flashing your lights.
c. using your turn signal.
d. doing both b and c.

b 13. When passing another vehicle, you move back into the lane
a. when the vehicle flashes its lights at you.
b. when you can see the vehicle's headlights in your mirror.
c. when you can see the entire vehicle in your mirror.
d. 15 seconds after you begin making your pass.

a 14. When another vehicle is passing you,
a. it is illegal to speed up.
b. it is illegal to slow down.
c. keep your car in the left side of the lane.
d. both a and c apply.

The following statements are procedures you follow when changing lanes. Number them in the order that you would perform them.

4 15. Adjust your speed up and down as necessary.

6 16. Steer smoothly into the next lane.

1 17. Check your mirrors.

5 18. Move only when you have the time and space to do so.

3 19. Check over your shoulder for vehicles in your blind spot.

2 20. Signal your intent to move.

21. When you are leaving a curb, you should consider visibility, time, and space. What are the factors that you need to be aware of in all three of these areas?

Visibility—Check your view of oncoming traffic and of traffic ahead of and behind you. Notice any traffic

signals, signs, and road markings. Time—Be aware of the speed limit and the speed of traffic. Space—

Check the space in front of and behind your vehicle to make sure you have space to enter the roadway

while still keeping clear of the vehicle ahead of you.

_____

_____

_____

NAME _____ DATE _____

CHAPTER 9 Basic Driving Skills

Moving from and to Curbs

A. Read the following account of a collision. You are the investigating police officer. Make a sketch of the collision scene in the space below. Explain how the collision could have been avoided.

Vehicle A was parked alongside the right curb just behind vehicle B. The driver of vehicle A came out of the dry cleaner's and hung the dry-cleaned clothes over the left rear window. The driver entered vehicle A and checked for traffic in the rearview mirror. Seeing none, the driver began to move the vehicle away from the curb and into the traffic lane. Vehicle C, traveling in the same direction and coming from behind vehicle A, crashed into the driver's side of vehicle A. The impact pushed vehicle A into the left side of vehicle B.
Review student's sketch.

The driver of vehicle A should have checked for traffic in the blind spot by looking over his or

her left shoulder and should have checked in the left sideview mirror. The driver would then

have seen vehicle C approaching. The driver of vehicle C should have been alert to the

possibility of vehicle A pulling into traffic and should have slowed or stopped.

B. FIND OUT MORE. Observe as a passenger in a car, bus, other vehicle, or even as a pedestrian, how people move from curb to curb. Keep notes on how the drivers that you observe manage visibility, time, and space. Can you draw any conclusions?

Review student's work.

_____

_____

_____

_____

_____

_____

NAME _____ DATE _____

Power and Speed on Hills and Mountains

A. Complete the sentences below by filling in the blanks with the correct words.

1. When you drive downhill, __gravity__ makes you go faster.

2. If you are behind a truck when going downhill, __increase__ your following distance.

3. When going from a flat highway to driving uphill, your vehicle needs __more__ power to maintain the same speed.

4. Going up a hill in a vehicle equipped with a manual transmission means that you have to __downshift__ to gain power.

5. As you drive downhill in a vehicle equipped with manual transmission, you may want to __downshift__ to help your vehicle slow down.

6. In high altitudes, there is __less__ oxygen in the air.

7. In high altitudes, a vehicle's engine may stall because at that altitude, gas can __vaporize__.

B. For driving on mountain roads, what are the differences between automatic and manual transmissions? What are some special problems that mountains present because of their high altitudes?

When you drive uphill in a vehicle with an automatic transmission, the shifting will be done

automatically, but going downhill, you will have to downshift manually if you need to slow

down. In a car with a manual transmission, you have to shift manually going either up or down.

At high altitudes, steep grades, sharp curves, bad weather conditions, and less oxygen can

make driving difficult.

C. FIND OUT MORE. Go to the library and look at a topographical road map of your state. Where are the roads in your state with the highest elevations? If your state has no roads at higher elevations, look at another state.

Review student's answers.

_____

_____

_____

NAME _____ DATE _____

Changing Lanes Safely

A. You should ask yourself the following questions before changing lanes or passing another vehicle. After each question, write an explanation of why it is an important consideration.

1. What is the path of travel like in the lane you are in? You need to know if the vehicles ahead of you are slowing down or stopping.

2. What is the path of travel like in the lane you want to enter? You need to know if the lane you are entering is clear next to you and also 20 to 30 seconds ahead of you.

3. Are other vehicles signaling to move into the lane you want to enter? It is important not to collide with other vehicles that are entering the same lane. The drivers may not see you.

4. What is happening in the lanes behind you? You should be aware of any vehicles tailgating or coming up fast behind you.

5. How fast are you going? Can you change lanes without exceeding the speed limit? You should not exceed the speed limit to change lanes.

6. Do you have room to make the move safely? For you to make a safe pass, there should be a large enough gap in the flow of oncoming and ongoing vehicles.

7. How much of a gap is there between vehicles in the lane you are moving into? You should have a safe gap between any vehicles ahead of you so that you can pull into it safely after the pass.

B. FIND OUT MORE. Using three separate situations, record your observations on the ways other drivers handle visibility, time, and space in changing lanes. Where were you? What time of the day was it? Could a collision have occurred because of what you saw?

Review student's work.

_____

_____

_____

_____

NAME _____ DATE _____

Passing Another Vehicle and Being Passed

A. For each sentence below, circle T if the statement is true and F if it is false. Correct each false statement in the space below.

1. You should not pass another vehicle in heavy fog.   (T)   F

2. You typically need to accelerate 25 miles per hour faster than the vehicle ahead of you if you are passing it on a two-lane highway.   T   (F)
You will typically need to accelerate 10 to 15 mph faster than the vehicle ahead of you.

3. You should exceed the speed limit only when passing a vehicle on a two-lane road.   T   (F)
You can never legally exceed the speed limit.

4. If you are driving a vehicle at 50 mph, it will take you about 6 seconds to pass another vehicle that is going 40 mph.   T   (F)
It will take you 16 seconds going 50 mph to pass a vehicle that is going 40 mph.

5. You should signal your intent to return to the right lane when passing a vehicle after you see both headlights in your sideview mirror.   T   (F)
You should signal your intent when you see both headlights in your rearview mirror.

6. It is illegal to accelerate when you are being passed by another vehicle.   (T)   F

B. FIND OUT MORE. Pay careful attention to the route from your home to your school. Are there any no-passing zones on this route? What is the evidence that they are no-passing zones? Why do you think they are there?

Location	Evidence	Reason
Review student's work.		

Basic Driving Skills

CHAPTER OVERVIEW

LESSON ONE

Basic procedures for moving away from a curb into traffic and out of traffic toward a curb are described.

LESSON TWO

Basic procedures for driving on hills and mountains are explained.

LESSON THREE

Factors involved in changing lanes safely are described.

LESSON FOUR

Procedures for safely passing a vehicle are described. What to do when a vehicle passes your vehicle is also discussed.

154

CONCEPT OF THE DRIVING TASK

Explain that patience plays an important part in responsible driving. Impatient drivers may drive too fast and may perform unsafe actions. Drivers should be mature enough to wait calmly and patiently in all traffic situations, from red lights to bumper-to-bumper traffic.

CHAPTER 9

Basic Driving Skills

Minimizing risk on the roadway depends on drivers' mastery of basic driving skills, such as passing, changing lanes, and moving to and from curbs. Understanding how to safely execute these skills is vital to all drivers.

CHAPTER 9   *Basic Driving Skills*   **155**

PRESENTING THE BIG IDEA

Drivers must learn to handle their vehicle under a variety of traffic and road conditions. Thinking ahead is one of the keys to safe driving under all conditions.

INTRODUCING THE CHAPTER

What's on the Road Ahead?

Have students look at the photographs and read the lesson titles and objectives. Briefly discuss the topic of each lesson. Tell students that in this chapter, they will be introduced to procedures for entering and leaving the flow of traffic, driving on hills and mountains, changing lanes, and passing vehicles.

Background: Violations and Collisions

All too many drivers pass vehicles improperly, exceed the speed limit, and commit other moving violations. Such violations are a good predictor of the likelihood of having a collision.

- Fewer than one in every seven drivers gets even one traffic ticket in a given year.
- Studies indicate that drivers with several tickets are three times more likely to be involved in a collision than drivers with a clean record.
- Statistics show that the average driver has a one-in-three chance of being injured in a lifetime of driving. However, drivers who tend to get tickets every year have about a one-to-one chance of being injured in a vehicle crash in their lifetime.

Relating to Prior Knowledge

Have students discuss what they know about driving on hills and mountains.

The Big Idea

Discuss students' reactions to the Big Idea statement. Suggest that they keep this idea in mind as they read Chapter 9.

Moving from a Curb into Traffic and out of Traffic to a Curb

(pages 156–158)

FOCUS

Objectives

• Describe procedures for steering away from the curb and entering traffic.

• Describe procedures for steering out of traffic and moving toward a curb.

Resources

 Study Guide, page 33

 Traffic charts

 Behind-the-Wheel Checklists 7 and 8

Motivator

Pose the following: You're parked at the curb on a busy street. You want to pull away from the curb and enter the flow of traffic. How can you manage visibility, time, and space to move away from the curb safely? (Sample answer: Be aware of how fast traffic is moving; check space in front of and behind your vehicle; decide whether you have enough room and time to pull out safely.)

TEACH

Explain

OBJECTIVE 1: Students should be reminded to look ahead just before moving away from a curb. A driver whose attention is focused solely on traffic flow may forget to check for the unexpected—such as a pedestrian walking in front of the vehicle.

LESSON ONE

OBJECTIVES

1. Describe procedures for steering away from the curb and entering traffic.
2. Describe procedures for steering out of traffic and moving toward a curb.

Moving from a Curb into Traffic and out of Traffic to a Curb

Basic driving skills include moving your vehicle away from the curb and into traffic, as well as moving the vehicle out of traffic and to the curb.

Anytime you are moving into or out of the flow of traffic, not with it, you face increased risks. You have to make judgments about visibility, time, and space. For example: Can you see well enough to make this move safely? How fast are other vehicles moving? Is there time enough and space enough to make the move?

What Is the Procedure for Leaving a Curb and Entering Traffic?

When you leave a curb, you are going from a stopped position to a moving position. This procedure involves planning how you will move, then actually making the move.

◆ As with any driving maneuver, you must plan ahead before leaving a curb and entering traffic.

Advance Planning

Visibility, time, and space are important factors in planning your move away from a curb.

Visibility Check your view of oncoming traffic and also of traffic ahead of you and behind you. Notice any traffic signals, signs, and road markings.

Time Be aware of the speed limit on the roadway and how fast the vehicles in the lane into which you want to move and the lanes next to it are moving. Will you have enough time to move into your lane? Will vehicles behind you have

156 UNIT 2 *Learning the Basics*

IT'S A FACT

Many fatal collisions occur when vehicles strike trees, utility poles, signposts, or other objects fixed in place along the road. One-third of such roadside hazard collisions occur on minor and local roadways. Twice as many fatal roadside hazard crashes take place at night as in the daytime.

to slow down or stop when you merge into traffic?

Space Check the space in front of and behind your vehicle. Decide whether or not you have room to pull out of your parked position in one smooth move or whether you will have to maneuver back and forth to clear a vehicle parked in front of you. Make sure you have room to enter the roadway and still keep a safe distance between your vehicle and the one in front of you.

Making the Move from the Right Curb

Once you've made your plan to leave the curb, follow these steps for making the move.

1. Using both your sideview and rearview mirrors, check the traffic around you.
2. When you have decided it is safe to move into traffic, signal your intention to leave the curb.
3. Turn to your left and look over your shoulder to check traffic in your blind spot.
4. Steer away from the curb and directly into the nearest lane of traffic, accelerating moderately. If traffic is heavy, you may want to use an arm signal. (See Chapter 11 for instructions on how and when to use arm signals.)

What Is the Procedure for Steering to the Curb?

Steering your car out of traffic and toward a curb also requires advance planning before you actually make the move.

◆ *Once you have prepared in advance, you are ready to move into the traffic flow.*

TIPS FOR NEW DRIVERS

Parking Beyond an Intersection

Be especially careful if you have decided to park in a space or make a turn just beyond an intersection. Follow these steps.

1. Do not signal right or left as you approach the intersection. Other drivers may think you're going to turn at the intersection.
2. If other vehicles are near the intersection, move carefully into the correct lane and slow down.
3. Use your signals only after you have entered the intersection.

OBJECTIVE 2: Students will benefit from a discussion of the need for caution when steering toward a curb. Two hazards to watch for are parked vehicles pulling out into traffic and pedestrians dashing into the street.

Teaching Model

Display this situation:

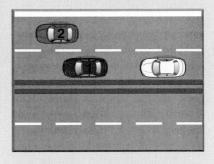

Tell students the following: You are in vehicle 1 traveling at 30 mph. You want to pull over to the curb as soon as it's safe to do so. Model the thinking process that you go through to manage visibility, time, and space. (You do the following.

• Check traffic ahead and behind you and to the sides.
• Consider the speed of your vehicle and of other vehicles.
• Signal your intent to move right.
• Gradually reduce speed.
• Wait until vehicle 2 is safely out of the way, then steer toward the curb.)

Ask

Ask students to discuss the dangers of moving toward the curb without checking traffic behind and to the side.

Read

Have students read Lesson 1 to learn how to manage visibility, time, and space when steering away from or toward a curb.

ASSESS

Guided Practice

Have students answer the Lesson 1 Review questions. The answers are provided below.

Driving Tip

Caution students always to check signs before stopping at a curb. Parking—or even stopping momentarily—at certain curbs is dangerous and often illegal. For example, drivers should not park next to fire hydrants or at bus stops.

TIPS FOR NEW DRIVERS

You may want to use a traffic chart to help students visualize why parking in a space just beyond an intersection requires extra care. Encourage students to restate the tips in their own words.

Reteaching

Pair a more able student with one who is having difficulty. Have them use the traffic chart to demonstrate management of visibility, time, and space when moving away from or toward a curb.

Enrichment

Assign the Study Guide for Lesson 1. The Find Out More section encourages students to expand their basic learning of the lesson concepts.

CLOSE

Summarize

Return to the Motivator question, and discuss the situation again in light of what students have learned about visibility, time, and space. Have them describe as specifically as possible how they would manage visibility, time, and space factors.

DRIVER'S LOG

How can managing visibility, time, and space help you reduce risk when moving toward or away from a curb?

WHAT WOULD YOU DO?

Sample answer: Use your mirrors to check traffic around you. Look over your shoulder to check blind spots. Do not move until you locate the emergency vehicle and are sure it has passed.

Advance Planning

You need to make plans in advance whenever you move your vehicle out of traffic.

As with moving away from a curb, visibility, time, and space are key factors in your plan to move *toward* the curb.

Visibility Pick out the spot where you want to stop. Scan the traffic scene in front of you, and use your mirrors to check traffic behind you and to your sides.

Time Note the speed of the traffic you're in. Consider how much you'll have to slow down to make the move.

Space Notice the amount of room available to you to move into another lane, if you need to do so to get to the curb. Is there space to move your vehicle directly into the parking place, or will you need to maneuver to parallel park?

Making the Move

After you have planned your move and decided it is safe to move toward the curb, follow these steps.

WHAT WOULD YOU DO?

You hear an emergency vehicle approaching as you are about to pull away from the curb. What steps would you take?

1. Signal your intent to move.
2. Tap your brakes lightly, signaling to drivers behind you that you are going to stop.
3. Apply gradual pressure on the brakes to reduce speed.
4. Steer out of the traffic lane to where you want to go, using your brakes as needed to stop the vehicle.

Lesson 1 Review

1. What are some factors to consider when moving your vehicle away from a curb and into the flow of traffic?
2. How can your wish to park near an intersection affect the way you exit from the flow of traffic?

Lesson 1 Review

Answers

1. You should consider traffic in front and in back of you, the speed of vehicles already on the road, and the space available to you.
2. You would use your signals only after you have entered the intersection, not as you approach it.

Managing Power and Speed on Hills and Mountains

OBJECTIVES

1. Describe how to drive uphill and downhill.
2. Describe safe procedures for driving on mountain roadways.

Whenever you drive, you always have an invisible passenger with you. That passenger is the force of gravity. Gravity works both inside and outside your vehicle at the same time.

If you drive uphill, gravity works against your vehicle, so you need to use more power. If you drive downhill, gravity is working with you, so you need to use less power, and you may have to use your brakes. For more information about how gravity affects your vehicle, see Chapter 15.

How Do You Drive Uphill and Downhill?

Driving on hills takes special effort, regardless of whether your vehicle has an automatic transmission or a manual transmission.

Driving Uphill

As you drive uphill, your vehicle needs more power in order to keep moving at the same speed. How you provide that power depends on whether your vehicle has an automatic or a manual transmission.

◆ *Whether you are driving uphill or downhill, the force of gravity is pulling on your car.*

THE INTERNATIONAL SCENE

Canada and Mexico

Gasoline and oil are sold by the liter in both Canada and Mexico. One liter equals just over $\frac{1}{4}$ gallon, or slightly more than 1 quart.

FOCUS

Objectives

- Describe how to drive uphill and downhill.
- Describe safe procedures for driving on mountain roadways.

Resources

- Study Guide, page 34
- Traffic charts
- Behind-the-Wheel Checklist 29

Motivator

Pose the following: You're driving along a rural highway. The road ahead slopes sharply upward. How can you drive up the hill smoothly if you're driving a vehicle with an automatic transmission? A vehicle with a manual transmission? (Students may respond that when driving with an automatic transmission, slowly increase pressure on the accelerator until your vehicle reaches the speed you want to maintain; when driving with a manual transmission, downshift to increase the engine's pulling power.)

TEACH

Explain

OBJECTIVE 1: Students should understand that the steeper and longer the hill they are ascending or descending, the more they may need to use the accelerator, brake, or gearshift to maintain their desired speed.

OBJECTIVE 2: Students may benefit from a discussion of the special visibility problems inherent in mountain driving, such as not being able to see around sharp curves or over the crest of hills.

Teaching Model

Describe the following situation: You're driving down a mountain road that has many sharp curves. It's hard for you to see oncoming traffic, so you know it's just as difficult for oncoming traffic to see you. Model the thinking process that you go through to minimize risk. (You do the following.

• Be certain that your headlights are on to help other drivers see your vehicle.

• Drive cautiously, at a reduced speed, and increase your following distance.

• Watch for signs warning of road conditions ahead.

• Reduce speed going into curves, and tap your horn to warn approaching drivers.)

Ask

Ask students to discuss the risks of driving down such a mountain road too fast.

Read

Have students read Lesson 2 to learn how to reduce risk when driving on hills and on mountain roads.

ASSESS

Guided Practice

Have students answer the Lesson 2 Review questions. The answers are provided below.

SAFETY TIPS

Be especially alert when you are driving through a falling rock zone. Be prepared to brake suddenly or to take other evasive maneuvers.

◆ *Shift to a lower gear to control speed when driving down a long, steep hill.*

Automatic transmission Before your vehicle begins to lose speed by moving uphill, slowly increase the amount of pressure you are putting on the gas pedal. Notice your speedometer. When you've reached the speed you want to maintain, keep your foot at that point until you near the crest of the hill or need to slow down for any reason.

Manual transmission Before your vehicle begins to lose power and speed, downshift to a lower gear in order to increase the engine's pulling power. (For more information on downshifting, see Chapter 8.)

Driving Downhill

As you drive downhill, your car will gain speed, so you need to decrease the engine power.

Automatic transmission Ease the pressure you are applying to the gas pedal. Your vehicle will begin to coast. If it begins to pick up too much speed, press the brake pedal lightly to slow down. If you're going to go down a long, steep hill, it is best to move the selector lever to a lower gear before starting down the hill. Doing so gives you better control of your speed and steering and saves on braking. If you need to use the brake, use periodic light pressure. Do not ride the brake pedal.

Manual transmission If you're going to go down a long, steep hill, it is best to downshift to a lower gear before you start down the hill. Doing so gives you more control over the speed of your vehicle by allowing you to use the engine to help slow the vehicle. If you wait to shift until you are moving downhill and picking up speed, you will need to apply the brakes lightly while shifting to the next lower gear. If the hill is steep, your engine's braking power may not be enough to slow the vehicle unless you continue to apply the brakes. If this is the case, quickly downshift again. Use the brakes to slow down even more if you need to.

How Do You Drive in the Mountains?

Driving up or down mountains presents special problems. The roads are curved and the grades may be steep. You need to use extra care to be able to control your vehicle under these conditions.

Special Roadway and Traffic Problems

Sharp curves, steep grades, and other vehicles limit how much of the road ahead you can see at one

---

Driving Tip

Advise students that they should try to avoid "riding" the brake pedal when traveling down long, steep hills. Doing so can cause the brakes to overheat, leading to "brake fade," a kind of temporary brake failure. Explain to students that if their brakes do overheat, they should pull off the roadway and allow the brakes to cool.

time. When you come to a curve where it is difficult to see oncoming traffic, slow down. If necessary, tap your horn and flash your lights to warn approaching drivers.

If you are behind a truck or vehicle with a trailer, increase your following distance. Pay attention to signs and pavement markings.

Effects of Weather and Altitude

Rain, snow, haze, and fog are especially dangerous when you are driving in the mountains. Try to find out about the weather conditions in the area before you begin a mountain drive.

In high altitudes, the air contains less oxygen. Lack of oxygen can cause you to feel short of breath and sleepy. Your heart may beat faster, and you may get a headache. If any of these symptoms occur, change drivers, stop driving, or find a route at a lesser altitude, if possible.

Mountain air also affects your vehicle's engine. It, too, gets less oxygen and loses power. It heats up faster, and gas may vaporize in the fuel line, causing the engine to sputter and stall. Keep an eye on the temperature gauge. If it shows red or hot, stop and allow the engine to cool.

Driving up a Mountain

If your vehicle has an automatic transmission, use the same procedure to drive up a mountain as you would use if you were driving up a hill. The transmission will downshift automatically. If you have a manual transmission, you may need to downshift often to go up steep inclines.

Driving down a Mountain

If you are driving with an automatic transmission, downshift manually for better control when going down a mountain. Do not ride the brake pedal. Use periodic light pressure on the brakes to slow down gradually. If you are driving with a manual shift, downshift as often as necessary to reduce speed, maintain control, and save on braking.

Lesson 2 Review

1. How are procedures for driving uphill different from those for driving downhill?
2. How can high altitude affect you and your vehicle if you are driving in the mountains?

Energy Tips

If your vehicle is equipped with cruise control, do not use it when you are driving uphill or downhill. It wastes gas. Save it for flat, straight roadways.

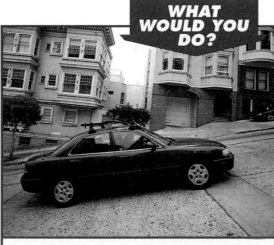

WHAT WOULD YOU DO?

Your vehicle has an automatic transmission, and you've been using the Drive gear. Describe your procedure as you are about to head up a hill.

Lesson 2 Review

Answers

1. As you drive uphill, you need to increase engine power; as you drive downhill, you need to decrease engine power.
2. You can become short of breath and sleepy. The engine may sputter and stall.

Reteaching

Have students work together in small groups to list risk management guidelines for driving on hills and mountains. Encourage them to make their lists as specific as possible and to include guidelines for both automatic and manual transmission vehicles. If students have trouble recalling risk management ideas, direct them to locate these ideas again in their books. You may also want to have students make explanatory drawings to accompany their lists.

Enrichment

Assign the Study Guide for Lesson 2. The Find Out More section encourages students to expand their basic learning of the lesson concepts.

CLOSE

Summarize

Return to the Motivator question, and discuss the situation again in light of the specific information students have gained from this lesson. Review the challenges of driving on hills and mountains and ways in which drivers can reduce risk.

DRIVER'S LOG

How can you manage visibility, time, and space when driving on hills and on mountain roads?

WHAT WOULD YOU DO?

Sample answer: Slowly increase the amount of pressure you are putting on the gas pedal.

Managing Visibility, Time, and Space When Changing Lanes

(pages 162–163)

FOCUS

Objectives

• Describe several factors involved in planning a lane change correctly.

• Understand the steps involved in making a lane change.

Resources

 Study Guide, page 35

 Traffic charts

 Behind-the-Wheel Checklist 9

 Information Master 16

Motivator

You're driving in the right lane of a four-lane roadway. You need to move to the left lane to make a left turn. How can you manage visibility, time, and space to change lanes safely? (Students may mention checking traffic ahead, behind, and to the sides; checking the speed of your vehicle and other vehicles; making sure there is enough room to move left; adjusting speed, signaling, checking blind spot, and moving left when it is safe to do so.)

LESSON THREE

OBJECTIVES
1. Describe several factors involved in planning a lane change correctly.
2. Understand the steps involved in making a lane change.

Managing Visibility, Time, and Space When Changing Lanes

TIPS — FOR NEW DRIVERS

Communicating with Other Drivers

Your safety, the safety of your passengers, and the safety of other roadway users depend to a large extent on how well you communicate with other drivers and with pedestrians. Good roadway communication involves giving clear signals and warnings, paying attention to signals and warnings given by other drivers, and noticing where pedestrians are and what they are doing.

Drivers exchange four basic kinds of communication.

Intentions
plan to turn left or right; slowing down; plan to pass (please move over); plan to back up

Warnings
trouble ahead in my lane; need to stop suddenly; danger in your lane; headlights are blinding

Presence
parked vehicle; disabled vehicle

Feedback
recognizing another driver's signal; recognizing the presence of a pedestrian; thanks to a driver for allowing you to pass

Here is how to communicate.

Electronic signals
turn-signal lights, brake lights, backup lights, emergency hazard flashers; horn (short, sharp, or steady blasts); headlights (flash on and off, switch from high to low beams)

Body gestures
hand signals; nodding up and down; shaking head sideways; smiling; puzzled or confused look; raised eyebrows

You have probably seen drivers who are constantly changing lanes, swooping between other vehicles on the highway. Chances are they're exceeding the speed limit and endangering lives. Of course, there are times when you and other drivers need to change lanes. You can minimize risk by learning the right way to do it.

What Is the Safest Way to Change Lanes?

As with other safe driving procedures, changing lanes involves two major phases: advance planning and making the change.

Advance Planning

You may have any of a number of reasons for changing lanes. You may need to change lanes to make a turn, pass another vehicle, avoid an obstacle in your lane, park, or exit a road. Whatever the reason for changing lanes, you need to plan ahead in order to make the move safely. Planning includes knowing where you are now, where you want to go, and what the road and traffic conditions are between the two. Check these items as you plan your move.

State BY State

Drivers with DWI convictions have in the past had their license suspended or revoked. In most states, however, drivers may now have their license taken away even before conviction if they fail or refuse to take a chemical test for alcohol. This procedure is known as *administrative license revocation* (ALR).

TIPS — FOR NEW DRIVERS

To check student understanding, you may want to discuss situations that require specific communication.

Visibility What is the path of travel like in the lane you are in? Note if there are vehicles in the path ahead and what they are doing. Use your mirrors to check for vehicles behind you. What is the path of travel like in the lane you want to enter? Search ahead 20 to 30 seconds and to the sides and rear.

Are other vehicles signaling to move into the lane you want to move to? If they are, wait until the other vehicles have changed lanes. Then check again.

Time How fast will you be going? You may need to increase or decrease speed to change lanes.

Space Do you have room to make the move safely? Make sure there is a 4-second gap between vehicles that you can move into.

◆ *You should take road conditions into account before you decide to change lanes.*

Making the Change

After you have checked out your plan to change lanes and are ready to make the move, follow these steps.

1. Check your mirrors again.
2. Signal your intent to move right or left.
3. Check over your shoulder on the side next to the lane you want to enter for vehicles in your blind spot.
4. Adjust your speed as necessary.
5. Move only when you have the time and space to do so.
6. Steer smoothly into the next lane. Push-pull-feed steering is best. After you have steered into the next lane, turn off your signal.

Lesson 3 Review

1. What factors are involved in planning a lane change?
2. What steps would you follow to make a lane change?

WHAT WOULD YOU DO?

You want to move into the right-hand lane. How will you manage visibility, time, and space?

WHAT WOULD YOU DO?

Sample answer: You should wait at a safe distance until there are no vehicles or pedestrians in your path or in your blind spots.

Lesson 3 Review

Answers

1. Advance planning: checking visibility, time, and space and making the change.
2. Check your mirrors again; signal your intent to change lanes; check over your shoulder; adjust your speed; move only when you have time and space to do so; steer smoothly into the next lane.

TEACH

Explain

OBJECTIVES 1 and 2: Students should be cautioned to watch for nearby drivers changing lanes at the same time they are.

Teaching Model

Describe the following situation: You're driving on a highway. You need to move into the right lane. Model your thinking process. (Check traffic conditions; adjust speed as needed; signal; steer into the right lane when safe.)

Ask

When might you increase rather than decrease speed before changing lanes?

Read

Have students read Lesson 3 to learn how visibility, time, and space come into play when one changes lanes.

ASSESS

Guided Practice

Have students answer the Lesson 3 Review questions. The answers are provided below.

Reteaching

Have small groups brainstorm factors to consider before changing lanes.

Enrichment

Assign the Study Guide for Lesson 3. The Find Out More section encourages students to expand learning of the lesson concepts.

CLOSE

Summarize

Reexamine the Motivator question in light of the information students gained from this lesson.

DRIVER'S LOG

How can managing visibility, time, and space help you change lanes safely?

Passing Another Vehicle and Being Passed

(pages 164–166)

FOCUS

Objectives

- Name conditions you should be aware of when you want to pass another vehicle.
- Describe the procedure for passing another vehicle.
- Describe what to do when another vehicle passes you.

Resources

 Study Guide, page 36

 Traffic charts

 Transparency 22

 Behind-the-Wheel Checklist 21

Motivator

Pose the following: You're driving on a two-lane, two-way highway. You're following a truck that is moving more slowly than you'd like to be going. How can you decide whether or not to pass the truck? (Sample answer: Consider whether passing is legal. You also have to consider traffic, weather, and road conditions as well as the speed at which your vehicle and the truck are traveling.)

TEACH

Explain

OBJECTIVE 1: Students will benefit from a discussion of visibility factors in the context of this statement from the student text: "If you cannot see ahead to the place where you will reenter the lane after passing, do not attempt to pass."

OBJECTIVES

1. Name conditions you should be aware of when you want to pass another vehicle.
2. Describe the procedure for passing another vehicle.
3. Describe what to do when another vehicle passes you.

Passing Another Vehicle and Being Passed

Passing another vehicle on a two-lane, two-way roadway can be one of the most dangerous movements in driving.

What Conditions Will Help You Decide Whether You Should or Should Not Pass?

Before you pass another vehicle on a road with one lane of traffic in each direction, you need to know whether or not passing is legal. If passing is legal, you then need to decide whether it makes sense to pass under existing traffic, weather, and road conditions. Finally, you need to decide whether your speed, the speed of the vehicle ahead of you, and the speed limit make it possible for you to pass safely.

Road Signs and Pavement Markings

Warning signs and roadway markings will tell you whether passing is allowed in the area in which you are driving. (See Chapter 5.)

Atmospheric Conditions

Bright sunlight, rain, snow, sleet, hail, and fog add to the danger of passing. If you're driving under these conditions, it is wiser to slow down, proceed with caution, and perhaps avoid passing even if road signs and markings indicate that passing is allowed.

Nighttime visibility and the condition of the road surface can also add to the danger of passing. If you cannot see ahead to the place where you will reenter the lane after passing, do not attempt to pass. If the road surface seems rough or in poor condition, avoid passing.

Your Speed and the Other Vehicle's Speed

As you approach a vehicle in front of you, note your speed. You may have to slow down to keep a margin of safety between your vehicle and the one ahead. Estimate how fast the other vehicle is moving. If it is going 5 to 10 miles per hour more slowly than you were before you began to slow down, you might decide to pass.

FYI

If you're driving a vehicle at 50 miles per hour, it will take you about 16 seconds to pass another vehicle traveling at 40 miles per hour. Longer vehicles, such as trucks and campers, take even more time to pass.

Driving Tip

Caution students to take special care when passing another vehicle while traveling up or down a hill. Vehicles moving in both directions may increase or decrease speed markedly, especially on steep inclines.

You must also be aware of the speed limit on the roadway. You will typically need to accelerate to 10 to 15 miles per hour faster than the vehicle in front of you in order to pass it. However, you cannot legally exceed the speed limit to pass another vehicle.

How Do You Pass Another Vehicle?

Once you know it is legal to pass and it makes sense to pass in the situation, follow this procedure.

1. Check the path ahead, the off-road areas, behind you, and the lane you want to enter. Make sure no other vehicles are signaling to move into the lane. If you are on a two-lane, two-way road, check that there are no oncoming vehicles. If there are, make sure that they are far enough away to allow you to complete the passing safely. If you have any doubt, do not pass.
2. If the way is clear, signal your intent to pass. Flash your headlights. Use your left turn signal.
3. Check over your left shoulder for vehicles in your blind spot. Adjust your speed upward as necessary, and steer smoothly into the passing lane. Use very slight controlled movement of the wheel—usually not more than one-eighth of a turn.
4. Accelerate firmly. If you are on a road with a single lane in each direction, keep watching for oncoming traffic.
5. Check your rearview mirror quickly. When you see both headlights of the vehicle you've passed in the rearview mirror, signal your intent to return to the right lane and steer gradually in that direction. Turn off your signal, and maintain an appropriate speed.

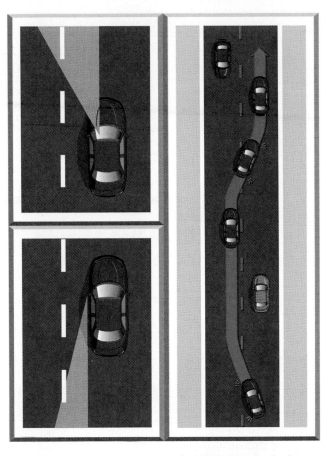

◆ **Before you pass, check your path ahead and to the sides and rear. Signal, pass, and signal again before returning to your lane. Keep in mind that if you're traveling 40 mph, you will need 10 to 13 seconds to pass a vehicle traveling 30 mph. However, if you're traveling 60 mph and the other vehicle is traveling 50 mph, the passing time increases to 16 to 19 seconds.**

MEETING STUDENT DIVERSITY

English as a Second Language

Students who have difficulty with English will benefit from an opportunity to act out the concepts. Use the traffic chart or arrange chairs in the classroom to allow students to role-play various situations. Encourage students to explain what visibility, time, and space factors they must consider as they go through each situation.

OBJECTIVE 2: Students should recognize how visibility, time, and space factors come into play when one is passing another vehicle.

OBJECTIVE 3: Students should be prepared for the unsafe actions of other drivers, such as cutting back into a lane too soon after passing.

Teaching Model

Display this situation:

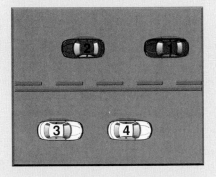

Tell students the following: You are in vehicle 1, and you want to pass vehicle 2. Model the thinking process you will use. (You will check lane markings to see if passing is legal; check traffic to see if it is safe to pass; determine that it is not safe; wait for vehicles 3 and 4 to go by; then check again.)

Ask

Ask what actions the driver of vehicle 2 should take when vehicle 1 passes.

Read

Have students read Lesson 4 to learn how to manage visibility, time, and space when passing or being passed.

ASSESS

Guided Practice

Have students answer the Lesson 4 Review questions. The answers are provided below.

ADVICE FROM THE EXPERTS

Encourage students to discuss the idea that a good driver is very predictable.

Reteaching

Have students work together in small groups to brainstorm questions drivers should ask themselves before passing a vehicle. After groups have completed this task, have them combine their questions into one class list and then discuss factors affecting the possible answers to each question.

Enrichment

Assign the Study Guide for Lesson 4. The Find Out More section encourages students to expand their basic learning of the lesson concepts.

CLOSE

Summarize

Return to the Motivator question, and discuss the situation again in terms of visibility, time, and space factors. Extend the discussion by asking students how the situation might change if the road surface was wet or the roadway was foggy.

DRIVER'S LOG

What factors should you consider before passing a vehicle?

WHAT WOULD YOU DO?

Sample answer: No, not until traffic thins out and there is more space.

ADVICE FROM THE EXPERTS

Barry Caruso
Coordinator, Traffic Safety Education,
Wayne County Public Schools, Ohio

Basic on-road procedures—such as moving to and from the curb, driving on grades, changing lanes, and passing—never change. The better you perform these procedures, the more predictable you are. A good driver is very predictable. A predictable driver communicates every move. Once you have perfected basic on-road procedures, you need to tell other drivers what you are doing.

Remember, as the driver you are responsible for the action of your vehicle. Be as good a driver as you can, and THINK!

What Should You Do If You Are Being Passed?

Drivers of vehicles that are passing you assume the responsibility for their safety and yours, but you can often protect yourself and be of help to the passing driver.

By regularly checking your sideview and rearview mirrors, you can remain aware of the movement of vehicles behind you and alongside of you. When you see that you're being passed, stay to the right in your lane. Do not speed up: It is illegal to do so when you're being passed.

Remain aware of the traffic situation around you. Sometimes a passing vehicle will decide to drop back rather than complete the pass. Do not accelerate unless it is necessary to give the vehicle more room to get back behind you.

Does it make sense for the driver of the car behind the van to try to pass the van?

Lesson 4 Review

1. What should you consider before deciding to pass another vehicle?
2. How are visibility, time, and space important when passing another vehicle?
3. How can you help another driver who is passing you?

Lesson 4 Review

Answers

1. You should consider visibility, weather, and road conditions; you should make sure passing is legal; you should consider the speed of your vehicle and of the other vehicle.
2. You must be able to see the roadway and other vehicles, and you must have sufficient time and space to pass the other vehicle.
3. You can help by regularly checking your mirrors, keeping to the right, and not increasing speed.

Using Prefixes and Combining Forms

The vocabulary describing vehicles and roadways is full of interesting words. Several of these words are formed by using a prefix and a root word.

A prefix is a word part that has a meaning of its own but cannot stand alone as a word. Here are some examples of prefixes and their meanings:

anti—not, against
de—removed, reversed
dis—apart, away from
inter—between, among
re—again
trans—across, beyond, or through
un—not

The vocabulary of driving also includes words that begin with a combining form. This is a word part that can act like a prefix, but it can also join another combining form to make a word, such as *photo* + *graphy*. Two common combining forms

are *auto,* meaning "self," and *semi,* meaning "half" or "partly."

Knowing the meanings and uses of prefixes and combining forms can help you figure out the meanings of new words.

Try It Yourself

Choose a prefix or combining form from those above in order to complete each word or term below. Define the words and terms, using what you already know and what you've learned about prefixes and combining forms. If you don't know what a word or term means, ask someone or look it up.

1. ___celeration
2. ___preciation
3. ___national symbols
4. ___action time
5. ___abled
6. ___protected left turn
7. ___change
8. ___section
9. ___alignment
10. ___lock brakes
11. ___freeze
12. ___fogger
13. ___theft device
14. ___tread
15. ___mission

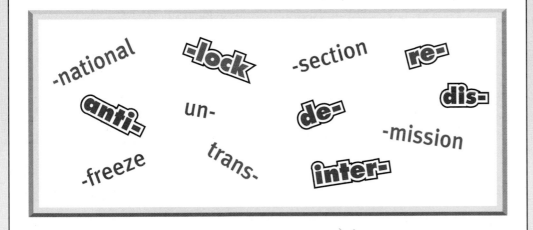

ANSWERS TO Try It Yourself Questions

1. deceleration
2. depreciation
3. international
4. reaction
5. disabled
6. unprotected
7. interchange
8. intersection
9. realignment
10. antilock
11. antifreeze
12. defogger
13. antitheft
14. retread
15. transmission

BUILDING SKILLS: LANGUAGE

Objective

Demonstrate an understanding of prefixes and combining forms.

Teaching the Skill

- Point out that there may be hundreds of words that have the same prefix or combining form. Knowing the meaning of common prefixes and combining forms can therefore be a great aid to vocabulary building.

- Explain to students that when a prefix is added to a root word, the spelling of the word itself does not change. Remembering this can help students correctly spell such potentially confusing words as *misspell* (*mis- + spell*).

- Explain that prefixes and combining forms come from various languages. *Anti-,* for example, comes from Greek, while *dis-* comes from Latin.

CHAPTER **9** REVIEW

CHAPTER SUMMARY

Key Points

Have students read the Key Points to review the major concepts of the chapter.

PROJECTS

Cooperative Learning:

Students will benefit by working with a partner on one or both projects. When the assignment is completed, the whole class will profit by sharing and comparing results.

KEY POINTS

Lesson One

1. To move your vehicle away from a curb and into the flow of traffic, check traffic in front and in back of you, the speed of vehicles already on the roadway, and the space available to you for moving away from the curb.
2. To move your vehicle out of traffic and toward the curb, prepare the move well in advance. Check traffic behind you, signal your intention, steer toward the curb, and brake as needed.

Lesson Two

1. To drive up or down hills, downshift and accelerate or brake as necessary.
2. Use your horn and lights to signal your presence when you cannot see around a sharp curve ahead. Increase your following distance, and be aware of the effects of low oxygen on your body and your vehicle.

Lesson Three

1. To change lanes correctly, plan your move in advance. Check your visibility, the time you will need to change lanes, and if you have room to make the move safely.
2. Communicate your intent to other drivers, check your blind spot, and begin and complete the move. Adjust your speed to meet the situation.

Lesson Four

1. Before you pass another vehicle, note whether passing is legal. Consider the effects of weather and road conditions on your ability to manage visibility, time, and space.
2. To pass another vehicle, make sure you have a clear path of travel, signal your intent, check your blind spot, and begin the pass. Accelerate and return to the lane when you see both headlights of the vehicle you've passed in your rearview mirror.
3. If you are being passed, pay particular attention to the movement of the passing vehicle. You can help a driver who is passing you by giving his or her vehicle enough time and space, remaining aware of the movement of other vehicles, and not speeding up.

PROJECTS

1. Take a ride as a passenger, and record the different forms of communication you notice between drivers. Include communication by mechanical or electronic signals and by body signals. What kinds of information do drivers communicate by each method?
2. Can you tell from reading your state's driver's manual whether your state is one that has many mountain roads? How much space does the manual devote to mountain driving?

*inter*NET CONNECTION

Explore the Web for more information on how to pass a vehicle safely. Find and study illustrations on correct and incorrect ways to pass a vehicle.
drivered.glencoe.com

*inter*NET CONNECTION

Visit Glencoe's Driver Education Web site for student activities that relate to this chapter.
drivered.glencoe.com

CHAPTER TEST

Write the letter of the answer that best completes each sentence.

1. When passing another vehicle, you must
   a. drive 5 mph above the speed limit.
   b. typically accelerate to at least 10 mph faster than the other vehicle.
   c. briefly flash your emergency lights.

2. To complete a pass safely, you should
   a. see the other vehicle's headlights in your rearview mirror.
   b. have at least 5 seconds total passing time.
   c. tap your horn lightly.

3. When you see a parking space you want across an intersection, you should
   a. enter the intersection, signal, and park.
   b. signal, cross the intersection, and park.
   c. cross the intersection, park, and signal.

4. When driving downhill in a vehicle with a manual transmission, you should
   a. downshift to gain more control.
   b. upshift to decrease engine power.
   c. ride the clutch to maintain an even speed.

5. Driving on mountain roads can cause you to
   a. become short of breath and feel sleepy.
   b. lose control of the gears.
   c. lose the effects of gravity.

6. When changing lanes,
   a. turn off the radio.
   b. make sure you are not on a one-way street.
   c. use push-pull-feed steering.

7. Drivers exchange information about
   a. intentions.   b. communications.
   c. markings.

8. You can help another driver pass you on a two-way, two-lane road by
   a. moving to the right.
   b. speeding up.
   c. putting on your high beams.

9. In moving from a curb, you must
   a. quickly accelerate and join the flow of traffic.
   b. avoid using hand signals.
   c. make judgments about visibility, time, and space.

10. When you come to a curve where you cannot see oncoming traffic, you should
    a. tap your horn and flash your lights.
    b. change lanes.
    c. use both your sideview and rearview mirrors.

Write the word or phrase that best completes each sentence.

communicate	altitudes
advance planning	gravity
atmospheric conditions	

11. You should avoid passing other vehicles in rain, snow, or other dangerous _____.

12. Driving at high _____ can affect the performance of your vehicle.

13. You can _____ with other drivers with electric signals or body gestures.

14. _____ causes a vehicle to speed up when it is traveling downhill.

15. Checking mirrors, the roadway, your path of travel, and traffic behind you are all part of _____.

DRIVER'S LOG

In this chapter, you have learned about some basic driving skills, such as moving to and from a curb, changing lanes, and passing and being passed. Which do you think will be hardest for you? Write two paragraphs explaining why and what you will do to gain confidence in your ability to execute the maneuver.

CHAPTER 9 REVIEW

CHAPTER TEST

Assign the Chapter Test to all students.

Answers
1. b
2. a
3. a
4. a
5. a
6. c
7. a
8. a
9. c
10. a
11. atmospheric conditions
12. altitudes
13. communicate
14. Gravity
15. advance planning

DRIVER'S LOG

Students' responses will reflect their personal viewpoints. However, their answers should provide an assessment of their understanding of the importance of mastering basic driving maneuvers.

Evaluate
- Test A, pages 17–18 or Test B, pages 17–18 📁
- Testmaker software

RETURN TO THE BIG IDEA ___

Discuss how thinking ahead can help drivers reduce risk when driving under the kinds of road and traffic conditions discussed in this chapter.

UNIT 2

This review tests students' knowledge of the material in Chapters 1 through 9. Use the review to help students study for their state driving test.

Answers

1. b
2. a
3. b
4. b
5. a
6. b
7. b
8. b
9. a
10. a
11. b
12. b
13. a
14. b

UNIT 2 CUMULATIVE REVIEW

This review tests your knowledge of the material in Chapters 1–9. Use the review to help you study for your state driving test. Choose the answer that best completes each statement.

1. A driver gathers the most information through
   a. hearing.
   b. vision.
   c. touch.
   d. memory.

2. Administrative laws require
   a. vehicle owners and drivers to be financially responsible.
   b. manufacturers to buy insurance.
   c. the governor to make traffic laws.
   d. the federal government to set vehicle prices.

3. When you are being passed on the left,
   a. speed up slightly.
   b. stay in the right side of the lane.
   c. stay in the left side of the lane.
   d. change lanes.

4. If you are involved in a collision,
   a. stop immediately.
   b. go home and call the police.
   c. find witnesses.
   d. sign documents at the scene.

5. Traffic control signals are typically located
   a. on expressways.
   b. at intersections.
   c. at interchanges.
   d. on the dashboard.

6. An extremely dangerous drug that changes the way you see, think, and act is a
   a. stimulant.
   b. hallucinogen.
   c. depressant.
   d. prescription.

7. Strong emotions can
   a. improve your driving ability.
   b. cause you to be inattentive.
   c. help you stay alert.
   d. improve your judgment.

8. A vehicle with a manual transmission has a
   a. clutch pedal.
   b. choke pedal.
   c. gear selector lever.
   d. Smith System.

9. When a license is taken away permanently,
   a. it is revoked.
   b. it is suspended.
   c. it is intoxicated.
   d. it is inhibited.

10. Traffic moving in opposite directions is separated by
    a. white lines.
    b. yellow lines.
    c. regulatory signs.
    d. shock absorbers.

11. Alcohol is absorbed into the bloodstream
    a. through the skin.
    b. through the stomach wall.
    c. through the adrenal gland.
    d. through the tongue.

12. The basic speed rule states that you should
    a. adjust your vehicle's speed to weather and road conditions.
    b. drive at one-half the posted speed limit.
    c. drive at the posted speed limit.
    d. check your vehicle's speedometer every few seconds.

13. The direction of a vehicle's front wheels is controlled by the
    a. accelerator.
    b. steering wheel.
    c. clutch.
    d. alternator.

14. Roadway warning signs are usually
  a. yellow or orange.
  b. blue and white.
  c. green or blue.
  d. black and white.

15. HOV lanes are for
  a. cyclists.
  b. pedestrians.
  c. vehicles carrying two or more occupants.
  d. emergency vehicles.

16. To start a vehicle with an automatic transmission, the gear selector lever should be in
  a. Park.
  b. choke.
  c. Neutral.
  d. First gear.

17. Using headlights during daylight
  a. can increase your visibility to others.
  b. is a waste of energy.
  c. is illegal in some states.
  d. can increase your risk of a collision.

18. You can prove ownership of a vehicle with a
  a. birth certificate.
  b. certificate of title.
  c. certificate of registration.
  d. driver's license.

19. A vehicle's engine will run more efficiently at high speeds when in
  a. Reverse gear.
  b. Low gear.
  c. First gear.
  d. Overdrive gear.

20. When driving down a mountain,
  a. shift to a lower gear.
  b. shift into Reverse.
  c. lock the brakes.
  d. exceed the speed limit.

21. A driver can usually sense a clutch's friction point best in
  a. First gear.
  b. Third gear.
  c. Reverse gear.
  d. Neutral gear.

22. To keep a parked vehicle from rolling, use
  a. cruise control.
  b. the accelerator.
  c. the parking, or emergency, brake.
  d. the SIPDE process.

23. Roadway regulatory signs
  a. control the flow of traffic.
  b. warn of changes in roadway conditions.
  c. are usually spaced 100 feet apart.
  d. are usually green or brown.

24. To prevent locking a vehicle's wheels, use
  a. the Smith System.
  b. threshold braking.
  c. the ignition switch.
  d. motor oil.

25. Recreational area signs on roadways are
  a. brown.
  b. blue.
  c. green.
  d. red.

26. To warn others that your vehicle is stopped on the side of the road, use
  a. the dome light.
  b. a dipstick.
  c. an emergency brake warning light.
  d. emergency flashers.

27. Large trucks
  a. gain speed slowly.
  b. gain speed quickly.
  c. frequently roll over.
  d. usually have 4-cylinder engines.

Answers

15. c
16. a
17. a
18. b
19. d
20. a
21. c
22. c
23. a
24. b
25. a
26. d
27. a

UNIT 3

Moving onto the Road

UNIT THEME

In Unit 3, as students progress to a consideration of the more intricate and complex driving maneuvers, they will develop an understanding of the influence of natural laws and different driving environments on the execution of these maneuvers. They will also recognize the importance of mastering safe driving techniques both for themselves and for others who share the roadway.

172

UNIT 3 Moving onto the Road

Once you are behind the wheel, you need to perform many complicated maneuvers. This unit will help you understand these maneuvers in order to become a responsible driver.

173

TEACHING YOUR TEENS TO DRIVE

AAA's *Teaching Your Teens to Drive: A Partnership for Survival* helps new drivers, with their parents' assistance, develop their driving skills. The program is available as a videotape or CD-ROM, both with a handbook.

Turning and Parking Overview

THEME DEVELOPMENT This chapter focuses on three essential skills that every driver must develop: making left and right turns, making turnabouts, and parking. These are complicated maneuvers that require practice and experience to master. By mastering these skills, however, drivers will be able to reduce driving risk greatly each time they get behind the wheel.

CHAPTER FEATURES	TCR COMPONENTS
	Study Guide, p. 37 Transparency 23 Lesson Plan, p. 21 Behind-the-Wheel Checklist 10
	Study Guide, p. 38 Transparencies 24 and 25 Lesson Plan, p. 21 Behind-the-Wheel Checklist 11
	Study Guide, p. 39 Transparencies 26, 27 Lesson Plan, p. 22 Behind-the-Wheel Checklists 13–16

TIPS   **FOR NEW DRIVERS**
 	
Learning how to leave a vehicle safely.
 	
ADVICE FROM THE EXPERTS
 	
The importance of turning maneuvers.
	Study Guide, p. 40
	Transparencies 28–31
	Lesson Plan, p. 22
	Behind-the-Wheel
	  Checklists 8, 17, 18, 19,
	  and 30

BUILDING SKILLS: READING MAPS Using Junctions and Interchanges **PROJECTS** **1.** Observe turnabouts and prepare a chart. **2.** Observe parked vehicles and record wheel positions.	Test A, pp. 19-20 Test B, pp. 19–20

OTHER PROGRAM RESOURCES

Testmaker software
Traffic charts
Teaching Your Teens to Drive: Lessons 2, 3, and 5, video or CD-ROM, AAA, 1998

NAME _____ DATE _____

CHAPTER 10 Turning and Parking

TEST A

Select the phrase that best completes each sentence below. Write the letter of the answer you have chosen to the left of each statement.

__c__ 1. You should signal for a turn at least
   a. 50 feet in advance of the turn.
   b. 100 feet in advance of the turn.
   c. 150 feet in advance of the turn.
   d. 500 feet in advance of the turn.

__a__ 2. When making a right turn from a two-way street, you should
   a. turn from the right lane.
   b. turn from the left lane.
   c. turn from either lane.
   d. always come to a complete stop before turning.

__d__ 3. When making a right turn at an intersection, make sure that
   a. your car is 3 to 5 feet from the curb.
   b. there are no cyclists on your right.
   c. there is no other traffic entering your path in the intersection.
   d. all of the above are true.

__b__ 4. When making a right turn, you should have a _____ gap in traffic to your left.
   a. 2- to 5-second
   b. 6- to 8-second
   c. 10- to 15-second
   d. 15- to 25-second

__b__ 5. A driver turning left
   a. always has the right-of-way at a light.
   b. must yield to cross traffic and to vehicles approaching from the opposite direction.
   c. must yield to cross traffic but not to oncoming traffic at a light.
   d. must do none of the above.

__a__ 6. The parking maneuver used most often along the side of a street is
   a. parallel parking.
   b. perpendicular parking.
   c. angle parking.
   d. double parking.

__b__ 7. When beginning a perpendicular parking maneuver, you should
   a. line up 3 to 5 feet from the vehicles you are parking next to.
   b. line up 7 to 8 feet from the vehicles you are parking next to.
   c. line up 10 feet from the vehicles you are parking next to.
   d. do none of the above.

__b__ 8. When parallel parking, you
   a. need a space at least 2 feet longer than your vehicle.
   b. need a space at least 5 feet longer than your vehicle.
   c. should drive into the space going 3 to 5 mph.
   d. both b and c.

© AAA and Glencoe/McGraw-Hill

◆ 19

NAME _____ DATE _____

__d__ 9. When parking downhill on a two-way road with a curb,
   a. turn the steering wheel to the right.
   b. set the parking brake.
   c. shift the car into Reverse if you have a manual transmission.
   d. do all of the above.

Read each statement below. If it is true, place a T in the space to the left of the statement. If the statement is false, place an F next to it.

__T__ 10. More than one-third of all collisions occur at intersections.

__F__ 11. A U-turn is a legal way to make a turnabout in all areas.

__F__ 12. A three-point turn is best done near the top of a hill or on a curve.

__T__ 13. A perpendicular parking space is 90 degrees to a curb or line.

The following steps describe how to make a turnabout heading into a driveway on the left. Number them in the order that you would perform them.

__3__ 14. Look in all directions for pedestrians and over your right shoulder for traffic. Back slowly and stop before crossing the curb.

__1__ 15. Signal a left turn, and when the driveway is clear, turn into it.

__4__ 16. Turn the wheel quickly all the way to the right. Halfway through the turn, start to straighten the steering wheel.

__2__ 17. When the rear bumper clears the roadway edge, stop with your front wheels straight. Shift into Reverse with your foot on the brake.

__5__ 18. Stop when your front wheels are straight. Check mirrors and over your shoulder. Signal, shift to Drive (or first gear), and accelerate.

19. It is illegal to park in bus zones in most states. In what other locations is it illegal to park in most states?

It is illegal in most states to park in loading zones; in the traffic lane beside another vehicle;

in a no-stopping or no-standing zone; on a sidewalk; half in, half out of a driveway; across

someone else's driveway; within a given distance of a fire hydrant; and in the fire zones of

certain buildings, such as schools.

_____

_____

_____

_____

20 ◆

© AAA and Glencoe/McGraw-Hill

NAME _____ DATE _____

CHAPTER 10 Turning and Parking

TEST B

Select the phrase that best completes each sentence below. Write the letter of the answer you have chosen to the left of each statement.

__c__ 1. You should begin to prepare for a turn
   a. 100 to 150 feet in advance.
   b. 150 to 200 feet in advance.
   c. 200 to 300 feet in advance.
   d. 300 to 400 feet in advance.

__a__ 2. When turning right at an intersection that allows two lanes to turn right,
   a. turn into the lane corresponding to the one you left.
   b. turn into the next lane.
   c. it does not matter what lane you turn into.
   d. you don't need to signal.

__d__ 3. When turning left, you should signal at least
   a. 50 feet in advance of the turn.
   b. 100 feet in advance of the turn.
   c. 500 feet in advance of the turn.
   d. 150 feet in advance of the turn.

__b__ 4. When parallel parking,
   a. you need a space at least 2 feet longer than your vehicle.
   b. you need a space at least 5 feet longer than your vehicle.
   c. you should drive into the space going 10 to 15 mph.
   d. both b and c apply.

__d__ 5. Making a turnabout heading into a driveway on the right is
   a. considered safer than most other turnabouts.
   b. illegal.
   c. called a three-point turn.
   d. dangerous.

__a__ 6. The kind of turnabout that you make when there are no driveways, traffic is very light, and the road is narrow and has no outlet is
   a. a three-point turn.
   b. a U-turn.
   c. a two-point turn.
   d. driving around the block.

__b__ 7. The parking maneuver used most often along the side of a street is called
   a. perpendicular parking.
   b. parallel parking.
   c. angle parking.
   d. double parking.

__d__ 8. When parking your vehicle uphill with a curb,
   a. turn your front wheels to the left.
   b. set your parking brake.
   c. leave your vehicle in First gear (if you have a manual transmission).
   d. do all of the above.

© AAA and Glencoe/ McGraw-Hill

◆ 19

NAME _____ DATE _____

__b__ 9. A vehicle turning left at an intersection
   a. always has the right-of-way.
   b. must yield to approaching traffic and to pedestrians in the intersection.
   c. must yield to cross traffic only.
   d. needs to do none of the above.

Read each statement below. If it is true, place a T in the space to the left of the statement. If the statement is false, place an F next to it.

__T__ 10. More than one-third of all collisions occur at intersections.

__T__ 11. A vehicle parked downhill with a curb on the right should have its front wheels turned sharply to the right.

__T__ 12. In most states, it is illegal to park half in and half out of a driveway.

__T__ 13. A three-point turn should not be started until you have a 20- to 30-second gap in traffic in both directions.

__F__ 14. A U-turn is a legal way to make a turnabout in all states.

The following steps for turning left from a two-way street onto a two-way street are in the wrong order. Write the correct order in the space to the left of each step.

__4__ 15. Look through the turn and begin the turn.

__2__ 16. Find a 9-second gap to your right and a 7-second gap to your left.

__5__ 17. Follow the path of travel to arrive in the lane just to the right of the center line.

__1__ 18. Check that there are no vehicles, pedestrians, or other obstacles in your intended travel path.

__3__ 19. Proceed into the intersection until you are about one lane width from its center. Yield to any approaching traffic and pedestrians.

20. Before making a turnabout, you must consider several things. What are they?

Are there signs or laws that prohibit the turnabout? Is there at least 500 feet of visibility in both

directions? Are you near hills or curves or within 200 feet of an intersection? Is there heavy traffic? Are

traffic and pedestrians in your path?

_____

_____

_____

20 ◆

© AAA and Glencoe/McGraw-Hill

NAME _____ DATE _____

CHAPTER 10 Turning and Parking

STUDY GUIDE FOR CHAPTER 10   LESSON 1

Right Turns

A. Beside each picture, describe the maneuver the driver has made. Be sure to mention the lane the vehicle is in and the lane it will enter. The first one is done as an example.

1. right turn from right lane of one-way street to right lane of one-way street

2. two-lane right turn from one-way street to another one-way street

3. right turn from two-way street to right lane of a one-way street

4. right turn from right lane of two-way street to a two-way street

B. FIND OUT MORE. Check out an intersection near where you live. What signs and markings give special information about turns, such as whether or not turns are allowed, or in which directions you can turn? Describe them below.

Review student's work.

NAME _____ DATE _____

STUDY GUIDE FOR CHAPTER 10   LESSON 2

Left Turns

A. Use a pencil or colored pencil to draw the path of each vehicle's intersection maneuver.

Review student's work.

B. Complete the following sentences by filling in the correct word in the space below.

1. A driver turning left must ___yield___ right-of-way to any cross traffic and to oncoming traffic.

2. When you are at an intersection and waiting to turn, your front wheels should be ___straight___.

3. You should signal your intentions to turn at least ___150___ feet in advance.

4. When turning left from a two-way street onto a two-way street, you should have a 9-second gap in traffic to your right and a ___7___-second gap to your left.

5. When turning left from a two-way street, ___position___ your car near the center line.

C. FIND OUT MORE. Find a safe spot from which to watch a fairly busy intersection with two turn lanes. Do most drivers finish a turn in the same lane they started in? What do the others do?

Review student's work.

NAME _____ DATE _____

STUDY GUIDE FOR CHAPTER 10   LESSON 3

Executing a Reverse in Direction

A. For each sentence below, circle T if the statement is true and F if it is false. Correct each false statement in the space below.

1. The safest turnabout is the three-point turn.   T   **F**
One of the hardest turnabouts is a three-point turn.

2. You should have at least 500 feet of visibility before you do a turnabout.   **T**   F

3. A three-point turn should be made when the street is narrow and there are no driveways to turn into.   **T**   F

4. A good location for three-point turn is on a curve.   T   **F**
You should not attempt to make a turnabout on a curve.

5. Driving around the block is often the easiest turnabout to make.   **T**   F

6. U-turns may not be legal in all areas.   **T**   F

7. You should not make a turnabout within 100 feet of an intersection.   T   **F**
You should not make a turnabout within 200 feet of an intersection.

8. A two-point turnabout heading into a driveway on the right is considered dangerous.   **T**   F

B. FIND OUT MORE. Are U-turns legal in your state? See if you can find the answer in your state driver's manual. See also if there are any restrictions on where you can and cannot make U-turns.
Review student's work.

NAME _____ DATE _____

STUDY GUIDE FOR CHAPTER 10   LESSON 4

How to Execute a Parking Maneuver

A. For each sentence below, circle T if the statement is true and F if it is false. Correct each false statement in the space below.

1. Angled parking spaces are set at an angle of 30 to 90 degrees to the curb or line.   **T**   F

2. When angle parking, stay at least 10 feet away from parked vehicles to give yourself room to maneuver.   T   **F**
When angle parking, stay 5 to 6 feet from parked vehicles to give yourself room to maneuver.

3. To parallel park, you need a space at least 10 feet longer than the length of your vehicle.   T   **F**
To parallel park, you need a space at least 5 feet longer than the length of your vehicle.

4. It is a good idea not to park your vehicle next to a poorly parked vehicle.   **T**   F

5. When parking downhill at a curb, park your vehicle with the wheels turned sharply to the left.   T   **F**
When parking downhill on a road with a curb, park with your wheels turned to the right.

6. When parking your vehicle downhill, leave it in Neutral if it has a manual transmission.   T   **F**
When parking downhill, leave your vehicle in Reverse if it has a manual transmission.

7. When parking uphill next to a curb, park your vehicle with the wheels turned sharply to the left.   **T**   F

8. If you are parking your vehicle uphill where there is no curb, your wheels should be turned sharply to the left.   T   **F**
If you are parking your vehicle on a road without a curb, turn your wheels to the right.

B. FIND OUT MORE. Find the following answers to parking questions in your state driver's manual.

1. Is it illegal to park at a bus stop? _____

2. Is it illegal to park in a loading zone? _____

3. How close to a fire hydrant can you park? _____

4. Can you park across someone else's driveway? _____

Review student's work.

Turning and Parking

CHAPTER OVERVIEW

LESSON ONE
The procedures and steps necessary for making a right turn are described, diagrammed, and explained.

LESSON TWO
The procedures and steps necessary for making a left turn are described, diagrammed, and explained.

LESSON THREE
Four methods of reversing direction are described, and the merits of each method are examined.

LESSON FOUR
Parking methods are described and diagrammed along with strategies for parking on hills, in garages, and in driveways.

VOCABULARY

angle parking
parallel parking
perpendicular parking
three-point turn
turnabout
two-point turn
U-turn

174

CONCEPT OF THE DRIVING TASK

Explain that driving involves performing basic maneuvers in a variety of different situations. Mastery of these maneuvers, however, does not guarantee that a person will be a good driver. A good driver is able to anticipate risk in all situations *and* has mastered basic driving maneuvers.

CHAPTER 10

Turning and Parking

The ability to execute turns and parking maneuvers properly requires practice, good judgment, and knowledge of traffic laws. It is important that you learn the techniques that will enable you to perform these maneuvers safely.

LESSON ONE
How to Prepare for and Execute a Right Turn

LESSON TWO
How to Prepare for and Execute a Left Turn

LESSON THREE
Planning and Executing a Reverse in Direction

LESSON FOUR
How to Prepare for and Execute a Parking Maneuver

PRESENTING THE BIG IDEA ━━━

Probably no one really enjoys studying and practicing lists of procedures. However, the correct—and safe—way to perform certain driving maneuvers, such as turning and parking, can be described in a simple, step-by-step way. Learning to carry out these procedures properly is critical for every driver and well worth the effort and concentration required.

INTRODUCING THE CHAPTER

What's on the Road Ahead?

Have students read the lesson titles and objectives. Briefly discuss the topic of each lesson. Tell students that in this chapter, they will be introduced to basic maneuvers that they will perform countless times when they drive—turning and parking.

Background: The Larger Picture

It is critical that new drivers understand the risks involved in driving and take these risks seriously. Statistics such as those below may help convince students that responsible driving means taking whatever actions are necessary to reduce risk.

• Teenagers comprised 6.7 percent of U.S. licensed drivers in 1997 but 14 percent of all drivers involved in fatal motor vehicle crashes.

• About twice as many male teenagers as female teenagers are killed in motor vehicle crashes.

• In 1997, the fatality rate for teen drivers (16 to 19 years old) was about four times as high as the rate for drivers 25 to 69 years old.

• Twenty percent of all passengers who die in motor vehicle crashes do so when a teenager is driving. Two-thirds of teen passenger deaths occur in crashes in which another teenager is driving.

Relating to Prior Knowledge

Have students discuss what they notice as pedestrians about drivers making turns at intersections. Ask what they think they will need to know about making turns in order to be good drivers.

The Big Idea

Discuss students' reactions to the Big Idea statement. Suggest that they keep this idea in mind as they read Chapter 10.

How to Prepare for and Execute a Right Turn

(pages 176–177)

FOCUS

Objectives

- List the procedures to follow when preparing to turn right at an intersection.
- Describe the steps needed to execute a right turn.

Resources

 Study Guide, page 37

 Traffic charts

 Transparency 23

Behind-the-Wheel Checklist 10

Motivator

Pose this situation: You are on a four-lane highway. You plan to turn right onto a two-lane, two-way highway. How will you prepare for this maneuver? (Students may mention checking for signs and road markings; choosing the correct lane; communicating your intentions; checking traffic.)

TEACH

Explain

OBJECTIVE 1: Encourage students to discuss advance preparation for turning.

OBJECTIVE 2: Students should recognize that as a rule of thumb, drivers turning from one street onto another should enter the first lane going in the direction they want to travel.

LESSON ONE

OBJECTIVES

1. List the procedures to follow when preparing to turn right at an intersection.
2. Describe the steps needed to execute a right turn.

How to Prepare for and Execute a Right Turn

Suppose that you are driving and want to turn right. What should you do? To answer that question, you need to learn the basics of control and visual search and make good use of time and space.

FYI

Manage risk. Be aware that more than one-third of all collisions occur at intersections.

◆ Make right turns from the lane closest to the right curb unless they are allowed from other lanes. Turn into the lane corresponding to the one you just left.

How Do You Prepare to Make a Right Turn?

Before you make a right turn, check the roadway, choose the correct lane, communicate your intentions, and position the vehicle correctly. Prepare for the turn 8 to 12 seconds in advance of reaching the intersection. This equals a distance of about 500 feet or 1 city block.

Check

Check for signs and markings that control your movement. Is a traffic signal, a yield sign, or a stop sign present? Are turns allowed? If so, are they restricted to certain times of day or to certain types of vehicles? Are there special turning lanes?

Choose

Choose the correct lane. Move into the lane if necessary, after you make sure that it is clear, and reduce your speed.

Communicate

Check your mirrors again, and signal early to let other drivers know that you intend to turn. Tap the brake pedal to flash your brake lights. Use your turn signal 3 to 4 seconds, or at least 150 feet, in advance of the turn in the city, and up to a quarter of a mile on a highway in the country.

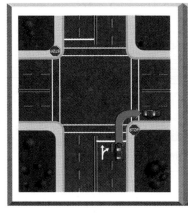
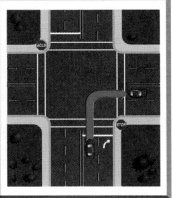

THE INTERNATIONAL SCENE

Great Britain

In the British Isles, drivers drive on the left, not on the right, as in the United States. British drivers need to be alert to foreign visitors unaccustomed to British traffic flow.

DRIVER'S LOG

How will you manage risk when making a right turn?

Position the Vehicle

Position your vehicle to the right side of the right lane, 3 to 5 feet from the curb or shoulder. Check other traffic in, at, and approaching the intersection. Make sure there are no cyclists to your right. If you are at a stop sign or red signal, stop before the crosswalk. Then slowly move up to a point where you can see cross traffic. Be prepared to yield to pedestrians.

◆ *Move to the right lane in advance of a right turn. Check for pedestrians and other vehicles, including those across the intersection, before turning.*

How Do You Execute a Right Turn?

The steps for executing a right turn are the same whether you are turning onto a one-way or a two-way street. After you have positioned yourself correctly and signaled your intentions, check again for cross traffic. Then follow these steps.

1. Find a 6- to 8-second gap in traffic to your left. Just before turning, search the intersection again to the left.
2. When your front wheels are opposite the point where the curb begins to curve, look through the turn along your intended path of travel. Begin the turn.
3. Follow the general curve of the curb as you turn. Stay in the right lane by looking through the turn along the intended driving path.
4. Complete the turn by reversing your steering as you accelerate. Make sure the turn signal is off.

Lesson *1* Review

1. What should you do before you turn right at an intersection?
2. How do you make a right turn?

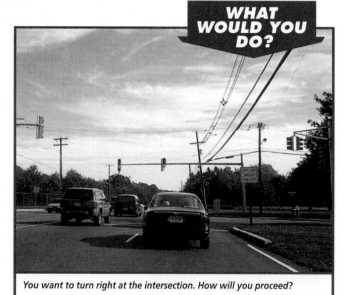

WHAT WOULD YOU DO?

You want to turn right at the intersection. How will you proceed?

WHAT WOULD YOU DO?

Sample answer: Reduce your speed and move into the proper lane. Check your mirrors and signal to other drivers that you are turning. Tap your brakes. Position your car 3 to 5 feet from the curb or shoulder.

Lesson *1* Review

Answers

1. Check the roadway, choose the correct lane, communicate your intentions by signaling in advance; position your vehicle to the right side of the right lane.
2. Look for signals or signs, find a gap in traffic, look along your intended path of travel, turn the vehicle.

Teaching Model

Display this situation:

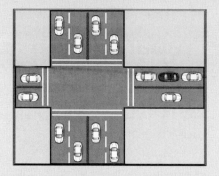

Explain the following: You are in vehicle 1 and want to turn right. Model your thinking process. (You check the roadway, signal your intention, position your vehicle properly, and watch for pedestrians.)

Ask

Why should you scan the intersection again before turning?

Read

Have students read Lesson 1 to find out how to manage risk when turning right.

ASSESS

Guided Practice

Have students answer the Lesson 1 Review questions. The answers are provided below.

Reteaching

Pair a student who had difficulty with this lesson with a more able student to walk through making a right turn. Have them act out the steps.

Enrichment

Assign the Study Guide for Lesson 1. The Find Out More section encourages students to expand their basic learning of the lesson concepts.

CLOSE

Summarize

Return to the Motivator question, and have students summarize how to make a right turn.

How to Prepare for and Execute a Left Turn

(pages 178–180)

FOCUS

Objectives

- Describe how to prepare for a left turn.
- State how to make a left turn from a one-way street and from a two-way street.

Resources

 Study Guide, page 38

 Traffic charts

 Transparencies 24 and 25

 Behind-the-Wheel Checklist 11

Motivator

Have students speculate on how preparing for and executing a left turn might be different from preparing for and executing a right turn. (Students may mention that drivers turning left must yield the right-of-way to any cross traffic and to vehicles approaching from the opposite direction; preparation and execution depend on whether the turn is made from or to a one- or two-way street.)

TEACH

Explain

OBJECTIVE 1: Students will benefit from recognizing that making a left turn is more dangerous than making a right turn because drivers cross the paths of both oncoming and approaching traffic from the left before entering the lane into which they are turning.

LESSON TWO

OBJECTIVES

1. Describe how to prepare for a left turn.
2. State how to make a left turn from a one-way street and from a two-way street.

How to Prepare for and Execute a Left Turn

When you make a left turn, you follow many of the same procedures you use to make right turns. However, be aware that a driver turning left *must* yield the right-of-way to any cross traffic and to vehicles approaching from the opposite direction. Drivers should also be alert for pedestrians and be prepared to yield to anyone in the crosswalks.

How Do You Prepare for a Left Turn?

To prepare for a left turn, check the roadway, choose the correct lane, communicate your intentions by signaling, and position your vehicle correctly. Remember to reduce speed before making your turn.

Check

Look through the turn on your intended path of travel. Check for traffic signs and signals and for traffic ahead and to the left and right. Be sure no one is about to pass you on your left side.

◆ *Position your car in advance of a left turn. Check for pedestrians and other vehicles in and across the intersection.*

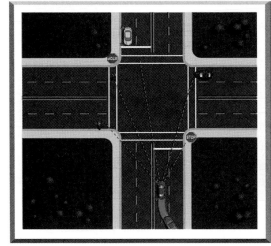
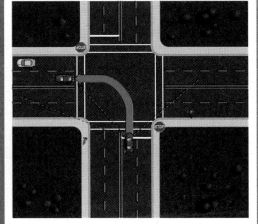

Driving Tip

Explain to students that to maintain a margin of safety behind their vehicle and avoid rear-end collisions, they should check their rearview and sideview mirrors and tap their brakes to warn following drivers of their intention to reduce speed and stop.

Choose the Correct Lane

Signal and move into the correct lane. Stop behind the stop line if there is one. Keep your wheels straight.

Communicate Your Intentions

Signal your turn 3 to 4 seconds, or at least 150 feet, in advance. Flash your brake lights by tapping the brake pedal before slowing. Use your turn signal.

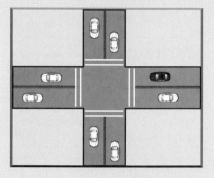

Left turn Right turn Stop

◆ *Use an arm (or hand) signal to communicate better with drivers behind you.*

Position the Vehicle

Position your vehicle just to the right of the center line or, on a one-way street, the left curb.

How Can You Execute a Left Turn?

The steps for executing a left turn depend on the type of street you are on and the type of street you are turning onto.

Turning Left from a Two-Way Street onto a Two-Way Street

1. Check that there are no vehicles, pedestrians, or other obstacles in your intended path of travel.
2. Find a 9-second gap to your right and a 7-second gap to your left.
3. Proceed into the intersection until you are about one lane width away from its center. Yield to any approaching traffic and pedestrians in the intersection. Keep your wheels straight.
4. Look through the turn along your intended path of travel. Begin the turn.
5. Follow the path of travel so that you arrive in the lane just to the right of the center line. Complete the turn by reversing your steering as you accelerate. Be sure the turn signal is off.

Turning Left from a Two-Way Street onto a One-Way Street

Turning onto a one-way street is like turning onto a two-way street except that you enter the lane of traffic closest to you.

SAFETY TIPS

When you are turning either right or left at an intersection, be very careful not to signal too early if there are other places to turn before the intersection. A driver on another roadway who believes you intend to turn somewhere else could pull out in front of you.

State BY State

Students should be aware that although most states accept either electric turn signals or hand signals, a few states require drivers to use hand signals when driving, or during the in-vehicle examination.

OBJECTIVE 2: Students should recognize that there are two key factors to consider when making a left turn: the type of roadway the driver is turning from and the type of roadway the driver is turning onto. Drivers must be aware of safe procedures for turning from and onto one-way and two-way roadways and single-lane and multiple-lane roadways.

Teaching Model

Display this situation:

Explain the following: You are in vehicle 1, traveling on a two-way street. You want to turn left onto another two-way street. Model your thinking process. (You do the following.

- Check for traffic signs and signals, and respond as required.
- Check for vehicles and pedestrians in, near, or approaching your intended path of travel; yield as required.
- Position your vehicle just to the right of the yellow center line.
- Move into the intersection until you are about one lane width from the middle of the intersection.
- Turn so that your vehicle ends up just to the right of the center line on the road you are turning onto.)

Ask

Why is it essential to remain alert for vehicles and pedestrians while in the process of making a turn?

Read

Have students read Lesson 2 to learn how to prepare for and make left turns.

Guided Practice

Have students answer the Lesson 2 Review questions. The answers are provided below.

Reteaching

Have students work in groups to set up and act out left-turn situations, walking through them and describing the maneuvers. You may want to have students create intersections on the floor of the classroom with tape or chalk.

Enrichment

Assign the Study Guide for Lesson 2. The Find Out More section encourages students to expand their basic learning of the lesson concepts.

CLOSE

Summarize

Return to the Motivator question. Have students discuss specific procedural differences for left and right turns. Encourage them to note ways in which they can minimize risk.

DRIVER'S LOG

How are the procedures for making a left turn and a right turn alike? How do they differ?

WHAT WOULD YOU DO?

Sample answer: Check for traffic and pedestrians, choose the correct lane, and communicate your intentions. Yield to cross traffic, oncoming vehicles, and pedestrians.

◆ *You need to learn which lane to enter when turning left from a one-way street onto another one-way street and onto a two-way street.*

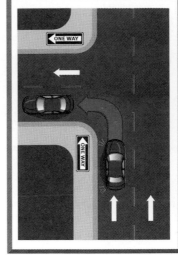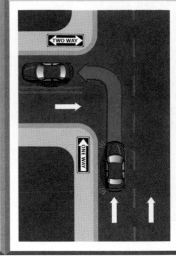

Turning Left from a One-Way Street onto a One-Way Street

Making a left turn from one one-way street onto another is similar to making other left turns. However, you will not have to cross a lane of traffic coming toward you.

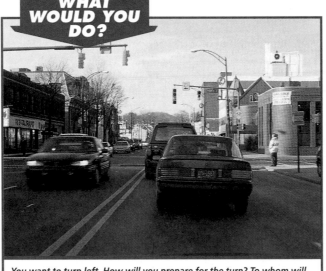

WHAT WOULD YOU DO?

You want to turn left. How will you prepare for the turn? To whom will you yield the right-of-way?

Turning Left from a One-Way Street onto a Two-Way Street

If you are turning left from a one-way street onto a two-way street, position your vehicle in the far left-hand lane. Turn into the first lane of traffic going in your direction.

Lesson 2 Review

1. What should you do *before* you make a left turn?
2. How would you make a left turn from a two-way street onto another two-way street?

Lesson 2 Review

Answers

1. Check for signs and signals, check for vehicles and pedestrians, position your vehicle properly, and signal.
2. Check for other vehicles and pedestrians; look for a 9-second gap to your right and a 7-second gap to your left; position your vehicle just to the right of the center of the road; move into the intersection until you are about one lane width from the middle; look through the turn, along your intended path of travel; turn so that your vehicle ends up just to the right of the center of the road.

Planning and Executing a Reverse in Direction

LESSON THREE

OBJECTIVES
1. Describe how to prepare to make a turnabout.
2. Describe four ways to make a turnabout.

KEY TERMS
turnabout
two-point turn
three-point turn
U-turn

No matter how skillful a driver you are, you may sometimes miss a street or building you are looking for. If so, you may have no choice but to turn around, or make a **turnabout.**

How Should You Prepare to Make a Turnabout?

As in all maneuvers you make with your vehicle, careful preparation is a key to managing risk. Before you make a turnabout, consider the following.
- Are there signs that prohibit the turnabout?
- Are there specific laws that prohibit the turnabout when there are no signs?
- Is there at least 500 feet of visibility in each direction?
- Are you near hills, curves, or within 200 feet of an intersection?
- Is there heavy traffic?
- Do you have enough space to complete the maneuver?
- Are there traffic and pedestrians in your path?

How Can You Make a Turnabout?

You can make a turnabout in one of four ways. Use the method that best suits traffic conditions, the street, and local traffic laws.

Two-Point Turns

The **two-point turn** is one method to use when making a turnabout. Either head into or back into a driveway to reverse direction.

Backing into a driveway Back into a driveway when there is no traffic close behind you in your lane and there is a clear driveway on your right.
1. Signal early. Flash your brake lights to alert following drivers. Check for objects or children in or near the driveway as you drive past.
2. Stop about 3 feet from the curb, with your rear bumper just beyond the driveway you will enter. With your foot on the brake, shift into Reverse. Check again for obstacles in your intended path.

◆ *If you can't go around the block, make a turnabout by backing into a driveway.*

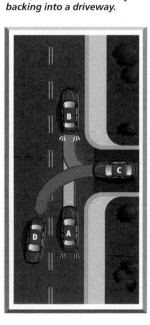

CHAPTER 10   *Turning and Parking*   **181**

MEETING STUDENT DIVERSITY

Hearing Impaired

Students who have a hearing impairment or total hearing loss can compensate for hearing difficulties by moving their eyes to pick up visual cues when driving. Encourage students to discuss kinds of visual cues.

FOCUS

Objectives
- Describe how to prepare to make a turnabout.
- Describe four ways to make a turnabout.

Resources
- Study Guide, page 39
- Traffic charts
- Transparencies 26 and 27
- Behind-the-Wheel Checklists 13–16

Vocabulary
turnabout
two-point turn
three-point turn
U-turn

Motivator

Pose the following situation: You are following instructions to drive to the home of a friend whom you have never visited. You make a mistake and have to turn around. What is the safest way to do so? (Students may mention making a U-turn, heading or backing into a driveway to reverse direction, making a three-point turn. The safest way to turn around, however, may be one students don't immediately think of—driving around the block.)

TEACH

Explain

OBJECTIVE 1: Encourage students to discuss each of the bulleted items on page 181 and the attendant risks. Be sure students recognize that turnabouts may seem easy, but they are more difficult—and dangerous—than they appear.

OBJECTIVE 2: Students may benefit from a discussion of the various turnabout options available to a driver and the situations that dictate one maneuver over another.

- **A two-point turn** is made by backing into or turning left or right into a driveway. It is best to avoid heading into a driveway on the right in order to turn about because the driver will then have to back across two lanes of traffic before driving forward. Two-point turns are recommended when there is no traffic close behind and when there is a clear driveway.

- **A three-point turn** is made when the street is narrow, there are no driveways to turn into, and there is good visibility and light traffic. This is the most difficult turn to make because it requires more maneuvering than either a U-turn or a two-point turn. For new drivers in particular, driving around the block is generally preferable.

- **A U-turn** is made on a wide street when there is not much traffic. This is the easiest turnabout, but it is often not legal.

- **Driving around the block** is the safest way to reverse direction. When this cannot be done because of a dead-end or one-way street, the other three options should be considered.

SAFETY TIPS

By backing into a driveway rather than heading in, you can see in both directions to better assess risk when you prepare to reenter traffic.

3. When it is clear, look over your right shoulder. Back up slowly, turning the wheel rapidly all the way to the right. As the rear of the vehicle enters the driveway, turn the wheel to the left, centering the vehicle in the driveway. Stop when the front of the vehicle is clear of the curb.
4. Shift to Drive or First gear, signal, check traffic, and leave the driveway when it is safe to do so.

Heading into a driveway on the left When you head into a driveway, you will have to back into the street. Select a driveway on the left that affords good visibility. Make sure there are no hedges or other objects along the driveway that will obscure your view of the road.

1. Signal a left turn. Check for traffic, flash your brake lights, and stop if necessary. When the driveway is clear, turn into it as close to the right side as you can. This allows more room for the front of the vehicle to swing left as you back out to the right.
2. When the rear bumper clears the edge of the roadway, stop with your front wheels straight. With your foot on the brake, shift into Reverse gear.
3. Look in all directions for pedestrians and over your right shoulder for traffic in your planned path. Back up slowly, rechecking traffic, and stop before crossing the curb.

◆ *You can make a turnabout by heading into a driveway on the left (below) or on the right (below right).*

IT'S A FACT

According to statistics compiled by the Insurance Institute for Highway Safety, the highest percentage of motor vehicle deaths occur on weekends: 16 percent on Friday, 19 percent on Saturday, and 16 percent on Sunday.

4. While slowly moving the vehicle back, turn the wheel quickly all the way to the right. Keep your vehicle in the first lane of traffic. Halfway through the turn, start to straighten the steering wheel.

5. Stop when the front wheels are straight. Check mirrors and over your shoulder, signal, shift to Drive or First gear, and accelerate to traffic speed.

Heading into a driveway on the right Heading into a driveway on the right in order to make a turnabout is very dangerous because a driver must back across at least two lanes of traffic before moving forward. You should make this maneuver only in low-speed, low-traffic residential areas. Follow the steps for heading into a driveway on the left, but reverse the directions in Steps 1, 3, and 4.

Three-Point Turns

One of the hardest turnabouts for the new driver is the **three-point turn.** To minimize risk, make a three-point turn only when the street is narrow, there are no driveways to turn into, you have very good visibility, traffic is very light, and you cannot drive around the block. To make a three-point turn, follow these steps.

1. Stop as close to the right edge of the curb as possible. Check for traffic in both directions. Wait until you have a 20- to 30-second gap to complete the turn.
2. Signal a left turn. Look over your left shoulder for any vehicles in your blind spot. Then move the vehicle slowly while turning the steering wheel rapidly to the left to bring the vehicle into the opposite lane. Hold this position.

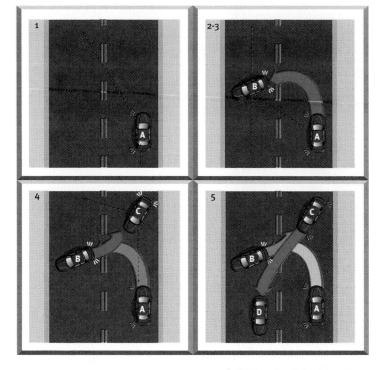

◆ You need to have a good sense of speed and steering control to make a three-point turn.

SAFETY TIPS

Never make a three-point turn near the top of a hill, on a curve, near an intersection, or near trees, hydrants, or other such objects near the road edge.

CHAPTER 10 *Turning and Parking* **183**

Driving Tip

Explain to students that a decision to go around the block is a viable turnabout maneuver and not a reflection on their ability to perform any of the other turnabout maneuvers. Point out that responsible drivers do not need to demonstrate their skill at executing difficult maneuvers when a simpler solution is available.

Teaching Model
Display this situation:

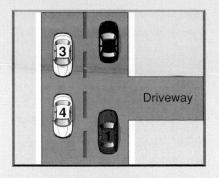

Explain the following: You are in vehicle 1 and need to turn around and travel in the opposite direction. Model your thinking process. (You do the following.

• Signal your intention to stop as you approach the driveway.
• Drive past the driveway and stop about 3 feet from the curb, with your rear bumper just beyond the driveway.
• Back up slowly while turning the steering wheel rapidly to the right so that the rear of the vehicle goes into the driveway.
• Stop when the front of the vehicle is clear of the traffic lane so there is no danger of being struck by another vehicle.
• Shift to Drive or First gear.
• Check traffic in all directions.
• Turn on the left-turn signal.
• Turn when the way is clear.)

Ask
Why is it more dangerous to head into this driveway in order to turn around than to back in?

Read
Have students read Lesson 3 to learn about ways in which drivers can turn their vehicle around. Have them read to find out which direction-reversing maneuvers are safest and easiest to perform.

ASSESS

Guided Practice
Have students answer the Lesson 3 Review questions. The answers are provided below.

Reteaching

Have students work in groups to role-play drivers, pedestrians, and other roadway users in situations that require a driver to make a turnabout. Encourage groups to set up situations in which a driver would have to make a U-turn, a two-point turn, or a three-point turn. For each situation, a different student should play the driver making the turn, while other group members take other parts. As the "driver" makes his or her maneuvers to reverse direction, have that student tell the others what he or she is doing. Encourage the other group members to comment on each decision. After students act out each maneuver, have the group discuss any risks they noticed.

Enrichment

Assign the Study Guide for Lesson 3. The Find Out More section encourages students to expand their basic learning of the lesson concepts.

CLOSE

Summarize

Return to the Motivator question, and review students' initial responses in light of what they have read in this lesson. Have students summarize in their own words the four different options available to them if they need to reverse direction when driving. Encourage them to evaluate each option and explain what factors they would consider when deciding which maneuver they would use. Also review the factors that a driver should consider before making a turnabout of any sort.

DRIVER'S LOG

What factors would prompt you to decide to drive around the block rather than attempt a turnabout maneuver?

◆ To make a U-turn, move your car slowly, but turn the steering wheel rapidly.

3. When the front wheels are almost to the curb (about 4 feet away), turn the steering wheel rapidly to the right. Then, stop the vehicle just short of the curb.
4. Check traffic to your left, then over your right shoulder. Shift into Reverse, and while backing slowly, turn the wheel to the extreme right position. About 4 feet before stopping, turn the wheel quickly to the left. Keep looking back until you have stopped the vehicle.
5. Shift into Drive or First gear. Check traffic. Signal, move into the proper lane, and accelerate to normal speed.

U-Turns

To make a **U-turn,** you do not back up, and therefore you need a wide street in which to make the turn. Be aware that U-turns are illegal in some places.

Here is how to make a U-turn on a two-lane road after first making sure the turn is legal.

1. Stop your vehicle close to the right edge of the curb. Check for traffic in both directions. Signal a left turn. Check over your left shoulder again before starting the turn. Do not start the turn if you will interfere with traffic.
2. Turn the steering wheel rapidly all the way to the left, moving the vehicle slowly until it is facing in the opposite direction.
3. When the turn is almost completed, straighten the wheels, and proceed in the proper lane at normal speed.

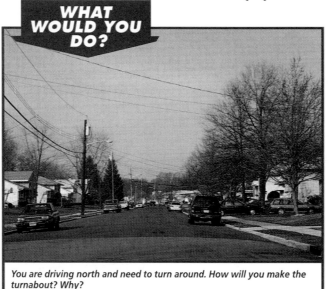

WHAT WOULD YOU DO?

You are driving north and need to turn around. How will you make the turnabout? Why?

Around the Block

The fourth way to reverse direction is to drive around the block. This method is often the easiest and safest to use.

Lesson 3 Review

1. What should you consider before making a turnabout?
2. How can you reverse your vehicle's direction?

WHAT WOULD YOU DO?

Sample answer: Drive around the block because that is the safest and easiest option.

Lesson 3 Review

Answers

1. Is it legal to make a turnabout? Is there sufficient visibility? Are you near hills, curves, or within 200 feet of an intersection? Is there heavy traffic? Is there enough space to maneuver? Are there vehicles or pedestrians in your path?
2. You can make a two-point turn, a three-point turn, or a U-turn, or you can drive around the block; the method used depends on legality, traffic, and roadway conditions.

How to Prepare for and Execute a Parking Maneuver

OBJECTIVES
1. Describe how to angle park and perpendicular park.
2. Describe how to parallel park.
3. Describe how to park in a driveway, in a garage, and on a hill.

KEY TERMS
angle parking
perpendicular parking
parallel parking

Parking can be one of the most exasperating experiences of driving. Sometimes you feel the only way you can get into a space is by bumping nearby vehicles out of the way. So how can you park easily?

Parking is an art. To park quickly, easily, and safely, you need good control of your vehicle, accurate judgment of space, a good understanding of steering, and continuous practice.

To park safely, you need to understand the different ways to park. They are angle parking, perpendicular parking, and parallel parking.

How Do You Angle Park and Perpendicular Park?

When you park at an angle, you have little room to maneuver and cannot see very well. You must therefore be very careful when entering and leaving angled and perpendicular parking spaces.

Right- or Left-Angle Parking

You may have seen angled parking spaces in parking lots or along the streets of towns and smaller cities. These spaces are set at an angle from 30 degrees to 90 degrees to the curb or line.

To execute **angle parking** on the right, follow these steps.

1. Stay 5 or 6 feet from parked vehicles to give yourself room to see and maneuver. Observe traffic in all directions and be alert for vehicles about to leave nearby spaces. Signal for a right turn.
2. Proceed until you can see along the left side of the vehicle to the right of the space you will enter. Steer sharply right. Creep ahead at 3 to 5 mph into the space midway between the lines. Check the left front and right rear of your vehicle to make sure you have clearance.
3. As you straighten the wheels, move forward until the front of your vehicle is aligned with those on both sides.

◆ *You need to position your car carefully before you enter an angled parking space.*

Begin to turn here

5 to 6 ft.

How to Prepare for and Execute a Parking Maneuver

(pages 185–190)

FOCUS

Objectives
- Describe how to angle park and perpendicular park.
- Describe how to parallel park.
- Describe how to park in a driveway, in a garage, and on a hill.

Resources

📁 Study Guide, page 40

📁 Traffic charts

🖱 Transparencies 28–31

📁 Behind-the-Wheel Checklists 8, 17, 18, 19, and 30

Vocabulary
angle parking
perpendicular parking
parallel parking

State BY State

Many states offer special oral knowledge tests for prospective drivers with low-level reading abilities. States may also provide information on test preparation for people with reading difficulties. Your state department of motor vehicles will have information on such options.

Motivator

Ask students why they think that many drivers find parking difficult and frustrating. Discuss student's ideas. Then ask students if they can name and describe some methods of parking. (Students may mention left- or right-angle parking—parking in spaces angled 30 to 90 degrees to the curb [this method offers little room to maneuver]; perpendicular parking—parking in spaces that are marked at 90 degrees to the curb [drivers find it difficult to see at this angle, and there is little room to maneuver]; parallel parking—parking along the side of the roadway in a space about 22 to 26 feet long.)

TEACH

Explain

OBJECTIVES 1 AND 2: Students should have little difficulty naming and describing different parking methods. However, they should be aware of the following points, which do not involve technique but are nonetheless very important.

- Do not block traffic behind you by driving too slowly or stopping in traffic to wait for a space to become vacant.
- Watch for signs and markings that tell whether parking is legal.
- Avoid places where parking is illegal, such as near fire hydrants, traffic controls, intersections, bus stops, in fire zones, and across driveways.

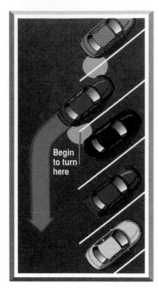

◆ **Check that your left front fender doesn't scrape the car on the left when you exit an angled space.**

◆ **Whether entering or leaving a perpendicular space, keep your car positioned 7 to 8 feet from the row of parked cars.**

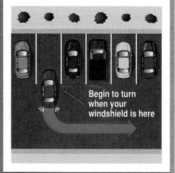

Angle parking on the left is similar to that on the right. In this case, start turning the steering wheel to the left when you can see along the right side of the vehicle parked to the left of your chosen space. Now you must keep track of the right front bumper and the left rear fender.

Perpendicular Parking

Many parking lots have parking spaces that are marked at a 90-degree angle to the curb or line. These are perpendicular parking spaces. **Perpendicular parking** is risky because it is hard to see at that angle and there is very little room for maneuvering. If possible select a perpendicular parking spot that allows you to drive forward rather than backing in order to exit.

To enter a perpendicular parking space on the right, follow these steps.

1. Stay 7 to 8 feet from parked cars for best visibility. Observe all traffic conditions, and check for vehicles about to back out of other spaces. Signal for a right turn.
2. Slow to 3 to 5 mph. Start turning right when you can look down the right side of the vehicle parked to the right of your chosen space. Steer sharply right. Proceed slowly, checking for clearance of your left front bumper. Check your right rear fender to see that it does not scrape the rear of the vehicle on your right.
3. As you straighten the wheels and center in your space, move forward slowly and stop just short of the curb or in line with the vehicles parked beside you.

Entering a perpendicular parking space on the left is similar to entering one on the right. In this case, you turn the steering wheel in the opposite direction and keep track of the right front bumper and the left rear fender.

Exiting an Angled or a Perpendicular Parking Space

To leave an angled or a perpendicular space, follow these rules.

1. Turn on your turn signal to alert drivers of your intentions. With your foot on the brake, shift into Reverse. Check all traffic

MEETING STUDENT DIVERSITY

Physically Challenged

Students should know that drivers who are physically challenged may apply to their state motor vehicle department for a special parking permit that allows them to park in otherwise restricted areas as well as in areas that are specifically set aside for people with physical challenges.

around you. Back very slowly with your wheels straight, looking to your left and over your right shoulder. Keep checking the back and sides for obstacles. Yield to any oncoming traffic.

2. To exit an angled space on the right, backing to the right, turn the steering wheel sharply right when your front bumper will clear the rear of the vehicle on your left.

3. When you exit from a perpendicular space, turn the steering wheel slightly right or left when your windshield lines up with the rear bumpers of the vehicles on both sides. Make sure your front fender clears the rear of the vehicle opposite to the direction in which you are turning.

4. As your vehicle enters the traffic lane, quickly turn the steering wheel in the opposite direction to straighten the front wheels. Keep looking out the rear window until the vehicle stops.

5. Shift into Drive or First gear, accelerate, and move into traffic.

How Do You Parallel Park?

You parallel park most often along the side of a street. **Parallel parking** may seem hard at first, and you'll have to practice to become expert at it. To parallel park, you need a space at least 5 feet longer than the length of your vehicle.

Parallel Parking

Here is how to parallel park.

1. Approach the parking space in the proper lane. Check traffic behind you. Signal in the direction of the curb and flash your brake lights to alert following drivers of your intention to stop.

2. Move parallel to the vehicle in front of the space, leaving about 3 feet between vehicles. Stop when the center door posts, or the backs of the front seats of the vehicles are even. Keep your foot on the brake, and shift into Reverse.

3. Back up, steering sharply to the right. Align the back of the front seat with the rear bumper of the vehicle in front. Continue backing slowly, straightening your front wheels, until your front bumper lines up with the rear bumper of the vehicle in front.

4. Back up, steering rapidly to the left. Stop before making contact with the bumper of the vehicle behind the space.

5. With your foot on the brake, shift into Drive or First gear. Move forward slowly, centering your vehicle in the parking space. Stop and set the parking brake.

To exit a parallel parking space on the right, follow these steps.

♦ *It takes a great deal of practice to be able to parallel park efficiently.*

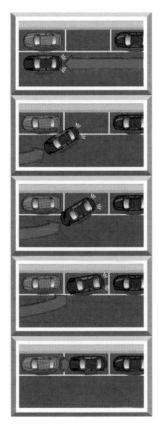

- Uphill with a curb—turn front wheels away from the curb so that if the vehicle starts to roll back, it will roll into the curb.

- Downhill with a curb—turn front wheels toward the curb so that if the vehicle starts to roll, the curb will stop it.

- Uphill or downhill with no curb—turn front wheels toward the side of the road so that if the vehicle starts to roll, it will roll away from the road.

Teaching Model

Display this situation:

Explain the following to students: You are in vehicle 1 and want to parallel park in the space between vehicles 2 and 3. Model your thinking process. (You do the following.

- Manage risk by checking for traffic behind you. If a vehicle is following too closely, find another parking space. This may be frustrating but it is far better than stopping suddenly and risking a rear-end collision.

- Give the hand signal for slowing down, then put on your turn signal to warn other drivers that you intend to park. If traffic permits, wave vehicles behind you to go around you.

continued on page 188

MEETING STUDENT DIVERSITY

Limited English Proficiency

For students who are having difficulty understanding a description of which way to turn the steering wheel when parking, go through the basic maneuvers slowly, step by step. Use models to aid student comprehension. Have students summarize in their own words what you say as they act out the steering maneuvers.

- Make sure the space is large enough for your vehicle by pulling up beside it and visually judging whether it is at least 5 feet larger than the length of your vehicle.
- Move parallel to the vehicle in front of the space (vehicle 2), leaving about 3 feet between your vehicle and the other vehicle.
- Check for traffic, then shift into Reverse.
- Look over your right shoulder and out the back window.
- Back the vehicle slowly while turning the steering wheel sharply to the right. Be alert for traffic and pedestrians.
- Straighten the front wheels as you back up until your front bumper lines up with the rear bumper of the vehicle ahead of your parking space.
- Continue to back slowly while turning your steering wheel sharply to the left.
- Check that you are parallel with the curb.
- Shift to Drive or First gear, and center the vehicle in the parking space. Set the parking brake.)

Ask

Why do you think that it is important for drivers to monitor both the front and back ends of their vehicle during the parallel-parking process? What possible risks do passing vehicles present? What possible risks do pedestrians present?

Read

Have students read Lesson 4 to learn about different ways to park a vehicle and also about techniques for parking on hills, in garages, and in driveways.

ASSESS

Guided Practice

Have students answer the Lesson 4 Review questions. The answers are provided below.

Energy Tips

Remember to adjust the driver's seat and all mirrors, lock the doors, and fasten your safety belt *before you start your car* in order to save fuel.

1. Shift into Reverse. Back slowly, with your wheels straight. When your vehicle is about 1 foot from the vehicle behind you, turn the steering wheel rapidly to the left and stop.
2. With your foot on the brake, shift into Drive or First gear. Check your mirrors. Signal a left turn. Move forward slowly, steering rapidly the rest of the way to the left.
3. Check your blind spots. Yield to approaching traffic. Then move forward slowly. When your center door post is even with the rear bumper of the vehicle in front of you, turn the steering wheel right until the front wheels point straight ahead.
4. Check the position of the vehicle to your right, being careful not to scrape it. When your rear bumper is opposite its rear bumper, accelerate gently and steer right as necessary into traffic.

How Would You Park in Other Areas?

Parking lots and city streets are not the only areas where you park. You might have to park in a driveway or a garage or on a steep hill.

TIPS **FOR NEW DRIVERS**

Leaving a Vehicle Safely

Don't be careless. Learn the safe way to leave your vehicle.
- With your foot firmly on the brake pedal, set the parking brake.
- Shift into Park (automatic) or Reverse (manual).
- Close all windows.
- Turn the key to the lock position, and remove it from the ignition switch. Turn your steering wheel slightly to lock it too.
- Check for approaching traffic. Look in your mirrors *and* check your blind spot.
- Wait for a break in traffic before opening the door. Then open it only far enough and long enough to get out of the vehicle.
- Lock the door. Then, keeping an eye on traffic, move quickly around the rear of the vehicle toward the curb.
- Whenever possible, have passengers exit from the curb side of the vehicle.

Parking in a Driveway

At times, you may have to park in a driveway. Driveways may have trees and shrubbery or fences and buildings on either side. Centering your vehicle is especially important in a narrow driveway. Furthermore, because many driveways are often sloped downward, you should make sure to set your parking brake.

Parking in a Garage

Parking in a garage is also similar to perpendicular parking. You must make sure to center your vehicle, either between the walls of the garage or between the sides of the garage door opening. Good positioning and the ability to judge space to your sides are important in parking in a garage. Remember to check both fenders for clearance as you back slowly out of the garage.

Parking on a Hill

Parking on a hill is similar to parking on a flat surface. However, you must make sure your vehicle will not roll into traffic after you leave it. The procedures described here are for parking on the right side of the street. To park on the left side, make appropriate right-left adjustments.

Parking downhill with a curb To make sure your vehicle does not roll, take these precautions.

1. Bring the vehicle to its normal parallel-parked position. Turn the steering wheel sharply right and move slowly forward.
2. Stop the vehicle when the front right wheel touches the curb. Set the parking brake. If your vehicle has a manual transmission, shift into Reverse.

Parking downhill without a curb You may need to park facing downhill on a roadway that has no curb. Follow the same procedure for parking downhill with a curb, but move as close to the inner edge of the shoulder as possible.

Parking uphill with a curb Follow these guidelines to park facing uphill when there is a curb at the edge of the roadway.

1. Bring the vehicle to a normal parallel-parked position.
2. Move forward slowly, turning the wheels sharply left as far as they will go. Move about 2 feet and stop.
3. In Neutral, with your foot covering the brake, allow the vehicle to roll back slowly with the wheels cramped left until the rear of the right front tire touches the curb. Set the parking brake. If your vehicle has a manual transmission, shift to First gear.

Parking uphill without a curb To park uphill on a road without a curb, follow the procedure for uphill parking with a curb. However, center the vehicle in the space with the front wheels turned to the right so that if the vehicle begins to roll, it will move off the roadway.

Restrictions on Parking

Every state has its own parking restrictions. Before you decide to park your vehicle anywhere, make sure that you will be parked legally. Parking laws may differ from state to state. However, in most states it is illegal to park in these areas:
- at a bus stop
- in a loading zone

SAFETY TIPS

Do not park just around a curve or just over the crest of a hill. Drivers approaching from the rear may not see you until it is too late. To avoid colliding with you, they may have to steer into the oncoming lane.

◆ *When you park on a hill, position the front wheels so that the car cannot roll into the roadway.*

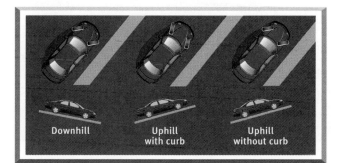

Downhill   Uphill with curb   Uphill without curb

Driving Tip

Explain to students that after parking on a hill, they should apply the parking brake and then shift to Park or Neutral (the opposite procedure to what is done when parking on level ground). Applying the parking brake before shifting to Park or Neutral reduces the strain on the transmission and keeps the vehicle from lurching when the gears are engaged.

Reteaching

Have students work in groups to demonstrate each parking method. Suggest that each group draw a diagram of an angled parking space, a perpendicular parking space, and a parallel parking space. Have students use erasers or similar objects to represent vehicles.

Encourage students to use their models to create parking situations and then demonstrate exactly what they would do in each situation. Have the student performing the demonstration describe each part of the parking procedure. Other group members should share their comments and suggestions with regard to technique as well as safety factors.

After group members have demonstrated pulling into a parking space, have them show how they would pull out of the space. Again, have the demonstrator say the steps aloud, and have other students comment. Be sure that students alternate roles so that everyone in the group has an opportunity to be both a demonstrator and an observer.

Enrichment

Assign the Study Guide for Lesson 4. The Find Out More section encourages students to expand their basic learning of the lesson concepts.

TIPS FOR NEW DRIVERS

To demonstrate their understanding, have students discuss how each tip can help them reduce risk when leaving a parked vehicle. For example, closing the windows and remembering to take their keys can reduce the risk of theft and vandalism to an unattended vehicle. Checking for approaching traffic and waiting for a break in traffic before exiting can reduce the risk of being hit by a passing vehicle.

ADVICE FROM THE EXPERTS

Students should realize that even at low speeds, collisions can result in injuries and property damage. Drivers must remain alert at all times and watch for vehicles and pedestrians approaching from all sides.

CLOSE

Summarize

Return to the Motivator question, and discuss with students how recognizing that parking is sometimes exasperating and difficult can help them manage risk by controlling their emotional reactions to their frustration.

Extend the discussion to include a description of the parking techniques that students have learned in this lesson. Ask students to describe each one in their own words. Discuss how knowing the problems inherent in each parking maneuver will help students carry out these maneuvers safely.

DRIVER'S LOG

Which parking maneuver do you think will give you the most trouble? What will you do to keep cool when you have to perform this maneuver?

WHAT WOULD YOU DO?

Sample answer: After parking, turn the steering wheel sharply right and slowly move forward until the front right tire touches the curb. Set the parking brake and shift to Park (automatic transmission) or Reverse (manual transmission).

ADVICE FROM THE EXPERTS

Carolyne Wilmoth
Classroom Driver Education Instructor, AAA Colorado

You use the same techniques to park, make turnabouts, and turn at intersections. The maneuvers you can make are not always the same. So, you need to understand signs, signals, and pavement markings. You must also practice proper techniques for visual search, steering, speed-control, and space management.

While low-speed and close-quarter maneuvers are rarely associated with serious injuries or deaths, it is still worthwhile always to use the correct procedures.

WHAT WOULD YOU DO?

What procedures will you follow in order to park on the hill?

- in the traffic lane beside another vehicle (double parking)
- on a sidewalk
- half in, half out of a driveway
- across someone else's driveway
- within a given distance of a fire hydrant
- in the fire zone in front of schools and in front of other public and private buildings
- in a no-stopping or no-standing zone

Lesson 4 Review

1. What should you do when entering an angled parking space?
2. How would you parallel park?
3. What should you do when parking on a hill or in a driveway or in a garage?

Lesson 4 Review

Answers

1. Stay 5 to 6 feet from parked vehicles; observe traffic in all directions; signal; proceed very slowly, steering carefully until the vehicle is properly aligned with surrounding vehicles.
2. Move parallel to the vehicle in front of the space; back up slowly and carefully; center the vehicle in the space, stop, and set the brake.
3. On a hill, position the front wheels so that the vehicle cannot roll into the roadway; in a driveway or garage, center the vehicle and set the parking brake.

Using Junctions and Interchanges

Roadways that are numbered routes meet, or intersect, at junctions. On a map, junctions may be marked by a ○, in the same way that towns are. On an expressway, junctions are interchanges, shown by a ◇ on the map. You need to know about junctions and interchanges to get from one roadway to another.

Suppose you are in Oswego and want to travel to Rome. You might drive south on Routes 81 and 481 until you reach the junction of Routes 481 and 90, at an interchange. Then you would drive east on Route 90 to the interchange that is the junction of Routes 90 and 365. You would drive north on Route 365 to Rome.

Try It Yourself

1. Is there a junction of Routes 20 and 90?
2. How would you drive from Chittenango to Eaton?
3. How would you drive from Florence to Parish, stopping in Williamstown? How many junctions are there? Where are they?
4. Describe the fastest and safest route from Hannibal to Syracuse. How many junctions are there? How many interchanges?

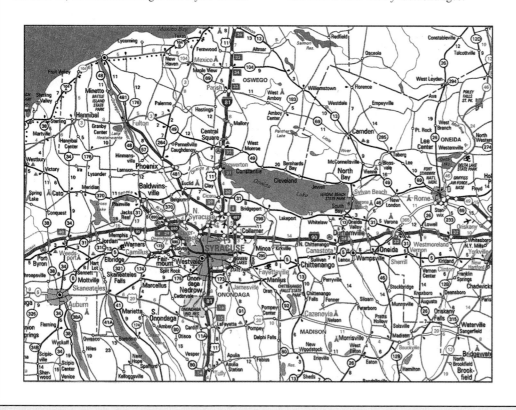

Objective

Demonstrate understanding and recognition of junctions and interchanges on a road map.

Teaching the Skill

- Be sure students understand that both junctions and interchanges represent points where roadways meet. Point out that both junctions and interchanges may have more than two roads intersecting.
- Help students locate several junction and interchange symbols on the map. Ask which roads meet at each junction and interchange identified.
- Explain that on some maps interchanges are numbered.

ANSWERS TO
Try It Yourself Questions

1. no
2. Route 13 south to Route 80 east to Eaton
3. possible answer: south to Camden, Route 13 to Williamstown, Route 183 to Amboy Center, west to Parish; three junctions
4. from Hannibal east on Route 3 to Route 481 at Fulton, turn southeast on Route 481 to Route 81 at North Syracuse, then southwest on Route 81 to Syracuse; two junctions and ten interchanges

CHAPTER SUMMARY

Key Points

Have students read the Key Points to review the major concepts of the chapter.

PROJECTS

Cooperative Learning:
Students will benefit by working with a partner on one or both projects. When the assignment is completed, the whole class will profit by sharing and comparing results.

CHAPTER 10 REVIEW

KEY POINTS

Lesson One

1. To prepare for a right turn, check the roadway, choose the correct lane, and communicate by signaling well in advance of the turn. Position your vehicle to the right side of the right lane.
2. To execute a right turn, find a gap in traffic to your left, look along your intended path of travel, and turn the vehicle, following the curve of the curb.

Lesson Two

1. To prepare for a left turn at an intersection, check the roadway, choose the correct lane, and communicate your intentions. Position your vehicle just to the right of the center line or, on a one-way street, the left curb.
2. When turning left, check for other vehicles and pedestrians across the intersection. Look for a 9-second gap to your right and a 7-second gap to your left. Look through the turn along your intended path of travel, and turn your vehicle.

Lesson Three

1. To prepare to make a turnabout, consider its legality in the situation, the amount of visibility, the amount and position of traffic, and the space available.
2. To turn your vehicle around, you can make a two-point turn by heading into or backing into a driveway, make a three-point turn, make a U-turn, or drive around the block. The method you use depends on its legality and on traffic and roadway conditions.

Lesson Four

1. To perform a perpendicular or angle parking maneuver, position your car correctly for best visibility; check for traffic and obstructions and signal; turn into the space when you have clearance on all sides.
2. To parallel park, move parallel to the vehicle in front of the space; back slowly into the space; and center your vehicle in the space.
3. Be aware of objects on either side when you park in a driveway or garage. Centering your vehicle is especially important. To park uphill or downhill, position the front wheels in such a way that your vehicle cannot roll onto the roadway.

PROJECTS

1. Observe a spot where turnabouts are permitted on a well-traveled road. Prepare a chart showing the kinds of turnabouts you observed drivers making and the frequency of each type of turnabout. Note any problems the drivers had in making the turnabouts. Discuss your observations with your class.
2. Observe several vehicles parked uphill and downhill. Record how each vehicle's front wheels are positioned. Make a diagram showing how each vehicle would move if it started to roll. Determine which vehicles had their wheels positioned correctly.

To learn more about reducing risk when making turns or parking, visit Glencoe's driver education Web site.
drivered.glencoe.com

Visit Glencoe's Driver Education Web site for student activities that relate to this chapter.
drivered.glencoe.com

CHAPTER TEST

Write the letter of the answer that best completes each sentence.

1. When you park uphill against a curb on the right, your vehicle's front wheels should be
   a. turned to the right.
   b. turned to the left.
   c. positioned straight ahead.

2. The safest way to reverse direction is to
   a. make a U-turn.
   b. drive around the block.
   c. make a three-point turn.

3. You should signal for a right or left turn
   a. 200 to 300 feet in advance.
   b. 7 to 8 feet in advance.
   c. at least 150 feet in advance.

4. To parallel park, move your vehicle parallel to the vehicle in front of the space, at a distance of
   a. 1 to 2 feet.
   b. about 3 feet.
   c. about 5 feet.

5. The steps for making a right turn
   a. are the same whether turning onto a one- or two-way street.
   b. depend on the kind of street you turn into.
   c. depend on the presence of traffic in the cross street.

6. Before you turn left, the traffic gap should be
   a. 7 to 8 seconds in both directions.
   b. 9 seconds to the right and 7 seconds to the left.
   c. 200 to 300 feet in either direction.

7. To make a two-point turn, you
   a. drive around the block.
   b. head into or back into a driveway.
   c. shift to Neutral.

8. To exit from an angled parking space, first
   a. turn the steering wheel sharply right.
   b. shift into Reverse.
   c. move parallel to the vehicle in front.

9. If you park downhill in a vehicle with a manual transmission,
   a. shift into Reverse.
   b. shift into Neutral.
   c. shift into First gear.

10. Your vehicle should be positioned next to the center line before you
    a. make a right turn from a one-way street.
    b. make a left turn from a two-way street.
    c. move straight across an intersection.

Write the word or phrase that best completes each sentence.

three-point turn	turnabout	right turn
perpendicular	roundabout	travel path

11. A _____ parking space is set at an angle of 90 degrees to the curb.

12. To make a _____, position your car to the right side of the right lane.

13. One example of a _____ is the U-turn.

14. Make a _____ only when the street is narrow, you have good visibility, and traffic is light.

15. When turning at an intersection, look through the turn along your intended _____.

DRIVER'S LOG

In this chapter, you have learned about preparing for and executing maneuvers such as making right and left turns and turnabouts and parking. Which of these maneuvers do you think will be hardest? What will you do to help you overcome the difficulty? Write two paragraphs to explain your ideas. You may draw a diagram to help you.

CHAPTER 10   *Turning and Parking*   **193**

CHAPTER 10 REVIEW

CHAPTER TEST

Assign the Chapter Test to all students.

Answers

1. b
2. b
3. c
4. b
5. a
6. b
7. b
8. b
9. a
10. b
11. perpendicular
12. right turn
13. turnabout
14. three-point turn
15. travel path

DRIVER'S LOG

Students' responses will reflect their personal viewpoints. However, their answers should provide an assessment of their understanding of basic driving maneuvers.

Evaluate

- Test A, pages 19–20 or Test B, pages 19–20 📁
- Testmaker software

RETURN TO THE BIG IDEA

Discuss reasons why mastering basic driving procedures, such as turning and parking, is critical for every driver.

Driving Environments Overview

THEME DEVELOPMENT Responsible drivers recognize that to minimize risk, they must effectively manage visibility, time, and space in a wide range of driving situations.

LESSON	PAGES	LESSON OBJECTIVES	STATE/LOCAL OBJECTIVES
1 Managing Visibility, Time, and Space	196–199	**1.** Describe how to manage visibility as a driver. **2.** Describe ways that you can manage time as a driver. **3.** Describe how to manage space as a driver.	
2 Visibility, Time, and Space on Urban Streets	200–203	**1.** Describe the special factors that affect driving on city streets. **2.** List ways to manage visibility, time, and space when driving in the city.	
3 Visibility, Time, and Space on Rural Roads	204–207	**1.** Describe the special factors that affect driving on rural roads. **2.** List ways to manage visibility, time, and space when driving on rural roads.	
4 Visibility, Time, and Space on Multiple-Lane Highways	208–212	**1.** Describe the special factors that affect driving on multiple-lane and limited-access highways. **2.** List ways to manage visibility, time, and space when driving on multiple-lane and limited-access highways.	
Building Skills	213		
Review: Chapter Summary	214		
Chapter Test	215		

CHAPTER FEATURES	TCR COMPONENTS
TIPS FOR NEW DRIVERS Developing strategies for effective time management.	Study Guide, p. 41 Transparency 32 Lesson Plan, p. 23 Information Master 17
TIPS FOR NEW DRIVERS Learning to identify problem behavior in other drivers.	Study Guide, p. 42 Transparency 33 Lesson Plan, p. 23
	Study Guide, p. 43 Lesson Plan, p. 24 Information Master 10
ADVICE FROM THE EXPERTS The importance of managing visibility, time, and space.	Study Guide, p. 44 Transparency 34 Lesson Plan, p. 24 Behind-the-Wheel Checklists 9, 20, and 22
BUILDING SKILLS: LANGUAGE Names and Meanings of Roadways	Test A, pp. 21–22 Test B, pp. 21–22

PROJECTS

1. Use a road map to plan a trip from one city to another.
2. Compare urban, rural, and highway driving.

OTHER PROGRAM RESOURCES

Testmaker software
Responsible Driving,
  Video 2: Lessons 1–4
Traffic charts
*Teaching Your Teens to
  Drive:* Lessons 3–12,
  video or CD-ROM, AAA,
  1998

ADDITIONAL RESOURCES

*Using Your Eyes
  Effectively,* Video 488,
  AAA Foundation
Night Driving, Video 453,
  AAA Foundation
Freeway Driving, Video
  431, AAA Foundation
*Managing Space and Time
  for Safe Driving,* Video
  449, AAA Foundation
Sharing the Road, Video
  468, AAA Foundation
*Breaking the Accident
  Chain of Events,* Video
  403, AAA Foundation
*Getting Safely Past the
  Orange Barrels,* Video
  433, AAA Foundation

NAME _____ DATE _____

CHAPTER 11 Driving Environments

TEST A

In each space below, write the word or words that best complete the sentence.

1. The distance your vehicle travels after you apply the brakes until it stops is the __braking__ distance.

2. If you double your speed, you will need __four__ times the distance to stop.

3. On most controlled-access highways, you enter and exit on the __right__ side.

Read each statement below. If it is true, place a T in the space to the left of the statement. If the statement is false, place an F next to it.

__T__ 4. Dirty headlights can reduce illumination by as much as 90 percent.

__T__ 5. To improve visibility, you should turn on your headlights during the day as well as at night.

__T__ 6. Braking distance is partially dependent on speed.

__F__ 7. Initial driver reaction time, or the time it takes a driver to see a problem and step on the brakes, is from 4 to 5 seconds.

__T__ 8. When you are driving, you should try to keep as much as 8 feet on either side of your vehicle to help manage space.

__F__ 9. A jackrabbit start saves fuel because you have much less idling time.

__F__ 10. To manage visibility, you should keep your eyes fixed on the path directly ahead of your vehicle.

__F__ 11. Speeding up to beat a changing traffic light is safe as long as you get through the light before it turns red.

__F__ 12. Speed limits in the city are usually higher than speed limits in rural areas.

__T__ 13. You can minimize risk by managing visibility, time, and space.

__T__ 14. Exit and entrance ramps for controlled-access highways usually have a speed limit range between 25 and 45 mph.

Select the phrase that best completes each sentence below. Write the letter of the answer you have chosen to the left of each statement.

__d__ 15. To help improve visibility, you can
a. clean the outside and inside of all windows.
b. make sure that all of your lights are clean and working.
c. keep sunglasses, a scraper, and a flashlight handy.
d. do all of the above.

NAME _____ DATE _____

__b__ 16. A factor that does not affect braking distance is
a. the kind of tires you have.
b. the acceleration power of your engine.
c. the condition of the road surface.
d. the size of your car.

__c__ 17. You should identify objects or conditions in your path of travel that could increase the level of risk
a. 2 to 3 seconds ahead.
b. 20 to 30 seconds ahead.
c. 12 to 15 seconds ahead.
d. 30 to 40 seconds ahead.

__d__ 18. Managing space when you drive means managing the distance between your car and the vehicle
a. ahead of you.
b. behind you.
c. to the sides of you.
d. in all of the above locations.

Match the following terms by placing the letter of the definition to the left of the item.

__c__ 19. controlled-access highway

__b__ 20. highway

__e__ 21. expressway

__a__ 22. turnpike

__d__ 23. beltway

a. a road that you pay a toll to drive on

b. a main public roadway

c. a road that allows vehicles to enter and exit only at specific places

d. a highway that goes around an urban area

e. a divided highway with limited access that has more than one lane running in each direction

24. What actions can you take to help manage visibility before starting your car?

Clean the inside and outside of all windows; make sure all car lights are clean and working. Make sure

the defroster and windshield wipers are working properly. Adjust all mirrors and the driver's seat.

Keep sunglasses, a flashlight, and a scraper handy. Remove any obstructions from inside the car.

_____

_____

_____

_____

_____

_____

NAME _____ DATE _____

CHAPTER 11 Driving Environments

TEST B

In each space below, write the word or words that best complete the sentence.

1. The distance traveled from the moment that you see a problem until you have stopped your vehicle is the __total stopping__ distance.

2. If moving at 30 mph on a dry road you need 37.5 feet to stop, you then will need about 150 feet to stop if you __increase__ your speed to 60 mph.

3. You can enter or leave an expressway at an __interchange__.

Read each statement below. If it is true, place a T in the space to the left of the statement. If the statement is false, place an F next to it.

__F__ 4. Collisions at high speeds are not as damaging as collisions at low speeds.

__T__ 5. On most controlled-access highways, vehicles enter and exit from the right side.

__T__ 6. Exit and entrance ramps for controlled-access highways usually have a speed limit ranging from 25 to 45 mph.

__F__ 7. On highways, identify threatening conditions 4 seconds ahead.

__T__ 8. Leave an additional 5 to 6 seconds following distance if the road is slippery.

__T__ 9. At a highway speed of 55 mph, it will take you between 4 and 5 seconds to react to a problem and stop your car.

__F__ 10. You can always assume that pedestrians will obey traffic rules.

Select the phrase that best completes each sentence below. Write the letter of the answer you have chosen to the left of each statement.

__b__ 11. The most fuel-efficient way to start moving your vehicle from a stop is
a. a fast jackrabbit start.
b. by gradually accelerating.
c. by starting out in Second gear.
d. none of the above.

__d__ 12. A clue that the driver of another vehicle could cause a problem is
a. the driver is using a cellular phone.
b. the vehicle has out-of-state license plates.
c. the driver is drifting from side to side.
d. all of the above.

NAME _____ DATE _____

__d__ 13. It is safe to follow a vehicle closely in
a. bumper-to-bumper traffic.
b. very slow traffic.
c. a medical emergency.
d. none of the above conditions.

__c__ 14. While driving on country roads,
a. you have a greater likelihood of a collision with another vehicle than in the city.
b. you have little likelihood of any kind of collision.
c. you have a greater chance of hitting a fixed object than another vehicle.
d. none of the above is true.

__a__ 15. When planning to pass another vehicle uphill on a rural road,
a. pass only when you have a clear path ahead in which to complete the pass.
b. pass as soon as you see no vehicles coming.
c. look for a gap of 6 to 7 seconds ahead.
d. first check for curve signs.

__c__ 16. In the city, your visibility can be limited by
a. double-parked vehicles.
b. buses.
c. both a and b.
d. none of the above.

Match the following terms by placing the letter of the definition to the left of the item.

__c__ 17. parkway

__d__ 18. deceleration lane

__a__ 19. limited-access highway

__e__ 20. expressway

__b__ 21. beltway

a. a road that allows vehicles to enter or exit only at a specific place

b. a highway that goes around an urban area

c. a wide landscaped highway

d. part of the road that allows vehicles to reduce speed to exit

e. a divided highway with limited access and more than one lane running in each direction

22. City driving has some special problems because of congestion and pedestrians. What can you do to better manage visibility in the city?

Search one to two blocks ahead and side to side; keep low beams on; check mirrors; signal intentions

well ahead of time; keep alert to other vehicles' taillights. Be ready for pedestrians coming onto the

road. Be alert for signs and signals and for sirens and flashing lights. Be aware of exits and entrances

for apartment buildings and parking lots.

_____

_____

_____

NAME _____ DATE _____

CHAPTER 11 Driving Environments

Managing Visibility, Time, and Space

A. For each sentence below, circle T if the statement is true and F if it is false. Correct each false statement in the space below.

1. Road grime can reduce headlight illumination up to 50 percent. T **(F)**

Road grime can reduce headlight illumination up to 90 percent.

2. Driving with your low beams on during the daylight hours makes your vehicle visible about 220 feet sooner than when you drive without them. T **(F)**

Low beams make your vehicle visible 2,200 feet sooner during daylight hours.

3. The amount of distance you need to stop the car increases with speed. **(T)** F

4. Braking distance is the distance your vehicle travels after you see a problem and before you apply the brakes. T **(F)**

Braking distance is how far your vehicle travels between when you first apply the brakes and when it stops.

5. Total stopping distance is the distance it takes from the moment you see a problem until your vehicle is stopped. **(T)** F

6. You should identify objects that could increase the level of risk 12 to 15 seconds ahead of you. **(T)** F

7. Between 20 and 30 seconds ahead equals about 1/, mile at 50 mph. **(T)** F

8. If you double your speed, your stopping distance will double. T **(F)**

If you double your speed, your stopping distance will multiply by four.

9. To get rid of a tailgater, slow down quickly to let the vehicle pass. T **(F)**

Increase the distance between your vehicle and the one ahead of you.

10. You should keep a minimum of 3 seconds of following distance, and 4 to 5 seconds at speeds of 40 mph or more. **(T)** F

B. FIND OUT MORE. During the next week, observe other people's driving while you are riding in the school bus or in another vehicle. Are people keeping safe following distances?

Review student's work.

NAME _____ DATE _____

Driving on Urban Streets

A. What are the guidelines for managing visibility, time, and space in city driving? Write at least three guidelines in each category.

Visibility Possible answers: Scan 1 to 2 blocks ahead, keep low beams on, signal turns well in advance, check all mirrors, watch taillights, be alert for pedestrians, and watch signs and signals.

Time Possible answers: Reduce speed, use SIPDE process, be alert in dense traffic, be ready to steer to avoid a collision, "cover" brakes in threatening situations, allow extra time, signal in advance.

Space Possible answers: Don't follow closely, always leave a margin of space between you and parked or moving vehicles, watch for people leaving parked vehicles, don't drive in another driver's blind spot.

B. What special factors affect city driving?

Traffic density, number of pedestrians, number of intersections, slow or irregular traffic flow, lower speed limits, sight obstructions, road defects.

C. FIND OUT MORE. The chapter lists some clues that indicate when the behavior of other drivers could be a potential problem or danger to you. What are they? Why would the actions listed be a hazard? During the next week, see how many of these clues you can spot. Report your findings below.

Review student's work.

_____

_____

_____

_____

_____

_____

NAME _____ DATE _____

Driving on Rural Roads

A. In the following sentences, two word choices are given. Circle the correct one.

1. Traffic is generally (heavier/**lighter**) on country roads.

2. Country roads generally have (**higher**/lower) speed limits than city roads.

3. Country roads have (more/**fewer**) traffic lights then city streets.

4. The greater risk of colliding with another vehicle is in the (country/**city**).

5. There is a greater risk of your car colliding with a fixed object in the (**country**/city).

6. If you are coming close to a rider on horseback, you (should/**should not**) use your horn to warn the rider.

B. For each sentence below, circle T if the statement is true and F if it is false. Correct each false statement in the space below.

1. Trees and shrubs growing near the roadway can limit visibility. **(T)** F

2. All country roads have shoulders. T **(F)**

Country roads may or may not have shoulders.

3. In the country, you should not drive with your headlights on during the day. T **(F)**

You should always drive with your low-beam headlights on during the day.

4. When approaching an animal near the road, you should drive slowly. **(T)** F

5. Never pass on an uphill grade when you don't have a clear path ahead. **(T)** F

C. FIND OUT MORE. Call your local law enforcement agency, your state patrol, or a local insurance agent. Ask them what they think the major differences are between city and country driving. Ask them where they think fatal collisions are more likely to occur, and why. Report your findings below.

Review student's work.

_____

_____

_____

_____

NAME _____ DATE _____

Driving on Multiple-Lane Highways

A. Finish each sentence below. Give as complete information as you can.

1. A limited-access, or controlled-access, highway allows vehicles to enter or to exit only at specific places.

2. An expressway is a divided highway with limited access that has more than one lane running in each direction.

3. A turnpike is a road or highway that requires drivers to pay a toll.

4. A beltway is a highway that goes around an urban area.

5. A parkway is a wide, landscaped highway that may be limited to noncommercial vehicles.

6. A deceleration lane allows vehicles to reduce speed in order to exit a controlled-access highway.

7. An acceleration lane lets vehicles increase speed to merge with traffic on a controlled-access highway.

8. An interchange is a place where vehicles can enter or leave the expressway or connect with a highway that goes in another direction.

B. FIND OUT MORE. Go to the library and look at a road atlas. Where are the limited-access roads in your state? Where do any interstate highways enter the state, and what routes do they take? How can you tell whether a road is a toll road by looking at the atlas?

Review student's work.

_____

_____

_____

Driving Environments

CHAPTER OVERVIEW

LESSON ONE

Ways for drivers to manage visibility, time, and space are described.

LESSON TWO

Special factors that affect city driving are described, and guidelines for managing visibility, time, and space when driving on city streets are explained.

LESSON THREE

Special factors that affect rural driving are described, and guidelines for managing visibility, time, and space in rural driving situations are provided.

LESSON FOUR

Special factors that affect driving on multiple-lane and limited-access highways are described along with strategies for managing visibility, time, and space in highway driving.

VOCABULARY

braking distance
interchange
limited-access highway
tailgate
total stopping distance
visibility

194

CONCEPT OF THE DRIVING TASK

Explain to students that driving requires constant mental alertness because the factors that contribute to risk are ever changing. Drivers must be prepared to deal with these factors in various driving environments: in cities, on rural roads, and on multiple-lane highways.

CHAPTER 11

Driving Environments

Whether you drive on a quiet country road or a busy four-lane highway, you must be alert to an increase in the level of risk. Learning how to manage visibility, time, and space in different environments will help you minimize risk.

CHAPTER 11   *Driving Environments*   **195**

PRESENTING THE BIG IDEA ——

Drivers who understand the various factors that affect driving on city streets, rural roads, and multiple-lane highways will be well prepared to manage visibility, time, and space so as to reduce risk in these driving environments.

INTRODUCING THE CHAPTER

What's on the Road Ahead?

Have students read the lesson titles and objectives. Briefly discuss the topic of each lesson. Tell students that in this chapter, they will learn strategies for managing visibility, time, and space when driving on city streets, rural roads, and highways.

Background: Highway Development

By 1920, the number of vehicles sold annually in the United States had increased from a few thousand to almost 2 million. A corresponding demand for better roads resulted in thousands of miles of road construction or improvement each year.

- The first scenic highway—the Bronx River Parkway in New York—was opened in 1923. By 1924, a grid of national highways was established.
- In 1956, Congress approved a 41,000-mile system of national interstate highways. The resulting construction turned rural areas into city suburbs.
- By the late 1960s, urban highways had become unpopular, and construction was delayed or cut.
- By 1987, only 10 percent of the nation's 3.9 million miles of road remained unsurfaced.

Relating to Prior Knowledge

Have students discuss what they know about the differences between city and rural driving conditions. Ask which kind of driving seems less stressful and why.

The Big Idea

Discuss students' reactions to the Big Idea statement. Suggest that they keep this idea in mind as they read Chapter 11.

Managing Visibility, Time, and Space

(pages 196–199)

FOCUS

Objectives

- Describe how to manage visibility as a driver.
- Describe ways that you can manage time as a driver.
- Describe how to manage space as a driver.

Resources

 Study Guide, page 41

Traffic charts

 Transparency 32

Information Master 17

Vocabulary

visibility
braking distance
total stopping distance
tailgate

Motivator

Pose this situation: You are driving on a multiple-lane highway. A considerable amount of traffic is traveling with you. What are some ways in which you can reduce the risk of collision? (Students may mention scanning the roadway; making sure you know the position of nearby and approaching vehicles; turning on your headlights to help other drivers see you; keeping a safe distance between your vehicle and vehicles ahead, behind, and to the sides.)

LESSON ONE

OBJECTIVES

1. Describe how to manage visibility as a driver.
2. Describe ways that you can manage time as a driver.
3. Describe how to manage space as a driver.

KEY TERMS

visibility
braking distance
total stopping distance
tailgate

Managing Visibility, Time, and Space

Whenever you drive, the risk of collision is always present. However, you can minimize that risk by learning to manage visibility, time, and space.

As you read about visibility, time, and space, keep in mind that they are closely related. To become a safe driver, you must understand how visibility, time, and space work together in all driving situations.

How Can You Manage Visibility?

Visibility refers to your ability to see and to be seen by other roadway users. You can take specific actions to maximize visibility both before you begin driving and once you are on the road.

Advance Preparations

Take these steps to manage visibility before you begin driving.

- Clear and clean the inside and outside of your vehicle windows.
- Make sure all vehicle lights are clean and in good working order.
- Make sure your defroster and windshield wipers and washer work properly.
- Adjust rearview and sideview mirrors for maximum visibility. Also adjust the driver's seat properly.
- Obtain and keep handy any items you might need to improve visibility, such as sunglasses, a flashlight, and a windshield scraper.
- Remove obstructions inside the vehicle, such as ornaments that hang from the rearview mirror or packages that block your view.

Behind-the-Wheel Actions

The first step in making your vehicle more visible while you are driving is to turn on your headlights whenever you drive, day or night. Driving with your low beams on in daylight makes your vehicle visible to drivers and pedestrians more than 2,200 feet sooner than it would be with no headlights.

Maximize your visibility to other roadway users by signaling your intentions well in advance. Also avoid driving in another driver's blind spot.

To help ensure your ability to see the roadway, always wear glasses or contact lenses if you need them. To shield your eyes from glare, put on sunglasses or use your sun visors.

◆ *To reduce risk and manage visibility, clean your headlights regularly.*

MEETING STUDENT DIVERSITY

Following Directions

Students who have difficulty following directions may be nervous about driving to places they have never been. Advise students to make sure they understand the directions *before* they begin driving, consulting a map when necessary. Also stress the need to leave plenty of travel time and, when appropriate, to make a trial run in advance. For example, finding one's way to an unfamiliar place is much easier during daylight hours than at night.

How Can You Manage Time?

By managing time wisely, you increase your control over driving situations and help reduce risk. Decreasing or increasing your vehicle's speed, for instance, can enable you to avoid colliding with other vehicles or a pedestrian.

To manage time effectively while driving, always keep in mind that time, speed, and distance are closely linked. For example, the amount of time and distance you need to stop your vehicle increases with your speed. Similarly, the time and distance required to pass depends on how fast your vehicle and the other vehicle are traveling.

Initial driver reaction time to a roadway problem, once the problem is spotted, is generally one-half to three-fourths of a second. During that time, your vehicle continues to move forward. The **braking distance** is the distance your vehicle travels until it stops, after you apply your brakes. **Total stopping distance** includes the distance traveled from the moment you recognize and respond to a problem plus the braking distance.

◆ *Drive with your low-beams on, even in the daytime, to enable other drivers to see you better.*

◆ *Stopping distance depends on many factors, including the size of your car, the condition of the road, and the car's speed.*

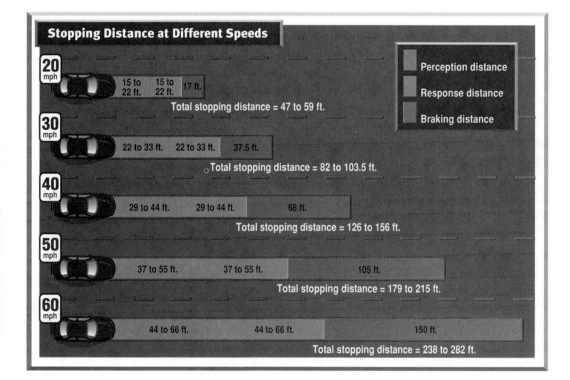

Stopping Distance at Different Speeds

20 mph — 15 to 22 ft. | 15 to 22 ft. | 17 ft.
Total stopping distance = 47 to 59 ft.

30 mph — 22 to 33 ft. | 22 to 33 ft. | 37.5 ft.
Total stopping distance = 82 to 103.5 ft.

40 mph — 29 to 44 ft. | 29 to 44 ft. | 68 ft.
Total stopping distance = 126 to 156 ft.

50 mph — 37 to 55 ft. | 37 to 55 ft. | 105 ft.
Total stopping distance = 179 to 215 ft.

60 mph — 44 to 66 ft. | 44 to 66 ft. | 150 ft.
Total stopping distance = 238 to 282 ft.

Legend:
- Perception distance
- Response distance
- Braking distance

Driving Tip

Explain to students that frequently they will have to make time and space adjustments to compensate for other drivers' poor judgment. For example, when another driver cuts in too soon after passing, the driver who was passed must slow down to increase following distance.

TIPS ▸ FOR NEW DRIVERS

Encourage students to share and discuss time management suggestions of their own.

TEACH

Explain

OBJECTIVE 1: Students will benefit from a discussion of the double significance of "visibility": being able to see and to be seen by drivers and pedestrians. Students should also keep in mind that visibility is affected by weather, amount of light, condition of the vehicle, and various other factors.

OBJECTIVE 2: Students may have difficulty understanding the concept of managing time when driving. Focus on the relative position of two vehicles traveling side by side. Discuss how the driver of either vehicle can alter the position by accelerating or braking—that is, traveling the same distance in less or more time. Stress the idea that time, speed, and distance are closely related and that by controlling these factors, drivers can manage risk.

OBJECTIVE 3: Students should recognize that a "safe margin of space" means room to maneuver on all sides of their vehicle.

Teaching Model

Display this situation:

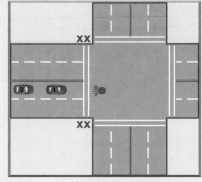

Tell students the following: You are in vehicle 1. Vehicle 2 is coming up rapidly behind you. As you approach the intersection, the light changes from green to yellow. You notice that people are waiting to cross the street. Model the thinking process for managing visibility, time, and space to reduce risk in this situation. (You do the following.

continued on page 198

- Observe the intersection ahead, the traffic light, and the pedestrians.
- Recognize that you will need to stop.
- Recognize that vehicle 2 is too close and may not have sufficient time to stop behind you.
- Check the right lane for vehicles.
- Signal and move into the right lane to put a safe margin of space between your vehicle and vehicle 2.
- Decrease speed and stop.)

Ask

Ask students to discuss the risks to drivers and pedestrians in the situation described and how changing lanes reduced those risks.

Read

Have students read Lesson 1 to learn how they can reduce driving risk by managing visibility, time, and space.

ASSESS

Guided Practice

Have students answer the Lesson 1 Review questions. The answers are provided below.

Reteaching

Have students work in small groups. Direct group members to take turns playing the role of the driver while other members describe specific driving situations. The driver should explain how he or she would manage visibility, space, and time in the situation. Other group members should then add any ideas or suggestions of their own. After everyone has had a chance to play the driver, have the class as a whole discuss any particularly challenging situations that were presented in the small-group discussions. Then brainstorm ways to reduce driving risk.

FYI

Dirty headlights limit visibility. Road grime on the headlights can reduce illumination as much as 90 percent.

In Chapter 1 you learned how you can use the SIPDE process to reduce risk. By helping you identify threatening objects or conditions as early as possible, the SIPDE process maximizes the amount of time available for you to take whatever evasive action may be required.

Here are some guidelines for managing time. Note how managing time and space, and distance are the same.

Search ahead 20 to 30 seconds as you drive for information that can help you select a safe path of travel. Twenty to 30 seconds equals about 1½ to 2 blocks at 25 to 30 mph in the city, and about ½ mile at 50 to 65 mph on the highway.

Identify objects or conditions within 12 to 15 seconds ahead that could increase the level of risk. Objects or conditions 12 to 15 seconds ahead are at a distance equal to about 1 city block or ¼ mile when you're on the highway.

Keep a minimum 3-second following distance between your vehicle and the vehicle ahead. You need at least 3 seconds to steer evasively. To figure the distance between your vehicle and the vehicle ahead, notice when the rear of the vehicle ahead passes a fixed point, such as a sign or tree. Count "one-second-one, two-seconds-two, three-seconds-three." If the front of your vehicle passes the point before you finish counting "three-seconds-three," you're following too closely.

How Can You Manage Space?

Managing space when you drive means managing the distance between your vehicle and the vehicles ahead, behind, and to the sides. Your goal is to allow yourself enough space to maneuver safely at all times. By managing space wisely, you also increase your ability to see and be seen.

TIPS **FOR NEW DRIVERS**

Managing Time

Effective time management begins before you get behind the wheel. Here are some tips.
- Make a conscious effort to understand and learn to judge time and speed factors. Try to develop a sense, for example, of how much longer it takes a vehicle to slow down and stop when moving at 50 mph than at 20 mph.
- Plan your route in advance, and always allow yourself plenty of time to reach your destination.
- Get traffic information from the radio or other source to help you plan the best route of travel.

Consider Time, Distance, and Speed

In learning to manage time, you have already learned a great deal about managing space. For example, by maintaining a minimum following distance of 3 seconds, you are managing both time *and* space.

The close link between managing time and space is also clear in terms of your vehicle's speed. The faster you're traveling, the more time *and* distance you need to brake to a stop.

THE INTERNATIONAL SCENE

Canada

Making a right turn on a red light is legal in some Canadian provinces, illegal in others. For example, you can turn right at a red light in Ontario but not in Quebec or New Brunswick. It is advisable to check with local authorities to find out what the law is in particular provinces.

In fact, if you double your speed, you need *four* times the distance to brake to a stop. Moving at 30 mph on a dry road after you apply the brakes, for instance, you need about 37.5 feet to stop. At 60 mph, however, you need at least 150 feet (4 × 37.5). In mathematical terms, the braking distance increase (in feet) equals the square of the increase in speed.

Assess and Adjust the Space Around Your Vehicle

Having ample space around your vehicle gives you time to observe, think, decide, and act or react. By adjusting your vehicle's position to maintain a safe margin of space, you can generally avoid the need to brake, accelerate, or swerve suddenly. A cushion of space also gives you room to steer in case of emergency.

Here are some guidelines for managing space.

Adjust your following distance as needed. Leave at least 3 seconds distance between your vehicle and the one ahead. Leave 4 to 5 seconds at speeds of 40 mph or more plus another 5 to 6 seconds if the road is slippery or you're behind a vehicle that blocks your view.

Try to keep a 3-second distance behind your vehicle. Distance behind your vehicle is the hardest to maintain because other vehicles may **tailgate,** or follow too closely. If you are being tailgated, *increase*—do *not* decrease—the space between you and the vehicle ahead to make up for the lack of space behind you. If possible, let the tailgater pass.

Whenever possible, try to keep as much as 8 feet on either side of you. At the very least, keep a vehicle's width to one side of you. The more room you have around your vehicle, the more space you have to react to threatening situations.

If there is insufficient space ahead, behind, or to the side of your vehicle, take prompt action to increase the space. For example, if you're boxed in by vehicles, adjust your speed to move away from the pack.

WHAT WOULD YOU DO?

What are some ways that you can manage visibility, time, and space before driving this vehicle? What steps will you take while driving?

Lesson 1 Review

1. In what ways can you manage visibility while driving?
2. How can you manage time while driving?
3. What actions can you take to manage space when you drive?

Lesson 1 Review

Answers

1. Turn on headlights; signal intentions well in advance; avoid driving in another driver's blind spot; wear glasses or lenses if needed; use sunglasses or sun visors against glare.
2. Scan ahead 20 to 30 seconds; identify threatening objects or conditions 12 to 15 seconds ahead; keep a following distance of at least 3 seconds.
3. Adjust following distance as needed; try to maintain a 3-second distance behind your vehicle and as much as 8 feet on either side; act promptly to preserve a safety margin of space.

Enrichment

Assign the Study Guide for Lesson 1. The Find Out More section encourages students to expand their basic learning of the lesson concepts.

CLOSE

Summarize

Return to the Motivator question. Recall students' initial responses, and discuss additional information they have gained from the lesson. Encourage students to be specific in describing ways to minimize risk by managing visibility, time, and space.

Extend the discussion by asking students how the illustration of braking and stopping distances on page 197 can help drivers manage time and space to reduce risk.

DRIVER'S LOG

Describe, with specific examples, how visibility, time, and space work together in driving situations. Which strategies discussed in this lesson do you think are most important for minimizing risk? Why?

WHAT WOULD YOU DO?

Sample answer: Before driving, clean windows and lights, make sure defroster and wipers work properly, adjust seat and mirrors, remove obstructions. While driving, turn on headlights, maintain a safe margin of space, scan the roadway, use SIPDE.

FOCUS

Objectives

• Describe the special factors that affect driving on city streets.

• List ways to manage visibility, time, and space when driving in the city.

Resources

 Study Guide, page 42

 Traffic charts

Transparency 33

Motivator

Emphasize that city driving presents its own unique challenges. Pose the following situation: You are driving in heavy city traffic. Blocks are short, but it seems to take forever to move from one street to the next. An upcoming light is green, but just as the vehicle ahead of you reaches the intersection, the light turns yellow. Pedestrians are already beginning to move into the crosswalk. What are some ways that you can manage visibility, space, and time to reduce risk at this and other such intersections? (Students may mention guarding against becoming impatient; being prepared for vehicles ahead to stop suddenly; watching for pedestrians who are in a hurry; driving with low beams on; signaling your intentions; trying to keep a safe margin of space around your vehicle; being alert for unsafe actions by other drivers.)

LESSON TWO

OBJECTIVES

1. Describe the special factors that affect driving on city streets.
2. List ways to manage visibility, time, and space when driving in the city.

SAFETY TIPS

Never speed up to "beat" a changing traffic signal. If an impatient driver accelerates into the intersection just as the red light turns green, your vehicles will collide.

◆ City streets, crowded with vehicles and pedestrians, demand an extra degree of driver alertness.

Visibility, Time, and Space on Urban Streets

The hustle and bustle of city streets can make driving a real challenge, especially for new drivers. By understanding the factors that affect driving in the city and by managing visibility, time, and space effectively, you can meet the demands of urban driving.

What Special Factors Affect City Driving?

Cities can be hectic places. Pedestrians fill the sidewalks and cross the street at any time, while cars, buses, and other vehicles crowd the streets. Double-parked vehicles often block visibility, and potholes may interrupt traffic flow.

Traffic Density

In city traffic, you will generally be driving among many more vehicles than you will in suburban or highway driving. The traffic is dense and often slow moving, and threatening situations can occur more frequently. Maintaining a margin of space around your vehicle can be difficult.

Number of Pedestrians

At times, large cities seem to overflow with people: workers, shoppers, children, and others. Expect to encounter pedestrians anywhere and everywhere. Never assume that pedestrians will see you or that they will obey traffic rules or signals.

Intersections

Cities are filled with intersections. In the city, intersections are frequently jammed with both vehicles and pedestrians moving in all directions. When approaching or crossing any intersection, you need to use maximum care.

Driving Tip

Caution students that the sound of horns in city driving can be distracting or intimidating. Explain that some drivers sound their horns out of frustration or impatience. Stress how important it is to concentrate on driving responsibly and safely and not let another driver's impatience goad students to unsafe action.

Slow or Irregular Traffic Flow

On congested city streets, vehicles often move in packs or lines. The movement may be in a steady stream or with frequent starts and stops.

Vehicles stopping to park or parked vehicles pulling away from the curb may interrupt the flow of traffic. Roadwork or construction can also slow traffic. While you may move more slowly than you'd like to when you drive in a city, it is usually dangerous to try to move any faster.

Lower Speed Limits

City speed limits are lower than suburban or highway speed limits. In addition, they may change in different parts of a city.

Sight Obstructions

Several factors tend to limit visibility in city driving. Double-parked vehicles as well as parked vehicles can partially block your view, as can buses, trucks, and vans.

Potholes and Other Road Defects

In cities with heavy traffic, streets take a lot of wear and tear. Potholes and rough surfaces may develop. They slow traffic and pose a potential danger to drivers, pedestrians, and cyclists.

How Can You Manage Visibility, Time, and Space in City Driving?

By knowing the special factors to be alert for when driving in the city, you can manage visibility, time, and space to minimize risk.

Guidelines for Managing Visibility in the City

Here is how you can manage visibility on urban streets.

- Search 1 to 2 blocks, or 20 to 30 seconds, ahead and from one side of the street to the other. Do not focus on any one object in your path.
- Keep your low-beam headlights on at all times.
- Check your rearview and sideview mirrors to monitor traffic every time you approach an intersection or when you intend to slow or stop.
- Signal your intention to turn or pull over well ahead of time.

◆ Congested city streets severely limit your ability to search ahead and manage time and space.

Energy Tips

Avoid "jackrabbit" starts when traffic signals first turn green. Search the intersection before proceeding on a fresh green light. Accelerating gradually saves fuel—and is safer.

State BY State

Traffic laws may vary from city to city within the same state. In New York City, for example, making a right turn on a red light is prohibited at all times. Elsewhere in New York State, however, it is lawful to turn right on a red light unless otherwise marked.

TEACH

Explain

OBJECTIVE 1: Students may benefit from a discussion of each of the special factors that affect city driving and how these factors add to risk. You may also want to explore how each factor contributes to driver stress and to discuss ways of combating such stress.

OBJECTIVE 2: Students may benefit from a discussion of how to manage visibility, time, and space in city driving by taking such actions as these.

- Scan ahead and from one side of the street to the other to identify movement of vehicles, pedestrians, and bicycles.
- Keep headlights on, and signal moves well ahead of time.
- Keep as much space around the vehicle as possible.
- Adjust speed as the situation requires.
- Be prepared to brake at any time.
- Allow extra time for city driving.

Teaching Model

Display this situation:

Tell students the following: You are in vehicle 1. Note that vehicle 2 is about to move away from the curb into traffic. Model the thinking process that you go through to manage visibility, time, and space in this situation. (You do the following.

continued on page 202

- Make sure your low-beam headlights are on so that other drivers and pedestrians can see you.
- Observe ahead, behind, and to either side, noting the position of vehicles 2, 3, and 4.
- Observe the intention of vehicle 2 to move out into traffic.
- Slow down gradually to give vehicle 4 plenty of time to note your intentions.
- Come to a stop to allow vehicle 2 to move into traffic.
- Do not move forward until vehicle 2 has moved ahead a safe distance.)

Ask

Ask students to discuss what other action the driver of vehicle 1 might take if vehicle 3 were not there. Also stress in this context the importance of remaining alert to the possible actions of drivers in parked or double-parked vehicles.

Read

Have students read Lesson 2 to understand the special challenges of city driving and how to cope with them by managing visibility, time, and space.

ASSESS

Guided Practice

Have students answer the Lesson 2 Review questions. The answers are provided below.

FOR NEW DRIVERS

To check students' understanding, have them discuss each of the tips listed and explain the potential risks.

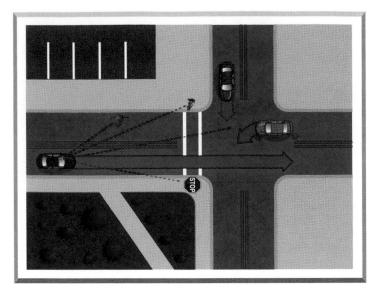

◆ *In the city, search carefully for pedestrians, cyclists, and other cars at intersections. Before entering an intersection, make sure nothing is blocking your intended path of travel.*

TIPS — FOR NEW DRIVERS

Problem Behavior

When you search the roadway, observe the behavior of other drivers for clues to potential problems. Watch for drivers:
- taking their eyes off the road while talking with others.
- using cellular phones.
- smoking, eating, reading, or looking at a map.
- with unusual postures at the wheel, which may indicate intoxication.
- signaling late or not at all.
- moving too slowly or too rapidly or following too closely (tailgating).
- drifting from side to side in their lane.
- whose view may be obstructed by packages, other objects, or tall passengers.
- with out-of-state license plates, who may be searching for an address or unaccustomed to driving in your area.

- Keep alert to the movement of vehicles four or five vehicles ahead of you so that you can anticipate when other drivers are braking or planning to turn. However, always be prepared for unexpected stops or turns.
- Be alert for pedestrians darting out from between parked vehicles or crossing streets illegally.
- Be on the lookout for warning signs and signals. Also be alert for the sirens and flashing lights of police vehicles, ambulances, fire engines, and other emergency vehicles.
- Be aware of entrances and exits for apartment buildings, parking lots, and the like. Often they are not visible until the last moment.

Guidelines for Managing Time in the City

Follow these guidelines for managing time while driving in the city.
- Drive at a moderate speed. Use the SIPDE process to help you identify objects or conditions that could increase the level of risk, particularly as you approach intersections.
- Dense traffic makes some drivers tense and impatient—and sometimes reckless. Always be ready to stop or steer to avoid a collision.
- Often braking is the only response you can make in city traffic to avoid a collision. When you spot a possible threatening condition but are not sure if you'll have to stop, take your

IT'S A FACT

Gridlock occurs when vehicles entering an intersection from one or more directions remain in the intersection when the light turns red, thereby preventing any other traffic from crossing the intersection. Traffic flow comes to a complete halt, and vehicles are unable to move in any direction. Many cities have posted signs in problem spots reminding motorists that blocking the intersection is against the law. Therefore, to prevent gridlock, do not enter the intersection until there is a space for your vehicle on the other side.

foot off the accelerator and place it just over the brake pedal without pushing down. By "covering the brake" in this manner, you reduce reaction time if you need to slow or stop.

- To give drivers and pedestrians maximum time to see and react to you, drive with your low-beam headlights on, and always signal your intentions well in advance.
- Give yourself extra time for driving in city traffic, particularly during rush hours and other busy periods. Know what route you'll be traveling, and listen to the radio for traffic information before setting out.

Guidelines for Managing Space in the City

Use these guidelines to manage space in city traffic.

- Do not follow other vehicles too closely, even in bumper-to-bumper traffic. Never follow less than 2 seconds behind.
- When stopping behind a vehicle, stop well back—20 to 30 feet—and watch the rearview mirror until two or three vehicles have stopped behind you. Then you can move up slightly. Always leave extra space in front in case the vehicle ahead stops suddenly or you have to steer out of your lane to avoid being struck from the rear. Wait for the vehicle ahead to move before you start moving forward.
- Keep as wide a margin of space as possible between your vehicle and parked vehicles. Watch for people leaving parked vehicles and for vehicles pulling out suddenly.
- Avoid driving in the blind spot of other vehicles on multiple-lane streets. Either move ahead of the other vehicles or drop back.
- Keep as much space as you can between your vehicle and vehicles in the oncoming lanes.

SAFETY TIPS

Rear-end crashes are more common than any other kind. Leave enough following distance. Too often drivers follow more closely than they should and are unable to stop in time. The increased chance of being struck in the rear while driving in the city makes it all the more important to monitor your mirrors effectively.

WHAT WOULD YOU DO?

You are driving through the city during rush hour. What steps will you take to manage visibility, time, and space?

Lesson 2 Review

1. What are some special factors that affect city driving?
2. What actions can you take to manage visibility, time, and space when you are driving in the city?

Reteaching

Have students work in small groups to make posters illustrating potential problems in city driving that involve visibility, time, and space factors. Along with each illustration, students should include specific strategies for minimizing risk. For example, students might illustrate a pedestrian crossing against the light and note the need always to search ahead, looking for sudden movements by pedestrians.

After groups have finished, display the posters in the classroom. Have students discuss the situations depicted and the strategies suggested.

Enrichment

Assign the Study Guide for Lesson 2. The Find Out More section encourages students to expand their basic learning of the lesson concepts.

CLOSE

Summarize

Return to the Motivator question. Discuss strategies that students have learned to manage visibility, time, and space in city driving. Help students summarize the basics of risk management in city driving by posing the following question: What advice would you give a new driver who is about to drive in city traffic for the first time?

DRIVER'S LOG

What factors contribute to the stress of city driving? What actions can you take to deal with each of these factors?

Lesson 2 Review

Answers

1. Dense traffic, many pedestrians, busy intersections, slow or irregular traffic flow, low-speed travel, sight obstructions, defects in street surface.
2. Search ahead and to the sides; use low beams; signal your intentions; reduce speed; try to keep a safe margin of space; stay calm and alert.

WHAT WOULD YOU DO?

Sample answer: Drive with your low beams on, watch for pedestrians, be prepared to steer evasively or stop, and allow a wide margin of space all around your vehicle.

Visibility, Time, and Space on Rural Roads

(pages 204–207)

FOCUS

Objectives

• Describe the special factors that affect driving on rural roads.

• List ways to manage visibility, time, and space when driving on rural roads.

Resources

 Study Guide, page 43

 Traffic charts

📁 Information Master 10

Motivator

Ask students if they think city or country driving is more challenging and why. (Students may respond that each type of driving can be challenging for different reasons. For example, city driving increases the chance that a crash will occur because of the higher number of vehicles, intersections, pedestrians, and bicyclists, while country driving involves higher risk of serious or fatal injury resulting from running off the road and striking a roadside object at high speed.)

Then pose the following: You are driving on a narrow, tree-lined country road that has many twists and turns. What possible hazards should you watch for? (Students may mention animals and objects on the road, unseen vehicles or objects around curves, rough road surfaces, slow-moving vehicles.)

LESSON THREE

OBJECTIVES
1. Describe the special factors that affect driving on rural roads.
2. List ways to manage visibility, time, and space when driving on rural roads.

Visibility, Time, and Space on Rural Roads

Country driving often seems easier than city driving. Traffic is generally lighter, and there are fewer pedestrians and not as many distractions. However, driving in rural areas poses a special challenge. A majority of occupant fatalities occur on country roads.

What Special Factors Affect Driving on Rural Roads?

When driving on rural roads, be especially alert for off-road conditions that limit your ability to see or maneuver.

Road Conditions

Many rural roads are two-lane, two-way roadways. Curves may be sharper and hills may be steeper than on many city streets. Roads may have concrete, asphalt, gravel, or dirt surfaces, with or without a shoulder. Many rural roads may even have drainage ditches close to both sides. At night, most rural roads are poorly lit—or not lit at all. Drivers must exercise special care, for example, when passing other vehicles and when driving on loose, low-traction road surfaces.

◆ *Snow on the road and a ditch alongside make maneuvering on this roadway difficult.*

Higher Speed, Fewer Controls

Sound judgment is more important than ever when driving in rural areas. Country roads typically have higher speed limits than city streets. You'll encounter fewer traffic lights and stop signs. At railroad crossings, there may be no signs, signals, or gates. Drivers must remain alert for traffic crossing the roadway.

Slow-Moving Vehicles

Tractors and other farm vehicles travel at much slower speeds than other vehicles. As a result, drivers on rural roads often have to pass such slow-moving vehicles. Some farm

204   UNIT 3   *Moving onto the Road*

IT'S A FACT

The vast majority (97 percent) of roadside hazard crashes involve only one vehicle. A vehicle may, for example, skid off the road and crash into a tree, utility pole, signpost, guardrail, or ditch. Sixty-five percent of the deaths in roadside hazard crashes occur on rural roads.

vehicles, such as harvesters, are very wide, limiting the visibility of following drivers and making passing extremely difficult, if not impossible.

Sight Obstructions

Trees, bushes, and tall crops growing close by the road all limit visibility for drivers on country roads. These obstructions can make driving even more challenging on narrow, winding, or sharply curving roads.

Hills, too, can reduce visibility. As you near the top of a hill, your view of the road ahead will be limited. The steeper the grade, the less you can see.

Animals and Objects on the Road

Deer, raccoons, cows, and other animals, both wild and domestic, frequently cross rural roads. To learn more about the very real dangers posed by animals on the roadway, see Chapter 13. Other possible threatening conditions on rural roads include fallen rocks, tree branches, and wet leaves.

◆ *You may encounter slow-moving vehicles more frequently in rural areas.*

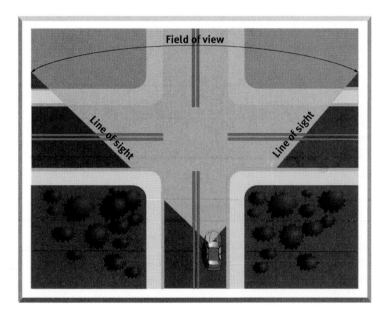

◆ *Trees close to the road limit visibility. To have a wider field of view, the driver must move closer to the intersection.*

SAFETY TIPS

Search the roadway and off-road area ahead. If you see a rider on horseback, reduce your speed and pass slowly, giving horse and rider as much leeway as possible. Never sound your horn to warn of your approach.

CHAPTER 11 *Driving Environments* **205**

Driving Tip

Caution students to avoid driving too far over to the left on curving, two-lane roads. Traffic moving in the opposite direction may drift toward the oncoming lane, increasing the risk of a head-on collision.

TEACH

Explain

OBJECTIVE 1: Students should understand that limited visibility and limited space to maneuver are problems of rural driving. Sharp curves, steep hills, narrow roadways, roadside obstructions to sight, and animals are difficulties drivers must deal with. These conditions are even more challenging at night or in poor weather.

OBJECTIVE 2: Students may benefit from a discussion of the similarities and differences in managing visibility, time, and space in rural and in city driving. Stress the idea that driver alertness is essential. Encourage students to identify specific risks in rural driving and to suggest ways to handle them.

Teaching Model

Display this situation:

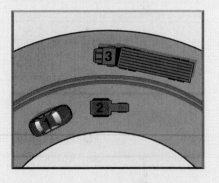

Tell students the following: You are in vehicle 1 traveling at 35 mph. You are approaching a slow-moving farm tractor, vehicle 2. Model the thinking process that you go through to manage visibility, time, and space in this situation. (You do the following.

• Slow down when you see the farm tractor, and leave a safe following distance.

• Wait until you get around the curve before checking to see if the way ahead is clear to pass.

• Check roadway markings and signs to see when it is safe and legal to pass.

• Put on your left-turn signal, and pass the tractor only when conditions allow.)

Ask students to discuss the risks posed by the oncoming truck (vehicle 3).

Read

Have students read Lesson 3 to learn what factors affect driving on rural roads and what strategies they can use to manage visibility, time, and space on rural roads.

ASSESS

Guided Practice

Have students answer the Lesson 3 Review questions. The answers are provided below.

Reteaching

Have students work together in small groups to list five factors that affect driving on rural roads. Then direct them to brainstorm different driving situations involving these factors and to discuss how they would manage visibility, time, and space.

After groups have finished, discuss with the class the benefits of using the SIPDE process to manage visibility, space, and time on rural roads.

◆ *When driving on low-traction roadways, lower your speed to manage risk.*

SAFETY TIPS

Do not underestimate the risks of rural driving. In the city, there is a greater danger of colliding with another vehicle. In the country, there is a greater chance of your vehicle going out of control and colliding with a fixed object or overturning. Drive cautiously at all times. Use low-beam headlights during daylight hours to make it easier for other vehicles to see you when trees and brush block visibility.

How Can You Manage Visibility, Time, and Space in Rural Driving?

Because of less traffic, many drivers are less attentive when driving on rural roads than on city streets. You must remain fully attentive at all times. Just as you would while driving on city streets, use the SIPDE process, and be ready to deal with the unexpected. More than 50 percent of occupant fatalities on rural roads and highways involve only one vehicle. The driver drifts or steers off the road and loses control.

Guidelines for Managing Visibility in Rural Areas

Here are some guidelines to help you manage visibility on country roads.

- During the day, always drive with low-beam headlights on. Use high beams at night on very dark roads when there are no other vehicles around.
- Search ahead 20 to 30 seconds, looking for vehicles, pedestrians, animals, and objects on or near the roadway. If road or weather conditions limit your ability to see, reduce your speed.
- Identify objects or conditions within 12 to 15 seconds ahead that may pose a danger. If you cannot see that far, slow down until your visual path clears.
- Drive at a speed that will let you respond safely to threatening conditions that may be just over a hill or around a curve.
- Follow at least 200 feet behind large vehicles so that they do not block your view of potential dangers.
- Always signal your intention to turn, to pull over, to pass, and to get back into your lane.

Guidelines for Managing Time in Rural Areas

Use these guidelines to help you manage time on rural roads.
- Watch for slow-moving vehicles. Adjust your speed as needed.
- Reduce your speed as you approach intersections, particularly those without traffic control devices. Be prepared to slow down further or even stop.

206   UNIT 3   *Moving onto the Road*

IT'S A FACT

Thirty-seven percent of pedestrians age 16 and older killed in crashes in 1994—and about 50 percent of those killed in nighttime crashes—had blood-alcohol concentrations (BACs) of 0.10 percent or higher.

- Allow extra time for driving on unfamiliar roads. Plan your route in advance.
- Reduce your speed when driving on gravel, dirt, or other low-traction road surfaces.
- When approaching or passing an animal on or near the road, drive slowly in case the animal bolts across your path.

Guidelines for Managing Space in Rural Areas

Follow these guidelines for managing space on rural roads.
- Adjust following distance for speed, traffic, roadway, and off-road conditions that affect your ability to see. Identify an escape path to which you can steer.
- If a vehicle is tailgating you, give it as much space as possible to pass and pull in front of you. If there is a vehicle ahead of you, increase your following distance.
- On two-lane roads, keep as much space as possible between your vehicle and oncoming traffic.
- Never pass on curves or hills when you do not have a clear path ahead in which to complete the pass.
- As you search the road for vehicles, animals, or objects that could threaten your safety, weigh the consequences of acting to avoid the threat against the danger of collision.

Lesson 3 Review

1. What are some special factors that affect rural driving?
2. What actions can you take to manage visibility, time, and space when you drive on rural roads?

WHAT WOULD YOU DO?

You are traveling on a two-way hilly road that has many sharp curves. What special factors affect visibility? What are some ways to manage time and space?

CHAPTER 11 *Driving Environments* **207**

Lesson 3 Review

Answers

1. Curves, hills, uneven road surfaces, poor lighting, limited number of signs and signals, slow-moving vehicles, sight obstructions, animals and objects on the roadway.
2. Use SIPDE; drive with low beams on; reduce speed; signal your intentions; keep a safe margin of space ahead, behind, and to the sides.

Enrichment

Assign the Study Guide for Lesson 3. The Find Out More section encourages students to expand their basic learning of the lesson concepts.

CLOSE

Summarize

Return to the Motivator questions. Recall students' initial responses, and then discuss what students have learned about the unique challenges of rural driving. Encourage students to be specific in comparing city and rural driving. Extend the discussion by having students describe how they would use the SIPDE process to cope with rural driving conditions.

DRIVER'S LOG

What factors can make rural driving difficult? What actions can you take to deal with each of these factors?

WHAT WOULD YOU DO?

Sample answer: Hills and curves limit your view of the road ahead; adjust speed to road and traffic conditions, adjust following distance for speed and road conditions, leave a safe margin of space.

Visibility, Time, and Space on Multiple-Lane Highways

(pages 208–212)

FOCUS

Objectives

• Describe the special factors that affect driving on multiple-lane and limited-access highways.

• List ways to manage visibility, time, and space when driving on multiple-lane and limited-access highways.

Resources

 Study Guide, page 44

 Traffic charts

 Transparency 34

 Behind-the-Wheel Checklists 9, 20, and 22

Vocabulary

limited-access highway

interchange

Motivator

Pose the following situation: You are traveling in the middle lane of a three-lane highway. Your exit is about a mile ahead on the right. There is a truck just behind you in the far right lane. What visibility, time, and space factors do you need to consider to exit the highway safely? (Students may mention the position of other vehicles ahead, on both sides, and behind you; the speed of the truck and other traffic; road signs and roadway markings; signaling to the truck driver your intention to move into the right lane and to exit.)

LESSON FOUR

OBJECTIVES

1. Describe the special factors that affect driving on multiple-lane and limited-access highways.
2. List ways to manage visibility, time, and space when driving on multiple-lane and limited-access highways.

KEY TERMS

limited-access highway
interchange

Visibility, Time, and Space on Multiple-Lane Highways

Traveling on multiple-lane highways and expressways is usually faster than traveling on local roads. Driving at higher speeds is demanding, however. You need to concentrate fully in order to manage visibility, time, and space.

This section focuses on expressways and other multiple-lane and limited-access highways, including freeways, interstate highways, parkways, and turnpikes and other toll roads. **Limited-access** or controlled-access **highways** allow vehicles to enter and exit only at specific places.

What Special Factors Affect Driving on Multiple-Lane Highways?

Driving on an expressway or other high-speed roadway is quite different from driving on urban streets or rural roads. There are usually two or more lanes of traffic moving in the same direction. Cars, trucks, buses and other vehicles pass you at high speeds. The scenery seems to whiz by—along with route markers and other road signs containing all sorts of information.

◆ *Traveling on multiple-lane, high-speed highways poses special challenges for the driver.*

Higher Speed Limits

Expressway speed limits are always higher than those on city streets and most rural roads. Higher speeds mean that drivers must manage time and space with particular care when following and passing vehicles, changing lanes, and reducing speed. High-speed collisions result in more damage and serious injuries than those occurring at lower speeds.

THE INTERNATIONAL SCENE

Europe

Visitors from the United States may be alarmed by the heavy, fast-moving traffic on Europe's major freeways, known as *autobahns* in Germany, *autoroutes* in France, and *autostrade* in Italy. Speed limits on these roads are much higher than those on similar roads in the United States—usually around 80 mph. Moreover, vehicles often travel 15 to 20 mph over these limits. In Germany, there is no officially posted speed limit, and drivers in the fast lane often exceed 100 mph.

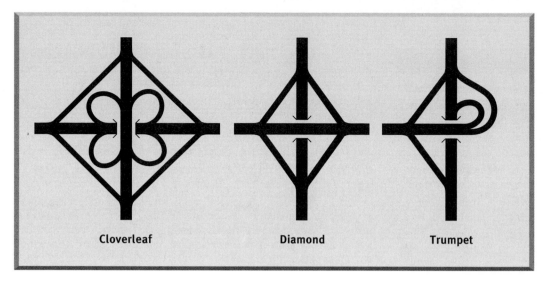

Cloverleaf   Diamond   Trumpet

◆ *Three common interchange designs are the cloverleaf, the diamond, and the trumpet.*

Limited Entrances and Exits

Entrance and exit ramps on limited-access highways may be many miles apart. Entrances and exits are usually made from the extreme right-hand lane. However, there are entrance and exit ramps located in the extreme left-hand lane.

Signs posted along the highway tell drivers when they are approaching an exit or interchange. **Interchanges** are points where you can enter or leave the expressway or connect with a highway going in another direction.

Interchanges are made up of through lanes, ramps, and speed-change lanes. Ramps are short, one-way roads connecting two highways. Speed limits on ramps typically range from 25 to 45 mph. Speed-change lanes are short lanes next to the main travel lanes of a highway. A deceleration lane allows vehicles to reduce speed to exit; an acceleration lane lets vehicles increase speed to merge with traffic.

Frequent Passing

Passing other vehicles and having other vehicles pass you is an integral part of driving on multiple-lane highways. Depending on the roadway and on your lane position and speed, you may find yourself being passed on your left, on your right, or on both sides simultaneously.

Trucks and Other Large Vehicles

Trucks, tractor-trailers, buses, and other large vehicles add additional challenges to driving on multiple-lane highways because they hamper

SAFETY TIPS

Sometimes the same lane is used for both entering and exiting a highway. It may be less rIsky to let the vehicle getting on the highway go first, but be prepared to yield whether you are the one who is exiting or the one who is entering.

TEACH

Explain

OBJECTIVE 1: Students will benefit from a discussion of each of the special factors that affect driving on multiple-lane highways. Stress that expressways require drivers to manage visibility, time, and space at much higher speeds than occur on city streets and rural roads. Students should also recognize that traveling too slowly on highways can be a hazard and that some highways have signs indicating minimum as well as maximum speeds.

OBJECTIVE 2: Students will benefit from a discussion of managing visibility, time, and space in highway driving, with emphasis on these and other important points.

- Search ahead for vehicles and objects on the road.
- Watch for passing vehicles.
- Stay alert to vehicles entering and exiting the highway.
- Signal your intentions to move.
- Drive with your headlights on low beam.
- Watch for road signs.
- Adjust your speed and distance from other vehicles under various driving conditions.
- Plan your travel route ahead of time.

MEETING STUDENT DIVERSITY

Limited English Proficiency

Some students may have trouble reading informational signs while driving at highway speeds. Suggest that students familiarize themselves in advance with place-names they are likely to encounter on road signs. Students should also know ahead of time the route numbers of highways they will have to travel.

Teaching Model

Display this situation:

Tell students the following: You are in vehicle 1 traveling at about 35 mph up the entrance ramp to the freeway. The freeway speed limit is 55 mph. Model the thinking process you go through to manage visibility, time, and space in order to merge into freeway traffic safely. (You do the following.

• Check traffic ahead, to the side, and behind as you move into the entrance or acceleration lane.

• Gradually accelerate to match the speed of the stream of other vehicles.

• Signal to other vehicles that you intend to enter the freeway.

• Check your blind spot, and allow traffic in the far right lane to pass before you move into that lane.

• Always be aware of what vehicles in the other lanes are doing; vehicle 5, for example, is moving into the right lane, which will affect vehicles 2 and 3.)

Ask

Ask students to discuss the risks that vehicle 5 is posing to other drivers. Also ask why merging onto a freeway without adequately checking traffic is extremely dangerous.

SAFETY TIPS

When passing a vehicle in the center lane of a highway that has three or more lanes of traffic traveling in the same direction, be careful of other vehicles passing on that vehicle's other side. They may wind up in your intended travel path.

◆ *Always signal while still in the acceleration lane and before merging into highway traffic.*

visibility. Large vehicles can also buffet smaller vehicles with wind gusts as they pass.

Because of their larger size, you need more time to pass a truck or bus than to pass another vehicle. If you're traveling at 60 mph, it takes you 5 to 7 seconds longer to pass a tractor-trailer traveling at 50 mph than it would to pass a car.

How Can You Manage Visibility, Time, and Space on Multiple-Lane Highways?

Safe and responsible driving on multiple-lane highways and expressways requires careful decision making on the part of every driver. You should focus on managing visibility, time, and space to reduce the risk of a collision or other mishap.

Guidelines for Managing Visibility on Highways

Here are some guidelines for managing visibility on multiple-lane and limited-access highways.

• Search 20 to 30 seconds ahead for vehicles, objects, animals, and even pedestrians on or near the roadway.

• Be alert for the dangers of entrances and exits. Drivers may merge too slowly or without looking or cut across lanes at the last moment.

• Check your rearview and sideview mirrors frequently to monitor the position of traffic around you, especially before changing lanes or exiting a highway.

• Always signal your intention to change lanes, merge, or exit well in advance of the move.

• Drive with your low beams on at all times. Use your high beams on very dark highways, but only when there are no other vehicles around.

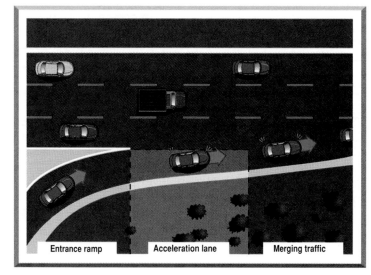

Entrance ramp   Acceleration lane   Merging traffic

Driving Tip

Caution students that driving at a constant high speed on a straight road for a long period of time can cause a driver to become drowsy. Drivers should make sure they are well rested before making a long drive, keep an adequate flow of fresh air in the vehicle, avoid eating heavy foods, and make frequent rest stops.

- Check the movement of vehicles several vehicles ahead to know when other drivers are slowing down or planning to pass or change lanes.
- Position your vehicle so that large vehicles do not block your view of the roadway ahead or to the sides.
- Look for road signs to learn what the speed limit is and to know when your exit is approaching and which side it is on.

Guidelines for Managing Time on Highways

Use these guidelines to help you manage time on highways.

- Use the SIPDE process to help you identify threatening conditions within 12 to 15 seconds ahead.
- Always adjust your speed and following distance so that you have at least 4 to 5 seconds to stop or steer evasively in case of an emergency.
- When you merge into traffic, try to enter the stream of vehicles at the speed they are traveling.
- When exiting an expressway, move over toward the exit lane as soon as you can. Wait until you're actually in the exit lane before reducing your speed.
- Adjust your speed to avoid traveling in packs of vehicles.
- Watch for vehicles that may have trouble keeping up with the speed of traffic. Adjust your speed or position in advance.
- Plan your route ahead of time. Know which highways you'll be traveling on and where to exit.
- Avoid driving on congested highways during peak traffic periods or in bad weather. Listen to the radio for roadway information before starting out. Allow extra time if you must drive.

Guidelines for Managing Space on Highways

Follow these guidelines to manage space on multiple-lane and limited-access roadways.

- Adjust your vehicle's position for the speed that you and other drivers are traveling and for road and weather conditions. Allow yourself a margin of space to accelerate, brake, and steer.
- Allow yourself a gap of at least 4 seconds when merging with other traffic, changing lanes, or entering an expressway from an entrance lane.
- To change lanes, turn the steering wheel slightly. Oversteering, or steering too sharply into another lane, can lead to loss of control at higher speeds.
- If you must cross several lanes, move over one lane at a time, signaling each time.

SAFETY TIPS

There may be more lanes at toll plazas than on the highway itself. Choose a lane with a green signal well in advance and stay in that lane. Be especially alert to drivers ahead of you who switch lanes suddenly.

SAFETY TIPS

At highway speeds of 40 to 65 mph, you'll need at least 4 to 5 seconds to react to a threatening situation and brake your vehicle to a stop. Therefore, you must be able to see ahead at all times an absolute minimum of 4 to 5 seconds. Furthermore, if a vehicle is tailgating you or a large vehicle is behind you, you should identify an escape path for evasive steering. Too often such vehicles cannot stop in time to avoid rear-ending the smaller vehicle in front of them.

Read

Have students read Lesson 4 to gain an understanding of the factors that affect driving on multiple-lane and limited-access highways and to learn how drivers can cope safely with these factors by managing visibility, time, and space.

ASSESS

Guided Practice

Have students answer the Lesson 4 Review questions. The answers are provided below.

Reteaching

Have students work together in small groups to list factors that contribute to driving risk on multiple-lane highways. Then have students take turns making up specific situations involving these factors and suggesting ways to manage visibility, time, and space to deal with each situation.

After groups have finished, have students take part in a class discussion focusing on what they consider to be the most difficult aspects of highway driving.

State BY State

Most state highways have a posted speed limit of 55 mph. However, most states have a posted limit of 65 mph on rural interstate highways. States that do not have the 65-mph limit are Alaska, Connecticut, Delaware, the District of Columbia, Rhode Island, and Hawaii. Fourteen states have a posted speed limit of 70 mph, while eight states have a 75-mph posted speed limit on rural interstates.

Have students suggest and discuss answers to each of the three questions.

Enrichment

Assign the Study Guide for Lesson 4. The Find Out More section encourages students to expand their basic learning of the lesson concepts.

CLOSE

Summarize

Return to the Motivator question. Have students explain in their own words the factors that they have learned to consider when driving on, entering, and exiting from a multiple-lane highway. To help students summarize important points, discuss the following questions: How can you manage visibility, time, and space to minimize risk when merging into highway traffic? When exiting from an expressway?

DRIVER'S LOG

What factors make highway driving challenging? What actions can you take to minimize risk when driving on a multiple-lane highway?

WHAT WOULD YOU DO?

Sample answer: If there is sufficient time to move safely, signal and change lanes. If not, get off the highway at the next exit.

ADVICE FROM THE EXPERTS

Bill Wen
Manager, Driver Training and Professional Development, AAA

Ask yourself three questions while driving: (1) What can I do to reduce the probability of a dangerous event? (2) How can I increase my opportunity to manage a dangerous event should one occur? (3) If a collision is unavoidable, how can I reduce its consequences?

Regardless of the driving environment, the first objective is to prevent a high-risk situation from developing by improving your visibility to others and by giving yourself enough time and space.

- Make room for vehicles entering expressways. If there are no vehicles in the lane next to you, move over a lane as you approach an entrance ramp.
- If a vehicle is tailgating you, change lanes—when it is safe—to let the vehicle pass. In the meantime, increase your following distance behind vehicles ahead.

- Never cut in too soon in front of a vehicle you are passing.
- When passing a large truck or other wide vehicle, keep in mind that you have less space to the side between your vehicle and the large vehicle than you do when passing a car.
- Be alert for places where highways may narrow—when approaching tunnels or bridges, for example. Reduce your speed and proceed cautiously.
- When crossing bridges or driving in hills and mountains, be alert for strong crosswinds that can buffet your vehicle.

WHAT WOULD YOU DO?

You are in the left lane of a crowded multiple-lane highway. Suddenly you realize you are approaching your exit, which is all the way over on the right. How will you handle this?

Lesson 4 Review

1. What factors affect driving on multiple-lane and limited-access highways?
2. What actions can a driver take to manage visibility, time, and space on an expressway?

Lesson 4 Review

Answers

1. High speed limits, limited number of entrances and exits, many passing vehicles, large vehicles.
2. Search ahead; know the position of traffic around you; signal your intentions; drive with low beams; use the SIPDE process; maintain a safe following distance; avoid traveling in a pack of vehicles; adjust speed to suit road and weather conditions.

Names and Meanings of Roadways

A route in a rural area is generally described as a road. A roadway within an urban area is usually called a street. Streets are usually paved and have more traffic, while rural routes are usually less traveled.

The roadways that connect cities and towns have many names, which vary somewhat in meaning. A highway is a main public roadway, especially one that runs between cities. An expressway is a high-speed divided highway with limited access that has more than one lane running in each direction. A freeway, sometimes called a superhighway, is generally a synonym for expressway, but usually refers to a highway that has no tolls.

A turnpike is a road, usually an expressway, that requires drivers to pay a toll. The word "turnpike" comes from early days when travelers on a road stopped at gates made of logs or pikes. When a toll was paid, the pike was opened or turned, allowing the travelers to pass through. A toll road may also be called a tollway.

A beltway is a highway that goes around an urban area. A parkway is a wide, landscaped highway that may be limited to non-commercial vehicles. Except for occasional rest stops, there may be few or no commercial establishments such as stores or office buildings on a parkway.

What Do You Think Now?

What do names and meanings of roadways tell you about the road systems in the United States?

BUILDING SKILLS: CRITICAL THINKING

Objective

Demonstrate an ability to analyze information and form an opinion.

Teaching the Skill

• Have students locate New Mexico on a map of the United States.

• To enhance student understanding, discuss elements that made Pueblo Bonito "the center of one of the most sophisticated settlements in the prehistoric southwest," such as the large, multistory dwelling and the network of roadways. Extend the discussion by asking students why it was essential to have an irrigation system to raise crops in the desert environment.

• Students may find it interesting to examine a road map of New Mexico, comparing the modern-day network of roads that makes up the state's highway system.

ANSWERS TO What Do You Think Now Question

Students' answers will vary but should reflect their understanding that a high level of civilization existed in parts of America before the arrival of Columbus.

CHAPTER SUMMARY

Key Points

Have students read the Key Points to review the major concepts of the chapter.

Cooperative Learning:
Students will benefit by working with a partner on one or both projects. When the assignment is completed, the whole class will profit by sharing and comparing results.

CHAPTER 11 REVIEW

KEY POINTS

Lesson One

1. In addition to making advance preparations, you can manage visibility by keeping your low beams on (even in daylight), signaling intentions well in advance, and avoiding driving in another driver's blind spots.
2. You can manage time by being aware of the link among time, speed, and distance and by using the SIPDE process.
3. You can manage space by allowing enough distance between your vehicle and other vehicles to the front, rear, and sides.

Lesson Two

1. Special factors that affect city driving are traffic density, number of pedestrians, number of intersections, slow or irregular traffic flow, lower speed limits, sight obstructions, and potholes and other road defects.
2. Some ways to manage visibility, time, and space on city streets are to search 1 to 2 blocks ahead, use your mirrors to monitor traffic, signal early, be ready for pedestrians and hidden exits, always be prepared to steer or stop, use the SIPDE process, and keep a margin of space around your vehicle.

Lesson Three

1. Factors that affect driving on rural roads are road conditions, higher speeds, fewer traffic controls, slow-moving vehicles, sight obstructions, and animals and objects on the road.
2. Among the ways to manage visibility, time, and space on rural roads are to identify dangerous objects 12 to 15 seconds ahead, drive slowly if an animal is nearby, avoid passing if your view is not clear, and use the SIPDE process.

Lesson Four

1. Special factors that affect visibility, time, and space on multiple-lane and limited-access highways are higher speed limits, limited entrances and exits, frequent passing, and the presence of trucks and other large vehicles.
2. Some ways to manage visibility, time, and space on multiple-lane and limited-access highways are to use the SIPDE process, signal when changing lanes, position your vehicle so that you can see and be seen, adjust your speed to avoid traveling in packs, and plan your route ahead of time.

PROJECTS

1. Use a road map to plan a trip from one city to another. List the highways you would travel on, and the numbers of the exits you would use. Take the trip as a driver or passenger, and compare the accuracy of your plan to what you actually experience on the trip.
2. Compare city driving and driving on a rural road. Observe differences in road surfaces, traffic signs and signals, density of traffic, and visibility.

*inter*NET CONNECTION

Use the Web to learn more about stopping distances at different speeds. Investigate how time is related to these total stopping distances.
drivered.glencoe.com

*inter*NET CONNECTION

Visit Glencoe's Driver Education Web site for student activities that relate to this chapter.
drivered.glencoe.com

CHAPTER TEST

Write the letter of the answer that best completes each sentence.

1. A limited-access highway
   a. allows vehicles to enter or exit only at certain places.
   b. does not permit trucks or buses.
   c. has no shoulders.

2. When you spot a threatening traffic condition in city traffic, you should
   a. shut your windows.
   b. cover the brake.
   c. use the total stopping method.

3. One way to manage time and space is to
   a. drive parallel to other vehicles.
   b. ride a bicycle.
   c. maintain a margin of space around your vehicle.

4. Speed limits on country roads are typically
   a. lower than those on urban roads.
   b. higher than those on urban roads.
   c. between 15 and 30 miles per hour.

5. Managing space while you drive means
   a. managing the distance between your vehicle and vehicles around you.
   b. reaching your destination safely.
   c. successfully passing other vehicles on multiple-lane highways.

6. As you near the top of a hill,
   a. your view of the road ahead is limited.
   b. your view of the road behind you is limited.
   c. you should accelerate.

7. When driving on a dirt road, you should
   a. pull over to the right side.
   b. increase your speed.
   c. reduce your speed.

8. The first step in managing visibility while driving is to

   a. stay away from large obstructions.
   b. turn on your low-beam headlights.
   c. look in your blind spots.

9. During urban driving, you should
   a. look at least 1 block ahead.
   b. look at least 5 blocks ahead.
   c. use your high-beam headlights.

10. On multiple-lane highways, passing other vehicles
    a. should be avoided.
    b. is an integral part of driving.
    c. is a method of staying alert.

Write the word or phrase that best completes each sentence.

distance	interchange	expressway
lead time	margin of space	rural road

11. The faster you travel, the more time and _____ you need to come to a stop.

12. Always keep a(n) _____ around your vehicle.

13. A(n) _____ may have drainage ditches alongside of it.

14. A freeway is one example of a(n) _____.

15. A(n) _____ is made up of through lanes, ramps, and speed-change lanes.

DRIVER'S LOG

In this chapter, you have learned about managing visibility, time, and space in different driving environments. Write two paragraphs in response to these questions:

In which driving environment do you think you will have the most difficulty managing visibility, time, and space? What steps will you take to overcome this difficulty?

RETURN TO THE BIG IDEA

Discuss the idea that a driver's understanding of the factors that affect different driving environments will prepare the driver to manage visibility, time, and space so as to reduce risk.

CHAPTER TEST

Assign the Chapter Test to all students.

Answers

1. a
2. b
3. c
4. b
5. a
6. a
7. c
8. b
9. a
10. b
11. distance
12. margin of space
13. rural road
14. expressway
15. interchange

DRIVER'S LOG

Students' responses will reflect their personal viewpoints. However, their answers should provide an assessment of their understanding of the relationship between different driving environments and the management of visibility, time, and space.

Evaluate

• Test A, pages 21–22 or Test B, pages 21–22 📁
• Testmaker software

Light and Weather Conditions Overview

THEME DEVELOPMENT Drivers must recognize how low light, glare from the sun, and adverse weather conditions affect visibility and otherwise increase driving risks. When driving with limited visibility or in bad weather, drivers need to manage visibility, time, and space wisely to minimize risk.

CHAPTER FEATURES	TCR COMPONENTS
TIPS FOR NEW DRIVERS Improving visibility during night driving.	Study Guide, p. 45 Lesson Plan, p. 25 Information Master 18
	Study Guide, p. 46 Lesson Plan, p. 25 Information Master 18
TIPS FOR NEW DRIVERS Learning to free a vehicle that has become stuck in snow.	Study Guide, p. 47 Lesson Plan, p. 26 Information Master 24
ADVICE FROM THE EXPERTS How to compensate for limited visibility at night or in poor weather conditions.	Study Guide, p. 48 Lesson Plan, p. 26
BUILDING SKILLS: READING MAPS Using a Triptik	Test A, pp. 23–24 Test B, pp. 23–24

PROJECTS

1. Investigate state laws.
2. Evaluate various products that are designed for use in winter driving.

OTHER PROGRAM RESOURCES

Testmaker software
Traffic charts
Teaching Your Teens to Drive, Lessons 6 and 13, video or CD-ROM

ADDITIONAL RESOURCES

Night Driving, Video 453, AAA Foundation
Driving in Bad Weather, Video 419, AAA Foundation
Get a Grip, AAA Foundation

CHAPTER 12

CHAPTER TEST

NAME _____ DATE _____

CHAPTER 12 Light and Weather Conditions

TEST A

Select the phrase that best completes each sentence below. Write the letter of the answer you have chosen to the left of each statement.

___d___ 1. All states require that you use your headlights
   a. from sunset to sunrise.
   b. between a half hour after sunset and a half hour before sunrise.
   c. 24 hours a day.
   d. when it is raining.

___b___ 2. When driving at dusk or dawn, you should
   a. use your parking lights.
   b. not use your parking lights.
   c. use your high beams.
   d. use your emergency flashers.

___c___ 3. You should use your high beams
   a. to see farther in dense fog.
   b. while it is snowing.
   c. only on dark roads with no other cars around.
   d. in all of the above situations.

___b___ 4. When you are driving at a speed that won't allow you to stop within the range of your headlights, you are
   a. going too slow.
   b. overdriving your headlights.
   c. underdriving your headlights.
   d. doing none of the above.

___a___ 5. When an oncoming vehicle's headlights are too bright, you should
   a. look at the right edge of the traffic lane beyond the oncoming vehicle.
   b. look at the spot just below the oncoming vehicle's headlights.
   c. turn on your high beams.
   d. cover your eyes, but for no more than 2 to 3 seconds.

___a___ 6. The sun's glare is most dangerous
   a. in the morning or late afternoon.
   b. in the morning or at noon.
   c. at noon.
   d. at noon or in the later afternoon.

___b___ 7. When the sun's glare is bad, you should
   a. stay at home.
   b. use hand signals in addition to taillight signals to communicate your intentions.
   c. use hand signals only.
   d. do none of the above.

© AAA and Glencoe/McGraw-Hill

NAME _____ DATE _____

___c___ 8. In a snowfall, you should drive in the tracks of the vehicle ahead of you so that you
   a. know which way to go.
   b. help to pack the snow down.
   c. can get better traction.
   d. can maintain momentum.

___a___ 9. When approaching a large vehicle on a slushy roadway, turn on your
   a. windshield washer and wipers 30 seconds before you meet.
   b. windshield washer and wipers 5 seconds before you meet.
   c. windshield wipers as you meet.
   d. emergency flashers.

Read each statement below. If it is true, place a T in the space to the left of the statement. If the statement is false, place an F next to it.

___T___ 10. If you must stop by the side of the road at night, you should turn on your emergency flashers to warn other drivers that you are there.

___T___ 11. If your windshield is badly scratched, you should replace it.

___F___ 12. Decreased visibility makes it easier to judge distances.

___T___ 13. Bad weather can reduce the ability of your tires to grip the road.

___F___ 14. When driving on snow or ice, it is essential to change direction quickly to minimize the risk of skidding.

___T___ 15. Roads are slickest in the early part of a rainstorm because the moisture mixes with dirt and oil on the road.

___F___ 16. Hydroplaning is what occurs when a large truck sprays water from its wheels during a rainstorm.

___T___ 17. The main thing you can do to prevent hydroplaning is to drive slowly.

___F___ 18. Using your high-beam headlights is essential in fog.

___T___ 19. A strong gust of wind can push a small vehicle out of its lane.

20. How does it happen that a bridge can freeze before a roadway?

In winter, the ground is usually warmer than the air surrounding it. A bridge has no ground

beneath it to keep it warmer, plus the air circulates freely around it. The bridge therefore

becomes colder faster, causing the bridge to freeze before the roadway.

_____

_____

_____

© AAA and Glencoe/McGraw-Hill

NAME _____ DATE _____

CHAPTER 12 Light and Weather Conditions

TEST B

Select the phrase that best completes each sentence below. Write the letter of the answer you have chosen to the left of each statement.

___b___ 1. If snow becomes so heavy that your windshield wiper's fastest speed can't keep up,
   a. turn your defroster on.
   b. pull off the road.
   c. keep on driving and let the wind blow off the snow.
   d. do none of the above.

___c___ 2. During a rainstorm, the roads are at their slickest
   a. toward the center of the road.
   b. in the last half hour.
   c. in the first 15 minutes.
   d. anytime after the first 20 minutes.

___a___ 3. Hydroplaning occurs
   a. when your vehicle is riding on a thin film of water.
   b. when your vehicle sprays water off its wheels.
   c. when a truck sprays water onto your vehicle.
   d. in none of the above circumstances.

___d___ 4. When driving in fog, it is essential that you
   a. have your high beams on.
   b. drive with your parking lights on.
   c. go the speed limit.
   d. drive with your low beams on.

___d___ 5. As the amount of light decreases,
   a. your chance of a collision decreases.
   b. it is more difficult to see other pedestrians and vehicles.
   c. other cars and pedestrians have trouble seeing you.
   d. both b and c are true.

___a___ 6. Parking lights were designed for
   a. use while you are parked.
   b. driving at dawn or dusk.
   c. driving during the day when cloudy.
   d. all of the above.

___c___ 7. A dirty or scratched windshield
   a. decreases glare.
   b. increases visibility.
   c. increases glare.
   d. is illegal.

© AAA and Glencoe/McGraw-Hill

NAME _____ DATE _____

___b___ 8. On a wet pavement, it is a good idea to drive in the tracks of the vehicle ahead of you because
   a. it will help to pack snow down better.
   b. the tracks are drier than the surrounding surface and offer better traction.
   c. you can maintain momentum.
   d. of none of the reasons above.

___a___ 9. The sun's glare is most dangerous
   a. in the morning and late afternoon.
   b. at noon.
   c. in the morning and at noon.
   d. at noon and in the late afternoon.

Read each statement below. If it is true, place a T in the space to the left of the statement. If the statement is false, place an F next to it.

___T___ 10. Although sometimes necessary, snow tires reduce fuel economy.

___F___ 11. At night, instead of looking directly at the oncoming car's headlights, you should look at the left side of your traffic lane.

___T___ 12. When you drive so fast at night that you cannot stop within the range of your headlights, you are overdriving your headlights.

___T___ 13. One problem with night driving is that your ability to see ahead is severely reduced.

___T___ 14. You should not use your parking lights while driving.

___T___ 15. If your car is stuck in snow, you may be able to free it by rocking it.

___T___ 16. You should replace a badly scratched windshield.

___T___ 17. While driving in glaring sun, you should use hand signals as well as your car's signals to communicate your intentions.

___F___ 18. During the daylight hours, you should drive with your high beams on.

19. In the glare of the sun, it is hard to see and to be seen. What precautions can you take to help other vehicles and pedestrians see you and to ensure that you see them?

Make sure windshield is clean; replace a badly scratched windshield; keep sunglasses handy; reduce

speed; increase following distance; adjust sun visor; use brake pedal to flash your taillights; use hand

signals when slowing, stopping, or turning; and drive with your low-beam headlights on.

_____

_____

_____

© AAA and Glencoe/McGraw-Hill

NAME _____ DATE _____

Light and Weather Conditions

STUDY GUIDE FOR CHAPTER 12 LESSON 1

Driving Safely in Low Light and at Night

A. For each sentence below, circle T if the statement is true and F if it is false. Correct each false statement in the space below.

1. As visibility decreases, your risk of being in an accident decreases. T **F**
As visibility decreases, your risk of being in an accident increases.

2. Headlights from an oncoming vehicle can have a blinding effect. **T** F

3. When driving during dusk and dawn hours, you should use your parking lights. T **F**
You should use your parking lights only for parking.

4. At night, you should decrease the distance between your vehicle and the vehicle ahead.
T **F**
At night you should increase the distance between your vehicle and the one ahead of you.

5. You can use your high beams on dark roads when there are no other vehicles around.
T F

6. When an oncoming vehicle's headlights are bright, you should look directly at the headlights.
T **F**
You should glance down at the right edge of your traffic lane beyond the vehicle to avoid the glare.

7. At night, you should not overdrive your headlights. **T** F

8. At dusk, you should keep your low-beam headlights on. **T** F

9. Overdriving your headlights means driving at a speed that will not allow you to stop within their range. **T** F

10. At night, you should get into the habit of looking for objects beyond your headlight beams.
T F

B. FIND OUT MORE. Keep a record of all traffic collisions reported in your local newspaper for one week. What percentage of the collisions happened between the hours of 9 p.m. and 6 a.m.?
Review student's work.

NAME _____ DATE _____

STUDY GUIDE FOR CHAPTER 12 LESSON 2

Visibility, Bright Light, and Glare

A. For each sentence below, circle T if the statement is true and F if it is false. Correct each false statement in the space below.

1. The sun's glare is most dangerous to drivers at noon. T **F**
The sun's glare is most dangerous in the morning or late afternoon, so you should wear sunglasses at those times.

2. A badly scratched windshield should be replaced. **T** F

3. Sunglasses are not effective against the glare of late afternoon sun. T **F**
Sunglasses are effective against the sun's glare.

4. During periods of extreme glare, you should decrease your following distance. T **F**
During periods of extreme glare, you should increase your following distance.

5. Driving with your low-beam headlights on does not help when the glare is strong. T **F**
Driving with low-beam headlights on helps others to see you when glare is strong.

B. What advance preparation can you make before driving when you know that you may be driving in glaring sun?
Examples of possible answers: Make sure windshield is clean, replace windshield if it is badly
scratched, keep sunglasses handy.

C. FIND OUT MORE. Call a local optometrist's office, the optical department of a local store, or a vision clinic, and ask what are some of the best kinds of sunglasses made to combat the effects of the sun's glare. Ask how much they cost. Report your findings below.
Review student's answers.

NAME _____ DATE _____

STUDY GUIDE FOR CHAPTER 12 LESSON 3

Minimizing Risk in Rain and Snow

A. For each sentence below, circle T if the statement is true and F if it is false. Correct each false statement in the space below.

1. When driving in snow, you should follow the tire tracks of the vehicle ahead of you because the tracks are drier and give better traction. **T** F

2. Driving with snow tires increases fuel economy. T **F**
Driving with snow tires reduces fuel economy.

3. To prevent skids, you should change speeds as rapidly as possible. T **F**
To prevent skids, you should change speeds gradually.

4. Roads are not very slick during the first 15 minutes of a rainfall. T **F**
Roads are at their slickest during the first 15 minutes of rainfall.

5. Hydroplaning happens when your vehicle rides on a thin film of water. **T** F

B. If your vehicle became stuck in the snow, what would you do to set it free?
Examples of possible answers: Keep front wheels as straight as possible, shift back and forth
between Drive (or First or Second gear with a manual transmission) and Reverse gear, release
the brake and accelerate with gentle pressure, and repeat as necessary.

C. FIND OUT MORE. Most states that allow the use of studded snow tires have restrictions on when they can be used. What does your state's driver's manual say about this?
Review student's work.

NAME _____ DATE _____

STUDY GUIDE FOR CHAPTER 12 LESSON 4

Other Hazardous Weather Conditions

A. What precautions should you take when driving in fog? What should you do when fog becomes very dense?
When driving in fog, keep low-beam headlights on, and if the fog is especially thick, turn on
your emergency flashers. Never turn on high beams. Reduce speed, increase following distance,
and remain alert for sudden movements. If fog is very dense, signal and pull off the road to a
safe area, and wait for the conditions to change.

B. What are the dangers of driving in high wind? What can you do to drive more safely in very windy situations?
The danger of driving in high wind is that the wind can buffet your vehicle around; if your
vehicle is lightweight, the wind can move it into another lane. You can be safer in these
situations by reducing your speed; gripping the steering wheel firmly; and leaving extra space
between your vehicle and any nearby vehicles, especially recreational vehicles, vans, and cars
pulling trailers.

C. FIND OUT MORE. The chapter says that in fog, your vehicle can collect moisture on the inside as well as on the outside of its windows. What can you do to prevent this? Visit or call a local auto parts store and ask if there are any products on the market that reduce moisture on the inside of your vehicle's windows.
Review student's work.

Light and Weather Conditions

CHAPTER OVERVIEW

LESSON ONE

How low-light conditions affect visibility is explained, and guidelines for driving safely in low light and at night are presented.

LESSON TWO

The conditions that create glare are discussed, and guidelines for driving safely in the glare of the sun are provided.

LESSON THREE

How to manage visibility, time, and space factors so as to minimize risk in rain and snow is explained.

LESSON FOUR

Hazardous weather conditions other than rain and snow are discussed, and suggestions for safe driving under these conditions are given.

VOCABULARY

hydroplaning
overdriving your headlights

2 1 6

CONCEPT OF THE DRIVING TASK

Explain that developing the ability to concentrate is essential to safe driving. Drivers must learn to tune out distractions—both inside and outside the vehicle—that are unrelated to their driving.

CHAPTER 12

Light and Weather Conditions

Good drivers are prepared for any kind of light or weather conditions. It is important for you to understand how to manage visibility, time, and space in order to minimize the risk caused by poor light or inclement weather.

LESSON ONE
Driving Safely in Low Light and at Night

LESSON TWO
Visibility, Bright Light, and Glare

LESSON THREE
Minimizing Risk in Rain and Snow

LESSON FOUR
Other Hazardous Weather Conditions

PRESENTING THE BIG IDEA

Drivers should be well prepared to cope with all sorts of weather conditions. They must know how to adjust their driving to meet the often combined challenges of reduced visibility and slippery roadways.

INTRODUCING THE CHAPTER

What's on the Road Ahead?

Have students read the lesson titles and objectives. Briefly discuss the topic of each lesson. Tell students that in this chapter, they will learn about reducing risk when driving with limited visibility or in bad weather.

Background: Wet-Weather Danger

Reduced visibility and wet weather are primary contributing factors to collisions. Of the 6.5 million vehicle crashes that occurred in 1994, about 17 percent occurred during wet weather conditions. Many such collisions don't involve other vehicles or pedestrians but occur when a vehicle crashes into a roadside hazard, such as a tree, barrier, ditch, pole, or signpost.

In fact, collisions on wet or slippery roads account for 18 percent of all deaths in roadside hazard crashes. Sixty-three percent of the deaths in crashes on slippery roads take place at night, 42 percent occur on curves, and 39 percent occur on hills.

Relating to Prior Knowledge

Have students discuss what they know about driving in rain, snow, fog, and other adverse weather conditions.

The Big Idea

Discuss students' reactions to the Big Idea statement. Suggest that they keep this idea in mind as they read Chapter 12.

Driving Safely in Low Light and at Night

(pages 218–219)

FOCUS

Objectives

* Describe how visibility is affected by low light conditions.
* Explain how to drive safely in low light and at night.

Resources

 Study Guide, page 45

 Information Master 18

Vocabulary

overdriving your headlights

Motivator

Pose the following: The sun has just set, and the twilight is making it hard for you to see the roadway ahead. What actions can you take to reduce driving risk? (Students may mention ensuring that headlights are on; increasing following distance; signaling well in advance; reducing speed; taking a break.)

TEACH

Explain

OBJECTIVE 1: Students should be aware that "visibility" signifies the ability to see and also to be seen.

OBJECTIVE 2: Students should recognize that reducing speed is essential when there is limited visibility.

LESSON ONE

OBJECTIVES

1. Describe how visibility is affected by low light conditions.
2. Explain how to drive safely in low light and at night.

KEY TERM

overdriving your headlights

Driving Safely in Low Light and at Night

Your ability to see is decreased at night and just before sunrise or after sunset. As visibility decreases, your risk of being in a collision increases. To lessen risk, you must understand how reduced light limits visibility and how to better manage the driving task in low light conditions.

How Do Low Light Conditions Affect Visibility?

Your ability to see and to be seen diminishes when the amount of available light is lessened.

Reduced sunlight during dusk and dawn hours makes it difficult to see the roadway and vehicles traveling on it. Other drivers as well as pedestrians have difficulty seeing your vehicle, particularly if you don't have your headlights on.

Night driving presents special challenges. At night, darkness limits your view of the road ahead and the surrounding area. Even with your headlights on, your ability to see ahead when turning or driving around a curve is severely reduced. In addition, the glare of other vehicles' headlights can be distracting—or blinding.

How Can You Drive Safely When the Amount of Light Is Low?

To drive safely in low light conditions, you must maximize visibility and manage time and space wisely.

When your view of the road is limited, slow down. Maximize your ability to see

FOR NEW DRIVERS

More Suggestions for Dealing with Visibility Problems at Night

Slow down. Remember that your visibility is limited. Avoid looking directly into the headlights of oncoming vehicles. When necessary to maintain your bearings, glance down at the right edge of your traffic lane beyond oncoming vehicles.

To remind an approaching driver that his or her high beams are on, quickly switch your own headlights from low to high and back again.

If you can, adjust your rearview mirror for night driving to cut glare from the headlights of vehicles behind you.

If you must stop along the road, use your emergency flashers to enable other drivers to see you.

Watch for animals, joggers, bicyclists, and obstacles in the road.

Always remove sunglasses once the sun sets.

TIPS FOR NEW DRIVERS

Have students add their own suggestions to the list of tips.

IT'S A FACT

At night, all drivers are affected by the glare of bright lights from the roadway and surroundings. While the average driver is blinded temporarily by the headlights of an oncoming vehicle, most people's eyes recover in 3 to 5 seconds. This recovery time usually increases with age.

and maneuver. Drive with your headlights on whenever you drive, day and night. Your headlights and taillights help illuminate your vehicle, making it easier for others to see you in all kinds of light.

During Dusk and Dawn Hours

All states require that you use your headlights either from sunset to sunrise or between a half hour after sunset and a half hour before sunrise. Using your headlights makes it easier to see and be seen in the dim light of dusk and dawn. Do *not* use your parking lights. They are not designed to light the road ahead but to indicate your position when you are parked safely off the roadway.

At dawn or dusk, increase the distance between your vehicle and the one ahead, and use your turn signals well in advance.

At Night

Night driving requires extra concentration and a greater level of awareness. With darkness limiting visibility, it is wise to drive more slowly at night than you do during the day and to leave more distance between your vehicle and the vehicle ahead.

Use low beams and high beams correctly. On very dark roads with no other vehicles around, use your high beams to increase visibility. Be sure to switch back to low beams as soon as you spot the headlights or taillights of a vehicle ahead of you. The glare of your high beams can momentarily blind another driver.

Do not overdrive your headlights. At night, drive at a speed that will allow you to stop within the range of your lights—that is, within the distance you can see. Driving faster than that is called **overdriving your headlights** and makes you vulnerable to unseen hazards.

Use the 3- or 4-second rules you have learned to help you judge a safe following distance.

Look beyond your headlights. Get into the habit of looking for objects just beyond your headlight beams to see possible threatening conditions. Looking beyond your headlights is essential when making turns or rounding curves.

Lesson 1 Review

1. Describe how visibility is affected by low light conditions.
2. What can you do to minimize risk when driving at night?

Fifty percent of all teenage motor vehicle fatalities occur between 9 P.M. and 6 A.M.

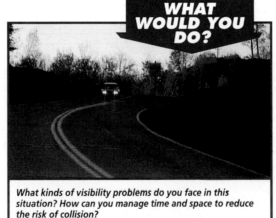

WHAT WOULD YOU DO?

What kinds of visibility problems do you face in this situation? How can you manage time and space to reduce the risk of collision?

WHAT WOULD YOU DO?

Sample answer: Your view of the road is limited, and the glare of headlights can be distracting or blinding; reduce speed and increase following distance.

Lesson 1 Review

Answers

1. Visibility decreases during dawn and dusk and at night; your ability to see and to be seen is reduced.
2. Reduce speed; increase following distance; use low and high beams correctly; don't overdrive your headlights; look beyond your headlights.

Teaching Model

Describe the following situation: You're driving on a winding rural road at night. Few other vehicles are on the road. Model the thinking process that you use to minimize risk. (You reduce speed; look beyond your headlights, especially on curves; drive at a speed so you can stop within the range of your lights; use high beams when no vehicles are near.)

Ask

Ask students to discuss the risks of driving when visibility is limited.

Read

Have students read Lesson 1 to learn how to reduce risk when driving with reduced visibility.

ASSESS

Guided Practice

Have students answer the Lesson 1 Review questions. The answers are provided below.

Reteaching

Have students work in small groups to list problems inherent in driving when visibility is limited and suggest solutions.

Enrichment

Assign the Study Guide for Lesson 1. The Find Out More section encourages students to expand their basic learning of the lesson concepts.

CLOSE

Summarize

Reexamine the Motivator question in terms of visibility, time, and space.

DRIVER'S LOG

How can you reduce risk when driving in low light and at night?

Visibility, Bright Light, and Glare

(pages 220–221)

FOCUS

Objectives

- Describe the conditions that create glare from the sun.
- Explain how you can drive safely in the glare of the sun.

> ### Resources
> Study Guide, page 46
> Information Master 18

Motivator

Pose the following: You're driving west, toward the setting sun. Glare is making it hard for you to see the highway. What can you do to reduce driving risk? (Students may mention cleaning the windshield; putting on sunglasses; adjusting the sun visor; slowing down; increasing following distance; turning on low beams.)

TEACH

Explain

OBJECTIVE 1: Students should be aware that the sun's reflection off snowy or wet surroundings also causes glare.

OBJECTIVE 2: Students should be cautioned not to search for their sunglasses while the vehicle is moving.

LESSON TWO

OBJECTIVES
1. Describe the conditions that create glare from the sun.
2. Explain how you can drive safely in the glare of the sun.

Visibility, Bright Light, and Glare

Think of a bright summer morning. The sky is cloudless and everything is bathed in sunlight. That's a pretty picture for a day at the beach, but it's not always so pretty when you're behind the wheel of a vehicle. The glow of that sunlight can turn to dangerous glare.

What Conditions Create Glare from the Sun?

Sunlight increases visibility, but the glare caused when the sun hits your windshield can act in the opposite way—it can reduce your ability to see. The sun's glare is most dangerous at certain times.

In the morning or late afternoon, for example, when the sun is low on the horizon, glare can make it hard to see the road ahead. Glare can also reduce your ability to see the brake lights of other vehicles, especially if you're driving toward the sun and its rays shine directly in your eyes.

◆ Glare decreases visibility and causes you to become more easily fatigued.

How Can You Drive Safely in the Glare of the Sun?

As in all driving situations, advance preparation can help you minimize the risk of glare. As part of your predriving check, you should always make sure that your vehicle's windshield is clean. As part of your overall vehicle maintenance, you should replace the windshield if it is badly scratched or pitted. Glare is worse through a dirty or scratched windshield.

THE INTERNATIONAL SCENE

Mexico

Knowing some basic Spanish words will help drivers understand road signs in Mexico. *Despacio* and *disminuya su velocidad* both warn drivers to reduce speed. *Entronque* signifies a highway junction. *Peligro* means "danger."

Have sunglasses handy. As soon as you begin to squint, slip them on to shield your eyes. Reduce speed, increase your following distance, and adjust your sun visor to block out the sun. However, be careful that the visor does not hinder your view of overhead signs and signals.

Use the SIPDE process to help you manage risk in glare situations. Give yourself an extra margin of safety by leaving more distance between your vehicle and other vehicles. Check carefully for pedestrians—remember, they are having trouble seeing too. Even if you have your sunglasses on and can see road signs and signals, keep in mind that others on the roadway may not be able to see as clearly. Always be alert for the sudden, careless, or unsafe actions of other drivers and pedestrians.

Keep in mind that if you are having trouble seeing, so are the drivers around you. The sun shining on the back of your vehicle may make it very difficult for the driver behind you to see your brake lights or directional signals. For this reason, it's wise to tap the brake pedal to flash your taillights, to use your turn signals well in advance, *and* to use hand or arm signals as well to communicate your intentions.

Keep in mind, too, that when the sun is behind you, oncoming drivers have the sun's glare in *their* eyes and may have trouble seeing you. Drive with your low-beam headlights on to make your vehicle more visible, and signal well in advance your intention to turn or change lanes.

◆ *The reflection of sunlight off snow and ice causes wide areas of glare.*

WHAT WOULD YOU DO?

The sun is shining behind you. What can you do to minimize risk for both yourself and the drivers behind and ahead of you?

Lesson 2 Review

1. Describe the circumstances in which the sun's light can create dangerous glare.
2. What steps would you take to minimize overall risk in a glare situation?

CHAPTER 12 *Light and Weather Conditions* **221**

WHAT WOULD YOU DO?

Sample answer: Flash brake lights, signal well in advance, use hand signals, and be sure low beams are on.

Lesson 2 Review

Answers
1. When the sun reflects off bright surfaces or hits your windshield or shines directly into your eyes.
2. Clean windshield; wear sunglasses; reduce speed; increase following distance; use sun visor; use SIPDE.

Teaching Model
Describe the following situation: Glare from the sun is making it hard to see. You plan to turn at the next corner. There is a vehicle behind you. Model the thinking process that you use to minimize risk. (You signal well in advance; use a hand signal; tap your brake pedal.)

Ask
Ask students to discuss how their driving risk increases when other drivers have reduced visibility.

Read
Have students read Lesson 2 to learn how to reduce risk when driving in the glare of the sun.

ASSESS

Guided Practice
Have students answer the Lesson 2 Review questions. The answers are provided below.

Reteaching
Have students work together in small groups to list problems of driving with the sun's glare and suggest solutions.

Enrichment
Assign the Study Guide for Lesson 2. The Find Out More section encourages students to expand their basic learning of the lesson concepts.

CLOSE

Summarize
Reexamine the Motivator question in terms of visibility, time, and space.

DRIVER'S LOG

How can you drive safely in the glare of the sun?

FOCUS

Objectives

- Explain how to manage visibility, time, and space in rain and snow.
- Explain how to minimize risk in snow and rain.

Resources

 Study Guide, page 47

 Information Master 24

Vocabulary

hydroplaning

Motivator

As you drive through the city, heavy rain is making it difficult for you to see vehicles and pedestrians. What actions can you take to help ensure the safety of yourself and others? (Students may mention driving with headlights on; reducing speed and increasing following distance; communicating intentions early; anticipating and preventing skidding and hydroplaning.)

LESSON THREE

OBJECTIVES

1. Explain how to manage visibility, time, and space in rain and snow.
2. Explain how to minimize risk in snow and rain.

KEY TERM

hydroplaning

Minimizing Risk in Rain and Snow

It might be pleasant if you could just stay indoors when it is raining or snowing outside. However, if you have to drive somewhere in rainy or snowy weather, you must understand and manage the risk that driving in such weather presents.

TIPS — FOR NEW DRIVERS

Stuck in the Snow?

If you get stuck in snow, you may be able to free your vehicle by "rocking" it. Follow the steps below.

1. Keep your front wheels pointed straight ahead, if possible. The vehicle will move more easily in a straight line.
2. Shift back and forth between Drive (or First gear) and Reverse. Accelerate forward slowly and steadily. When the vehicle will move forward no farther, press firmly on the brake to stop and hold the vehicle while you quickly shift to Reverse.
3. Release the brake and accelerate with gentle pressure as far back as the vehicle will go until the wheels start to spin. Step on the brake again and hold it while shifting to Drive or First gear.
4. Repeat as necessary. Do *not* spin your wheels: You'll only dig yourself in more deeply.

Repeat these shifts as quickly and smoothly as possible, but be sure to use the brake to hold the vehicle at a stop while shifting gears. Each forward-and-backward movement should take the vehicle a little farther in one direction or the other.

When rocking a vehicle, proceed cautiously. If the tires do suddenly grip, the vehicle may lurch forward, backward, or sideways. Warn bystanders to keep their distance, and take care not to strike nearby vehicles or objects.

How Can You Manage Visibility, Time, and Space in Rain and Snow?

Rain and snow decrease your ability to see ahead, to the sides, and to the rear. Decreased visibility, in turn, makes it more difficult than usual for you to judge distances and to manage time and space well. Bad weather conditions also make it much harder for other drivers and pedestrians to see your vehicle.

Heavy rain or snow can limit your view so much that you can't see very far ahead or even the edges of the roadway. Snow and sleet collecting on your windshield can produce blind areas that your windshield wipers can't reach. Snowy or rainy weather can also make the roadway slick, reducing the ability of your tires to grip the road and increasing your risk of collision. Here are some steps you can take to control the level of risk.

Prepare in advance. Start by cleaning your vehicle's windows and lights. Check the tread and pressure of your tires. Check the headlights, windshield wipers, defroster, and other equipment to make sure they are in good working condition.

222 UNIT 3 *Moving onto the Road*

State BY State

California, Texas, and Florida accounted for about 24 percent of the 41,967 motor vehicle deaths that occurred in 1997. Motor vehicle death rates that year ranged from 7 to 30 per 100,000 people. Mississippi and Wyoming had the highest rate; Rhode Island and Massachusetts had the lowest.

Allow an extra margin of safety. Drive more slowly and leave extra space between your vehicle and other vehicles.

On a wet pavement, drive in the tracks of the vehicle ahead of you. Those tracks are drier than the surrounding surface and offer better traction.

Give other drivers plenty of advance notice. When you intend to slow down or turn, communicate your intentions early so that other drivers have time to react accordingly.

Be alert. Be on the watch for pedestrians dashing for shelter, or with umbrellas restricting their view of traffic.

Keep your low-beam headlights on. Increase the distance you can see, and make your car more visible to other drivers and pedestrians.

Ease your way into turns and curves. Avoid sudden acceleration, starts, or stops.

If rain becomes so heavy that even your windshield wipers' highest speed cannot keep up with the downpour, signal, then pull well off the road in a protected area and wait for the storm to lessen in intensity. Remember to switch on your emergency flashers so that other drivers can see your vehicle.

You may also need to pull over if, in snow or sleet, your windshield wipers become crusted with ice or if accumulating snow or sleet creates blind areas on your windshield. Use a scraper and brush to remove all of the buildup, and run your defroster before you resume driving.

How Can You Minimize Risk in Snow and Rain?

If you've ever gone sledding, skiing, or ice-skating, you know just how slippery a snow- or ice-covered surface can be. Imagine trying to maneuver a heavy, fast-moving vehicle on such a surface. One way to reduce the level of risk is to postpone driving until the weather clears. Whenever possible, wait until the roads are plowed and sanded or salted before venturing out on them.

Sometimes you cannot postpone a trip. If you do have to drive under snowy or icy conditions, be aware that there is a great danger of skidding. Drive slowly and extremely cautiously. Allow yourself an extra large margin of safety. When you do want to slow down, stop, or turn, maneuver the vehicle gently and gradually.

Keep on hand cold-weather items such as a windshield scraper and brush, a shovel, jumper cables, emergency flares, and gloves.

Energy Tips

Even though snow tires may be necessary during winter months, they reduce fuel economy. Remove them as soon as winter is over.

SAFETY TIPS

If you are approaching a large vehicle on a slush-covered roadway, turn on your windshield washers and wipers about 2 to 3 seconds before you meet. This gets the glass wet and will help clean the glass quickly after you pass.

Driving Tip

Advise students to remove all snow, ice, and frost from vehicle windows, outside mirrors, headlights, and taillights before starting to drive. They should also clear snow from the hood, roof, and body of the vehicle so that it won't melt or blow onto the windows while the vehicle is moving.

TEACH

Explain

OBJECTIVE 1: Students may benefit from a discussion of the special hazards of city driving during a sudden downpour.

OBJECTIVE 2: Students will benefit from a discussion of the risks of driving on a wet roadway when temperatures drop near the freezing point.

Teaching Model

Describe the following situation: You're driving on the highway when it begins to snow. Before long, the roadway becomes wet and slippery. Model the thinking process that you use to reduce risk in this situation. (You drive slowly and with extra care; allow an extra margin of safety; maneuver the vehicle gently and gradually; anticipate and try to prevent skidding and hydroplaning.)

Ask

Ask students to discuss the risks of driving too fast on a wet roadway.

Read

Have students read Lesson 3 to learn how to minimize risk when driving in rain and snow.

TIPS **FOR NEW DRIVERS**

If rocking alone won't free the vehicle, find a way to create traction under both drive wheels. You might, for example, put sand, gravel, or cat litter under the wheels.

ASSESS

Guided Practice

Have students answer the Lesson 3 Review questions. The answers are provided below.

Reteaching

Pair a more able student with one who is having difficulty. Have students use the clingboard to demonstrate management of visibility, time, and space when driving in rain or snow.

Enrichment

Assign the Study Guide for Lesson 3. The Find Out More section encourages students to expand their basic learning of the lesson concepts.

CLOSE

Summarize

Reexamine the Motivator question in terms of managing visibility, time, and space. Encourage students to discuss ways to reduce risk to themselves, to other drivers, and to pedestrians. Stress the need to be especially alert and the importance of driving defensively when the weather is bad.

DRIVER'S LOG

How can you drive defensively in rain or snow?

WHAT WOULD YOU DO?

Sample answer: Straighten the front wheels, and use traction materials under both drive wheels; try "rocking" the vehicle forward and backward.

Anticipate and Prevent Skids

If you change speed or direction gradually and smoothly rather than abruptly, you will minimize the chance of skidding. In Chapter 14 you will learn what to do if your vehicle starts to skid.

Anticipate situations in which skids are likely, and take steps to maintain control of your vehicle. For example, when driving on a wet road when the temperature is near freezing, allow yourself extra time and space to brake and steer. If you're approaching a sharp curve or steep hill, slow down well in advance and keep a firm grip on the steering wheel. When you have to turn the wheel, do so slowly and only as much as necessary.

When you know that you'll have to stop for a stop sign or red signal light on an ice- or snow-packed roadway, shift to Neutral and press the brake pedal down gently. Shifting to Neutral helps you brake and prevent skidding by eliminating the thrust effect of the wheels.

Anticipate and Prevent Hydroplaning

During the first 10 to 15 minutes of a rainfall, the roads are at their slickest. This occurs because the rain's moisture mixes with surface dirt and oil to form a slippery film. This film greatly reduces the ability of your tires to grip the road.

Additionally, at speeds as low as 35 mph, the tires of a vehicle can begin to skim along the wet surface of the road, much like a water-skier zipping across the surface of a lake. The vehicle's tires may completely lose contact with the road and be moving on a thin film of water. This is called **hydroplaning.** Hydroplaning is very dangerous because it severely limits your ability to control your vehicle. To reduce the chance of hydroplaning, reduce speed by about one-third when driving on wet roadways. Be sure your tires have plenty of tread and are properly inflated.

SAFETY TIPS

Avoid using your high beams in heavy rain, sleet, or snow. Under such conditions, light is reflected back into your eyes, decreasing your ability to see.

WHAT WOULD YOU DO?

How would you get your vehicle out of the snowdrift?

Lesson 3 Review

1. What strategies can you use to manage visibility, time, and space in rainy or snowy weather?
2. What risks can you anticipate when driving in rain or snow? What steps can you take to minimize them?

Lesson 3 Review

Answers

1. Check and prepare your vehicle in advance, increase following distance, drive in the tracks of the vehicle ahead, communicate your intentions well in advance, remain alert, use your low beams, ease into turns and curves, slow early and gradually for stops.
2. Skidding and hydroplaning; drive slowly and carefully, allow an extra margin of safety, maneuver gently and gradually, anticipate high-risk situations.

Other Hazardous Weather Conditions

LESSON FOUR

OBJECTIVES
1. Describe five hazardous weather conditions other than snow and rain.
2. Understand the risks involved in driving under each condition.

Fog, industrial smog, or a sudden dust storm or sandstorm can diminish the light of a bright, clear day. Strong gusts of wind can blow your vehicle off the road. You can minimize risk under these conditions.

How Can You Minimize Risk in Other Hazardous Weather Conditions?

Just as you must understand and learn how to manage risk when driving in rain and snow, you must also understand and learn how to manage risk posed by other weather hazards.

Fog or Smog

Dense fog poses hazards. Scattered patches of fog may suddenly occur, cutting your field of vision without warning. If humidity is too high, moisture can form on both inside and outside the windshield, further reducing visibility. Turn on the windshield wipers and defogger as necessary.

Low-beam headlights are essential when driving in fog. You may also want to switch on your emergency flashers to further increase the ability of other highway users to see you. Resist the temptation to put on your high beams. The small droplets of water in fog reflect light back into your eyes, making visibility worse with high beams than with low beams.

To better manage time and space when driving in fog, reduce speed, increase your following distance, and remain alert for sudden movements.

If fog is very dense, the wisest thing to do is to signal, pull off the road, and wait for conditions to improve. Do *not* stop on the road. Stop outside a guardrail if possible, and turn off all lights.

In some areas, industrial smoke and other kinds of air pollution create smog that decreases drivers' visibility as much as does fog. Methods described for driving in fog are equally useful for smog conditions.

Sand and Dust

In some parts of the country, sand and dust cause serious visibility problems. In desert areas, for example, these storms can cause a severe decrease in visibility that greatly increases the risk of a collision.

MEETING STUDENT DIVERSITY

Learning Disabled

Use photographs from books, magazines, and newspapers to help students visualize driving under various conditions of limited visibility. Encourage students to describe their own experiences with fog, strong wind, sandstorms, and the like.

LESSON FOUR

Other Hazardous Weather Conditions

(pages 225–226)

FOCUS

Objectives

- Describe five hazardous weather conditions other than snow and rain.
- Understand the risks involved in driving under each condition.

Resources

 Study Guide, page 48

 Traffic charts

Motivator

Pose the following: Patches of fog have reduced visibility along the road. What actions can you take to improve visibility and lessen driving risk? (Use low-beam lights and emergency flashers; reduce speed; increase following distance; turn on wipers and defogger.)

TEACH

Explain

OBJECTIVES 1 AND 2: Students may benefit from a discussion of how certain visibility-reducing conditions can occur together, such as fog and rain.

Teaching Model

Describe the following situation: The wind is so strong that you can feel it push against your vehicle. Model the thinking process that you use to minimize risk. (You reduce speed; grip the steering wheel firmly; increase the margin of space around your vehicle.)

ADVICE FROM THE EXPERTS

Gary Guzouskas
Administrator, New Hampshire Department of Education

As you drive you may encounter various conditions that affect your ability to see and operate your car safely. To reduce risk, use your head-lights every time you drive and keep them clean and aligned. Be alert to changing environmental and roadway conditions. When buying a car, consider one whose design limits blind spots and whose color enhances its ability to be seen.

Whenever visibility becomes limited, adjust your speed and position to provide more space between your car and other highway users.

Ask

Discuss the risks of driving near a vehicle pulling a trailer in strong wind.

Read

Have students read Lesson 4 to learn how to reduce risk when driving in hazardous weather conditions.

ASSESS

Guided Practice

Have students answer the Lesson 4 Review questions. The answers are provided below.

Reteaching

Have small groups describe how to deal with hazardous weath-er conditions.

Enrichment

Assign the Study Guide for Lesson 4. The Find Out More sec-tion encourages students to expand their basic learning of the lesson concepts.

CLOSE

Summarize

Return to the Motivator ques-tion, and discuss risk reduction techniques.

Advice from the Experts

Stress the importance of always using your head-lights when you drive, par-ticularly in bad weather.

If you're caught in such a storm, signal, pull off the road, turn on your flashers, and wait for the storm to pass. If you must drive, use your low-beam headlights, and proceed slowly and very cautiously.

Wind

Depending on the size and weight of the vehicle you're driving, high winds can be a nuisance—or dangerous. Wind can buffet vehicles travel-ing on a highway like boats tossed in stormy seas. A strong enough gust of wind can actually push a lightweight vehicle right out of its lane!

Under windy conditions, reduce speed and grip the steering wheel firmly to maintain control of your vehicle. Leave extra space between your vehicle and nearby vehicles, especially those that are likely to be affected by the wind, such as vans, recreational vehicles, and vehi-cles pulling trailers.

Nature is not the only source of wind. When a bus, truck, or tractor-trailer speeds by you—in either direction—you'll feel a powerful blast as it passes. Always allow as much distance as possible to the side between your vehicle and a passing large vehicle. In this way, you can mini-mize the force of the resulting wind gust.

WHAT WOULD YOU DO?

Explain how you would manage risk in this situation.

Lesson 4 Review

1. What weather conditions other than snow and rain pose dangers for drivers?
2. What risks would you anticipate in these conditions?

DRIVER'S LOG

How can you reduce risk when driving in fog? In wind?

WHAT WOULD YOU DO?

Sample answer: *Use low-beam headlights and, if needed, emergency flash-ers; reduce speed; increase following distance; stay alert.*

Lesson 4 Review

Answers

1. Fog, smog, sand, wind, and dust.
2. Reduced visibility; wind blowing your vehicle out of its lane or off the roadway.

Using a Triptik

A *Triptik* is a continuous series of strip maps in booklet form put out by AAA. A Triptik provides detailed routing from one place to another. All you have to do is flip the strips.

The front page of each strip map shows a section of a through, cross-country route and all necessary highway details (Map A). The centerfold contains an area map (Map B). It shows the area surrounding the major route so that you can deviate from the marked route if you choose. The back page ordinarily shows detailed maps of cities along the marked route (Map C).

Try It Yourself

1. On which map would you find the route highlighted for best travel through Baltimore? What route is this? What else does the map tell you about this route?

2. You are at the corner of Bentwood Avenue, heading west on Chase Street. Describe how you would get to the Baltimore Arena. Which map would you use?

3. Suppose you are north of Baltimore, traveling south on Route 83. You want to take Route 45 into the city. Which map would you use? How would you get to Route 45?

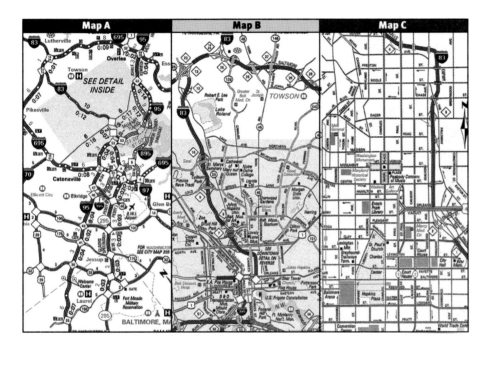

BUILDING SKILLS: READING MAPS

Objective

Demonstrate an ability to use a Triptik.

Teaching the Skill

• Be sure students understand that the maps vary in scale and in total area shown.

• Explain that for some information, drivers use such maps individually. At other times, drivers use two or more maps in combination.

• Point out that the compass arrow indicates direction and makes it easier to compare maps.

• You may want to have students locate a common feature on more than one map. Route 83, for example, appears on all three maps.

ANSWERS TO
Try It Yourself Questions

1. Map A; Route 95; repairs are in progress; the route is an interstate

2. possible answer: take Howard Street south; Map C

3. Map B; travel east to connect with Route 45

CHAPTER SUMMARY

Key Points

Have students read the Key Points to review the major concepts of the chapter.

Cooperative Learning:

Students will benefit by working with a partner on one or both projects. When the assignment is completed, the whole class will profit by sharing and comparing results.

CHAPTER 12 REVIEW

KEY POINTS

Lesson One

1. Reduced light during dusk and dawn and at night makes it harder for you to see and harder for others to see you. At night, your view of the roadway is limited, and you have to cope with glare from the lights of oncoming vehicles.
2. When driving in low light, reduce speed, increase following distance, signal turns well in advance, and use your low or high beams as appropriate.

Lesson Two

1. When the sun is low on the horizon, glare makes it hard to see the road and the brake lights of other vehicles.
2. To minimize the risk from sun glare, wear sunglasses and use your sun visor. Reduce speed and increase your following distance.

Lesson Three

1. Steps you can take to manage visibility, time, and space in rain or snow are to prepare in advance, leave an extra margin of safety, drive in the tracks of the vehicle ahead of you, signal other drivers early, keep your low-beam headlights on, ease your way into turns and curves, and slow down gradually for stops.
2. To minimize risk in rain or snow, maneuver the vehicle gently and gradually to prevent skids, allow extra time for braking and steering, and drive slowly to avoid hydroplaning.

Lesson Four

1. Five hazardous weather conditions other than snow and rain are smog, fog, sandstorms, dust storms, and wind.
2. Fog and smog decrease visibility. Keep on low-beam headlights, reduce speed, and increase following distance. If the fog or smog is very dense, pull off the road and wait for driving conditions to improve.

   In a sandstorm or dust storm, pull off the road. Use emergency flashers to alert others of your presence. If you must drive, use low-beam headlights and proceed with caution.

   In heavy winds, reduce speed and grip the steering wheel firmly; increase the distance between your vehicle and other vehicles. When being passed by a large vehicle, allow as much distance as possible to minimize the force of the resulting wind gust.

PROJECTS

1. Laws governing the use of headlights and parking lights vary from state to state. Find out what the rules are in your state. Take an informal survey of drivers you know. How many are aware of your state's regulations?
2. Stores sell products designed to help drivers cope with winter driving. Visit a store and evaluate several such products. Which would you buy? Which would you avoid? Why? Discuss your findings with the class.

*inter*NET CONNECTION

Look forward to becoming an experienced driver! Use the Internet to learn more about minimizing risk while driving in poor light and weather.
drivered.glencoe.com

*inter*NET CONNECTION

Visit Glencoe's Driver Education Web site for student activities that relate to this chapter.
drivered.glencoe.com

CHAPTER TEST

Write the letter of the answer that best completes each sentence.

1. You can lessen the risk of sun glare by
   a. opening your sunroof.
   b. using your high beams.
   c. wearing sunglasses.

2. You should keep your low-beam headlights on
   a. at all times, day or night.
   b. from dusk until dawn.
   c. only when you cannot see.

3. As visibility decreases,
   a. your risk of being involved in a collision decreases.
   b. your risk of being involved in a collision increases.
   c. the barometer rises.

4. Using your high beams in fog can
   a. increase visibility by as much as 250 feet.
   b. decrease your ability to see.
   c. warn other drivers of your approach.

5. A dirty or scratched windshield
   a. can cause you to skid in bad weather.
   b. can worsen the effects of glare.
   c. has no effect on glare.

6. During dusk and dawn hours, it is
   a. more difficult for other drivers and pedestrians to see you.
   b. easier to hydroplane.
   c. easier to see the roadway.

7. To brake safely on a snow-packed road,
   a. quickly press the brake all the way to the floor.
   b. shift to Neutral and press the brake gradually.
   c. shift to Overdrive and press the brake.

8. Dense fog can
   a. permanently affect the surface of your windshield.
   b. cause moisture to accumulate on the inside of your windshield.
   c. cause elevated roadways to freeze.

9. If you are caught in a sandstorm, you should
   a. use your windshield wipers.
   b. pull off the road and put on your emergency flashers.
   c. use your high beams.

10. A car traveling on a wet road at 35 mph can
    a. get increased gas mileage.
    b. lose contact with the road entirely.
    c. develop engine trouble.

Write the word or phrase that best completes each sentence.

sun visor	temperature	smog
hydroplane	windshield	taillights

11. When you _____, your car skims along the surface of water on the roadway.

12. Your headlights and _____ help illuminate your car.

13. One way to avoid glare is to use your _____.

14. Air pollution and smoke can create _____, which decreases drivers' visibility as much as fog does.

15. Glare caused when the sun hits your _____ can diminish visibility.

DRIVER'S LOG

In this chapter, you have learned how different light and weather conditions affect the driving task. Imagine that the temperature is between 25°F and 35°F and that it is beginning to rain. Write a weather advisory for drivers that gives hints on driving safely in these conditions and what conditions drivers might expect later in the day.

RETURN TO THE BIG IDEA

Discuss how drivers can prepare themselves for driving under the kinds of adverse conditions discussed in this chapter.

CHAPTER 12 REVIEW

CHAPTER TEST

Assign the Chapter Test to all students.

Answers

1. c
2. a
3. b
4. b
5. b
6. a
7. b
8. b
9. b
10. b
11. hydroplane
12. taillights
13. sun visor
14. smog
15. windshield

DRIVER'S LOG

Students' responses will reflect their personal viewpoints. However, their answers should provide an assessment of their understanding of the relationship between weather conditions and the steps a driver must take to minimize risk.

Evaluate

- Test A, pages 23–24 or Test B, pages 23–24
- Testmaker software

Sharing the Roadway Overview

THEME DEVELOPMENT Responsible drivers recognize and are prepared to cope with the special problems posed by pedestrians, cyclists, animals, all types of vehicles, and railroad crossings.

LESSON	PAGES	LESSON OBJECTIVES	STATE/LOCAL OBJECTIVES
1 Sharing the Roadway with Pedestrians and Animals	232–236	**1.** Describe problems that pedestrians can pose. **2.** Explain how to avoid collisions with pedestrians. **3.** Describe pedestrian responsibilities. **4.** Identify ways drivers can avoid collisions with animals.	
2 Sharing the Roadway with Motorcycles and Bicycles	237–239	**1.** Identify situations involving cyclists, and explain actions that drivers can take to reduce the risk of collision with them. **2.** Describe the responsibilities of motorcyclists on the roadway.	
3 Sharing the Roadway with Other Vehicles	240–244	**1.** Describe ways to share the roadway with vehicles other than cars and cycles. **2.** Describe at least three precautions you should take around slow-moving vehicles.	
4 Safe Driving Procedures at Railroad Crossings	245–246	**1.** Explain how to drive safely through a railroad crossing. **2.** Describe what to do if your vehicle stalls on railroad tracks.	
Building Skills	247		
Review: Chapter Summary	248		
Chapter Test	249		

CHAPTER FEATURES	TCR COMPONENTS
TIPS FOR NEW DRIVERS Identifying pedestrians who require drivers to pay special attention.	Study Guide, p. 49 Lesson Plan, p. 27 Information Masters 12 and 16
	Study Guide, p. 50 Transparency 35 Lesson Plan, p. 27 Information Masters 3 and 11
TIPS FOR NEW DRIVERS Learning how to share the roadway safely with a truck. **CONNECTIONS** *CULTURAL CROSSROADS* History Learning about the Japanese Processions of the Lords.	Study Guide, p. 51 Transparency 36 Lesson Plan, p. 28 Information Masters 9, 14, and 19
ADVICE FROM THE EXPERTS Sharing the roadway safely with other drivers, pedestrians, and bicyclists.	Study Guide, p. 52 Lesson Plan, p. 28
BUILDING SKILLS: MATH Figuring Travel Time **PROJECTS** **1.** Observe pedestrians and motor vehicles. **2.** Locate products that enhance visibility.	Test A, pp. 25–26 Test B, pp. 25–26

OTHER PROGRAM RESOURCES

Testmaker software
Teaching Your Teens to Drive: Lessons 8–11, video or CD-ROM, AAA, 1998

ADDITIONAL RESOURCES

Managing Space and Time for Safe Driving, Video 449, AAA Foundation
Sharing the Road, Video 468, AAA Foundation
Using Your Eyes Effectively, Video 488, AAA Foundation
Dangerous Crossings: A Second Thought, Video 412, AAA Foundation

---

NAME _____ DATE _____

CHAPTER 13 Sharing the Roadway

TEST A

Select the phrase that best completes each sentence below. Write the letter of the answer you have chosen to the left of each statement.

_c_ 1. Every year,
  a. about 5,300 pedestrians are killed in the United States.
  b. about 77,000 pedestrians are injured in the United States.
  c. both a and b occur.
  d. none of the above occurs.

_a_ 2. Of all the collisions between vehicles and pedestrians, most
  a. occur in urban areas.
  b. occur in rural areas.
  c. occur near playgrounds.
  d. result in a fatality.

_a_ 3. Pedestrians jaywalk when they
  a. cross a street without regard for traffic rules or signals.
  b. walk along the side of the road.
  c. cross the street at a crosswalk.
  d. walk in between cars in a parking lot.

_c_ 4. When waiting at a red signal at an intersection,
  a. you should begin driving the second the light turns green.
  b. after the light turns green, you should lightly tap on your horn before driving away.
  c. do not start driving until the light turns green and you have checked for pedestrians.
  d. you should wait 3 seconds before leaving the intersection after the light turns green.

_b_ 5. When backing up your vehicle where children may be present,
  a. honk your horn before backing.
  b. look behind and next to your car first.
  c. look in your mirror and back up.
  d. do none of the above.

_a_ 6. When driving on a two-lane road in an area where animals might cross into traffic, drive
  a. with your headlights on and close to the center line.
  b. toward the right side of the road.
  c. with your lights off and toward the right edge of the roadway.
  d. quickly to get out of the area.

_b_ 7. At dusk, there is more danger of hitting a deer because
  a. deer cannot see very well at dusk.
  b. deer move around to feed at dusk.
  c. deer are naturally sleepy at dusk.
  d. there is more traffic at that time.

_d_ 8. Motorcycles and bicycles are a safety risk because
  a. they are less stable than cars.
  b. drivers tend not to look for cyclists.
  c. they can easily be in a driver's blind spot.
  d. all of the above apply.

NAME _____ DATE _____

_a_ 9. After passing a truck, you should not pull in closely in front of it because
  a. you need to have plenty of room between you and the truck in case you have to hit the brakes.
  b. you will block the truck driver's view of the road.
  c. you could get a ticket for tailgating.
  d. all of the above apply.

_c_ 10. When driving a small car, you
  a. need less time and space than a larger vehicle to pass another vehicle.
  b. have greater visibility than you would in a larger car.
  c. need more time and space than a larger vehicle to pass another vehicle.
  d. should never pass another car.

_c_ 11. At a railroad crossing, stop
  a. 15 feet or closer to the crossing.
  b. no closer than 10 feet from the crossing.
  c. no closer than 15 feet from the crossing.
  d. anywhere as long as it is before the crossing.

In each space below, write the word or words that best complete the sentence.

12. Never pass a truck on its _____right_____ side.

13. When approaching and passing a stopped bus, you should be alert for _____pedestrians_____.

14. If you come upon a school bus with flashing red lights on a two-lane nondivided road, you should _____stop_____.

15. If your vehicle stalls on a railroad track and a train is coming, you should _____leave_____ your vehicle.

16. In rural areas, the likelihood of a fatal car-pedestrian collision is _____greater_____ than in the city.

17. The chapter discusses clues that children may be present in an area. What are these clues?

    Clues that children may be nearby are playground and school- crossing signs, toys in the front yard, or

    a tricycle in the driveway.

    _____

    _____

    _____

    _____

    _____

NAME _____ DATE _____

CHAPTER 13 Sharing the Roadway

TEST B

Select the phrase that best completes each sentence below. Write the letter of the answer you have chosen to the left of each statement.

_b_ 1. The chance of a death occurring in a vehicle-pedestrian collision is
  a. greater in the city.
  b. greater in the country.
  c. 1 in 20.
  d. greater at noon.

_a_ 2. Jaywalking happens when a pedestrian
  a. crosses a street without regard for traffic rules or signals.
  b. walks along the side of the road and not on the sidewalk.
  c. crosses the street at a crosswalk.
  d. walks between cars in a parking lot.

_d_ 3. Children are at a disadvantage as pedestrians because they are
  a. smaller and less visible than adults to drivers.
  b. less capable than adults of judging where it's safe to cross a street.
  c. less likely to fully understand the consequences of making a bad judgment.
  d. all of the above.

_b_ 4. A clue that children may be playing nearby is
  a. parked vehicles on the side of the road.
  b. toys in the front yard.
  c. a 35-mph-speed sign.
  d. all of the above.

_c_ 5. When waiting for a red signal to change at an intersection,
  a. begin driving the second the light turns green.
  b. lightly tap on your horn before driving away.
  c. do not start driving until you have checked for pedestrians.
  d. wait 3 seconds before leaving the intersection.

_a_ 6. When walking or jogging near a roadway,
  a. wear reflective clothing.
  b. wear headphones.
  c. do both a and b.
  d. do none of the above.

_b_ 7. One way to help avoid a collision with an animal at night is to
  a. drive to the right side of the lane.
  b. look for the reflections of your headlights in the animal's eyes.
  c. always try to steer around it.
  d. drive more quickly than usual.

_c_ 8. In 1997, over _____ motorcyclists were killed in collisions in the United States.
  a. 250
  b. 850
  c. 2,100
  d. 10,000

NAME _____ DATE _____

_b_ 9. You need to drive very carefully near a motorcycle carrying a passenger because
  a. the cyclist is going too slow as a result of the added weight.
  b. the weight of a passenger leaning can throw the motorcycle off balance.
  c. the added weight can make the motorcycle impossible to stop.
  d. all of the above apply.

_d_ 10. Driving just below the right-side passenger window of a truck is dangerous because
  a. the gust of air created by the mass of the truck could pull you into the truck's path.
  b. the truck could pull over.
  c. it takes a truck a long time to stop.
  d. you could be in the truck's blind spot.

_a_ 11. If you come to a railroad crossing with warning lights flashing,
  a. do not attempt to cross.
  b. cross quickly after you have checked both directions.
  c. cross slowly after you have checked both directions.
  d. cross only after you have gotten out of your vehicle to see whether or not a train is really coming.

In each space below, write the word or words that best complete the sentence.

12. More than 70 percent of collisions with pedestrians happen in _____urban_____ areas.

13. When walking on or near a roadway, walk on the side of the roadway _____facing_____ traffic.

14. The time that animals on the roadway can be a particular problem is between _____sunset_____ and _____sunrise_____.

15. You should allow a following distance of at least _____4_____ seconds when following a truck.

16. What kinds of pedestrians require you as a driver to pay more attention to them?

    You need to pay more attention to elderly pedestrians, physically challenged pedestrians, pedestrians

    with strollers or carriages, joggers, and people who walk on their jobs, such as mail carriers and

    roadway maintenance workers.

    _____

    _____

    _____

NAME _____ DATE _____

CHAPTER 13 Sharing the Roadway

STUDY GUIDE FOR CHAPTER 13   LESSON 1

Sharing with Pedestrians and Animals

A. Some people have never learned to drive, so they do not understand problems related to vehicle control. Their ignorance or carelessness as pedestrians can cause loss of life, and it makes sense for drivers to be extra careful around them. Label each pedestrian error listed below with the letter in the picture that illustrates it.

_F_	1. Playing in the street	_E_	5. Ignoring traffic
_H_	2. Taking a shortcut from sidewalk to corner	_A_	6. Walking in traffic when intoxicated
_D_	3. Crossing between intersections	_G_	7. Walking diagonally across an intersection
_B_	4. Stepping out from between parked vehicles	_C_	8. Crossing against a signal

B. FIND OUT MORE. Ask ten people who drive often what they do when they see an animal in the road. What action do they take to avoid hitting it? Sometimes colliding with an animal when driving is unavoidable. If any of the people you talk to have had this experience, ask them what happened and what they did.

Review student's work.

_____
_____
_____

NAME _____ DATE _____

STUDY GUIDE FOR CHAPTER 13   LESSON 2

Sharing with Motorcycles and Bicycles

A. For each sentence below, circle T if the statement is true and F if it is false. Correct each false statement in the space below.

1. On the roadway, motorcycles are less visible than cars.   (T)   F

_____

2. When driving behind a cyclist, reduce your following distance.   T   (F)

When driving behind a cyclist, increase your following distance.

3. The risk of a serious or fatal injury to a driver of a motorcycle involved in a collision is low.   T   (F)

The risk of a fatal injury to a driver of a motorcycle involved in a collision is high.

4. Since a motorcycle is smaller than a car, it is safe to pass one in a tight space.   T   (F)

It is dangerous to pass a motorcycle in a tight space.

5. Two-wheeled vehicles are most difficult to spot when they approach from behind on a highway.   (T)   F

_____

B. FIND OUT MORE. Look through local newspapers for a week, collecting as many articles as possible about bicycle and motorcycle collisions. What were the causes? Was weather a factor? What were the results?

Review student's work.

_____
_____
_____
_____
_____
_____
_____
_____
_____

NAME _____ DATE _____

STUDY GUIDE FOR CHAPTER 13   LESSON 3

Sharing with Other Vehicles

A. For each sentence below, circle T if the statement is true and F if it is false. Correct each false statement in the space below.

1. Trucks on the road today can be up to 60 feet long.   T   (F)

Trucks on the road today can be up to 120 feet long.

2. Truck drivers have excellent visibility ahead.   (T)   F

_____

3. A truck tends to lose speed when going downhill.   T   (F)

A truck tends to gain speed when going downhill.

4. You should decrease your following distance when driving behind a truck.   T   (F)

You should increase your following distance when following a truck.

5. You should pass a truck on the right side of the roadway.   T   (F)

Never pass a truck on the right side of the roadway.

6. You should use the 2-second rule when following a bus.   T   (F)

You should use the 4-second rule when following a bus.

7. When driving a small, low-powered vehicle, you should allow extra space and time to pass another vehicle.   (T)   F

_____

8. If you see an emergency vehicle with its lights flashing, you should pull to the left and let it pass.   T   (F)

You should pull to the right to let an emergency vehicle pass if its lights are flashing.

B. FIND OUT MORE. In some states, you must stop for an ice cream truck that has lights flashing. Look at your state driver's manual, or any other resource that you can find, and see what the law says about this.

Review student's work.

_____
_____
_____
_____
_____

NAME _____ DATE _____

STUDY GUIDE FOR CHAPTER 13   LESSON 4

Driving Safely at Railroad Crossings

A. For each sentence below, circle T if the statement is true and F if it is false. Correct each false statement in the space below.

1. When you come to any railroad crossing, you should always slow down.   (T)   F

_____

2. You should stop no closer than 5 feet from a railroad crossing.   T   (F)

You should stop no closer than 15 feet from a railroad crossing.

3. If the lights at a railroad crossing are flashing, you can cross the tracks only if you do not see a train and after looking carefully.   T   (F)

If the lights at a railroad crossing are flashing, you must stop.

4. A railroad crossing with no lights flashing does not necessarily mean that it is safe to cross without looking first.   (T)   F

_____

5. You should stop on railroad tracks only if the vehicle ahead of you has stopped.   T   (F)

You should never stop on railroad tracks.

6. As soon as a train has passed, you should look and listen to see if there is another train before moving.   (T)   F

_____

B. FIND OUT MORE. Choose a nearby railroad crossing and describe it in as much detail as you can. Are the warning signs leading up to it adequate and visible? How far ahead of the crossing are the signs? Does the crossing have a gate and warning lights? Overall, in your opinion, is it a safe crossing?

Review student's work.

_____
_____
_____

CHAPTER 13

Sharing the Roadway

CHAPTER OVERVIEW

LESSON ONE
Problems that pedestrians and animals pose for drivers are described, and strategies for minimizing the risk of collision are provided.

LESSON TWO
High-risk situations involving drivers and cyclists are identified, and strategies for avoiding collisions are described.

LESSON THREE
Strategies for drivers to share the roadway safely with vehicles other than cars and cycles are described.

LESSON FOUR
Safe procedures for driving through a railroad crossing are explained.

VOCABULARY

ground viewing
jaywalking
moped

230

CONCEPT OF THE DRIVING TASK

Explain that an awareness of the characteristics and limitations of various kinds of vehicles—bicycles, motorcycles, trucks, buses, vans, and sport utility vehicles, for example—enhances drivers' ability to anticipate and deal with problems involving other roadway users.

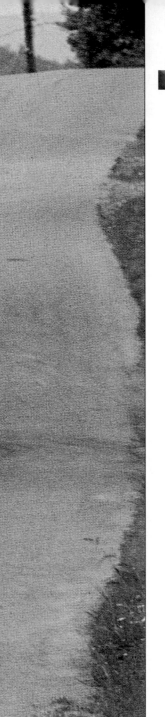

CHAPTER 13

Sharing the Roadway

The society of roadway users includes motorists, pedestrians, and cyclists. It is important to learn how to interact safely with others on the roadways. Good drivers do this by communicating with and anticipating the actions of others.

CHAPTER 13   *Sharing the Roadway*   **231**

PRESENTING THE BIG IDEA ——

Essential parts of risk management are remaining constantly alert to the actions of all roadway users and trying to anticipate problems that these users might pose.

INTRODUCING THE CHAPTER

What's on the Road Ahead?

Have students read the lesson titles and objectives. Briefly discuss the topic of each lesson. Tell students that in this chapter, they will learn strategies for sharing the roadway safely with pedestrians, cyclists, and vehicles other than cars.

Background: The Larger Picture

The following statistics for 1997 will help students realize the importance of learning to drive defensively.

- More than 5,300 pedestrians were killed in motor vehicle collisions. Two-thirds of the fatalities were males.
- More than 2,100 motorcyclists were killed in crashes.
- More than 800 bicyclists were killed in crashes.
- Light trucks, such as pickups, vans, and sport utility vehicles were involved in more than 18,500 fatal crashes. This is about one out of three fatal crashes; one out of two fatal crashes involves a passenger car.
- Ninety-five percent of the 12 million vehicles involved in motor vehicle crashes in 1997 were passenger cars or light trucks.

Relating to Prior Knowledge

Have students discuss factors that may contribute to pedestrian-motor vehicle collisions and suggest ways in which pedestrians and drivers might interact safely.

The Big Idea

Discuss students' reactions to the Big Idea statement. Suggest that they keep this idea in mind as they read Chapter 13.

LESSON ONE

Sharing the Roadway with Pedestrians and Animals

(pages 232–236)

FOCUS

Objectives

- Describe problems that pedestrians can pose.
- Explain how to avoid collisions with pedestrians.
- Describe pedestrian responsibilities.
- Identify ways drivers can avoid collisions with animals.

Resources

 Study Guide, page 49

 Traffic charts

 Information Masters 12 and 16

Vocabulary
jaywalking
ground viewing

Motivator

Pose the following: You are driving through a crowded residential neighborhood on a weekday morning. You see a sign ahead indicating a school zone. Just beyond the sign is a busy intersection. How can you reduce risk to yourself and to other people in this situation? (Students may mention slowing down; being alert for children and other pedestrians, especially near the intersection; searching the roadway continuously for vehicles and people; driving as far from parked vehicles and from the curb as you can; searching beneath parked vehicles.)

LESSON ONE

OBJECTIVES
1. Describe problems that pedestrians can pose.
2. Explain how to avoid collisions with pedestrians.
3. Describe pedestrian responsibilities.
4. Identify ways drivers can avoid collisions with animals.

KEY TERMS
jaywalking
ground viewing

Sharing the Roadway with Pedestrians and Animals

Drivers must be alert to all roadway users, not just other motorists. Other roadway users such as pedestrians and animals can present special problems. Anticipating these problems can help you protect yourself and others.

What Problems Do Pedestrians Pose to Drivers?

In 1997, some 5,300 pedestrians were killed and about 77,000 injured in the United States.

Intersections are the most common scene of collisions with pedestrians. Drivers concentrating on traffic, signs, and signals, as well as other roadway users, often fail to see pedestrians until it is too late.

Moreover, pedestrians may be distracted and cross streets without looking. They often run across streets either against a red light or just as a light is turning red.

◆ Be on the lookout for pedestrians who cross the street illegally or who may need extra time to cross the street.

Jaywalking, crossing without regard for traffic rules or signals, is a common pedestrian error, as is walking into the street from between parked vehicles.

When traffic is light, pedestrians sometimes cross at places other than intersections because they assume no vehicles are coming. In areas without sidewalks, pedestrians walk in the street or roadway, posing an additional risk to drivers.

Children

Children are at a disadvantage as pedestrians because they're smaller and less visible than adults to drivers. They are also less capable than adults

232   UNIT 3 *Moving onto the Road*

IT'S A FACT

Twenty-nine percent of children age 12 and under who were killed in motor vehicle collisions in 1994 were pedestrians. The pedestrian death rate per 100,000 children was highest for 2- to 7-year-olds.

of judging when it's safe to cross a street and less likely to understand fully the consequences of their misjudgment.

In many urban and suburban areas, children use the street as their playground. When playing on sidewalks, children tend to forget about traffic and dart into the street, often between parked vehicles.

Children on skateboards, sleds, roller skates, or bicycles sometimes lose control and shoot over the edge of a sidewalk into the street.

Adults

Adults should know better than children, but they don't always act that way. Adults commonly jaywalk, particularly when rushing to get somewhere or to escape harsh weather. Adults often assume not only that drivers will see them but that the drivers will always grant them the right-of-way. Making these two assumptions can prove fatal.

How Can You Avoid Collisions with Pedestrians?

The SIPDE procedure—particularly the first step, Search—is essential to drivers in avoiding and preventing collisions with pedestrians.

Search the roadway and sides of the road continuously as you drive. Watch for children on or near the roadway. Also look for clues that children may be present. Playground and school-crossing signs, toys in a front yard, or a tricycle in a driveway all indicate that children may be nearby.

In residential areas, reduce speed and drive as far away from the curb or parked vehicles as you safely can. Use **ground viewing,** which means searching beneath parked vehicles, for any sign of movement.

Exercise special care at intersections, particularly when you're making a turn. Be alert for people crossing against the light, stepping off a curb prematurely, or rushing to beat a changing light. Watch, too, for pedestrians who need more time to cross a street than the "Walk" signal allows them. Although not exactly a pedestrian, someone riding a skateboard or on roller skates should deserve your attention, especially near intersections.

◆ *Be on the alert for children on bicycles in suburban areas.*

More than 120 people are killed each year in the United States in collisions with deer and other animals. An equal number are killed when drivers try to avoid striking an animal and instead crash into another vehicle or an object or cause their own vehicle to roll over.

Driving Tip

Sudden rain showers send pedestrians scurrying for shelter. Caution students to drive with special care under such conditions. Not only does the rain limit visibility for both drivers and pedestrians, but people may dart across streets, showing less caution than they normally would.

TEACH

Explain

OBJECTIVES 1 AND 2: Students should recognize the importance of making no assumptions about pedestrian behavior. Drivers should never assume that a pedestrian sees a vehicle approaching, for example, and should never assume that a child on skates or on a bike will stop before crossing a street. Emphasize that a driver must yield to a pedestrian even if the pedestrian is jaywalking. Students should also note the need for extra alertness to pedestrians when driving during dawn and dusk, at night, and in bad weather.

OBJECTIVE 3: Students should recognize the importance of obeying traffic rules and regulations and following the basic safety guidelines given in the text in order to minimize risk. Advise students also to be as cautious and observant as pedestrians as they are as drivers.

OBJECTIVE 4: Stress the point that if one deer or other animal appears on the road, others may well be nearby. Be sure students do not underestimate the great potential risk that a collision with an animal weighing hundreds of pounds poses to driver, passengers, and vehicle.

TIPS ➤ **FOR NEW DRIVERS**

To enhance student understanding, you may want to discuss the different categories of pedestrians, focusing on the risks each particular group poses for drivers. Stress the need for drivers to be observant and patient.

Describe this situation: You are driving along a rural road as the sun is setting. You pass a deer-crossing sign. Model the thinking process you go through to manage risk in this situation. (You do the following.

- Be aware that some animals begin searching for food at sundown.
- Be aware of decreased visibility at dusk.
- Make sure your headlights are on.
- Slow down and be alert for movements of animals on the sides of the road.)

Ask

Ask students to discuss under what conditions a collision with an animal might be the only possible course of action. How might the consequences of such a collision be minimized?

Read

Have students read Lesson 1 to develop an understanding of problems that pedestrians and animals can pose for drivers and to learn strategies for avoiding and dealing with these problems.

◆ Because of their size, buses can block your view of pedestrians who are about to cross the street.

FYI

Most pedestrians who are hit at intersections are struck just as they step onto the street. Many walk into the side of a moving vehicle that they fail to see.

Be alert for adults and children near bus stops, train stations, in school zones, near parks, and in shopping areas.

When backing up, never rely on your rearview mirror alone. Before backing, make certain there is no one behind or next to your vehicle. This is particularly important with regard to children, who may be too small for you to see them when you are behind the wheel.

Never assume a pedestrian can see your vehicle. A pedestrian who is preoccupied, or who has been drinking, may not notice your approach. You should always be ready to take evasive action. To warn a pedestrian that you are approaching, tap your horn. Blasting a horn loudly could frighten a pedestrian into doing something dangerous. You should always yield to pedestrians. They have the right-of-way, even if they are crossing the road illegally.

What Responsibilities Do Pedestrians Have?

Like drivers, pedestrians, too, must pay attention to rules, signals, and signs. Pedestrians must learn to judge gaps in traffic and then cross streets only when and where it is safe—and legal—to do so.

- Never assume that a driver will see you and stop.
- Cross only at intersections.
- Cross only when the light is green or when a pedestrian signal shows a "walk" symbol.
- Do not step off the curb while waiting for the light to change.
- Pause before crossing to look and listen for approaching traffic.
- When walking on or near a roadway, walk facing traffic.
- When walking or jogging on or near a roadway, wear reflective clothing, especially when visibility is reduced. In addition, do not wear headphones.
- When walking with young children, always take them by the hand when crossing streets.

THE INTERNATIONAL SCENE

Canada

In Canada, speed limits are stated in kilometers per hour rather than miles per hour. One kilometer equals about five-eighths of a mile. Thus, a speed limit of 100 kilometers per hour is equal to just over 60 miles per hour.

How Can Drivers Avoid Collisions with Animals?

The dangers posed by animals on the roadway should not be taken lightly. Smashing into a 150-pound deer at 50 miles per hour, for example, will not only kill the animal but will also wreck the vehicle and may well kill the passengers.

The problem of animals on the roadway is particularly severe during the hours between sunset and sunrise, when light conditions limit visibility. Fog can also contribute to vehicle–animal collisions.

Small Animals

Whether it's a cat darting across a city street or a raccoon crossing a highway, small animals cause a surprising number of collisions. In trying to avoid the animal, the driver might swerve and strike another vehicle or a fixed object along the road. Or the driver might slam on the brakes— and be struck in the rear by the vehicle behind. Violent evasive action is not advisable.

Large Animals

Hitting a large animal can prove fatal for both the animal and the vehicle's occupants. Deer are the large animals most often struck, but drivers also have collisions with horses, cows, and other farm animals.

Using SIPDE to Avoid Collisions with Animals

Whether you're driving on city streets or along country roads, using the SIPDE procedure will help you avoid having a collision with an animal.

Be especially cautious when driving through farmland or any wooded areas where you are more likely to encounter deer or other animals alongside or in the road. Search for movement along the sides of the road. At night, search for sudden, unusual spots of light that may be identified as the reflection of your headlights off animals' eyes.

As you're driving, think about what you could do if an animal suddenly darted onto the road and into the path of your car.

FYI

Each year, motor vehicles kill hundreds of thousands of deer, antelope, and other large wild animals.

TIPS

FOR NEW DRIVERS

Pedestrians to Watch For

Certain pedestrians require drivers to pay special attention.

- Elderly pedestrians may have impaired eyesight or hearing. They may move and react slowly and require extra time to cross streets.
- The physically challenged, such as people who are blind and people in wheelchairs, may need extra time to cross streets.
- Pedestrians with strollers or carriages may need extra time to move onto or off a sidewalk.
- Joggers running with their backs to traffic can pose a hazard. Many do not wear reflective clothing, which makes them difficult to see when visibility is low.
- People on the job, such as mail carriers, delivery people, or roadway maintenance workers, may be distracted by their work and step out into the roadway without checking traffic.
- Umbrellas and hooded parkas may impair pedestrians' ability to notice traffic.

CHAPTER 13 *Sharing the Roadway* **235**

ASSESS

Guided Practice

Have students answer the Lesson 1 Review questions. The answers are provided below.

Reteaching

Pair a more able student with one who is having difficulty with this lesson. Use a traffic chart to display the situation shown below. Have students study the situation and describe how and where they would scan for pedestrians. Encourage students to be specific.

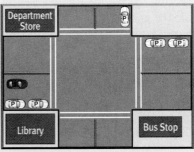

P = parked car

After student pairs have completed this task, they should compare their observations and strategies with the rest of the class.

MEETING STUDENT DIVERSITY

Limited English Proficiency

Substitute simple words for more difficult vocabulary to help students with language problems. Speak of "people walking" instead of "pedestrians," for example, and "look" instead of "scan." You may also want to make an audio recording of driver and pedestrian safety guidelines for students who have limited reading ability.

Enrichment

Assign the Study Guide for Lesson 1. The Find Out More section encourages students to expand their basic learning of the lesson concepts.

CLOSE

Summarize

Return to the Motivator question, and discuss the students' initial responses in light of what they've learned in this lesson. Help students summarize basic safety precautions for both drivers and pedestrians. In this context, also review the use of the SIPDE process to minimize risks posed by pedestrians and animals.

DRIVER'S LOG

Why do you think collisons between pedestrians and vehicles occur most frequently in intersections? What can drivers do to reduce the risk of intersection collisions? What can pedestrians do?

WHAT WOULD YOU DO?

Sample answer: The cyclists may be getting ready to cross the street. Children may be running or playing in the street. People may jaywalk. Use the SIPDE process: reduce speed; move left to increase space margin; tap horn; flash lights.

SAFETY TIPS

While hitchhiking may be legal in some areas, it is not a safe practice. The hitchhiker has no idea what kind of person the driver is, and there is no guarantee that the hitchhiker will not be robbed or assaulted by the driver, or the driver by the hitchhiker.

WHAT WOULD YOU DO?

What possible unseen hazards may be present in this situation? How can you manage risk?

What you can do, if you encounter an animal, will depend on the kind of road you're on, traffic conditions, and other factors. As a general rule, try to position yourself so that you have extra room to manuever. If you're driving on a two-lane road, drive with your headlights on, and when there is no oncoming traffic, move toward the center line to improve visibility. That way, you'll have more room to spot an animal on the side of the road without having to swerve immediately to avoid it. However, always avoid swerving to the left into the path of oncoming vehicles.

Be especially careful when driving at night and in fog. At dusk and dawn, deer move around to feed, and these are also the times during the day when visibility is reduced. If you do spot an animal near or on the road, slow down and be prepared to adjust speed or position as necessary. Leave as wide a safety margin as you can when driving around or past an animal. If you spot one animal, assume that others are nearby.

If it appears impossible to avoid striking a large animal, brake firmly and steer to strike it at an angle. Let up on the brake pedal just before hitting the animal. This will cause the front of the car to rise and reduce the chance that the animal will come through the windshield.

If you see signs that say "Cattle Crossing" or "Open Range" or signs that warn of horseback riders, keep a lookout for animals on or near the roadway. Reduce speed as soon as you see an animal.

Always drive past any animal slowly and cautiously; a frightened animal may bolt in any direction.

Finally, keep in mind that in certain situations your best choice is to strike an animal rather than try to evade it. For example, if a small animal darts in front of your vehicle, and swerving or hard braking might cause a collision with a pedestrian or other vehicle, you must choose the less serious of the collisions.

Lesson 1 Review

1. What are some pedestrian behaviors that lead to collisions with vehicles?
2. What precautions can drivers take to avoid collisions with children?
3. What are some of the basic safety rules pedestrians should follow?
4. If you can't avoid hitting a large animal, what steps should you take to minimize the damage to your vehicle?

Lesson 1 Review

Answers

1. Jaywalking, darting into the street between parked vehicles, playing in the street, rushing to beat a changing light.
2. Use the SIPDE process; be alert for signs of children; position the vehicle for maximum visibility; reduce speed; scan continuously; take special care when backing the vehicle up.
3. Obey all rules, signals, and signs; never assume drivers will see you; don't step off the curb while waiting for a light to turn green; before crossing a street, look and listen for vehicles; take young children by the hand when crossing streets.
4. Brake firmly; steer to strike the animal at an angle.

Sharing the Roadway with Motorcycles and Bicycles

In 1997, 813 bicyclists and more than 2,100 motorcyclists were killed in collisions in the United States. As the number of people riding bikes and motorcycles increases, the number of collisions with cars and other large vehicles may increase too.

As a driver, you should recognize the potential risk of collisions posed by cyclists and take precautions to minimize the risk.

How Can You Recognize and Reduce the Risk of Problems Caused by Cyclists?

Both motorcycles and bicycles are smaller, less stable, and less visible than other vehicles. Two wheels provide less stability than four, making motorcycles and bicycles harder to steer and handle than many people realize. As a driver, you need to be aware of cyclists and of how the roadway problems they face are different from yours.

Watching Out for Cyclists

Two-wheeled vehicles are much more difficult than other vehicles for drivers to spot, especially when they approach from behind or from the side. A **moped** is a low-powered, two-wheeled vehicle that shares some of the same visibility problems as a bicycle or motorcycle and is most commonly driven on city streets. On highways, a motorcycle does not take up an entire lane and may not be seen. In addition, drivers tend not to look for cyclists.

◆ *Cyclists should be especially careful to stay out of a driver's blind spots.*

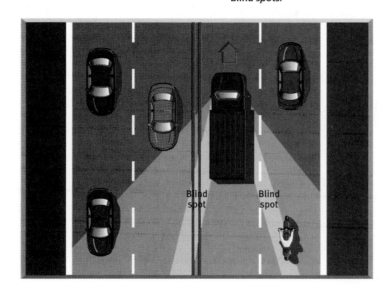

CHAPTER 13 *Sharing the Roadway* **237**

State BY State

Colorado, Iowa, and Illinois are the only states that do not have laws requiring motorcyclists to wear helmets. Some states that had previously repealed their helmet laws later reinstated them, often with dramatic results. When Louisiana reenacted its helmet-use law, for example, the death rate among motorcyclists immediately decreased almost 24 percent.

LESSON TWO

OBJECTIVES
1. Identify situations involving cyclists, and explain actions that drivers can take to reduce the risk of collision with them.
2. Describe the responsibilities of motorcyclists on the roadway.

KEY TERM
moped

LESSON TWO

Sharing the Roadway with Motorcycles and Bicycles

(pages 237–239)

FOCUS

Objectives

- Identify situations involving cyclists, and explain actions that drivers can take to reduce the risk of collision with them.
- Describe the responsibilities of motorcyclists on the roadway.

Resources

 Study Guide, page 50

Traffic charts

Transparency 35

Information Masters 3 and 11

Vocabulary
moped

Motivator

Pose the following: You are driving through an area of the city where bicyclists and motorcyclists are common. What precautions can you take to reduce the risk of collision? (Students may mention making cyclists aware of your presence and intentions by using your turn signals, horn, and lights; watching for road conditions that might cause problems for cyclists; allowing cyclists as much room as possible; not trying to pass a cyclist in a tight space; using rearview and sideview mirrors to check for cyclists and checking blind spots; being prepared to take evasive action.)

TEACH

Explain

OBJECTIVE 1: Students may already have some knowledge of high-risk situations from a bicyclist's perspective. Encourage them to share relevant biking experiences they may have had. Students will benefit from a discussion of the special vulnerability of motorcyclists and bicyclists to road and weather conditions. A discussion of reckless behavior on the part of cyclists can also help students appreciate the need for caution when they are driving.

OBJECTIVE 2: Students will benefit from a reminder not to rely solely on their mirrors because mirrors cannot show the entire roadway. Advise students, too, to listen as well as look for nearby vehicles.

Teaching Model

Display this situation:

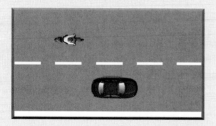

Describe this situation: You are traveling at 35 mph in the right lane of a two-lane, one-way road. You want to move into the left lane to make a left turn but notice a motorcyclist in your left rear blind spot. Model the thinking process you use to minimize risk in this situation. (You do the following.

- Use your turn signal to indicate your intention to change lanes.
- Check your left-side mirror.
- Check over your left shoulder to continue to observe the cyclist.
- Either increase speed to give yourself sufficient space to change lanes safely or else decrease speed to allow the cyclist to pass before you change lanes.)

Motorcycles have a shorter stopping distance than other motor vehicles. This means you need to increase your following distance when there is a motorcycle in front of you.

Motorcycles and bicycles also are easily hidden from drivers' sight by larger vehicles sharing the roadway. The small handlebar mirrors on both motorcycles and bicycles offer their drivers only a limited view to the rear. In addition, some motorcycles have no windscreen or windshield wipers to aid visibility in case of a sudden shower.

Always make cyclists aware of your intentions and position. Drive with your headlights on, and signal well in advance when turning, changing lanes, or stopping. Tap your horn early to warn a cyclist of your approach.

Dangerous Roadway Conditions

Drivers must be aware of the problems that cyclists face in order to anticipate situations in which a cyclist might veer or skid into the path of a vehicle, or might suddenly slow down, steer widely left or right, or stop suddenly.

Cyclists must make a much more major adjustment in speed or position than a driver in situations such as these:
- encountering a storm drain, a gravel surface, or a pothole
- driving on a rain-slicked road or through a large puddle
- getting caught in an unexpected rain or snow shower
- being blown by a sudden strong gust of wind

To minimize risk, search the roadway ahead for problems that may cause a cyclist to change speed or direction, skid, or make a sudden stop. Anticipate potential risk by allowing cyclists as much maneuvering space as possible. When driving behind a cyclist, increase your following distance. *Never* try to pass a cyclist in a tight space.

If a cyclist is carrying a passenger, be especially careful. A passenger leaning the wrong way can throw a motorcycle or bicycle off balance.

Use your mirrors to check for cyclists approaching from the rear. They often squeeze between vehicles traveling in parallel lanes. Always check your blind spots, too, before changing lanes. Be on the lookout for cyclists approaching intersections and coming around curves.

Lack of Protection

Unlike drivers, who have the protection of their vehicle's shell, cyclists are unprotected. In the event of a mishap—collision, skid, blowout—the risk of serious or fatal injury is high to the cyclist. Keep this in mind when dealing with cyclists.

When driving through residential areas, watch for bicycles and motorcycles entering the roadway from driveways and side streets.

Failure to Obey Traffic Laws

Human error or ignorance accounts for countless collisions involving cyclists. Although motorcycles are subject to the same laws that other

IT'S A FACT

More than 800 bicyclists were killed in crashes with motor vehicles in 1997. Eighty-two percent of the riders killed were between the ages of 5 and 20 and the ages of 25 and 54.

motor vehicles are, some cyclists seem to break every rule. They ride between lanes, weave in and out of traffic, ride in drivers' blind spots, and fail to signal their intentions.

Some bicyclists show an equal disregard for safety. They shoot through stop signs and red lights, and cut in front of vehicles. Children on bikes may ride the wrong way on one-way streets or sail through intersections with barely a glance to either side.

Such careless riding poses a danger not just to the cyclist but to all roadway users. You should be alert to the possibility that cyclists may not follow traffic laws, and you should always be prepared to take evasive action if necessary.

On the other hand, you should follow all traffic laws so that you do not endanger cyclists and other users of the roadway.

Irresponsible Drivers

Many collisions involving cyclists occur because drivers have difficulty seeing motorcycles and bicycles. However, some cyclists become the victims of careless or inconsiderate drivers. These drivers may tailgate cyclists, cut them off, or pass too close for safety. Such reckless actions put both driver and cyclist at risk.

What Special Responsibilities Do Motorcyclists Have?

Motorcyclists have the same rights on the roadways as any other drivers. They also have the responsibility of driving safely and watching out for drivers of other vehicles.

Motorcyclists should not take advantage of the smaller size of their vehicles to weave in and out of lanes of traffic at high speeds. This behavior is highly dangerous to the cyclist. Motorcyclists should take care to stay out of other drivers' blind spots. Other drivers might not be as aware as they should be about looking in their mirrors for motorcycles to begin with, so it is important that a motorcyclist never be in a spot that is not visible to nearby vehicles.

Lesson 2 Review

1. Describe problems that cyclists can cause for a driver. Explain how you would manage risk in each circumstance.
2. What should motorcyclists do to avoid risks on the roadway?

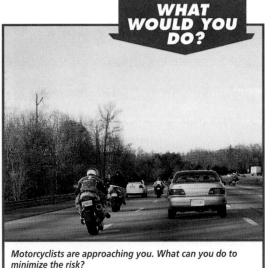

WHAT WOULD YOU DO?

Motorcyclists are approaching you. What can you do to minimize the risk?

Ask

Ask students to discuss the specific risks in this situation.

Read

Have students read Lesson 2 to become familiar with problems that cyclists pose for drivers and with strategies drivers can use to minimize the risk of collisions with cyclists.

ASSESS

Guided Practice

Have students answer the Lesson 2 Review questions. The answers are provided below.

Reteaching

Have students work together in small groups to make charts of safety rules for bicyclists and motorcyclists and for drivers who encounter cyclists. Have students compare their work and discuss the rules they included.

Enrichment

Assign the Study Guide for Lesson 2. The Find Out More section encourages students to expand their basic learning of the lesson concepts.

CLOSE

Summarize

Return to the motivator question, and discuss students' initial responses in light of what they've learned in the lesson. Help students summarize the guidelines in the lesson by discussing this question: How do scanning and communication help drivers and cyclists avoid collisions?

DRIVER'S LOG

What actions can a driver take to reduce the risk of colliding with a motorcyclist? With a bicyclist? What actions can cyclists take to reduce risk?

WHAT WOULD YOU DO?

Sample answer: Search the roadway for problems that may cause a cyclist to change speed, change direction, skid, or make a sudden stop; give the cyclist as much maneuvering space as possible.

Lesson 2 Review

Answers

1. Cyclists are difficult to see: search the roadway and check blind spots. Cyclists may fail to obey traffic laws: be alert and ready to take evasive action. Cyclists may have difficulty coping with road conditions: allow them extra space to maneuver, and try to anticipate adjustments they may have to make.
2. Cyclists should keep out of drivers' blind spots, avoid weaving in and out of lanes, and obey all traffic laws.

Sharing the Roadway with Other Vehicles

(pages 240–244)

FOCUS

Objectives

• Describe ways to share the roadway with vehicles other than cars and cycles.

• Describe at least three precautions you should take around slow-moving vehicles.

Resources

  Study Guide, page 51

Traffic charts

 Transparency 36

Information Masters 9, 14, and 19

Motivator

You are in the center lane of a three-lane, one-way highway. You are approaching a tractor-trailer traveling in the same lane. You decide to pass. How will you manage visibility, time, and space to minimize risk in this situation? (Students may mention being aware of the driver's inability to see vehicles behind and to the side; allowing a 4-second following distance; not attempting to pass on the right; checking your mirrors for traffic behind you and to your left; keeping in mind that it will take more time and space to pass the truck than it would to pass a car; not getting too close to the truck before you begin to pass; leaving as much space as possible between your vehicle and the truck; leaving plenty of space between you and the truck before you pull back into the lane in front of the truck; signaling your intentions.)

LESSON THREE

OBJECTIVES

1. Describe ways to share the roadway with vehicles other than cars and cycles.
2. Describe at least three precautions you should take around slow-moving vehicles.

Sharing the Roadway with Other Vehicles

When driving on any street or highway, you'll share the road with vehicles that range in size from 2-wheel, 30-pound bicycles to 18-wheel, 80,000-pound tractor-trailers. You've already explored some problems you might encounter with bicycles and motorcycles. To manage time and space near larger vehicles, you need to understand their characteristics and limitations.

Energy Tips

Save fuel by using public transportation, such as buses, or riding a bicycle whenever possible.

How Can You Safely Share the Roadway with Other Vehicles?

Keep in mind that differences in the size, shape, and weight of vehicles affect handling ability as well as the amount of visibility a driver has.

Trucks and Tractor-Trailers

Trucks on the road today can be up to 120 feet long and weigh up to 60 tons. That's about 8 times as long as the average car and 40 to 60 times

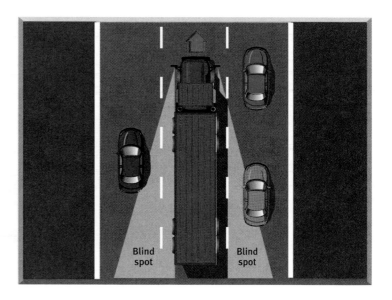

◆ *Tractor-trailer mirrors are mounted high, so the driver loses sight of your car if you travel alongside the trailer.*

Blind spot   Blind spot

State BY State

In 1997, 29 percent of motor vehicle deaths involved occupants of pickups, vans, and sport utility vehicles. States with the highest number of fatalities included Texas (1,095), California (821), Florida (518), Georgia (432), and Missouri (345).

heavier. Put yourself in the truck driver's place. Being aware of problems he or she faces will help you better manage risk.

Visibility Truck drivers sit high above the roadway and have excellent visibility ahead. However, it is hard for them to see to the side and behind the truck. Despite the use of sideview mirrors, some vehicles may be all but invisible to a truck driver.

Trucks create visibility problems for other drivers. With a truck blocking your view, you can't see other traffic or the roadway ahead.

Time Handling a truck is more difficult than handling a car. Weighed down with cargo, a truck accelerates slowly and tends to lose speed when climbing an uphill road. Going downhill, however, a truck's momentum causes it to pick up speed. See Chapter 14 for more on momentum.

When you're passing a truck, allow much more time than you'd need in order to pass a car. Not only is the truck longer, but its bulk creates a wind factor that you'll also have to be aware of as you steer around the vehicle.

Space Trucks, of course, take up much more room on the roadway than do cars. As a result, it's much harder to see around one when you're following it. Increase your following distance when you're behind a truck. Remember that a truck requires a wide turning space and more time and space to stop than cars do. When you approach a truck in an oncoming lane, leave as much space as possible between the truck and your vehicle.

Buses

The same visibility and handling factors that pertain to trucks also apply to buses. Allow buses an equal amount of "elbow room," and follow the same 4-second distance rule when following a bus. Remember that local buses stop frequently to pick up and discharge passengers, often disrupting traffic flow in the process.

TIPS **FOR NEW DRIVERS**

How to Safely Share the Roadway with a Truck

Always allow at least a 4-second following distance to make yourself visible to a truck driver and to allow you to see more of the roadway.

When stopping behind a truck stopped at a sign or signal, allow extra distance in case the truck rolls back when starting off.

Allow yourself extra time and space when passing. When a large truck is about to pass you, steer to adjust to the gust of air caused by the truck.

If a truck is bearing down on you as you drive downhill, move into another lane or pull over to let the truck pass.

Try not to drive on the right side of a truck, especially just below the right-front passenger sIde. This is a blind spot for the truck driver.

Never try to drive by the right side of a truck at an intersection if the truck's right-hand signal is on, even if the truck is in the left lane. Large trucks make very wide right-hand turns.

Never pass a truck on the right side on the roadway.

After passing a truck, do not pull right in front of it after you clear it. Leave plenty of room in case you have to apply your brakes.

THE INTERNATIONAL SCENE

Europe

New tractor-trailers in the European Union countries were required to have antilock brakes before those in the United States. In the United States, few older tractor-trailers have antilock brakes. However, antilock brakes have been required on new tractors since 1997 and on new trailers since 1998.

TEACH

Explain

OBJECTIVE 1: Encourage students to brainstorm the various kinds of vehicles they have seen. Then discuss differences in size, weight, and ease of handling of the vehicles named. Point out that parked or double-parked vehicles often pose visibility problems for drivers and that such problems are particularly great when the parked vehicle is a truck or other oversize vehicle. Also stress the special problems posed by local buses disrupting traffic flow and the danger of children (and adults) running to an ice-cream truck. Finally, discuss proper procedures for drivers to follow when emergency vehicles approach.

OBJECTIVE 2: Caution students to show patience when "caught" behind a slow-moving vehicle. Point out that many collisions occur because drivers who are in a hurry fail to show good judgment in passing a slow-moving vehicle. Stress, too, that large, slow-moving vehicles pose visibility problems to drivers traveling in both directions on a two-way road, particularly if the road has curves or hills.

TIPS **FOR NEW DRIVERS**

To check student understanding, discuss how each tip reduces risk. For example, never passing a truck on the right prevents you from being trapped or forced off the road by a truck whose driver is unaware of your presence and suddenly moves right.

Teaching Model

Display this situation:

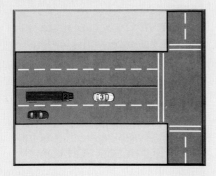

Tell students the following: You are in vehicle 1. A truck (vehicle 2) is passing you in the lane to your left. As you and the truck approach the intersection, you notice that the truck driver has switched on the right-turn signal. Model the thinking process you will go through to manage risk in this situation. (You will do the following.

- Be prepared for the gust of wind caused by the passing truck.
- Anticipate that the truck driver is going to move into your lane and possibly make a right turn.
- Be aware that the truck driver may lose sight of your vehicle.
- Honk your horn to alert the driver if necessary.
- Slow down and give the truck driver time and space to change lanes.
- Leave plenty of room between your vehicle and the truck if the truck is turning.)

A truck weighing 80,000 pounds traveling at 55 mph takes about 300 feet, or the length of a football field, to brake to a stop. This does not include the distance covered during the time the driver identifies a need to stop. A car typically requires less than half this distance.

You should be especially careful when you approach or pass a stopped bus. Reduce speed and keep alert for pedestrians rushing to catch the bus and discharged passengers hurrying across streets in front of the bus. Always be ready to stop.

Remember, drivers traveling in either direction on a nondivided roadway must stop for a school bus that has flashing red lights to indicate it is picking up or dropping off children.

Small Cars

There are more small cars on the road today than ever before. While these vehicles may cost less to buy and operate than larger vehicles, they have some drawbacks.

Small cars may have less power than larger vehicles. As a result, a small car may take a lot longer to pass other vehicles. Small cars may also lose speed when climbing a steep hill. In many small cars, the driver also sits lower and therefore has reduced sight distance.

When driving a small car, allow yourself extra space and time to pass another vehicle. If a small car is passing you, give the driver ample space and time to maneuver.

Also give small cars extra room when roads are slippery or there are strong winds. Lightweight cars tend to skid more easily than heavier vehicles on slick roadways.

CONNECTIONS
History

CULTURAL CROSSROADS

In Japan in the year 1635, a law was passed that caused Japanese lords and thousands of their household staff to take to the roadways of that island nation. The law required that the nation's lords, known as *daimyo,* or "great names," build mansions in the capital city of Edo, now known as Tokyo. The lords were to keep their families in Edo and spend every other year at the court of the ruler, or *shogun.*

Because of this law, the daimyo had to travel once a year to or from their country estates and Edo. Moreover, the daimyo were told how many of their household staff must travel with them, what equipment to take, and what route to follow. The wealthiest daimyo had to take 1,000 or more of their household staff both to and from Edo.

Since there were more than 250 daimyo to which the law applied, there would be many great processions criss-crossing Japanese roads in all seasons. These groups, known as *Daimyo Gyoretsu* or "Processions of the Lords," were on the roadways for several weeks. Each night they would stop at one of a huge network of inns established along the national roadways to accommodate the travelers in these processions. In no other country of the world was there such an extensive and elaborate system of overnight accommodations at the time.

IT'S A FACT

Vehicle size and weight matter in collisions. According to statistics compiled in 1997, the fatality rate per million registered vehicles one to three years old was highest in mini cars, small cars, and small sport utility vehicles. The rate was lowest in large cars and large sport utility vehicles. Moreover, small sport utility vehicles had a very high rate of fatal rollover crashes—more than five times the rate of the largest cars.

Other Kinds of Vehicles

You may encounter other kinds of vehicles on the roadway.

Emergency vehicles When you meet ambulances, police vehicles, and fire trucks with lights flashing or sirens blaring, you should yield the right-of-way. Pull to the right and stop, or otherwise provide a clear path for the emergency vehicle.

Snowmobiles Snowmobiles are allowed on certain roads in some states. They can come onto the roadway in unexpected places. They are often hard to see and can be difficult for their drivers to handle and to stop. Allow extra time and space to adjust to any maneuver that a snowmobile makes.

Sport utility vehicles Sport utility vehicles (SUVs) are taller than the average passenger car. This gives the driver a better view of the traffic ahead. It also means that a driver following an SUV will have an obstructed view of the traffic ahead. Keeping an extra distance behind an SUV may help you to see around the vehicle. Also remember that sport utility vehicles need extra stopping distance.

Ice-cream trucks Approach ice-cream trucks cautiously. Watch for children darting into the street and emerging from between parked vehicles. In some states, drivers must stop for an ice-cream truck equipped with flashing red lights and must yield the right-of-way to pedestrians going to and from the truck. Check your state driver's manual.

Maintenance vehicles Roadwork involves vehicles of many sizes and shapes with the potential to disrupt traffic. Drivers need to be alert to such vehicles and to adjust speed and position to accommodate sudden changes in traffic flow.

How Do You Deal with Slow-Moving Vehicles?

Slow-moving vehicles, such as farm tractors, horse-drawn wagons, and various special-purpose vehicles, move at a much slower speed than other traffic.

Try to spot a slow-moving vehicle as early as possible, because your vehicle will approach it

◆ You may encounter slow-moving maintenance vehicles in city traffic.

How can the driver of vehicle 3 minimize the risk of being struck from behind by the truck?

Read

Have students read Lesson 3 to gain an understanding of how to manage visibility, time, and space when sharing the roadway with vehicles other than cars and cycles.

ASSESS

Guided Practice

Have students answer the Lesson 3 Review questions. The answers are provided below.

Reteaching

Have students work in small groups or pairs, taking turns asking each other how to minimize risk when encountering each of the vehicles discussed in this lesson: trucks and tractor-trailers, buses, small cars, emergency vehicles, snowmobiles, sport utility vehicles, ice-cream trucks, maintenance vehicles, and slow-moving vehicles, such as tractors and horse-driven wagons.

After the groups or pairs have completed their questions and answers, have students take part in a class discussion of the benefits of understanding the characteristics and limitations of vehicles of all sizes.

Driving Tip

Explain to students that when they hear an emergency vehicle siren, they should try to identify the direction from which the vehicle is coming as soon as possible. Knowing this will help them determine how nearby traffic will move and what action to take to provide a clear path

CONNECTIONS
History

To add to students' understanding, have students locate Japan and Tokyo on a map.

Assign the Study Guide for Lesson 3. The Find Out More section encourages students to expand their basic learning of the lesson concepts.

CLOSE

Summarize

Return to the Motivator question, and reexamine the situation in light of what students have learned about risk management in this lesson. Encourage students to be specific in their answers. Extend the discussion by having students discuss the use of the SIPDE process to minimize risk when encountering trucks, buses, small cars, sport utility vehicles, and slow-moving vehicles. Also discuss what additional safety precautions a driver should take when encountering such vehicles under bad weather conditions.

DRIVER'S LOG

Have students divide a page into three columns. Ask them to list as many different kinds of vehicles as they can think of in the first column. In the second column, students should note any special problems each of the vehicles listed in the first column might pose. In the third column, have students write strategies for coping with the specific problems posed.

WHAT WOULD YOU DO?

Sample answer: Allow yourself more time than you would need if passing a passenger vehicle.

◆ *Allow a wide vehicle more room to maneuver, especially on turns.*

WHAT WOULD YOU DO?

You are passing this truck. What should you do?

more rapidly than a vehicle traveling at a normal rate of speed. Slow-moving vehicles often, but not always, display special signs identifying them as slow-moving. If a vehicle is especially wide, it may carry a "wide load" sign on the rear. Once you identify such a vehicle, reduce speed immediately and follow at a safe distance.

Before passing, consider the driver's likely actions. For example, the driver of a construction vehicle may drive on the roadway for only a short distance before turning off. A road maintenance or utility truck may stop or pull over to the side.

If you decide to pass, do so safely and only where it is legal to pass. Be especially careful on narrow, single-lane country roads, where you're more likely to encounter a slow-moving vehicle. Visibility and space are limited on such roads, and if the vehicle you're following is large, you'll have added difficulty seeing past it.

If you see a slow-moving vehicle traveling in the opposite direction, be alert for oncoming vehicles moving into your path as they pass the vehicle.

Lesson 3 Review

1. Name three types of motor vehicles with which you might share the roadway. Explain how you can reduce risk when interacting with these vehicles.
2. When you are sharing the roadway with a slow-moving vehicle, what are three precautions you should take?

Lesson 3 Review

Answers

1. Sample answers: trucks and buses—increase following distance; allow extra time and space when passing; emergency vehicles—pull over to the right side of the road and stop, or otherwise provide a clear path; sport utility vehicles—allow an extra margin of safety.
2. Reduce speed; follow at a safe distance; before passing, try to anticipate the driver's actions.

Safe Driving Procedures at Railroad Crossings

Despite warning signs, crossing gates, and signals, many collisions occur at railroad crossings each year. Among the causes of these crashes are driver impatience, driver inattention, and poor judgment.

How Can You Drive Through a Railroad Crossing Safely?

Too many drivers forget, or ignore, safe-driving procedures at railroad crossings, often with fatal consequences. This lesson describes those procedures.

Determine When It Is Safe to Cross

Slow down as you approach a railroad crossing. Look for warning lights or signals or lowered crossing gates.

Stop no closer than 15 feet from a railroad crossing if a train is approaching. *Never* attempt to cross a track if warning lights are flashing.

Even if warning lights are not flashing, look both ways and listen to make sure no train is coming before you cross a track. Never rely solely on mechanical warning equipment—it could be broken.

If there are no lights or crossing gates present at a railroad crossing, proceed with extra caution. If there is any question about safety, stop, look, and listen for approaching trains before moving ahead.

After a train has passed, check in both directions to see that no other trains are coming, especially before you start across multiple sets of tracks.

Always wait for the vehicle ahead of you to clear the tracks before you start across. Never stop on the railroad tracks.

(pages 245–246)

◆ *Be patient and very cautious at railroad crossings. Never think you can beat the train to the crossing.*

CHAPTER 13   *Sharing the Roadway*   **245**

Driving Tip

Caution students that impatience can be fatal when driving. Drivers have been killed trying to "beat" a light or attempting to drive across railroad tracks ahead of an approaching train. Risking your life and the lives of others is too high a price to pay to save a small amount of time.

Safe Driving Procedures at Railroad Crossings

(pages 245–246)

FOCUS

Objectives

- Explain how to drive safely through a railroad crossing.
- Describe what to do if your vehicle stalls on railroad tracks.

Resources

📁   Study Guide, page 52

📁   Traffic charts

Motivator

Pose the following: You are approaching a railroad crossing. How can you determine if it's safe to cross? (Look for warning lights, signals, or lowered crossing gates; look both ways and listen for a train.)

TEACH

Explain

OBJECTIVES 1 AND 2: Stress that warning equipment can malfunction. Drivers should check the tracks in both directions before crossing.

Teaching Model

Pose this situation: You are crossing the tracks when your vehicle stalls. Model your thinking. (Check in both directions for trains; leave your vehicle, and move far away if a train is coming; try to restart the vehicle if no train is coming; try to push the vehicle off the tracks if it won't start and there are no trains coming.)

OBJECTIVES

1. Explain how to drive safely through a railroad crossing.
2. Describe what to do if your vehicle stalls on railroad tracks.

*Have students discuss
how thinking ahead helps
drivers anticipate danger
and reduce risk.*

Ask

How would you proceed once you got your vehicle started?

Read

Have students read Lesson 4 to learn the safe procedure for driving through a railroad crossing.

ASSESS

Guided Practice

Have students answer the Lesson 4 Review questions. The answers are provided below.

Reteaching

Have students work in small groups to create a chart or poster detailing the procedure for driving safely through a railroad crossing.

Enrichment

Assign the Study Guide for Lesson 4. The Find Out More section encourages students to expand their basic learning of the lesson concepts.

CLOSE

Summarize

Return to the Motivator question. Discuss how following the proper safety procedures helps drivers manage risk in this situation.

DRIVER'S LOG

What precautions should a driver take to minimize risk when driving through a railroad crossing?

ADVICE FROM THE EXPERTS

Bruce J. Oliver
Manager of Driver Training, AAA Mid-Atlantic
Remain alert to share the roadway safely:
- *Bicyclists are expected to obey all traffic laws and regulations. Bicyclists have the same rights, privileges, and responsibilities as drivers.*
- *Think ahead. Drivers can often anticipate dangers involving pedestrians.*
- *Even if you obey all traffic laws, unexpected events can and do occur. Managing time and space effectively will help minimize risk should an emergency occur.*
- *Maintain respect for all roadway users to aid in the safe, smooth flow of traffic.*

Stay Alert

Drivers who travel the same route day after day tend to pay less attention to their surroundings. Such inattention can have tragic consequences at a railroad crossing.

Don't take familiar crossings for granted. Never assume that the track is clear: be alert, look, and listen for trains.

Do Not Panic If Your Vehicle Stalls

Never stop your vehicle on railroad tracks for any reason whatsoever. In the rare event that your vehicle stalls on the tracks, don't panic.

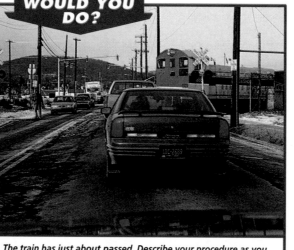

WHAT WOULD YOU DO?

The train has just about passed. Describe your procedure as you get ready to resume movement.

Immediately check in both directions for approaching trains. If a train is coming, leave your vehicle at once, walk in the direction the train is coming from, but move away from the tracks. If no train is approaching and you have a clear view of the tracks in both directions, try to restart your engine. Continue to check for trains.

If you can't start your vehicle and you're sure no trains are coming, try to push your vehicle off—and well away from—the tracks.

Lesson 4 Review

1. What must you do to negotiate a railroad crossing safely?
2. What would you do if your vehicle stalled on railroad tracks?

WHAT WOULD YOU DO?

Sample answer: Wait until the signal is no longer red. Stop, look, and listen for another train. Wait for the vehicle ahead to clear the tracks.

Lesson 4 Review

Answers
1. Slow down and look for warning lights, signals, or lowered gates. Before crossing the tracks, stop, look, and listen for trains in both directions.
2. Check for approaching trains; if a train is coming, leave your vehicle, and move away from the tracks, walking in the direction the train is coming from. If you can't start the vehicle and no train is coming, try to push the vehicle off the tracks.

Figuring Travel Time

Travel involves rate of speed, distance, and time. To find how long it will take you to get somewhere when you know your distance and speed, divide the distance by the speed. (To get an exact answer, you may have to change miles per hour to miles per minute by dividing mph by 60.)

$T = D \div S$, where T = time,
D = distance, and S = speed.

For example, suppose you will drive 270 miles at an average speed of 45 mph. How long will the trip take?

$$T = 270 \div 45$$
$$T = 6$$

The trip will take 6 hours.

Figure the time for each distance and speed below.

TIME	DISTANCE	SPEED
(a)	20 miles	30 mph
(b)	40 miles	35 mph
(c)	115 miles	50 mph

To estimate distance when you know speed and time, multiply the speed and the time.

$$D = S \times T$$

How far can you travel in 5 hours at an average speed of 35 mph?

$$D = 35 \times 5$$
$$D = 175$$

You can travel about 175 miles.

Figure the distance for each speed and time below. Round your answer to the nearest whole mile.

DISTANCE	SPEED	TIME
(d)	25 mph	30 minutes
(e)	45 mph	2¼ hours
(f)	30 mph	1 hour 20 minutes

Now look back at each problem. If you wanted an estimate instead of an exact answer, what shortcuts could you take?

Try It Yourself

1. Traveling at local speeds, about how many miles away is someplace 20 minutes from your home?
2. Use a map to plan a trip from one city to another. Estimate the amount of time it will take to travel the distance between the two cities.
3. Use a map to figure out which cities or towns are about 3 hours away from your home.

Objective

Demonstrate an ability to figure travel time and distance traveled.

Teaching the Skill

- Make sure students understand the relationship between speed, distance, and time.
- You may want to give students additional practice in converting miles per hour to miles per minute.
- Provide students with hints to help them estimate distance. For example, 30 minutes is half an hour, so if you're driving at 50 miles an hour, in 30 minutes you'd travel about 25 miles; in 20 minutes, or one-third of an hour, at 45 mph, you'd travel about 15 miles.
- Point out that travel time estimates must be adjusted for road, weather, and traffic conditions.

ANSWERS TO
Try It Yourself Questions

1. Answers will vary, depending on local speeds.
2. Answers will vary. Encourage students to include time for resting and for urban traffic congestion. Point out that they should not drive more than 8 hours in a day.
3. Answers will vary. Students should recognize that travel time and distance will also depend on travel conditions and directness of travel route.

ANSWERS TO
Figuring Travel
Time and Distance

(a) 40 minutes;
(b) about 1 hour and 8 minutes;
(c) about 2 hours and 20 minutes;
(d) 12½ miles;
(e) 101 miles;
(f) 40 miles.

CHAPTER SUMMARY

Key Points

Have students read the Key Points to review the major concepts of the chapter.

Cooperative Learning:

Students will benefit by working with a partner on one or both projects. When the assignment is completed, the whole class will profit by sharing and comparing results.

CHAPTER 13 REVIEW

KEY POINTS

Lesson One

1. Pedestrian problems may be caused by people who cross a roadway without regard for rules or signals, children who run into or play in the street, people who need extra time to cross, and joggers.
2. To prevent collisions with pedestrians, use the SIPDE process to develop effective visual search habits.
3. Pedestrians should obey all rules, signals, and signs; walk facing traffic if walking on the road; wear reflective clothing when jogging; hold children by the hand; cross streets only when and where it is safe and legal to do so.
4. To avoid collisions with animals, be careful when driving through wooded areas, especially when visibility is reduced.

Lesson Two

1. Motorcycles and bicycles have less stability and protection than other vehicles. To reduce the risk of collision with cyclists, anticipate problems they may have, and adjust your speed or position. Always make cyclists aware of your position and intentions.
2. Cyclists should not weave in and out of traffic and should make themselves visible to drivers.

Lesson Three

1. Trucks and tractor-trailers: when passing allow extra time; when you approach a truck or tractor-trailer in an oncoming lane, leave plenty of space between it and your vehicle. Buses: react as you would to a truck, but remember that approaching and passing requires special care because buses may be picking up or discharging passengers. Small cars: allow extra room on slippery roads or windy days.
2. Try to spot a slow-moving vehicle early. Reduce your speed, and follow at a safe distance. Pass only where it is legal and safe to do so.

Lesson Four

1. Slow down as you approach a railroad crossing. Look for warning lights or signals or lowered gates. Before you cross, stop, look, and listen for trains. Never assume the track is clear.
2. If your vehicle stalls on a railroad track and a train is approaching, leave the vehicle and walk in the direction the train is coming from, but away from the track. If no train is coming, try to restart the engine or push the vehicle off the track.

PROJECTS

1. Observe the interaction between pedestrians and traffic at a busy intersection for about 15 minutes. Make note of unsafe actions taken by both pedestrians and drivers. Discuss your observations with the class.
2. Visit a bicycle shop or sporting goods store. What products does the store sell to help make cyclists, joggers, and others more visible in dim light?

*inter***NET** **CONNECTION** To learn more about safety on the road, visit Glencoe's driver education Web site for the most current Traffic Safety Facts from the U.S. Department of Transportation. **drivered.glencoe.com**

*inter***NET** **CONNECTION**

Visit Glencoe's Driver Education Web site for student activities that relate to this chapter. **drivered.glencoe.com**

CHAPTER TEST

Write the letter of the answer that best completes each sentence.

1. When driving behind a tractor-trailer,
   a. allow at least a 4-second following distance.
   b. attempt to pass.
   c. tap your horn lightly.

2. Collisions with pedestrians occur most often
   a. at intersections.
   b. on highways.
   c. on weekends.

3. Drivers who travel the same route every day
   a. have fewer collisions than other drivers.
   b. pay less attention to their surroundings.
   c. fall asleep at the wheel more often.

4. As the use of cycles increases,
   a. collisions with other vehicles will decrease.
   b. air pollution will decrease.
   c. the number of collisions with other vehicles might also increase.

5. Drivers use ground viewing to
   a. search the road for animals.
   b. search beneath parked vehicles for signs of movement.
   c. avoid large puddles.

6. Because truck drivers sit high above the surface of the roadway, they
   a. don't have any blind spots.
   b. have great visibility of the road ahead.
   c. are able to see above fog.

7. If it appears impossible to avoid striking a large animal, you should
   a. accelerate and move forward.
   b. turn off your vehicle's engine.
   c. steer to strike it at an angle.

8. When driving behind a cyclist, you should
   a. increase your following distance.
   b. pass at the first opportunity.
   c. turn on your high beams.

9. Most small cars have
   a. more power than larger cars.
   b. the ability to pass easily.
   c. less power than larger cars.

10. If you approach a railroad crossing when a train is coming, you should
    a. stop at least 15 feet from the crossing.
    b. stop directly in front of the crossing signal.
    c. try to cross the tracks if the gate is open.

Write the word or phrase that best completes each sentence.

traffic flow	parallel	hazard
stability	stalls	jaywalking

11. Crossing a street without regard for traffic rules or signals is called _____.

12. Motorcycles are harder to steer than many people realize because two wheels provide less _____ than four.

13. If your vehicle _____ on railroad tracks while a train is coming, you should leave the vehicle at once.

14. Cyclists often squeeze between vehicles traveling in _____ lanes.

15. Local buses stop frequently to pick up and discharge passengers, often disrupting _____ in the process.

DRIVER'S LOG

In this chapter, you have learned about the responsibilities and risks of sharing the roadway with motorists, pedestrians, cyclists, and animals. Write what you think are the five most important responsibilities a driver has when sharing the roadway.

CHAPTER 13 REVIEW

CHAPTER TEST

Assign the Chapter Test to all students.

Answers

1. a
2. a
3. b
4. c
5. b
6. b
7. c
8. a
9. c
10. a
11. jaywalking
12. stability
13. stalls
14. parallel
15. traffic flow

DRIVER'S LOG

Students' responses will reflect their personal viewpoints. However, their answers should provide an assessment of their understanding of the responsibilities of sharing the roadway with others.

Evaluate

- Test A, pages 25–26 or Test B, pages 25–26 📁
- Testmaker software

RETURN TO THE BIG IDEA

Discuss the idea that constant driver alertness and forethought are essential to minimizing risk when interacting with various roadway users.

Natural Laws and Driving Overview

THEME DEVELOPMENT The natural laws of inertia, friction, momentum, kinetic energy, and gravity are among the factors that affect a vehicle's movement. Understanding the effects of natural laws can help drivers steer, stop, and otherwise control their vehicle. Knowledge of natural laws can also help drivers minimize the risk and consequences of a collision.

LESSON	PAGES	LESSON OBJECTIVES	STATE/LOCAL OBJECTIVES
1 Natural Laws and the Movement of Your Vehicle	252–256	**1.** Describe the natural laws of inertia, friction, momentum, kinetic energy, and gravity. **2.** Explain the relationship of these natural laws to driving.	
2 Natural Laws and Steering and Braking	257–259	**1.** Explain how natural laws affect a vehicle's stopping distance. **2.** Identify the factors that affect steering. **3.** Name the ways that natural laws affect steering around a curve. **4.** Describe how gravity and the contour of the road affect steering.	
3 Using Natural Laws to Manage Skids	260–262	**1.** List factors that can cause your vehicle to skid. **2.** Name and describe the kinds of skids there are. **3.** Describe how to manage risk in responding to a skid.	
4 Natural Laws, Risk Management, and Collisions	263–266	**1.** Explain how speed control can help you avoid a collision. **2.** Describe how knowledge of natural laws can help you avoid a collision. **3.** Tell how to minimize the risks of a collision.	
Building Skills	267		
Review: Chapter Summary	268		
Chapter Test	269		

CHAPTER FEATURES	TCR COMPONENTS
TIPS FOR NEW DRIVERS Learning how to dry the brakes. **CONNECTIONS** Math Learning how to calculate braking distance.	Study Guide, p. 53 Lesson Plan, p. 29 Information Master 22
	Study Guide, p. 54 Transparencies 37, 38, and 39 Lesson Plan, p. 29
TIPS FOR NEW DRIVERS Dealing with skids.	Study Guide, p. 55 Lesson Plan, p. 30 Information Master 21
ADVICE FROM THE EXPERTS Natural laws and vehicle control.	Study Guide, p. 56 Lesson Plan, p. 30
BUILDING SKILLS: READING MAPS Using the Distance Numbers **PROJECTS** 1. Make a photo display of potential low-traction areas. 2. Check shoulders and off-road areas of local highways.	Test A, pp. 27–28 Test B, pp. 27–28

OTHER PROGRAM RESOURCES

Testmaker software
Responsible Driving, Video 2: Lesson 1
Traffic charts
Teaching Your Teens to Drive: Lessons 3, 6, and 13, video or CD-ROM, AAA, 1998

ADDITIONAL RESOURCES

Don't Let Up!, Video 377, AAA Foundation
Driving in Bad Weather, Video 419, AAA Foundation

CHAPTER 14

CHAPTER TEST

NAME _____ DATE _____

CHAPTER 14 Natural Laws and Driving

TEST A

Match the following terms by placing the letter of the definition to the left of the item.

d	1. crowned road	a. friction between a tire and the road
f	2. safety belt	b. the ability of a car to hold a straight line
h	3. total stopping distance	c. pushes a moving object out of a curve and into a straight line
c	4. centrifugal force	d. a road higher in the center than on either edge
e	5. inertia	e. a force that keeps objects moving in a straight line
a	6. traction	f. reduces the effects of inertia
i	7. kinetic energy	g. the force with which a moving vehicle hits another object
g	8. force of impact	h. perception distance, reaction distance, and braking distance
b	9. directional control	i. energy of motion

Read each statement below. If it is true, place a T in the space to the left of the statement. If the statement is false, place an F next to it.

T 10. Inertia causes your books on the car seat to continue moving forward even after you brake.

T 11. Tires with little or no tread do not have good traction on a wet, snowy, or icy road.

T 12. When driving on ice and snow, traction is poorest when the temperature is near 32°F.

F 13. The more energy of motion that a car has, the less time and distance it will take to stop.

T 14. To help slow a car using engine braking, just take your foot off the accelerator.

Select the phrase that best completes each sentence below. Write the letter of the answer you have chosen to the left of each statement.

b 15. Your car speeds up going down a steep hill because
    a. it takes longer to apply the brakes when going downhill.
    b. gravity makes the car go faster.
    c. higher elevations reduce traction.
    d. all of the above apply.

a 16. One way you can reduce the effects of inertia in a car is by
    a. wearing safety belts.
    b. using chains.
    c. using studded tires.
    d. braking hard.

© AAA and Glencoe/McGraw-Hill

◆ 27

NAME _____ DATE _____

d 17. A banked curve is one that
    a. is higher in the inside of the curve than the outside.
    b. has at least a 30-degree turn.
    c. curves and goes downhill at the same time.
    d. is higher on the outside of the curve than the inside.

d 18. Skids can be caused by
    a. reduced traction.
    b. driving too fast.
    c. changing directions too quickly.
    d. all of the above.

c 19. The first thing to remember to do in a skid is
    a. brake hard.
    b. steer in the opposite direction of where you want the car to go.
    c. do not brake.
    d. none of the above.

c 20. If your wheels lock,
    a. reduce traction.
    b. increase stopping distance.
    c. ease up on the pedal and squeeze down again.
    d. turn off the ignition.

c 21. If you are driving in the rain on tires that have been properly inflated and have good tread,
    a. you will never skid.
    b. you will hydroplane at 10 mph.
    c. much of the water will go into the grooves between the tread.
    d. you will increase your inertia.

22. Describe the four different types of skids. How is each caused?

A braking skid is caused by applying the brakes too hard. A power skid occurs when you press too fast

or hard on the accelerator. A cornering skid occurs when tires lose traction in a turn. A blowout skid

occurs when a tire suddenly loses pressure.

_____

_____

_____

_____

_____

_____

_____

_____

28 ◆

© AAA and Glencoe/McGraw-Hill

NAME _____ DATE _____

CHAPTER 14 Natural Laws and Driving

TEST B

Match the following terms by placing the letter of the definition to the left of the item.

d	1. inertia	a. energy of motion
f	2. friction	b. ability of a vehicle to hold a straight line
h	3. traction	c. force that pulls you out of a curve back to a straight path
e	4. momentum	d. force that keeps objects moving in a straight line
a	5. kinetic energy	e. the product of weight and speed
g	6. banked road	f. a force between two surfaces that resists movement
i	7. center of gravity	g. a road that is higher on the outside of curves than on the inside
b	8. directional control	h. friction between the tire and the road
c	9. centrifugal force	i. the point around which the weight of an object is evenly distributed

Read each statement below. If it is true, place a T in the space to the left of the statement. If the statement is false, place an F next to it.

T 10. Inertia tends to make a vehicle go in a straight line.

T 11. You need enough friction to successfully overcome centrifugal force when turning.

F 12. If you begin to skid, you are helpless to control the outcome.

F 13. If you hit the brakes so hard that the wheels lock, you are achieving top braking efficiency.

Select the phrase that best completes each sentence below. Write the letter of the answer you have chosen to the left of each statement.

a 14. One way you can reduce the effects of inertia in a car is by
    a. wearing seat belts.
    b. using chains.
    c. using studded tires.
    d. braking hard.

d 15. Underinflated tires grip the road unevenly,
    a. but are better on rainy surfaces.
    b. and only the middle of the tire grips the road.
    c. but don't wear out as fast.
    d. and only the outer edges of the tire grip the road.

© AAA and Glencoe/McGraw-Hill

◆ 27

NAME _____ DATE _____

b 16. Tire tread should be a minimum of
    a. 1 inch deep.
    b. $\frac{1}{16}$ inch deep.
    c. $\frac{1}{12}$ inch deep.
    d. $\frac{1}{32}$ inch deep.

c 17. If you are driving in the rain on tires that have been properly inflated and have good tread,
    a. the tread will push the water away.
    b. you will hydroplane on a watery surface.
    c. most of the water will go into the grooves between the tread.
    d. you will increase your inertia.

d 18. When you are driving on ice and snow,
    a. you have less traction than when driving in rain.
    b. your traction is poorest when the temperature is near 32° Fahrenheit.
    c. your chances of skidding are greater.
    d. all of the above are true.

b 19. Driving on a bouncy, rough road that has potholes
    a. increases your inertia.
    b. makes your traction worse.
    c. increases your vehicle's kinetic energy.
    d. does all of the above.

a 20. If a vehicle's weight doubles, then its _____ also doubles
    a. momentum
    b. center of gravity
    c. kinetic energy
    d. friction

b 21. A vehicle's center of gravity
    a. needs to be high to be safe.
    b. needs to be low to be safe.
    c. does not change the way that a vehicle drives.
    d. does none of the above.

22. What can you do to lessen the force of impact in a head-on collision?

To lessen the force of a head-on collision, you should reduce your speed as much as possible and drive

into a snowbank, bush, or anything else that is movable.

_____

_____

_____

_____

_____

28 ◆

© AAA and Glencoe/McGraw-Hill

250C   CHAPTER 14

STUDY GUIDE

NAME _____ DATE _____

CHAPTER 14 Natural Laws and Driving

STUDY GUIDE FOR CHAPTER 14 LESSON 1

Natural Laws and the Movement of Your Vehicle

A. Match the following terms by placing the letter of the definition or a description of what the item does to the left of the item.

__c__	1. inertia	**a.**	friction between your tires and the road
__e__	2. friction	**b.**	energy of motion
__a__	3. traction	**c.**	causes objects to continue moving in a straight line
__f__	4. momentum	**d.**	the point about which weight is evenly distributed
__b__	5. kinetic energy	**e.**	force between two surfaces that resists the movement of one surface across the other
__d__	6. center of gravity	**f.**	the product of weight and speed

B. Complete the following sentences by writing in the natural law each sentence is describing.

1. When you brake quickly and your books and packages on the backseat fall onto the floor, the force at work is __inertia.__

2. The force that makes your tires "stick" to the surface of the road is called __friction.__

3. Two vehicles going at the same speed hit the same brick wall, but the one that weighs more sustains much more damage. This is an example of __momentum.__

4. The faster a vehicle moves, the more __kinetic__ energy it has.

5. The force that slows your vehicle going uphill is called __gravity.__

C. FIND OUT MORE. What is kinetic energy? Look in your library and find out more about what the effects of kinetic energy are. Summarize your findings below.

__Review student's work.__

_____

_____

_____

_____

NAME _____ DATE _____

STUDY GUIDE FOR CHAPTER 14 LESSON 2

Natural Laws and Steering and Braking

A. For each sentence below, circle T if the statement is true and F if it is false. Correct each false statement in the space below.

1. Perception distance, reaction distance, and braking distance make up total stopping distance.
   (T)   F

2. Braking is a result of friction between the brake linings and your foot.   T   (F)
   Braking is a result of friction between the brake linings and wheel drums or discs.

3. Braking distance is greater on a smooth road.   T   (F)
   Braking distance is reduced when you drive on a smooth road.

4. Your braking distance decreases if you are going downhill.   T   (F)
   Your braking distance increases if you are going downhill.

5. Your ability to steer a vehicle depends partly upon the condition of the vehicle's suspension.
   (T)   F

6. Directional control is a vehicle's ability to hold a straight line.   (T)   F

7. A banked road is higher on the inside of curves than on the outside.   T   (F)
   A banked road is higher on the outside of curves than on the inside.

8. A crowned road is higher in the center of the road than on the edges.   (T)   F

B. FIND OUT MORE. Go to the library. Look up centrifugal force and centripetal force. What are they, and what are the differences between them?
   Review student's work.

_____

_____

_____

_____

_____

NAME _____ DATE _____

STUDY GUIDE FOR CHAPTER 14 LESSON 3

Using Natural Laws to Manage Skids

A. Complete the following sentences.

1. A __blowout__ skid occurs when a tire suddenly loses pressure.

2. A __braking__ skid occurs when you apply the brakes so hard that one or more wheels lock.

3. When driving on slick roads, you should make __gradual__ and smooth changes in your speed.

4. When __traction__ is reduced, your tires lose their grip on the road's surface.

5. The kind of skid in which you lose steering control while making a turn is called a __cornering__ skid.

6. A __power__ skid occurs when you press on the accelerator suddenly, too hard.

B. What is the correct and safe way to steer out of a skid?
   Ease off the gas pedal, steer in the direction you want the vehicle to go each time the skid

   changes direction, turn the steering wheel smoothly in the direction you want to go, keep

   steering until you are out of the skid. Concentrate, do not panic, do not brake.

C. FIND OUT MORE. Talk with someone whose job involves a lot of driving. Ask this person to describe what happens when a driver brakes in a skid. Diagram what happens in the space below.
   Review student's diagram.

NAME _____ DATE _____

STUDY GUIDE FOR CHAPTER 14 LESSON 4

Natural Laws, Risk Management, and Collisions

A. For each pair of vehicles, put an X next to the one that would experience the greater force of impact in a collision.

____	1.	Vehicle A is moving at 35 mph.
__X__		Vehicle B is moving at 45 mph.
__X__	2.	Truck X hits a tree.
____		Truck Y hits a wooden fence.
__X__	3.	Vehicle Y is carrying five passengers.
____		Vehicle C is carrying only the driver.
____	4.	Motorcycle A runs into a haystack.
__X__		Motorcycle B runs into a concrete divider.

B. With a ruler, measure the tread depth of some tires in your neighborhood or at school. Make sure that you have the permission of the owners to do this. What percentage of cars had all four tires with a tread depth of at least $\frac{1}{16}$ inch? How many cars had tread depths of between $\frac{1}{16}$ and $\frac{1}{8}$ inch?
   Review student's work.

_____

_____

_____

C. FIND OUT MORE. The chapter briefly discusses what an antilock brake system (ABS) is. Use any resource that you can find, such as a mechanic, literature from the library, or an advertisement. Find out as much as you can about an antilock brake system. How does it work? How much extra does it cost? Would you want one in your vehicle?
   Review student's work.

_____

_____

_____

_____

_____

_____

Natural Laws and Driving

CHAPTER OVERVIEW

LESSON ONE
The natural laws of inertia, friction, momentum, kinetic energy, and gravity are explained, and examples of their effects are discussed.

LESSON TWO
The effects of natural laws and other factors on stopping distance and steering are explained.

LESSON THREE
Factors that cause skidding are described, and ways to manage risk in response to a skid are explained.

LESSON FOUR
Minimizing the risk and consequences of a collision are explained in the context of understanding the effects of natural laws.

VOCABULARY

adhesion
antilock brake system (ABS)
banked curve
blowout skid
braking distance
braking skid
center of gravity
centrifugal force
cornering skid
crowned road
directional control
force of impact
friction
gravity
inertia
kinetic energy
momentum
perception distance
power skid
reaction distance
skid
total stopping distance
traction

250

CONCEPT OF THE DRIVING TASK

Explain that the more a driver knows about the factors that affect a vehicle's movement, the better able that driver is to minimize driving risk.

CHAPTER 14

Natural Laws and Driving

Natural laws, which include the laws of inertia, gravity, and momentum, affect a driver's ability to perform the driving task. It is important to understand natural laws so that you can use your knowledge of them to help you manage risk in different driving situations.

CHAPTER 14   *Natural Laws and Driving*   **251**

PRESENTING THE BIG IDEA ——

Drivers who understand what causes a vehicle to move as it does are better prepared to maintain control of their vehicle than drivers who do not.

INTRODUCING THE CHAPTER

What's on the Road Ahead?

Have students read the lesson titles and objectives. Briefly discuss the topic of each lesson. Tell students that in this chapter, they will learn how natural laws affect the movement of a vehicle and how understanding these laws can help them maintain control of their vehicle and reduce driving risk.

Background: Tires

Students will learn in this chapter that *traction* (or *adhesion*)—friction between tires and road—holds a vehicle on the roadway. In this context, the following facts may be of interest.

- Most modern tires are made of synthetic rubber, backed by nylon or rayon. Early tires were made of natural rubber, but the synthetics are stronger and more durable.

- Most modern tires are tubeless. That is, they have no inner tube for holding air. Instead, the tire itself holds the air. The tire's tight fit around the wheel rim is what keeps the air from leaking out.

Relating to Prior Knowledge

Have students discuss what they know about the natural laws of inertia, friction, momentum, kinetic energy, and gravity.

The Big Idea

Discuss students' reactions to the Big Idea statement. Suggest that they keep this idea in mind as they read Chapter 14.

Natural Laws and the Movement of Your Vehicle

(pages 252–256)

FOCUS

Objectives

• Describe the natural laws of inertia, friction, momentum, kinetic energy, and gravity.

• Explain the relationship of these natural laws to driving.

Resources

 Study Guide, page 53

 Information Master 22

Vocabulary

inertia
friction
traction
adhesion
momentum
kinetic energy
gravity
center of gravity

Motivator

Explain to students that knowing certain basic principles of science can help them understand the various physical factors that affect a moving vehicle. Ask students how understanding these factors might help a driver. (Accept all reasonable answers. Possible response: Drivers who understand the physical factors that affect their vehicle are better able to reduce risk when driving.)

LESSON ONE

OBJECTIVES

1. Describe the natural laws of inertia, friction, momentum, kinetic energy, and gravity.
2. Explain the relationship of these natural laws to driving.

KEY TERMS

inertia
friction
traction
adhesion
momentum
kinetic energy
gravity
center of gravity

Natural Laws and the Movement of Your Vehicle

Does this sound familiar? You're in a vehicle and the driver applies the brakes. The vehicle stops, but your books on the backseat of the vehicle continue moving forward onto the floor. Why did this happen? A natural law is the culprit.

What Are Natural Laws?

Natural laws are always at work. Some of these laws are inertia, friction, momentum, kinetic energy, and gravity.

Inertia

Inertia caused your books on the backseat to continue moving forward even after the driver braked. Two properties govern inertia. One is that objects at rest do not move unless some force acts on them. The other is that moving objects continue to move in a straight line unless some force acts on them.

All things have inertia. As the vehicle was moving, so were your books. When the driver braked, a force was exerted to make the vehicle stop, but unrestrained, your books kept moving forward in a straight line. Then they fell to the floor.

You have to understand inertia when you drive because you and your passengers have inertia. If you brake a vehicle hard, everyone in it will tend to keep moving forward. Drivers must manage risk by anticipating how to reduce inertia's effects.

One way to do this is to wear safety belts. These belts provide a force that acts against inertia. If you brake hard and are not wearing a safety belt, you may be thrown forward against the windshield or dashboard.

Another way to manage risk is to be sure to secure all loose objects, such as your books, luggage, or boxes.

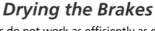 **FOR NEW DRIVERS**

Drying the Brakes

Wet brakes do not work as efficiently as dry brakes. After you have driven through heavy rain or deep puddles, always check for wet brakes. If you apply the brakes lightly and the vehicle pulls to one side or does not slow as quickly as normal, your brakes are probably wet. Dry the brakes by driving slowly and applying light pressure on the brake pedal with your left foot. The friction created will generate heat, which will dry the brakes.

252   UNIT 3   *Moving onto the Road*

IT'S A FACT

Braking tests show that tractor-trailers may need twice the braking distance of cars to stop. Traveling at 55 mph, for example, the braking distance for a car may be 150 feet, while the braking distance for a tractor-trailer may be 300 feet or more.

FOR NEW DRIVERS

Point out to students that to keep brakes from getting wet when driving through a deep puddle, apply light pressure to the brake pedal as you drive slowly through the water.

Friction

Press your foot down hard on a carpeted floor. Keep it pressed down as hard as you can and try to move across the carpet. Does it feel as if some kind of force is trying to stop your foot from moving, almost as if your foot and the carpet are sticking together?

The force that seems to try to make the surface of your shoe "stick" to the surface of the carpet is friction. **Friction** is a force between two surfaces that resists the movement of one surface across the other. You can make your foot move across the carpet by applying more force than friction can resist or overcome.

Just as friction tries to make your foot stick to the carpet, it tries to make the surface of your tires "stick" to the surface of the road. Your vehicle has to overcome friction in order to move. Your vehicle stays on the road, however, because a certain amount of friction is always present.

Friction between the road and your tires is called **traction,** or **adhesion,** which means "sticking together." Adhesion, or traction, holds your vehicle on the road. Here are some factors affecting traction.

Tire pressure Tires are made with grooved surface treads that are designed to grip the road in a wide variety of conditions. For best traction, inflate tires to the maximum pressure recommended by the manufacturer. Properly inflated tires grip the road evenly. Under- or overinflation reduces traction. If you underinflate your tires, only the outer edges grip the road. If you overinflate them, only the centers tend to make contact with the road.

Tire condition Would you try to walk on slippery packed snow or ice with rubber boots worn smooth? Of course not! You would slide all over. The same concept applies to tires. Bald tires—tires with very little or no tread—provide almost no traction on wet, icy, or snow-covered roads. Even on dry roads, bald tires reduce directional control, particularly if there is sand or debris on the road, and are more apt than treaded tires to get punctured.

Rain When the road is wet, water gets between the surface of the road and the tires. At 55 mph, tires can lose contact with the road surface if the water is as shallow as ½ inch. Water provides a smooth, nearly frictionless, surface for the tires to move across, and it does not provide good traction. If tires are properly inflated and have good tread, much of the water will go into the grooves between

◆ *The minimum legal—though not necessarily safe—tread depth for your tires is ¹⁄₁₆ inch. To check your tire's tread depth, examine the tread-wear bars that are built into the tire. When the tread-wear bars are even with the surface of the tread at more than two spots around the tire, the tire is no longer legal or safe to use.*

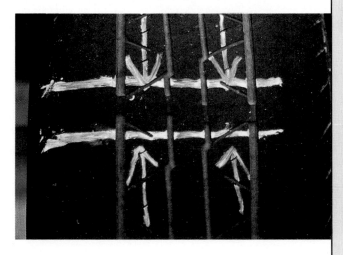

Pose the following situation: You're driving along the highway when it begins to rain. To reduce risk, you drive more slowly. What physical factors have you taken into consideration? (Students may mention that friction is a force between two surfaces that resists the movement of one surface across the other. Friction between roadway and tires—called *traction* or *adhesion*—holds the vehicle on the road. On a wet roadway, water gets between the surface of the road and the tires. The tires move along this smooth surface, which provides less traction, thereby increasing driving risk.)

TEACH

Explain

OBJECTIVES 1 AND 2: Students should recognize that natural laws work in combination with one another. For example, when driving a vehicle down a hill in the rain, the driver must contend with both reduced friction and the pull of gravity. If the driver allows the vehicle's speed to increase as the vehicle moves downhill, the vehicle's increased momentum and kinetic energy cause the braking distance to increase.

Students will benefit from a discussion of additional examples of the interaction of natural laws: inertia, friction, momentum, kinetic energy, and gravity.

Driving Tip

Advise students to use a tire pressure gauge to check the air pressure in their vehicle's tires. Tell students that for accuracy, they should check tire pressure before driving the vehicle, when the tires are cold.

Teaching Model

Describe the following situation: It's winter, and you're preparing to take a two-day drive into the mountains to visit your uncle. Knowing how important tire traction is to driving safety, you check your tires carefully. Model the thinking process that you use to check your tires. (You do the following.

- Check tire pressure because to grip the road evenly, tires must be neither underinflated nor overinflated.
- Check tire condition because bald or badly worn tires provide less traction than tires with adequate tread.
- Prepare for snowy or icy mountain roads by equipping your vehicle with snow tires, chains, or studded tires if necessary.)

Ask

Ask students to discuss the risks of driving under conditions of reduced traction.

Read

Have students read Lesson 1 to learn about the natural laws that are always at work—inertia, friction, momentum, kinetic energy, and gravity—and how these laws affect the movement of a vehicle.

◆ Snow and ice make a roadway slick, reducing friction between your car and the road's surface.

the treads. This means that the treads themselves will maintain contact with the road surface.

Ice and snow Ice and snow can reduce traction more than rain. Traction is poorest near 32°F, when snow and ice start to become a slippery, watery slush. Any road is dangerous when covered with ice or snow, so adjust your driving habits accordingly.

Snow tires help increase traction in snow but not necessarily on ice. Chains are helpful in increasing traction on ice, but they provide poor traction on pavement. In states where studded tires are allowed, they can help on ice but are not as effective as chains. All-weather tires are a good choice for most drivers.

Road condition Road condition also affects traction. Rough roads and potholes make your vehicle's tires bounce up and down, reducing traction. Wet leaves on the road also reduce friction, causing the tires to lose traction and slide.

Momentum

If a 12-pound bowling ball and a 16-pound bowling ball were rolling toward an object at the same speed, which ball would cause more damage? Because it is heavier, the 16-pound bowling ball would.

Momentum is the product of weight and speed. It provides an explanation for what seems obvious in the bowling ball example. All objects in motion have momentum. The greater the momentum of the vehicles, the greater the damage in a collision will be.

A vehicle's momentum depends on its weight and its speed. If either the weight or the speed doubles, so does the vehicle's momentum. If the weight or the speed triples, so does the momentum.

In short, as speed increases, so does the likelihood of damage in case of a collision. Lighter vehicles may cause less damage because of reduced momentum. However, the lighter your vehicle, the greater the likelihood that it will be damaged when in a collision.

Kinetic Energy

All objects in motion have kinetic energy as well as momentum. **Kinetic energy** is the energy of motion. The faster a vehicle moves, the more energy of motion it has.

MEETING STUDENT DIVERSITY

Limited English Proficiency

Words such as *inertia, adhesion,* and *kinetic energy* can be especially challenging for students with limited English proficiency. Try to explain such words as simply as possible. Whenever possible, provide concrete, visual examples.

What does this mean to you as a driver? You need to know that the more energy of motion a vehicle has, the more time and distance it will take to stop.

The faster a vehicle moves, the more energy of motion it has. If a vehicle's speed doubles, its stopping distance increases by an amount equal to the square of the difference in speed.

Here is what kinetic energy and momentum can mean when you are accelerating or braking.

Acceleration Suppose that you drive a van or sport utility vehicle (SUV) and usually carry one or two passengers and light packages. You are aware of how your vehicle accelerates when you enter an expressway. Now suppose that you are going on a trip with four other people, and the back of the van or SUV is fully packed. You have increased the weight of your vehicle. It will not accelerate as quickly. Thus, you will not be able to enter an expressway as quickly as you usually do. You may need to manage time and space differently. You might want to press down more on the accelerator to compensate for the extra weight and wait for a larger gap in traffic before entering the roadway.

Braking Once you are moving on the expressway, the van or SUV's momentum and kinetic energy have increased because its weight and speed have been increased. Its stopping distance has also increased. Reduce risk by leaving a greater distance between your vehicle and the one in front of you.

Gravity

If you toss a ball into the air, it comes down. The ball falls because of gravity. **Gravity** is a force that pulls all objects toward the center of the Earth. Because gravity affects all objects, it can make a vehicle speed up or slow down.

Energy Tips

Do not overload your vehicle. Every 100 miles that you travel with extra weight costs you 1 mile per gallon.

CONNECTIONS
Math

It's a mathematical fact that the faster you drive, the more braking distance you will need to have.

Use the following formula to demonstrate this. If S is the speed, the formula is:

$(S \times \frac{1}{10} S) \div 2.4$ = braking distance in feet

Braking distance at a speed of 50 miles per hour can be calculated as follows:

$(50 \times \frac{1}{10} \times 50) \div 2.4$
$(50 \times 5) \div 2.4$
$250 \div 2.4 = 104$ feet

You don't have to do the calculations as you drive to realize that the faster you are traveling, the more space you have to leave in front of you in case you have to brake suddenly.

CHAPTER 14 *Natural Laws and Driving* **255**

CONNECTIONS
Math

To check students' understanding, you may want to have them calculate and compare the braking distances for other speeds.

IT'S A FACT

In 1997, teenagers between the ages of 15 and 20 represented 7 percent of all licensed drivers but 14 percent of motor vehicle fatalities. Seventy-five percent of the teens killed were occupants of cars, pickups, sport utility vehicles, and vans. Thirteen percent were pedestrians, 5 percent were motorcyclists, 2 percent were bicyclists. The rest were occupants of other vehicles.

Guided Practice

Have students answer the Lesson 1 Review questions. The answers are provided below.

Reteaching

Divide students into five groups if possible. Have the students in each group work together to create a poster explaining and illustrating one of the natural laws discussed in this lesson: inertia, friction, momentum, kinetic energy, and gravity. After groups have completed their posters, have them share their work with the class. Encourage discussion of driving risk factors associated with each of the natural laws. What can drivers do to minimize the risks?

Enrichment

Assign the Study Guide for Lesson 1. The Find Out More section encourages students to expand their basic learning of the lesson concepts.

CLOSE

Summarize

Reexamine the first Motivator question. Ask students how understanding the natural laws described in this lesson can help them drive more safely. Encourage students to provide specific examples and to express their answers in terms of managing visibility, time, and space.

Discuss the situation described in the second Motivator question. Recall students' initial responses, and have students expand their original answers in terms of what they have learned in this lesson.

DRIVER'S LOG

Have students create a section focusing on natural laws. Direct them to include in this section definitions of such key terms as inertia, friction, momentum, kinetic energy, gravity, traction, and center of gravity.

Ask students also to list in this section risk management strategies linked with the natural laws they've studied and to expand their list of risk management strategies as they continue reading this chapter.

WHAT WOULD YOU DO?

Sample answer: Safety belts are essential protection because they keep you from being thrown around in the vehicle—or out of the vehicle—in the event of a collision.

◆ *Overpacking can make a vehicle less stable by changing its center of gravity.*

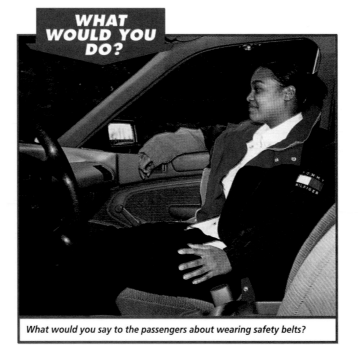

WHAT WOULD YOU DO?

What would you say to the passengers about wearing safety belts?

When you drive uphill, gravity acts to slow your vehicle. To maintain speed, accelerate just before the vehicle begins to climb the hill. When you drive downhill, gravity acts with your vehicle, so your speed increases. To keep the vehicle from moving too fast, ease up on the accelerator. You may also have to use your brakes or downshift.

Center of Gravity

Gravity gives objects their weight. The weight of an object, such as your vehicle, is distributed evenly about a point. This point is called the object's **center of gravity.**

The lower an object's center of gravity, the more stable the object. Most vehicles are designed to have a low center of gravity in order to handle well in turns and during quick maneuvers. Changes in a vehicle's center of gravity affect how well the vehicle handles. A roof carrier loaded with heavy objects raises the vehicle's center of gravity, making it less stable and difficult to control on turns and curves and during sudden changes in braking, acceleration, and direction. Vehicles that have a high center of gravity, such as sport utility vehicles, some types of vans, and pickup trucks, also have these problems.

Lesson 1 Review

1. What affects traction? How?
2. How would changes in a vehicle's center of gravity affect its stability?

Lesson 1 Review

Answers

1. Tire pressure: properly inflated tires grip the road evenly; tire condition: tread helps grip the road; rain, snow, and ice: wet roads create a slick surface; road condition: rough roads or wet leaves reduce traction.
2. If a vehicle's center of gravity is raised, it will be less stable and more difficult to control on turns and curves and during sudden changes in braking, acceleration, and direction.

Natural Laws and Steering and Braking

Natural laws affect stopping distance, braking, and steering. Understanding the relationships between natural laws and driving can help you to be a better and a safer driver.

How Do Natural Laws Influence Braking Distance?

The distance your vehicle takes to stop is its **total stopping distance.** Perception distance, reaction distance, and braking distance make up total stopping distance. For estimating stopping distance use the 3- or 5-second rule. See Chapter 10 for more information.

In order to stop, you must (1) identify a need to stop (this is your **perception distance**), (2) react by braking (your **reaction distance**), and (3) slow your vehicle to a stop (your **braking distance**).

Natural Laws and Braking

Braking is a result of friction between the brake linings and the wheel drums or wheel discs and pads. This friction slows the rotation of the wheels and tires. The adhesion between the tires and the road increases. As you brake, you decrease your vehicle's momentum and kinetic energy.

Factors Affecting Braking Distance

The following factors can increase braking distance.

Speed The greater the speed, the longer the braking distance.

Condition of the vehicle Worn brakes, tires, or shock absorbers reduce traction. Reduced traction increases braking distance.

Condition of the roadway Braking distance is greater when roadway friction is reduced, such as during bad weather or if the road is unpaved.

Hills and mountains Gravity affects the time and space needed to stop a vehicle going downhill. Because a vehicle going downhill has the added force of gravity contributing to its inertia, the braking distance increases.

LESSON TWO

OBJECTIVES

1. Explain how natural laws affect a vehicle's stopping distance.
2. Identify the factors that affect steering.
3. Name the ways that natural laws affect steering around a curve.
4. Describe how gravity and the contour of the road affect steering.

KEY TERMS

total stopping distance
perception distance
reaction distance
braking distance
directional control
centrifugal force
banked curve
crowned road

FYI

Telephone poles usually are 100 feet apart. Use this measure to help you estimate distance while you are driving.

THE INTERNATIONAL SCENE

Central America

Advise students that before driving in other countries, they should always find out whether they need to purchase local automobile insurance. In the Central American countries of Guatemala and Belize, for example, neither U.S. nor Mexican motor vehicle insurance coverage is considered valid.

LESSON TWO

Natural Laws and Steering and Braking

(pages 257–259)

FOCUS

Objectives

- Explain how natural laws affect a vehicle's stopping distance.
- Identify the factors that affect steering.
- Name the ways that natural laws affect steering around a curve.
- Describe how gravity and the contour of the road affect steering.

Resources

📁 Study Guide, page 54
📁 Traffic charts
🖨 Transparencies 37–39

Vocabulary

total stopping distance
perception distance
reaction distance
braking distance
directional control
centrifugal force
banked curve
crowned road

Motivator

Pose the following: You're driving on a narrow one-way street. Vehicles are parked along both sides of the street. A short distance ahead, a vehicle pulls out in front of you. You step on the brake. What factors will determine the distance and time you will need to stop? (Factors include speed of the vehicle, condition of brakes and tires, condition of the roadway, and whether the road is level.)

TEACH

Explain

OBJECTIVE 1: Students should recognize that if a driver is distracted, both perception distance and reaction distance increase.

OBJECTIVE 2: Students should be cautioned to keep both hands on the steering wheel for effective control.

OBJECTIVE 3: Students should recognize the need to reduce speed even further when steering around a curve on a wet roadway.

OBJECTIVE 4: Students should note that with experience, drivers learn to compensate automatically for changes in road contour.

Teaching Model

Describe the following situation: You're driving on a two-lane country road when you spot a sign ahead warning that you're approaching a sharp curve. Model the thinking process that you will use to minimize risk. (You will hold the steering wheel firmly; slow down as you enter the curve; turn the steering wheel as needed, being careful not to oversteer or understeer.)

Ask

Ask students to discuss the added risks in this same situation at night and in wet weather.

Read

Have students read Lesson 2 to learn how natural laws and other factors affect braking and steering.

ASSESS

Guided Practice

Have students answer the Lesson 2 Review questions. The answers are provided below.

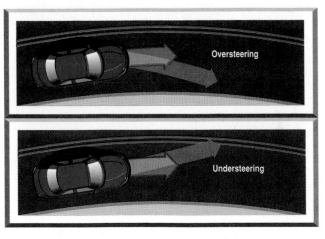

◆ *Monitor your speed as you enter a curve so that you neither oversteer nor understeer.*

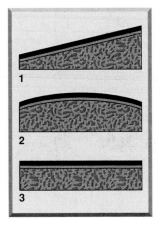

◆ *A car handles differently on (1) banked roads, (2) crowned roads, and (3) flat roads.*

What Factors and Natural Laws Affect Steering?

Your ability to steer a vehicle depends on many factors. The steering mechanism, tires, and suspension are three mechanical factors. Wheel alignment and road conditions are also important in steering, as is the way you load the vehicle.

Friction helps to keep your vehicle on the road. When a driver turns the steering wheel, the front tires provide the friction, or traction, to turn the vehicle.

Because of inertia, a moving vehicle will tend to go in a straight line. The vehicle, however, may wander, and regular steering corrections will be necessary. **Directional control** is a vehicle's ability to hold a straight line. You will have an easy time keeping the vehicle moving in the direction in which you steer it.

Hand position is another factor that affects vehicle control. Hold the steering wheel firmly, but with your fingers rather than the palms of your hands. Keep your thumbs along the face of the steering wheel, not wrapped around it. This gives you better control.

How Do Natural Laws Affect Steering Around a Curve?

Inertia tends to keep a vehicle moving in a straight path. As you enter a curve or turn, you must overcome the effects of inertia by turning the steering wheel. You are moving the vehicle out of its straight path. At the same time, you feel as if you are being pulled toward the door into the curve. What you feel is **centrifugal force** pushing you in the direction opposite to the way you are turning.

As you slow down and enter the curve or turn, you turn the wheel. Friction between the tires and the road acts against centrifugal force and allows the vehicle to follow a curved path. As long as there is enough friction to overcome centrifugal force, you can make the turn. As you turn the wheel, the front tires provide the traction needed to turn the vehicle.

Slow your vehicle as you approach a curve or turn. The faster you go, the more difficult it is for traction to overcome inertia.

Driving Tip

Explain to students that to avoid a collision, it is generally wiser to steer evasively (or combine evasive steering with braking) than simply to apply the brakes. Evasive steering is preferable to braking—especially at speeds over 25 mph—because less distance is needed to steer around an object than to brake the vehicle to a stop.

How Do Gravity and the Contour of the Road Affect Steering?

Gravity in relation to the contour of the road affects how well a vehicle will take a curve.

Banked Roads

Have you ever seen the Indy 500 auto race? The track is banked, or higher on the outside of curves than on the inside. On a properly **banked curve,** the roadway tilts down toward the inside of the curve. Although a vehicle tends to move toward the outside of a curve, the downward tilt of a banked curve improves steering control by working with the force of gravity. If the banking or downward tilt were toward the outside of the curve, gravity and inertia would tend to pull the vehicle off the road, making steering more difficult.

Crowned Roads

Crowned roads are higher in the center than at either of the edges to facilitate drainage. When driving in the right lane on a two-way crowned road, gravity will tend to pull your vehicle to the right, off the roadway. You must counteract the effect of gravitational pull by exerting more force on the steering wheel to keep the vehicle on the road. Slowing down will give you more control on this type of roadway.

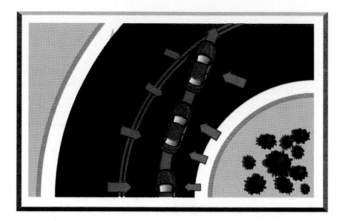

◆ *Turning the steering wheel enables friction to overcome centrifugal force.*

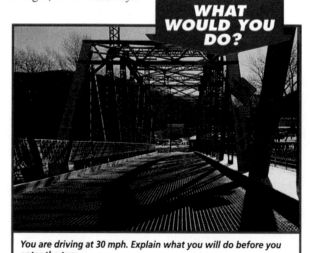

WHAT WOULD YOU DO?

You are driving at 30 mph. Explain what you will do before you enter the turn.

Lesson 2 Review

1. How do speed, traction, and gravity affect braking distance?
2. Describe how steering is affected by traction and inertia.
3. What role do friction and centrifugal force play in steering around a curve?
4. How does gravity affect steering on a banked or crowned road? How should you respond?

Lesson 2 Review

Answers

1. The greater the speed or the less the traction, the longer the braking distance; gravity increases speed on a decline, increasing braking distance.
2. When you turn the steering wheel, you are working against inertia, which tends to keep a vehicle moving straight; traction allows the tires to grip the road and follow a curved path.
3. Friction between tires and roadway overcomes the pull of centrifugal force.
4. On a banked road, the downward tilt works with gravity to improve steering control; on a crowned road, gravity may tend to pull your vehicle off the road, so you must exert more force on the steering wheel and/or reduce speed to counteract its effects.

Reteaching

Have students work in small groups to identify the natural laws that affect braking and steering on a winding road.

Enrichment

Assign the Study Guide for Lesson 2. The Find Out More section encourages students to expand their basic learning of the lesson concepts.

CLOSE

Summarize

Return to the Motivator question. Recall students' initial responses, and have them summarize additional information they have gained from this lesson. In the discussion, emphasize that a combination of factors determines stopping distance and time. Extend the discussion by having students distinguish between braking distance and total stopping distance.

DRIVER'S LOG

How can knowing how natural laws and other factors affect braking and steering help you minimize driving risk?

WHAT WOULD YOU DO?

Sample answer: Slow down and turn the wheel gradually as the roadway requires.

FOCUS

Objectives

- List factors that can cause your vehicle to skid.
- Name and describe the kinds of skids there are.
- Describe how to manage risk in responding to a skid.

Resources

 Study Guide, page 55

 Traffic charts

 Information Master 21

Vocabulary

skid
braking skid
power skid
cornering skid
blowout skid

Motivator

You're driving on an expressway just after a rainstorm. What can you do to minimize the likelihood of skidding? (Avoid abrupt changes in speed or direction; slow down; drive in the tracks of vehicles ahead.)

TEACH

Explain

OBJECTIVE 1: Students should note that traction is especially reduced in the first 10 to 15 minutes of a rainfall.

LESSON THREE

OBJECTIVES

1. List factors that can cause your vehicle to skid.
2. Name and describe the kinds of skids there are.
3. Describe how to manage risk in responding to a skid.

KEY TERMS

skid
braking skid
power skid
cornering skid
blowout skid

Using Natural Laws to Manage Skids

Understanding the natural laws that affect the control of your vehicle can help you regain that control when you lose it through skidding. When you **skid,** you lose control of the direction and speed of your vehicle's movement because of reduced traction. If you skid, you are not helpless. Once you understand what causes a skid, you're already on your way to dealing with one.

What Can Make Your Vehicle Skid?

Whenever you skid, one of three things has happened: traction was reduced, you tried to change speed too quickly, or you tried to change direction too quickly.

Reduced Traction

A loss of traction or a reduction in traction can be frightening and dangerous even for experienced drivers. When traction is reduced because of a change in conditions, your tires can lose their grip on the road's surface and the vehicle can begin to slide. Drivers should always be aware of conditions that could result in reduced traction. See Chapter 12 for more information on driving in conditions of reduced traction.

Changing Speed Too Quickly

You are on a slippery road, and you want to slow down. You step firmly on the brake pedal, and your vehicle starts to skid. What happened? You tried to change speed too quickly. Traction could not overcome the vehicle's kinetic energy and momentum as fast as you wanted it to.

Changing Direction Too Quickly

Turning a vehicle quickly is like a large football player trying to make a sharp turn at

FOR NEW DRIVERS

Dealing with Skids

Skidding can be frightening. You can minimize trouble, however, by remembering the following points.
- The most important thing you must do is respond quickly and correctly. Concentrate. Do not panic.
- Do not brake. This will only make the skid worse.
- Look and steer in the direction in which you want the front of the vehicle to go.
- Make steering corrections quickly but smoothly.
- Do not give up. Keep steering.

TIPS FOR NEW DRIVERS

To reinforce students' understanding, have them restate and explain the tips in their own words.

IT'S A FACT

Recent studies show that in head-on collisions, 25 percent fewer driver deaths and significantly fewer injuries occurred in vehicles with air bags than in vehicles without them. Today air bags for drivers and front passengers are standard in almost all new vehicles.

a full gallop. Sometimes it works, but sometimes it doesn't. If you're driving at a high speed, your vehicle has a tremendous amount of momentum and kinetic energy. Inertia is also at work, trying to force your vehicle to move in a straight path. Tire traction may not be great enough to compensate for momentum, kinetic energy, and inertia when you turn or enter a sharp curve.

How fast is a high speed? It depends on the road. Look at the speed limit signs posted just below the warning signs as you near a curve. They tell you the maximum safe speed you should use to enter the curve. Then you need to adjust speed downward according to conditions.

What Are the Kinds of Skids?

Knowing the kind of skid you are experiencing will help you manage the risk involved, and it may even help you prevent skidding.

KINDS OF SKIDS

Type	Braking skid	Power skid	Cornering skid	Blowout skid
Reason	The brakes are applied so hard that one or more wheels lock.	The gas pedal is pressed suddenly and too hard.	The tires lose traction in a turn.	A tire suddenly loses air pressure.
Conditions	A sudden stop A wet, slippery, or uneven road	A sudden, hard acceleration A slippery road surface	A turn made too fast Poor tires or a slippery road surface	A punctured, worn, or overinflated tire An overloaded vehicle
What can happen	Steering control is lost. If the front wheels lock, the vehicle skids straight ahead. If only the rear wheels lock, the rear of the vehicle slides sideways. The vehicle may spin around.	A vehicle with front-wheel drive plows straight ahead. In a vehicle with rear-wheel drive, the back end can skid to the side. The vehicle may spin around.	Steering control is lost. The rear wheels skid away from the turn. The vehicle keeps going straight ahead.	There is a strong pull toward the side on which a front tire has blown out. A rear-tire blowout may cause a pull toward the blowout, side-to-side swaying, or fishtailing.
What to do	Take your foot off the brake pedal. Steer. When the wheels start turning again and moving forward, steering control will return.	Ease up on the gas pedal until the wheels stop spinning. Steer to straighten the vehicle. Countersteer if the vehicle starts to spin.	Take your foot all the way off the accelerator. Steer to straighten the vehicle.	Do not brake. Make firm, steady steering corrections. Do not change speed suddenly. Slow down gradually, and drive off the road.

Driving Tip

Advise students to take special note of their surroundings when driving on wet or icy roads. If their vehicle does go into a skid—or if they must steer to avoid another skidding vehicle—they may need to steer around roadside obstacles.

OBJECTIVE 2: Students will benefit from a comparison of similarities and differences between types of skids. The chart on page 261 will help focus the discussion.

OBJECTIVE 3: Students should recognize the danger of oversteering. They should also understand the importance of remaining calm if their vehicle goes into a skid. In this situation, as in any emergency, panicking can only make matters worse.

Teaching Model

Describe the following situation: Your vehicle begins to skid. Model the thinking process that you will use to manage risk. (You will do the following.

- Stay calm.
- Ease off the accelerator.
- Shift into Neutral.
- Avoid stepping on the brake.
- Steer in the direction you want the vehicle to go.
- Make necessary steering adjustments smoothly and quickly.
- Continue steering until your vehicle recovers from the skid.)

Ask

Ask students to discuss why they should not apply the brakes when a vehicle begins to skid.

Read

Have students read Lesson 3 to learn how to avoid and manage skids.

ASSESS

Guided Practice

Have students answer the Lesson 3 Review questions. The answers are provided below.

Reteaching

Have students work in small groups to discuss different kinds of skids and list strategies for preventing and managing them. After the groups have completed their lists, have the class work together to create a chart of do's and don'ts for coping with skids.

Enrichment

Assign the Study Guide for Lesson 3. The Find Out More section encourages students to expand their basic learning of the lesson concepts.

CLOSE

Summarize

Return to the Motivator question. Discuss with students how their ideas about minimizing the likelihood of a skid may have changed. Extend the discussion by focusing on strategies for responding to different kinds of skids.

DRIVER'S LOG

How can you drive so as to minimize the chance of skidding? What are the four basic kinds of skids? How should you respond to each of them?

WHAT WOULD YOU DO?

Sample answer: The vehicle will probably pull toward the side of the blowout, or it may fishtail. You should slow down gradually without stepping on the brake. Braking can make the skid worse.

◆ *Accelerate and brake gradually to reduce the risk of skidding on snowy roadways.*

You have a blowout. What is likely to happen? What should you do? Why?

There are four basic kinds of skids: braking, power, cornering, and blowout. If you know the causes and results of these kinds of skids and the conditions under which they occur, you can deal with them safely.

- A **braking skid** occurs when you apply the brakes so hard that one or more of the wheels lock.
- A **power skid** occurs when you suddenly press on the accelerator too hard.
- A **cornering skid** occurs when you lose steering control in a turn, curve, or lane change.
- A **blowout skid** occurs when a tire suddenly loses air pressure.

How Do You Respond to a Skid?

Suppose you are driving carefully on an ice-covered roadway. Vehicles are parked alongside the traffic lane, and traffic is heavy in both directions. Suddenly your vehicle begins to skid. How can you manage the risk of a skid and safely drive out of it?

1. Ease off the gas pedal and shift into Neutral. Stay off the brake.
2. With your foot off the pedals, look well ahead and steer in the direction in which you want the front of the vehicle to go.
3. As the skid starts to change direction, turn the wheel smoothly and quickly in the direction in which you want the front of the vehicle to go.
4. Keep steering until you are out of the skid.

Lesson 3 Review

1. What conditions can make your vehicle skid?
2. Describe four kinds of skids.
3. Describe how to safely steer out of a skid.

Lesson 3 Review

Answers

1. Reduced traction; abrupt change in speed; sudden change in direction.
2. Braking skid: brakes applied so hard that wheels lock; power skid: accelerator pressed hard and suddenly; cornering skid: steering control lost in turn; blowout skid: tire suddenly loses pressure.
3. Ease off accelerator; shift into Neutral; steer in direction you want the vehicle to go.

Natural Laws, Risk Management, and Collisions

The goal of any driver is to avoid collisions and injuries. Good drivers understand how to use accelerating, braking, and steering to help them achieve this goal.

LESSON FOUR

OBJECTIVES
1. Explain how speed control can help you avoid a collision.
2. Describe how knowledge of natural laws can help you avoid a collision.
3. Tell how to minimize the risks of a collision.

KEY TERMS
antilock brake system (ABS)
force of impact

How Can You Use Speed Control to Avoid a Collision?

Braking is a natural reaction to avoid a collision. However, it is not always the correct evasive action.

Accelerating

Accelerating may sometimes be your only means of reducing risk. Such situations occur most often at intersections or in merging traffic. A vehicle may be coming at you from one side. Braking may leave you in the vehicle's path. Steering to the side may be impossible if there are objects on both sides of you. If the road ahead is clear, a quick burst of speed may take you to safety, or at least move the crash farther back on the vehicle.

Braking

Steering to the side or accelerating may not be possible. Under 25 mph, it takes less time and distance to stop than to steer into another lane.

When braking, you want to stop fast without making the wheels lock, or stop turning. Locking of the wheels reduces traction and will cause loss of steering control. To brake quickly, use the threshold/squeeze braking method. Use your body to sense how the brakes are working. Keep your heel on the floor and your foot on the brake. "Squeeze" the pedal down with a

◆ *The driver in the left lane accelerated to avoid the possible collision in the right lane.*

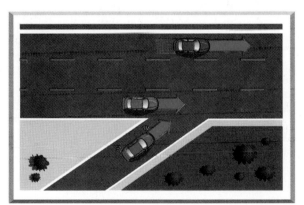

CHAPTER 14 *Natural Laws and Driving* **263**

IT'S A FACT

More motor vehicle collisions occur in urban areas than in rural areas. However, more motor vehicle deaths occur on rural roads than on urban roads.

LESSON FOUR

Natural Laws, Risk Management, and Collisions

(pages 263–266)

FOCUS

Objectives
- Explain how speed control can help you avoid a collision.
- Describe how knowledge of natural laws can help you avoid a collision.
- Tell how to minimize the risks of a collision.

Resources

📁 Study Guide, page 56

📁 Traffic charts

Vocabulary
antilock brake system (ABS)
force of impact

Motivator

Have students review the natural laws they studied in Lessons 1 and 2: inertia, friction, momentum, kinetic energy, and gravity. Ask students to give examples of how these laws affect the movement of a vehicle. Tell students that in Lesson 4, they will learn how understanding these natural laws can help them avoid or minimize the risks of a collision.

Pose the following situation: You're driving through a rural area at 45 mph on a gently winding two-lane highway. Just as you come around a curve, you spot a vehicle broken down in your lane. What defensive-driving options do you have? What factors should you consider to decide which

continued on page 264

option to take? (Students may mention such defensive-driving options as braking, steering to the left or right, a combination of braking and evasive steering; factors to consider include speed, distance between your vehicle and the other vehicle, oncoming traffic, following traffic, availability of highway shoulders.)

TEACH

Explain

OBJECTIVE 1: Students will benefit from a discussion of how using the threshold/squeeze braking method is different from "slamming on the brakes." Students should, however, recognize the serious limitations of relying on braking alone to avoid a collision, especially when driving at high speeds.

OBJECTIVE 2: Students may find it interesting and enlightening to discuss how race car drivers put their knowledge of natural laws to use during a race.

OBJECTIVE 3: The majority of vehicle crashes in which someone is killed or seriously injured are head-on collisions. Students should recognize the extreme danger of head-on collisions and realize that they can take actions to avoid them. For example, they may be able either to adjust their vehicle's position to alter the angle of collision or to steer toward a movable object to reduce the force of impact.

◆ *For best braking control, squeeze the brake pedal with steady, firm pressure.*

FYI

More than 39 percent of all vehicle occupant fatalities involve a single vehicle. The driver leaves the roadway, brakes hard, or oversteers. The driver loses control. The vehicle skids, rolls over, or strikes an object.

steady, firm pressure until just before the brakes lock. If they lock, ease up about 2 or 3 degrees. Immediately squeeze down again, but not as firmly. Continue until you reach your desired speed. This type of braking allows you to maintain steering control. An **antilock brake system (ABS)** eliminates the problem of locked brakes. Sensors detect when a wheel stops turning. Pressure on the wheel's brakes is reduced until the wheel starts turning again. This action is independent of the pressure the driver applies to the brake pedal. Antilock brakes permit maximum brake pressure while retaining steering control. Do *not* pump these brakes.

How Can Knowledge of Natural Laws Help You Avoid a Collision?

A knowledge of natural laws is vital to vehicle control. Knowing how natural laws work is also important when making evasive maneuvers.

Steering to Avoid a Collision

You are driving at 55 mph. At the top of a hill, you see a vehicle with a flat tire stopped in your lane about 3 seconds ahead. You are going too fast to stop in time. With normal traction, it takes about 4 to 5 seconds to stop your vehicle. You have only 3 seconds. What can you do?

You should steer to the right, if possible. Take the following steps.

1. Turn the steering wheel just enough to get onto the shoulder.
2. Once past the disabled vehicle, immediately turn the steering wheel back about twice the amount you turned it to the right.
3. Turn the wheel right to bring your vehicle back into its original path.

You use what you know about traction to steer out of trouble. If you turn the wheel more than half a turn, your speed may be too high for traction to overcome centrifugal force.

Controlled Off-Road Recovery

You see a passing vehicle coming toward you. It will not return to its lane in time. You steer to the right. The vehicle passes on the left, but now your two right wheels are on the unpaved shoulder. You want to get back on the road.

Tires rolling on different surfaces have different amounts of grip. Paved areas give more traction than unpaved areas. Braking may cause

Driving Tip

Caution students to recognize that changing weather conditions can raise the level of risk rapidly. For example, falling temperatures can turn a wet road into an icy road, reducing traction from little to virtually none. Similarly, sudden wind gusts coupled with rain can cause vehicles to swerve and skid out of control.

your vehicle to skid. Turning the wheel sharply could cause your vehicle to skid, flip over, or shoot back across the roadway. Do the following.

1. Let the vehicle move right until the wheels on the shoulder are about 12 to 18 inches from the road edge.
2. Look for a spot where the road edge appears to be no more than 2 inches higher than the shoulder.
3. Signal your intention to return to the roadway.
4. Move the steering wheel ⅟₁₆ to ⅛ of a turn to the left. As soon as you feel the right front tire contact the road edge, steer back to the right ¼ to ½ of a turn.
5. Turn the steering wheel straight without braking or accelerating.

This maneuver is called controlled off-road recovery.

How Can You Minimize the Risk and Consequences of a Collision?

It is not always possible to avoid a collision. Knowing what to do before a collision happens will help minimize its effects. You should understand the factors that contribute to the force of impact of a collision.

Force of Impact

The force with which a moving vehicle hits another object is called the **force of impact.** Three factors affect the force of impact.

Speed of the vehicle The force of impact at 20 mph is four times that at 10 mph. And the force of impact at 30 mph is nine times that at 10 mph.

Weight of the vehicle The heavier a vehicle is, the harder it will hit any other object.

Impact distance The force of impact also depends on the distance a moving vehicle travels between first impact with an object and the point where the vehicle comes to a full stop. When a vehicle hits an unmoving solid object, the impact distance is short. The object does not "cave in" at impact, and so kinetic energy is spent immediately on impact. The shorter the impact distance, the greater the damage.

Reducing the Force of Impact

These energy-absorbing features help increase impact distance.

Sand canisters You often see canisters filled with sand in front of concrete barriers on highways. If a vehicle hits these canisters, they break apart. The sand helps reduce the vehicle's force of impact.

Vehicle features New vehicles include a number of features that help increase impact distance by absorbing energy. These features include

---

SAFETY TIPS

When you are making a left turn across oncoming traffic, do not turn your steering wheel to the left until the traffic clears. If you did turn the wheel and then were bumped from behind, you could be pushed into a head-on collision with traffic in the oncoming lane.

FYI

In the 1400s, the Inca Empire stretched from the border between Colombia and Ecuador to central Chile in South America. From Cuzco, the empire's capital, roads that were well-constructed ran to all parts of the empire. The total length of this road system was about 9,500 miles, and it was designed for people on foot. Relay runners were stationed at posts along the road to carry messages and parcels quickly to and from the capital.

State BY State

Twenty-five states now require all motorcyclists and passengers to wear protective helmets. Twenty-two other states require only certain motorcycle riders to wear helmets. Only three states—Colorado, Illinois, and Iowa—have no helmet laws for motorcyclists. In states with universal helmet laws, the helmet use rate is almost 100 percent. In states without these laws, the helmet use rate is only 50 percent.

Teaching Model

Describe the following situation: You're driving in the right lane of a rural highway at about 50 mph. Suddenly a boy on a dirt bike seems to appear out of nowhere, cutting across your path of travel. You swerve and successfully avoid him. However, your front and rear right wheels slip off the paved highway onto the dirt shoulder. Model the thinking process that you use to maintain control of your vehicle in this situation. (You avoid applying the brakes suddenly, turning the steering wheel sharply, or accelerating. Instead, you let your vehicle move right until the wheels on the shoulder are about 12 to 18 inches from the pavement edge; move the steering wheel about a quarter turn to the left until you feel the right front tire climb the road edge; steer to the right about half a turn, then immediately steer straight ahead.)

Ask

Ask students to discuss the dangers of applying the brakes suddenly or turning the steering wheel sharply in an unequal traction situation such as the one described.

Read

Have students read Lesson 4 to learn how a knowledge of natural laws can help minimize the risk and consequences of a collision.

To add to students' understanding, have them locate Colombia, Ecuador, Chile, and Cuzco on a map.

ASSESS

Guided Practice

Have students answer the Lesson 4 Review questions. The answers are provided below.

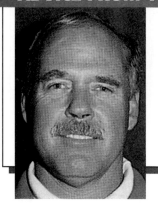

Stress the idea that eva-sive steering, not braking, is often the best way to avoid a collision, especially at speeds over 25 mph.

Reteaching

Pair a more able student with one who is having difficulty. Have students brainstorm and analyze driving situations in which having a knowledge of natural laws can help the driver reduce risk. Encourage students to recognize how the natural laws work in combination with one another.

Enrichment

Assign the Study Guide for Lesson 4. The Find Out More section encourages students to expand their basic learning of the lesson concepts.

CLOSE

Summarize

Return to the situation described in the Motivator section. Encourage students to evaluate each of the possible defensive-driving options and carefully work through the thought process they would use to decide which option to take.

DRIVER'S LOG

Have students return to the section on natural laws they began at the end of Lesson 1. Ask them to add to their list other risk management strategies studied in this lesson.

Bruce Reichel
Driving Instructor, Bill Scott Racing (BSR), Inc.

If you understand the factors involved when a vehicle is in motion, you can learn how to adjust the speed and position of the vehicle to work with the natural laws.

Controlling a vehicle is controlling its energy, and its weight and speed determine the vehicle's energy. A car weighing 2,000 pounds traveling at 30 mph has half the energy of a 4,000-pound car traveling at the same speed. A 2,000-pound car traveling at 60 mph has four times the energy of the same car traveling at 30 mph.

air bags; crumple zones; automatic safety belts; head restraints; and padded dashboards. See Chapter 7 for more information about energy-absorbing features.

If a Collision Is Unavoidable

Suppose a collision seems unavoidable. What should you do? If you can increase the impact distance, you will lessen the force of impact, which in turn will reduce the risk of serious damage or injury.

Head-on A head-on collision with a vehicle or an immovable object, such as a large tree, is the worst type of collision. If you can reduce speed, the force of impact will be less. Driving into something that is movable, such as a bush or a snowbank, will also reduce the force of the impact.

Side Suppose you are about to be broadsided in an intersection and cannot avoid it. How can you minimize the damage? You can accelerate to make impact behind the passenger compartment or with the rear end of your vehicle. This will help minimize damage or injury because impact will occur behind the passengers.

WHAT WOULD YOU DO?

A driver has lost control of a vehicle, and it is swerving into your lane. What should you do?

Lesson 4 Review

1. Under what conditions can accelerating or braking help you avoid a collision?
2. How can traction and steering help you avoid a collision?
3. How would you use knowledge of force of impact to respond to a head-on or side collision?

WHAT WOULD YOU DO?

Sample answer: Steer to the right to avoid a head-on crash; if necessary, drive into something movable to reduce the impact.

Lesson 4 Review

Answers

1. Accelerating: when braking would leave your vehicle in the path of an oncoming vehicle; braking: at low speeds, when it takes less time and distance to stop than steer evasively.
2. By enabling you to maintain control of your vehicle while avoiding a vehicle or object.
3. By increasing impact distance, reducing speed, or driving into something movable.

Using the Distance Numbers

The distance numbers shown on a map can give you a more accurate idea than the map scale of how far apart two places are. On this map, distance numbers are either black or red. The numbers indicate the distance in miles between towns, junctions, and interchanges.

Here's an example of how the numbers work. Find Lake Butler and Starke on the road map. Along the highway running between the two cities, you'll see a red number 15. This means that Lake Butler and Starke are 15 miles apart.

Along Route 301 between Starke and Waldo, you'll see the red number 11. It tells you that it is about 11 miles from Starke to Waldo.

If you add the numbers—15 + 11—the sum is 26. The distance by road from Lake Butler to Waldo, going through Starke, is about 26 miles.

In general, you can estimate driving time more accurately by using distance numbers rather than the map scale, especially if the road to be driven has many curves and loops. Keep in mind, though, that distance numbers indicate only the mileage, not the condition of the road. Six miles of travel along a twisting back road can take twice as long as 10 miles of highway driving!

Try It Yourself

1. How many miles is it from Otter Creek to Trenton along Routes 98 and 129?
2. You're going from Jasper to Branford along Route 129. How far is it?
3. What is the shortest route between Greenville and Branford?

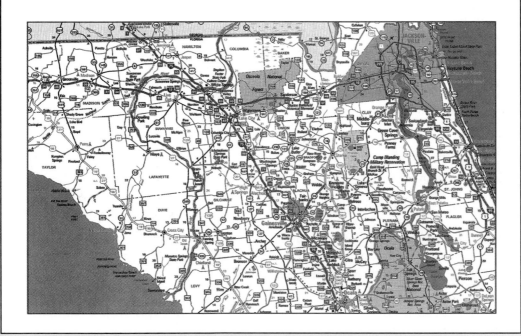

BUILDING SKILLS: READING MAPS

Objective

Demonstrate an ability to use the distance numbers shown on a road map.

Teaching the Skill

- Explain that some road maps have distance numbers in two colors, the second color indicating cumulative mileage. For example, a red number 12 on such a map may represent the total of a black number 7 plus a black number 5.

- Discuss why distance numbers are more accurate than the map scale for estimating driving time and distance on roads that are not straight. Stress the importance of taking into consideration the type of road in order to make a valid estimate.

- Remind students that in addition to using the map scale and the distance numbers to determine distance, they can also use mileage charts (see the Building Skills section in Chapter 3).

ANSWERS TO
Try It Yourself Questions

1. 23 miles
2. 41 miles
3. south on Route 221 to Route 10, east on Route 10 to Route 129, south on Route 129 to Branford

CHAPTER SUMMARY

Key Points

Have students read the Key Points to review the major concepts of the chapter.

PROJECTS

Cooperative Learning:

Students will benefit by working with a partner on one or both projects. When the assignment is completed, the whole class will profit by sharing and comparing results.

CHAPTER 14 REVIEW

KEY POINTS

Lesson One

1. Natural laws include the laws of inertia, friction, momentum, kinetic energy, and gravity.
2. Inertia causes passengers to keep moving forward when a vehicle is stopped abruptly. Friction between the road and tires holds a vehicle on the road. Momentum determines the extent of damage in a collision. Kinetic energy affects braking and acceleration. Gravity can slow your vehicle when you are driving uphill or increase its speed when going downhill.

Lesson Two

1. Braking is a result of friction between the brake linings and the wheel drums or wheel discs and pads.
2. Friction and inertia affect steering, as do road conditions and a vehicle's tires, steering mechanism, suspension, and wheel alignment.
3. As you enter a curve, inertia and centrifugal force can be overcome by the friction between the tires and roadway, allowing you to change direction.
4. Gravity pulls a vehicle into the curve on an inwardly banked curve, thus aiding steering control. If the banking is toward the outer part of the curve, gravity pulls the vehicle away from the curve, making steering more difficult.

Lesson Three

1. Reduced traction and too rapid changes in either speed or direction can cause skidding.
2. Four kinds of skids are braking, power, cornering, and blowout.
3. To respond to a skid, do not brake. Look well ahead in the direction in which you want to go. Steer smoothly and quickly in that direction.

Lesson Four

1. It is possible to avoid some collisions by accelerating and steering if the roadway is clear. At speeds under 25 mph, braking can help avoid a collision.
2. You may be able to avoid a collision by understanding the relationship between steering, speed, and friction.
3. Reducing speed, choosing something that will "cave in," and protecting the passenger compartment from impact are three ways to reduce the force of impact in a collision.

PROJECTS

1. Make a photo display of potential low-traction areas in your community. Label each photo, and list the potential danger. Return to the area to check out your suspicion. Make sure to position yourself so that you are safe and will not become a danger to traffic.
2. Check the shoulders and off-road areas of some local highways. Are they well designed and maintained? Do they provide an escape path in an emergency? What dangers do they pose to drivers? How could they be improved?

*inter*NET CONNECTION Pick two of the natural laws studied in the chapter. Use Glencoe's driver education Web site to gather more information on these natural laws. Learn more about how each law will help you maintain control of your vehicle and reduce driving risk.
drivered.glencoe.com

*inter*NET CONNECTION

Visit Glencoe's Driver Education Web site for student activities that relate to this chapter.
drivered.glencoe.com

CHAPTER **14** REVIEW

CHAPTER TEST

Write the letter of the answer that best completes each sentence.

1. A vehicle's momentum depends on its
   a. kinetic energy.
   b. speed and weight.
   c. center of gravity.

2. If only the outer edges of a tire grip the road,
   a. the tire is properly inflated.
   b. the tire is overinflated.
   c. the tire is underinflated.

3. Three factors that affect braking distance are
   a. car and roadway conditions and speed.
   b. steering ability, centrifugal force, and ocular tracking.
   c. tread depth, controlled recovery, and the motion of energy.

4. If you are trying to get out of a skid,
   a. look for wet leaves to slow you down.
   b. keep your foot off the pedals and steer in the direction that you want the vehicle to go.
   c. slam on the brakes.

5. If your vehicle has good directional control,
   a. you can decrease total stopping distance by 3 seconds.
   b. you will be able to keep the vehicle moving in the direction in which you steer it.
   c. you can make sharp turns at high speed.

6. After driving through a deep puddle,
   a. only use engine braking for a while.
   b. apply light pressure to the brake pedal.
   c. stop at the nearest service station for brake fluid.

7. A power skid occurs when you
   a. apply the brakes too hard.
   b. press the accelerator too hard.
   c. downshift too quickly.

8. A driver can turn successfully as long as there is enough
   a. friction to overcome centrifugal force.
   b. centrifugal force to overcome friction.
   c. adhesion to overcome friction.

9. Because of inertia,
   a. objects at rest move in a straight line.
   b. moving objects continue to move in a straight line.
   c. moving objects continue to move along a curved path.

10. A vehicle's speed and weight both affect
    a. the center of gravity.
    b. friction.
    c. force of impact.

Write the word or phrase that best completes each sentence.

skidding	kinetic energy	inertia
centripedal	center of gravity	

11. Any object in motion has _____.

12. Safety belts work against _____ to keep you from being thrown forward.

13. A higher _____ makes a vehicle less stable and harder to control on turns and curves.

14. _____ is loss of control over the direction in which your vehicle is moving because of reduced traction.

DRIVER'S LOG

In this chapter, you have learned about the effect that natural laws have on a variety of driving situations. Summarize, in a few sentences for each, the meaning of inertia, gravity, and momentum. Explain how these laws help you anticipate and manage risk.

CHAPTER TEST

Assign the Chapter Test to all students.

Answers

1. b
2. c
3. a
4. b
5. b
6. b
7. b
8. a
9. b
10. c
11. kinetic energy
12. inertia
13. center of gravity
14. Skidding

DRIVER'S LOG

Students' responses will reflect their personal viewpoints. However, their answers should provide an assessment of their understanding of the relationship between the effects of natural laws and risk management.

Evaluate

- Test A, pages 27–28 or Test B, pages 27–28 📁
- Testmaker software

RETURN TO THE BIG IDEA

In the context of what they have learned in this chapter, have students discuss the idea that drivers who understand what causes a vehicle to move as it does are better prepared to maintain control of their vehicle than are drivers who do not. Encourage students to give specific examples.

Responding to an Emergency Overview

THEME DEVELOPMENT Drivers must be prepared to respond to brake failure, engine stalling, steering failure, tire blowouts, and various other driving-related emergencies. Drivers should also know what to do at the scene of an emergency and be familiar with basic first aid guidelines and procedures.

CHAPTER FEATURES	TCR COMPONENTS

 **FOR NEW DRIVERS**

Identifying emergency items to keep in the vehicle's trunk.

Study Guide, p. 57
Lesson Plan, p. 31
Car Care Manual

 **FOR NEW DRIVERS**

Learning to do a periodic 15-minute checkup.

Study Guide, p. 58
Lesson Plan, p. 31
Car Care Manual
Information Master 20

Study Guide, p. 59
Lesson Plan, p. 32

CONNECTIONS
History

Learning about the American National Red Cross.

Study Guide, p. 60
Lesson Plan, p. 32

ADVICE FROM THE EXPERTS

How to minimize the consequences of a roadside emergency.

BUILDING SKILLS: CRITICAL THINKING

Benjamin Banneker

Test A, pp. 29–30
Test B, pp. 29–30

PROJECTS

1. Learn how to respond to vehicle failures and emergencies.
2. Interview an emergency medical technician or member of a first aid squad.

OTHER PROGRAM RESOURCES

Testmaker software
Traffic charts

ADDITIONAL RESOURCES

Driving in Bad Weather, Video 419, AAA Foundation
On the Scene: A Guide to Bystander Care at Roadside Emergency, Video 458, AAA Foundation
First on the Scene, Video 428, AAA Foundation

NAME _____ DATE _____

CHAPTER 15   Responding to an Emergency

TEST A

Select the phrase that best completes each sentence below. Write the letter of the answer you have chosen to the left of each statement.

__b__ 1. The first thing to do in the event of brake failure is to
   a. use the parking brake to stop your car.
   b. pump the brake pedal rapidly.
   c. shift to a lower gear.
   d. steer against the curb.

__d__ 2. Engine failure can be caused by
   a. a broken timing gear.
   b. a lack of fuel.
   c. extreme heat.
   d. all of the above.

__c__ 3. If your engine stalls,
   a. your power brakes won't work at all.
   b. your power steering won't work at all.
   c. your power brakes and power steering won't work very well.
   d. you should pump your power brakes.

__a__ 4. If your engine is flooded, you will probably
   a. smell gasoline.
   b. see steam coming out from under the hood.
   c. have your engine stall after going through a large puddle of water.
   d. experience all of the above.

__b__ 5. The most common kind of steering failure is
   a. total system failure.
   b. power-assist failure.
   c. both a and b.
   d. none of the above.

__d__ 6. In case of total steering failure,
   a. stop quickly using the foot brake.
   b. stop as quickly as possible using the parking brake.
   c. downshift.
   d. do both b and c.

__d__ 7. If your tire loses pressure while you are driving, you should
   a. keep a firm grip on the steering wheel with both hands.
   b. release the accelerator pedal slowly.
   c. brake hard and pull over.
   d. do both a and b.

__a__ 8. If you change a flat tire for an undersized or low-mileage spare, you should drive
   a. no faster than 50 mph to the nearest repair station.
   b. no faster than 15 mph to the nearest repair station.
   c. no faster than 25 mph to your destination.
   d. no farther than 6 miles to the nearest repair station.

© AAA and Glencoe/McGraw-Hill   ◆ **29**

NAME _____ DATE _____

__c__ 9. A stuck accelerator pedal could be caused by
   a. a clogged fuel injector.
   b. a bad fuel pump.
   c. a broken engine mount.
   d. all of the above.

__d__ 10. Engine fires are usually
   a. electrical.
   b. fuel-fed.
   c. smoky.
   d. all of the above.

Match the following terms by placing the letter of the definition to the left of the item.

__c__ 11. blowout   a. a neck injury

__d__ 12. jumper cables   b. a condition caused by a lack of oxygen to the brain

__a__ 13. whiplash   c. sudden loss of tire pressure

__e__ 14. hemorrhaging   d. a device that helps start a car with a dead battery

__f__ 15. direct pressure   e. severe bleeding

__b__ 16. shock   f. a method to help stop bleeding

In each space below, write the word or words that best complete the sentence.

17. When brake failure occurs, the brake pedal may yield little or no ____resistance____.

18. To treat shock, it is important to keep the victim ____warm____.

19. If you apply the ____parking____ brake too abruptly in an emergency situation, you may lock the wheels.

20. What is a flooded engine?

   An engine that has flooded has had too much gas pumped to it. Not enough air has gotten to the engine, so the car will not start.

21. How do you start a flooded engine?

   You start a flooded engine by pressing the accelerator pedal to the floor and keeping it there while turning the ignition for 5 to 10 seconds.

30 ◆   © AAA and Glencoe/McGraw-Hill

NAME _____ DATE _____

CHAPTER 15   Responding to an Emergency

TEST B

Select the phrase that best completes each sentence below. Write the letter of the answer you have chosen to the left of each statement.

__b__ 1. In case of a vehicle engine fire,
   a. open the hood and spray water directly on the fire.
   b. open the hood release and spray the fire extinguisher at the fire through the small opening.
   c. go to a service station and spray water on the fire with the hood fully open.
   d. drive fast and let the wind extinguish the flames.

__c__ 2. Before you jump-start your vehicle's battery,
   a. make sure that both vehicles are touching slightly.
   b. attach the red (positive) cables to the negative posts on the battery.
   c. make sure the battery fluids are not frozen or low.
   d. do all of the above.

__a__ 3. Headlight failure is usually caused by
   a. a burned-out low-beam headlamp.
   b. an electrical short.
   c. overuse of high beams.
   d. a rock sprayed from another vehicle's tire.

__d__ 4. Going without breathing for only _____ minutes can cause permanent brain damage.
   a. 12 to 15
   b. 10 to 12
   c. 6 to 10
   d. 2 to 3

__c__ 5. If the engine temperature is becoming hot, your first step should be to
   a. drive to a service garage.
   b. turn off your heater.
   c. turn off your air conditioner and any other accessories.
   d. turn on your flashers.

__a__ 6. If your engine is flooded, you will probably
   a. smell gasoline.
   b. see steam coming out from under the hood.
   c. have your engine stall after going through a large puddle of water.
   d. experience all of the above.

__c__ 7. When your engine stalls because it is wet, you should steer off the road and
   a. keep the ignition turned on.
   b. open the hood.
   c. keep the hood closed and the ignition off.
   d. do none of the above.

__d__ 8. When you have to change a flat tire on the side of the road,
   a. try to position your vehicle on a flat, hard surface.
   b. set out flares or warning triangles.
   c. use wheel blocks.
   d. do all of the above.

© AAA and Glencoe/McGraw-Hill   ◆ **29**

NAME _____ DATE _____

__b__ 9. The first thing to do in the event of a brake failure is to
   a. use the parking brake to stop your vehicle.
   b. pump the brake pedal rapidly.
   c. shift to a lower gear.
   d. steer against the curb.

__c__ 10. If your engine stalls,
   a. your power brakes won't work at all.
   b. your power steering won't work at all.
   c. your power brakes and power steering won't work very well.
   d. you should pump your power brakes.

Match the following terms by placing the letter of the definition to the left of the item.

__d__ 11. brake fade   a. a condition caused by a lack of oxygen to the brain

__e__ 12. lug wrench   b. a sudden loss of tire pressure

__a__ 13. shock   c. a way to stop bleeding

__b__ 14. blowout   d. temporary brake failure

__f__ 15. hemorrhaging   e. a tool used to help change a tire

__c__ 16. direct pressure   f. severe bleeding

In each space below, write the word or words that best complete the sentence.

17. The pulse of a person who is in shock will be weak and ____fast____.

18. Six minutes without breathing can cause ____death____.

19. To treat shock, it is important to keep the victim ____warm____.

20. Briefly describe the steps you should take in the event of sudden brake failure.

   Rapidly pump the brake pedal. If that does not work, use the parking brake. Shift to a lower gear; look for a place to steer against the curb. If you can't avoid a collision, steer so that you sideswipe an object rather than hit it head-on.

30 ◆   © AAA and Glencoe/McGraw-Hill

NAME _____   DATE _____

CHAPTER 15 Responding to an Emergency

STUDY GUIDE FOR CHAPTER 15   LESSON 1

Brake, Engine, and Steering Failures

A. The three procedures listed below are possible ways of slowing your car in case of total brake failure. Match each procedure with its result.

_b_ **1.** Shift to a lower gear.

_c_ **2.** Pump the brake pedal rapidly.

_a_ **3.** Use the parking brake, keeping your hand on the release button or handle.

a. slows the rear wheels

b. slows the engine and forward movement of the vehicle

c. may build up pressure in the brake-fluid lines

B. Suppose you have tried the above methods without success. Study the picture. Explain what you might do to stop yourself at each numbered spot if you were driving vehicle X and your brakes were not working. Then add one more emergency measure you might try.

1. hit barrier or curb

2. drive into open area (parking lot)

3. drive into open area (road)

4. drive uphill

5. Another measure to try when the brakes fail is:

turn ignition to Off position, sideswipe an

object such as parked car rather than hit it

head-on

C. FIND OUT MORE. The chapter lists several emergency items to keep in the trunk of your vehicle. Ask someone you know who drives what her or his family keep in their vehicle for emergencies. How is this person's answer different from what the chapter lists?
Review student's work.

NAME _____   DATE _____

STUDY GUIDE FOR CHAPTER 15   LESSON 2

Tire Failure and Other Serious Problems

A. The following steps outline what you should do if a tire loses pressure, but they are in the wrong order. In the space next to each step, write a number to show where in the order it should appear.

_3_ **a.** Check the traffic around you. When you find a gap, signal and steer off the roadway as far as you can.

_5_ **b.** Get out of the vehicle, and have any passengers get out also.

_1_ **c.** Keep a firm grip on the steering wheel with both hands.

_4_ **d.** Shift into Park (or Reverse in a manual-shift vehicle), and put on your emergency flashers.

_2_ **e.** Release the accelerator slowly. Don't brake.

B. For each sentence below, circle T if the statement is true and F if it is false. Correct each false statement in the space below.

1. Between 300 and 400 people are killed yearly while changing tires, when the vehicle falls off the jack or they are hit by other vehicles.   Ⓣ   F

2. An engine fire cannot be put out with water.   Ⓣ   F

3. Jump-starting a battery whose fluid is frozen can cause the battery to explode.   Ⓣ   F

4. Check the brake-fluid level once a month if you drive 10,000 miles or more a year.   Ⓣ   F

C. FIND OUT MORE. Tires are rated by their safety features to help you make good purchasing decisions. Go to a library and look up articles in *Consumer Reports*, or call a local tire store; find out what features tires are rated on, what the possible "grades" are, and what a good rating is. Summarize your findings below.

Review student's work.

NAME _____   DATE _____

STUDY GUIDE FOR CHAPTER 15   LESSON 3

Protecting the Scene

A. Read the following paragraph that describes a situation in which a vehicle you are driving breaks down. In the space below the paragraph, write down what was done correctly under the "Right" heading and what was not correctly done, under "Wrong."

You are driving down the interstate highway when you notice your vehicle's temperature gauge beginning to climb. You decide to wait to see if it gets any worse. Finally, the temperature gets very high and you decide to pull over. You are now driving in a road construction area where there is very little shoulder available. You get out of your vehicle, tie a scarf on the right-hand side door handle, and open the vehicle's trunk. You then turn on the vehicle's emergency flashers, and since it is very cold outside, you get back into the vehicle and wait for help. You are careful to close the window all the way, since your heater is keeping you warm and you do not want to waste the heat. Soon someone sees you and pulls over. The person comes over to your vehicle, and you get out.

RIGHT	WRONG
turned on emergency flashers	did not stop right after temp. began to climb,
	pulled off near construction area, tied scarf to
	shoulder side of vehicle, raised trunk lid,
	waited inside vehicle, closed window
	completely, got out of vehicle to meet
	stranger who stopped.

B. FIND OUT MORE. Call a local emergency road service. Ask them about the costs associated with road service.
Review student's work.

1. Do they bill insurance companies? _____

2. How much do they charge to fix a flat tire? _____

3. How much do they charge to help someone who runs out of gas? _____

4. How much is the towing charge per mile? _____

5. How much is the basic charge just to come to help somebody? _____

NAME _____   DATE _____

STUDY GUIDE FOR CHAPTER 15   LESSON 4

First Aid Guidelines and Procedures

A. For each sentence below, circle T if the statement is true and F if it is false. Correct each false statement in the space below.

1. The Good Samaritan Law states that you must stop and give aid to the injured in a road emergency.   T   Ⓕ
The Good Samaritan Law says that you cannot be held liable for civil damages if you help an injured person.

2. When you help somebody who has been injured in a collision, it is important to move the person off the roadway as quickly as possible.   T   Ⓕ
You should never try to move an injured person unless you do so for his or her safety.

3. It is important to speak calmly when helping injured people.   Ⓣ   F

4. To stop bleeding, apply direct pressure to the wound.   Ⓣ   F

5. Somebody who is hemorrhaging can die within minutes.   Ⓣ   F

6. When a person is in shock, his or her pulse rate is slow.   T   Ⓕ
When a person is in shock, the pulse is weak and fast.

7. To treat shock, you should keep the person's temperature as close to normal as possible.   Ⓣ   F

8. As little as 2 or 3 minutes without breathing can cause permanent brain damage.   Ⓣ   F

B. FIND OUT MORE. The chapter lists several items that you should carry in your car in a first aid kit. Go to a local drugstore or department store and look at their first aid kits. (The contents are listed on the outside of each kit.) What items on the list in the chapter are not in the kits in the store? What do the kits in the store cost? Would it be cheaper to make up a kit on your own?

Review student's work.

Responding to an Emergency

CHAPTER OVERVIEW

LESSON ONE
Procedures for responding to brake failure, steering failure, and various kinds of engine failure are explained.

LESSON TWO
Procedures for responding to tire failure and other serious driving-related difficulties are described.

LESSON THREE
Basic guidelines for what to do at the scene of an emergency are discussed.

LESSON FOUR
Basic first aid guidelines and procedures are described, and items to be included in a first aid kit are suggested.

VOCABULARY

blowout
first aid
hemorrhaging
jump-start
mouth-to-mouth resuscitation
shock

270

CONCEPT OF THE DRIVING TASK

Explain to students that experience teaches drivers to expect the unexpected. The more time a person spends driving, the greater the chance that the person will encounter such unexpected events as engine malfunctions, flat tires, collisions, and the like. Wise drivers prepare themselves to deal with such problems and emergencies.

CHAPTER 15

Responding to an Emergency

Emergencies happen even to the most experienced and careful drivers. It is important to learn how to assess and respond to emergencies safely, efficiently, and calmly. When you can do this, an emergency need not turn into a disaster.

LESSON ONE
Brake, Engine, and Steering Failures

LESSON TWO
Tire Failure and Other Serious Problems

LESSON THREE
Waiting for Help and Protecting the Scene

LESSON FOUR
First Aid Guidelines and Procedures

What's on the Road Ahead?

Have students read the lesson titles and objectives. Briefly discuss the topic of each lesson. Tell students that in this chapter, they will learn how to deal with a wide range of driving-related emergencies. They will also learn what to do at the scene of an emergency and what basic first aid procedures to follow.

Background: Automobile Clubs

Automobile clubs provide their members with towing, battery charging, and other kinds of emergency road service. By far the largest automobile club is the American Automobile Association (AAA), founded in 1902. In fact, the AAA has more members—over 35 million—than any other national association in America.

Relating to Prior Knowledge

Have students discuss experiences they have had with vehicle breakdowns or other driving-related emergencies.

The Big Idea

Discuss students' reactions to the Big Idea statement. Suggest that they keep this idea in mind as they read Chapter 15.

PRESENTING THE BIG IDEA

Remaining calm and thinking clearly are essential in coping effectively with an emergency situation. "Freezing" or reacting with panic can only make a bad situation worse.

Brake, Engine, and Steering Failures

(pages 272–276)

FOCUS

Objectives

- Describe what to do in case of brake failure.
- Explain what to do in case of engine stalling or other engine failure.
- Describe what to do in case of steering failure.

Resources

 Study Guide, page 57

 Traffic charts

📁 Car Care Manual

Motivator

Write the word *emergency* on the chalkboard, and have students brainstorm a working definition. (Suggested definition: An emergency is a sudden, usually unexpected occurrence or situation demanding immediate action.)

Ask students for examples of emergencies, other than collisions, they might encounter while driving. (Students may mention brake failure, engine stalling, steering failure, flat tires.) For the examples that students provide, refer back to the definition of *emergency*, stressing the sudden and unexpected nature of the occurrence and the need for immediate action. Explain that in the first two lessons of this chapter, students will learn about a variety of driving-related emergencies and how to respond to them.

Pose the following situation: You're stopped at a red light.

LESSON ONE

OBJECTIVES

1. Describe what to do in case of brake failure.
2. Explain what to do in case of engine stalling or other engine failure.
3. Describe what to do in case of steering failure.

◆ *Learn how to deal with emergency vehicle failures to manage risk.*

Brake, Engine, and Steering Failures

You see the stop sign at the intersection ahead and step on the brake. The pedal goes all the way to the floor, but your vehicle doesn't slow down. Two teenagers start across the street. Your mind races: "What should I do?"

Emergencies can occur suddenly and without warning. Brakes can fail, engines can stall, steering systems can malfunction. If you are prepared to deal with such emergencies, however, you can keep a dangerous situation from becoming a tragedy.

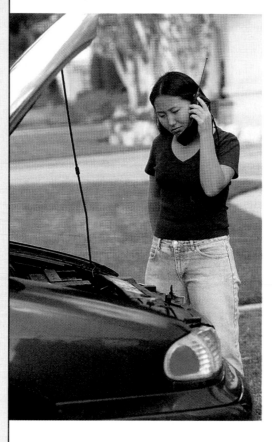

What Actions Can You Take When Your Brakes Fail?

All new vehicles have a dual-service brake system. Some vehicles have separate systems for the front and back wheels. Other vehicles use an "X" brake system, which links each front wheel with its diagonal rear wheel. Total failure of both systems at once is very unlikely, although partial or temporary brake failure does happen occasionally.

In Case of Brake Failure

When brake failure occurs, the foot brake may have no resistance. The brake pedal may sink to the floor and the brake warning light may come on. Here is what to do.

1. Rapidly pump the brake pedal. Doing so may build up pressure in the brake-fluid lines, providing some braking force. After a few pumps you'll know whether or not you've restored braking power. If power is restored, stop pumping.
2. Shift down to a lower gear to slow the movement of the vehicle.
3. If pumping the brakes does not work, use the parking brake. Either keep your thumb on the release button or hold the brake handle so that you can alternately apply and release brake pressure. Applying

---

IT'S A FACT

About nine out of ten American households have a motor vehicle. More than half of the households in the United States have two or more vehicles.

---

the parking brake too abruptly may lock the rear wheels—usually the only ones the parking brake affects—and send the vehicle into a spin. Use an apply-release-apply-release pattern with the parking brake to slow down the vehicle.

4. If you still have little or no brake control, look for a place to steer against the curb if there is one. Scraping the tires against a curb can help reduce speed.

5. Other ways to slow the vehicle after you've applied the parking brake and downshifted include steering into an open area, such as a parking lot and shifting into lower gears as quickly as possible; steering onto an uphill road; and turning the ignition to the off position, *not* the lock position, which would lock the steering wheel. After you have brought the vehicle to a stop, put the gear selection in Park to keep the vehicle where it is.

6. If you cannot avoid a collision, steer so that you sideswipe an object rather than hit it head-on. If possible, steer your vehicle into bushes or scrape along a guardrail or even parked vehicles rather than move toward pedestrians or occupied vehicles.

Note: If your vehicle has power brakes, engine failure may cause brake malfunction. If that is the case, your brakes will still work, but you'll have to press harder on the pedal.

Other Brake Problems

If you apply your brakes hard for a long time, such as when traveling down a long mountain slope, you could overheat them and cause "brake fade," a kind of temporary brake failure. To help prevent this, shift to a lower gear before starting down the slope. You can also pull off the road to let your brakes cool.

Drive more slowly through puddles. Driving at normal speeds through deep puddles or on flooded roadways can make your brakes wet and lead to temporary brake failure as well as cause hydroplaning. To dry your brakes, drive slowly with your left foot gently on the brake pedal. The friction will produce heat that will dry the brakes.

SAFETY TIPS

In an emergency situation, try to stay calm, think clearly, and act quickly. Learning what to do in case of vehicle failure will help you avoid panic.

TIPS   FOR NEW DRIVERS

Emergency Items

It is wise to keep emergency items in the trunk of your vehicle. Include such items as these:
- flashlight with extra batteries
- jumper cables (for starting a dead battery)
- flares, warning triangles, or reflectors
- coolant
- windshield-washer fluid
- wiping cloth
- ice scraper, snow brush, and snow shovel
- jack with flat board for soft surfaces
- lug wrench (for changing a flat tire)
- screwdriver, pliers, duct tape, and adjustable wrench (for making simple repairs)
- extra fan/alternator belt
- extra fuses (if needed for your car)
- fire extinguisher
- heavy gloves
- blanket
- drinking water
- first aid kit
- pencil and notebook (for recording emergency information)
- spare headlamp and bulb

CHAPTER 15 *Responding to an Emergency*   **273**

When the light changes, you step on the accelerator. Your vehicle moves forward, slowly gaining speed. Then, suddenly, the engine stops running. What actions can you take to deal with this situation in a safe manner? (Shift to Neutral, and try to restart the engine. If the engine won't start, check traffic, signal, and steer off the roadway. Once off the roadway, turn on emergency flashers, raise the hood, put out flares or warning triangles, and get help.)

TIPS   FOR NEW DRIVERS

Advise students to check periodically the flashlight, fire extinguisher, first-aid kit, and other emergency items to make sure they remain functional.

TEACH

Explain

OBJECTIVE 1: Students should recognize the importance of acting promptly but without panic. Brake failure poses great danger not only to driver and passengers but also to other drivers as well as pedestrians. When brakes fail, the driver must act responsibly to minimize danger to all concerned.

Driving Tip

Explain to students that drivers who are new to vehicles with a manual transmission sometimes have engine-stalling problems when they try to move forward after having come to a complete stop, as at a traffic light. Caution students to show patience until the driver gets the vehicle moving again.

OBJECTIVE 3: Students should note that most steering-related problems appear gradually. Advise students to have a mechanic check out their vehicle at the first signs of a steering problem rather than wait until a true emergency occurs.

Teaching Model

Describe the following situation: You're driving at 50 mph on an expressway. As you approach your exit, you step on the brake. The pedal goes down with very little resistance. Your vehicle's speed does not decrease. Model the thinking process that you will use in response to this situation. (You will do the following.

- Rapidly pump the brake pedal.
- Use the parking brake if pumping doesn't help.
- Shift down to a lower gear.
- If necessary, look for an open place to steer toward or something safe to steer against.)

Energy Tips

Power equipment and accessories add to the total weight and energy requirements of a vehicle. This extra weight and load on engine power, in turn, leads to reduced fuel efficiency.

◆ *Your car's engine may stall and your brakes may get wet in rainy weather.*

How Can You Respond to Engine Failure?

Engine failure occurs more often than any other kind of vehicle failure. Engines fail for many different reasons, such as a broken timing gear, a fuel system problem, lack of fuel, an electrical system malfunction, or problems caused by extreme heat or cold.

If Your Vehicle's Engine Stalls

If your vehicle's engine stalls (stops suddenly) while you are driving, check traffic around you and determine the best point at which to leave the roadway. Signal, then steer off the road or to the curb as quickly as possible while you still have momentum. Keep in mind that if your engine stalls and you have power brakes and power steering, the brakes and steering will still work, but they will be much harder to operate. If your vehicle has power brakes, do not pump the brake pedal. Use firm, steady pressure instead. When you are off the road, shift to Neutral, and try to restart the engine. If the engine starts, shift into Drive and continue driving. If you're driving a vehicle with a manual transmission, shift into First gear and continue moving forward.

If the engine won't start, make sure your flashers are on, and raise the hood. Place flares or warning triangles 100 feet in front of your vehicle and at least 100 feet behind it. Signal or wait for help.

If You Flood the Engine

If you pump the accelerator more than once when trying to start your vehicle, too much gas and not enough air may be supplied to the engine. The result is a flooded engine that won't start. When your engine is flooded, you can often smell gas. In vehicles with fuel injection, there is no need to pump the accelerator before starting; in fact, a flooded engine may result.

To start a flooded engine, press the accelerator pedal all the way to the floor and hold it there. At the same time, turn on the ignition switch, and hold it on for 5 to 10 seconds. If the vehicle starts, slowly release the accelerator. If the vehicle doesn't start, wait about 10 minutes and try again.

274   UNIT 3 *Moving onto the Road*

THE INTERNATIONAL SCENE

Canada

U.S. citizens do not need a passport to drive into Canada. They should, however, have a birth certificate or other proof of citizenship, a driver's license, and proof of insurance, as well as their vehicle registration card and, if the vehicle is not registered in the driver's name, a letter from the owner authorizing use of the vehicle. It is also advisable for teenagers under age 18 unaccompanied by a parent or guardian to take a letter indicating their parent's or guardian's permission for them to be traveling in Canada. Demerit points for moving violations are now exchanged between certain locales, such as New York and Ontario.

If the Engine Overheats

Your engine may overheat for any of various reasons: driving in slow-moving traffic during hot weather, with the air conditioner running; driving up long, steep hills; a loose or broken fan belt; a broken water pump or hose; not enough coolant or antifreeze in the cooling system; a stuck or broken thermostat; or a clogged radiator.

When engine temperature is too high, the temperature gauge or warning light on your instrument panel indicates that the engine is overheating. You may also see steam or smoke rising from under the hood.

If your engine overheats, follow these steps.

1. Turn off all accessories, especially the air conditioner.
2. If the temperature gauge continues to show hot or the warning light stays on, signal and pull off the road. Raise the hood, let the engine cool, and get professional help.

   If you can't pull off the road immediately, turn on the heater to draw heat from the engine. Doing so will not solve the problem, but it will help temporarily until you can get off the road safely.
3. If there is no steam or smoke coming from the engine, carefully open the hood (wear gloves to protect your hands). Look for such problems as a broken hose or belt. Note whether the radiator overflow tank is empty, but do not touch the radiator.
4. When the engine has cooled completely, check the fluid level in the radiator overflow tank again. If the fluid level is low, you need to add coolant. Many overflow tanks have a fill line to help you determine the proper level of fluid. Start the engine, and let it run at idle speed as you add the coolant.

If the Engine Is Wet

If you drive through water, your vehicle's engine may get wet, start to sputter, and stall. The water may short out your vehicle's electrical system or be drawn into the combustion chamber by way of the air filter and the carburetor.

If your engine gets wet and stalls, steer off the road and turn off the ignition. Wait a few minutes, keeping the hood closed to let the heat of the engine compartment dry out the moisture. Then try to restart the engine. If it doesn't start, the engine may need more time to dry. If it's a hot, sunny day, you may speed up the process by raising the hood.

◆ *Let the temperature cool before you check an overheated engine.*

Ask

Ask students to discuss where, or against what, they might steer in order to minimize risk in the situation described.

Read

Have students read Lesson 1 to learn what to do in response to brake failure, engine failure, or steering failure.

ASSESS

Guided Practice

Have students answer the Lesson 1 Review questions. The answers are provided below.

Reteaching

Have students work together in small groups to create "What Do I Do If . . ." posters. Posters should contain brief, step-by-step guidelines for coping with each of the vehicle failure situations described in this lesson.

After groups complete their posters, have them share their work with the class. Extend the discussion by encouraging students to describe visibility, time, and space factors associated with each situation.

Driving Tip

Explain to students that when they must drive through water—as on a flooded highway—they should first observe the contour of the road. Often roadways are higher at the center than at the edges; on such roads, the water level will be lower near the center line.

Assign the Study Guide for Lesson 1. The Find Out More section encourages students to expand their basic learning of the lesson concepts.

CLOSE

Summarize

Return to the situation described in the Motivator section. Recall students' initial responses, and have students expand their original answers in terms of what they have learned in this lesson. Encourage students to be as specific as possible in their answers. Extend the discussion by asking how they might handle the situation differently if the vehicle had stalled on a highway or an expressway.

DRIVER'S LOG

Have students create a section focusing on driving-related emergencies. Have them include each emergency situation studied along with specific response strategies. Have students expand their list of strategies as they continue reading this chapter. Have students compile a list of basic emergency-related tips, such as remaining calm and getting the vehicle off the road.

WHAT WOULD YOU DO?

Sample answer: The brakes have failed; try pumping the brake pedal; use the parking brake if necessary; downshift.

SAFETY TIPS

To prevent your brakes from getting wet when driving through deep water, apply pressure to the brake pedal as you move slowly through the water.

What Actions Can You Take When Your Steering Fails?

Two kinds of steering failure are possible: power-assist failure and total steering system failure. The former is far more common than the latter.

If Power Steering Fails

Power-steering failure can occur if your engine stalls or the power-assist mechanism fails. When power steering fails, your steering wheel suddenly becomes very difficult to turn.

If your vehicle's power steering fails, grip the steering wheel firmly and turn it with more force. Check surrounding traffic, signal, and when it's safe to do so, steer off the road and stop. As soon as you possibly can, have a mechanic check your steering system.

Total Steering Failure

Sudden and total steering failure is a rare occurrence. However, if a breakdown in either the steering or suspension system does happen, your ability to control your vehicle will be drastically reduced.

In case of total steering failure, bring your vehicle to a stop as quickly and safely as possible, using the parking brake, not the foot brake. If you step on the foot brake it might cause your vehicle to pull sharply to one side. Just as when responding to brake failure, keep hold of the parking brake release button or handle to avoid locking the rear wheels and going into a spin. Downshift.

WHAT WOULD YOU DO?

As you prepare to slow your vehicle, you find that the brakes don't work and the vehicle does not slow down. What do you suppose has happened? How will you handle this situation?

Lesson 1 Review

1. What actions would you take if your vehicle's brakes failed?
2. What would you do if your engine stalled while you were driving? What if the engine overheated?
3. What would you do if your vehicle's power steering suddenly failed?

Lesson 1 Review

Answers

1. Pump the brake pedal; if necessary, use parking brake; shift to lower gear; if necessary, steer against curb, into an open area, or onto an uphill road.
2. Stalling: steer safely off roadway and try to restart engine; overheating: turn off accessories, pull off road, raise hood, let engine cool; look for obvious problems, such as low coolant level; get help.
3. Grip the wheel firmly, and turn it with more force; safely steer off road; have steering system checked.

Tire Failure and Other Serious Problems

A motor vehicle is a complex machine that must endure years of stop-and-go driving, rough roads, and harsh weather. No matter how well you maintain your vehicle, there's always the possibility that a part may break or a system may malfunction.

In addition to the major vehicle failures you read about in the previous lesson, you should be prepared to deal with a number of other serious problems.

What Actions Can You Take in Case of a Blowout or Flat Tire?

A blowout and a flat tire are similar but not the same. A **blowout** is an explosion in a tire while the vehicle is in motion. The tire suddenly loses air pressure, and the vehicle may become difficult to control.

A tire can also lose pressure gradually through a slow leak. If you don't detect the leak in time, the tire is likely to go flat. A tire can go flat either while the vehicle is parked or when it is moving.

If Your Tire Loses Pressure

When a tire fails while you are driving, you may feel a strong pull to the right or left. The rear of your vehicle may shimmy or swerve back and forth. You may even hear a thumping sound. The effect may be gradual if the tire has a slow leak or sudden if the tire blows out.

If a tire loses pressure, take these steps:

1. Keep a firm grip on the steering wheel with both hands. Look well ahead along your intended path. Maintain or slightly increase pressure on the accelerator until your steering is stable.
2. Release the accelerator slowly. Do not brake—you could make the vehicle swerve out of control.
3. Check the traffic around you. When you find a gap, signal and steer off the road. You'll have to change the tire, so move as far off the main

◆ *Tire failures are fairly common. You should become familiar with emergency procedures for handling tire failure.*

LESSON TWO

OBJECTIVES

1. Explain what actions to take if your vehicle has a blowout or flat tire.
2. Tell what to do if the accelerator pedal sticks.
3. Describe what to do if the hood flies up.
4. Explain what to do if your vehicle catches fire.
5. Tell how to jump-start a dead battery.
6. Tell what to do in case of headlight failure.

KEY TERMS

blowout
jump-start

LESSON TWO

Tire Failure and Other Serious Problems

(pages 277–282)

FOCUS

Objectives

- Explain what actions to take if your vehicle has a blowout or flat tire.
- Tell what to do if the accelerator pedal sticks.
- Describe what to do if the hood flies up.
- Explain what to do if your vehicle catches fire.
- Tell how to jump-start a dead battery.
- Tell what to do in case of headlight failure.

Resources

📁 Study Guide, page 58
📁 Traffic charts
📁 Information Master 20
📁 Car Care Manual

Vocabulary

blowout
jump-start

IT'S A FACT

John P. Dunlop invented the pneumatic tire in Ireland about 100 years ago. First used for bicycles, it has become indispensable for motor vehicles.

Motivator

Review with students the working definition of the word *emergency* established in Lesson 1: a sudden, usually unexpected occurrence or situation demanding immediate action. You may want to have students recap the driving-related emergencies they studied in Lesson 1.

Explain that in Lesson 2, students will learn about various other driving-related emergencies and how to respond to them. While these emergencies do not involve major system failures, they can be extremely serious, even life-threatening. Pose the following situation: You're driving along the expressway at 55 mph in light traffic. Ahead you see a sign telling drivers to reduce speed. You ease your foot off the accelerator, but the vehicle continues to move at the same speed. You realize that the accelerator pedal is stuck. What actions can you take to deal with this situation in a safe manner?

(Step on the brake and shift into Neutral; check traffic and signal a lane change; when safe, steer off the road, continuing to apply the brakes; once off the road, turn off the ignition and apply the parking brake; with the vehicle stopped, try to unstick the pedal; test the pedal before reentering traffic; if the problem is mechanical, have it repaired before driving again.)

roadway as you can. As the vehicle slows, brake gradually and come to a stop on a flat surface.

4. Shift to Park (Reverse in a manual-shift vehicle), set the parking brake, and put on your emergency flashers.
5. Get out of the vehicle, and have passengers get out too, on the side away from traffic.

How to Change a Tire

Changing a tire requires caution and may require more strength than some people possess. Between 300 and 400 people are killed yearly while changing tires when the vehicle falls off the jack and onto them or they are struck by passing vehicles.

Position your vehicle on a flat, hard surface as far from traffic as possible. Set out flares or warning triangles at least 100 feet in front and back to alert other drivers.

Use two rocks, bricks, or pieces of wood (each at least 4 inches by 8 inches by 2 inches) to block the wheel that is diagonally across from the flat tire. Put one block in front of the wheel and another behind it. The blocks will keep the vehicle from rolling when it is jacked up.

You'll find complete instructions for changing a tire in your owner's manual or inside the trunk of your vehicle. Here are the basic steps.

1. After the wheel blocks are in place, remove the jack, lug wrench, and spare tire from your vehicle and place them near the flat tire.
2. Assemble the jack, and position it according to instructions in the owner's manual. Jack up the vehicle until the flat tire is just in contact with the ground.

◆ When you change a tire, get as far from traffic as possible. Then continue to watch for traffic approaching you.

3. Remove the hubcap or wheel cover from the wheel. Use the lug wrench to loosen the lug nuts enough so that they'll move easily, but do not remove them.
4. Jack up the vehicle until the tire clears the ground.
5. Take off the lug nuts and put them inside the hubcap or in some other safe place.
6. Pull off the wheel with the flat tire. Replace it with the spare tire. Put the lug nuts back on by hand, and tighten them slightly with the wrench.
7. Carefully let the vehicle down, and remove the jack. Tighten the lug nuts with the lug wrench.
8. Put the flat tire, jack, wrench, and other equipment back in the vehicle.
9. If the spare is an undersized tire or limited-mileage tire, drive no faster than 50 mph to the nearest service station. Have the flat tire repaired or replaced right away.

278   UNIT 3   *Moving onto the Road*

Driving Tip

Caution students to avoid driving over seemingly harmless items on the roadway. A flat piece of wood lying on the street, for example, may contain nails that could puncture a tire. Similarly, an apparently empty paper bag may contain glass bottles.

What Should You Do If Your Accelerator Pedal Sticks?

As you're driving along, you decide to decrease speed. You lift your foot from the accelerator pedal but nothing changes; the vehicle keeps moving at the same speed. The problem is a stuck accelerator: The engine does not return to idle when you take your foot off the pedal.

A stuck accelerator pedal may be caused by a sticking linkage or accelerator spring, a broken engine mount, a crumpled floor mat, or ice or snow on the floor around the pedal. Here's what to do.

1. Apply the brakes, and shift to Neutral. The engine will race, but power will be disengaged from the wheels.
2. Check traffic, and signal a lane change.
3. Choose a safe path, and steer off the road, continuing to apply the brakes.
4. When you are off the roadway, shift to Park, turn off the ignition, and apply the parking brake.
5. Do not attempt to unstick the pedal until after you've steered off the road and come to a stop. Test the pedal before reentering traffic. If the pedal problem is mechanical, have it repaired before driving again.

What Should You Do If the Hood Flies Up?

Anything that blocks your forward view is a threat to your safety. If the hood of your vehicle suddenly flies up while you're driving, you must take action to avoid a collision and get off the road.

1. Lean forward and look through the space between the dashboard and the hood. If this view is blocked or limited, roll down your side window and look around the hood. Continue to steer in the direction in which you were moving.
2. Check your mirrors to see what traffic is behind you. Check the traffic to either side of you.
3. Signal to indicate the direction you want to move. Maintain your lane position while waiting for a gap in traffic. Then steer off the road.

TIPS FOR NEW DRIVERS

15-Minute Checkup

To keep your vehicle in good working order, follow the suggestions in your owner's manual for periodic checkups and maintenance. In addition, if you drive 10,000 or more miles a year, do a 15-minute check of the following items every month:

- all lights for burned-out bulbs
- the battery fluid level or, if your vehicle has a sealed battery, the green battery-charge indicator
- the engine oil level and transmission fluid level
- the brake pedal for firmness and proper operation
- the brake fluid level
- the air pressure in all tires
- the tires for uneven wear
- the cooling system
- the hoses and belts that operate the fan, compressor, and the like
- the windshield washer and wipers
- the power-steering fluid level

MEETING STUDENT DIVERSITY

Learning Disabled

The procedure for jump-starting a dead battery confuses some students. Review the sequence of steps—using visual aids or models if possible—as often as needed until students understand how to carry out the procedure safely.

TIPS FOR NEW DRIVERS

For review and reinforcement, you may want to have students discuss the dangers of *not* checking each of these items regularly.

TEACH

Explain

OBJECTIVE 1: Advise students to check their spare tire periodically to make sure it is properly inflated. Also, if wheels are equipped with lock-on wire caps, students should store the key needed to remove the caps in a safe place—preferably with the spare tire or in the glove compartment.

OBJECTIVE 2: Students should recognize the importance of not trying to unstick a stuck accelerator pedal until after they have steered off the road and turned off the engine.

OBJECTIVE 3: Caution students not to let panic cause them to drive unsafely if the hood flies up. They should reduce speed but not change lanes abruptly without looking. They should use the center line or the lane marking to help guide them.

OBJECTIVE 4: Students should recognize the danger of a fuel fire causing the vehicle's gas tank to explode. If a vehicle fire is burning out of control, driver and passengers should move a minimum of 100 feet away from the vehicle.

OBJECTIVE 5: Students should recognize that winter weather is hard on batteries. Caution students to be alert for increasing difficulty starting their vehicle as temperatures drop. It is better to replace an old battery before it goes dead than to be stranded on a freezing winter night.

continued on page 280

OBJECTIVE 6: Students should note that, on most vehicles, replacing a burned-out headlamp is more complicated and time consuming than it might seem. In general, having a service station replace the headlamp is more practical.

Teaching Model

Describe the following situation: You're driving on a highway at 45 mph in light traffic. Suddenly, you hear a loud thunk. The vehicle wobbles, then pulls sharply to the right. You realize that one of your tires has probably lost pressure. Model the thinking process that you will use in response to this situation. (You will do the following.

- Firmly grip the steering wheel with both hands.
- Look well ahead in your intended path.
- Once steering is stable, slowly ease your foot off the accelerator pedal.
- Check traffic, signal, and steer off the road, moving as far off the roadway as possible.
- Apply the brakes gradually as the vehicle slows, stopping on a flat surface.
- Shift into Park (Reverse in a vehicle with a manual transmission), set the parking brake, and put on the emergency flashers.
- Have everyone get out of the vehicle on the side away from traffic.
- Put out flares or warning triangles.
- Change the tire.)

Ask

Ask students to discuss why it would not be a good idea to step hard on the brake pedal as soon as a tire blows out.

Read

Have students read Lesson 2 to learn what actions to take in response to tire failure and other driving-related emergencies.

◆ *Get out of the vehicle as soon as you safely can if your car catches fire.*

What Actions Can You Take If Your Vehicle Catches Fire?

Vehicle fires don't occur often, but when they do, prompt action minimizes risk to people and property.

If the Engine Catches Fire

Engine fires are usually fuel-fed or electrical. You'll see and smell smoke coming from under your hood. Follow these steps.

1. Steer off the road to an open space. Turn off the ignition.
2. Get out of the vehicle, and have all passengers get out too. Move far away from the vehicle. Call for help.
3. Decide how serious the fire is. If it is serious—high heat and flames around the hood—do not attempt to put the fire out yourself. Wait for the fire department.
4. If the fire is not serious and you have a fire extinguisher, you can try to put it out yourself. *Do not use water;* it is not effective against fuel, electrical, and oil fires. Wear gloves, or wrap your hands in cloth. Face away from the vehicle, and crouch down so that your head is at the level of the hood. Do not open the hood. Just pull the hood release to create a small space into which you can spray the extinguishing agent.

If There Is a Fire in the Passenger Compartment

A fire in the passenger compartment is usually caused by carelessness of a passenger or the driver. A common cause of such fires is a burning cigarette or match that drops to the floor or gets blown into the backseat.

If there's a fire in the passenger compartment, steer off the road and stop clear of traffic. Turn off the ignition. Get out of the vehicle, and have all passengers get out. Use a fire extinguisher or water to put out the fire.

What Should You Do If Your Vehicle's Battery Is Dead?

It's a freezing-cold winter night. You turn the ignition switch to start. Nothing happens—no sound, no engine turnover, nothing. Your vehicle's battery is dead.

A battery may go dead if you keep your headlights on or play the radio for a long time while the engine is not running. An old battery may no longer have enough power to start a vehicle in very cold weather.

IT'S A FACT

Early tires did not last nearly as long as present-day tires. In fact, in the early days of the automobile, providing and replacing tires was the single greatest expense of vehicle ownership. A set of four tires could cost as much as $1,500.

If the battery is dead, you can't start the engine. However, you may be able to restore power to your battery by using jumper cables.

Jump-Starting Your Vehicle

The most common way to recharge your battery is to **jump-start** it. To do this, you need another vehicle with a working battery that is the same voltage as yours and a pair of jumper cables.

Before you decide to jump-start your battery, make sure the battery fluid is not frozen or the level of fluid low. If it is, do *not* attempt to jump-start your battery because it might explode.

To jump-start your vehicle, follow these steps.

1. Position the vehicle so that the cables can reach between the two batteries. Do not let the vehicles touch.
2. Turn off ignition and electrical equipment in both vehicles. Shift both vehicles into Park or Neutral. Put on their parking brakes.
3. Double-check to make sure both vehicle batteries have the same voltage (usually 12 volts).
4. If either battery has cell or vent caps, remove them. Check again to make sure your dead battery is not frozen.
5. Cover each battery with a heavy cloth to protect against splashing of boiling battery fluid.
6. Attach the positive jumper cable (red, or marked P or +) to the positive terminal of the good battery. Clamp the other end of the same cable to the positive terminal of the dead battery.
7. Attach the negative jumper cable (black, or marked N or –) to the engine or frame of the vehicle with the good battery. Be sure the cable does not touch the fan or drive belts.
8. Attach the other end of the negative cable to the engine or frame of the vehicle with the dead battery. Connect as far as possible from the battery or moving parts, such as the fan.
9. Start the engine of the vehicle that has the good battery. Hold down the accelerator so that the engine runs at a high idle.
10. Start the engine of the vehicle with the dead battery, and with the cables still attached, run it for several minutes.
11. With both engines still running, remove the cables in reverse order from the order in which you attached them.
12. Replace battery caps if they've been removed, and dispose of the cloth covers in case they contain acid.

◆ *It's a good idea to keep jumper cables in the trunk of your car.*

ASSESS

Guided Practice

Have students answer the Lesson 2 Review questions. The answers are provided below.

Reteaching

As students did in Lesson 1, have them work together in pairs or small groups to create "What Do I Do If . . ." posters. These posters should contain brief, step-by-step guidelines explaining what to do if:

- a tire blows out or goes flat.
- the accelerator pedal gets stuck.
- the hood flies up.
- the engine catches fire.
- there is a fire in the passenger compartment.
- the battery goes dead.
- headlights fail.

After students finish their posters, have them share their work with the class. Extend the discussion by asking students to describe the risks associated with each problem and to explain how they can manage visibility, time, and space factors to reduce these risks.

Enrichment

Assign the Study Guide for Lesson 2. The Find Out More section encourages students to expand their basic learning of the lesson concepts.

Driving Tip

Caution students that vehicle breakdowns and emergencies can be doubly dangerous at night and in bad weather because of reduced visibility. Tell students that if they are forced to pull over under such circumstances, they should do all they can—set up flares, turn on flashers, raise the hood—to increase their vehicle's visibility to other drivers. Moreover, if driver or passengers must leave the vehicle, they should keep a safe distance off the roadway.

CLOSE

Summarize

Return to the Motivator question. Recall students' initial responses, and have students expand or modify their original answers with additional information that they have learned from this lesson.

Extend the discussion by asking how this situation is similar to and different from the various other emergency situations studied in Lessons 1 and 2. Encourage students to come up with general conclusions or guidelines regarding how to respond to driving-related emergencies.

DRIVER'S LOG

Have students add to the section on driving-related emergencies that they began in Lesson 1. Direct them to include each of the driving-related emergencies studied in this lesson along with the specific response strategies they learned. Also have students make note of any general conclusions or guidelines regarding how to deal with driving-related emergencies.

WHAT WOULD YOU DO?

Sample answer: Look through the space between the dashboard and hood or open the window and look around the hood; steer off the road when it is safe to do so.

What Should You Do If Your Headlights Fail?

Headlight failure at night is dangerous because without lights, your ability to see is reduced, as is the ability of other drivers to see your vehicle.

Rarely do both headlights fail at the same time. However, if one headlight goes out, you may not notice it until the other also goes out. Headlight failure is usually the result of a burned-out low-beam headlamp.

If you're driving at night and suddenly your lights flicker or die, you have to get off the road, but without making any sudden, possibly dangerous moves. Here's what to do.

1. Slow down and continue in the same direction you were going. Be aware of the traffic around you.
2. Try switching to high beams. Headlights seldom burn out on both high and low beams at the same time. If switching to high beams gives no light, try turning on parking lights, turn indicators, and the emergency flashers. These can give you enough light to help you get off the road.
3. When you see a gap in traffic, steer off the roadway. If you have no lights at all, look for the side-lane markers on the pavement. You can also use available light from other vehicles on the roadway.
4. If possible, stop your vehicle off the roadway near a lighted place, such as a lighted sign, building, or streetlight. Call for help.

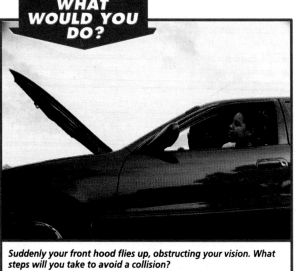

WHAT WOULD YOU DO?

Suddenly your front hood flies up, obstructing your vision. What steps will you take to avoid a collision?

Lesson 2 Review

1. What would you do if one of your vehicle's tires suddenly lost pressure while you were driving?
2. How would you deal with a stuck accelerator pedal while driving?
3. What would you do if your vehicle's hood flew up while you were driving?
4. How would you respond to an engine fire? To a fire in the passenger compartment?
5. List the steps for jump-starting a dead battery.
6. What would you do if your headlights failed while you were driving at night?

Lesson 2 Review

Answers

1. Grip wheel firmly; once steering is stable, release accelerator; steer safely off road.
2. Brake and shift to Neutral; steer off road; turn off engine, apply parking brake, shift to Park.
3. Look through space between dashboard and hood or open window and look around hood; steer off road.
4. Engine: steer off road; shut off engine; move away from vehicle; get help; inside: steer off road; turn off engine; use fire extinguisher.
5. Connect positive terminal of good battery to positive terminal of dead battery; attach negative cable to engine or frame of vehicle with good battery, then to engine or frame of vehicle with dead battery; start vehicle with good battery; start other engine.
6. Reduce speed; try high beams and other lights; steer off road and get help.

Waiting for Help and Protecting the Scene

OBJECTIVES

1. Describe how you would get help if your vehicle broke down.
2. Explain how you would protect yourself at the scene.

In an emergency, you may need assistance even though you may be miles from a phone. You may be able to correct a minor mechanical problem yourself. You might also choose to call on passing vehicles and pedestrians to get the help you need.

What Should You Do at the Scene of a Vehicle Breakdown or Other Emergency?

If your vehicle breaks down, you may be able to remedy the problem yourself—by changing a flat tire, for example. If you can't fix the problem, you'll need to get help.

After pulling completely out of traffic, you'll have to communicate your situation to passing drivers or pedestrians in a way that keeps you and other roadway users safe.

Make Others Aware of Your Problem

If you have a cellular phone, you'll be able to call for help immediately from your vehicle.

If you have no cell phone and must pull off the road at a place where there's no telephone within safe walking distance, you'll need to get the attention of other drivers. To do this safely—in a way that protects you as well as other drivers—raise the hood of your vehicle, and tie a handkerchief or scarf to the antenna or left door handle. You can also hold the handkerchief or scarf in place by closing a window on it. Set out flares or warning triangles to alert other drivers. Stay in the vehicle if you have pulled well off the roadway. Otherwise,

◆ *Raising the hood of your car is one action you can take to let others know you need help.*

CHAPTER 15 *Responding to an Emergency* **283**

IT'S A FACT

Almost 60 percent of all teenage motor vehicle deaths occur on weekends. More than twice as many male teenagers as female teenagers are killed in motor vehicle crashes.

LESSON THREE

Waiting for Help and Protecting the Scene

(pages 283–284)

FOCUS

Objectives

• Describe how you would get help if your vehicle broke down.
• Explain how you would protect yourself at the scene.

Resources

📁 Study Guide, page 59
📁 Traffic charts

Motivator

You thought you could make it to the next exit on the highway. You were wrong. Your vehicle is running out of gas. How can you reduce risk to yourself and others after you pull off the road? (Raise the hood; tie a handkerchief or scarf to the antenna or outside left door handle; switch on emergency flashers; set out flares or other warning devices.)

TEACH

Explain

OBJECTIVE 1: Caution students to keep young children close to the vehicle and not let them wander near the roadway.

OBJECTIVE 2: Explain to students the dangers of carbon monoxide poisoning if they wait in the vehicle with the engine running.

Teaching Model

Describe the following situation: Engine trouble forces you to pull onto the shoulder. Model the thinking process that you would use if you could not fix the problem. (You would make other drivers aware of your situation; take steps to protect yourself and your passengers; be prepared to make decisions once help arrived.)

Ask

Ask students to discuss the risks of stopping along the shoulder.

Read

Have students read Lesson 3 to learn what to do at the scene of an emergency while awaiting help.

ASSESS

Guided Practice

Have students answer the Lesson 3 Review questions. The answers are provided below.

Reteaching

Have students work in small groups to create a "Safety at the Scene" checklist.

Enrichment

Assign the Study Guide for Lesson 3. The Find Out More section encourages students to expand their basic learning of the lesson concepts.

CLOSE

Summarize

Return to the Motivator question, and discuss the importance of maximizing visibility.

DRIVER'S LOG

How can you minimize risk while waiting for assistance?

SAFETY TIPS

If your vehicle breaks down on a highway, your immediate goal is to get the vehicle safely off the roadway and onto the shoulder. Then set out flares or other warning devices to increase your vehicle's visibility to other drivers.

WHAT WOULD YOU DO?

Your vehicle has broken down and you have moved it to the side of the road. What actions will you take to find assistance?

get as far away from the road as you can. Switch on your emergency flashers to alert passing drivers to your situation.

Protect Yourself

You can wait inside your vehicle if the weather is bad and you're far enough off the road. Keep the windows almost closed and the doors locked. Do not sit in a stopped car with windows closed, engine running, and heater on. You could be putting yourself and your passengers at risk of carbon monoxide poisoning.

It is very dangerous to lower your window or open your vehicle door to strangers. If a stranger does stop to offer help, just ask the person to call for emergency road service.

If your vehicle is not far enough from roadway traffic or if you think it might be struck from behind by another vehicle, leave your vehicle and walk to a safe place. Proceed carefully—especially at night or in bad weather, when visibility is limited.

Never stand behind or directly in front of your vehicle. Other roadway users will have trouble seeing you, and you could be struck by an oncoming vehicle.

Make Decisions When Help Comes

Emergency road service operators can usually change a flat tire or do minor repairs on the spot. They may also have gasoline and a booster battery in case you've run out of gas or have a dead battery.

If you need to be towed to a service garage, you should know whether or not your insurance covers all or part of the towing charge. You should also find out how many miles away the service garage is and what the charge is for towing.

If your vehicle is towed, you'll have to arrange transportation for yourself and your passengers. Passengers are not allowed to ride in a vehicle when it's being towed.

Lesson 3 Review

1. What steps would you take to get help if your vehicle broke down?
2. How would you protect yourself at the scene?

WHAT WOULD YOU DO?

Sample answer: Raise hood, tie handkerchief to outside door handle, and switch on emergency flashers.

Lesson 3 Review

Answers
1. Raise hood; tie handkerchief or scarf to antenna or door handle; put on flashers; set out flares or other warning devices.
2. Wait inside vehicle; keep windows almost closed and doors locked; leave vehicle and walk to safe place if possible; don't stand directly in front of or directly in back of vehicle.

First Aid Guidelines and Procedures

First aid is emergency treatment given to a person who is injured or ill, before professional medical care arrives. Learning about first aid procedures may help you prevent further injury or even save someone's life in an emergency.

What Are Some Basic First Aid Guidelines?

Because it is usually another motorist and not a medical professional who is first on the scene, all drivers should have some knowledge of first aid. You can learn first aid by taking a course given by the American National Red Cross. You can also read about first aid procedures in a manual or book. However, to really know what you're doing, you need both training and practice in first aid.

Here are some basic first aid guidelines for emergency situations.

- Quickly search the scene and decide if you can help. If you feel confused and uncertain, do not try to give first aid. Call for help.
- The person with the most experience should give first aid. If there are other uninjured people nearby, quickly find out who among you has the most experience with first aid.
- If more than one person is injured, care for the most seriously injured person first.
- Keep calm and act quickly and quietly. Speak in a normal tone of voice. Try not to worry the injured.
- Check that the injured person is breathing. If not, start mouth-to-mouth resuscitation. (See page 286.)
- Find out if the injured person is bleeding. Try to stop any serious bleeding as quickly as possible.
- *Never* move an injured person unless you must do so for his or her safety. Moving an injured person can worsen the injury. Try to keep injured people from moving.
- Get trained medical help as soon as possible. However, if you are the only uninjured person at the scene, do not leave the victim in order to get help unless you have no other choice.

OBJECTIVES

1. List several basic first aid guidelines.
2. Describe procedures for controlling bleeding, treating shock, and restoring breathing.
3. List the items that should be in a first aid kit.

KEY TERMS

first aid
mouth-to-mouth resuscitation
hemorrhaging
shock

◆ *First aid can be given to injured persons before an ambulance arrives on the scene.*

CHAPTER 15   *Responding to an Emergency*   **285**

Driving Tip

Advise students that they may want to keep a first aid manual handy in their vehicle. Various manuals of this sort are available in paperback at low cost.

FOCUS

Objectives

- List several basic first aid guidelines.
- Describe procedures for controlling bleeding, treating shock, and restoring breathing.
- List the items that should be in a first aid kit.

Resources

📁 Study Guide, page 60

Vocabulary

first aid
mouth-to-mouth resuscitation
hemorrhaging
shock

Motivator

Pose the following: While driving on a suburban highway, you come upon the scene of a two-vehicle collision. Apparently, the crash just occurred because neither police nor medical personnel are at the scene. What should you do? (Remain calm; decide if you can help; provide necessary first aid care if you are capable; obtain medical assistance as soon as possible.)

TEACH

Explain

OBJECTIVE 1: Students should realize that moving an injured person unnecessarily can cause the person serious, even permanent damage.

OBJECTIVE 2: Students may benefit from a discussion of the value of taking a first aid course. Such courses can prepare students to deal with driving-related as well as other types of emergencies. A first aid course may be of special value to students who baby-sit, those with elderly relatives, and students who participate in such outdoor activities as camping and boating.

OBJECTIVE 3: Students should be aware that some of the contents of a first aid kit may dry out or otherwise deteriorate over time, particularly when subjected to temperature extremes. Students should also note the value of having a blanket and flashlight in the vehicle for emergency use.

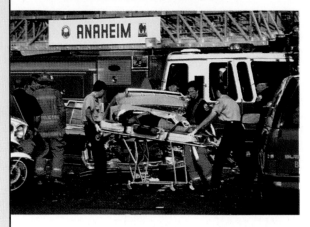

◆ *Professional medical personnel are the only ones who should move an injured person.*

SAFETY TIPS

Wear protective equipment when giving first aid to a seriously injured person. For example, disposable gloves will decrease the risk of contracting an infectious disease. Keep one or two pairs of disposable gloves in your vehicle's first aid kit. Consult a first aid manual for additional information.

- A person who looks uninjured but is unable to move may have an injury to the spine. Do *not* try to move the person. Cover him or her with a blanket if available, and go for help.
- Take precautions to protect yourself against exposure to an injured person's blood or body fluids.

What Are Some Specific First Aid Procedures?

You should learn procedures for restoring breathing, controlling bleeding, and treating shock. They could help you save a life.

Restoring Breathing

Two or three minutes without breathing can cause permanent brain damage. Six minutes without breathing can cause death. To try to restore breathing, apply **mouth-to-mouth resuscitation.**

1. Place the person faceup. Then kneel down and clear the victim's mouth with your fingers.
2. Put one hand under the victim's neck. Gently tilt the head backward, pushing the chin up. Using your thumb and index finger, pinch the victim's nostrils closed.
3. Put your mouth right over the victim's mouth. Blow air into the victim's mouth until you see his or her chest rise. Remove your mouth. Let air escape from the victim's lungs while you take another breath.
4. Repeat the procedure. You should blow air into an adult's mouth at a rate of about 12 times per minute. For children, the rate should be about 20 times per minute. Continue until you are sure the victim is breathing independently or until medical help arrives.

Controlling Bleeding

Someone who is bleeding heavily, or **hemorrhaging,** can die within minutes, so it is very important to try to stop heavy bleeding as quickly as possible.

You can control heavy bleeding by applying direct pressure. Remember to wear protective equipment, such as disposable gloves. Put a clean cloth—such as a folded handkerchief or piece of a shirt—directly over the wound and press down firmly. If you don't have a clean cloth, press directly on the wound with your gloved hand. Keep pressing, without lifting your hand, until medical help arrives.

286   UNIT 3   *Moving onto the Road*

State BY State

A growing number of communities are requiring bicycle riders to wear protective helmets. Injury statistics across the country indicate that this is a wise trend. In one North Carolina study, for example, 99 percent of young bicyclists (under age 15) treated in emergency rooms had not been wearing helmets. In a Dade County, Florida, study, the head or the neck was the most seriously injured part of the body for 96 percent of fatally injured bicyclists.

Other means of stopping heavy bleeding are to apply arterial pressure or to use a tourniquet. Do not use either of these methods unless you are fully trained to do so.

Treating Shock

Serious injury, bleeding, or burns can cause shock. When a person is in a state of **shock,** the blood does not circulate properly. As a result, the brain and other tissues fail to get enough oxygen. Shock can cause death if it is not treated.

A shock victim usually feels faint, weak, cold, and often nauseated. The person's skin will feel cold and clammy and may look pale—even blue. Breathing is irregular, and the pulse is weak and fast.

It is wise to treat seriously injured people for shock even if they do not show signs of it. Keep the victim warm with a blanket or coat. Try to keep the body temperature near normal. Control any bleeding, and loosen tight clothing. Do not give the injured person anything to eat or drink. This could induce vomiting and aggravate any internal injuries.

FYI

A rear-end vehicle collision may cause a whiplash injury, in which the victim's head snaps backward, then abruptly whips forward. Such an injury can cause severe neck damage. This type of injury can be minimized by ensuring that your headrest is properly adjusted at all times.

What Items Should You Include in a First Aid Kit for Your Vehicle?

Always keep a first aid kit in your vehicle. The contents of the kit may enable you to save a life—or enable someone else to save your life.

CONNECTIONS
History

In 1881 Clara Barton founded the American Red Cross in Washington, D.C. It is a nonprofit humanitarian organization with the express purpose of preventing and easing human suffering. In 1905 the organization was renamed the American National Red Cross. It made a commitment to provide a worldwide network of emergency relief.

Throughout the 20th century, the American National Red Cross has been a pioneer in the field of emergency relief and medical assistance. The organization provided assistance during World Wars I and II, contributing medical supplies, blood plasma, and able-bodied volunteers. Following

World War II, the organization launched a program to provide blood to people of all races, colors, and creeds who need it.

During the past 40 years, the American National Red Cross has become deeply involved in the field of public health. The organization offers many instructional programs in first aid, lifesaving, nurse's aide training, baby care, and home nursing. Many people serve in first aid stations and mobile units along highways.

There are now more than 2 million Red Cross volunteers nationwide. In addition, more than 20 million Junior Red Cross members participate in activities geared toward helping people in their communities as well as underprivileged children in other countries.

MEETING STUDENT DIVERSITY

Learning Disabled

As an aid to comprehension, provide students with an actual first aid kit to examine. Give students time to study the contents and ask questions.

CONNECTIONS
History

Point out that the American National Red Cross offers first aid instructional programs for people of all ages in communities all across the country.

Teaching Model

Describe the following situation: A driver loses control of his vehicle and crashes into a tree. You are the first person to arrive at the scene of the collision. The driver is conscious and breathing and does not seem to be severely injured. However, a cut on his arm is bleeding heavily. Model the thinking process that you will use in this situation. (You will keep calm and act quickly; not move the person and try not to let him move; use a clean cloth to apply direct pressure to the wound until medical help arrives.)

Ask

Ask students to discuss how they might handle this situation if more than one person were injured.

Read

Have students read Lesson 4 to learn some basic first aid guidelines and procedures they could apply at the scene of an emergency.

ASSESS

Guided Practice

Have students answer the Lesson 4 Review questions. The answers are provided below.

Reteaching

Have students work in small groups to create charts or posters of first aid do's and don'ts. After groups have completed their charts or posters, have them share their work with the class.

Enrichment

Assign the Study Guide for Lesson 4. The Find Out More section encourages students to expand their basic learning of the lesson concepts.

CLOSE

Summarize

Reexamine the Motivator question. Recall students' initial responses, and have students summarize the additional information that they have gained from this lesson. To extend the discussion, suggest different variables for the situation, such as multivehicle involvement or limited visibility conditions.

DRIVER'S LOG

In the students' section on driving-related emergencies, have students write basic guidelines for what to do—and what not to do—with regard to first aid in emergency situations.

WHAT WOULD YOU DO?

Sample answer: Use a clean cloth to apply direct pressure.

ADVICE FROM THE EXPERTS

Loretta J. Martin
Coordinator, Safety and Driver Education, Chicago Public Schools

Roadside emergencies can happen anytime. You can minimize their consequences if you mentally prepare for them, know how to handle common vehicle failure, and know what to do at the scene of an emergency.
- *Don't drive unless you are fit.*
- *Wear your safety belt.*
- *Carry an emergency car kit.*
- *Carry a good first-aid kit and know how to use it.*
- *Protect the scene.*
- *Know how to get help quickly.*

The American National Red Cross suggests that the following items be included in a first aid kit:
- bottle of syrup of ipecac; bottle of activated charcoal (both for use only on advice of a medical professional)
- change for phone calls
- pencil and notebook
- disposable gloves
- plastic adhesive bandages (25, in various sizes)
- gauze dressings (12, 4 inches square)
- roller gauze bandages (2 rolls, 3 inches wide)
- safety pins (10, in various sizes)
- adhesive tape (1 roll, 1 inch wide)
- scissors
- triangular bandages (5)
- moist towelettes (6)
- combine dressings (3)
- tweezers

Check the contents of your first aid kit regularly, and replace any items as needed. Be sure to keep the kit out of children's reach.

WHAT WOULD YOU DO?

You have been involved in a collision with another vehicle. You are uninjured, but the other driver is bleeding. How can you help?

Lesson 4 Review

1. What first aid guidelines should you follow in an emergency?
2. What are the first aid procedures for restoring breathing, controlling bleeding, and treating shock?
3. What items should you include in a first aid kit for your vehicle?

Lesson 4 Review

Answers
1. Scan the scene; decide if you can help; give first aid if you are capable; never move an injured person unless you must; get medical help.
2. Breathing: ensure airway is clear, give mouth-to-mouth resuscitation; bleeding: apply direct pressure; shock: keep victim warm, loosen tight clothing, give no food or drink.
3. Bandages, dressings, safety pins, tape, scissors, towelettes, tweezers, syrup of ipecac, activated charcoal, change for phone, pencil and notebook.

Benjamin Banneker

To drivers traveling through the United States, it seems as though many major cities just grew, without any plan at all. In many cases, this is true. However, our capital city, Washington, D.C., is one of the few cities in this country that was designed before it was built. This is particularly evident in the area surrounding the United States Capitol, which is located near the center of Washington. Like the spokes of a wheel, broad streets extend out from the Capitol in all directions. This roadway pattern can also be seen near Union Station, the Lincoln Memorial, and Mt. Vernon Square.

President George Washington chose Pierre L'Enfant, a French engineer, to draw up the plans for the new capital. Benjamin Banneker helped L'Enfant to work out the city's plan and to survey, or measure, the size, shape, and area of the land. Banneker was the first African American ever to be appointed to work for the government.

L'Enfant left the United States before the building of Washington, D.C., was completed, taking the plans with him. However, Benjamin Banneker stepped in and finished laying out the city from memory.

Benjamin Banneker was the son of a free woman and a slave father. He was born free in 1731 on a farm in Maryland. Banneker was educated in a Quaker school, where he became interested in mathematics and science. He later taught himself astronomy.

Banneker used his knowledge to make astronomical and tidal calculations in order to write a yearly almanac predicting weather conditions. He sent a copy of his almanac to Thomas Jefferson along with a letter urging the abolition of slavery. Those against slavery held Banneker up as an example of the talents and abilities of African Americans.

What Do You Think Now?

What do you think was Benjamin Banneker's most important accomplishment? Why?

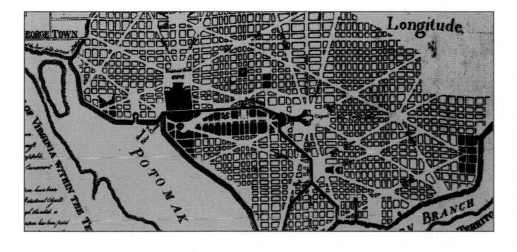

BUILDING SKILLS: CRITICAL THINKING

Objective

Demonstrate an ability to analyze information and form a conclusion.

Teaching the Skill

- Direct students' attention to the map of Washington, D.C. Have students note which features the map does and does not show. Ask what purpose such a map might serve.

- Encourage students to think about the spokelike arrangement of streets. Have students discuss what the advantages and disadvantages of such a design might be.

- Have students list and discuss Benjamin Banneker's accomplishments. Ask students to think about which accomplishment may have posed the greatest challenge to Banneker and why.

ANSWERS TO
What Do You Think Now Questions

Students' answers may vary, but they should reflect students' understanding that Banneker's role in helping to lay out Washington, D.C., had long-range significance.

CHAPTER SUMMARY

Key Points

Have students read the Key Points to review the major concepts of the chapter.

PROJECTS

Cooperative Learning:
Students will benefit by working with a partner on one or both projects. When the assignment is completed, the whole class will profit by sharing and comparing results.

CHAPTER 15 REVIEW

KEY POINTS

Lesson One

1. In case of brake failure, rapidly pump the brake pedal. If that doesn't work, use the parking brake. Downshift.
2. If your engine stalls while you're driving, signal and steer off the road. If your vehicle is in motion, shift to Neutral and try to restart the engine. If the engine won't start, steer near the curb or onto the shoulder and stop.
3. If your vehicle's power steering fails, grip the steering wheel firmly and turn it with more force than usual. Steer off the road and stop. In case of total steering failure, use the parking brake to stop.

Lesson Two

1. If your vehicle has a blowout or flat tire, keep a firm grip on the steering wheel. When steering is stablized, release the accelerator slowly but do not brake. Steer off the road.
2. If the accelerator pedal sticks, brake and shift to Neutral. Carefully steer off the road.
3. If the hood flies up, look through the space between the dashboard and the hood or out of the driver's side window. Continue to steer in the direction in which you were moving until you can leave the road.

4. In case of a vehicle fire, steer off the road to an open space. Turn off the ignition. Get out and move away from the vehicle. Call for help.
5. To jump-start a dead battery, turn off the ignition in both vehicles, and shift both into Park. Attach the jumper cables properly. Start the engine of the vehicle with the good battery, then the engine of the other vehicle.
6. If your headlights fail, slow down and switch to high beams. If that doesn't work, turn on the parking lights, turn indicators, and flashers to see how to get off the road.

Lesson Three

1. If your vehicle breaks down, get off the road. Let other drivers know you need help.
2. Protect yourself at the scene. Wait inside your vehicle. Don't open your vehicle to strangers.

Lesson Four

1. If you encounter an injured motorist, see if you can help. Give first aid if necessary. Never move an injured person.
2. To restore breathing, give mouth-to-mouth resuscitation. To control bleeding, apply direct pressure to the wound. To treat shock, keep the victim warm.

PROJECTS

1. Look over a vehicle owner's manual. What special directions does the manual contain for avoiding and responding to vehicle failures and emergencies? What preventive maintenance tips does the manual offer?
2. Interview a member of a first aid squad. Ask what collision-related injuries occur most frequently. Also find out what kinds of first aid treatments are given most frequently.

*inter*NET
CONNECTION
Use the Internet to gather more information on AAA and the educational and other services they provide in addition to emergency road service.
drivered.glencoe.com

*inter*NET
CONNECTION

Visit Glencoe's Driver Education Web site for student activities that relate to this chapter.
drivered.glencoe.com

CHAPTER TEST

Write the letter of the answer that best completes each sentence.

1. If your vehicle breaks down, you should
   a. phone for help or get the attention of passing drivers.
   b. stand directly in front of your vehicle until help arrives.
   c. stand in the road and wave your arms.

2. If your steering wheel suddenly becomes very hard to turn, the problem probably is
   a. power-steering failure.
   b. engine overheating.
   c. wet brakes.

3. If one of your tires suddenly loses pressure,
   a. release the accelerator slowly.
   b. brake hard.
   c. immediately shift into Park.

4. A collision victim who looks uninjured but cannot move
   a. should try to get up and walk around.
   b. may have a spinal injury.
   c. should be moved as quickly as possible.

5. If the fluid in your battery is frozen and the engine won't start,
   a. use jumper cables.
   b. do not use jumper cables.
   c. turn on the heater and use jumper cables.

6. If the hood flies up while you're driving,
   a. stop immediately.
   b. honk your horn and move right.
   c. look through the space between the hood and the dashboard.

7. If your foot brake suddenly loses power,
   a. turn the ignition to the lock position.
   b. shift into Reverse.
   c. rapidly pump the brake pedal.

8. A victim who feels faint, weak, and cold
   a. needs artificial respiration.
   b. should be kept as cool as possible.
   c. may be suffering from shock.

9. To dry wet brakes,
   a. drive slowly with your left foot pressing gently on the brake pedal.
   b. stamp down on the pedal several times.
   c. drive in low gear.

10. To put out a minor engine fire, use
    a. a fire extinguisher.
    b. water.
    c. a heavy cloth.

Write the word or phrase that best completes each sentence.

engine flooding   first aid   hemorrhaging
cooling system   brake fade   resuscitation

11. A person who is _____ can die in minutes.

12. Applying your brakes hard for a long time may cause _____.

13. Your engine may overheat if there is not enough coolant in the _____.

14. _____ is emergency treatment given to a person who has been injured.

15. Pumping the accelerator repeatedly when trying to start your vehicle can result in _____.

DRIVER'S LOG

In this chapter, you have learned about how to deal with emergency situations caused by vehicle failures and those in which personal injury is involved. Write two paragraphs giving your ideas on the most important factors to keep in mind when confronted with both types of emergency.

CHAPTER TEST

Assign the Chapter Test to all students.

Answers

1. a
2. a
3. a
4. b
5. b
6. c
7. c
8. c
9. a
10. a
11. hemorrhaging
12. brake fade
13. cooling system
14. First aid
15. engine flooding

DRIVER'S LOG

Students' responses will reflect their personal viewpoints. However, their answers should provide an assessment of their understanding of how to deal with an emergency situation.

Evaluate

- Test A, pages 29–30 or Test B, pages 29–30 📂
- Testmaker software

RETURN TO THE BIG IDEA ———

Discuss why it is essential to remain calm in an emergency, using driving-related examples studied in this chapter. Also explore the idea that "freezing" or reacting with panic can only make a bad situation worse.

UNIT 3

This review tests students' knowledge of the material in Chapters 1–15. Use the review to help students study for their state driving test.

Answers

1. b
2. c
3. b
4. d
5. c
6. c
7. b
8. a
9. b
10. b
11. c
12. b
13. b
14. d

UNIT 3 CUMULATIVE REVIEW

This review tests your knowledge of the material in Chapters 1–15. Use the review to help you study for your state driving test. Choose the answer that best completes each statement.

1. The penalties for DWI and DUI
   a. are the same in all states.
   b. differ from state to state.
   c. are set by the National Highway Safety Act.
   d. are not very severe.

2. When driving at 55 mph, your following distance should be at least
   a. 10 seconds.
   b. 6 seconds.
   c. 4 seconds.
   d. 1 minute.

3. When turning left from a two-way street,
   a. yield the right-of-way to traffic behind you.
   b. yield the right-of-way to oncoming traffic.
   c. use hand signals.
   d. shift into Reverse gear.

4. While driving, you should
   a. aim low and look down.
   b. keep your head moving.
   c. keep your windows open.
   d. keep your eyes moving.

5. Lane-use lights are mounted
   a. on slow-moving vehicles.
   b. below warning signs.
   c. above reversible lanes.
   d. on telephone poles.

6. The best way to avoid becoming a problem drinker is to
   a. drink only on weekends.
   b. drink beer only.
   c. avoid drinking in the first place.
   d. drink at home.

7. A problem common to rural roads in spring and fall is the presence of
   a. busy intersections.
   b. slow-moving vehicles.
   c. HOV lanes.
   d. smog.

8. A driver can avoid skidding in the rain by
   a. changing speed gradually instead of abruptly.
   b. driving between 45 and 60 mph.
   c. frequently changing gears.
   d. riding the clutch.

9. Inertia, friction, and kinetic energy are
   a. difficult to manage.
   b. natural laws.
   c. different terms for visibility, time, and space.
   d. culprits.

10. Vehicles made since 1986 are required to have
    a. air bags and safety belts at all seats.
    b. a third, centered, high-mounted brake light.
    c. power windows.
    d. antilock brakes.

11. To make a turnabout safely, you need
    a. 100 yards of visibility.
    b. 1,000 feet of visibility in each direction.
    c. 500 feet of visibility in each direction.
    d. at least 1 minute.

12. Friction between the road and tires is
    a. latex.
    b. adhesion.
    c. centrifugal force.
    d. gravity.

13. If your accelerator sticks, you should
    a. reach down and grab it.
    b. shift to Neutral and steer off the road.
    c. jump out of the vehicle.
    d. pump the brakes.

292

14. Crosswalks are most frequently located at
    a. bridges.
    b. steep grades.
    c. campsites.
    d. intersections.

15. A good driver is one who has learned
    a. to eliminate risk completely.
    b. how to manage risk.
    c. to drive very fast.
    d. to read a map while driving.

16. Parking at an angle of 90 degrees to the curb is called
    a. parallel parking.
    b. illegal parking.
    c. double parking.
    d. perpendicular parking.

17. *Jaywalking* refers to the act of
    a. walking across a street without regard for traffic rules.
    b. smoking marijuana in public.
    c. obeying traffic rules.
    d. yielding the right of way to others.

18. Gravity pulls objects
    a. toward a collision.
    b. across a banked road.
    c. toward the Earth's center.
    d. into kinetic energy.

19. When making a right turn, you should wait until there is a
    a. 2-second gap to your left.
    b. 6- to 8-second gap to your left.
    c. 7- to 9-second gap to your right.
    d. 12-second gap to your right.

20. You can reduce glare in snowy weather by wearing
    a. sun visors.
    b. sunglasses.
    c. a defroster.
    d. a hat.

21. Points at which you can safely enter or exit a limited-access highway are called
    a. intersections.
    b. HOV lanes.
    c. crosswalks.
    d. interchanges.

22. As you enter a turn or a curve, you should
    a. decrease speed.
    b. increase speed.
    c. maintain an even speed.
    d. apply centrifugal force.

23. A way to restore breathing is using
    a. direct pressure.
    b. mouth-to-mouth resuscitation.
    c. a tourniquet.
    d. an air bag.

24. A vehicle with a manual shift has
    a. an automatic transmission.
    b. two brake pedals.
    c. a selector lever.
    d. a clutch and a gearshift.

25. A vehicle's rate of acceleration is
    a. lower at high speeds.
    b. lower at low speeds.
    c. perception distance.
    d. set by the Uniform Vehicle Code.

26. Truck drivers have poor visibility
    a. behind a car.
    b. in daylight.
    c. at speeds of 55 mph.
    d. to the sides.

27. Engine fires are often
    a. caused by cigarette smoking.
    b. electrical in nature.
    c. best ignored.
    d. easily extinguished by water.

Answers

15. b
16. d
17. a
18. c
19. b
20. b
21. d
22. a
23. b
24. d
25. a
26. d
27. b

Planning for Your Future

UNIT THEME

In Unit 4, students will begin to consider their future as drivers. They will investigate priorities to take into account in the eventual purchase of a vehicle and explore the basics of vehicle care and maintenance. Students will also examine the planning involved in using their vehicle.

294

UNIT 4

Planning for Your Future

As a driver, you will make many important decisions. This unit will help you develop guidelines so that your decisions will be based on understanding your needs, intelligent planning, and informed judgment.

295

TEACHING YOUR TEENS TO DRIVE

AAA's *Teaching Your Teens to Drive: A Partnership for Survival* helps new drivers, with their parents' assistance, develop their driving skills. The program is available as a videotape or CD-ROM, both with a handbook.

Buying a Vehicle Overview

THEME DEVELOPMENT Buying and owning a vehicle require the maturity to accept responsibility, the knowledge to make wise choices, and the ability to afford the costs involved. Although vehicle ownership is a responsibility that generally should not be undertaken until after high school graduation, it is important for students to understand the factors involved in choosing and owning a vehicle.

CHAPTER FEATURES	TCR COMPONENTS
	Study Guide, p. 61
	Lesson Plan, p. 33
	Information Masters 7, 9, 23, and 26
TIPS FOR NEW DRIVERS Checking the condition of a used vehicle.	Study Guide, p. 62 Transparency 40 Lesson Plan, p. 33 Information Masters 7, 9, 23, and 26
CONNECTIONS Math Calculating interest on a loan.	Study Guide, p. 63 Lesson Plan, p. 34 Information Masters 7, 9, 23, and 26
ADVICE FROM THE EXPERTS Safety factors to consider when buying a vehicle.	Study Guide, p. 64 Lesson Plan, p. 34
BUILDING SKILLS: READING MAPS Understanding Map Symbols **PROJECTS** **1.** Visit several vehicle dealerships. **2.** Interview a local insurance agent.	Test A, pp. 31–32 Test B, pp. 31–32

OTHER PROGRAM RESOURCES

Testmaker software

ADDITIONAL RESOURCES

AAA Autograph '99
Consumer Reports

CHAPTER 16

CHAPTER TEST

CHAPTER 16 Buying a Vehicle

TEST A

Read each statement below. If it is true, place a T in the space to the left of the statement. If the statement is false, place an F next to it.

_F_ 1. A new vehicle costs more to maintain than a used vehicle.

_T_ 2. Most fatalities occur in head-on collisions in which the driver hits the steering wheel.

_F_ 3. Death rates in crashes involving large vehicles are higher than in ones involving the smallest vehicles.

_F_ 4. The more cylinders in the engine, the less fuel is needed.

_T_ 5. A vehicle with a manual transmission uses less fuel when driven correctly than a vehicle with an automatic transmission.

_F_ 6. Power steering leads to lower fuel use as a result of increased efficiency.

_F_ 7. A burnt smell on the transmission dipstick may indicate that the vehicle has been driven too fast.

_F_ 8. Insurance companies will pay for damages to a vehicle based on what the owner proves it is worth.

In each space below, write the word or words that best complete the sentence.

9. There are two kinds of liability insurance: bodily injury liability and __property__ damage liability.

10. The kind of insurance policy in which you pay a fixed amount of damage first and the insurance company pays the rest is called a __deductible__ policy.

11. The costs for on-road repairs when your vehicle breaks down on the road is paid for by __towing__ insurance.

12. Carpooling will __decrease__ the cost of your insurance.

13. Antilock brakes __decrease__ the time and distance it takes for a vehicle to stop.

Select the phrase that best completes each sentence below. Write the letter of the answer you have chosen to the left of each statement.

_a_ 14. A vehicle with a death rate greater than 2 per 10,000 is
 a. probably not a good vehicle to buy.
 b. safe enough to buy.
 c. safer than most other vehicles on the road.
 d. none of the above.

_b_ 15. A _____ vehicle is considered a high-visibility vehicle.
 a. navy blue
 b. mint green
 c. black
 d. brown

_d_ 16. Fuel consumption depends on
 a. the vehicle's weight.
 b. the type of engine.
 c. the type of transmission.
 d. all of the above.

_c_ 17. An advantage of selecting a vehicle with an automatic transmission is
 a. it offers increased fuel savings.
 b. it has increased power going up hills.
 c. it is easier to use.
 d. all of the above.

_a_ 18. The axle-gear ratio is
 a. the number of times the drive shaft revolves to make the wheels turn once.
 b. the number of times the wheels revolve to make the drive shaft turn once.
 c. the number of axles on your vehicle divided by the number of gears.
 d. none of the above.

_d_ 19. When looking over a vehicle, you should check the radiator for
 a. green coolant.
 b. clean coolant.
 c. leaks.
 d. both b and c.

_c_ 20. The *Blue Book* is a guide that shows
 a. the true value of any vehicle.
 b. the top value for any vehicle.
 c. the average price paid to dealers for different vehicles.
 d. none of the above.

21. Why do men have higher insurance rates than women?

Statistics show that men drive more often and farther than women and are involved in more collisions.

22. Why do young married men pay less for insurance than single men the same age?

Statistics show that young married men are involved in fewer collisions than single men.

CHAPTER 16 Buying a Vehicle

TEST B

Read each statement below. If it is true, place a T in the space to the left of the statement. If the statement is false, place an F next to it.

_T_ 1. Insurance companies rely on statistics to determine the rates that they charge.

_F_ 2. If you carpool to work, you will most likely see an increase in your car insurance.

_F_ 3. Automotive insurance costs are greater if you live in the country.

_T_ 4. A sports sedan that costs less than a larger, nonsports sedan will cost more to insure.

_T_ 5. Many insurance companies offer discounts to students who complete a driver education course.

_T_ 6. Most fatalities in head-on collisions are due to chest injuries from hitting the steering wheel.

_F_ 7. Air conditioners do not increase fuel use because today's models are built very efficiently.

_T_ 8. Uneven wear on tires can indicate a front-end problem.

In each space below, write the word or words that best complete the sentence.

9. A new vehicle usually is __less__ expensive to maintain than a used vehicle.

10. Antilock brakes __decrease__ the amount of time it takes for a vehicle to stop.

11. A __warranty__ is a written guarantee that the seller will repair the vehicle if something goes wrong in a given amount of time.

12. When you step hard on the accelerator at a slow speed and __blue__ exhaust smoke comes out, you may need an engine overhaul.

13. As a vehicle increases in weight, its safety __increases__.

Select the phrase that best completes each sentence below. Write the letter of the answer you have chosen to the left of each statement.

_b_ 14. Shaky steering and a wobbly ride can mean
 a. a low gear-axle ratio.
 b. misaligned front wheels.
 c. a low level of power-steering fluid.
 d. none of the above.

_d_ 15. Your monthly vehicle payments to the lending institution are determined in part by
 a. your income.
 b. the interest on the loan.
 c. the amount of money that you borrow.
 d. both b and c.

_d_ 16. The most important kind of insurance you can buy for driving is
 a. life insurance.
 b. comprehensive insurance.
 c. collision insurance.
 d. liability insurance.

_d_ 17. Uninsured motorist insurance protects you if
 a. you hit a vehicle that is uninsured.
 b. you are hit by an uninsured driver.
 c. you are the victim of a hit-and-run driver.
 d. both b and c occur.

_b_ 18. If your deductible amount is at a high level,
 a. your insurance rates will be relatively high.
 b. your insurance rates will be relatively low.
 c. you are a high-risk driver.
 d. you have to carry proof you can pay the deductible amount.

_d_ 19. A feature of antilock brakes is that they
 a. allow you to steer if you brake too fast.
 b. decrease the amount of time it takes to stop.
 c. decrease the distance it takes to stop.
 d. do all of the above.

_a_ 20. A low-visibility color for a vehicle is
 a. navy blue.
 b. white.
 c. mint green.
 d. fire-engine red.

21. What kinds of data does the Insurance Institute for Highway Safety analyze to rate the safety of cars?

It studies death rates per 10,000 registered vehicles of the same make and model for most models sold

in the United States. It also studies the death rate in single-vehicle crashes compared with multivehicle

crashes.

NAME _____ DATE _____

STUDY GUIDE FOR CHAPTER 16   LESSON 1

CHAPTER 16 | Buying a Vehicle

Determining Personal Need for a Vehicle

A. What particular features should you look for in a vehicle to meet your personal needs? How many passengers will you be carrying? What are their ages? Will you have to carry heavy loads?

Review student's work.

_____

_____

B. You have read many statistics about the higher rate of accidents and fatalities among young drivers. How do you evaluate your own maturity? What concerns, if any, do you have regarding the responsibility of driving?

Review student's work.

_____

_____

C. FIND OUT MORE. Talk to three or four people who drive and who pay their own vehicle expenses. Ask them to list their monthly vehicle expenses: the vehicle payment, insurance, fuel, oil, maintenance, and any other related expenses. What is the total? Would you have to work to be able to own a vehicle? How many hours per week would it take to do this? What would happen to your schoolwork?

Expenses	Driver 1	Driver 2	Driver 3	Driver 4
Vehicle payment				
Insurance				
Fuel				
Oil				
Maintenance				
Other vehicle expenses				
Total Expenses				

Review student's work.

_____

NAME _____ DATE _____

STUDY GUIDE FOR CHAPTER 16   LESSON 2

Factors Involved in Selecting a Vehicle

A. Complete each sentence below with one or more words.

1. Since most fatalities in head-on collisions occur when the driver hits the steering wheel, a good safety device to prevent this from happening is <u>an air bag.</u>

2. If you are evaluating a vehicle and discover that this particular make and model has a death rate of 4 per 10,000 registered vehicles, you should <u>not buy the vehicle.</u>

3. Examples of low-visibility colors are <u>brown, navy blue, and black.</u>

4. The death rate in the smallest vehicles is almost <u>twice as much</u> as in the largest vehicles.

5. As vehicles increase in weight, their safety usually <u>increases.</u>

6. The number of times the drive shaft revolves to make the wheels turn once is called the <u>axle-gear ratio.</u>

7. A vehicle with 6 cylinders uses <u>more</u> fuel than a vehicle with 4 cylinders.

B. FIND OUT MORE. The chapter lists items you should check in a new vehicle before purchasing it. What are they? Ask someone who drives to let you and other students make this check on his or her vehicle. How does the vehicle look? Would you buy it? How does your evaluation compare with other students' evaluations?

Review student's work.

_____

_____

_____

_____

_____

_____

_____

_____

NAME _____ DATE _____

STUDY GUIDE FOR CHAPTER 16   LESSON 3

Obtaining Financing for a Vehicle

A. Complete the chart by calculating the amount of the monthly payments for the following examples.

	Amount of Loan	Interest Rate	Loan Period	Total Amount of Loan	Monthly Payment
1.	$3,000	12%	12 months	$3,360	$208.00
2.	$4,000	12.4%	24 months	$4,992	$208.00
3.	$9,000	12.4%	24 months	$11,232	$468.00
4.	$3,000	10%	12 months	$3,300	$275.00

B. From the above exercise, what advantage do you see in shopping around for lower interest rates?

Lower monthly payments for the same vehicle or the ability to purchase a better vehicle for the

same amount of money.

_____

In the situations above, what advantage would there be if you had saved $1000 for a down payment?

The amount of the loan would be less; therefore the monthly payment would be lower.

_____

_____

C. FIND OUT MORE. Call at least three local lending institutions and find out what their interest rates are for loans to buy a new vehicle.

Review student's answers.

Is there any difference between the rates for a new vehicle and for a used one?

_____

Do finance companies have different rates from banks?

_____

_____

NAME _____ DATE _____

STUDY GUIDE FOR CHAPTER 16   LESSON 4

Choosing Insurance for a Vehicle

A. Read each description below. Fill in the blank with the letters of any type or types of insurance you think will cover each accident. You may have to list more than one type of insurance.

LI = liability   MP = medical payment
CM = comprehensive   CL = collision

<u>CL,LI</u> 1. You see a red light ahead and begin to slow down. A driver behind you does not realize that you are stopping. The vehicle hits yours and damages a fender. The other driver admits to not having watched the road carefully.

<u>CM</u> 2. You are driving on a country road on a windy night. Suddenly you hear a loud noise and feel a jolt. You stop the vehicle and find that a large tree limb has fallen onto your roof, leaving a big dent.

<u>LI,CL,MP</u> 3. You are driving along a street in your town. You are worried that a carton of groceries on the back seat is about to slide onto the floor. Reaching back to steady it, you take your eyes off the road for a moment. You hit a vehicle that is parked on the street. You have made a big dent in the other vehicle's side. Your vehicle has a broken light and a collapsed fender. In addition, your left arm hurts—the jolt of the accident has wrenched your left shoulder.

<u>CM</u> 4. You look for your vehicle one morning and discover that it is not where you left it. You are sure that you parked it right in front of your house. Someone has stolen your vehicle.

B. Complete each sentence by filling in the blank with the type of insurance that applies.

1. <u>No-fault</u> insurance pays for losses without determining who is to blame for an accident.

2. <u>Comprehensive</u> insurance covers damage to your vehicle by a tornado.

3. <u>Uninsured motorist</u> insurance covers victims of hit-and-run drivers.

4. <u>Property damage liability</u> insurance pays for damage that you have caused.

5. <u>Collision</u> insurance will pay if your vehicle is damaged while parked on the road.

C. FIND OUT MORE. Look in your state driver's manual and see what is said about automobile insurance. Do you have to carry proof of insurance? Do you have to prove that you are insured before you can register your vehicle? What kinds of insurance are required?

Review student's work.

_____

_____

_____

Buying a Vehicle

CHAPTER OVERVIEW

LESSON ONE

Factors to consider in determining whether a driver needs to own a vehicle are explored, and ways to determine what kind of vehicle is needed are introduced.

LESSON TWO

Guidelines for selecting a vehicle are presented with specific emphasis on safety considerations, fuel efficiency, and comfort factors. Information about choosing a used vehicle is also provided.

LESSON THREE

The alternatives available for financing a vehicle are described, and suggestions for deciding on loan terms are provided.

LESSON FOUR

The need for automotive insurance is explained, the various kinds of available coverage are described, and factors influencing insurance costs are discussed.

VOCABULARY

Blue Book
collision insurance
comprehensive insurance
deductible
liability insurance
no-fault insurance
uninsured motorist insurance
warranty

296

CONCEPT OF THE DRIVING TASK

Explain to students that deciding whether or not to buy a vehicle is not a decision to be made lightly. Both practical and personal factors, ranging from financial responsibility to the driver's degree of maturity, must be considered honestly.

CHAPTER 16

Buying a Vehicle

Purchasing a vehicle requires mature judgment, evaluation of needs, and ability to manage expense. It is important to learn how to assess safety features, fuel efficiency, comfort, and insurance needs to make a wise choice.

PRESENTING THE BIG IDEA

Buying and owning a vehicle require careful evaluation and handling of many different factors and a willingness to accept serious ongoing responsibility.

INTRODUCING THE CHAPTER

What's on the Road Ahead?

Have students read the lesson titles and objectives. Briefly discuss the topic of each lesson. Tell students that in this chapter, they will be introduced to guidelines that will help them when they are ready to buy their own vehicle.

Background: The Larger Picture

The following statistics will give students some perspective on vehicle ownership.

- The average price of an automobile first passed the $10,000 mark in 1983. Fifteen years later, the average price had risen to more than $20,400.
- In 1998, the average age of a vehicle in the United States was 8.7 years.
- Automobile consumer installment credit in the United States totaled about $418 billion in 1997.
- Insurance premiums paid on vehicle policies of all types in the United States total more than $95 billion a year.
- In 1997, the motor vehicle industry throughout the world produced about 53.5 million cars, buses, and trucks.

Relating to Prior Knowledge

Discuss with students what they know about buying a vehicle. Encourage them to suggest reasons why a teenager should or should not own a vehicle. Ask how they think a driver education course will help them make decisions about vehicle ownership.

The Big Idea

Discuss students' reactions to the Big Idea statement. Suggest that they keep this idea in mind as they read Chapter 16.

Determining Personal Need When Considering Buying a Vehicle

(pages 298–299)

FOCUS

Objectives

- List factors to consider that may determine your need to buy a vehicle.
- Describe what you should consider in determining the kind of vehicle you need.

Resources

 Study Guide, page 61,

 Information Masters 7, 9, 23, and 26

Motivator

Pose the following question: What should you consider in choosing a vehicle? (Cost of vehicle, cost of insurance, vehicle size, estimated number of miles to be driven, cost of maintenance.)

TEACH

Explain

OBJECTIVE 1: Students should understand that owning a vehicle is both a financial and a legal responsibility.

OBJECTIVE 2: Students should recognize the consequences of choosing a vehicle that is ill-suited to their primary needs.

LESSON ONE

OBJECTIVES

1. List factors to consider that may determine your need to buy a vehicle.
2. Describe what you should consider in determining the kind of vehicle you need.

Determining Personal Need When Considering Buying a Vehicle

If you are considering buying a vehicle, the first question you should ask yourself is not about the vehicle—it's about you. The question is "Am I responsible enough to own and drive a vehicle?" Examine the reasons you are considering the purchase—including both your wants and your needs.

There are many reasons to *want* your own vehicle.

- A vehicle makes you more independent.
- A vehicle saves you time in getting from one place to another.
- Owning a vehicle makes you feel more mature.
- Going places in your own vehicle is fun.

Make your own *want list*. Why do you really want a vehicle? Then think about another question: "Do I really *need* to own a vehicle?"

How Can You Tell Whether You Need Your Own Vehicle?

The following questions may help you focus on your needs.

- How close to your home are the places that you go to most often?
- How do you get to these places now?
- How available is public transportation?
- Is there a family vehicle, and if so, how available is it to you?

Think about your answers. If you live close to the places you normally go to, if public transportation is convenient, or if the family vehicle is available to you, you may not need to own a vehicle at all.

You still have other questions to consider.

Can you afford a vehicle? You will need to examine all of the costs involved in buying and owning a vehicle. In addition to the purchase price, you'll have to pay for fuel, oil, maintenance, repairs, insurance, licensing, registration, tolls, and often, parking.

How will a vehicle affect your schedule? For students who have to earn the money to pay for buying and operating a vehicle, the cost can be measured in hours as well as dollars. Working to pay vehicle expenses takes away time needed for studies, and a balanced social life.

298   UNIT 4   *Planning for Your Future*

IT'S A FACT

The library is an excellent source of information for anyone wanting to buy, repair, or maintain a vehicle or learn more about how a vehicle engine works. Magazines such as *Consumer Reports* also provide up-to-date information about vehicle safety and reliability.

Are you mature enough to manage the responsibilities of owning a vehicle? Often, increased responsibility means increased stress. Can you cope with that stress? Are you mature enough to distinguish your wants from your needs? Are you able to evaluate honestly all of the costs (both in time and in money) involved in vehicle ownership?

Can you deal in a mature way with the social pressures of driving and owning a vehicle? Driving a vehicle always involves risk to yourself and to others. If you're not mature enough to manage that risk responsibly, you shouldn't buy—or drive—a vehicle, regardless of your age.

What Personal Factors Influence the Kind of Vehicle You Need?

Be prepared when you shop for a vehicle. Think about how your vehicle will be used and what your needs are. The following questions will help you sort out what *you* should be looking for in a vehicle.

How many passengers will you usually have? The answer may help you decide what size vehicle you should buy.

What age are your passengers? Considering your passengers' comfort and space needs can help you decide what size vehicle you need and whether it should be a two- or four-door model. For example, if your regular passengers include elderly people, you need to think about the ease with which they can enter or leave the vehicle.

How many miles do you expect to drive each day, month, or year? Consider your expected mileage to help you determine how fuel efficient your vehicle needs to be.

What is the cost of the vehicle plus the cost of insurance? Expensive vehicles cost more to insure than less expensive ones. Insurance rates are also higher for sports vehicles than for family-type sedans.

How much will you have to spend to maintain the vehicle? A new vehicle usually costs much less to maintain than a used vehicle. You need to make sure that you can afford repairs and maintenance.

Lesson 1 Review

1. How can you tell if you really need a vehicle?
2. How should passenger comfort and maintenance costs influence the kind of vehicle you buy?

WHAT WOULD YOU DO?

How would you explain to the drivers what factors they should think about before buying a vehicle?

WHAT WOULD YOU DO?

Sample answer: Suggest considering number of passengers, cost of ownership and maintenance, and anticipated number of miles driven.

Lesson 1 Review

Answers
1. Consider how much traveling you normally do, how you can get to the places you need to get to, and whether you have access to a family vehicle.
2. Passenger comfort influences your decisions about vehicle size and number of doors; maintenance costs influence your decision about the age and condition of the vehicle you choose.

Teaching Model

Describe the following situation: You need a vehicle to transport items you sell at flea markets. One vehicle that you are considering buying has a powerful engine but a small trunk. The other vehicle has a less powerful but more fuel-efficient engine and a large trunk. Model your thinking process for making a purchase decision. (You decide on the second vehicle because it has a greater capacity and will cost less per mile to drive.)

Ask

Ask students to discuss other features they might consider in comparing vehicles.

Read

Have students read Lesson 1 to learn how to decide whether they need to own a vehicle and, if so, how to choose a vehicle.

ASSESS

Guided Practice

Have students answer the Lesson 1 Review questions. The answers are provided below.

Reteaching

Have students work in pairs to list reasons for *wanting* and for *needing* a vehicle. Have them discuss features to consider.

Enrichment

Assign the Study Guide for Lesson 1. The Find Out More section encourages students to expand their basic learning of the lesson concepts.

CLOSE

Summarize

Return to the Motivator question. Ask students how their ideas about factors to consider have been affected by this lesson.

DRIVER'S LOG

Have students list their own personal wants and needs for a vehicle.

FOCUS

Objectives

- List several considerations for selecting a safe vehicle.
- Describe how to select a comfortable vehicle.
- Name several factors affecting a vehicle's fuel efficiency.
- Explain what you should know about buying a used vehicle.

Resources

 Study Guide, page 62

 Transparency 40

Information Masters 7, 9, 23, and 26.

Vocabulary

warranty
Blue Book

Motivator

Pose the following situation: Your older brother has found a vehicle that he thinks will meet his needs. What factors would you suggest that he consider before buying the vehicle? (Students may mention safety features, comfort, engine power, fuel efficiency, design features, availability of a warranty.)

LESSON TWO

OBJECTIVES

1. List several considerations for selecting a safe vehicle.
2. Describe how to select a comfortable vehicle.
3. Name several factors affecting a vehicle's fuel efficiency.
4. Explain what you should know about buying a used vehicle.

KEY TERMS

warranty
Blue Book

Factors That Are Involved in Selecting a Vehicle

You have decided that you really need to own a vehicle. You've thought carefully about how your vehicle will be used and what your needs are. Now you need to know what to look for in a vehicle in order to choose one that is safe, comfortable, and fuel efficient.

There's a great deal to think about when you really get down to choosing a vehicle. However, the very first thing you should check out is the vehicle's safety. In fact, if safety is *not* your first concern, you shouldn't be buying a vehicle.

How Can You Select a Vehicle That Is Safe?

You should ask a number of questions about safety before purchasing a vehicle. To find the answers, you may have to do a little research.

Does the vehicle have air bags? In head-on crashes, most fatalities occur when the driver hits the steering wheel and suffers head or chest injuries. Air bags help prevent such injuries. Passenger-side air bags help protect front-seat occupants.

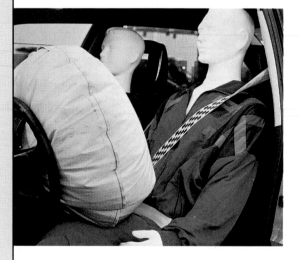

◆ *The presence of air bags is a safety factor you should consider when buying a car.*

How does the vehicle hold up in a crash test? Crash test data are available from the U.S. Department of Transportation's National Highway Traffic Safety Administration.

Does the vehicle have an antilock brake system (ABS)? Vehicles with antilock brakes can stop in a shorter distance on slick surfaces than can vehicles without such brakes. However, the main advantage of antilock brakes is that they let you steer around an obstacle even if you panic and slam on the brakes.

What is the size of the vehicle? Most recent studies show death rates in the smallest vehicles to be more than twice as high as those in the largest vehicles.

What is the death rate per 10,000 registered models of the vehicle? Getting all of the information you can about your potential vehicle's safety record could

---

MEETING STUDENT DIVERSITY

Limited English Proficiency

Students who have difficulty speaking or understanding English may feel uneasy about talking with a vehicle dealer or other seller. Suggest that these students write or have someone help them write a list of questions they want to have answered when they look for a vehicle. Encourage them to practice asking the questions beforehand and to anticipate the range of possible answers.

save your life. Vehicle models differ by as much as 800 percent in their safety records. The Insurance Institute for Highway Safety analyzes the safety records of most vehicles sold in the United States.

The institute examines the death rate by manufacturer and model. Vehicle death rates range from 0.5 to 4 deaths per 10,000 registered vehicles. Generally, the higher the death rate, the less safe the vehicle. If the death rate of a particular model is more than 2 per 10,000 registered vehicles, think twice before buying.

The institute also examines the death rate in single-vehicle crashes compared to multivehicle crashes. If more than 50 percent of the deaths occurred in single-vehicle crashes, the particular vehicle model may encourage unsafe driving.

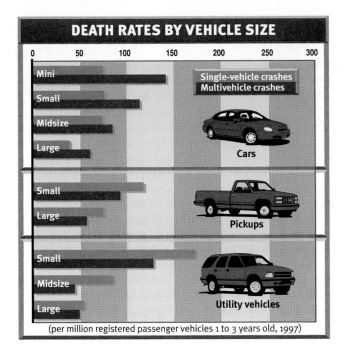

DEATH RATES BY VEHICLE SIZE

0   50   100   150   200   250   300

Single-vehicle crashes
Multivehicle crashes

Cars: Mini, Small, Midsize, Large

Pickups: Small, Large

Utility vehicles: Small, Midsize, Large

(per million registered passenger vehicles 1 to 3 years old, 1997)

◆ *You can see by the graph that small two-door cars are the least safe.*

How Can You Check a Vehicle's Comfort Features?

You will spend a lot of time in your vehicle, so check to be sure that it's comfortable for you. Get into the vehicle. Does it fit you? Are the seats adjustable? Can you adjust the steering wheel height so that the top of the wheel is at or below the top of your shoulders? Do the seat and steering wheel positions give you maximum control of the vehicle?

Ask to take the vehicle for a test drive. Be sure that you can reach all accessory switches and dials easily. Be sure the seat is comfortable enough so that a long drive won't leave you with an aching back.

How Can You Determine Whether a Vehicle Is Fuel Efficient?

Fuel consumption is an important consideration when choosing a vehicle. An energy-efficient vehicle can save you money, reduce pollution, and help conserve this planet's energy resources.

Energy Tips

If you are buying a new vehicle, look carefully at the dealer's sticker. It contains information about miles per gallon of gasoline. The greater the number of miles per gallon, the more fuel efficient the vehicle.

Driving Tip

Point out to students that many vehicle experts recommend taking a test drive of at least 20 minutes. The salesperson or vehicle owner usually accompanies the prospective buyer. The test drive should include driving in slow-moving traffic and on a highway, where the vehicle can be run at a higher speed. The vehicle should also be backed and parked.

TEACH

Explain

OBJECTIVE 1: Most students should be aware of such basic safety features as safety belts, head restraints, and air bags. Students may also benefit from a discussion of design factors that add to safety, such as steel door reinforcements, safety glass, padded dashboard and steering wheel, and side marker lights.

OBJECTIVE 2: Students should understand that comfort depends largely on the size and height of the driver in relation to the size and design of a particular vehicle. Therefore, vehicle buyers need personally to try out seats, steering wheel, and other features to see whether they can be adjusted as required. Emphasize, too, that in addition to comfort considerations, students should check visibility. Comfort is irrelevant if the driver does not have a clear view of the roadway.

OBJECTIVE 3: Students will benefit from a discussion of the factors that affect fuel efficiency and how those factors may relate to safety or comfort. Students should also realize that the highway/city fuel estimates shown on new-vehicle stickers are averages for the model. Individual driving styles and use of the vehicle will affect fuel consumption.

OBJECTIVE 4: Students should benefit from a discussion comparing what to look for when buying a used vehicle versus a new vehicle. Stress the fact that owners frequently have a good reason for selling their vehicle, such as wanting to avoid having to make a major repair. Therefore, it is essential to have a mechanic check out a used vehicle before you buy it.

Teaching Model

Describe the following situation: You are comparing two new vehicles. One is larger and more expensive than the other. The salesperson lists the features of both vehicles. The larger vehicle has more safety and luxury features; the smaller vehicle is more fuel efficient and sportier looking. Model the process you would use to make a wise decision. (You would research safety and repair records for both vehicles; compare fuel efficiency; test-drive each vehicle for comfort and ease of use; consider which features are important enough to pay extra for.)

Ask

Ask students to discuss which features they would consider most important in making their purchase decision.

Read

Have students read Lesson 2 to understand what important safety, comfort, and efficiency factors to consider when buying a new or used vehicle.

ASSESS

Guided Practice

Have students answer the Lesson 2 Review questions. The answers are provided below.

Reteaching

Have students work in groups of three. Have them take turns role-playing a vehicle dealer or other seller, a vehicle buyer, and an observer who makes sure the buyer asks the questions necessary to obtain sufficient information to make a wise purchase decision.

After each student has played all parts, discuss with the class the importance of taking time to research and learn as much as possible about a vehicle before buying it.

The Insurance Institute for Highway Safety provides free information on death rates and crash test data. You can write to the institute at 10005 N. Glebe Road, Arlington, Virginia 22201.

Fuel consumption depends on a vehicle's weight, type of engine, design, and type of transmission, among other factors.

The Weight of the Vehicle

The less weight an engine pulls, the more efficiently it works. This saves fuel. In general, however, the heavier the vehicle, the more protection it provides you in a crash.

The Type of Engine

The more cylinders in the engine the more fuel it uses. A 4- or 6-cylinder engine probably will meet the needs of most intermediate-size vehicles. This size engine is also fuel efficient.

The Design of the Vehicle

One key to fuel economy is how well the vehicle overcomes air resistance. A streamlined vehicle has less air resistance than a vehicle with a boxy design.

The Type of Transmission

A manual transmission consumes less fuel than an automatic one. A vehicle with a manual transmission also is less expensive to buy. However, again there are trade-offs. An automatic is easier to use and to learn to drive than a manual one, and more models are available.

In addition, most drivers have more control driving vehicles with automatic transmissions.

The Power Train

The power train powers the wheels that move the vehicle. The number of times that the driveshaft revolves to make the wheels turn once is known as the axle-gear ratio. The higher the axle-gear ratio, the greater the fuel consumption.

TIPS

FOR NEW DRIVERS

Used-Vehicle Checks

When purchasing a used vehicle, check the following.

The condition of the paint New paint can indicate collision damage.

For rust Don't buy a vehicle with rusted-out areas unless you can afford repairs.

For worn tires, including the spare Uneven wear on any tire may indicate front-end problems.

The tailpipe A light gray color indicates proper combustion.

The radiator Remove the radiator cap. Is the coolant clean? Is there caked-on rust on the cap? Are there signs of leaks on the back of the radiator?

The transmission Pull out the transmission dipstick and sniff it. A burned smell may indicate an overheated transmission. Feel the oil on the crankcase dipstick. If it is gritty, there may be dirt in the engine.

The service stickers Service stickers tell you how often a vehicle has been tuned and had the oil changed.

All windows and door locks Check for ease of operation.

The engine Listen for loud or unusual noises when you start the vehicle. Check all gauges and warning lights.

The headlights, taillights, brake lights, and turn indicators

For slamming sounds or lurching as the vehicle starts An automatic transmission should take hold promptly when in gear.

Safety belts, air bags, and head restraints

State BY State

All but two states have some form of "lemon law" that requires a dealer or manufacturer to refund the purchase price or replace a vehicle that has a critical defect. Vehicle owners can check with their state's attorney general's office to learn the procedures for filing a complaint.

TIPS

FOR NEW DRIVERS

To enhance student understanding, you may want to discuss how each tip can avert possible problems. For example, a leaky radiator could cause a vehicle to overheat.

Power Equipment

Power equipment and accessories add extra weight and energy requirements to a vehicle, which leads to higher fuel use. When choosing a vehicle, evaluate whether ease of operation is worth extra fuel cost to you.

What Should You Know About Buying a Used Vehicle?

Many consumers decide to buy a used vehicle, usually for economic reasons. You should consider many of the same factors when buying a used vehicle that you would when buying a new one. However, there are other considerations as well.

You can buy a used vehicle from a private owner or a used vehicle dealer. Buying from the owner can cost less, but you will not get a **warranty,** a written guarantee that the seller will repair the vehicle if something goes wrong within a given period of time. Dealers, on the other hand, often offer warranties.

The *Blue Book* is a guide to the average price paid to dealers for different makes and models of used vehicles. Actual price may differ from the "book" price depending on the condition of the vehicle and its mileage.

Before buying a used vehicle, test-drive it. Shaky steering and a wobbly ride may mean front wheels are misaligned or need balancing. Make several sharp turns at a low speed. Steering should not stiffen up. If the vehicle has power steering, there shouldn't be any squeaks or other noises.

Slow down from 50 mph to 15 mph without braking. Step hard on the accelerator. If there is blue exhaust smoke, the vehicle may need an engine overhaul. Having diagnostic tests performed on the vehicle you choose *before* you buy it may save you money in the long run.

SAFETY TIPS

The color of a vehicle affects how visible it is to other drivers. White, fire-engine red, mint green, and yellow are high-visibility colors. Brown, gray, navy blue, and black are low-visibility colors.

WHAT WOULD YOU DO?

You want some of these features, but you also want fuel economy. What will you do?

Lesson 2 Review

1. How can information from the Insurance Institute for Highway Safety help you evaluate a vehicle's safety?
2. Describe how test-driving a vehicle can help you evaluate how comfortable it is.
3. How does the type of engine a vehicle has affect its fuel efficiency?
4. What should you check when you select a used vehicle?

Enrichment

Assign the Study Guide for Lesson 2. The Find Out More section encourages students to expand their basic learning of the lesson concepts.

CLOSE

Summarize

Return to the Motivator question. Recall students' initial responses, and discuss what additional considerations for buying a vehicle they've learned about in this lesson. Extend the discussion by asking: Why are safety and comfort more important than a vehicle's appearance?

DRIVER'S LOG

Have students make a priority list of features they would look for in a new or used vehicle. Suggest they obtain crash test data for their favorite model vehicle by writing to the Insurance Institute for Highway Safety, then sharing the information with the class and recording it in their logs.

WHAT WOULD YOU DO?

Sample answer: See whether another make or model vehicle offers both the features desired and fuel economy.

Lesson 2 Review

Answers

1. The institute provides data on death rates in crashes by make and model.
2. You can see whether switches, controls, and dials are within easy reach and whether the seat feels comfortable; you can judge how smoothly the vehicle rides.
3. The more engine cylinders, the more fuel consumed.
4. Paint condition, presence of rust, tire condition, tailpipe, radiator, transmission, engine, lights, turn indicators, windows and door locks, service stickers, safety belts, air bags, and head restraints.

How to Obtain Financing for a New or Used Vehicle

(pages 304–305)

FOCUS

Objectives

- Explain where to get financing for a vehicle.
- Discuss the process of making monthly payments for your vehicle.

Resources

📁 Study Guide, page 63

📁 Information Masters 7, 9, 23, and 26

Motivator

Pose the following situation: You've found a vehicle you want to buy, but you don't have the full purchase price. How will you pay for it? (Students may mention borrowing the money from a family member, finance company, or bank.)

TEACH

Explain

OBJECTIVES 1 and 2: Students may benefit from a discussion of loan sources and the range of interest rates charged.

Teaching Model

Pose the following situation: You have your eye on a vehicle that costs more than you planned to spend. Model the process you will use to decide what to do. (You will figure out how much you can afford to put down on the vehicle. Then you will check with different lending institutions to compare interest rates and monthly payments for the loan

LESSON THREE

OBJECTIVES

1. Explain where to get financing for a vehicle.
2. Discuss the process of making monthly payments for your vehicle.

How to Obtain Financing for a New or Used Vehicle

Once you have chosen the vehicle you want to buy, you have to decide how to pay for it. Very few people can afford to pay cash for a new vehicle or for a late-model used vehicle. Most people have to take out a loan to pay for the vehicle. How do you get a loan?

What Should You Know About Financing a Vehicle?

To finance the purchase of a vehicle, you need to know where to get a loan and the amount of the monthly payments.

Where to Get Financing

If you are a full-time high school student, you will not be able to obtain financing on your own. The lending institution will require that an adult be responsible for loan repayment. You may be able to get a loan if you are 18 years old and work full-time. In most cases, however, a responsible adult will need to co-sign the loan.

Drivers finance their vehicles through banks, credit unions, finance companies, and if buying a new vehicle, often through the dealer. You

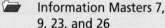 CONNECTIONS
Math

Calculate the interest on a vehicle loan to estimate the monthly payments. Suppose that you want to buy a used vehicle for $6,000. You've saved $2,000 and want to borrow the rest. Further suppose that a bank will lend you $4,000 for 24 months (2 years) at 12 percent interest. Follow these steps to estimate the amount you'll pay in interest and what your monthly payments will be.

1. Multiply the amount of the loan by the interest: $4,000 × 0.12 = $480.

2. Multiply the interest by the number of years: $480 × 2 = $960.
3. Add the interest to the amount of the loan: $4,000 + $960 = $4,960.
4. Divide the total by the number of months to find out how much you'll pay per month: $4,960 ÷ 24 = $206.66.

Amount of loan	$4,000
Interest on loan	12%
Total amount of loan	$4,960
Loan period	24 mos.
Monthly payments	$206.66

MEETING STUDENT DIVERSITY

Learning Disabled

Some students may be confused by the concept of interest. Explain that interest is money that a borrower pays to a lender in return for being able to use the lender's money.

 CONNECTIONS
Math

Students should understand that several factors affect the amount of monthly payment: amount borrowed, loan period, and interest rate.

should check out each possible source of financing as carefully as you've checked out the vehicle you want to buy.

◆ *In order to finance a vehicle, you can ask about a loan at the bank where you have a checking or savings account. Dealerships may also offer financing at low interest rates as part of their sales promotions.*

The Amount of Monthly Payments

Loan agencies lend money to make money. They make money by charging interest on the money they lend. Different sources of financing often charge different interest rates. Compare rates to get the best deal.

The amount of the loan is based on the cost of the vehicle. The amount of time you have to pay back the loan is based on whether the vehicle is new or used. Used vehicle loans have to be repaid more quickly than new vehicle loans.

You should try to pay as much as you can toward the purchase of the vehicle—the down payment—and then borrow the rest. The lender will give you a schedule of monthly payments. The amount of these payments will depend on how much money you borrow, the interest rate on your loan, and whether or not your vehicle's insurance is included in the loan.

WHAT WOULD YOU DO?

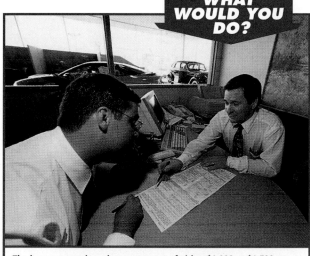

The buyer can make a down payment of either $1,000 or $1,500 on a used vehicle. Which should he choose to do? Why?

Lesson 3 Review

1. Where would you go to get financing for a vehicle?
2. What advice would you give someone about financing a vehicle?

WHAT WOULD YOU DO?

Sample answer: Put down $1,500; a higher down payment means you need to borrow less money.

Lesson 3 Review

Answers

1. A bank, credit union, finance company, the dealer.
2. Check various financing sources to find the best terms; know what your monthly payments will be.

---

term you want. If you cannot afford the payments, you will have to increase the down payment, find a lower interest rate, or consider a cheaper vehicle.)

Ask

Have students discuss factors to consider when deciding whether they can afford to take out a loan.

Read

Have students read Lesson 3 to understand what a vehicle loan is and how to obtain one.

ASSESS

Guided Practice

Have students answer the Lesson 3 Review questions. The answers are provided below.

Reteaching

Have students work in small groups to list questions they would ask a bank or finance company about a vehicle loan.

Enrichment

Assign the Study Guide for Lesson 3. The Find Out More Section encourages students to expand their basic learning of the lesson concepts.

CLOSE

Summarize

Return to the Motivator question, and discuss with students the responsibility involved in financing and paying for a vehicle.

DRIVER'S LOG

Have students describe how they might budget for vehicle payments.

Choosing and Purchasing Insurance for a Vehicle

(pages 306–310)

FOCUS

Objectives

- Describe the types of motor vehicle insurance.
- List the factors that determine the cost of insurance.

Resources

 Study Guide, page 64

Vocabulary

liability insurance
uninsured motorist insurance
collision insurance
deductible
comprehensive insurance
no-fault insurance

Motivator

Pose the following situation: You live in a state where motor vehicle insurance coverage is required by law. How can such coverage protect you financially? (It can protect you by paying for most of the cost of injuries or damage resulting from a collision; by paying medical costs; by paying for your vehicle if it is stolen or damaged.)

OBJECTIVES

1. Describe the types of motor vehicle insurance.
2. List the factors that determine the cost of insurance.

KEY TERMS

liability insurance
uninsured motorist insurance
collision insurance
deductible
comprehensive insurance
no-fault insurance

Choosing and Purchasing Insurance for a Vehicle

In most states, when you buy a vehicle, you must purchase insurance. Many different kinds of vehicle insurance policies are available, and you should investigate each kind carefully before deciding what you will need. It should be noted that insurance laws sometimes vary from state to state.

What Kinds of Insurance Might You Need?

Suppose you are involved in a collision that results in property damage and serious injury. How will you pay the costs involved? Unless you're very rich, you'll need automobile insurance. That's why many states require anyone who owns a vehicle to have one or more kinds of motor vehicle insurance.

Liability Insurance

The word *liable* means "responsible." **Liability insurance** is proof that you will be financially responsible if you cause damage to property or injure other people. Many states require drivers to prove that they have a certain amount of liability insurance before their vehicles can be registered.

Liability insurance is the most important motor vehicle insurance protection you can have. It protects you against claims if you are at fault in a collision. It helps you pay for any injury or property damage caused by your actions. Liability insurance not only protects you, it also protects anyone else who has your permission to drive your vehicle. (Check your policy first to see if there are restrictions on who can and who cannot drive your vehicle.)

Most drivers have two kinds of liability insurance: bodily injury liability insurance and property damage liability insurance. Both are usually sold in amounts of $10,000 to $500,000.

◆ *Liability insurance provides coverage if you cause injury or property damage.*

THE INTERNATIONAL SCENE

Canada

All provinces and territories in Canada require motor vehicle insurance. Visiting motorists need to prove they can financially cover the costs of any collision in which they may be involved. U.S. citizens who plan to drive in Canada should get a Canadian Non-Resident Inter-Provincial Motor Vehicle Liability Insurance Card to show financial responsibility. This card can be obtained through insurance companies in the United States.

Bodily injury liability insurance covers you if your driving causes injury to or the death of another person or persons. It also covers legal fees, court costs, and lost wages.

Property damage liability insurance covers you if your driving causes damage to the property of other people. It covers damage to their vehicles and property in their vehicles and damage to buildings, telephone poles, and traffic lights.

Of course, you are covered only for the amount of insurance you have purchased. If a court determines that you have caused more damage than your insurance will pay, you are held personally liable.

Uninsured Motorist Insurance

Although many states require that vehicle owners have liability insurance and show proof of it before their vehicles can be registered, some drivers allow their policies to lapse or cancel their policies after registration. If you are involved in a collision with such a driver, or if you are involved with a hit-and-run driver, **uninsured motorist insurance** protects you. Uninsured motorist insurance also protects you in states where no liability insurance is required. It pays for any bodily injury that you may suffer. Generally, it does not pay for damage to your vehicle.

Collision Insurance

Collision insurance pays for damage to your vehicle even if you are to blame in a crash or are involved with an uninsured driver. Collision insurance also covers repairs if your vehicle is damaged in a parking lot or in a parking space on the street.

Because of the increasing cost of repairing collision damage, very few insurance companies offer full-coverage collision insurance that pays the entire amount of any damages. Most drivers have a deductible policy. With this kind of policy, you agree to pay a fixed amount, such as the first $50, $100, $250, or $500 worth of damages. The insurance company pays the rest. The greater the fixed amount, or **deductible,** you pay, the less this insurance costs.

Banks and companies that finance motor vehicle loans usually require a vehicle's owner to have collision insurance with a deductible of no more than $250. However, once the vehicle loan is repaid, it is a good idea to raise the deductible to $500 in order to lower the cost of the insurance.

FYI

Although most vehicle owners buy insurance, some states only require that owners show proof of their ability to pay if they injure other people or damage their property. Some states permit an owner to put up a deposit in the form of cash, a bond, or stocks of a fixed amount.

◆ Collision insurance covers the cost of damage to a vehicle no matter who is at fault.

Explain

OBJECTIVE 1: Students should recognize the need for financial protection in case of collision, theft, or other mishap and understand that motor vehicle insurance meets this need. Students should realize that the cost of insurance is relatively small compared with the huge expenses that may result from a collision with a vehicle, pedestrian, or roadside hazard. Too many drivers underestimate the risk and consequences of a collision, not fully realizing that even a "minor" crash can cost a driver years of financial hardship. Students should become familiar with the specific insurance requirements in their own state.

OBJECTIVE 2: Students may benefit from discussing why various factors affect the cost of vehicle insurance. Students should be aware that insurance companies charge more to insure a vehicle that is especially expensive to fix, such as a luxury car or sport utility vehicle; more to insure drivers who drive more than the average number of miles driven by the typical driver; more in areas that have heavier traffic or a high rate of collisions or vehicle thefts; and more to drivers who belong to high-risk groups. Drivers should shop around before purchasing insurance, comparing rates, coverage, and service of several insurance companies. Insurance buyers should also note that they can lower policy costs by accepting higher deductibles and, in many instances, by installing discount-eligible antitheft devices. Graduates of a driver education program may receive premium discounts.

MEETING STUDENT DIVERSITY

Physically Challenged

Explain to students that shopping around for vehicle insurance is especially important for drivers who are physically challenged because different companies vary in their approach to insuring these drivers. Suggest that students ask drivers who are physically challenged what insurance company they use. Rehabilitation agencies are also a good source of information.

Teaching Model

Describe the following situation: You have caused a collision that has damaged your vehicle and another driver's vehicle, as well as a property owner's fence. No one is seriously hurt, but you and the other driver do need some medical attention. Model the thinking process that demonstrates that you understand what costs you will have to pay and what kinds of vehicle insurance protect you in such a situation. (You recognize that liability insurance helps pay the costs of bodily injury and property damage—in this case, the other driver's injuries, the damage to his or her vehicle, and the damage to the property owner's fence; collision insurance covers repairs to your vehicle; medical payment insurance covers medical and hospital costs; and towing insurance covers the cost of having your vehicle towed, if necessary. You must pay the amount of the deductible shown in your insurance policy, and the insurance company pays the rest. You are personally responsible for expenses that exceed your insurance coverage limits.)

Ask

Ask students to discuss the advantages and disadvantages of having a high deductible.

Read

Have students read Lesson 4 to become familiar with the kinds of motor vehicle insurance available and the factors that affect the cost of insurance.

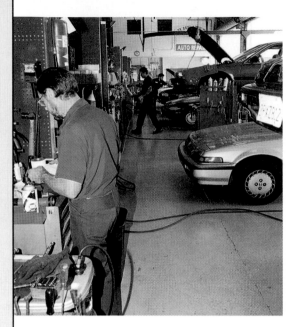

◆ *You are responsible for the cost of repairs up to and including the deductible amount.*

Comprehensive Insurance

If your vehicle is damaged by anything other than a collision, **comprehensive insurance** pays the bills. For example, comprehensive insurance covers theft or damage caused by fire, explosions, natural disasters, falling objects, or vandalism.

Medical Payment Insurance

Medical payment insurance covers medical, hospital, or funeral costs regardless of who is at fault. It pays a fixed amount if you or passengers in your vehicle are injured or killed in a collision. It also pays if you or a member of your family is injured or killed while riding in someone else's vehicle. Very often, medical payment insurance pays if you or a member of your family is struck as a pedestrian or the rider of a bicycle, bus, or taxicab. The amount paid is determined by the policy.

No-Fault Insurance

An increasing number of states have no-fault insurance laws. In this system, your insurance company pays your medical bills and any other costs resulting from a collision-related injury. The system is called **no-fault insurance** because blame is not considered before the insurance company pays your bills. In very serious crashes, the injured parties can still go to court and sue the person responsible for damages.

Towing Insurance

Towing insurance covers the costs of on-road repairs and the cost of having your vehicle towed.

What Factors Determine the Cost of Insurance?

You purchase vehicle insurance by paying a premium, or a set amount of money, to an insurance company, usually every six months. How is this premium determined?

Insurance companies rely on statistics to determine their rates. The statistics indicate the likelihood that people of a certain age, gender, or marital status will be involved in a crash. They also indicate the likelihood of certain types of vehicles being involved in a crash. Insurance companies use the following factors to determine rates.

IT'S A FACT

Many insurance companies cancel a driver's insurance policy if he or she is involved in numerous collisions, especially ones that are determined to be the driver's fault. Even if an insurance company does not cancel a policy, insurance rates for drivers who have several collisions or make several insurance claims, especially in a short period of time, may rise dramatically.

Your age Drivers under the age of 25 pay the highest premiums.

Your driving record Traffic-violation convictions, collisions, and insurance claims can increase your insurance costs. Some companies offer discounts to those who drive a specified number of years without a collision or traffic ticket.

Mileage per year The farther you drive, the more your vehicle insurance will cost.

If you drive to work Carpooling reduces the cost of insurance.

Where you live If you live in a city, your insurance costs will be greater than those of a person who lives in the country.

Your gender Women pay lower insurance rates than men. Statistics show that men drive more often and farther and are involved in more collisions.

FYI

Insurance companies usually pay damages only up to a vehicle's "book" value. This amount can be less than an owner thinks the vehicle is worth. Any special or custom equipment may not be covered either unless specifically noted in your policy.

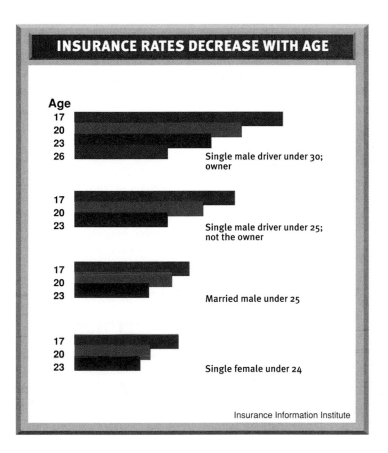

INSURANCE RATES DECREASE WITH AGE

Age
17
20
23
26
Single male driver under 30; owner

17
20
23
Single male driver under 25; not the owner

17
20
23
Married male under 25

17
20
23
Single female under 24

Insurance Information Institute

◆ *Many drivers receive minimum coverage at a base rate. You can see that single males pay the highest insurance premiums.*

CHAPTER 16 *Buying a Vehicle* **309**

ASSESS

Guided Practice

Have students answer the Lesson 4 Review questions. The answers are provided below.

Reteaching

Have students work in groups to brainstorm situations in which motor vehicle insurance would help protect drivers and others, such as single- and multiple-vehicle collisions, auto theft, vandalism, and fire and flood damage. Have students determine the kind of insurance that would pertain in each situation. If students have difficulty remembering the types of insurance, suggest that they review the information in their textbooks.

After groups have completed this task, have them take part in a class discussion about the importance of having adequate motor vehicle insurance. Invite students to share any news reports that they may have read about court cases involving vehicle-related damages or injuries.

State BY State

After receiving numerous consumer complaints, some state governments have investigated the rates that motor vehicle insurance companies charge their customers. As a result of these investigations, some drivers in New York, for example, received refunds on their insurance payments because the insurance companies had failed to offer discounts for safety features on certain vehicles.

To check students' understanding, have them summarize the key points in their own words. Stress the importance of protecting both driver and passengers.

Enrichment

Assign the Study Guide for Lesson 4. The Find Out More section encourages students to expand their basic learning of the lesson concepts.

CLOSE

Summarize

Return to the Motivator question, and review the various kinds of insurance and the protection they offer. You may want to extend the discussion by having students debate the fairness of linking insurance rates to each of the cost factors described on pages 306–310 of the student textbook.

DRIVER'S LOG

Direct students to write in their logs their ideas on the following question: How does learning about motor vehicle insurance help young people become more responsible drivers?

WHAT WOULD YOU DO?

Sample answer: Obtain liability insurance whether it is required or not.

ADVICE FROM THE EXPERTS

David Van Sickle
Director, Auto and Consumer Information, AAA International

Shopping for a car? Consider safety features first. Safety belt systems, air bags, antilock brakes, and traction control should top your list.

Stick to basics with your first car. Features like a 4-cylinder engine and a manual transmission can make a vehicle more affordable to buy, operate, and maintain.

Try to stay away from high-performance vehicles. Even though they can be affordable to buy, high insurance rates for young drivers can make them unaffordable to operate.

Your marital status Young married men pay less than men of the same age who are single. Young married men are involved in fewer collisions than young single men.

The value of your vehicle The more expensive the vehicle, the greater the cost of insurance.

The type of vehicle A sports car or sport utility vehicle costs more to insure than a larger sedan.

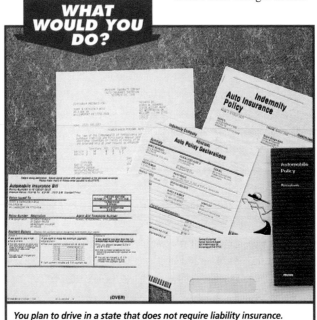

WHAT WOULD YOU DO?

You plan to drive in a state that does not require liability insurance. What will you do to be sure you are adequately covered?

Other factors Many insurance companies offer discounts to students who have completed a driver education program and to students whose grade average is B or higher. Companies may also offer discounts to drivers whose vehicles have air bags or antilock brakes. Discounts may be given as well to drivers who garage their vehicles. Those who buy cars with antitheft devices, or who have antitheft devices installed in their vehicles, may also qualify for a discount.

Lesson 4 Review

1. How is liability insurance different from other kinds of motor vehicle insurance?
2. How does being male or female play a role in the amount you pay for motor vehicle insurance?

Lesson 4 Review

Answers
1. Liability insurance protects against injury or property damage that you may cause to other people; other kinds of insurance protect against injury or property damage that you may sustain.
2. Men pay higher rates than women because statistically they are involved in more collisions.

Understanding Map Symbols

Look at the symbols and the legend on a map to learn about the area you are traveling through.

You can see that there is an airport near Great Falls, Montana, at D, 7, and a campground near Choteau at C, 6.

Try It Yourself

1. At what coordinates can ski areas be found?
2. How many campgrounds can you find in the Blackfeet Indian Reservation?
3. What does ✦ stand for at A, 4?

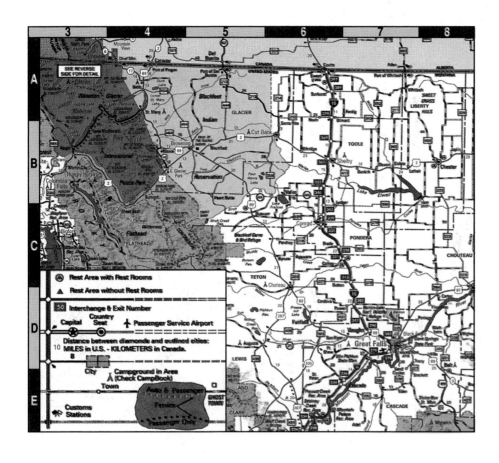

BUILDING SKILLS: READING MAPS

Objective

Demonstrate an ability to use map symbols to locate places of interest.

Teaching the Skill

- Be sure students understand what each symbol on the legend represents before they locate symbols on the map.
- Point out the letter coordinates along the side of the map and the number coordinates across the top. You may want to have students use their fingers to locate and trace the areas identified by the coordinates.
- Advise students that they should always check the map legend before using a map. Symbols may vary from map to map.

ANSWERS TO
Try It Yourself Questions

1. B, 3; B, 4; C, 5
2. three (one at A, 4, and two at B, 5)
3. Customs Station

CHAPTER SUMMARY

Key Points

Have students read the Key Points to review the major concepts of the chapter.

PROJECTS

Cooperative Learning:

Students will benefit by working with a partner on one or both projects. When the assignment is completed, the whole class will profit by sharing and comparing results.

CHAPTER 16 REVIEW

KEY POINTS

Lesson One

1. To determine your need for a vehicle, think about how close you are to places that you go to most often, how available public transportation is for you, how available the family vehicle is, and whether you are mature enough to take on the responsibilities of owning a vehicle.
2. Before buying a vehicle, think about the number of passengers you will have and their age; the number of miles you expect to drive; and the cost of the vehicle plus the cost of maintenance and insurance.

Lesson Two

1. To select a safe vehicle, consider its equipment; what its death rate per 10,000 models is, how it holds up in crash tests, and its size.
2. To select a comfortable vehicle, sit in the driver's seat and adjust the seat and steering wheel (where possible), making sure you can reach accessory switches and dials easily.
3. Factors that affect fuel efficiency are a vehicle's weight, engine and transmission type, design, power train, and whether it has power equipment and other fuel-consuming accessories.

4. If you're thinking of buying a used vehicle, find out if a warranty is available, know the *Blue Book* value, test-drive the vehicle, and have it checked by an independent professional.

Lesson Three

1. You can get financing through banks, credit unions, finance companies, or the vehicle dealer.
2. Shop around to get the best interest rates, and know what your monthly payments will be.

Lesson Four

1. The basic types of insurance are liability (bodily injury and property damage), uninsured motorist, collision, comprehensive, medical payment, no-fault, and towing insurance.
2. Factors that determine insurance cost include age, driving record, mileage per year, where you live, gender, marital status, and the vehicle's value. Insurers may offer discounts to students who have completed a driver education course and to drivers who have safety devices, keep their vehicle in a garage, and have antitheft devices.

PROJECTS

1. Visit several vehicle dealerships in your area. Talk to salespeople and compare prices, safety features, and service facilities. Select a vehicle that you might want to own. Interview a mechanic certified by the National Institute for Automotive Service Excellence (NIASE) about the vehicle you have selected.
2. Interview a local insurance agent to find out if there are differences in rates for new drivers under the age of 25. Use what you learn to propose ways a new driver can

reduce insurance costs. Share your information and ideas with your class.

Cruise Glencoe's Web site to investigate how vehicles for sale are advertised over the Internet.
drivered.glencoe.com

Visit Glencoe's Driver Education Web site for student activities that relate to this chapter.
drivered.glencoe.com

CHAPTER TEST

Write the letter of the answer that best completes each sentence.

1. A driver interested in fuel efficiency would
   a. buy a vehicle with 4 cylinders.
   b. buy a vehicle with 8 cylinders.
   c. buy a vehicle with 16 cylinders.

2. When buying a vehicle, most people
   a. pay with a credit card.
   b. pay cash.
   c. take out a loan.

3. Before buying a vehicle, consider
   a. how clean it is.
   b. how many passengers you will have.
   c. whether it is a convertible.

4. A driving record and marital status can affect
   a. the cost of your insurance.
   b. the purchase price of a vehicle.
   c. your concentration at the wheel.

5. Expensive vehicles
   a. cost more to insure than inexpensive vehicles.
   b. cost less to insure than inexpensive vehicles.
   c. use less fuel than inexpensive vehicles.

6. The death rate in the smallest vehicles is
   a. lower than that in the largest vehicles.
   b. the same as that in the largest vehicles.
   c. twice as high as that in the largest vehicles.

7. The *Blue Book* is a guide to
   a. vehicle dealerships in the United States.
   b. the average price paid to dealers for various used vehicles.
   c. different types of vehicle engines.

8. Liability insurance
   a. protects you against claims if you are at fault in a collision.
   b. is available to drivers over 21 years of age.
   c. protects you if you are accused of lying.

9. The purchase price of a vehicle is
   a. one of the many expenses associated with owning a vehicle.
   b. the only expense in owning a vehicle.
   c. generally lower than it was ten years ago.

10. Bodily injury insurance covers
    a. any damages to the body of your vehicle.
    b. the death or injury of other people while you are driving.
    c. only the driver of a vehicle.

Write the word or phrase that best completes each sentence.

fuel consumption	warranty
comprehensive insurance	financing
uninsured motorist insurance	deductible

11. A(n) _____ is a written guarantee that the seller will repair your vehicle.

12. If your vehicle is damaged by anything other than a collision, _____ will pay the bills.

13. There can be large differences in _____ among different vehicle models.

14. Vehicle dealers can offer you a(n) _____ arrangement when you buy a new vehicle.

15. If you are involved in a collision with a hit-and-run driver, _____ can protect you.

DRIVER'S LOG

In this chapter, you have learned some considerations to keep in mind when you are ready to buy a vehicle. Write a paragraph in response to each of the following questions.
- Describe the guideposts you use to measure maturity. Which do you need to work on?
- What will you look for when you buy a vehicle? What do you think your choice will say about your maturity? Why?

CHAPTER TEST

Assign the Chapter Test to all students.

Answers

1. a
2. c
3. b
4. a
5. a
6. c
7. b
8. a
9. a
10. b
11. warranty
12. comprehensive insurance
13. fuel consumption
14. financing
15. uninsured motorist insurance

DRIVER'S LOG

Students' responses will reflect their personal viewpoints. However, their answers should provide an assessment of their understanding of the maturity needed to own a vehicle.

Evaluate
- Test A, pp. 31–32 or Test B, pp. 31–32
- Testmaker software

RETURN TO THE BIG IDEA

Discuss the idea that buying and owning a vehicle require an individual to evaluate and handle a variety of factors and to accept serious ongoing responsibility.

CHAPTER 17   Vehicle Systems and Maintenance Overview

THEME DEVELOPMENT Keeping a vehicle in safe and efficient operating condition requires regular maintenance checks, periodic servicing, and attention to warning signs of mechanical problems.

CHAPTER FEATURES	TCR COMPONENTS
TIPS FOR NEW DRIVERS Having a vehicle serviced or repaired.	Study Guide, p. 65 Car Care Manual Lesson Plan, p. 35 Behind-the-Wheel Checklist 3
	Study Guide, p. 66 Transparency 41 Car Care Manual Lesson Plan, p. 35 Information Master 20
CONNECTIONS **Science** How to avoid carbon monoxide poisoning.	Study Guide, p. 67 Transparencies 42–46 Car Care Manual Lesson Plan, p. 36
ADVICE FROM THE EXPERTS The importance of your vehicle's tires.	Study Guide, p. 68 Transparencies 47 and 48 Car Care Manual Lesson Plan, p. 36
BUILDING SKILLS: SCIENCE Graphing Braking Distances	Test A, pp. 33–34 Test B, pp. 33–34

PROJECTS

1. Learn how to maintain a vehicle by reading the owner's manual.
2. Report on various types of tires.

OTHER PROGRAM RESOURCES

Testmaker software
Teaching Your Teens to Drive: Lesson 1, AAA, 1998

CHAPTER 17 Vehicle Systems and Maintenance

TEST A

Select the phrase that best completes each sentence below. Write the letter of the answer you have chosen to the left of each statement.

__b__ 1. After turning the key in the ignition, power is drawn from the battery directly to the
   a. ignition.
   b. starter motor.
   c. crankshaft.
   d. spark plugs.

__c__ 2. A piston in each car cylinder turns the
   a. starter motor.
   b. carburetor.
   c. crankshaft.
   d. flywheel.

__d__ 3. The wheels that receive the power from the engine are called
   a. front wheels.
   b. rear wheels.
   c. power wheels.
   d. drive wheels.

__a__ 4. The function of the differential is to
   a. allow each of the rear wheels to turn at a different speed when turning a corner.
   b. keep the coolant in the engine moving.
   c. stop your car from losing control when you brake too hard.
   d. do all of the above.

__b__ 5. Check your vehicle's oil
   a. every time you fill the fuel tank.
   b. every second time you fill the fuel tank.
   c. once a month.
   d. once every three months.

__d__ 6. The purpose of the car's exhaust system is to
   a. carry away harmful gases from the engine.
   b. muffle engine noise.
   c. ignite the fuel.
   d. do both a and b.

__d__ 7. A warning sign of steering trouble is
   a. too much play in the steering wheel.
   b. vibrations in the steering wheel.
   c. a wobbly front end to your vehicle.
   d. all of the above.

__a__ 8. As the engine is running, the battery is charged by
   a. the alternator, or generator.
   b. the distributor.
   c. the carburetor.
   d. none of the above.

© AAA and Glencoe/McGraw-Hill

Match the following terms by placing the letter of the definition to the left of the item.

__c__ 9. spark plug   a. an odorless, poisonous gas

__e__ 10. power train   b. grooved outer surface of a tire

__h__ 11. battery   c. causes the fuel-air mixture to explode

__i__ 12. muffler   d. reduces amount of harmful gases emitted

__d__ 13. catalytic converter e. transmits power from engine to drive wheels

__a__ 14. carbon monoxide   f. supplies a constant charge for the battery

__f__ 15. alternator   g. has a lower freezing point and higher boiling point than water

__j__ 16. engine-control module h. provides power to start engine

__b__ 17. tread   i. absorbs noise

__g__ 18. antifreeze   j. controls electrical and other systems

Read each statement below. If it is true, place a T in the space to the left of the statement. If the statement is false, place an F next to it.

__F__ 19. Engine oil should always be checked with the engine running.

__T__ 20. The starter turns the flywheel of the engine.

__T__ 21. The transmission is a part of the power train.

__F__ 22. Stop-and-go city driving is easier on a vehicle than highway driving.

__T__ 23. In a vehicle that has a catalytic converter, you should use unleaded gasoline.

24. When checking out your tires, what are the warning signs of trouble?

   less than $1/16$ inch of tread; bald areas; uneven wear; bulges; embedded nails, glass, or metal; and

   frequent pressure loss
   _____
   _____
   _____
   _____
   _____
   _____

   © AAA and Glencoe/McGraw-Hill

CHAPTER 17 Vehicle Systems and Maintenance

TEST B

Select the phrase that best completes each sentence below. Write the letter of the answer you have chosen to the left of each statement.

__d__ 1. To keep your battery in top condition,
   a. keep the terminals clean.
   b. keep battery cables firmly connected.
   c. keep the battery fluid level up if you have an older type of battery.
   d. do all of the above.

__b__ 2. Coolant is circulated throughout the radiator and engine block by
   a. induction.
   b. the water pump.
   c. the radiator fan.
   d. all of the above.

__b__ 3. Check your vehicle's oil
   a. every time you fill the fuel tank.
   b. every second time you fill the fuel tank.
   c. every six weeks.
   d. once every six months.

__c__ 4. The kind of force that slows or stops a vehicle's brakes is
   a. air pressure.
   b. water pressure.
   c. hydraulic pressure.
   d. none of the above.

__a__ 5. To minimize the risk of brake failure, brake systems are designed so that
   a. front and rear brakes work independently.
   b. front and rear brakes work together.
   c. rear brakes stop harder than front brakes.
   d. the left side and the right side operate independently.

__c__ 6. Tires should be rotated
   a. every year.
   b. every two years.
   c. every 5,000 to 6,000 miles.
   d. every 10,000 to 12,000 miles.

__b__ 7. With power steering, you should have _____ play in the steering wheel.
   a. no more than 2 inches of
   b. almost no
   c. no more than 1 inch of
   d. no more than 15 degrees of

__a__ 8. Fuel is ignited in the engine by the
   a. spark plugs.
   b. starter.
   c. camshaft.
   d. distributor.

© AAA and Glencoe/McGraw-Hill

Match the following terms by placing the letter of the definition to the left of the item.

__e__ 9. catalytic converter   a. controls the electrical and engine systems

__c__ 10. tread   b. controls bouncing

__f__ 11. alternator   c. grooved outer surface of a tire

__h__ 12. muffler   d. transmits power from the engine to the wheels

__b__ 13. shock absorber   e. reduces the amount of harmful gases coming from the tailpipe

__g__ 14. differential   f. provides a constant charge for the battery

__a__ 15. engine control module g. allows rear wheels to turn at different speeds when the vehicle turns

__d__ 16. power train   h. absorbs noise from the cylinders

Read each statement below. If it is true, place a T in the space to the left of the statement. If the statement is false, place an F next to it.

__T__ 17. Change your vehicle's oil according to the recommendations in your owner's manual.

__F__ 18. Antifreeze has a higher freezing point than water.

__T__ 19. One way heat is removed from your engine is through the lubricating system.

__F__ 20. All automobile engines are cooled by water.

__F__ 21. The minimum legal depth of tread is $1/26$ of an inch.

22. What are the individual parts of the power train?

   The drive wheels, transmission, clutch, drive shaft, differential, and axle are the parts of the power

   train.
   _____
   _____
   _____
   _____
   _____
   _____

   © AAA and Glencoe/McGraw-Hill

NAME _____ DATE _____

STUDY GUIDE FOR CHAPTER 17   LESSON 1

CHAPTER 17 Vehicle Systems and Maintenance

Checking Your Vehicle Before You Drive

A. For each sentence below, circle T if the statement is true and F if it is false. Correct each false statement in the space below.

1. You should check the engine oil level only when the engine is running.   T   Ⓕ
You should check the engine oil level when the engine is not running.

2. The radiator cap should be opened only when the radiator is cool.   Ⓣ   F

3. A fan belt should be replaced every 5000 miles.   T   Ⓕ
A cracked or frayed fan belt should be replaced as soon as possible.

4. Your vehicle's brake warning light will make you aware of any brake problems the vehicle may have.   T   Ⓕ
The brake warning light will make you aware of some, not all, brake problems.

5. Brakes should be tested once a month.   T   Ⓕ
You should check your brakes every time you begin driving your vehicle.

6. You should check your vehicle's headlights and turn signals every week.   T   Ⓕ
You should test your headlights and turn signals every time you drive your vehicle.

7. You can't know the specific guidelines for servicing your vehicle.   T   Ⓕ
Specific guidelines for servicing your vehicle can be found in its owner's manual.

8. You should ask a mechanic for an estimate before work begins on your vehicle.   Ⓣ   F

9. With newer vehicles, many repairs are covered under the vehicle's warranty.   Ⓣ   F

10. You should check your vehicle's battery cables to make sure that they are not too tight.   T   Ⓕ
You should check battery cables to make sure that they are not loose.

B. FIND OUT MORE. Talk to a friend or relative who owns a vehicle. Ask if you can check the vehicle out as a part of your driver's training. Check the battery terminals, oil level, transmission fluid level, coolant level, hoses, wires, and fan belts. Let the owner know what you found, and write your findings below.
Review student's work.

NAME _____ DATE _____

STUDY GUIDE FOR CHAPTER 17   LESSON 2

The Engine and Power Train

A. Briefly describe the function of each of the following parts of a vehicle.

1. spark plug   Produces a spark that causes the fuel/air mixture to explode.

2. crankshaft   Transmits power to the wheels, making the car move.

3. starter motor   Receives electricity from the battery to start the car, and turns the flywheel.

4. drive wheels   The wheels that receive the power from the engine.

5. differential   Allows each of the rear wheels to turn at a different speed when you turn a corner.

6. drive shaft   Connects the transmission and differential.

7. clutch pedal   Used to help shift gears, breaks the connection between the transmission and the engine.

8. ignition   Causes power to be drawn from the battery to the starter motor.

B. FIND OUT MORE. Using three separate situations, record your observations on the ways other drivers handle visibility, time, and space in changing lanes. Where were you? What time of the day was it? Could a collision have occurred because of what you saw?
Review student's work.

NAME _____ DATE _____

STUDY GUIDE FOR CHAPTER 17   LESSON 3

Understanding and Maintaining Vehicle Systems

A. Match the following terms by placing the letter of the definition or the description of what the item does to the left of the item.

e	**1.** coolant	**a.** protects vehicle's electrical circuits from overloading
c	**2.** exhaust manifold	**b.** pumps coolant through radiator and engine
h	**3.** muffler	**c.** collects unburned gasses
k	**4.** tailpipe	**d.** another name for alternator
n	**5.** catalytic converter	**e.** mixture of water and antifreeze
l	**6.** carbon monoxide	**f.** key is used here to start vehicle
o	**7.** battery	**g.** supplies electricity needed to keep engine running
f	**8.** ignition switch	**h.** quiets engine noise
g	**9.** alternator	**i.** moves oil to all moving engine parts
m	**10.** engine control module	**j.** controls flow of coolant
d	**11.** generator	**k.** where exhaust gases exit vehicle
a	**12.** fuse	**l.** an odorless, deadly gas
i	**13.** oil pump	**m.** controls electric and other vehicle systems
b	**14.** water pump	**n.** reduces harmful gas emissions
j	**15.** thermostat	**o.** provides energy to start the engine

B. FIND OUT MORE. Go to your library and find out how a catalytic converter works. Describe your findings below. You may also make a diagram in the space below to show how the catalytic converter works.
Review student's work.

NAME _____ DATE _____

STUDY GUIDE FOR CHAPTER 17   LESSON 4

Suspension, Steering, Brakes, and Tires

A. For each sentence below, circle T if the statement is true and F if it is false. Correct each false statement in the space below.

1. The main parts of a suspension system are the springs and the tires.   T   Ⓕ
The main parts of a suspension system are the springs and the shock absorbers.

2. Springs are designed to soften the impact of bumps in the roadway.   Ⓣ   F

3. Tire tread depth should be at least $\frac{1}{20}$ inch.   T   Ⓕ
Tire tread depth should be no less than $\frac{1}{16}$ inch.

4. Your vehicle's tires should be rotated at least every 5000 to 6000 miles.   Ⓣ   F

5. There should be no more than two inches of play in the steering wheel if your vehicle has power steering.   T   Ⓕ
There should be no play at all in the steering wheel if the vehicle has power steering.

B. There are several clues that a vehicle's front end is out of alignment or that the tires need balancing. What are they?
The steering wheel vibrates or is hard to turn, the front end wobbles, the car pulls to one side, the vehicle bounces too much after going over a bump, and tire treads wear unevenly.

C. FIND OUT MORE. Ask somebody you know who has a vehicle if you may inspect their tires. What did you check for, and what did you find?
Review student's work.

Vehicle Systems and Maintenance

CHAPTER OVERVIEW

LESSON ONE

Maintenance and performance checks a driver should perform before entering a vehicle and after starting the engine are explained. Guidelines for vehicle servicing are also discussed.

LESSON TWO

The operation of a vehicle's engine and power train is explained along with guidelines for maintenance.

LESSON THREE

The operation of several vehicle systems—fuel and exhaust systems, electrical and light systems, and lubricating and cooling systems—is explained along with guidelines for maintenance.

LESSON FOUR

Four comfort and safety systems—suspension, steering, brakes, and tires—are described and guidelines for maintenance are provided. Warning signs of possible problems are discussed.

VOCABULARY

alternator
antifreeze
battery
catalytic converter
coolant
crankshaft
cylinder
differential
disc brake
drive wheel
drum brake
electronic fuel injection (EFI) system
engine control module (ECM)

exhaust manifold
hydraulic pressure
internal combustion engine
muffler
piston
power train
radiator
shock absorber
spark plug
strut
tread

CONCEPT OF THE DRIVING TASK

Explain that maintaining a reliable and safe vehicle is the responsibility of the driver. Responsible drivers remember to make regular maintenance checks and have their vehicle serviced as required. They also know what warning signs indicate a mechanical problem that should be checked by a reputable mechanic.

CHAPTER 17

Vehicle Systems and Maintenance

Good drivers make sure that their vehicles are safe to drive. Good drivers understand their vehicles' different systems and make sure that those systems are properly maintained.

PRESENTING THE BIG IDEA

Understanding how a vehicle's component systems function and what signs to watch for to learn of system malfunctions can help drivers maintain their vehicles in peak operating condition and reduce driving risk.

INTRODUCING THE CHAPTER

What's on the Road Ahead?

Have students look at the photographs and read the lesson titles and objectives. Briefly discuss the topic of each lesson. Tell students that in this chapter, they will learn how various vehicle systems operate and how to check and maintain these systems.

Background: Engineering and Design Improvements

From the time the relatively simple automobiles first appeared on America's roads long ago, vehicles have become increasingly sophisticated. A few years ago fuel-injection systems began to replace carburetors on many vehicle models, making starting easier. Today many vehicles have high-technology features such as computers that coordinate the atmospheric conditions within the engine to make a vehicle more efficient. New synthetic oils have also been developed to reduce friction and increase resistance to heat. These new oils contain no natural petroleum products. Future vehicle designs will incorporate more new ideas to make vehicles safer and more comfortable, reliable, and environmentally friendly.

Relating to Prior Knowledge

Discuss with students what they know about how various vehicle systems operate. Invite students to share what they know about vehicle maintenance and reasons for having a vehicle serviced. Ask students if they would be able to identify mechanical problems from the way a vehicle sounded or handled on the road.

The Big Idea

Discuss students' reactions to the Big Idea statement. Suggest that they keep this idea in mind as they read Chapter 17.

Checking Your Vehicle Before and After You Start the Engine

(pages 316–318)

FOCUS

Objectives

- List several things on your vehicle that you can inspect before entering it.
- List what to check after starting the engine.
- Explain when to have your vehicle serviced.

Resources

📁 Study Guide, page 65

📁 Behind-the-Wheel Checklist 3

📁 Car Care Manual

Motivator

Pose the following situation: You are planning to take a long driving trip. What actions can you take in advance to avoid having vehicle problems on the road? (Make sure vehicle is running well—have it serviced if necessary; check all fluid levels; test brakes; inspect wires, belts, and hoses; check all signals and lights; check gauges; test horn.)

LESSON ONE

OBJECTIVES
1. List several things on your vehicle that you can inspect before entering it.
2. List what to check after starting the engine.
3. Explain when to have your vehicle serviced.

◆ Before you enter your vehicle, check under the hood for items such as the coolant level.

Checking Your Vehicle Before and After You Start the Engine

You've probably heard the old saying that an ounce of prevention is worth a pound of cure. That maxim is especially important for drivers.

Inspecting and caring for your vehicle before something goes wrong can save you both money and aggravation. More important, maintaining your vehicle can save your life.

Different makes and models are alike in some ways, different in others. To be able to check your particular model properly, you should refer to the owner's manual. If you don't have the manual for your vehicle, obtain a copy from a dealer or order one from the manufacturer. Manuals are also available in many bookstores. Keep the manual in your glove compartment so you'll have it handy when you need it.

What Can You Inspect Before Entering Your Vehicle?

You don't need to be a mechanic to inspect your vehicle. You can check many items quickly and easily before driving. Make these checks at least once a month and before long drives.

In addition to the guidelines below, refer to Chapter 7 for other important predriving checks and procedures.

Fluid Levels

You can inspect the different fluid levels. Check:
- the engine oil (when the engine is cool and not running).
- the level of coolant in the radiator overflow tank or radiator.
- the transmission fluid and the fluid level in the power-steering and master-brake-cylinder reservoirs.
- the battery fluid (if necessary for your battery).
- the windshield-washer fluid.

State BY State

Twenty-three states and the District of Columbia require annual safety inspections for registered vehicles at an official inspection station. Thirty-two states and the District of Columbia require motorists in certain parts of the state to bring in their vehicles for an annual emissions test. A sticker placed on the inside of the windshield shows that a vehicle has been inspected.

Belts, Hoses, and Wires

Before you enter your vehicle, inspect belts, hoses, and wires.

- Check the fan belt and the belts that run the power-steering and air-conditioning units. Many new vehicles have only one belt that drives these units. Belts may need tightening or adjustment. Replace frayed or cracked belts as soon as possible.
- Check all hoses and hose connections for leaks.
- Look for loose, broken, or disconnected wires. Also check for cracked insulation on wires.
- Make sure the battery cables are tightly connected and the terminals are free of corrosion.

◆ *Learning how to do your own maintenance can save you the cost and inconvenience of repairs.*

What Can You Check After Starting the Engine?

Once your engine is running, you should make several routine checks to ensure that your vehicle is operating properly and safely.

Gauges and Warning Lights

You have already read about the various gauges and warning lights that provide information about your vehicle. Check these gauges and lights regularly as you drive. They will warn you of a wide range of problems, such as low oil pressure or fuel level, engine overheating, and alternator malfunction.

Brakes

Your vehicle's brake-warning light will make you aware of some—but not all—problems with your brake system.

For this reason, always test your brakes as soon as you begin driving. When you step on the brake pedal, you should feel firm resistance, and your vehicle should come to a smooth, straight stop. The pedal should stay well above the floor.

Specific warning signs of a brake system malfunction are discussed later in this chapter.

FOR NEW DRIVERS

Having Your Vehicle Serviced or Repaired

- To find a reliable mechanic or garage, ask friends and relatives for their recommendations. You can also call your local American Automobile Association.
- Ask the mechanic for a cost estimate of the work to be done.
- Find out for how long the mechanic will guarantee any work done. Save your bill or receipt.
- Know what you're paying for. If there's something you don't understand, ask for an explanation.
- If the mechanic replaces a part, ask to see the old part.
- Warranties may cover many repairs. Know what your warranty does and does not cover.

MEETING STUDENT DIVERSITY

Learning Disabled

Students who have trouble remembering which items to check before and after entering a vehicle may find it helpful to create their own checklist to keep in the glove compartment of the vehicle they normally drive.

TIPS FOR NEW DRIVERS

To check student understanding, discuss how choosing a reliable mechanic can save needless expense. Also stress the importance of knowing what your warranty covers and for what period of time.

TEACH

Explain

OBJECTIVE 1: Students will benefit from a discussion and demonstration of the various advance checks, including checks of engine oil, radiator coolant, transmission fluid, brake fluid, battery fluid, windshield washer fluid, and the condition of belts, hoses, and wires. Use an actual vehicle if possible, or else use illustrations.

OBJECTIVE 2: Students should recognize the importance of checking gauges and warning lights regularly and taking prompt action when required.

OBJECTIVE 3: Students may benefit from a discussion of the reliability and cost savings of a vehicle that is well-maintained. They should also recognize the importance of keeping accurate service records. Emphasize, too, the advisability of getting a second opinion from another mechanic before having major repair work done.

Teaching Model

Describe the following situation: As you are about to enter your vehicle, you remember you need to refill the windshield wiper fluid. Model the additional checks you will make after adding the fluid. (If you have not checked the oil level within the past month, you will check the engine oil; level of radiator coolant; steering, brake, and transmission fluids; belts, hoses, wires; battery cable connections.)

Ask

Ask students what might happen if these checks were not regularly performed.

Read

Have students read Lesson 1 to learn the inspection checks to make before and after entering a vehicle and to recognize when to have a vehicle serviced.

ASSESS

Guided Practice

Have students answer the Lesson 1 Review questions. The answers are provided below.

Reteaching

Encourage students to work in small groups to create a predriving checklist, discussing the importance of each item listed. After groups have completed this task, lead a class discussion focusing on the benefits of preventing vehicle problems.

Enrichment

Assign the Study Guide for Lesson 1. The Find Out More section encourages students to expand their basic learning of the lesson concepts.

CLOSE

Summarize

Return to the Motivator question. Discuss with students the importance of keeping a vehicle well maintained, and have them explain how they can accomplish this. Help students summarize by asking: What advance checks can save you time, trouble, and money in the long run?

DRIVER'S LOG

With the aid of an owner's manual, have students create a chart showing a theoretical schedule for making vehicle maintenance checks.

SAFETY TIPS

Always check radiator coolant level by looking at the radiator overflow tank. If additional coolant is needed, add it to the overflow tank, not to the radiator. Rarely should it be necessary to remove the radiator cap. If you do have to remove the radiator cap, do so *only when the radiator is cool.* If you remove the cap when the radiator is hot, boiling water could spurt out and scald you.

WHAT WOULD YOU DO?

A friend has agreed to let you use her car while she's on vacation. What checks will you make before getting into her car? What checks will you make after starting the engine?

WHAT WOULD YOU DO?

Sample answer: Before entering the vehicle, check fluid levels, belts, hoses, and wires. After entering the vehicle, check gauges and warning lights, brakes, lights, signals, and the horn.

Horn

Periodically check to make sure your horn works. If you're driving an unfamiliar vehicle, always locate and try the horn *before* you begin driving. Horn position on the steering wheel varies from vehicle to vehicle.

Lights and Turn Signals

Vehicle safety checks find that nearly one out of four vehicles has at least one lightbulb or headlight burned out. Check all exterior lights and turn signals before you drive. Periodically have a friend or family member stand outside the vehicle and tell you if your brake lights work when you press the brake pedal.

How Do You Know When Your Vehicle Should Be Serviced?

Your owner's manual contains guidelines for servicing and maintaining your vehicle. The guidelines vary, depending on the kind and amount of driving you do and on the manufacturer's recommendations.

Some systems and parts require more frequent attention than others. Recommended intervals for servicing may be based either on time or on miles driven. For example, your manual might recommend checking tire pressure once a month, changing the oil every few months, and having the suspension checked every 20,000 miles.

Keeping complete records will help you maintain a schedule of care. An easy way to keep track of repairs and maintenance is to keep a small notebook in your vehicle. Each time you or a mechanic services or repairs the vehicle, jot down exactly what was done and the date. Save your receipts in an envelope in the glove compartment.

Lesson 1 Review

1. What kinds of problems might you spot as you check your vehicle before entering it?
2. What can you check after you start the engine?
3. What can help you determine when to have your vehicle serviced?

Lesson 1 Review

Answers

1. You might spot low fluid levels, loose or cracked belts, disconnected hoses or wires, or a loose battery cable connection.
2. Check gauges and warning lights, lights and turn signals, brakes, and the horn.
3. Consult your owner's manual; keep records to develop a schedule.

Becoming Familiar with the Engine and Power Train

Many parts work together to produce a vehicle's power and motion. By keeping these parts operating smoothly, you help your vehicle run safely and fuel efficiently.

How Does the Engine Work?

Your vehicle's engine is known as an **internal combustion engine.** It is called that because the power it produces comes from burning a mixture of fuel and air inside, rather than outside, the engine.

When you start your vehicle's engine, you're setting off a chain of events.

1. Turning the key in the ignition causes power to be drawn from the battery to a small electric starter motor, commonly called the starter.
2. The starter turns the flywheel of the engine. When the flywheel turns, it turns the crankshaft.
3. A piston in each **cylinder** of the vehicle is attached to the crankshaft. Most vehicles have 4, 6, or 8 cylinders. The more cylinders in a vehicle, the more power the engine has, but also the more gasoline the engine uses.

OBJECTIVES
1. Explain how a typical vehicle engine works.
2. Tell what the power train is and what it does.
3. Describe four guidelines for maintaining the engine and power train.

KEY TERMS
internal combustion engine
cylinder
spark plug
piston
crankshaft
power train
drive wheel
differential

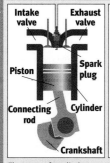

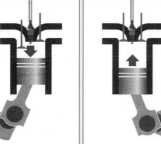
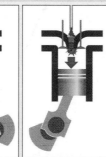

The parts of a cylinder. Most cars have four, six or eight cylinders. The piston in each cylinder is attached to a part of the crankshaft.

Step 1. As the piston moves down, the air-fuel mixture is drawn into the cylinder through the intake valve or valves.

Step 2. The piston moves up and compresses the air-fuel mixture. (The intake and exhaust valves are both closed.)

Step 3. A spark explodes the compressed air-fuel mixture. This pushes down the piston, which turns the crankshaft.

Step 4. The piston moves up and forces the burned gas out the exhaust valve or valves. The cycle begins again.

CHAPTER 17 *Vehicle Systems and Maintenance* **319**

MEETING STUDENT DIVERSITY

Limited English Proficiency

Engine-related terminology can be particularly challenging for students with limited English proficiency. Use drawings, models, and other visual aids to help students understand how the parts of an engine work together.

FOCUS

Objectives
- Explain how a typical vehicle engine works.
- Tell what the power train is and what it does.
- Describe four guidelines for maintaining the engine and power train.

Resources
 Study Guide, page 66

 Transparency 41

 Information Master 20

Car Care Manual

Vocabulary
internal combustion engine
cylinder
spark plug
piston
crankshaft
power train
drive wheel
differential

Motivator

Pose the following situation: You get into a vehicle, fasten your safety belt, and turn the key in the ignition. What happens inside the engine to produce the familiar sound of a vehicle motor starting and running? (Turning the key brings power from the battery to the starter motor, which turns the flywheel. The flywheel turns the crankshaft, which moves the pistons in the cylinders. Sparks from
continued on page 320

the plugs cause a fuel-air mixture to explode, pushing down the pistons and turning the crankshaft. The up-and-down movement of the pistons keeps the crankshaft turning.)

TEACH

Explain

OBJECTIVE 1: Students may benefit from a step-by-step discussion tracing the engine start-up sequence on a diagram.

OBJECTIVE 2: In the context of the transmission being a key part of the power train, you may want to refer back to what students learned about manual and automatic transmissions in Chapter 8.

OBJECTIVE 3: Students may benefit from a discussion of the importance of regular oil changes; tune-ups, if necessary; and other regular maintenance.

Teaching Model

Describe this situation: You have had your vehicle for about six months and have driven approximately 4,000 miles. Most of your driving has been in city traffic. Your own regular 15-minute monthly checkups have revealed nothing wrong. Model the procedures you need to follow to continue to maintain the vehicle. (Have the oil changed; take the vehicle in for a tune-up if your vehicle manual says it is due for one—this may include having an oil change; replacing filters; cleaning or replacing spark plugs; checking fuel-injection system; checking ignition system and battery; checking pollution-control devices and exhaust system.)

Ask

Ask students to discuss problems oil changes and tune-ups may prevent.

Read

Have students read Lesson 2 to understand how a vehicle's engine and power train work and to learn how to maintain these components.

4. In each cylinder, a **spark plug** produces a spark. This spark causes the fuel-air mixture inside the cylinder to explode. The explosion pushes down the **piston,** which turns the **crankshaft.**
5. The continuous up-and-down motion of the pistons keeps the crankshaft turning. Power sent from the crankshaft is transmitted to the wheels, making the vehicle move.

What Is the Power Train and What Does It Do?

Several parts of your vehicle work together to transmit power from the engine to the wheels. These parts make up the **power train.**

In most vehicles, the power train sends power from the engine to only two of the four wheels. The wheels that receive the power are called the **drive wheels.** If the two front wheels are the drive wheels, the vehicle has front-wheel drive. If the two rear wheels receive the power, the vehicle has rear-wheel drive. A vehicle has four-wheel drive if all four wheels receive power.

The transmission is part of the power train. Gears in the transmission allow it to transfer power to the drive wheels. With a manual transmission, the driver uses the clutch pedal and the gearshift lever to shift gears and change the amount of power that goes to the drive wheels. With an automatic transmission, the clutch works automatically, so the gears are shifted automatically too.

In a vehicle with rear-wheel drive, the transmission is connected by a driveshaft to the differential, rear axle, and rear wheels. The **differential** allows the rear wheels to turn at different speeds when the vehicle turns.

◆ *Power is transmitted differently to vehicles with rear-wheel drive, front-wheel drive, and four-wheel drive.*

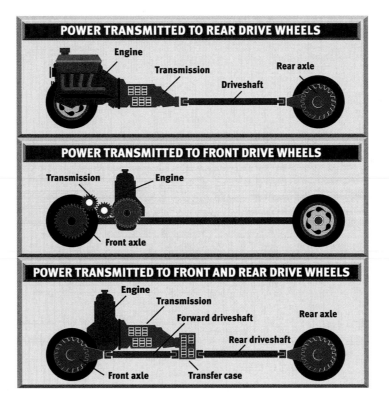

POWER TRANSMITTED TO REAR DRIVE WHEELS
Engine — Transmission — Rear axle — Driveshaft

POWER TRANSMITTED TO FRONT DRIVE WHEELS
Transmission — Engine — Front axle

POWER TRANSMITTED TO FRONT AND REAR DRIVE WHEELS
Engine — Transmission — Forward driveshaft — Rear axle — Rear driveshaft — Front axle — Transfer case

THE INTERNATIONAL SCENE

Mexico

Vehicle repairs may cost less in Mexico than in the United States because of the exchange rate. However, finding a reliable mechanic in Mexico can be just as difficult as it is in the United States, and a language barrier may compound the problem. Local residents may help in finding a good mechanic.

In a vehicle with front-wheel drive, engine power is sent to a combination transmission and differential and then directly to the front wheels.

How Can You Maintain the Engine and Power Train?

Vehicles that are well maintained perform better, are more fuel efficient, and last longer than vehicles that are neglected.

Here are some basic guidelines for keeping your vehicle's engine and power train in top condition. Your owner's manual will give you additional specific recommendations.

Check and Change the Oil Regularly

Check your vehicle's oil every second time you fill the fuel tank. Change the oil according to the recommendations in your owner's manual. Most manufacturers give two schedules for oil changes: one for normal use and one for severe use. Severe use is often described as plenty of short trips, stop-and-go driving, or regular travel in dusty conditions. Failure to follow the recommended schedule can void your warranty.

Have Regular Tune-Ups

Some older vehicles require regular tune-ups, but most new ones do not have any need for such attention beyond regular checks and replacement of fluids and filters. Emission regulations require a vehicle's computer to make the necessary "tune-ups" as the vehicle ages to ensure the most complete combustion of fuel and to prevent pouring unburned hydrocarbons into the atmosphere. Consult your vehicle manual to determine your recommended tune-up intervals. Do a visual check of belts, hoses, and wires under the hood for any obvious signs of wear or problems as you check the oil—every second time you fill the vehicle's fuel tank.

Lesson *2* Review

1. What is an internal combustion engine, and how does it work?
2. What parts make up the power train, and how do they supply power to the wheels?
3. What are some of the tasks a mechanic might do when giving your vehicle a tune-up?

WHAT WOULD YOU DO?

The used car you've just bought is running beautifully. You'd like to keep it that way. Describe the actions you will take to maintain your car in top shape.

WHAT WOULD YOU DO?

Sample answer: Check and change oil regularly. Check your vehicle manual and take the vehicle to a mechanic for regular tune-ups as recommended.

Lesson *2* Review

Answers

1. An internal combustion engine powers the vehicle by burning a fuel-air mixture inside the engine.
2. The power train includes the transmission and clutch; gears in the transmission allow it to send power to the drive wheels.
3. A mechanic might change the oil filter; check the carburetor or fuel-injection system; clean or replace spark plugs; check filters; check alternator, battery, and voltage regulator; check the ignition and exhaust systems.

ASSESS

Guided Practice

Have students answer the Lesson 2 Review questions. The answers are provided below.

Reteaching

Pair a more able student with one who is having difficulty with this lesson. Have them work together to describe and illustrate how a vehicle's engine and power train function and then explain how to keep these components in good operating condition.

After pairs have finished, have them share their descriptions and illustrations with the class. Encourage students to explain the meaning of key terms in their own words.

Enrichment

Assign the Study Guide for Lesson 2. The Find Out More section encourages students to expand their basic learning of the lesson concepts.

CLOSE

Summarize

Refer back to the Motivator question. Have students explain in their own words what they have learned in this lesson about how a vehicle's engine operates and how power is transmitted by the power train. Help students summarize main points with the aid of illustrations or models. Extend the discussion by asking students how they can keep their vehicle in peak operating condition.

DRIVER'S LOG

Have students list the parts of a vehicle's engine and power train and describe how these parts function.

Understanding and Maintaining Vehicle Systems

(pages 322–327)

FOCUS

Objectives

• Explain how the fuel and exhaust systems work and how to maintain them.
• Explain how the electrical and light systems work and how to maintain them.
• Describe how the lubricating and cooling systems work and how to maintain them.

Resources

 Study Guide, page 67

 Transparencies 42–46

Car Care Manual

Vocabulary

electronic fuel-injection (EFI) system
exhaust manifold
muffler
catalytic converter
battery
alternator
engine control module (ECM)
coolant
antifreeze
radiator

Motivator

Pose the following situation: You have trouble getting your vehicle started, and when you do, it soon overheats. In addition, the engine sounds very loud. Which part of your vehicle might be causing these problems? (Students may mention the exhaust system, the electrical system, the cooling system; a bad muffler, a weak battery, a leaking radiator.)

LESSON THREE

OBJECTIVES

1. Explain how the fuel and exhaust systems work and how to maintain them.
2. Explain how the electrical and light systems work and how to maintain them.
3. Describe how the lubricating and cooling systems work and how to maintain them.

KEY TERMS

electronic fuel-injection (EFI) system
exhaust manifold
muffler
catalytic converter
battery
alternator
engine control module (ECM)
coolant
antifreeze
radiator

◆ *The fuel system both stores fuel and delivers the correct air-fuel mixture to the engine.*

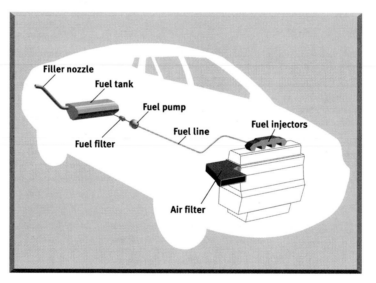

Filler nozzle
Fuel tank
Fuel pump
Fuel line
Fuel injectors
Fuel filter
Air filter

Understanding and Maintaining Vehicle Systems

Today it's easy to take motor vehicles for granted. But they are still among the most complicated machines ever invented. Every time you get behind the wheel, you take control of a network of many different systems that work together to make your vehicle work the way it does.

How Do the Fuel and Exhaust Systems Work?

The fuel and exhaust systems in a vehicle must operate properly to maximize engine efficiency and minimize pollution.

The Fuel System

Your vehicle's fuel system includes the fuel tank, fuel lines, fuel pump, fuel filter, **electronic fuel-injection (EFI) system,** and air filter. Fuel is stored in the tank, where in some cases the fuel pump resides. The pump forces fuel through the fuel lines and filter. The air-fuel mixture forms a vapor that is injected at a specific time into each cylinder, where it is ignited by a spark plug.

Most vehicles now have electronic multipoint fuel-injection systems. Multipoint means that there is a separate nozzle or injector fed by a separate fuel line for each cylinder.

IT'S A FACT

Lead-free gasoline was introduced to the United States in 1973 as a result of regulations to reduce nitrous oxide and hydrocarbons in the environment. Today all new vehicles require the use of lead-free fuel. Since 1975, catalytic converters have been required on new vehicles as well, reducing the amount of pollutants emitted through the tailpipe. Using leaded gasoline would destroy a catalytic converter.

The Exhaust System

The exhaust system serves two main purposes. First, it carries off carbon monoxide and other harmful gas by-products of combustion. Second, it muffles engine noise.

The pipes that make up the **exhaust manifold** collect unburned gases from the engine and carry them to the muffler. The **muffler** absorbs noise created from the explosions in the cylinders. Exhaust gases exit through the tailpipe. Pollution-control devices, such as the **catalytic converter,** reduce the amount of harmful gases coming from the tailpipe.

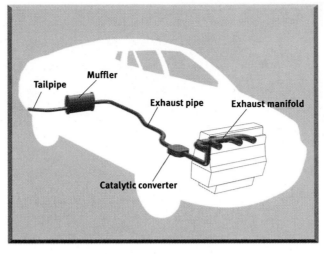

◆ *The exhaust system carries off poisonous gases and muffles engine noise.*

How Can You Maintain the Fuel and Exhaust Systems?

To maintain your vehicle's fuel system, replace the air and fuel filters as needed.

Most vehicles today operate on lead-free gasoline. Using leaded gasoline will destroy the catalytic converter.

How much maintenance or repair the exhaust system requires varies with the conditions under which you drive. Short trips, for example, are harder on a vehicle than long highway drives. Be on the lookout for loose, rusting, or damaged parts. Always have your exhaust system thoroughly inspected as part of a tune-up.

◆ *The electrical system supplies energy to start the vehicle and sends electrical current to the spark plugs.*

How Do the Electrical and Light Systems Work?

The electrical and light systems help keep your vehicle running smoothly and safely.

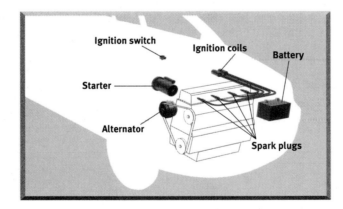

CONNECTIONS
Science

To check student understanding, ask: What should you do before running a vehicle in a closed garage? (Open the garage door.)

Driving Tip

Explain that visible smoke coming from the tailpipe of a running vehicle is a trouble signal. White smoke means coolant is being burned, which may signal a problem with the head gasket. Blue smoke means the engine is burning engine oil. Black smoke means the engine is receiving more fuel than it needs. All of these problems require a mechanic's attention.

TEACH
Explain

OBJECTIVE 1: Students may be familiar with many of the terms for parts of the fuel and exhaust systems, but they will profit from a discussion of the function served by each part. Students should be aware that the exhaust system needs to be checked more frequently in areas that experience snow and ice because salt on roads can increase rust problems.

OBJECTIVE 2: Students should recognize the importance of the parts of the electrical system and understand how they interact. Students should also be aware that a fully functioning battery can be drained or damaged by a faulty alternator.

OBJECTIVE 3: Students should understand the different and crucial functions of oil and antifreeze in the lubricating and coolant systems. Students may benefit from a discussion of the possible problems caused by faulty maintenance of these systems and the importance of regular checks.

Teaching Model

Describe the following situation: The weather has been especially cold, wet, and snowy. You must drive your vehicle several evenings after dark. Model your thinking about which of your vehicle's operating systems you would pay particular attention to in order to make sure the vehicle operates smoothly and safely. (You would do the following.

- Make sure that all lights operate, including headlights, taillights, brake lights, side-marker lights, signal lights, parking lights, and emergency flashers.
- Clean the headlights frequently, and make sure they are properly aligned so that there is full visibility after dark.
- Make sure the battery is in top condition by checking the terminals and cables and the fluid levels if the battery is not maintenance-free.
- Check the antifreeze level to ensure that the liquid in the cooling system will not freeze up.
- Check the exhaust system for loose, rusting, or damaged parts.)

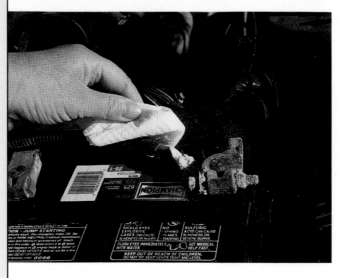

◆ *In order to keep your battery in top working condition, keep terminals free of corrosion.*

FYI

If the "check engine" light comes on, make sure the gas cap or lid is fully tightened to the point of at least one click or notch. The emission control equipment is so sensitive that it can detect if the cap is not correctly tightened and will cause the warning light to come on. You may or may not need to computer reset it.

The Electrical System

The heart of your vehicle's electrical system is the battery. The **battery** provides the power to start the engine. It also enables you to operate, for a short time, such equipment as your radio and lights when the engine is not running.

After you turn the ignition key and start the vehicle, the battery supplies the electricity to fire the spark plugs, operate the stereo, air-conditioning, and other systems. The **alternator,** or generator, provides a constant charge for the battery. The **engine control module (ECM)** controls the electrical and other engine systems.

To prevent electrical overloads and damage to delicate electronic components, the electrical system is equipped with fuses, usually located in a clearly labeled pod beneath the instrument panel or under the hood.

The Light System

Your vehicle's light system enables you to see and be seen.

Exterior lights include headlights, taillights, side-marker lights, brake lights, signal lights, parking lights, and emergency flashers. Interior lights include the dome light on the inside roof of the vehicle and the various dashboard lights that provide you with information about the vehicle or warn you of malfunctions.

How Can You Maintain the Electrical and Light Systems?

The first step in maintaining the electrical and light systems is to keep your battery in top working condition. Keep the battery terminals free of corrosion and the battery cables firmly connected. Most current batteries are maintenance-free, but if you have an older one, check the fluid level at least once a month, and add water when needed.

The electrical system is constantly monitored by the engine control module or computer. If it detects a problem, the "check engine" light on the instrument panel may come on.

Keep headlights clean and properly aligned. Even a thin layer of dirt can cut light output by as much as 90 percent. Misaligned lights

Driving Tip

Students need to be careful when checking levels of possibly harmful vehicle fluids. For example, batteries contain sulfuric acid, which is highly corrosive. Students should be advised to wear rubber gloves and eye protection when checking battery fluid levels and warned never to smoke near a battery. A cigarette or a spark could cause hydrogen gas discharged by a battery to explode.

can reduce your ability to see the roadway and can momentarily blind oncoming drivers.

Check exterior lights at least once a week, and promptly replace any burned-out bulbs.

How Do the Lubricating and Cooling Systems Work?

As the parts of your vehicle's engine move rapidly and rub against each other, they produce friction and heat. At the same time, the fuel-air explosions in the cylinders create more heat. Small wonder then that the engine temperature may exceed 4,000°F.

Too much heat can destroy your vehicle's engine. The lubricating and cooling systems are designed to keep that from happening.

The Lubricating System

Oil is the key element in your vehicle's lubricating system. Coating engine parts with oil reduces friction, heat, and wear. Oil also helps clean internal engine surfaces and prevent rust and corrosion.

An oil pump moves oil from the oil pan, where it is stored, to all moving engine parts. The oil filter cleans the oil as it circulates.

In addition to oil, grease is used to lubricate parts of the vehicle, such as the steering system. Like oil, grease reduces friction and helps parts move smoothly.

Energy Tips

The engine control module or computer in a modern vehicle automatically adjusts the engine's systems for whatever grade of fuel you use. Some engines will perform better with higher, more expensive grades of fuel, but most will not. See your owner's manual for the manufacturer's recommendations.

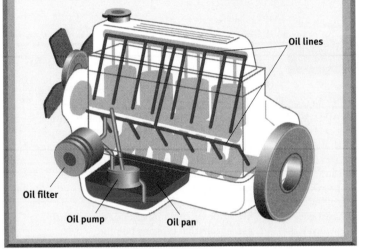

FYI

Each year, electrical system failures disable more vehicles than the combined next two causes of vehicle breakdowns.

◆ *The lubricating system reduces heat by coating the parts of the engine with oil.*

Ask

Ask students to discuss why extra attention to checking and maintaining a vehicle's operating systems is especially important during very hot or cold weather.

Read

Have students read Lesson 3 to learn how a vehicle's various systems function and how to check and maintain these systems.

ASSESS

Guided Practice

Have students answer the Lesson 3 Review questions. The answers are provided below.

IT'S A FACT

Used motor oil removed from vehicles during an oil change can be recycled. Drivers who change their own oil are advised to contact a local service station or repair shop to see who collects used oil. Local recycling centers also schedule times for residents to bring in old oil.

Reteaching

Have students work in small groups. Direct them to write the names of the parts of the various vehicle systems on one set of index cards and the names of the systems themselves on a second set of cards. Have students quiz each other by drawing a system card, identifying the cards naming parts of this system, and discussing the function of each part named. Encourage students to extend the activity by describing the maintenance checks that apply to each system.

After groups have finished, discuss with the class the benefits of getting used to a regular routine of checking a vehicle's operating systems. Have students give reasons why each system is important to the function and safety of a vehicle.

Enrichment

Assign the Study Guide for Lesson 3. The Find Out More section encourages students to expand their basic learning of the lesson concepts.

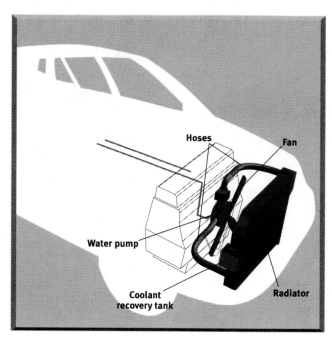

Hoses

Fan

Water pump

Coolant recovery tank

Radiator

◆ *The so-called water-cooled engine actually uses a coolant in its cooling system.*

The Cooling System

The purpose of the cooling system is to keep your vehicle's engine from overheating. To do this, the cooling system circulates **coolant**—a mixture of water and antifreeze—through the engine by means of a network of pipes, channels, and connecting hoses.

Antifreeze has a lower freezing point and higher boiling point than pure water. Without it, the liquid in the cooling system would freeze in very cold weather and could boil over in hot weather, especially in traffic jams and on long trips. Frozen or boiling coolant does not circulate, and this can cause the engine to overheat.

Your vehicle's coolant is stored in the radiator and in the radiator overflow tank. A water pump pumps the coolant through the radiator and the circulating network. A fan forces the air through the **radiator** to cool the liquid. A thermostat in the system works to control the flow of the coolant in order to maintain the best operating temperature.

CONNECTIONS
Science

Carbon monoxide is an odorless, colorless, and tasteless gas. Small amounts of carbon monoxide can make you sleepy or nauseated or give you a headache by interfering with the ability of your red blood cells to carry oxygen. Large amounts of carbon monoxide can kill you.

Avoid driving a vehicle that has an exhaust leak or a broken tailpipe. Such defects allow carbon monoxide and other harmful exhaust gases to be trapped beneath the vehicle, even when it is

moving. These gases may leak up into the vehicle's interior.

To guard against carbon monoxide poisoning, also avoid:
- running a vehicle's engine in a closed garage.
- sitting in a parked vehicle with the windows closed, the engine running, and the heater on.
- driving with the trunk lid up.
- driving with the rear window of a station wagon open.
- stopping so close to the vehicle ahead that your heater or air conditioner draws in exhaust gases from that vehicle's tailpipe.

IT'S A FACT

A faulty thermostat valve can greatly affect a vehicle's fuel efficiency. If an engine is running too cold, it may waste one out of every ten gallons of gas. Replacing a thermostat is inexpensive and relatively easy to do.

How Can You Maintain the Lubricating and Cooling Systems?

Checking and changing the oil and oil filter regularly is the key to maintaining your vehicle's lubricating system. Low oil pressure allows the engine to become too hot, which may cause excessive wear of moving parts.

Keep in mind that the oil-pressure gauge or warning light does not indicate how much oil is in the engine, but it will signal a drop in oil pressure. To check the actual level of oil, use the oil dipstick. *Never* drive your vehicle with insufficient oil: you could destroy the engine. The engine oil level can only be checked after the engine has been turned off for some period of time, preferably an hour or more. This is necessary to give the oil time to drain back into the oil pan from throughout the engine. Checking it before that has happened will give you a false low reading.

Driving with an overheated engine can also damage your vehicle. If the temperature gauge or warning light indicates overheating, stop driving as soon as possible. Let the engine cool before you look for the cause of the problem.

To maintain the cooling system, use the proper coolant, and check the fluid level whenever the vehicle is serviced. Also check the fan belt and connecting hoses. Have the cooling system completely drained, flushed, and refilled every two years.

◆ *You can learn to use a dipstick to check whether or not your vehicle needs more oil.*

Lesson 3 Review

1. Why is it important to keep the fuel and exhaust systems of your vehicle in good condition?
2. Explain how your vehicle uses electricity, and name the source of electrical power in your vehicle.
3. How do the lubricating and cooling systems work?

WHAT WOULD YOU DO?

You've been stuck in bumper-to-bumper traffic for nearly an hour on a hot summer day. The temperature warning light has just come on. How will you handle this situation? What safety precautions will you take?

CLOSE

Summarize

Return to the Motivator question. Recall students' initial responses. Then review what they have learned about a vehicle's operating systems and how to maintain each system. Help them summarize main points of the lesson by discussing how a vehicle's various systems work together.

DRIVER'S LOG

Encourage students to draw their own diagrams of the systems studied in this lesson. Have students label key parts and describe briefly why the system is important and how to maintain it.

WHAT WOULD YOU DO?

Sample answer: Stop driving as soon as possible. Find a place to pull off the road or exit; let the engine cool.

Lesson 3 Review

Answers

1. The fuel and exhaust systems must operate properly to maximize engine efficiency and to minimize pollution.
2. The battery provides the power to start the engine; the alternator supplies electricity to keep the engine running, to operate equipment, and to recharge the battery, which is the source of electrical power in the vehicle.
3. The lubricating system coats the internal moving engine parts with oil, thus reducing friction, heat, and wear; the cooling system circulates coolant through the engine by means of a network of pipes, channels, and hoses to keep the engine operating at optimum temperature.

Suspension, Steering, Brakes, and Tires

(pages 328–332)

FOCUS

Objectives

• Describe four systems that are important for comfort and safety.

• Describe warning signs of possible problems with the suspension, steering, or tires.

Resources

 Study Guide, page 68

Transparencies 47 and 48

Vocabulary

strut
shock absorber
hydraulic pressure
disc brake
drum brake
tread

Motivator

Pose the following situation: When your vehicle was new, the ride was smooth and comfortable. Now the vehicle is three years old, and the ride seems to be much harder and less comfortable. Is there anything you can do to increase your comfort, or is this just a sign of an older vehicle? (Students may say that you can have the springs and shock absorbers checked and replaced if necessary.)

OBJECTIVES

1. Describe four vehicle systems that are important for comfort and safety.
2. Describe warning signs of possible problems with the suspension, steering, or tires.

KEY TERMS

strut
shock absorber
hydraulic pressure
disc brake
drum brake
tread

Suspension, Steering, Brakes, and Tires

Your comfort and safety in a vehicle depend not only on how well you drive but also on how your vehicle handles. To protect yourself and others, make sure your vehicle's suspension, steering, and brake systems as well as all four tires are in good operating condition.

What Vehicle Systems Are Important for Comfort and Safety?

The suspension, steering, and brake systems, and tires, work together to give you control over your vehicle and to provide a comfortable ride.

The Suspension System

The suspension system supports your vehicle's weight, cushions the ride, and helps keep the vehicle stable when you drive over bumps or uneven roadway surfaces.

Most vehicles today use suspensions—especially in the front of the vehicle—where the spring and shock absorber are contained in one unit called a **strut**.

◆ *The suspension system cushions the vehicle's frame against bumps in the road.*

Coil springs
Shock absorbers
Upper control arms
Chassis
Lower control arms

The springs soften the impact of bumps in the roadway. If your vehicle had only springs, however, it would continue bouncing after hitting a bump. This bouncing would reduce the contact between the tires and the road and make it harder for you to control the vehicle.

The **shock absorbers**—or shocks, as they're commonly called—work to control bouncing. By absorbing the shocks of driving, they make the ride smoother and help you maintain steering and braking control.

Driving Tip

If a vehicle equipped with power brakes and power steering stalls while moving, the brake system and steering system will still work but will require considerably more effort on the part of the driver. Advise students to apply firm, steady pressure on the brake pedal rather than pump the brake.

The Steering System

The steering system enables you to turn the front wheels. The steering wheel is connected to the front wheels by a steering shaft and movable rods.

The front wheels are designed to remain in an upright position and move up and down over bumps, even when they are turned.

The Brake System

Brakes slow or stop a vehicle by applying **hydraulic pressure**—pressure created by the force of a liquid—against the four wheels. Stepping on the brake pedal forces brake fluid from the master brake cylinder through the brake-fluid lines to the wheel cylinders. There are two types of brakes: disc brakes and drum brakes.

Disc brakes In a **disc brake,** pressure squeezes the brake pads against a flat metal wheel disc, producing the friction needed to stop the wheel from turning.

All new vehicles now have disc brakes on the front wheels. Many have them on the rear wheels as well. All new vehicles now also have power brakes, which require less pressure on the brake pedal than older non-power systems. Power brakes do *not,* however, shorten a vehicle's stopping distance.

Drum brakes In a **drum brake,** the fluid pressure causes the brake shoes to push against the brake lining. The lining then presses against the round hollow metal drum inside the wheel. Friction slows and stops the wheel's turning motion.

SAFETY TIPS

You can check for sufficient tread depth by inserting a quarter in the tread. It should at least come to the top of Washington's head. If there is less tread than this, the tire will not function safely in even a light rain.

◆ *A hydraulic brake system gives all four wheels stopping power.*

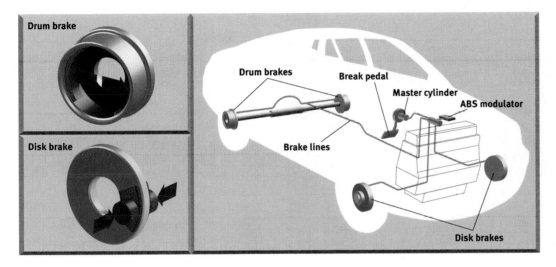

Drum brake

Disk brake

Drum brakes

Break pedal

Master cylinder

ABS modulator

Brake lines

Disk brakes

Explain

OBJECTIVE 1: Students should understand both the safety and comfort aspects of a vehicle's suspension, steering, brakes, and tires. Students should also be aware that different sizes of vehicles require different sizes of tires. Students may also benefit from a discussion of government requirements for mileage and safety ratings on tires. These ratings grade tread wear, traction, and heat resistance.

OBJECTIVE 2: Students will benefit from a discussion of various warning signs a driver may encounter while driving at low or high speeds. Here are some points to stress.

- Steering problems are indicated by vibration in the steering wheel or an increase in play.
- Suspension system problems are indicated by increased bumpiness of the ride.
- Alignment problems are indicated when the vehicle pulls to one side or the front end shimmies.
- Traction or fuel-efficiency problems are caused by under- or overinflation of the tires or indicated by tread wear.

State BY State

In many states, the state police often stage impromptu roadside checks for legal registrations and inspection stickers. At the same time, police officers may check for tire wear and, if necessary, warn drivers to replace or check their tires in the near future.

Teaching Model

Describe the following situation: Lately your vehicle has been harder to steer around corners, the tires sometimes spin when the vehicle starts to move, and your fuel efficiency has gone down. Model the thinking process you go through to decide what the problem might be and what you can check or have a mechanic check and fix. (You do the following.

- Check the air in the tires to see if they are overinflated or underinflated.
- Check the tire tread to see if it is worn; buy new tires if necessary.
- Have a mechanic check the steering to be sure all possible problems have been covered.)

Ask

Ask students to discuss the risks of ignoring warning signals and failing to have a vehicle checked.

Read

Have students read Lesson 4 to become familiar with the parts and functions of the suspension, steering, brakes, and tires and to recognize warning signals that indicate problems with them.

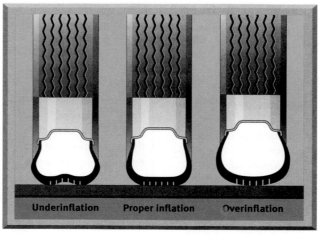

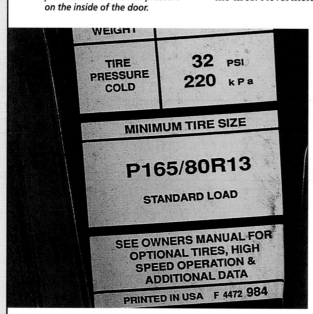

◆ It is important for fuel efficiency and traction that a vehicle's tires be properly inflated.

◆ The vehicle manufacturer often places maximum tire air pressure on the inside of the door.

To minimize the risk of brake failure, brake systems are designed so that front and rear brakes are controlled independently. If one pair of brakes fails, the other pair will still work to stop the vehicle.

Antilock brakes Many newer vehicles have an antilock brake system (ABS), which is designed to keep the wheels from locking when the driver presses too hard on the brake pedal in an emergency. Since the wheels do not lock, the driver can continue to steer the vehicle. Antilock brakes do not shorten the stopping distance of a vehicle.

Parking brake A parking brake is a mechanically operated brake that is separate from the hydraulic brake system. Attached by cable to the rear wheels, it is used to prevent a parked vehicle from rolling.

The Tires

A driver's control of a vehicle depends largely on the condition of the tires. Nevertheless, more than 40 percent of nearly 250,000 vehicles inspected between 1982 and 1993 had defective tires.

Tire inflation Tires must be inflated properly to provide maximum traction and control. Too little tire pressure (underinflation) or too much tire pressure (overinflation) reduces traction, makes a vehicle harder to handle, and lowers fuel efficiency.

Most vehicles require different pressures for the front and rear tires. To find the recommended maximum air pressures for your vehicle, check your owner's manual or look for a sticker that may be affixed to a doorpost or inside the fuel filler door. Usually two tire pressures are listed—one for normal and a higher number for long trips or when carrying heavy loads. The lower number may result in a softer ride but will likely mean lower tread life. The higher number will improve both handling and wear at the cost of some ride quality.

IT'S A FACT

Tires come in three types: bias ply, bias belted, and radial. More expensive tires are not necessarily better tires. Radial and bias-belted tires have a greater tread life than bias ply tires. Radial tires are also good for long-distance highway driving and for all-season use. Radials should never be mixed with other types of tires.

Tire tread The grooved outer surface of a tire is its **tread.** On wet or slippery surfaces, the amount of tread on your tires determines how much traction your vehicle will have. Compared with tires that have good tread, overly worn tires have double the risk of skidding and are also more likely to go flat or blow out.

Tires should be replaced when the depth of the tread is ¹⁄₁₆ inch. To help you judge tread depth, all tires have tread wear bars that run across the tire.

Tire rotation Front tires generally wear faster than rear tires. To equalize tire wear, have your vehicle's tires rotated about every 5,000 to 6,000 miles. Rotating tires means switching their position from front to rear and sometimes from one side to the other. Check your owner's manual for the recommended tire-rotation pattern.

When tires are rotated, they often need to be balanced. This helps ensure that weight is evenly distributed as the wheel turns. Balanced tires provide better steering control, a smoother ride, and longer tire life.

What Are Some Warning Signs of Vehicle Problems?

Sometimes vehicle problems appear unexpectedly. More often, though, advance warnings signal that a part or system needs attention.

Suspension and Steering Problems

Most problems affecting the suspension and steering system develop gradually as a result of wear. Watch for the following warning signs.

- There is too much play (free movement) in the steering wheel. With rack and pinion power steering, there should be virtually no play in the wheel. In a manual system, there should be no more than 2 inches of play.
- The steering wheel vibrates or is difficult to turn.
- The front end of the vehicle wobbles or shimmies.
- The vehicle bumps as you turn the wheel while driving on a smooth road.
- The vehicle pulls to one side as you drive.
- The vehicle bounces too much after hitting a bump.
- Tread wear on the front tires is uneven.

Have a mechanic check your vehicle if any of these warning signs appear. The front end of your vehicle may need aligning, the tires may need to be balanced, or some other problem may need correction.

◆ *Have a mechanic check the vehicle if any warning signs of suspension or brake problems appear.*

CHAPTER 17   *Vehicle Systems and Maintenance*   **331**

ASSESS

Guided Practice

Have students answer the Lesson 4 Review questions. The answers are provided below.

Reteaching

Divide students into small groups. Have group members take turns describing a driving situation in which there is a warning signal of trouble in the suspension, steering, brakes, or tires. Encourage other members to identify what the problem might be and how it might be checked and fixed.

Then ask groups to review which problems were the hardest to assess or which situations may have indicated problems that might be traced to more than one system.

Driving Tip

Explain to students that besides checking for tread wear, they should check tires for cracks and bulges in the sides. The rubber in tires that remain motionless for long periods of time and are exposed to climate extremes can dry out and lose its elasticity. As a result, the rubber may crumble, a condition sometimes called dry rot. The tread may look fine, but the tire is still unsafe.

ADVICE FROM THE EXPERTS

Stress the importance of having properly inflated tires. This maximizes tire life and ensures proper traction on the road.

Enrichment

Assign the Study Guide for Lesson 4. The Find Out More section encourages students to expand their basic learning of the lesson concepts.

CLOSE

Summarize

Return to the Motivator question, and discuss how students' ideas may have changed about how much control a driver has over the comfort and safety of a vehicle as it ages. Stress the importance of regular maintenance. Extend the discussion by having students describe how the four systems discussed in this lesson interact.

DRIVER'S LOG

How does knowing what a vehicle's warning signals mean help someone become not only a safer driver but also a more informed consumer when dealing with a mechanic?

WHAT WOULD YOU DO?

Sample answer: *There may be a problem with the steering or brake system. Consult a mechanic before making a decision.*

ADVICE FROM THE EXPERTS

Richard Russell
Member, Society of Automotive Engineers, nationally certified Master Driving Instructor, and consultant to AAA

Tires are arguably the most important safety feature on your vehicle. The four small patches of rubber in contact with the road determine how you stop, steer, and go. Don't think of buying new tires as a "grudge buy." Tires are the one area where a purchase decision can directly affect the safety of your vehicle. This is not an area to try to save money. Generally speaking, the more you spend on a tire, the better the grip it will provide and the safer you will be.

Brake Problems

See Chapter 14 for a description of brake failure. Neglecting a problem with the brake system can have fatal consequences. Check with a mechanic if any warning signs appear.

Tire Problems

Inspecting your tires regularly *before* you drive will help avoid problems on the road. Watch for the following warning signs of tire troubles:

WHAT WOULD YOU DO?

- tread wear bars appear, indicating less than ⅟₁₆ inch tread
- areas of little or no tread—"bald" spots
- uneven wear
- bulges
- embedded nails, glass, or metal
- frequent pressure loss in one particular tire, suggesting a slow leak

You just test-drove this car. As you stepped on the brake, the car pulled to the right. What could cause this problem? Would you buy the car?

Lesson 4 Review

1. How are the steering, suspension, brakes, and tires important to your safety?
2. What are some warning signs that indicate tire problems?

Lesson 4 Review

Answers

1. The steering system enables the driver to turn the front wheels; the suspension system supports the vehicle's weight, cushions the ride, and helps keep the vehicle stable; the brakes slow or stop the vehicle; the tires enable the vehicle to grip the road.
2. Warning signs of tire problems include insufficient tread, bald spots, uneven wear, bulges, embedded objects, and frequent loss of air pressure.

Graphing Braking Distances

After you apply the brakes, the distance it takes to come to a stop depends in part on the speed at which your vehicle is moving.

The formula for figuring out braking distance is

$$D = S \times {}^1\!/_{10}S \div 2.4$$

where S = speed and D = distance in feet.

Here is how you would figure braking distance at 35 mph.

$$D = 35 \times ({}^1\!/_{10} \times 35) \div 2.4$$
$$D = 35 \times 3.5 \div 2.4$$
$$D = 51.04$$

Thus, braking distance at 35 mph is 51.04 feet, or a little more than 17 yards.

Make a graph to show how braking distance changes in relation to speed.

Try It Yourself

1. First, use the formula to figure the stopping distance for these speeds:
   20 mph 30 mph 40 mph 50 mph 60 mph
2. On a sheet of graph paper, write the speeds along the bottom of the graph at regular intervals, as shown below.
3. On the left side of the graph, write distances in regular intervals, as shown below.
4. For each distance you figure, put a dot at the appropriate place on your graph.
5. Finally, draw a line from the first dot to the second, from the second to the third, and so on, beginning with the dot at the shortest braking distance.

What conclusion can you draw from your graph?

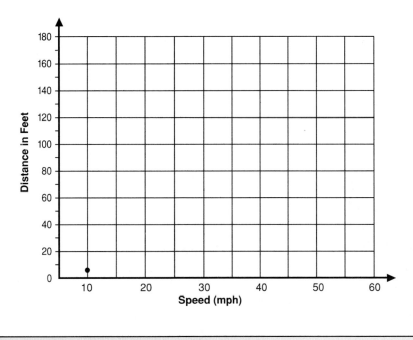

CHAPTER 17 *Vehicle Systems and Maintenance* **333**

BUILDING SKILLS: SCIENCE

Objective

Demonstrate an ability to graph braking distances at different speeds.

Teaching the Skills

- Be sure students understand how to use the formula for computing braking distance. You may want to work through several examples with the class before students work on their graphs.
- Recommend that students use a ruler to align the points on the graph with the distances on the left. Suggest that they also use the ruler to connect the points.
- Remind students that power brakes allow the driver to stop with less effort but that the distance required to stop is the same.

ANSWERS TO
Try It Yourself Questions

Graph should reflect these stopping distances: about 17 ft at 20 mph, 37.5 ft at 30 mph, about 68 ft at 40 mph, 100 ft at 50 mph, 150 ft at 60 mph. A conclusion that can be drawn from the graph is that the greater the speed of the vehicle, the greater the distance needed to stop the vehicle.

CHAPTER SUMMARY

Key Points

Have students read the Key Points to review the major concepts of the chapter.

PROJECTS

Cooperative Learning:
Students will benefit by working with a partner on one or both projects. When the assignment is completed, the whole class will profit by sharing and comparing results.

CHAPTER 17 REVIEW

KEY POINTS

Lesson One

1. At least once a month, before entering your vehicle, check fluid levels, belts and hoses, and connections.
2. After starting the engine, check gauges and warning lights, and test your brakes and horn.
3. Service your vehicle according to the kind and amount of driving and manufacturer recommendations.

Lesson Two

1. An internal combustion engine burns a mixture of fuel and air. In each cylinder, a spark causes the mixture to explode, pushing down the piston, turning the crankshaft.
2. The power train sends engine power to the wheels through the transmission.
3. Regularly check and change the oil, check the transmission fluid, and change filters.

Lesson Three

1. The fuel pump forces fuel from the tank to the fuel-injection system to mix with air. The vapor is ignited in the cylinders. Unburned gases from the engine exit through the tailpipe. Replace filters as needed. Have your exhaust system inspected at least twice a year.
2. The battery is the source of electrical power. Keep headlights clean and aligned, and replace any burned-out bulbs.
3. Lubricating and cooling systems keep heat from destroying the engine by sending oil to moving engine parts. A mixture of fluid and antifreeze cools the engine.

   Change oil and oil filters regularly. Use coolant, and check the fluid level when the vehicle is serviced.

Lesson Four

1. The suspension supports a vehicle's weight, cushions the ride, and stabilizes the vehicle; the steering system enables the front wheels to turn; brakes stop the vehicle; tires help it grip the road.
2. Warnings of possible suspension problems include too much play in the wheel; front-end wobble; and pulling to one side.

PROJECTS

1. In an owner's manual, find the sections that deal with the vehicle systems discussed in this chapter. What information does the manual provide that applies specifically to the particular make and model vehicle? In what other ways does the manual help the owner maintain the vehicle?
2. Research and report on the various types of tires, including summer, all-season, and winter or snow tires. What are the advantages and limitations of each? Where should you put two new tires or snow tires on a vehicle with front-wheel drive?

*inter*NET CONNECTION

To learn how car systems have changed with the use of computers, visit Glencoe's Web site.
drivered.glencoe.com

*inter*NET CONNECTION

Visit Glencoe's Driver Education Web site for student activities that relate to this chapter.
drivered.glencoe.com

CHAPTER 17 REVIEW

CHAPTER TEST

Write the letter of the answer that best completes each sentence.

1. A catalytic converter is part of a vehicle's
   a. transmission.
   b. exhaust system.
   c. fuel system.

2. You should check your engine oil
   a. while your engine is running.
   b. before starting your engine.
   c. every 12,000 miles.

3. Springs and shock absorbers are parts of a vehicle's
   a. transmission.
   b. front-end alignment.
   c. suspension system.

4. Most vehicles' engines are
   a. turbine engines.
   b. external combustion engines.
   c. internal combustion engines.

5. When you step on your brake pedal, you should feel
   a. firm resistance.
   b. no resistance.
   c. the floor.

6. The temperature of a vehicle's engine may exceed
   a. 212°F.
   b. 500°F.
   c. 4,000°F.

7. You should rotate your vehicle's tires to
   a. equalize tire wear.
   b. increase fuel efficiency.
   c. improve suspension.

8. Most vehicles today operate on
   a. lead-free gasoline.
   b. leaded gasoline.
   c. diesel fuel.

9. Many vehicles are equipped with
   a. a power clutch.
   b. drum brakes on the front wheels and disc brakes on the back wheels.
   c. disc brakes on the front wheels and drum brakes on the back wheels.

10. Your vehicle's alternator
    a. controls suspension.
    b. mixes oxygen with gasoline.
    c. supplies electricity to run the engine.

Write the word or phrase that best completes each sentence.

| pistons | hydraulic pressure | power train |
| muffler | electrical system | owner's manual |

11. The parts of a vehicle that transmit the engine's power to the wheels make up the _____.

12. The heart of a vehicle's _____ is called the battery.

13. Brakes slow or stop a vehicle by applying _____ against the four wheels.

14. A(n) _____ contains specific guidelines for servicing and maintaining a vehicle.

15. The pipes that make up the exhaust manifold collect unburned gases from the engine and carry them to the _____.

DRIVER'S LOG

In this chapter, you have learned how the systems that operate a vehicle function and what the maintenance requirements of these systems are. Based on your observations, do most drivers pay attention to these maintenance requirements? Write a paragraph about what you would tell those who do not.

CHAPTER TEST

Assign the Chapter Test to all students.

Answers

1. b
2. b
3. c
4. c
5. a
6. c
7. a
8. a
9. c
10. c
11. power train
12. electrical system
13. hydraulic pressure
14. owner's manual
15. muffler

DRIVER'S LOG

Students' responses will reflect their personal viewpoints. However, their answers should provide an assessment of their understanding of the safety risks inherent in an improperly maintained vehicle.

Evaluate

• Test A, pages 33–34 or Test B, pages 33–34
• Testmaker software

RETURN TO THE BIG IDEA

Discuss the idea that understanding how a vehicle works and what signs indicate system malfunctions can help drivers maintain their vehicles in peak operating condition and reduce driving risk.

Planning a Trip Overview

THEME DEVELOPMENT Drivers should prepare in advance for both short and long vehicle trips. Drivers should recognize the special challenges and risks they face when driving a vehicle with a trailer attached or driving a pickup truck, sport utility vehicle, or van.

CHAPTER FEATURES	TCR COMPONENTS
TIPS FOR NEW DRIVERS Learning how to work a self-service gas pump.	Study Guide, p. 69 Lesson Plan, p. 37
	Study Guide, p. 70 Lesson Plan, p. 37
	Study Guide, p. 71 Transparencies 49 and 50 Lesson Plan, p. 38 Information Master 24
ADVICE FROM THE EXPERTS How to plan for a trip.	Study Guide, p. 72 Lesson Plan, p. 38
BUILDING SKILLS: READING MAPS Reading City Maps	Test A, pp. 35–36 Test B, pp. 35–36

OTHER PROGRAM RESOURCES

Testmaker software
Traffic charts

PROJECTS

1. Compare state laws regarding trailers and light trucks.
2. Plan a trip to the place in which your ancestors lived.

NAME _____ DATE _____

CHAPTER 18 Planning a Trip

TEST A

Read each statement below. If it is true, place a T in the space to the left of the statement. If the statement is false, place an F next to it.

T 1. Most traffic fatalities happen within 25 miles of the driver's home.

F 2. Because of the extra weight when a trailer is hooked to a vehicle, the stopping distance is actually reduced.

T 3. You should prepare yourself and your vehicle even for short trips.

F 4. It is acceptable to read your map while driving as long as you do it only in short intervals.

T 5. Overloading a vehicle can have ill effects on the vehicle's fuel efficiency.

F 6. When driving a vehicle with a trailer, you should allow less distance between you and the vehicle ahead if you are planning to pass it.

F 7. To activate the brakes of a trailer you are pulling, you need to hit the second brake pedal at the same time you step on the main brake pedal.

F 8. Roads leading into urban areas are busiest during the evening rush hours.

T 9. You need to check your transmission's oil more often when you are towing a trailer.

F 10. If your vehicle is pulling a trailer and you pack too much weight in the back of the vehicle, the front end of the vehicle will rise.

Select the phrase that best completes each sentence below. Write the letter of the answer you have chosen to the left of each statement.

a 11. You should always add a little time to your trip plan because
    a. hurrying can make you nervous and careless.
    b. you need to manage space wisely.
    c. you need to plan extra time for vehicle breakdowns.
    d. of none of the reasons above.

b 12. Limited-access roadways
    a. are more scenic than other roads.
    b. have fewer stops and starts than other roads.
    c. are hard to maintain a steady speed on.
    d. all of the above.

d 13. A good plan to keep alert on a long trip is to
    a. drink lots of coffee.
    b. drive in 2-hour stretches with 15-minute breaks in between.
    c. drive no more than 8 hours a day.
    d. follow both b and c.

© AAA and Glencoe/McGraw-Hill

NAME _____ DATE _____

c 14. Before a long trip, a mechanic should check your exhaust system for
    a. proper fluid level.
    b. worn shock absorbers.
    c. leaks.
    d. proper alignment.

a 15. When you pack your vehicle for a trip, the heaviest items should be
    a. in the bottom of the trunk.
    b. in the center of the vehicle.
    c. placed in the vehicle-top carrier.
    d. in the front seat if possible.

b 16. To tow a trailer, a vehicle will need
    a. an oversized fuel tank.
    b. a hitch and safety chains.
    c. a towing license.
    d. all of the above.

a 17. If you are towing a trailer, you may need to
    a. increase the air pressure in your vehicle's tires.
    b. have a towing license.
    c. increase your engine oil by 4 quarts.
    d. add larger air filters.

d 18. Because of the additional height of pickups, vans, and sport utility vehicles,
    a. headlights are above the rest of traffic.
    b. the driver can see over surrounding traffic.
    c. the vehicle's center of gravity is higher.
    d. all of the above are true.

d 19. After packing your trailer, you should
    a. check that the vehicle's back springs are not extended.
    b. stop frequently to check that the load and hitch are secure.
    c. check to see if the vehicle and trailer are parallel to the ground.
    d. do all of the above.

20. What special problems do drivers of light trucks face on the road?

The additional height of pickups, sport utility vehicles, and vans creates problems when the vehicle

turns or stops suddenly. Because of extra height and weight, they handle less securely in emergencies.

Their stopping distance is longer. They have a greater surface area to the wind. Because of the vehicle's

increased size, the driver may tire more quickly.

© AAA and Glencoe/McGraw-Hill

NAME _____ DATE _____

CHAPTER 18 Planning a Trip

TEST B

Read each statement below. If it is true, place a T in the space to the left of the statement. If the statement is false, place an F next to it.

T 1. If you are driving a vehicle with a trailer, you will need more time and space to pass another vehicle.

F 2. To activate the brakes of a trailer you are pulling, you need to hit the second brake pedal at the same time that you step on the main brake pedal.

F 3. A typical trailer has six tires.

T 4. A sport utility vehicle is higher than a car and affords good visibility ahead.

F 5. Most traffic fatalities happen 50 miles or more from the driver's home.

T 6. The most popular vehicles on American roads today are light trucks.

T 7. When you are packing a vehicle, the heaviest items should go in the bottom of the trunk.

F 8. Automotive insurance automatically covers your driving a trailer.

T 9. After packing a vehicle and trailer, they both should be nearly parallel to the ground.

F 10. When backing a vehicle with a trailer, it is easier if your trailer turns to the right side of your vehicle.

F 11. Because of the extra weight when a trailer is hooked to a vehicle, the stopping distance is actually reduced.

T 12. When driving a sport utility vehicle, you need more stopping distance than you do with a passenger car.

F 13. Roads leading out of an urban area will be busiest in the morning hours.

Select the phrase that best completes each sentence below. Write the letter of the answer you have chosen to the left of each statement.

d 14. After packing your trailer, you should
    a. check that the vehicle's back springs are not extended.
    b. stop frequently to check that the load and hitch are secure.
    c. check to see if the vehicle and trailer are parallel to the ground.
    d. do all of the above.

c 15. To help prevent the chance of a trailer slipping off its jack,
    a. purchase a heavy-duty jack.
    b. park downhill.
    c. put a block between the frame of the trailer and the ground.
    d. chain the trailer to the back of the vehicle.

© AAA and Glencoe/McGraw-Hill

NAME _____ DATE _____

b 16. When driving a trailer or a recreational vehicle in a curve to the right,
    a. keep in the center of the lane.
    b. keep to the left of the lane.
    c. keep to the right of the lane.
    d. begin the turn in the left side and then switch to the right side of the lane.

c 17. Driving a pickup, sport utility vehicle, or van will make you more tired than driving a car because
    a. the vehicle has a gentle rolling motion.
    b. the vehicle is so comfortable you will get sleepy.
    c. the vehicle is more difficult to maneuver than a car.
    d. the headlights are higher than on a car.

c 18. Limited-access roadways
    a. are more scenic than other roads.
    b. are harder to maintain a steady speed on than other roads.
    c. have fewer stops and starts than other roads.
    d. have all of the above.

d 19. A good plan to keep alert on a long trip is
    a. to drink lots of coffee.
    b. to drive in 2-hour stretches with 15-minute breaks in between.
    c. to drive no more than 8 hours a day.
    d. both b and c.

a 20. When you pack your vehicle for a long trip, the heaviest objects should be
    a. in the bottom of the trunk.
    b. at the most center point of the vehicle.
    c. placed in the vehicle-top carrier.
    d. placed in the front seat if possible.

21. If you are going on a long road trip, what should you have a mechanic check on your vehicle before you leave?

brake shoes and pads; exhaust system for leaks; front-end alignment; tire condition; fluid levels;

condition of belts, hoses, and wires; battery fluid level; and shock absorbers

© AAA and Glencoe/McGraw-Hill

NAME _____ DATE _____

STUDY GUIDE FOR CHAPTER 18   LESSON 1

Preparing for a Short Trip

A. Complete each sentence below.

1. Most traffic fatalities happen within _____ 25 _____ miles of the driver's home.

2. Roads leading into an urban area are busiest during the _____ morning rush _____ hours.

3. In case your planned route is blocked, you should have an _____ alternate _____ plan ready.

4. Anticipate delays by listening to the _____ radio _____.

5. Use a _____ map _____ to be sure that you know how to get to your destination.

B. What does "enough time" mean to you when you plan a trip?

Review student's work.

_____

_____

_____

_____

_____

_____

C. FIND OUT MORE. Ask someone you know who drives if you may give his or her vehicle a predriving check. What did you find out about the following?

Review student's work.

1. Tires _____

2. Signal lights _____

3. Front and back lights _____

4. Oil and fuel levels _____

NAME _____ DATE _____

STUDY GUIDE FOR CHAPTER 18   LESSON 2

Getting Ready for a Long Trip

A. For each sentence below, circle T if the statement is true and F if it is false. Correct each false statement in the space below.

1. Driving on a road with a lot of stops, hills, and curves is more fuel efficient than driving on an expressway because you travel faster on expressways.   T   **F**

   Driving on expressways is more fuel efficient because there are fewer stops, hills, and curves.

2. If you need to look at a map while you are on the road, use quick glances to get your information.   T   **F**

   If you need to look at a map, you should pull the vehicle over safely first.

3. A good plan to keep yourself alert while driving is to take 15-minute breaks every 2 hours.   **T**   F

4. It is safe to drive for up to 15 hours a day.   T   **F**

   It is safe to drive for up to 8 hours a day.

5. Overloading a vehicle can have an adverse effect on its headlight aim.   **T**   F

6. Heavy items should be placed in the vehicle-top carrier if you have one.   T   **F**

   You should put only lighter items in a vehicle-top carrier.

B. FIND OUT MORE. Call a local repair garage. Ask what they check out in vehicles that are going on long trips. Find out, specifically, what they look for in the following items.

Review student's work.

1. brake shoes and pads _____

2. exhaust system _____

3. front-end alignment _____

4. tire condition _____

5. fluid levels _____

6. hoses _____

7. belts _____

8. wires _____

NAME _____ DATE _____

STUDY GUIDE FOR CHAPTER 18   LESSON 3

Loading and Driving with a Trailer

A. Complete the following sentences. You may have to use more than one word in the space.

1. To tow a trailer, a vehicle needs a _____ hitch _____ and properly installed safety chains.

2. The back springs of the vehicle should not be extended so that its front end _____ rises _____.

3. When you load a trailer, the heaviest items should be loaded _____ on the bottom _____ of the trailer.

4. It is easier to turn while backing a vehicle and trailer if the trailer turns to the _____ left _____ side of the vehicle.

5. When making a right turn, you should position the vehicle _____ farther away _____ from the curb than you would if you didn't have a trailer.

6. When you swerve, you may cause the trailer to _____ tilt, sway, or lose control _____.

7. Do not follow another vehicle closely when pulling a trailer because you need _____ more _____ space to stop than you would without one.

8. A hitch that is welded or _____ bolted _____ to your vehicle's frame is better than a hitch that you hook to the bumper.

B. Your vacation plans just changed! Your family has decided to rent a trailer to sleep in on the way. Your trip is a long one—1800 miles each way. Adding the trailer will increase your fuel use by 50 percent; your vehicle gets 29 miles per gallon without the trailer. How much extra will the trailer cost your family for fuel at an average of $1.19 per gallon?

about $74.00 extra in gas

C. FIND OUT MORE. Look at your state driver's manual. What does it say about trailers? Do people need a permit to pull a trailer? Are there any speed limits that are different when you have a trailer attached? What other regulations about trailers does your driver's manual discuss?

Review student's work.

_____

_____

_____

NAME _____ DATE _____

STUDY GUIDE FOR CHAPTER 18   LESSON 4

Traveling Safely in a Light Truck: A Pickup, Sport Utility Vehicle, or Van

A. For each sentence below, circle T if the statement is true and F if it is false. Correct each false statement in the space below.

1. Drivers of pickups, sport utility vehicles, or vans can see farther ahead than drivers of cars.   **T**   F

2. Vehicles driving behind a pickup, sport utility vehicle, or van will have no trouble seeing ahead.   T   **F**

   The extra height of most light trucks means that other vehicles often cannot see over or past them to determine what lies ahead.

3. Driving one of these larger vehicles can make you more tired than driving a car.   **T**   F

4. Higher headlights on a sport utility vehicle can cause more glare.   **T**   F

5. The center of gravity is lower on these larger vehicles.   T   **F**

   The center of gravity is higher on these vehicles.

6. Light trucks tend to be easier to drive in heavy winds because they are bigger than cars.   T   **F**

   Light trucks are harder to drive in heavy winds because they are taller and square in shape.

7. You can manage the added risk of driving a larger vehicle by increasing your following distance to give you more time to maneuver and stop.   **T**   F

B. FIND OUT MORE. Look in the automotive section of your newspaper for advertisements from vehicle dealers. Read ads for passenger cars as well as ads for larger vehicles such as pickups, sport utility vehicles, and vans. Compare vehicle prices. Do you think that you would buy one of these larger vehicles?

Review student's work.

_____

_____

_____

Planning a Trip

CHAPTER OVERVIEW

LESSON ONE

Preparations to make for a short vehicle trip are explained.

LESSON TWO

Advance preparations for a long vehicle trip are described.

LESSON THREE

Factors to consider when planning to tow a trailer are explained, and procedures for driving a vehicle with a trailer attached are described.

LESSON FOUR

Factors to consider when driving a light truck such as a pickup, sport utility vehicle, or van are described.

VOCABULARY

hitch
sport utility vehicle (SUV)

336

CONCEPT OF THE DRIVING TASK

Explain that advance planning is a wise habit for drivers to develop. By knowing ahead of time exactly where they are going, how to get there, and what roadway conditions to expect, drivers can help eliminate unanticipated distractions that contribute to driving risk.

CHAPTER 18

Planning a Trip

Planning is essential to travel, whether it is to a local supermarket or across the country. Vehicle preparation, wise route decisions, and time management are key ingredients to responsible planning.

LESSON ONE

Preparing Yourself and Your Vehicle for a Short Trip

LESSON TWO

Getting Ready for a Long Trip

LESSON THREE

Loading and Driving with a Trailer

LESSON FOUR

Traveling Safely in a Light Truck: A Pickup, Sport Utility Vehicle, or Van

PRESENTING THE BIG IDEA ———

Be prepared is a phrase that serves drivers well in a wide range of contexts, from planning alternate travel routes to practice-driving before driving in traffic.

INTRODUCING THE CHAPTER

What's on the Road Ahead?

Have students read the lesson titles and objectives. Briefly discuss the topic of each lesson. Tell students that in this chapter, they will learn about the usefulness of planning in advance for trips. They will also learn about procedures for driving a vehicle with a trailer attached and for driving a light truck.

Background: Americans and Their Vehicles

The following facts may interest or surprise students.

• Ninety-two percent of U.S. households own a motor vehicle. Sixty percent own two or more motor vehicles.

• The most prevalent reason for travel is family and personal business. One out of every two trips is for this purpose, which includes shopping, health appointments, and dropping off or picking up others.

• About one-third of the world's vehicles are in the United States.

• Social and recreational activities, including vacations, visiting friends, and trips taken for entertainment, account for one out of every four trips.

• Travel related to work is the third most frequent trip purpose, accounting for one out of every six trips.

Relating to Prior Knowledge

Have students discuss driving (or other) trips they have taken, describing how they prepared for their trips.

The Big Idea

Discuss students' reactions to the Big Idea statement. Suggest that they keep this idea in mind as they read Chapter 18.

Preparing Yourself and Your Vehicle for a Short Trip

(pages 338–339)

FOCUS

Objectives

- Describe how you would prepare yourself for a short trip.
- Discuss how you would prepare your vehicle for a short trip and the reasons for doing so.

> ### Resources
>
> Study Guide, page 69

Motivator

Pose this situation: You plan to meet a friend at a movie theater in a town about 10 miles away. Before getting into your vehicle, what preparations should you make? (Find out exactly where the theater is and how to get there; plan an alternate route just in case; bring whatever items you may need; allow enough time; check your vehicle.)

TEACH

Explain

OBJECTIVES 1 AND 2: Students should recognize the need to allow extra time for driving at night, in bad weather, and when trying to find a place for the first time.

Teaching Model

Describe the following situation: You're driving into the city to visit your aunt. Model the thinking process that you will use

---

LESSON ONE

OBJECTIVES

1. Describe how you would prepare yourself for a short trip.
2. Discuss how you would prepare your vehicle for a short trip and the reasons for doing so.

Preparing Yourself and Your Vehicle for a Short Trip

Most traffic fatalities happen within 25 miles, or a short trip's distance, of the driver's home. Have you thought about ways to reduce your chances of being in a collision when you take a short trip away from home?

What Steps Should You Take When Planning a Short Trip?

A short trip can be a 5-mile drive to a neighborhood shopping center, a 2-mile drive to work or school, or a 45-mile trip to visit a relative who lives in another town. Even if you make the same trip every day, being prepared can help you reduce the risk of being in a collision.

> **TIPS** **FOR NEW DRIVERS**
>
> ### Working a Self-Service Gas Pump
>
> To operate a self-service gas pump, pull up to the pump that dispenses the kind of fuel your vehicle uses. If a sign says "Pay Cashier Before Pumping," the pumps will not operate until you pay. Otherwise, pump the amount you need, and pay when you are done.
>
> 1. Open the fuel filler door, and take off the gas cap.
> 2. Take the pump nozzle off its cradle, and place the nozzle in the fuel tank opening.
> 3. Turn on the pump switch. It is usually located near the pump nozzle cradle.
> 4. Squeeze the lever on the pump nozzle to begin pumping the fuel.
> 5. If you have prepaid or when the tank is full, the pump will shut off automatically. Otherwise, release the lever, and put the nozzle back on its cradle. Turn off the pump switch. Then put the gas cap back on, and shut the fuel filler door.

Prepare Yourself

You need to make advance preparations for a trip even if you'll only be driving a short distance. Ask yourself these questions before you get into the car.

Do I know how to get where I'm going? If you are going someplace you have never been before, work out your route in advance. Make sure that you have specific directions to follow, and use a map to check them out. Know the names of the streets and roads that you have to follow. Make sure that you are able to drive on them in the direction you want to go.

Do I know another way to get there? Sometimes even the best plans just don't work out. Your planned route may be

---

Driving Tip

Explain to students that when they prepare for a short trip, they should also plan the return trip. Traffic patterns, roadwork, and other factors can sometimes cause travel problems in one direction that do not exist in the other direction.

> **TIPS** **FOR NEW DRIVERS**
>
> Caution students never to smoke or light matches near gasoline.

blocked for many reasons, so it's smart to have alternative plans to get where you're going by another route.

Do I have everything I need? Even though you will probably not take any luggage on a short trip, you may need some or all of the following items: identification, money, addresses, directions or a map, and a list of things to do, see, or buy.

Have I given myself enough time? Hurrying can make you nervous and careless. First figure out how long the trip should take, then add some time for the unexpected. You can anticipate some delays by listening to the radio for weather conditions and traffic reports.

Am I going at a good time? Try to avoid rush-hour traffic. There's no reason to get involved in a traffic jam if you don't absolutely have to. As you plan your route, remember that roads leading into urban areas will be busiest during the morning rush hours and roads leading out will be busiest in the evening rush hours.

◆ *Use a map to make sure you know how to get where you're going.*

Prepare Your Vehicle

Every time you use your vehicle, you should check to be sure that it is in proper condition to be driven. (See Chapter 7 for predriving checks.) You should check to see that:

• tires are properly inflated.
• signal lights are working.
• front and back lights are working.
• you have enough fuel and oil.

Preparing yourself and your vehicle for a trip does not take much time. However, the time you spend in preparation will save you time and trouble in the long run.

WHAT WOULD YOU DO?

You had last-minute errands and are going to be late for an appointment. What will you do next time to avoid this situation?

Lesson *1* Review

1. What are some helpful questions to ask yourself as you prepare for a short trip?
2. What items should you check as you prepare to drive your vehicle?

---

to prepare for your trip. (You will plan your route in advance; make sure to take a map along; decide on the best time of day to go; estimate how long the drive will take, and allow extra time; make sure the vehicle is in good working condition.)

Ask

Ask students to discuss how advance trip planning can reduce driving risk.

Read

Have students read Lesson 1 to learn how to prepare for a short trip.

ASSESS

Guided Practice

Have students answer the Lesson 1 Review questions. The answers are provided below.

Reteaching

Have students work in pairs or small groups to create an advance-planning checklist for short trips.

Enrichment

Assign the Study Guide for Lesson 1. The Find Out More section encourages students to expand their basic learning of the lesson concepts.

CLOSE

Summarize

Return to the Motivator question, and discuss advance planning step-by-step.

WHAT WOULD YOU DO?

Sample answer: Plan ahead to allow sufficient time.

Lesson *1* Review

Answers

1. Do I know how to get where I'm going? Do I know another way to get there? Do I have everything I need? Have I given myself enough time? Am I going at a good time?
2. See that tires are properly inflated; signal lights are working; front and back lights are working; there is enough fuel and oil.

DRIVER'S LOG

How can planning a trip in advance reduce your driving risk?

FOCUS

Objectives

• Explain how you would prepare yourself for a long trip.
• Describe how you would prepare your vehicle for a long trip.

Resources

 Study Guide, page 70

Motivator

Pose this situation: You are planning to go camping on your vacation. It's a three-day drive to your destination, through a scenic part of the country. Before starting out, what preparations should you make for your trip? (Obtain a map; plan your travel route; decide where you will spend your nights while on the road; make a budget; plan your driving time; check the condition of your vehicle; pack the vehicle carefully.)

TEACH

Explain

OBJECTIVE 1: Students should be aware that travel books available at the library contain useful information about places to stay, restaurants, sights and attractions, and weather conditions. Many of these books also offer approximate costs of lodging and restaurants. However, it is wise to add at least 15 percent to these costs when planning a budget. In addition to providing practical guidance, travel books can also make a trip more interesting by

LESSON TWO

OBJECTIVES

1. Explain how you would prepare yourself for a long trip.
2. Describe how you would prepare your vehicle for a long trip.

Getting Ready for a Long Trip

You face risk when you take a long trip, just as you do when you take a short trip. Fatigue, unfamiliarity with the area, and uncertain weather conditions are some factors that can increase driving risk on a long trip. Long trips also present you and your vehicle with some different needs.

What Should You Do to Prepare for a Long Trip?

If you plan to take a long trip, some of the preparations you should make are similar to those you make for a short trip. Others, however, are important only when you are traveling long distances.

Prepare Yourself

Here are some questions that you should ask yourself to prepare for a long trip.

How will I get to where I want to go? You may choose the most direct route to your destination, or you may choose to drive on a more leisurely route through scenic country. Whichever you choose, plan your route carefully. Use a map, and keep in mind the risks that each route may pose. The most direct route may involve expressway driving, where high speeds and large trucks present special problems. On the other hand, a scenic route may lead through congested towns or wilderness areas with no gas stations or places to stay.

Plan your route before you start the trip. Don't try to read a map while you're moving on the roadway. If you need to check the map, pull into a rest area or onto the shoulder when it is safe to do so.

You may want to write to or visit an auto club or travel agency to obtain maps, route suggestions, and recommendations on places to stay.

◆ Call ahead to make reservations at hotels or motels along your route and at your destination.

340   UNIT 4   *Planning for Your Future*

THE INTERNATIONAL SCENE

Mexico

U.S. vehicle insurance coverage is *not* valid in Mexico. When driving in Mexico, it is absolutely essential to obtain *Mexican* insurance, which can be purchased near border crossings (on either side of the border). A driver without Mexican motor vehicle insurance may be jailed in the event of a collision and have his or her vehicle impounded!

Where will I spend the night while I am on the road? Plan where you will spend each night, and make your reservations in advance. Ask about rates and parking facilities, and figure this information into your budget and schedule.

Will I have had enough sleep the night before driving? Be sure that you get enough rest before getting behind the wheel. If you become tired while driving, pull over at a rest stop.

A good plan is to drive in 2-hour stretches with 15-minute breaks in between. Don't try to drive more than a total of 8 hours in a day. If you're traveling with another person who also drives, share the driving task.

Budgeting Your Money and Planning Your Time

A long trip can be expensive. To figure out how much money you'll need, make a budget. Use the categories above, adding others if you need to. Figure your budget by the day or by the week. Your emergency supplies should include an extra set of vehicle keys as well as replacements for or additions to supplies you normally carry in your trunk or other vehicle storage area. (See Chapter 15 for a list of emergency supplies.)

BUDGET

	Food	Lodging	Gas	Tolls	Parking	Recreation
Day 1	$75	$95	$18	$5	—	$20
Day 2	$120	$70	$15	—	$5	—
Day 3	$70	$80	$15	$3	—	$15

SCHEDULE

	Depart		Average	Arrive		
	Place	**Time**	**Speed**	**Place**	**Time**	
Day 1	Holyoke	7 A.M.	40 mph	Boston	9 A.M.	
Day 2	Boston	2 P.M.	45 mph	NYC	6 P.M.	
Day 3	NYC	6 A.M.	45 mph	Washington, D.C.	11 A.M.	

BEFORE-THE-TRIP CHECKLIST

Emergency supplies	Professional vehicle checkup	Maps and travel books
Extra fuses	Brakes	City maps
Gloves	Transmission	State maps
Duct tape	Shocks	Places of interest
Flashlight		
First aid kit		
Keys		

Energy Tips

Although a scenic route may be more enjoyable, a limited-access highway tends to be much safer and more energy efficient. You'll have fewer stops, starts, curves, and hills, and you'll be able to maintain a steady speed for longer periods of time.

giving background information on the history and economy of towns and cities.

OBJECTIVE 2: Explain to students that in spite of careful vehicle preparation, something might go wrong on a long trip. Discuss how to prepare for this—for example, by having extra cash available for a vehicle emergency.

Teaching Model

Describe the following situation: You're visiting a friend who lives in another state. The drive will take at least two days. Model the thinking process that you will use to prepare for your trip. (You will plan the route you will take; choose a place to stay overnight along the way; figure out your budget; plan your travel time; make sure your vehicle is in good operating condition; pack your vehicle carefully.)

Ask

Ask students how planning for a long trip is different from planning for a short trip.

Read

Have students read Lesson 2 to learn how to prepare for a long trip.

ASSESS

Guided Practice

Have students answer the Lesson 2 Review questions. The answers are provided below.

MEETING STUDENT DIVERSITY

Limited English Proficiency

Travel-related terminology can be especially confusing for students with limited English proficiency. You may want to define such common terms as *hotel, motel, motor inn, resort, inn, American Plan, Modified American Plan, European Plan,* and the like.

Reteaching

Have students work together in pairs or small groups to create a checklist for planning long trips. After students complete this task, have them use their checklist to discuss the preparations they would make for an imaginary four-day trip.

Enrichment

Assign the Study Guide for Lesson 2. The Find Out More section encourages students to expand their basic learning of the lesson concepts.

CLOSE

Summarize

Return to the Motivator question, and have students describe the tasks involved in planning a long trip. Then have students discuss this statement: The longer a trip is, the more planning that is required. Encourage students to share any relevant experiences they may have had.

DRIVER'S LOG

In what ways is preparing for a long trip similar to preparing for a short trip? In what ways is it different? Why is advance planning important?

WHAT WOULD YOU DO?

Sample answer: Do not overload vehicle; check manual for maximum recommended weight load per tire. Have a mechanic check brakes, exhaust system, alignment, fluid levels, shock absorbers, belts, and hoses.

FYI

To find the recommended air pressures for your tires, check your vehicle owner's manual or look for a sticker that may be affixed to a doorpost or to the inside of the fuel filler door. *Never exceed the maximum tire pressure recommended for your vehicle.*

Planning your travel time by making a schedule is also helpful. In making up your schedule, consider such factors as rush-hour traffic, speed limits, the kind of route you want to take, how far you want to drive at a time, and occasional stops for stretching, eating, and relaxing. Plan your driving time so that you avoid morning and early-evening rush-hour traffic.

Prepare Your Vehicle

Your vehicle should always be in good condition. However, before a long trip, you should have a mechanic check the following:

- brake shoes and pads
- exhaust system for leaks
- front-end alignment
- tire condition
- fluid levels in the engine, transmission, and battery
- shock absorbers
- belts and hoses

Pack the vehicle carefully. Overloading can have an adverse effect on your vehicle's handling, acceleration, and fuel efficiency.

Before you load your vehicle, consult your owner's manual for the maximum weight load recommended per tire. Then be sure that your tires are inflated to the tire pressure recommended to carry any extra weight.

When you pack the vehicle, follow these additional guidelines.

- Pack the heaviest objects at the bottom of the trunk or storage area.

- If you use a vehicle-top carrier, be sure to place only lighter objects in it.
- Do not put anything on the rear-window shelf that will obstruct your view of the roadway behind you or that can be thrown forward in a sudden stop. Do not obstruct the back seat windows by hanging clothes over them.

You and your family are about to take a three-week driving trip. What will you do to make this vehicle trip-worthy?

Lesson 2 Review

1. How can you prepare yourself and your vehicle for a long trip?
2. How can making a budget and a schedule help you with your plans for a long trip?

Lesson 2 Review

Answers

1. Preparations are similar to those for a short trip; additional checks include checks of brake shoes and pads; exhaust system for leaks; front-end alignment; tires; fluid levels in engine, transmission, and battery; shock absorbers; belts and hoses.

2. Making a budget and a schedule will help ensure you have enough money and time for your trip; to prepare yourself, get a good night's sleep; to prepare your vehicle, have a mechanic check it; also, pack it carefully.

Loading and Driving with a Trailer

Many drivers tow boats, campers, or other kinds of trailers behind their vehicles. Towing a trailer, however, can make driving more difficult.

What Do You Need to Know About Trailers?

Knowing some of the special features and needs of trailers can help you minimize the risk when driving with one attached to your vehicle.

Weight of the Trailer and Its Load

Many vehicles are limited in the amount of weight they can pull in a trailer. Consider the weight of your vehicle, the weight of the trailer you're planning to haul, and the weight of the load. Check your owner's manual for recommended factory load limits.

Necessary Equipment

If you tow a trailer frequently, your vehicle may need additional equipment, such as a heavy-duty suspension, anti-sway bars, a large-capacity radiator, transmission cooler, and heavy-duty shock absorbers. You will need to add mirrors on your vehicle to increase visibility. You also need extra emergency equipment for heavier trailers, including a hydraulic jack, blocks for holding on grades, and tow ropes.

To tow a trailer, you need a **hitch,** a device that attaches to the back of the vehicle, and safety chains. For ordinary loads, use a hitch that is welded or bolted to the frame of the vehicle. For heavier loads, there are special hitches for load equalizing. When your hitch is installed, also install an electrical outlet for the trailer's taillights, stoplights, and turn signals.

Preparing to Tow a Trailer

The increased load that a trailer puts on your vehicle means that you will need to check your oil and transmission fluid more often than

LESSON THREE

OBJECTIVES
1. Describe factors you should be aware of when planning to use a trailer.
2. Explain the procedures for driving a vehicle with a trailer attached.

KEY TERM
hitch

FYI

The poorest trailer hitch is a bumper attachment unit. Do not use this kind of hitch for anything except the very lightest loads.

◆ *Pack a trailer so that 60 percent of the load is in the front half.*

Driving Tip

Advise students to check with their insurance agent before driving with a trailer to make sure their motor vehicle insurance policy covers such use. Additional endorsements to the policy may be required.

IT'S A FACT

The greatest use of trailers on the road today involves the hauling of large and small private boats. Aside from boats, trailers of varying sizes and shapes are used to haul everything from furniture to horses.

FOCUS

Objectives

- Describe factors you should be aware of when planning to use a trailer.
- Explain the procedures for driving a vehicle with a trailer attached.

Resources

📁 Study Guide, page 71

📁 Traffic charts

🕹 Transparencies 49 and 50

📁 Information Master 24

Vocabulary

hitch

Motivator

Pose this situation: You are helping a friend move to a new home. Your friend has asked you to attach a trailer to your vehicle in order to transport some of her belongings. What are some factors you must consider when attaching and loading the trailer? (Consider the weight of the vehicle, the trailer, and the load to be carried; add any necessary equipment, such as additional mirrors; consider how to attach the trailer to the vehicle safely; make any adjustments to the vehicle that may be required, such as increasing air pressure in the tires.)

TEACH

Explain

OBJECTIVE 1: Students should be aware that many states require that all loaded trailers weighing
continued on page 344

more than 40 percent of the weight of the towing vehicle be equipped with brakes as well as other safety devices. States may prohibit the use of trailers on certain roads and during high-wind conditions.

OBJECTIVE 2: Students will benefit from a discussion of how to manage visibility, time, and space when driving a vehicle with a trailer attached. Cautious driving is particularly important to reduce risk when backing up, slowing and stopping, making turns, merging into traffic, passing another vehicle, and being passed by a heavy vehicle.

Teaching Model

Describe the following situation: Your vehicle is towing a trailer, and you want to back into a driveway. Model the thinking process that you will use to back up. (You will do the following.

- Get out and check behind the trailer before backing up.
- If possible, back up so that the trailer turns to the left side of your vehicle in order for you to see it over your left shoulder.
- Back up slowly and cautiously.
- Turn the steering wheel to the right to move left, to the left to move right.
- Do not turn the steering wheel too far or hold it too long, thereby causing the trailer to jackknife.)

Ask

Ask students to discuss the risks involved in backing up with a trailer attached.

Read

Have students read Lesson 3 to learn what factors to consider when planning to use a trailer and what procedures to follow when driving a vehicle with a trailer attached.

ASSESS

Guided Practice

Have students answer the Lesson 3 Review questions.

344 CHAPTER 18

FYI

The wheel may be civilization's most important technological development. The wheel is believed to have been invented in about 3500 B.C. Its invention is credited to the Sumerians, a civilization that developed in the Tigris-Euphrates Valley in the area that is now Iraq.

◆ *Practice backing with a trailer before you actually need to do it.*

Turn wheel this way to make trailer go right.

Turn wheel this way to make trailer go left.

usual. You will also need to replace air, oil, and fuel filters sooner than you ordinarily would. You may need to increase the air pressure in your tires.

Packing a Trailer

The rear end of your vehicle will have to support 10 to 15 percent of the trailer load. Therefore, the vehicle itself should carry 10 to 15 percent less than the maximum weight recommended by the owner's manual. Too much weight in the back of the vehicle will cause its front to rise and will affect steering, braking, and the aim of the headlights.

When you pack the trailer, follow manufacturer's guidelines. Load the heaviest items at the bottom, over the trailer wheels. About 60 percent of the weight should be packed in the front half of the trailer, and the total weight should be about equal from side to side. Be sure to pack all items tightly or tie them down so that they cannot shift during driving maneuvers.

Check what you have done. The bottoms of both the vehicle and the trailer should be nearly parallel to the ground.

How Do You Drive a Vehicle with a Trailer Attached?

Towing a trailer requires new driving skills and plenty of practice.

Starting

Maneuverability and acceleration are limited when you tow a trailer. Check traffic carefully. Signal before moving. Allow a large gap before entering traffic. Start slowly, and check traffic in the mirrors frequently.

Backing

Backing is a difficult maneuver. Use these guidelines to back with a trailer: back slowly; to go left, turn the steering wheel to the right and then straighten it; to go right, turn the steering wheel to the *left* and then straighten it. Do not turn the steering wheel too much or hold it in the turned position too long. Doing so can cause the trailer to jackknife.

Making a Right Turn

To turn right, follow these steps.

1. Check traffic and signal for the right turn in advance of the intersection.
2. Position farther from the curb than if you didn't have a trailer attached.

IT'S A FACT

Towing a trailer can decrease a vehicle's fuel efficiency by as much as 50 percent. Thus, if a vehicle normally gets 24 miles per gallon of gas, the same vehicle may get only 12 miles per gallon when pulling a trailer.

Driving Tip

Caution students to beware of drivers towing trailers. To minimize risk, allow an extra margin of safety when following or passing a vehicle towing a trailer.

3. Steer the vehicle straight ahead until the front wheels are well beyond the curb line.
4. Turn the steering wheel sharply right.
5. Complete the turn by straightening the steering wheel.

Making a Left Turn

To turn left, follow these steps.

1. Check traffic and signal early.
2. Proceed farther into the intersection than usual to allow for the trailer.
3. Swing wide enough so that the trailer will not cut the corner.
4. Complete the turn and move into traffic.

Overtaking, Passing, and Being Overtaken

When you plan to overtake and pass another vehicle, allow much more time and space because of the length and weight of the trailer.

When you are being passed by a light vehicle, observe the same rules that you do in a car. (See Chapter 9.) However, if a heavy vehicle is passing you, the air that it displaces will tend to push the trailer to the side. Be ready to adjust your steering.

Slowing and Stopping

If your trailer does not have brakes, the brakes on your vehicle control all slowing and stopping. If the trailer does have brakes, then your vehicle's brakes control the trailer's brakes.

The additional weight and length of the trailer mean that you will need more time and space to stop. When you do enter traffic, allow a greater following distance than you ordinarily would.

Before driving with a trailer, check your insurance to be sure that you are covered for towing a trailer. Also check the laws about trailers in states that you will be traveling through.

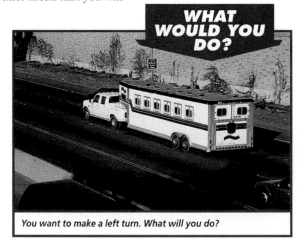

◆ A draft from large vehicles can make a trailer move from side to side. Be ready to adjust steering.

SAFETY TIPS

If you are pulling a trailer, you will need twice the usual distance to merge into traffic, to pass another vehicle, or to stop.

WHAT WOULD YOU DO?

You want to make a left turn. What will you do?

Lesson 3 Review

1. Why is it important to pack a trailer carefully?
2. In what ways is driving with a trailer different from driving without one?

CHAPTER 18   *Planning a Trip*   **345**

WHAT WOULD YOU DO?

Sample answer: As you proceed to the next intersection, signal and move to the proper turn lane when it is safe to do so.

Lesson 3 Review

Answers
1. Too much weight in the back of the vehicle will cause the front end to rise, affecting steering, braking, and the aim of the headlights.
2. Your vehicle must work harder to pull the extra load; you may need to increase tire pressure; you need more time and distance to maneuver and stop; backing up is much more difficult; your visibility to the sides and rear is restricted.

The answers are provided below.

Reteaching

Have students work together in small groups to create charts or posters of procedural do's and don'ts for operating a vehicle with a trailer attached. Separate charts might focus on backing up, making left and right turns, or passing another vehicle. Encourage students to illustrate their charts.

Have groups share their work with the class. Encourage discussion of risk factors in each situation and what drivers can do to reduce risk.

Enrichment

Assign the Study Guide for Lesson 3. The Find Out More section encourages students to expand their basic learning of the lesson concepts.

Encourage students to think about why the wheel has been so important to technological advancement.

CLOSE

Summarize

Return to the Motivator question. Recall students' initial responses, and have students summarize the additional information that they have gained from this lesson.

Review the challenges and risks of driving a vehicle with a trailer attached. Discuss how drivers can help ensure safety by managing visibility, time, and space.

DRIVER'S LOG

What did you learn about attaching and loading a trailer that you didn't know before? What aspects of driving a vehicle with a trailer attached seem most challenging to you? Where could you practice driving a vehicle and trailer to develop the necessary skills?

CHAPTER 18   **345**

Traveling Safely in a Light Truck: A Pickup, Sport Utility Vehicle, or Van

(pages 346–348)

FOCUS

Objectives

• Explain the importance of visibility and vehicle size when traveling in a pickup truck, sport utility vehicle, or van.

• Describe how you can protect yourself and other motorists when driving a large vehicle.

Resources

📁 Study Guide, page 72

📁 Traffic charts

Vocabulary

sport utility vehicle (SUV)

Motivator

Pose this situation: You are learning to drive a light truck. What factors make driving a light truck different from driving a car? (Students may mention that drivers of light trucks can see farther ahead than drivers of cars because they sit higher; because light trucks are higher than cars, rear visibility may be limited; a light truck's greater size can be problematic in strong wind and when parking in garages or enclosed parking spaces; because of their weight, light trucks take longer than cars to stop, turn, and accelerate.

LESSON FOUR

OBJECTIVES

1. Explain the importance of visibility and vehicle size when traveling in a pickup truck, sport utility vehicle, or van.
2. Describe how you can protect yourself and other motorists when driving a large vehicle.

KEY TERM

sport utility vehicle (SUV)

Traveling Safely in a Light Truck: A Pickup, Sport Utility Vehicle, or Van

The most popular vehicles on American roads today are light trucks. This category includes pickups, vans, and **sport utility vehicles (SUVs).** An SUV is designed for a variety of uses and usually incorporates four- or all-wheel drive. It features increased ground clearance and a cargo area included within the interior of the vehicle. Driving a light truck or sharing the road with light trucks requires consideration for their size and limitations.

How Do You Drive a Pickup, Sport Utility Vehicle, or Van?

A number of factors make light trucks more difficult than cars to drive and more difficult to share the road with.

Visibility

A taller vehicle allows the driver to see over surrounding traffic and take advantage of that height to search farther down the road for pending problems. This gives the driver an advantage in planning driving strategy.

◆ Because you sit higher in a van or sport utility vehicle, you can see farther ahead than you do in a car.

Vehicle Size

Most pickups, SUVs, and vans are wider and higher than cars. This greater width and height, along with a greater weight, pose special problems that you must learn to deal with in order to manage risk.

Know the height of your vehicle. The extra height of most light trucks means that vehicles sharing the road with them often cannot see through, around, or past them to determine what lies ahead. While you can see through the glass area of a car, the same cannot always be said for these taller vehicles. When following one, stay farther behind to increase your ability to see around it.

State BY State

Restrictions on the driving privileges of teenagers vary from state to state. For example, in some states, such as Florida, Ohio, and Texas, teenagers under 18 must be enrolled in or have completed high school to be eligible for a license. Similarly, some states allow unsupervised night driving, while others limit the hours that teenagers can drive at night or specify a minimum age at which they may drive at night.

Because these vehicles are taller than cars, the headlights and bumpers are above the rest of the traffic. In case of a collision, the bumpers will not match up with those of surrounding cars but will more likely strike the cars' bodies above their bumpers, resulting not only in more damage to the vehicles but also an increased possibility of injury to the cars' occupants.

Because headlights are higher they cause more glare when approaching or following other traffic. As the driver of the taller vehicle, you should be aware of this and stay farther back from vehicles you are following and pay strict attention to keeping your lights on low beam when approaching other vehicles.

Additional height also causes problems when you are trying to turn or stop suddenly. The center of gravity is higher, and the vehicle will roll to the side or pitch forward more easily than a car. The additional size and weight makes pickups, SUVs, and vans handle much less securely than cars in emergency situations.

Don't forget to check the height of your vehicle, especially a van, which might not fit into some garages or enclosed parking spaces.

Know the weight of your vehicle. Pickups, vans, and sport utility vehicles, because of their construction and additional components, weigh more than cars. Weight is the enemy of fuel mileage, handling, and braking. Being larger, these vehicles take longer to stop, turn, or accelerate than does a lighter vehicle.

Be alert for wind. The square shape and taller height mean that light trucks present a greater surface to the wind and are more susceptible to it.

Know about your vehicle's tires. Tires determine how well any vehicle can stop, turn, or accelerate. Tires used on pickups, SUVs, and vans have a more open and rugged tread design to allow them to deal with off-road use. However, this makes them less efficient on wet or dry pavement because they place less rubber on the road, limiting the ability of these larger, heavier vehicles to stop or turn. On average, a pickup or sport utility vehicle will take between 10 percent and 20 percent more distance to stop from highway speeds than a passenger car.

Protecting Other Motorists

Adjust your driving to take into account that you are driving a larger and wider vehicle than

SAFETY TIPS

Larger vehicles are capable of carrying more passengers. This means more opportunity for distraction. Don't allow others in the vehicle to take your mind away from the very important job of driving.

◆ *Look for signs on underpasses that tell you what the maximum clearance is.*

Driving Tip

Caution students to beware of crosswinds when driving a light truck across open areas and bridges and in stormy weather. Because of their size, pickups, SUVs, and vans are much more liable than cars to be rocked by wind gusts.

TEACH

Explain

OBJECTIVE 1: Students should be cautioned about visibility problems while driving behind all large vehicles, including trucks and buses.

OBJECTIVE 2: Students should be cautioned about the different tires used on four-wheel-drive SUVs and many pickup trucks and how they will require additional stopping distances.

Teaching Model

Describe this situation: You are driving a sport utility vehicle in congested traffic. Model the thinking process needed to minimize risk to both yourself and other vehicles sharing the road with you. (Increase following distance between your vehicle and others; allow extra time and space to maneuver and stop; be aware that the large size of your SUV can create problems for drivers behind you.)

Ask

How does the greater size and weight of a pickup, an SUV, or a van increase risk?

Read

Have students read Lesson 4 to learn what factors to consider when driving a pickup, an SUV, or a van.

ASSESS

Guided Practice

Have students answer the Lesson 4 Review questions. The answers are provided below.

Reteaching

Have students work together in pairs or small groups to make a poster describing visibility, time, and space factors that the driver of a large vehicle must consider.

Stress the importance of maintaining an adequate level of fuel to avoid running out of gas and getting stranded.

After students complete this task, have them discuss and compare how a driver's thinking would change in a given situation, depending on whether he or she were driving a car, a larger vehicle, such as a pickup, an SUV, or a van, or a vehicle towing a trailer.

Enrichment

Assign the Study Guide for Lesson 4. The Find Out More section encourages students to expand their basic learning of the lesson concepts.

CLOSE

Summarize

Return to the Motivator question. Recall students' initial responses, and have students summarize the additional information that they have gained from this lesson. You may also want to have students draw parallels between driving a pickup, an SUV, or a van and driving a vehicle with a trailer attached.

DRIVER'S LOG

What special risks are involved in driving a light truck? How can you protect yourself and others against these risks?

WHAT WOULD YOU DO?

Sample answer: Maintain a greater margin of space; remember that you may be blocking the visibility of other drivers.

ADVICE FROM THE EXPERTS

Bill Hughes
Director, National Travel, AAA

Allow sufficient time to get to your destination to avoid feeling rushed and making last-minute decisions. Keep a sufficient amount of fuel in your vehicle—you may not know how long it is to the next service station. Plan your stops so that you don't find yourself in an area where suitable accommodations cannot be found. Select a map that offers the proper level of detail to ensure that you can find your way safely. Check the map for toll roads to make certain you have enough cash to get to your destination.

many others on the road. Maintain a greater margin of space around the vehicle. Keep in mind that you may be blocking the visibility of other drivers. Take this into consideration when you spot potentially threatening conditions ahead that cars behind you may not see.

Increase your following distance to give yourself more time to maneuver and stop. Manage the risk to yourself and to others by staying alert and allowing extra time and space to accomplish driving maneuvers.

Protecting Yourself

Driving long distances is always strenuous and requires frequent rest stops and careful planning. Because of size and the increased difficulty in maneuvering a pickup, sport utility vehicle, or van, you may get tired more quickly than when you are driving a car. Manage risk to yourself and to your passengers by planning to drive shorter distances and resting more often than you would if you were driving a car. If possible, share driving duties.

WHAT WOULD YOU DO?

Since you're driving a vehicle larger and wider than many others, how should you adjust your driving to protect other motorists?

Lesson **4** Review

1. How would the size, weight, and height of a pickup, sport utility vehicle, or van make driving more difficult than driving a car?
2. How do you protect yourself and other motorists when driving a light truck?

Lesson **4** Review

Answers

1. Visibility to the rear might be restricted; wind might cause such a vehicle to sway; you would need to beware of objects above the roadway, of weight limits on bridges, and of height limits for tunnels and underpasses.

2. Take into account that you are driving a larger and wider vehicle; maintain a greater margin of space around the vehicle; increase following distance; on trips, plan to drive shorter distances and take frequent rests; share driving duties if possible.

Reading City Maps

Driving in a new city is often very confusing. Most maps have insets that show major cities in larger scale. Below is an inset map of Wichita, Kansas.

Suppose you are coming into Wichita from the north, on Interstate 135. To get to Wichita State University, you would leave Route 15 at the interchange for 13th Street. Then you would head east to Hillside Avenue. To get from Washington Road to the Historical Museum, you would drive about 1 mile east on Douglas Avenue.

Try It Yourself

1. How would you get from Wichita State University to Friend University?
2. Suppose you are at the airport. How would you drive to Planeview Park?
3. How would you get from the corner of 25th Street and Amidon Avenue to the Wichita Center for the Arts?

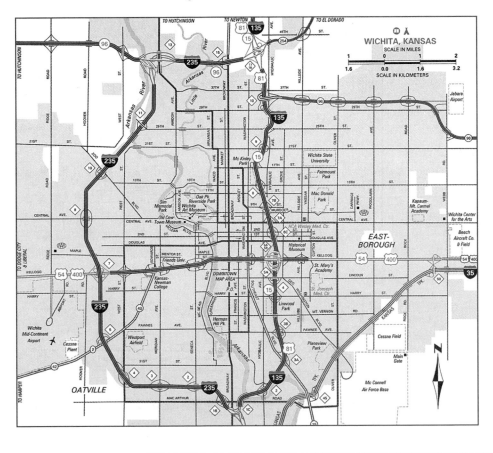

Objective

Demonstrate an ability to read and use city maps.

Teaching the Skill

- Point out to students that the mileage scale on the inset map is different from the scale on the large state map.
- Point out that the city map does not indicate whether or not streets are one-way. Therefore, drivers will need to look for this information on traffic signs.
- Alert students to the fact that inset maps show only major streets. If more detail is needed, drivers can often purchase a more extensive city map.

ANSWERS TO
Try It Yourself Questions

1. possible answer: travel west on 21st Street to West Street, then travel south on West Street and east on Douglas Ave. to the university
2. possible answer: take Route 54 to George Washington Boulevard, which travels south to Oliver Street and the park
3. possible answer: go south to 21st Street, then east to Rock Road; take Rock Road south to Central Avenue; take Central Avenue east

CHAPTER SUMMARY

Key Points

Have students read the Key Points to review the major concepts of the chapter.

PROJECTS

Cooperative Learning:

Students will benefit by working with a partner on one or both projects. When the assignment is completed, the whole class will profit by sharing and comparing results.

KEY POINTS

Lesson One

1. To prepare yourself for a short trip, have good directions or a map, know an alternate route, take all the items you need, allow extra time, and avoid rush-hour traffic.
2. To prepare your vehicle, be sure that tires are properly inflated, signal lights are working, front and back lights are in order, and that you have enough gas and oil.

Lesson Two

1. Prepare yourself for a long trip by planning your route, making a budget and schedule, making reservations, and getting enough rest.
2. Prepare your vehicle by having it checked by a mechanic and making sure you have adequate emergency equipment.

Lesson Three

1. When planning to use a trailer, consider the weight of the trailer and its load, the weight of your vehicle, and whether your vehicle can tow and control the loaded trailer. Be sure you have any necessary additional equipment to help you tow the trailer safely. Pack the trailer so that 60 percent of the load is in the front half and the heaviest items are on the bottom, making sure the load is secure.
2. To start out in a vehicle with a trailer attached, check traffic, signal, allow a very large gap when entering traffic, and begin slowly. To back with a trailer, move slowly and turn the wheel left when going right and right when going left. To turn, signal early, position the vehicle beyond the curb line, and turn the steering wheel so that the trailer does not cut the corner. Allow extra time and space to pass, to be passed, and to slow and stop.

Lesson Four

1. Although drivers of pickups, sport utility vehicles, and vans sit higher and can see farther ahead and around them than other drivers, this additional height means that people following them will not see as much as they would otherwise.
2. When you are driving a light truck, allow extra stopping distances by following farther behind vehicles. Allow an extra margin of space in all directions at all times.

PROJECTS

1. Choose four neighboring states through which you might take a long trip. Find out what their laws are regarding driver licensing for pickups, SUVs, vans. Compare other state laws with the laws in your own state. Prepare a report on their differences and similarities.
2. Find out where your ancestors lived or where they entered this country. Plan a trip to that place. Plot out your route, and make a budget and schedule. Mark your route on a map for display, and report on your travel plans.

*inter*NET
CONNECTION

Explore the Glencoe Web site to find more information on the advantages and disadvantages of driving an SUV. Find out which SUVs are the safest.
drivered.glencoe.com

*inter*NET
CONNECTION

Visit Glencoe's Driver Education Web site for student activities that relate to this chapter.
drivered.glencoe.com

CHAPTER TEST

Choose the letter of the answer that best completes each sentence.

1. When packing a trailer, 60 percent of the load should be
   a. over the wheels.
   b. in the front half of the trailer.
   c. at the bottom of the trailer.

2. You should not drive more than a total of
   a. 8 hours a day.
   b. 5 hours a day.
   c. 12 hours a day.

3. Most traffic fatalities occur
   a. within 50 miles of the driver's home.
   b. within 25 miles of the driver's home.
   c. when a vehicle is changing lanes.

4. If you are going someplace you have never gone before, you should
   a. use a road map while you are driving.
   b. stop periodically to ask directions.
   c. plan your route ahead of time.

5. If you tow a trailer frequently, you may need a
   a. hydraulic jack.
   b. vehicle-top carrier.
   c. boat.

6. You can anticipate some delays by
   a. using a map.
   b. having an alternate route.
   c. listening to the radio for traffic and weather reports.

7. Before starting on a long trip, you should
   a. choose the quickest route.
   b. choose the most leisurely route.
   c. keep in mind the risks that each route may have.

8. You can make a schedule to
   a. know when to exceed the speed limit.
   b. plan your travel time.

   c. keep track of how much money you spend on a trip.

9. When backing a trailer,
   a. turn right to go left.
   b. turn left to go left.
   c. look over your right shoulder.

10. Drivers of taller vehicles can see farther ahead because they
    a. have better eyesight.
    b. have bigger mirrors.
    c. can see over smaller vehicles.

Write the word or phrase that best completes each sentence.

overloading   shock absorbers
restrictions   following distance
trailer hitch   urban areas

11. Roads leading into _____ are busiest during the morning rush hour.

12. _____ can have an adverse effect on your vehicle's acceleration.

13. Have a mechanic check for worn _____ before a long trip.

14. Use a(n) _____ that is welded or bolted to the frame of your vehicle.

15. When you drive a vehicle heavier or taller than a car, you should increase your _____.

DRIVER'S LOG

In this chapter, you have learned how to plan long and short trips, how to tow trailers safely, and how to drive pickups, sport utility vehicles, and vans. Make a personal checklist to remind you of considerations that you would take into account when planning a cross-country trip in such vehicles.

RETURN TO THE BIG IDEA

Discuss how drivers can "be prepared" when taking a short or long trip, when driving a vehicle with a trailer attached, and when driving a pickup truck, an SUV, or a van.

CHAPTER 18 REVIEW

CHAPTER TEST

Assign the Chapter Test to all students.

Answers

1. b
2. a
3. b
4. c
5. a
6. c
7. c
8. b
9. a
10. c
11. urban areas
12. overloading
13. shock absorbers
14. trailer hitch
15. following distance

DRIVER'S LOG

Students' responses will reflect their personal viewpoints. However, their answers should provide an assessment of their understanding of the factors involved in planning a long trip.

Evaluate

- Test A, pages 35–36 or Test B, pages 35–36
- Year-End Test A, pages T1–4
- Year-End Test B, pages T1–4
- Testmaker software

UNIT 4

This review tests students' knowledge of the material in Chapters 1–18. Use the review to help students study for their state driving test.

Answers

1. d
2. c
3. c
4. b
5. b
6. a
7. c
8. c
9. a
10. c
11. b
12. d
13. a
14. a

UNIT 4 CUMULATIVE REVIEW

This review tests your knowledge of the material in Chapters 1–18. Use the review to help you study for your state driving test. Choose the answer that best completes each statement.

1. To stop heavy bleeding, use
   a. an air bag.
   b. shock.
   c. adhesion.
   d. direct pressure.

2. At a flashing red traffic signal, you must
   a. slow down.
   b. yield to an emergency vehicle.
   c. come to a full stop.
   d. reverse direction.

3. A vehicle's weight, body design, and engine type all contribute to
   a. the driver's popularity.
   b. oil consumption.
   c. fuel efficiency.
   d. night vision.

4. Plan your time on a trip by
   a. making a budget.
   b. making a schedule.
   c. taking a scenic route.
   d. wearing a watch.

5. At least once a month, check your vehicle's
   a. brake linings.
   b. fluid levels.
   c. shock absorbers.
   d. front-end alignment.

6. At a four-way stop, yield to the
   a. vehicle at your right.
   b. vehicle behind you.
   c. truck at your left.
   d. oncoming car.

7. To prove your identity at the department of motor vehicles, you can take
   a. a phone bill.
   b. your parent's tax return.
   c. a birth certificate.
   d. a report card.

8. Coolant is stored in the
   a. glove compartment.
   b. power train.
   c. radiator.
   d. steering column.

9. Vehicle financing can be obtained through
   a. a bank.
   b. your school.
   c. an insurance company.
   d. the federal government.

10. Tires should be rotated every
    a. 50 miles.
    b. 500 to 600 miles.
    c. 5,000 to 6,000 miles.
    d. two years.

11. You should pack a trailer so that
    a. 25 percent of the load is in the front half.
    b. 60 percent of the load is in the front half.
    c. the load is evenly distributed.
    d. your vehicle's rear bumper touches the ground.

12. Narcotics
    a. stimulate the central nervous system.
    b. are safe and easy to use.
    c. are often used by truck drivers.
    d. can cause death.

13. One problem common to urban driving is
    a. busy intersections.
    b. large animals on the road.
    c. high altitudes.
    d. interchanges.

352

14. Driving through deep puddles can lead to
    a. brake failure.
    b. front-end alignment.
    c. engine lock.
    d. clutch fade.

15. You are responsible for providing a vehicle for the
    a. in-vehicle test.
    b. knowledge test.
    c. Smith System.
    d. visual acuity test.

16. A factor in the cost of motor vehicle insurance is
    a. ethnic background.
    b. age.
    c. parents' driving records.
    d. number of school years completed.

17. The night before your knowledge test,
    a. stay awake and study.
    b. get plenty of rest.
    c. take a stimulant.
    d. go out with your friends and relax.

18. Driving faster than the posted speed limit is
    a. sometimes necessary.
    b. legal on country roads.
    c. always illegal.
    d. legal but irresponsible.

19. You can increase visibility in dense fog by using
    a. your dome light.
    b. brake lights.
    c. low-beam headlights.
    d. high-beam headlights.

20. The catalytic converter
    a. is a pollution-control device.
    b. is an optional feature.
    c. is attached to the battery.
    d. converts miles to kilometers.

21. Think twice about buying a vehicle if its passenger death rate is
    a. less than 1 per 10,000 registered vehicles.
    b. more than 2 per 10,000 registered vehicles.
    c. less than 2 per 10,000 registered vehicles.
    d. more than 1 per 100,000 registered vehicles.

22. To relax during the in-vehicle test,
    a. chat with the examiner.
    b. admit that you are nervous.
    c. hold your breath.
    d. wear loose clothing.

23. The odometer tells you
    a. the speed of the vehicle.
    b. how far you have driven.
    c. the engine temperature.
    d. how much fuel is in the tank.

24. One step of the Smith System is
    a. the SIPDE process.
    b. risk.
    c. angle parking.
    d. keep your eyes moving.

25. To start a vehicle, insert a key in the
    a. steering wheel.
    b. dashboard.
    c. ignition switch.
    d. carburetor.

26. Traction is poorest at about
    a. 32°F.
    b. 112°F.
    c. 40°F.
    d. the equator.

27. The air filter is part of the
    a. cooling system.
    b. exhaust system.
    c. protection system.
    d. fuel system.

Answers

15. a
16. b
17. b
18. c
19. c
20. a
21. b
22. b
23. b
24. d
25. c
26. a
27. d

acceleration An increase in speed.

accelerator The gas pedal; controls speed by adjusting the flow of gasoline to the engine.

adhesion Sticking together; in automotive terms, traction or friction.

administrative laws Laws that regulate driver licensing, vehicle registration, financial responsibility of drivers and vehicle owners, or minimum equipment and vehicle standards.

advisory speed limit A speed limit that interrupts normal driving speed for a limited time and provides guidelines for adjusting speed.

air bag A safety bag that automatically inflates upon impact in a collision.

alternator A generator that produces the electricity needed to run a vehicle and its electrical devices.

angle parking Parking so that a vehicle is positioned at a 30- to 90-degree angle with a curb or other boundary.

antifreeze A substance with a low freezing point, usually added to the liquid in a vehicle's radiator to prevent freezing.

antilock brake system (ABS) A braking system that is designed to keep a vehicle's wheels from locking when the driver brakes abruptly.

antitheft device Any device used to protect a vehicle from being stolen or entered.

area of central vision The area of vision directly ahead of a person.

automatic transmission A system that transmits power to the drive wheels. Gears are changed automatically in a vehicle with this type of transmission.

axle The shaft or rod connecting two opposite wheels on which the wheels revolve.

banked curve A curve that slopes up from the inside edge.

battery A unit that stores an electrical charge and furnishes current.

beltway A highway that passes around an urban area.

blind spot An area outside a vehicle that is not visible to the driver in the rearview or side-view mirrors.

blood-alcohol concentration (BAC) The percentage of alcohol in a person's blood.

blowout A sudden loss of air pressure in a tire.

blowout skid A skid occurring when a tire suddenly loses air pressure.

Blue Book A guide to the average price paid to dealers for different makes and models of used vehicles.

brake pedal A pedal that enables a driver to slow or stop a vehicle.

brake system The system that enables a vehicle to slow down and stop by means of hydraulic pressure.

braking distance The distance a vehicle covers from the time the driver applies the brakes until the vehicle stops.

braking skid A skid caused when the brakes are applied so hard that one or more wheels lock.

carbon monoxide A colorless, odorless, highly poisonous gas; a by-product of burning fuel.

catalytic converter An antipollution device, part of the exhaust system, that reduces harmful emissions.

center of gravity The point around which all the weight of an object is evenly distributed.

centrifugal force The force that tends to push a moving object out of a curve and into a straight path.

clutch In a vehicle with a manual transmission, a device that engages and disengages the engine and is connected to the drive shaft; the pedal by which the device is operated.

collision A crash; the result of one object hitting another with sudden force.

collision insurance Insurance that covers the cost of repairs to your vehicle even if you are to blame in a crash or are involved with an uninsured driver. It also covers repairs to your vehicle if it is damaged in a parking lot or in a parking space on the street.

color blindness The inability to distinguish between certain colors.

comprehensive insurance Insurance that covers the cost of repairs for vehicle damage caused by anything other than a collision, such as theft, fire, explosions, natural disasters, falling objects, or vandalism.

contrast sensitivity A person's ability to see details in the driving environment in situations such as facing the glare of headlights or driving when it is dark.

controlled-access highway See **limited-access highway.**

coolant A liquid added to a motor vehicle's radiator to reduce heat.

cooling system The system that keeps the engine cool by forcing air over metal cooling vanes that surround the cylinders. It includes the radiator, overflow tank, water pump, and thermostat.

cornering skid A skid on a turn or curve.

crankshaft The shaft that is turned as the pistons move up and down in the cylinders of the engine.

crowned road A road that is higher in the center than at either edge.

cruise control A vehicle feature that allows a driver to maintain a desired speed without manually pressing the accelerator; intended for highway driving.

cylinder A part of the engine that houses a piston; most vehicles have four, six, or eight cylinders.

deceleration A decrease in speed.

deceleration lane An expressway lane used for slowing down before an exit.

deductible A fixed amount of money that an insured person must pay for damages before the insurance company pays the rest, usually the first $100, $250, or $500 worth of damage.

defogger See **defroster.**

defroster A heating unit that clears moisture from the inside of the front and/or rear windows and ice from the outside surfaces.

depth perception Vision that gives objects their three-dimensional appearance and that enables a person to judge the relative distance between two objects.

differential An arrangement of gears that allows each drive wheel to turn at a different speed when a vehicle goes around a curve.

directional control The ability of a motor vehicle to hold to a straight line.

directional signal A device that allows drivers to communicate their intentions to move right or left by means of a blinking light; an arm or a hand signal.

disc brake A brake in which pressure squeezes the brake pads against a flat metal wheel disc, producing the friction needed to stop the wheel from turning.

downshift To shift to a lower gear from a higher one.

Drive The most frequently used forward gear in a vehicle with an automatic transmission.

drive train See **power train.**

drive wheel A wheel that moves a vehicle.

driver evaluation facility A special center where individuals with physical disabilities undergo a comprehensive medical assessment to determine their potential to drive.

driving under the influence (DUI) See **driving while intoxicated.**

driving while intoxicated (DWI) An offense with which drivers may be charged if their blood-alcohol concentration at the time of arrest is above a certain percent.

drum brake A brake in which fluid pressure causes the brake shoes to push against the brake lining, which then presses against the round hollow metal drum inside the wheel. This creates friction, which slows and stops the wheel's turning motion.

electrical system The system that carries electricity throughout the vehicle and consists of the battery, the alternator or generator, the voltage regulator, and wires.

electronic fuel-injection (EFI) system A system that times and measures fuel flow and injects gasoline into the engine.

emergency brake See **parking brake.**

emergency flashers A signaling device that makes all four turn signals flash at once; used to warn other drivers that a vehicle has stopped or is moving slowly.

engine See **internal combustion engine.**

engine control module (ECM) A computerized system that controls the electrical and other engine systems in a vehicle.

exhaust manifold A collecting system for unburned gases as they exit from the cylinders.

exhaust system The system that gets rid of waste gases and vapors from the engine and reduces the noise of the explosions within the engine cylinders.

expressway A divided highway with limited access that has more than one lane for traffic moving in the same direction; designed for high-speed travel.

field of vision The area ahead and to the left and right that can be seen when one looks straight ahead.

first aid Emergency treatment given to an injured or ill person before professional medical personnel arrive.

fixed speed limit A posted speed limit that cannot legally be exceeded.

flywheel The part of the engine that is turned by the starter and, as a result, turns the crankshaft.

following distance The time-and-space gap between vehicles traveling in the same lane of traffic.

force of impact The force with which a moving vehicle hits another object.

freeway An expressway; a highway that is not a toll road.

friction Resistance to motion between two objects when they touch.

friction point The point at which the clutch pedal and other parts of the power train begin to work together as the driver releases the clutch pedal.

fuel system A system that consists of the fuel tank, fuel pump, fuel filter, fuel-injection system, and air filter.

fuses Safety devices, usually located beneath the dashboard, that protect a car's electrical circuits from overloading.

gas pedal See **accelerator.**

gear Toothed wheels that mesh with each other to transmit motion or change a vehicle's speed or direction.

gear selector lever The lever in a vehicle with an automatic transmission that allows the driver to choose a gear.

gearshift The lever in a vehicle with a manual transmission that permits gears to be changed.

graduated driver licensing (GDL) A driver training program based on the idea that a teen with a new driver's license needs time and guidance to gain the necessary driving experience and skills in reduced-risk settings.

gravity The invisible force that pulls all objects on Earth toward its center.

ground viewing Searching beneath parked vehicles and other objects for signs of movement.

guide sign A sign, including a route marker or destination, mileage, recreational area, or roadside service sign, used to guide and direct drivers.

hand brake See **parking brake.**

hand-over-hand steering A steering method in which the driver's hands cross when turning.

hazard flashers See **emergency flashers.**

head restraint A safety device attached to the back of the seat that is designed to prevent injury to the head and neck.

hemorrhaging Bleeding heavily.

high-occupancy vehicle (HOV) lane A lane reserved for use by vehicles having two or more occupants.

highway A main public roadway, especially one that runs between cities.

highway hypnosis A drowsy state that may occur during long hours of highway driving.

highway transportation system (HTS) A system made up of roadways, motor vehicles, and people.

hitch A device attached to the back of a vehicle to haul a trailer.

hydraulic pressure The pressure created by a liquid being forced through an opening or tube.

hydroplaning Skimming on top of a film of water.

idle To operate the engine without engaging the gears or applying pressure on the accelerator.

implied consent A law stating that any licensed driver charged with driving under the influence or while intoxicated cannot legally refuse to be tested for blood-alcohol concentration.

inertia The tendency of an object in motion to stay in motion and for an object at rest to stay at rest.

inhibitions Personality elements that stop a person from behaving without regard to possible consequences.

interchange A point at which a driver can enter or exit an expressway or connect with a highway going in another direction.

internal combustion engine The part of a vehicle that produces its power by exploding an air-fuel mixture within its cylinders.

international sign A road sign that conveys meaning through symbols, not words.

intersection The place where two or more roadways cross.

jaywalking The pedestrian practice of crossing a roadway without regard for traffic rules or signals.

jump-start To attach a vehicle's dead battery by cables to a charged battery to start the vehicle.

kinetic energy The energy of motion.

lane-use light An electronic signal mounted above a reversible lane that indicates whether the lane can or cannot be used at a particular time.

liability insurance Insurance that protects you against claims if you are at fault in a collision and helps pay for any injury or property damage you cause.

limited-access highway A highway that has fixed points of entry and exit.

lubricating system A system that reduces heat by coating the engine parts with oil; consists of the oil pump, oil pan, and oil filter.

manual shift A system in which the driver changes gears by moving the gearshift and depressing the clutch.

margin of space The amount of space that should be allowed in front of, behind, and to both sides of a vehicle, giving it room to maneuver in threatening situations.

momentum The energy of motion; the product of weight and speed.

moped A low-powered, two-wheeled vehicle most commonly driven on city streets.

mouth-to-mouth resuscitation A method of restoring breathing to a victim.

muffler A device in the exhaust system that reduces engine noise.

multiple-lane highway A highway that has more than one lane for traffic moving in each direction.

Neutral A gear position in which the gears are not engaged and cannot transmit power.

night blindness The inability to see well at night.

no-fault insurance A system in which one's insurance company pays one's medical bills and any other costs resulting from a collision-related injury regardless of who is at fault.

odometer A device that measures distance traveled by a vehicle; its gauge.

overdrive The highest forward gear in many newer vehicles with automatic transmissions; it allows a vehicle to travel more efficiently at higher speeds. In a vehicle with a manual transmission, the fourth and fifth gears are sometimes identified as overdrive gears.

overdriving one's headlights Driving so fast at night that the driver is unable to stop within the range of the headlights.

parallel parking Parking parallel and close to the edge of the road.

Park Gear setting on a vehicle that locks the transmission.

parking brake The brake that holds the rear wheels. It is used to keep a parked vehicle from moving.

parkway A broad highway that may be limited to noncommercial vehicles.

passive safety device A device, such as an air bag or head restraint, that functions without the user having to operate it.

pedestrian A person traveling on foot.

peer pressure The influence of friends who are in your age group.

perception distance The distance a vehicle covers during the time in which its driver identifies a need to stop.

peripheral vision The area of vision to the left and right of the area of central vision.

perpendicular parking Parking so that a vehicle forms a 90-degree angle with a curb or line.

piston A cylinder enclosed in another cylinder within the engine. Its up-and-down movement turns the crankshaft.

point system A system used to keep track of traffic violations by individual drivers.

power brakes Brakes that make it easier to slow or stop without intense foot pressure on the brake pedal.

power skid A skid caused when the accelerator is pressed too hard and suddenly.

power steering A vehicle steering system designed so that it takes little effort to turn the steering wheel.

power train The parts of a motor vehicle that transmit power from the engine to the wheels; the engine, transmission, and clutch.

push-pull-feed steering A steering method in which the driver's hands do not cross even when changing lanes or turning.

radiator A cooling device that air-cools liquid pumped from the engine.

rate of acceleration The time it takes to speed up from a stop or from one speed to a higher one.

rate of deceleration The time it takes to slow down from one speed to a lower one or to a stop.

reaction distance The distance a vehicle covers between the time a driver identifies a situation that requires braking and the moment that the brakes are applied.

regulatory sign A sign that controls the flow of traffic.

Reverse The gear used to back a vehicle.

reversible lane A lane on which the direction of traffic changes at certain times of day.

revoke To cancel a person's license to drive a vehicle, usually for the period of a year or more, after which time the driver can apply for another license.

right-of-way The right of one roadway user to go first or to cross in front of another; right-of-way must be yielded to others in many situations.

risk The chance of injury to oneself or others and of damage to vehicles and property.

safety belt A restraining belt designed to protect the driver and riders in a motor vehicle; a seat belt.

shared left-turn lane A lane that drivers moving in either direction use to make a left turn.

shift To change gears by means of a mechanism; the mechanism itself.

shock A physical disorder often accompanying serious injury; characterized by faintness, weakness, feeling cold, and nausea.

shock absorber A device that cushions a vehicle's frame against the impact of bumps in the road.

shoulder The strip of land along the edge of a roadway, sometimes referred to as a berm.

SIPDE process A five-step driving strategy (search, identify, predict, decide, execute) that enables drivers to process information in an organized way.

skid A driver's loss of control over the direction in which the vehicle is moving.

Smith System A set of five principles that help drivers operate safely and defensively.

space margin See **margin of space.**

spark plug A device in an engine's cylinder that ignites the fuel-air mixture by means of an electric spark.

speedometer A device that measures the speed of a vehicle in miles per hour or kilometers per hour; its gauge.

sport utility vehicle (SUV) A vehicle designed for a variety of uses, usually incorporating four- or all-wheel drive, and featuring increased ground clearance and a cargo area included within the interior.

steering system The system that enables a driver to turn a vehicle's front wheels.

strut A suspension unit that contains both a spring and a shock absorber.

suspend To take away a person's driver's license for a specified period of time, usually 30 to 90 days.

suspension system The system, including shock absorbers, that protects the body of a vehicle from road shocks.

tailgate To drive too closely behind another vehicle.

three-point turn A turnabout made by turning left, backing to the right, then moving forward.

threshold braking A braking technique in which the driver firmly presses the brake pedal to a point just before the wheels lock.

total stopping distance The distance covered by a vehicle from the perception distance to the moment that the vehicle comes to a stop.

tracking Steering; keeping a vehicle steadily and smoothly on a desired course.

traction The friction between a vehicle's tires and the road surface.

traffic control signal An electronic signal, such as a colored light, used to keep traffic moving in an orderly manner.

transmission The gears and related parts that carry power from the engine to the driving axle.

tread The outer surface of a tire, with its pattern of grooves and ridges.

turnabout Any turning maneuver by which a driver moves a vehicle to face in the opposite direction.

turnpike A road, usually an expressway, that requires a driver to pay a toll.

turn signal See **directional signal.**

two-point turn A turnabout made by first backing or heading into a driveway or alley and then heading or backing into the street.

uninsured motorist insurance Protection from financial losses resulting from a collision involving a driver who does not have insurance protection or from a hit-and-run driver; also protects you in states where no liability insurance is required.

U-turn A turnabout carried out by making a U-shaped left turn.

vertical field of vision The area extending upward and downward that allows you when driving to see traffic lights overhead and pavement markings below.

visibility The distance and area a driver can see and the ability of a vehicle or pedestrian to be seen.

visual acuity The ability to see clearly.

warning lights and gauges Dashboard lights and gauges that provide information to the driver about the vehicle; include oil pressure, alternator, and fuel gauges and brake, safety belt, and temperature warning lights.

warning sign A sign that alerts drivers to potential dangers or conditions ahead.

warranty A written guarantee that a motor vehicle dealer will repair a vehicle, within a certain amount of time, at no charge to the customer.

yield sign A road sign at which you must slow and give the right-of-way to traffic on the crossroad or the road onto which you are merging.

END-OF-YEAR TEST

NAME _____ DATE _____

FORM A   Driver's Education

END-OF-YEAR TEST

Select the phrase that best completes each sentence below. Write the letter of the answer you have chosen to the left of each statement.

a 1. Ideally, the in-vehicle test should be taken in
a. the same vehicle you have practiced in.
b. a vehicle with a manual transmission.
c. a vehicle with an automatic transmission.
d. your family's car.

d 2. For the in-vehicle test, your state may require you to present
a. your driver's permit.
b. the vehicle's registration.
c. the vehicle's insurance identification card.
d. all of the above.

a 3. Inhaling too much carbon monoxide while in your car can
a. have fatal results.
b. make you feel drowsy.
c. make you sick to your stomach.
d. do all of the above.

b 4. The best remedy for driving fatigue is
a. fresh air.
b. rest.
c. singing loudly.
d. coffee.

c 5. The vision that enables you to detect movement to the side is
a. field of vision.
b. central vision.
c. peripheral vision.
d. color vision.

c 6. The alcoholic content of a 5-ounce glass of wine, a 12-ounce bottle of beer, or 1½ ounces of whiskey is
a. greatest in whiskey.
b. least in the glass of wine.
c. about the same.
d. greatest in the bottle of beer.

d 7. The way to sober up a person who has had too much to drink is to
a. give the person black coffee.
b. make the person take a cold shower.
c. make the person exercise.
d. give the alcohol time to wear off.

c 8. A regulatory sign that has a red circle with a red slash means
a. detour.
b. railroad crossing.
c. no.
d. yield.

NAME _____ DATE _____

b 9. If you come to a stop sign and there is no white stop line,
a. stop 10 feet in front of the stop sign.
b. stop even with the stop sign or just in front of it.
c. stop 10 feet behind the stop sign.
d. stop anywhere as long as you stop.

b 10. To determine whether or not to suspend a driver's license, most states use
a. accident reports.
b. a point system.
c. a judge's discretion.
d. the federal government.

a 11. A certificate of title proves
a. who owns a car.
b. you have insurance.
c. the car is registered in the state.
d. your license plate is not stolen.

a 12. When turning left at an intersection, yield
a. to all oncoming vehicles until you have the time and space to turn.
b. just to traffic on the right.
c. just to traffic on the left.
d. only to emergency vehicles.

a 13. The air conditioner is used to
a. lower humidity.
b. raise humidity.
c. dispel carbon monoxide.
d. make the interior smell nice.

a 14. The function of an odometer is to
a. keep track of the number of miles the vehicle has been driven.
b. keep track of miles per gallon.
c. show how fast you are going.
d. tell you when your electrical system is failing.

d 15. You set a vehicle's automatic choke by
a. pressing the brake pedal once to the floor and then releasing it.
b. pressing the clutch pedal once to the floor and then releasing it.
c. having a mechanic give your vehicle a tune-up.
d. pressing the accelerator once to the floor and then releasing it.

d 16. Locking your wheels in an emergency braking situation
a. decreases braking effectiveness.
b. can make you go into a skid.
c. increases your stopping distance.
d. can do all of the above.

b 17. The friction point is
a. the place where the wheels meet the pavement.
b. the point where, as you let up on the clutch pedal, the transmission and engine engage.
c. the point where, as you push down on the brake, the car begins to slow down.
d. the place where the brake shoes rub against the wheel drum.

d 18. The first thing to do before changing lanes is to
a. steer smoothly into the next lane.
b. adjust your speed.
c. signal your intentions.
d. check your mirrors.

NAME _____ DATE _____

c 19. You should signal for a turn
a. no sooner than 50 feet before the turn.
b. no sooner than 100 feet before the turn.
c. at least 150 feet before the turn.
d. at least 500 feet before the turn.

b 20. A driver turning right
a. always has the right-of-way at a red signal.
b. must yield right-of-way to cross traffic.
c. does not need to yield to pedestrians.
d. should position the car to the left of the roadway.

b 21. When parallel parking, you
a. need a space at least 2 feet longer than your vehicle.
b. need a space at least 5 feet longer than your vehicle.
c. should drive into the space at 10 to 15 mph.
d. should check the sidewalk for pedestrians.

a 22. When an oncoming vehicle's headlights are too bright, you should
a. look at the right edge of the traffic lane beyond the oncoming vehicle.
b. look at the spot just below the oncoming vehicle's headlights.
c. turn on your high beams.
d. cover your eyes, but for no more than 2 to 3 seconds.

c 23. In a snowfall, you should drive in the tracks of the vehicle ahead of you so that you
a. know which way to go.
b. help to pack the snow down.
c. can get better traction.
d. can maintain momentum.

a 24. Of all the collisions between vehicles and pedestrians, most
a. occur in urban areas.
b. occur in rural areas.
c. occur near playgrounds.
d. result in a driver fatality.

b 25. At dusk, there is more danger of hitting a deer because
a. deer cannot see very well at dusk.
b. deer move around to feed at dusk.
c. deer are naturally sleepy at dusk.
d. there is more traffic at that time.

a 26. After passing a truck, you should not pull in closely in front of it because
a. you need to have plenty of room between you and the truck in case you have to hit the brakes.
b. you will block the truck driver's vision of the road.
c. you could get a ticket for tailgating.
d. all of the above apply.

d 27. A banked curve is one that
a. is higher in the inside of the curve than the outside.
b. has at least a 30-degree turn.
c. curves and goes downhill at the same time.
d. is higher on the outside of the curve than the inside.

b 28. The first thing to do in the event of brake failure is to
a. use the parking brake to stop your car.
b. pump the brake pedal rapidly.
c. shift to a lower gear.
d. steer against the curb.

NAME _____ DATE _____

c 29. If your engine stalls,
a. your power brakes won't work at all.
b. your power steering won't work at all.
c. your power brakes and power steering won't work very well.
d. you should pump your power brakes.

a 30. If your engine is flooded, you will probably
a. smell gasoline.
b. see steam coming out from under the hood.
c. have your engine stall after going through a large puddle of water.
d. have wet brakes as well.

c 31. An advantage of selecting a vehicle with an automatic transmission is
a. it offers increased fuel savings.
b. it has increased power going up hills.
c. it is easier to drive.
d. it will have power steering.

d 32. Uninsured motorist insurance protects you if
a. you hit a car that is uninsured.
b. you are hit by an uninsured driver.
c. you are the victim of a hit-and-run driver.
d. both b and c occur.

d 33. The wheels that receive the power from the engine are called
a. front wheels.
b. rear wheels.
c. drum wheels.
d. drive wheels.

a 34. The function of the differential is to
a. allow each of the rear wheels to turn at a different speed when turning a corner.
b. keep the coolant in the engine moving.
c. stop your car from losing control when you brake too hard.
d. remove exhaust gases from the vehicle.

d 35. A warning sign of steering trouble is
a. too much play in the steering wheel.
b. vibrations in the steering wheel.
c. a wobbly front end to your vehicle.
d. all of the above.

a 36. When you pack your vehicle for a long trip, the heaviest items should be
a. in the bottom of the trunk.
b. toward the center of the car.
c. placed in the vehicle-top carrier.
d. in the front seat.